The Management of Innovation
Volume II

The International Library of Critical Writings on Business and Management

1. Cross-Cultural Management (Volumes I and II)
   Gordon Redding and Bruce W. Stening
2. The Management of Innovation (Volumes I and II)
   John Storey

Future titles will include:

Negotiation, Decision Making and Conflict Management
Max H. Bazerman

Strategic Management
Julian Birkinshaw

Human Resource Management
Paul R. Sparrow

International Marketing
Stanley J. Paliwoda and John K. Ryans, Jr.

Wherever possible, the articles in these volumes have been reproduced as originally published using facsimile reproduction, inclusive of footnotes and pagination to facilitate ease of reference.

For a list of all Edward Elgar published titles visit our site on the World Wide Web at www.e-elgar.com

The Management of Innovation Volume II

Edited by

John Storey

Professor of Management
Open University, UK

THE INTERNATIONAL LIBRARY OF CRITICAL WRITINGS ON BUSINESS AND MANAGEMENT

An Elgar Reference Collection
Cheltenham, UK • Northampton, MA, USA

Published by
Edward Elgar Publishing Limited
Glensanda House
Montpellier Parade
Cheltenham
Glos GL50 1UA
UK

Edward Elgar Publishing, Inc.
136 West Street
Suite 202
Northampton
Massachusetts 01060
USA

A catalogue record for this book is available from the British Library.

Library of Congress Cataloguing in Publication Data

The management of innovation / edited by John Storey.
p. cm. — (The international library of critical writings on business and management ; 2)
(The Elgar reference collection)
Includes bibliographical references and index.
1. Technological innovations—Management. 2. Industrial management. I. Storey, John, 1947- II. Series. III. Series: The Elgar reference collection

HD45.M3248 2004
658.5'14—dc22

2004045461

ISBN 1 84376 429 6 (2 volume set)

Printed and bound in Great Britain by MPG Books Ltd, Bodmin, Cornwall

Contents

Acknowledgements

The editor and publishers wish to thank the authors and the following publishers who have kindly given permission for the use of copyright material.

Academy of Management and the Copyright Clearance Center, Inc. for articles: Deborah Dougherty and Cynthia Hardy (1996), 'Sustained Product Innovation in Large, Mature Organizations: Overcoming Innovation-to-Organization Problems', *Academy of Management Journal*, **39** (5), October, 1120–53; Katherine J. Klein and Joann Speer Sorra (1996), 'The Challenge of Innovation Implementation', *Academy of Management Review*, **21** (4), October, 1055–80; Wenpin Tsai (2001), 'Knowledge Transfer in Intraorganizational Networks: Effects of Network Position and Absorptive Capacity on Business Unit Innovation and Performance', *Academy of Management Journal*, **44** (5), October, 996–1004.

Administrative Science Quarterly for article: Jane M. Howell and Christopher A. Higgins (1990), 'Champions of Technological Innovation', *Administrative Science Quarterly*, **35** (2), June, 317–41.

Blackwell Publishing Ltd for articles: K. Pavitt (1991), 'Key Characteristics of the Large Innovating Firm', *British Journal of Management*, **2** (1), April, 41–50; Maxine Robertson, Jacky Swan and Sue Newell (1996), 'The Role of Networks in the Diffusion of Technological Innovation', *Journal of Management Studies*, **33** (3), May, 333–59; John Coopey, Orla Keegan and Nick Emler (1998), 'Managers' Innovations and the Structuration of Organizations', *Journal of Management Studies*, **35** (3), May, 263–84; Stephen K. Markham and Abbie Griffin (1998), 'The Breakfast of Champions: Associations Between Champions and Product Development Environments, Practices and Performance', *Journal of Product Innovation Management*, **15** (5), 436–54; Urs S. Daellenbach, Anne M. McCarthy and Timothy S. Schoenecker (1999), 'Commitment to Innovation: The Impact of Top Management Team Characteristics', *R & D Management*, **29** (3), July, 199–208; Graeme Salaman and John Storey (2002), 'Managers' Theories About the Process of Innovation', *Journal of Management Studies*, **39** (2), March, 147–65; Denis Harrisson and Murielle Laberge (2002), 'Innovation, Identities and Resistance: The Social Construction of an Innovation Network', *Journal of Management Studies*, **39** (4), June, 497–521.

Elsevier for articles: Eric von Hippel (1976), 'The Dominant Role of Users in the Scientific Instrument Innovation Process', *Research Policy*, **5** (3), July, 213–39; Paul L. Robertson and Richard N. Langlois (1995), 'Innovation, Networks, and Vertical Integration', *Research Policy*, **24**, 543–62; Rod Coombs and Richard Hull (1998), '"Knowledge Management Practices" and Path-Dependency in Innovation', *Research Policy*, **27** (3), 237–53; Michael D. Mumford (2000), 'Managing Creative People: Strategies and Tactics for Innovation', *Human Resource Management Review*, **10** (3), 313–51.

Emerald MCB University Press Ltd for article: Jacky Swan, Sue Newell, Harry Scarbrough and Donald Hislop (1999), 'Knowledge Management and Innovation: Networks and Networking', *Journal of Knowledge Management*, **3** (4), 262–75.

Institute for Operations Research and the Management Sciences (INFORMS) for articles: John Seely Brown and Paul Duguid (1991), 'Organizational Learning and Communities-of-Practice: Toward a Unified View of Working, Learning, and Innovation', *Organization Science*, **2** (1), February, 40–57; Eric von Hippel (1994), '"Sticky Information" and the Locus of Problem Solving: Implications for Innovation', *Management Science*, **40** (4), April, 429–39; Deborah Dougherty and Trudy Heller (1994), 'The Illegitimacy of Successful Product Innovation in Established Firms', *Organization Science*, **5** (2), May, 200–218.

Sage Publications Ltd for articles: Darren McCabe (2002), '"Waiting for Dead Men's Shoes": Towards a Cultural Understanding of Management Innovation', *Human Relations*, **55** (5), May, 505–36; Denis Harrisson and Murielle Laberge (2002), 'Innovation, Identities and Resistance: The Social Construction of an Innovation Network', *Journal of Management Studies*, **39** (4), June, 497–521.

Taylor and Francis Ltd (http://www.tandf.co.uk) for articles: Jaap J. Boonstra and Maurits J. Vink (1996), 'Technological and Organizational Innovation: A Dilemma of Fundamental Change and Participation', *European Journal of Work and Organizational Psychology*, **5** (3), 351–75; Jeremy Howells (1996), 'Tacit Knowledge, Innovation and Technology Transfer', *Technology Analysis & Strategic Management*, **8** (2), 91–106.

John Wiley and Sons, Inc. for article: Randall S. Schuler (1986), 'Fostering and Facilitating Entrepreneurship in Organizations: Implications for Organization Structure and Human Resource Management Practices', *Human Resource Management*, **25** (4), 607–29.

John Wiley and Sons Ltd for article: Dorothy Leonard-Barton (1992), 'Core Capabilities and Core Rigidities: A Paradox in Managing New Product Development', *Strategic Management Journal*, **13**, Special Issue, Summer, 111–25.

World Scientific Publishing Co. Pte. Ltd for articles: John Storey (2000), 'The Management of Innovation Problem', *International Journal of Innovation Management*, **4** (3), September, 347–69; Ian McLoughlin, Christian Koch and Keith Dickson (2001), 'What's This "Tosh"?: Innovation Networks and New Product Development as a Political Process', *International Journal of Innovation Management*, **5** (3), September, 275–98.

Every effort has been made to trace all the copyright holders but if any have been inadvertently overlooked the publishers will be pleased to make the necessary arrangement at the first opportunity.

In addition the publishers wish to thank the Marshall Library of Economics, Cambridge University, the Library of the University of Warwick and the Library of Indiana University at Bloomington, USA for their assistance in obtaining these articles.

Part I
Barriers and Enablers

[1]

The Illegitimacy of Successful Product Innovation in Established Firms

Deborah Dougherty • Trudy Heller
Faculty of Management, McGill University, 1001 Sherbrooke Street West, Montreal, Quebec, Canada H3A 1G5
The Wharton School, University of Pennsylvania, 2000 Steinberg–Dietrich Halls, Philadelphia, Pennsylvania 19104-6370

Why is new product development so difficult in established firms? This paper takes us deep into the development process to show both why and how successful new product creation requires as much organizational as technical innovation. The rich details point out the multitude of small barriers that inhibit "sensible" action and the necessity for managers at all levels to creatively redefine organizational routines.

Dorothy Leonard-Barton

Abstract

This paper reports on a theory building effort to understand the persistent difficulties with successful product innovation in large, established firms. Drawing on an institutional approach, we suggest that the constituent activities of effective product innovation either violate established practice or fall into a vacuum where no shared understandings exist to make them meaningful. Product innovation, therefore, is illegitimate. This means that to enhance their innovative abilities, managers must weave the activities of product innovation into their institutionalized system of thought and action, not merely change structures or add values. We use insights from 134 innovators to identify the different ways that product innovation is illegitimate, and to consider alternate ways to overcome these problems. Exploratory results suggest that successful product innovators experience as many instances of illegitimacy as others, but creatively reframed their activities more often to legitimate their work. We conclude with some new insights for why barriers to innovation exist in large, established firms, and how those barriers can be managed.

(*Product Innovation*; *Institutions*; *Organizational Change*)

The ability to generate commercially successful new products on a regular basis can be important to large, established firms. Product innovation is one way that such firms can gain market share in both mature and new markets (Kerin, Mahajan, and Varadarajan 1990), and discover new wealth-creating synergies among their resources (Burgelman 1983). While many large firms product successful new products occasionally, they have difficulties doing so in a sustained fashion, according to a recent survey by Arthur D. Little (1991). Studies indicate that product innovators in large firms often do not learn about customer needs (Cooper 1979, Dougherty 1990), develop products that are seriously flawed (Burgelman 1984), and do not integrate departments (Souder 1987).

The purpose of this research is to develop a better understanding of the organizational problems with effective product innovation. There are two views on why these difficulties persist and what can be done about them. One view is that big old firms may too rigid and inert to accommodate the learning and creativity necessary to innovation. Their emphasis on routine output makes them "machine bureaucracies" (Mintzberg 1979), where structures are too fixed and the work is too segmented for innovation. Galbraith (1982) argues that managers need to separate new product efforts from the noninnovative firm rather than attempt to change the firm. Others suggest that sustained innovation is only possible during short periods of revolution when the configurations or deep structures are altered (Miller and Friesen 1984, Tushman and Romanelli 1985). These tendencies toward rigidity and inertia may keep established firms from adopting new technologies

1047-7039/94/0502/0200/$01.25

(Tushman and Anderson 1986), or even new generations of familiar technologies (Henderson and Clark 1990).

A second view is that managers indeed can enhance the innovativeness of big old firms. The difficulties are not inherent but rather reflect a lack of know-how or inappropriate organization. Writers suggest that managers alter the firm's culture to be more integrative and enable learning and experimentation (Kanter 1983), institutionalize innovation by tying it systematically to every unit's performance and evaluation (Jelinek 1979), and organize projects to include overlapping problem solving and "heavy weight" managers (Clark and Fujimoto 1991). Moreover, some argue that change not only can be made incrementally, but ought to be (Quinn 1978, Nelson and Winter 1982). This view is also supported empirically, in that firms sometimes become more innovative (Miles and Cameron 1982), and, at least in the semiconductor industry, are innovative over time (Jelinek and Schoonhoven 1990).

We develop another theory about the difficulties with product innovation that combines the reality of bureaucratic inertia with the possibility of change. The views above differ because they encompass various kinds of "innovation." To overcome this problem, we focus on the day-to-day practices of product innovation (described below) in one kind of organization, the large old firm. The views also differ because they focus on different levels of analysis, ranging from macroscopic evolutionary forces to microscopic activities of individuals. To overcome this problem, we use an institutional approach, since it allows us to focus on everyday social practice but still consider the larger context of the work organization (Berger and Luckmann 1967, Perrow 1986). Others have used an institutional approach to study change by encompassing the micro world of everyday social action and macro patterns. For example, Kimberly (1979) details how the institution of medical education withheld legitimacy from a new kind of medical school at the micro level by inhibiting new ways to evaluate students or recruit faculty, and Powell (1985) shows how the everyday actions of editors at scholarly presses fit with the institution of "good editing," which produced considerable conformity even though editors worked with considerable autonomy.

By focusing on day-to-day practices within the institution of the large established organization, we develop a middle range conception of barriers to product innovation in this setting and what can be done about them, not a grand theory of "innovation" (see Mohr 1982, Nord and Tucker 1987 on the need for such focused research). We develop the idea that the necessary activities of product innovation do not fit into the institutionalized practices in large old firms. These activities either violate the existing system of thought and action, or fall into a vacuum where no shared understandings exist to make them meaningful. Therefore, while managers may support "innovation" in general, product innovation is in fact illegitimate at the level of everyday thought and action. The idea of illegitimacy suggests new insights into the difficulties with product innovation. To develop those insights, we first describe the necessary activities of product innovation, and consider how institutional dynamics of stability and change can affect them. These ideas are then explored empirically through the experiences of 134 product innovators from 15 large old firms.

Conceptual Background

The Constituent Activities of Effective Product Innovation

Research on the process of new product development suggests that its constituent activities can be grouped into three sets of linkages.[1] First, innovators need to link the market and technological possibilities in the design. Successful new products meet user needs, are seen as superior by customers, have technological and production synergy, and are marketed more effectively (Cooper 1979, 1983; Zirger and Maidique 1990). A product is not just a technology or a business, it constitutes the integration of a variety of attributes (Dougherty 1992b). Customer needs may be hard to discern, however, so the product's attributes cannot be specified easily, and the mix of attributes may change as customers learn to use the product. The manufacturing processes may be new or the product technology may be unfamiliar, which means that technical problems may crop up unexpectedly. Linking market and technology possibilities thus requires a creative process that is even more complex than that described by Allen (1977) for developing technology alone. Product innovators must experiment with different attributes, work closely with customers, pursue multiple development paths at once, and at times make discontinuous leaps in imagination.

Second, product innovators must link the expertise of different functions within the firm. According to Dougherty (1992a) each department comprises a distinct "thought world" regarding customer needs and how products should be designed to meet those needs. Each thought world has a vital yet unique piece of the market-technology linkage puzzle, so the thought worlds must be integrated to create the comprehensive understanding of the product. Equally important, collaborative interdepartmental relationships speed up learning (Souder 1987, Adler 1990), while their mutual adaptation enhances coordination and implementation (Mintzberg and McHugh 1985, Leonard-Barton 1988).

Third, product innovators need to link their product to the firm's strategy and resources. Burgelman (1983) argues that new products need to be connected to the strategic context of the firm so they can draw on resources and be incorporated into management's understanding of what the firm is about. A product-firm linkage is also suggested by those who argue that new products should relate to the firm's capacities and resources (cf. Ansoff 1965, Rumelt 1974, Prahalad and Hamel 1990). Empirical work shows that such strategic linkages enhance the likelihood of a new product's success (Nord and Tucker 1987, Cooper and Kleinschmidt 1990).

Institutional Concepts and Product Innovation in Large Firms

Why do product innovators in large established firms have difficulty carrying out the necessary design, collaborative, and strategic linkages? An institutional approach suggests an answer. By definition, an institution is an enduring system of belief and behavior that is "imposed" by society upon the conduct of individuals. That is, although institutions are constructed and maintained by human interaction, we experience them as having an external reality, as something objectively real that exists outside our individual thoughts (Berger and Luckmann 1966, Berger and Berger 1975, Scott 1987). Institutionalized practices provide a common understanding of appropriate behavior, facilitate coordination, make behavior understandable and predictable, and can be repeated with a minimum of effort.

Organizations with a long history of stability are crisscrossed with institutionalized practices that come from without, such as labor-management relationships and "rational" decision making (Collins 1987, Meyer 1990), and from within, such as emergent standards and roles (Zucker 1977). Such organizations emphasize bureaucratic routinization and control to support high volume production of standard products (Mintzberg 1979). These practices endure through dynamics of institutional conformity. External actors such as customers, banks, and regulatory agencies expect organizations to "act right," so managers conform to standards to signal their legitimacy (DiMaggio and Powell 1983, Scott 1987). Internally, at the level of day-to-day thought and action, people infuse these practices with value beyond technical requirements of the task, making them "the right thing to do" (Selznick 1957). These practices become rooted in the conformity of the taken-for-granted aspects of everyday life, so other practices can be "literally unthinkable," according to Zucker (1977).

The Illegitimacy of Product Innovation. According to DiMaggio (1988): "institutional theory recognizes that the taken-for-granted nature of much of organizational life and the intractability and opacity of organizational systems have been underestimated by ultilitarian... theorists..." (1988, 5). As outlined above, our ultilitarian theories say much about how product innovation *ought* to be carried out, but difficulties with product innovation persist nonetheless. This persistence suggests that the three linkage activities do not fit into the institutionalized thoughts and actions in large old firms. They either violate prevailing practice, inside and outside the firm, or require ways of thinking and acting that are "undoable" or "unthinkable," albeit in intractable or opaque ways. The activities of product innovation, therefore, are illegitimate.

Institutional Dynamics for Change. To say that the activities are illegitimate does not mean that organizations can never incorporate them. Institutions do adapt over time—even the French language changes occasionally. But the idea of illegitimacy suggests that problems with product innovation will not be overcome simply by adding skills or altering structures. Rather, the linkage activities need to be woven into the established practices, that is, legitimated. The strong pressures for conformity suggest that new activities cannot "come out of the blue," but rather must be connected in some way to already legitimate practices or understandings. Three different modes of legitimation can be extrapolated for product innovation.

One mode of institutional change or legitimation is to make new activities conform with existing institutionalized practices. The basic dynamic is that "new" practices can be adopted readily if they seem familiar, as illustrated by Hinings and Greenwood's (1988) study of reforms in local government practice that readily occurred when a "new" practice was already in existence, and as elaborated theoretically by Dimaggio and Powell's (1983) discussion of institutional isomorphism. To extend this idea to product innovation, we can suggest that product innovators overcome legitimacy problems by conforming to the usual practices in the firm. For example, innovators may link technologies and markets by drawing on established product conceptualizations, link departments by relying on existing roles, and link the product with the firm by following the usual chain of command.[2]

Another mode of institutional change is that new activities can be legitimated "ceremonially," by associating an innovation with a legitimate practice, but continuing to behave in the old way. Meyer and Rowan (1977) argue that US public schools used ceremonial legitimacy to respond to federal regulations in the late 1960s. Schools did not change their classroom behavior, but simply added legitimate, rational-seeming bureaucratic structures to appear to conform to government expectations. Ritti and Silver (1986) likewise suggest that sponsors of the Polaris weapon system used PERT (program evaluation and review technique) in a ceremonial fashion to legitimate the system. By espousing PERT but not actually using it, the sponsors gave Congress the impression that their program was well managed and efficiently run. Similarly, product innovators could espouse legitimate innovation mechanisms such as champions or venture units, or simply by claiming to be "innovative," but not change how they actually work. As we use the term, ceremonial legitimation provides external legitimation but does not alter innovators' day-to-day practices.

A third mode of institutional change is to use legitimate practices to reframe new activities, which is to reconceive them so people can now understand how to carry them out. Hirsch (1986) shows how reframing works in the case of the hostile corporate takeover, which was an illegitimate form of ownership transfer until the early 1980s, one not used by established members of the business community. The hostile takeover required people to make sense out of experience for which existing vocabularies were inadequate. According to Hirsch: "Without concrete terms, metaphors, and contexts in which to describe and interpret new, unexpected events, it is unlikely that they can become conceptualized as normal, routine, and acceptable" (1986, 821). The hostile takeover became legitimated through a "micro-cultural-subjective" (1986, 821) reframing, in which legitimate metaphors such as cowboys and knights of the round table were used to reframe it. Reframing gave people familiar roles and scripts to play out, like "corporate raider," "damsel in distress," and "white knight."

In a study of a factory's change from authoritarian to participatory management, Westley (1990) similarly suggests that change did not happen until individuals could reconceive their roles and relationships, from "boss" to "coach" for example, as if they were "converted." "(I)t may be argued that the conversion moment is *achieved* through metaphor, when for an instant a parallel is seen between the familiar and the unfamiliar experiences" (Westley 1990, 289). Product innovators could also draw on legitimate practices or ideas such as "the venture" or "teamwork" to help them metaphorically see how to carry out the three linkages. These and other ways to reframe the linkage activities can provide innovators with concrete terms and roles with which to make sense of these unfamiliar and heretofore illegitimate actions.

Research Questions

To develop the idea of illegitimacy, we explore two descriptive questions. First, how are the three linkage activities illegitimate? In what sense are they "unthinkable" and in what sense is the organization intractable when it comes to new product development? Exploring this question will pinpoint the deficiencies as well as the categories of behavior and practice that need development if the organization is to become innovative. Second, which of the three modes of legitimation enables product innovation? Each has different implications. If successful innovators conform to usual practice, then a firm can enhance its innovativeness by incrementally expanding already legitimate practices for market definitions, integrating work, and so forth. In contrast, if reframing relates to success, then innovativeness can be enhanced if people learn to use principles of innovation management to reframe their day-to-day innovation practices. However, if successful innovators rely on ceremonial solutions, then a simple display of legitimacy may be all that is needed.

Methods

To gain insight into the effects of institutionalized practices on product innovation, we needed people's accounts of how an actual product innovation effort clashed with established routines, expectations, and shared understandings in their firm. We approached firms through the aegis of sponsoring associations (The Marketing Science Institute, The Industrial Research Institute, the Wurster Center of International Management), and asked to interview employees involved with a new product. We concentrated on large established firms, but multiple industries, to focus on a single institution. The 15 firms who gave access averaged 96 years of age, 54,000 employees, and $9.4 billion annual revenue.

Next, we selected products in consultation with a firm's representative that were still in progress or recently completed. Innovative products were defined as those that embodied unfamiliar technology, were intended for unfamiliar markets, or both. The focus of this research is on people's perceptions of the innovation activity, not on the merits of a particular product. However, having people talk about an actual rather than a hypothetical event allowed us to ground their perceptions in actual experiences.

Table 1 shows the products by success status and degree of innovativeness. The number of firms represented in each category of success status is shown at the bottom. The products ranged from fairly incremental investment bonds or food products to state of the art communication devices and expert systems. We determined a product's success or "current" status through follow-up phone calls two years later.[3] When the interviews were held none of the products had achieved commercial success, defined as generating enough revenues to cover costs and produce a profit (Cooper 1979). Three had already been introduced to the market and then cancelled. Two years later, several more products had been cancelled while still in development, some were not yet in the market, some were in the market but whether or not they would succeed was not clear, and some were generating profits as planned. These five categories of *current status* are shown in Table 1. For degree of product innovativeness, the project director of each was asked to describe how unfamiliar the product was in five areas: applications, market segments, distribution, product technology, and manufacturing. Three categories of innovativeness were devised: low—unfamiliar in one or two areas; medium—unfamiliar in three areas; high—unfamiliar in four or five areas.

Table 1 New Product Cases by Current Status and Innovativeness[a]

	Current Status				
Innovativeness[b]	Success	In Market Success not Clear	In Development	Cancelled in Development	Failed
Low unfamiliar in one or two ways	Bond (3)[a]	Bond (8)	Bond (1)		Bond (4)
	Food Item (7)	Information Package (2)	Information Package (1)		
	Document System (2)				
Medium unfamiliar in three ways	Food Item (3)	Rock Crusher (2)	Specialty Chemical (1)	Chemical (3)	Specialty
	Chemical (4)	Document System (5)	Lubricant (3)		
		Office Product (4)	Building Product (1)		
		Chemical (2)	Machine (4)		
		Chemical (3)	Solvent (4)		
		Information Package (1)	Office Machine (1)		
		Food Item (5)			
		Chemical (3)			
		Communication System (4)			
		Plastic (6)			
High unfamiliar in four or fives ways		Medical System (2)	Medical Product (3)	Communication System (2)	Operating System (4)
		Expert System (4)	Computing System (2)	Site Mgt System (2)	
		Expert System (7)	Robot (5)	Waste-fix (4)	
		Warehouse System (1)	Office Machine (1)	Food Item (10)	
no. products:	5	16	12	4	3
no. firms in cat:	5	10	8	4	3
	(shows that results not due to data coming from only one or two firms)				

[a] = number of individuals interviewed

[b] = five different ways to be innovative: new users, new uses, new product technology, new manufacturing, new distribution.

In face-to-face interviews, people were asked to tell the story of the product, and then describe what they knew about the market and technology, how they knew, how they worked with other departments, and how strategic decisions were made. To provide more data on problems *and* solutions, they were asked to describe two problems and how those problems were solved. We also asked if the firm had "gotten in the way" and how people had responded. The interviews lasted about an hour on the average. We tried to talk to at least two people for each product to get multiple views. Due to difficulty in contacting people, only one person was interviewed for six of the forty products. The people were all white collar professionals or scientists in operating level positions from different departments, and averaged nine years of tenure with the firm. Eleven people described products that had already been cancelled, so they were speaking retrospectively. The rest described products that were still in development.

The interviews provide multiple insights from informed people who work within a similar institution about the institutional constraints on their innovation activities. The data's variety and breadth meet the needs of our exploratory purpose by allowing us to explore different settings and develop categories that are more broadly grounded empirically. The variety of products allows us to consider whether certain product attributes such as success status, degree of innovativeness, or stage of development affect the experience of illegitimacy. The data are also limited in important ways. First, we explore which mode of legitimation is more effective by comparing the experiences of people whose products became successful with those whose products did not. There are a number of explanations for a product's success that may have nothing to do with overcoming illegitimacy, but we control only for factors that we have measured. Second, we look primarily at the microscopic aspects of institutional practice, and measure those only through the interviews. Appendix A details how we took these limitations into account in our analysis.

Findings

In What Ways Are the Linkages Illegitimate?

To discover how the activities of product innovation are illegitimate, we content-analyzed the interviews, noting passages that concerned the failure of established practices, the imposition of procedures that did not fit, the violation of usual practices, or the lack of shared knowledge regarding how to carry out a linkage activity. Instances of illegitimacy were described spontaneously as well as in response to questions about problems.

In order to create a descriptive summary of illegitimacy problems without inferring possible motives (e.g., a search for power or stability), or imposing our own interpretations on the events, we used Strauss's (1987) methodology for searching interpretive data for underlying themes.[4] The first step was to analyze illegitimacy passages to identify a variety of possible themes, so we met together and with others in numerous coding sessions to generate and discuss possible themes. The second step was to reduce the list but still capture qualitatively different issues. Here, passages from a variety of interviews about the same type of illegitimacy were clustered and examined to identify that theme more sharply. Multiple interviews for some products helped develop a deeper appreciation for a theme, since sometimes people discussed the same instance of illegitimacy from different perspectives. Multiple products helped to develop a broader appreciation since we could explore each kind of illegitimacy in different contexts. This process resulted in eight different ways that the linkage activities were illegitimate.

The final step was to clarify the illegitimacy categories by classifying each of the grand total of 1,024 illegitimacy passages across the 134 interviews into one of the eight types. We iteratively coded and discussed our decisions, since the illegitimacy types were complex themes which had to be evaluated in context of each interview. All illegitimacy passages were coded three times, and each time decision rules for coding were sharpened. There are no independent measures of rater reliability, but we feel that this collaborative approach produced a reliable summary of illegitimacies discussed by the product innovators. Table 2 outlines the steps, decision rules, and the final typology.

This is not the only way to classify institutional constraints on innovation since another analysis may find fewer or more types, or highlight other aspects. However, this analysis shows that the constituent activities of product innovation do not fit into the established order in *multiple* ways. Institutionalized practices in these firms kept innovators from engaging in a creative design process (ILL1), evaluating their product effectively (ILL2), overcoming departmental barriers (ILL3), understanding different perspectives (ILL4), maintaining team commitment (ILL5), and fitting the product into the structure (ILL6), strategy (ILL7), or climate (ILL8) of the firm.[5]

Because we coded the illegitimacy problems as part of our category development, we can count up how

Table 2 Illegitimacy Problems in New Product Development: The Coding Process and Final Typology of Illegitimacies

Step One: Open coding of interviews to identify variety of possible types of illegitimacy.

↓

Step Two: Axial coding for each preliminary type to develop typology of descriptions that fit across interviews, and to see if types fit entire data set;

A. compare within multi-interview cases and across cases to define illegitimacies: rule is to stick to what people say, and to not impose our own interpretations

B. then sort illegitimacy types into one of three linkage activities.

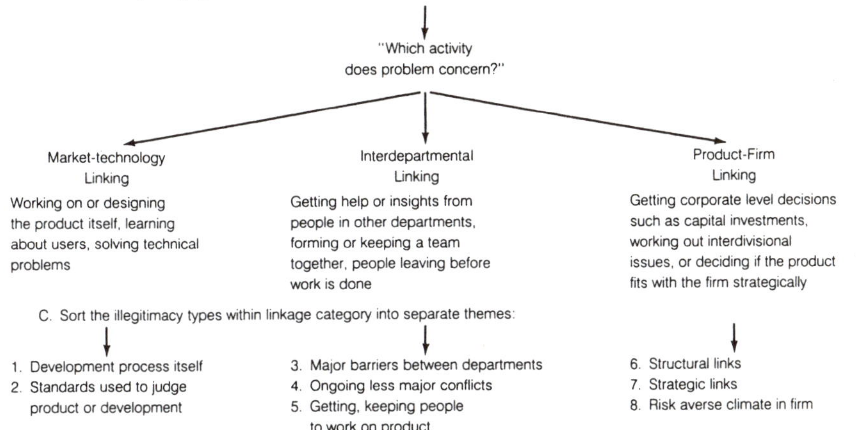

Step Three: Selective coding to finalize illegitimacy typology:

A. Develop specific coding rules to distinguish between illegitimacy types:

ILL1 concerns developing the specific product; ILL6 concerns connecting product to firm.
ILL2 is about evaluating the product itself; ILL7 is about whether the firm should do the product.
All major capital allocation decisions are ILL6.
All management of the product's development issues are ILL1.
Use ILL8 only if the illegitimacy does not fit into another category.
ILL3 is a barrier between departments that is so strong the people cannot fix by themselves; all others are ILL4.

Final Illegitimacy Typology

Market-Technology Linking	Interdepartmental Linking	Product-to-Firm Linking
ILL1: cannot follow emergent or discontinuous development process; get resources for design, learn about users	ILL3: barriers between departments that cannot be worked out by product innovators	ILL6: cannot determine how to locate product in firm's structure, or make budget decisions, or get senior approval
ILL2: inappropriate or not helpful standards are imposed on product	ILL4: ongoing misperceptions, conflicts between departments, from thought world differences	ILL7: cannot determine if firm should have product, or if it fits with firm strategy
	ILL5: cannot get people to work on product, or people are moved away, or other team problems	ILL8: risk averse climate in firm

Table 3 A Summary of the Illegitimacy Problems in the Interviews and Product Cases

Problems	Percent of all people who experienced the problem one or more times $n = 134$	Average number of instances of problem by individual $n = 134$	Average number of instances of problem by products $n = 40$
ILL1: no creativity in design	76%	1.84	1.88
ILL2: inappropriate prod. evaluation	41	0.68	0.71
ILL3: departmental barriers	28	0.51	0.51
ILL4: departmental clashes in view	64	1.28	1.36
ILL5: team commitment maintenance problems	46	0.71	0.67
ILL6: no structural fit	57	1.12	1.11
ILL7: no strategic fit	42	0.74	0.88
ILL8: no climate fit	28	0.40	0.47.

many people experienced what kinds of illegitimacies and compare those counts by different groups of people and products to explore our data further. Table 3 shows how many of the 134 people interviewed mentioned at least one instance of an illegitimacy, and the average number of instances of each illegitimacy. The ILL1 problems (no creativity) were discussed most by the most people, followed by ILL4 (clashing functional perspectives) and ILL6 (no structural fit). The table also shows the average number of illegitimacies by case. Note that the averages by person and by case are virtually the same, even though we interviewed more people for some products. This makes sense in theory; everyone is in a similar institution and thus should have similar experiences with illegitimacy, all else being equal, of course. The number and kind of illegitimacies may vary by certain product attributes, but before we consider those data let us consider the illegitimacies themselves.

Description of Illegitimacy Problems

The Creative Linkage of Market and Technological Issues. As discussed in the conceptual background, linking uncertain market and technology issues may require early contact with customers, simultaneous exploration of multiple options, and discontinuous leaps of imagination. We found two kinds of illegitimacy which made it difficult for innovators to carry out this linkage: the inability to respond creatively to market and technical insights to design the product (ILL1 in Table 2), and the inability to evaluate or monitor the product's development effectively (ILL2).

Creative design problems (ILL1) arose because institutionalized practices could not tolerate or forbade the experimenting that innovators needed to carry out to learn about the product's development or design. For example, in the passage below, a planner anticipated that surprises would crop up as he and his team developed their new plastic material. However, he noted that such surprises would seem like failures against the backdrop of normal events in the firm and was worried about the team's ability to deal with the organizational backlash:

> Another problem is that the speed at which you commercialize becomes an issue because of all the related issues you attract... As you go, certain events won't happen the way you project. In development these events are like failures, but they have to happen. These technical obstacles always come up, but the question is, how can you handle those most efficiently with the least aggravation to the organization?... [I worry about whether] the team can handle them.

Another aspect of creative design constraints (ILL1) was the inability to get resources to develop critical pieces of a product's overall package. While acquiring resources is always a problem, the use of the resources in innovation did not fit with usual practice, so the need was ignored, not simply delayed. For example, a software product needed a technical support component, but that need was virtually denied, according to this manager:

> Our technical people are not into bits and bytes. There is no recognition here for the cost of technical support to release a software product. Management laughs at us and says "What do you mean you need technical support?"

A lack of knowhow regarding how to incorporate market insights into the design process was also an aspect of ILL1 illegitimacies. For example, this sales director for a new specialty chemical to clean surfaces understood that he *ought* to assess his markets, but he didn't see how he could in practice:

> We haven't done any formal market research for this product. The product is based on a gut feel—we know there is a market. But we don't know whether or not the product will work.... If there were one or two applications, OK, I could evaluate them. But I have twelve or fifteen different applications, and to evaluate them all would take too much time. So, we take opportunities as they come...

He explained that this linear, technology push approach was how they normally developed new products. Unfortunately, the product was uncertain because their haphazard approach to market development had produced a small level of sales.

Inappropriate product evaluation (ILL2 illegitimacies) reflected a similar lack of flexibility or capability in product development. Others in the firm tended to view the new product through the lens of existing, often inapplicable standards, such as time or financial returns. Sometimes keeping to a schedule seemed more important than adequate design, so people felt pressured to introduce their product prematurely. For example, a marketing person cancelled an analysis she felt was necessary because: "Our management kept saying 'get it out! get it out!'" Other standards dictated that a new product look like conventional products, or meet conventional accounting criteria:

> We have to constantly defend the product. They [division management] look on it as an operating expense.

> This product violates the payback rules. Usually we expect a two-year payback, but this is a four.

The Collaborative Linkage of Different Departments. These three illegitimacies concerned bringing in *and* maintaining necessary expertise from across departmental lines. As already outlined, effective collaboration among departments is vital to new product success. However, the roles, relationships, and commitment necessary to innovation either conflicted with the establishment practice for task allocation, work relationships, and career progression, or there were no guidelines for this kind of collaboration.

Departmental barriers (ILL3) concerned innovators' inability to breach functional boundaries. Roles and tasks were often narrowly construed. For example, in one firm the engineering department was responsible for designing new products and managing their transfer to manufacturing, while the research department's charge was to develop new technologies. These roles were enforce through written procedure and tradition. However, a new rock drilling machine was initiated by the research department. To produce the product, they went to an outside vendor rather than their own manufacturing department:

> We did not involve manufacturing because we knew what they would say. This product is difficult to make and we knew they wouldn't want to do it. I did contact a manufacturing manager and he agreed to meet me out here one Saturday morning, but then he cancelled.

Strong prior expectations and the lack of established means to interact outside of entrenched roles seriously limited collaboration in this case, reducing people to an almost illicit assignation. The manufacturing department eventually became involved, but perhaps too late. While initial sales were good, the vendor's drill shaft was of low quality. Customers were returning the machines, so the product's status had become uncertain.

Another example of how normal work roles did not map onto the work of innovation came from a bank. The project manager of a new bond explained her continuing challenge to foster collaboration:

> At meetings we say this and that were resolved, but then finance says: "We can't change our rules to go along with that." Then marketing says: "You must for our customers." Finance is starting to back off from their water torture where they always say they can't do it. Now, they say OK, but then down the road we find that they have priced the security so high that we can't sell them.... We have to figure out a way to get these trade-offs done up front. In their heads they know it has to happen, but I can't figure out how to get them to go along and participate in the process.

Again, we can see a disjuncture between the needs of innovation and the routine practices. The manager said that people conceptually understood the need to collaborate, but did not know how to actually do it. A comment by the finance person showed that he did not see such collaboration as part of his "real" work:

> There has only been a couple of meetings for this product. We have had one concept thinktank and one follow-up that I missed. It is hard to go to those meetings so I try to avoid them if I can. You get 30 pages to read and then the meeting drifts off to some isolated thing. There is some value to knowing what another department is up to, but I have better things to do with my time.

Even when people were able to establish working relationships across departments, departments still conflicted over their understanding of the work (ILL4). Such problems reflected conflicting thought worlds, as exemplified by this sales person's frustration that research people ignored his insights on customer needs:

> The big issue is when I tell research people what I need in the marketplace, they don't believe it. I kept telling them that I couldn't sell that polymer in this market, and they kept coming back with the same polymer. Finally, I wrote out a three-page memo detailing all the attributes I needed. Then I took Fred and Bob out and introduced them to customers, and sat down with customers... Suddenly everything I've been saying they now say we need.

In contrast, Fred the researcher felt the marketing issues were taken care of:

> The key problem was where to enter the marketplace with this material and how? We resolved that problem as I got teamed up with George... .

Fred did not that there were a few disagreements with marketing, but he did not seem to appreciate George's agony.

Overcoming ILL3 problems would require that barriers be torn down and roles be redefined, but overcoming ILL4 problems would require an ongoing effort to work out differences between specialized groups. Problems with developing or maintaining team commitment (ILL5) are also qualitatively distinct. Even if the barriers are breached and thought world conflicts worked out, collaboration problems may exist if people are not assigned in a timely fashion, or the team falls apart before its work is finished. With ILL5 problems, innovators could not get people assigned to a project in a timely fashion, as in this example:

> Getting personnel is a problem. You have to get borrowed resources at the right time and within an effective time frame, but it takes three months to yank them out of the existing organization... .

Or they could not keep people on the project. For example:

> So many of the team members are no longer dedicated. It is a constant challenge to keep people informed. I send documents, but this is a verbal company. So I send paper and then call them to check, and I also call them to remind them about meetings. Keeping the team together and involved is difficult... .

Getting human resources is always a problem. It is an illegitimacy problem when the needs for flexible assignment and commitment in an innovation activity are either ignored or denied by the established practices.

The Strategic Linkage of the Product with the Firm. The third set of illegitimacies concern the difficulties innovators had in connecting their product with the firm's structure or strategy. These illegitimacies differ from the first two sets, which concern how the product should be developed or who should work on it. The first product-to-firm illegitimacy reflected difficulties with connecting new products to the firm's structure (ILL6). This meant that the new products could not connect to the established authority, decision making, and communication flows and relationships, and thus could not tap into resources. This also meant that the established system ignored the special management needs of the innovations. For example, some firms had no structure to nurture innovations. They had "venture units" to create a new product, but as soon as the product was introduced to the market, it was passed on to an established business, which managed the product like all other routine products. This structural void ignored the need for ongoing change in response to customer feedback after market launch. This manager worried that a product would not be finalized once it was transferred out of the new products group:

> We still have a number of uncertainties. But Nancy [boss] wants me to move onto another product and transfer this one over to project management [out of the new products unit]. This product will not get the attention it has in the past. I don't know what will happen once it moves over.. They are totally bogged down now, so once they take this product, I don't know what will happen to it.

The structural problems (ILL6) also included an inability to work out interdivisional clashes. For example, a corporate level planning committee approved a product and promised the innovator that resources would be assigned to him from different divisions in the firm. The various managers among the divisions were very slow to release those resources, however, because they did not want to buy equipment that another division might keep, or insisted that another division was responsible for certain expenditures. Meanwhile, the innovator got a low performance evaluation because he had not met his commitments. This instance may have reflected political conflict, lack of competence, or managers' opinion that the product was not viable. We also suggest that there were few legitimate interdivisional practices to guide the management of new products.

Structural illegitimacies included an inability to relate with senior managers as well. Some innovators felt that they had no way to discuss their special needs with managers, and described elaborate machinations they devised to get the approval of senior people. This person explained how revealing problems to senior managers was "not done" in his firm:

> Big companies like fairy tales. I have identified a funny thing that goes on in this company. We view managers as adversaries, and we hide our real issues from them. The idea is, let me prove that I know more than anyone else. We will not reveal our concerns... because we assume management won't like it.

A second product-to-firm problem was an inability to determine *whether* the product fit with the firm (ILL7). ILL7 problems were evaluative like ILL2 problems, but concerned the strategic question of should the firm be in that business, not what the product should be. Many products raised this strategic question since they took the firm to unfamiliar markets or drew on the firm's resources in an unusual way. Yet the question was often unresolved, which frustrated the innovators. For example, a new chemical product remediated toxic industrial wastes, a "hot" market in the 1980s. However, some said the firm should not get into that market because 20 years before they had failed with a similar product. This criterion for strategic choice ignored the real possibility that the market had changed significantly:

> XCO developed [a remediation technique] some time ago. We tried to market it but failed miserably, so we sold the technology. So there are a lot of people in the company who think that waste treatment is not a good fit for XCO. There is a real bias against it.

Another firm had widely trumpeted innovation, but this innovator could not get management to support innovation with real funds:

> You have to hold a gun to management's head. They like to have solid proof of a commercial opportunity before they will invest. But they can't tell a hairbrained idea from a solid opportunity, because innovations all look the same to them. So they tend to pursue what everyone else is doing. When you come with a new idea, they say: "We'll if it's so good, why isn't everyone else doing it?"

In both cases the criteria for whether the products fit strategically did not seem sensible. People at different levels apparently had no shared cognitive map of the firm's competencies and how new products related to them.

The final kind of illegitimacy concerned more general problems about the firm's overall atmosphere (ILL8). As noted in Table 2, we used this category only when problems did not fit elsewhere. These included a risk-averse climate as suggested in these three examples: "There is not a lot of stomach here for new products..., "This company is very conservative. It is not acceptable to make a lot of noise..." and "We have the same mentality as the phone company... ."

The anti-innovative climate illegitimacies also reflected a general lack of commitment from the firm, as in statements that there was no firm-wide commitment, or in discussions of seemingly capricious resource removal, as this example illustrates:

> The biggest problem for us is the weekly battles we have to fight for our survival.... The company is trying to sell off a very important piece of technology and the VP... is doing this for his own personal profitability so it will look good on his bottom line.... It's a message that the company isn't serious about the project. I take it very personally. It's not like we work forty hour weeks around here.

Summary Statistics on the Illegitimacies. Table 4 shows the average number of illegitimacy problems by current status.[6] Analyses of variance are used to reinforce the qualitative analysis and identify noteworthy differences between groups. Innovators whose products had failed tended to describe more instances of ILL1, no creativity ($p = .13$). Those whose products ultimately became successful described no instances of ILL3 (department barriers), but more of ILL5 (maintaining team commitment). This finding can be interpreted in a number of ways, but since the successful efforts relied on good teams, we think it suggests that maintaining a team over the several years it may take to develop, launch, and revise a new product is especially problematic in these firms. Since the total number does not seem to differ, we infer that the innovators we interviewed experienced roughly similar numbers of illegitimacy problems, regardless of the ultimate success status of their product.

We find a number of differences by the product's degree of innovativeness, however, as shown in Table 5. Innovators whose products were more innovative described more instances of illegitimacy in the four problem types shown in the table, as well as for the total number of problems.[7] However, when we control for the length of time in development, the difference in total number of problems disappears. This suggests that the longer a product is in development, the more illegitimacies that accrue, although we cannot say which causes which. There are no differences in illegitimacy type by stage of development, which suggests that all illegitimacies crop up throughout development.

Institutional Dynamics of Change and Innovativeness

Next, we analyzed whether and, if so, how the 1,024 illegitimacies described by the 134 innovators were solved. Coding rules were developed to categorize the three types of solution, as summarized in Table 6. The

Table 4 Average Number of Illegitimacy Problems by Current Status

	Current Status of Product					
Problem	Successful $n = 19$	Out, uncertain $n = 60$	Still in development $n = 26$	Cancelled in development $n = 18$	Failed $n = 11$	Results of oneway ANOVA
IL1 no creativity in design	1.42	1.97	1.54	1.60	2.9	$p = 0.13$
ILL2 inappropriate product evaluation	0.74	0.7	0.5	0.5	1.18	$p = 0.41$
ILL3 departmental barriers	00	0.83	0.35	0.06	0.73	**
ILL4 departmental clashes in view	1.00	1.18	1.54	1.17	1.91	$p = 0.32$
ILL5 team commitment maintenance problems	1.26	0.65	0.5	0.89	0.27	$p = 0.03$
ILL6 no structural fit	1.47	1.25	0.89	0.94	0.64	$p = 0.31$
ILL7 no strategic fit	0.47	0.67	0.73	1.17	0.91	$p = 0.34$
ILL8 no climate fit	0.37	0.40	0.35	0.72	0.09	$p = 0.26$
Total Average Number of Problems	6.74	7.65	6.40	7.06	8.6	7.64 $p = 0.53$

**No statistic, since one group has no variance.
Based on individuals whose products fit each category.

first decision was whether or not the problem was solved. Solved problems were typically expressed as follows: "*X* occurred, so we did *Y*." Since sometimes people mentioned a problem and described how they worked it out later in their story, the entire interview was examined for solutions to each problem. If people described what they *might* do, such hypothetical solutions were included in the "not solved" category. We had originally also coded failed solutions. Most of these were either usual or ceremonial types. However, only 7% of the total were failed, and most were described by the failed innovators, which raises the possibility of bias in our failure measure. Therefore, we recoded failures as not solved.

Once a solved problem was identified, the solution was coded as one of the three approaches to legitimation, according to the decision rules in Table 6. Each author separately coded 20 interviews, and our inter-rater reliability was 84%. Differences were discussed, and the coding scheme was sharpened. Half of the remaining interviews were coded jointly, and half separately.

Table 5 Illegitimacy Problems That Vary by Product Innovativeness
average number of instances of problem by individual

Problems	Degree of Innovativeness: Low: unfamiliar in one or two ways $n = 29$	Medium: unfamiliar in three ways $n = 58$	High: unfamiliar in four or five ways $n = 47$	Total: $n = 134$
ILL1 no creativity in design	1.24	2.05	1.93	1.88 *$p = 0.10$
ILL2 inappropriate product evaluation	0.38	0.67	0.87	0.71 *$p = 0.13$
ILL6 no structural fit	0.66	1.14	1.38	1.11 *$p = 0.06$
ILL7 no strategic fit	0.48	0.50	1.19	0.88 *$p = 0.00$

*Based on oneway ANOVAS.

Usual solutions followed the usual practices in the firm to carry out the linkage activity, based on how the person presented the solution. To legitimate a new product idea, for example, innovators in a heavy equipment firm followed a process that had been developed for customized machinery. As one said: "that gave us a conduit to follow." Other innovators overcame resistance to their new idea by selling some of the products, because in their firms a usual criterion of legitimacy was sales. In another example, the people redefined their new products in terms of the firm's typical product line. To overcome collaboration problems via usual solutions, some innovators went up the hierarchy to get someone in authority to "order" another department to cooperate, or relied on the usual communication processes to keep people involved in a project. In overcoming product-to-firm illegitimacies, usual solutions included arranging to have a project assigned to corporate managementrather than to a division to give it a structural home, or "visiting all the camps" to work an interdivisional conflict, as one described the normal political practices in his firm.

Ceremonial solutions relied on practices that were legitimate in the larger environment such as venture units, project management, team training, champions, and skunkworks. Innovators associated their project with these legitimate practices, *but they did not actually use the practices* to carry out the linkage activities. For example, in one firm some people objected to a new product because it did not meet usual standards for quality, an ILL2 problem. The innovators solved this problem by declaring the product a "venture" that did not have to meet quality standards, *not* by fixing the product or by developing new quality standards that fit this product. They worked around the illegitimacy problem. In other examples, innovators claimed that they overcame illegitimacies because they were able to "sell" the idea or persuade others to just go along. Note that we operationalized "ceremony" by distinguishing the form of the innovation structure from the substance of the innovation activity, and coded use of the form only as ceremonial legitimation. When ventures, teams, and so forth were used to redefine the linkages the instances were coded as reframed.

Reframed solutions used legitimate practices or understandings as metaphors to alter how people think about the particular linkage activity. For example, this person explains how his group reconceived product design to overcome the firm's standard process that dictated set steps in set time periods:

> We have bent the rules, shortening the product development cycle. We're using a pilot plant, which is unusual. We are also developing a different kind of relationship with the retailer. The time line is longer for introduction...

Reframing to solve collaboration illegitimacies typically involved redefined work roles and relationships. For example, in this case the innovators used the principle of a venture unit to rework career progression problems:

> At (XCO) there is a lack of continuity on developing businesses. People move every nine months... From the beginning we created a radically new organization. It has two concepts. The first is that we did not want turnover, the theory being that if you are going into a business that you know nothing about, you don't want to keep retraining people. Second, we had a long term incentive system installed [to compensate for loss of career moves].

Product-to-firm reframing included ventures or project teams that invoked a new kind of authority relationship within which innovators and senior managers had different kinds of responsibility than usual. An example was the creation of an open two-way dialogue with senior managers rather than sending the proposal up the hierarchy (usual solution). In one case the innovators arranged to meet with senior people informally to discuss the pros and cons of the innovation openly. Again, this sounds ordinary, but several people

Table 6 Solutions to Illegitimacy Problems: The Coding Process and Examples

Decision 1: was problem solved?

Yes	No
Described how problem was overcome or stated that a certain process solved several problems; includes all solutions, even partial or seemingly temporary ones	No solution mentioned in interview, a solution was tried but it failed, or person described only what they might do

Decision 2: which a priori defined legitimation approaches were used?

	Usual	Ceremonial	Reframed
Decision criteria:	Action consistent with typical patterns in firm, no mention of uniqueness, AND linking problem was addressed	Action described as special for project, or recently implemented in firm for innovations, and comprised ventures, project management, champions, entrepreneuring; AND linking problem was not addressed	Action described as special for project, or consisted of a new way of thinking, or concerned breaking rules; AND linking problem was addressed
Examples	Put product in the market to show it works; redefine it as a familiar product; work the system in the usual way to get decisions made; assign product to corporate	Invoke project management techniques and have people assigned to project or assign project to a venture; act like a champion or sponsor to get attention; use persuasion, guile to keep idea alive	Generate careful product definition in the beginning; make multiple visits to users; redefine work roles and take broader responsibility for product; negotiate realistically with senior managers; take teaching role

pointed out this unusual kind of meeting enabled them to truly interact with management.

In the instances of reframing people noted a "change in thinking," or a "whole new perspective," but drew on metaphors that were less colorful than Hirsch's "cowboys" or "knights." Instead, they used more mundane and seemingly ordinary ideas like pilot production or changing the reward systems, more in line with Westley's (1990) description of change at a factory. These were reframings nonetheless, since they involved a reconceptualization of day-to-day practice based on existing ideas as metaphors.

Table 7 shows the proportion of illegitimacies that were solved, and the proportion of solutions that were usual, ceremonial, and reframed by success status. First, solving problems with illegitimacy is associated with success in our data, since the innovators whose products ultimately became successful solved more problems than those in all other success status groups. Those whose products were cancelled solved very few problems, but this result may be biased by retrospection if these innovators dwelled on unsolved problems more than the others. The number of illegitimacies that were solved is not associated with degree of innovativeness or stage of product's development.

Second, the mode of legitimation used is also associated with success in our data. When we consider only solved illegitimacy problems, innovators whose products ultimately became successful solved 70% of them through reframing. However, innovators whose products were ultimately cancelled also had a high rate of reframed solutions, which suggests that reframing is not enough to assure product success.[8] We checked to see if these two results might be affected by other variables. Within each category of innovativeness, stage of development, and organizational structure for which we had successful innovators, the successful innovators always had a higher proportion of solved problems and reframed solutions.

Discussion

In this paper we have tried to understand why people *in practice* have trouble with product innovation, even though *in theory* we know a great deal about it. To

Table 7 Solution of Illegitimacy Problems
average rate of solution by individual in success categories

	Current Status					
Solutions	Successful $N = 19$	Out, uncertain $N = 60$	Still in development $N = 26$	Cancelled in development $N = 18$	Failed $N = 11$	Total $N = 134$
Average percent of individual's problems that were solved	57	36	34	42	.09	37*
Of the solved problems: Average percent solved with USUAL solutions	19	55	52	27	50	44*
Average percent solved with CEREMONIAL solutions	10	17	28	12	50	20
Average percent solved with REFRAMED solutions	70	29	20	61	00	37*

*Significantly different at $p < .05$ without the failed group, oneway ANOVA.
All group variances are homogeneous.
Columns add to 100% (some rounding error).

explain this divergence, we explored the possibility that the constituent activities of product innovation are illegitimate in large, established firms. Our analysis suggested that the thesis of illegitimacy provides a number of new and useful implications for managing innovation in these firms, and is worthy of the resources needed to test it and explore it further.

First, we found eight different ways that institutionalized practices impeded product innovation. Obviously, additional research is necessary to develop this typology and to see if the kinds of illegitimacies are different in different types of organizations. However, our findings indicate that the constituent activities of new product development *do not fit into*, or *are not a part of*, the legitimate system of thought and action in multiple, if subtle, ways. The typology reveals some of the intractability of the institutional practices with regard to product innovation, because even if product innovators managed to carry out a creative design (overcome ILL1 and ILL2), they might have difficulty acquiring human resources (ILL5) or locating a structural home (ILL6). Our typology also suggests a preliminary inventory of the thought and action that needs to be developed to become more proficient with new product development.

Second, our findings suggest that the specific processes used to legitimate innovation activities are important. By looking closely at the microdynamics of change, we found that *reframing* was associated with the more successful innovation efforts. Obviously, this too must be explored and confirmed in further research. To reframe a linkage activity, innovators used a legitimate practice or understanding to reconceive how they worked at the micro level of day-to-day action.

These reframing ideas already had some meaning and so provided the innovators and their colleagues or managers with some guidance for action. At least in our data, following usual practices or simply displaying legitimacy ceremonially did not contribute to innovation success. Reframing incorporates both revolutionary and incremental change, in that old ideas are used for new action. Many of the reframed solutions were not only consistent with what the literature says innovators *ought* to do, they were rather ordinary, sensible actions. However, innovators often had to reframe thought and action for themselves and their managers to use these actions, which suggests how difficult effective innovation was in these firms. Our micro and short term data do not allow us to see if these reframed actions survived as part of the firms' legitimate practices, or if they withered away and had to be created anew for subsequent product efforts. In addition, other research suggests that more "macro" level reframings such as strategic reorientations, major changes in personnel policies, or leadership change are also necessary to break out of dynamics of conformity (Jelinek 1979, Miles and Cameron 1982). More research on the relationships on reframings from micro and macro levels is needed.

These descriptive findings lead us to hypothesize that change needs to occur on two levels. At the particular level of day-to-day action, people need to become adept with and practiced at the specifics of linking markets and technologies in a product conceptualization, at working effectively with diverse thought worlds, and at creating a connection between a new product and the existing set of resources. These activities must be institutionalized, or made a part of the taken-for-granted system of thought and action. At a more general level people need practices to help them frame the complexities of specific product development activities. These, too, need to be institutionalized so that people understand them in a similar way. People would draw on institutionalized frames for action to carve out domains of work, and then draw on the specific skills to carry out day-to-day innovation activities within those frames.

This is an important if perhaps subtle point. People need to *connect* the various principles for innovation to their day-to-day practices. For example, "the voice of the customer" or "quality function deployment" are frames that can be meaningless unless coupled with specific actions for making sense of customer needs and incorporating them with technology. Specific activities such as visiting customers with a multidisciplinary team and jointly learning from that experience (especially when customers cannot articulate needs precisely), and experimenting with alternate options, are ways to act within these frameworks. In the same way, "teams" or "participative decision making" can be empty notions unless people can adopt broadened work roles and anticipates one another's problems and needs. A redefinition of career practices is an example of a more macro reframing that may be necessary to resolve the difficulties with sustaining commitment over time. People cannot become committed if narrow jobs and individual achievement are reinforced by the reward and career structure (cf. Bailyn 1985, Kanter 1989).

Third, the thesis of illegitimacy raises an interesting question about some of the mechanisms that are widely touted for innovation, such as the champion, the sponsor, and the skunkworks (see Roberts 1988, Kanter 1988 for reviews). Do these mechanisms actually facilitate development of a new product, or are they simply means to overcome the illegitimacy of product innovation? For example, is the champion vital to a product's design, or is it a legitimate way to allow for illegitimate behavior? This is an important question, because many of the popular solutions to problems with innovation emphasize use of these mechanisms in a recipe fashion. We do not argue that these mechanisms are not important. However, by relying on them instead of changing the institutionalized practices in their firms, managers actually perpetuate the illegitimacy of innovation.

This exploratory study has only scratched the surface of this problem, and a number of important research questions remain. First, we assume that all firms in the study represented a similar institution. However, there may well be variation in the styles and patterns of illegitimacy in large firms based on, perhaps, strategic emphases, technology, and history that our methods did not detect. To look for these differences, subsequent research should gather more detailed data on firms. Second, we would expect to find interesting differences in the patterns of illegitimacy across types of organizations based on factors such as technology or history. For example, perhaps the science basis of biotechnology firms would make the marketing aspects of product design illegitimate, while firms with a long history of hierarchy might find strategic linkage especially illegitimate. Third, the dynamics of legitimacy and institutional change should be studied over time, since reframing may be important only as firms begin to transition. Or, perhaps reframing can become institutionalized as an ongoing process, in which case a wider array of innovative activities would be possible. Fourth, by emphasizing the everyday level of activities, we have not resolved whether or not big old organizations can actually become more innovative. We have, however, suggested a theoretical basis for exploring that issue in depth.

In conclusion, an emphasis on the constituent activities of successful product innovation and the institutional dynamics that constrain them suggests that the constraints are deeply entrenched in the way people work. But making large established firms more innovative may not require bizarre, exotic, or radical types of employees, leaders, cultures, or structures, since practices which enable the linkage activities are both straightforward and ordinary (see Jelinek and Schoonhoven 1990). We speculate, however, that institutionalizing these practices will require that managerial practice itself be reframed. Perhaps the most important next research question is to explore the change in managerial ideology that may be necessary for product innovation to become truly legitimate, that is, truly a part of the institutional order of large old firms.

Appendix A

Our data contain variation on the kinds of products and people, so we can examine whether or not these factors affect the results reported in Tables 4, 5, and 7. For example, we looked at the percent of problems that are solved by current status *within* all products that were low, medium, and high in innovativeness to make sure that the successful innovators still had the highest percentage—they did. The effects of the following factors were examined:

(1) *Individual Effects.* Since the products were not randomly selected, and since we could not contact everyone associated with a product, we may have interviewed a peculiar sample of product innovators. Two factors were examined to see if they affected the illegitimacies and solutions people discussed:

(a) *Person's Department.* Department had no effects on the illegitimacies and solutions except that planners were less likely to report collaboration problems. (b) *Person's Tenure with the Firm:* Based on people's reports of when they began with the firm, in five categories: (1) 20 or more years; (2) 10–19 years; (3) 5–9 years; (4) 0–4 years; (5) not reported. People with more tenure reported fewer product-to-firm illegitimacies and more solved problems. Neither affected the findings of Tables 4 and 7 since both were distributed across our data.

(2) *Stage of Product's Development.* Stage of development codes: (1) already cancelled; (2) still in development; (3) out in the market. Innovators whose products were in the market had more solutions and more reframed solutions, which indicates some effects of time in development. Successful innovators still had more solutions and reframings than those whose products were in the same development stage.

(3) *Retrospection Bias.* Stage of development results suggest that retrospection bias in stories that reflected back do not affect our results. We also deleted those whose product was already cancelled because they are most likely biased, and reran the analyses for Tables 4 and 7. The results were still significant. Third, we compared projects that were started at different times (initiated in 1983 or 1984; in 1985 or 1986; and in 1987 or 1988). Those whose products began most recently had fewer illegitimacies in total, fewer ILL5 problems, and more reframed solutions. The successful cases were started more recently, so our results could reflect retrospection bias. Or, perhaps innovators whose products took longer to develop encountered more illegitimacy problems. A longitudinal study is necessary to sort out these possibilities.

(4) Seven of the 134 people did not describe any illegitimacies. We found nothing noteworthy about these people, since they did not fall primarily into any success status, department, or product type.

(5) *Product Innovativeness.* We also checked to see if the findings in Tables 4 and 7 came from different degrees of product innovativeness rather than success status. Once all the other variables were controlled for (including current status), the most innovative projects had more ILL7 problems (strategic fit) and a lower proportion of usual solutions. As reported, within each category of innovativeness, those whose products became successful had more solutions and more reframed solutions.

Acknowledgements

This research has received support from the Marketing Science Institute, the Industrial Research Institute, and the Reginald Jones Center, Sol C. Snider Center and Management Department, all of the University of Pennsylvania. We thank Steve Barley, Hans Pennings, Paul Olk, Peter Sherer, and Sarah Corse for their helpful comments. We are also grateful to editor Dorothy Leonard-Barton and the anonymous reviewers for their assistance.

Endnotes

[1]This typology of the constituent activities of new product development is similar to those used by several organization theorists, but it includes insights from the marketing (e.g., Cooper 1983) and technology management (e.g., Souder 1987, Roberts 1988) literatures. For example, Van de Ven (1986) uses four types of activity: managing attention, managing ideas into good currency (similar to our first linkage activity), managing parts-whole relationships (similar to our second linkage activity), and institutional leadership (similar to our third linkage activity). Burgelman (1983) has a more complex model of 12 activities but his dimensions are technology-needs linking (similar to our first linkage activity), organizational championing, and strategic context connections (similar to our third linkage activity). Kanter's (1988) typology includes idea generation (similar to our first linkage activity), coalition building (similar in part to our second linkage activity), and technology transfer (similar to our third linkage activity).

[2]Focusing on usual practices within the firm may seem strange to those organization theorists who see institutional forces operating solely at the "macro" level, on organizations rather than in them. However, firms the size and age of those we study are institutions in their own right and have embodied many usual practices to which innovators may need to conform in order to legitimate their new product.

[3]We could not contact someone for five of the forty products, since people had left the firm and others would not return our calls. These five cases were placed in the "still in development" or "out but uncertain" current status categories, based on our best guess. Since

this could affect our findings, all of the results reported here were rerun with the people from these five cases deleted, and the results were the same. The categories of success status are descriptive. "Failed" means in the market but then cancelled, while "cancelled during development" means that the product did not go to market, but was cancelled. "Out but uncertain" means that the product is in the market but not yet making money to any significant degree, and not making the cash flow that had been expected during development. "Success" means that the product is making the cash flow at least that was expected at the time of the follow-up interview. Most studies compare successes and failures by relying entirely on retrospective data, but as can be seen the commercial status of a vast majority of our products is still indeterminant.

[4]A number of systematic approaches for analyzing qualitative data have been described (e.g., Miles and Huberman 1983, Yin 1989). We use Strauss' (1987) explication of such a methodology because it builds on his earlier work in grounded theory building (Glaser and Strauss 1967) and provides a very detailed explication of *how* to develop categories, not only rules of thumb to follow. In addition, we relied on the logic of analysis described by Bailyn (1977).

[5]We focus only on large established firms. The idea of illegitimacy suggests that other kinds of organizations with different institutional histories and experiences would have different kinds of illegitimacies, or perhaps different amounts of these kinds of illegitimacies.

[6]Table 4 reports results by product innovators. We also did the same analysis with case means, to see if the different numbers of people interviewed by case affected the results. The product means for the cancelled in development group for ILL6, ILL7, and ILL8, respectively, were 1.19, 1.31, and 0.99; versus 0.94, 1.17, and 0.72 for the individual means. The large number of people in one case in this group might have suppressed the number of strategic problems, although in both cases this group's numbers for ILL7 and ILL8 are the highest. There are no other differences.

[7]Again, the same results were analyzed by case means. The product mean for ILL7 was 1.46, versus 1.19 for individuals. All other means were about the same.

[8]When we look at the means by product, we find that the cancelled while in development group has a much lower proportion of reframed solutions—42% versus 62% for the individuals. Again, the one large case with ten people interviewed may be skewing the results. However, the 42% average is still high, so our inference that reframing is not enough still seems reasonable.

References

Adler, P. (1990), "Shared Learning," *Management Science*, 36, 938–957.

Ansoff, H. I. (1965), *Corporate Strategy*, New York: McGraw-Hill.

Allen, T. (1977), *Managing the Flow of Technology*, Cambridge, MA: MIT Press.

Arthur D. Little (1991), "Worldwide Survey and Product Innovation," ADL, 25 Acorn Way, Cambridge, MA.

Bailyn, L. (1977), "Research as a Cognitive Process: Implications for Data Analysis," *Quality and Quantity*, 11, 97–117.

____ (1985), "Autonomy in the R&D Lab," *Human Resource Management*, 24, 129–146.

Berger, P. and T. Luckman (1967), *The Social Construction of Reality*, Anchor Books Ed., Garden City, NY: Doubleday.

____ and B. Berger (1975), *Sociology: A Biographical Approach* (2nd Ed.), NY: Basic Books.

Burgelman, R. (1983), "A Process Model of Internal Corporate Venturing in the Diversified Major Firm," *Administrative Science Quarterly*, 28, 223–244.

____ (1984), "Managing the Internal Corporate Venturing Process," *Sloan Management Review*, Winter, 33–48.

Burns, T. and G. Stalker (1961), *The Management of Innovation*, London: Tavistock.

Clark, K. and T. Fugimoto (1991), *Product Development Performance: Strategy, Organization, and Management in the World Auto Industry*, Boston: Harvard Business School Press.

Collins, R. (1986), *Weberian Social Theory*, Cambridge: Cambridge University Press.

Cooper, R. (1979), "The Dimensions of Industrial New Product Success and Failure," *Journal of Marketing*, 43, 93–103.

____ (1983), "A Process Model for Industrial New Product Development," *IEEE Transactions on Engineering Management*, 30, 2–11.

____ and E. Kleinschmidt (1986), "An Investigation Into the New Product Process: Steps, Deficiencies, and Impact," *Journal of New Product Development*, 3:71–85.

____ and E. Kleinschmidt (1990), "New Product Success Factors: A Comparison of Kills Vs. Successes and Failures," *R&D Management*, 20:47–63.

DiMaggio, P. (1988), "Interest and Agency in Institutional Theory," in L. Zucker (Ed.), *Institutional Patterns and Organizations*, Cambridge: Ballinger.

____ and W. Powell (1983), "The Iron Cage Revisited: Institutional Isomorphism and Collective Rationality in Organizational Fields," *American Sociological review*, 48, 147–160.

Dougherty, D. (1990), "Understanding New Markets for New Products," *Strategic Management Journal*, 11, 59–78.

____ (1992a), "Interpretive Barriers to Successful Product Innovation in Large Firms," *Organization Science*, 3, 179–202.

____ (1992b), "A Practice-Centered Model of Organizational Renewal Through Product Innovation," *Strategic Management Journal*, 13, 77–92.

Galbraith, J. (1982), "Designing the Innovative Organization," *Organizational Dynamics*, Winter, 5–25.

Glaser, B. and A. Strauss (1967), *The Discovery of Grounded Theory*, Chicago: Aldine.

Henderson, R. and K. Clark (1990), "Architectural Innovation: The Reconfiguration of Existing Product Technologies and the Failure of Established Firms," *Administrative Science Quarterly*, 35 (March), 9–31.

Hinings, B. and R. Greenwood (1988), "The Normative Prescription of Organizations," in L. Zucker (ed.), *Institutional Patterns and Organizations*, Cambridge, MA: Ballinger.

Hirsch, P. (1986), "From Ambushes to Golden Parachutes: Corporate Takeovers as an Instance of Cultural Framing and Institutional Integration," *American Journal of Sociology*, 91, 800–837.

Jelinek, M. (1979), *Institutionalizing Innovation*, New York: Praeger.

____ and C. Schoonhoven (1990), *The Innovation Marathon: Lessons from High Technology Firms*, Cambridge, MA: Basil Blackwell, Inc.

Kanter, R. M. (1988), "When a Thousand Flowers Bloom," in B. Staw and L. Cummings (Eds.), *Research in Organizational Behavior*, Greenwich CT: JAI Press, 10, 169–211.

____ (1989), "The New Managerial Work," *Harvard Business Review*, November-December.

Kerin, R., V. Mahajan and P. Varadarajan (1990), *Conceptual Perspectives on Strategic Market Planning*, Boston: Allyn and Bacon.

Kimberly, J. (1979), "Issues in the Creation of Organizations: Initiation, Innovation, and Institutionalization," *Academy of Management Journal*, 22, 437–457.

Leonard-Barton, D. (1988), "Implementation as Mutual Adaptation of Technology and Organization," *Research Policy*, 17, 251–267.

Meyer, J. and B. Rowan (1977), "Institutionalized Organizations: Formal Structure as Myth and Ceremony," *American Journal of Sociology*, 83, 340–363.

Meyer, M. (1990), "The Weberian Tradition in Organization Research," in C. Calhoun et al. (Eds.), *Structures of Power and Constraint*, Cambridge: Cambridge University Press, 191–217.

Miles, M. and M. Huberman (1983), *Qualitative Data Analysis*, Beverly Hills, CA: Sage.

Miles, R. H. and K. Cameron (1982), *Coffin Nails and Corporate Strategies*, Englewood Cliffs, NJ: Prentice Hall.

Miller, D. and P. Friesen (1984), *Organizations: A Quantum View*, Englewood Cliffs, NJ, Prentice Hall.

Mintzberg, H. and A. McHugh (1985), "Strategy Formation in an Adhocracy," *Administrative Science Quarterly*, 30, 160–197.

Mohr, L. (1982), *Explaining Organizational Behavior*, San Francisco: Jossey-Bass.

Nord, W. and S. Tucker (1987), *Implementing Routine and Radical Innovations*, Lexington, MA: Lexington Books.

Perrow, C. (1986), *Complex Organizations: A Critical Essay*, New York: Random House.

Powell, W. (1985), *Getting Into Print: The Decision-Making Process in Scholarly Publishing*, Chicago: University of Chicago Press.

Accepted by Dorothy Leonard-Barton December 23, 1992.

Quinn, J. B. (1978), "Strategic Change: Logical Incrementalism," *Sloan Management Review*, 20, 7–21.

Ritti, R. and J. Silver (1986), "Early Processes of Institutionalization: The Dramaturgy of Exchange in Interorganizational Relations," *Administrative Science Quarterly*, 31, 25–42.

Roberts, E. (1988), "What We've Learned: Managing Invention and Innovation," *Research—Technology Management*, January-February, 11–29.

Rumelt, R. (1974), *Strategy, Structure, and Economic Performance*, Dissertation, Harvard University, Graduate School of Business.

Scott, W. R. (1987), "The Adolescence of Institutional Theory," *Administrative Science Quarterly*, 32, 493–511.

Selznick, P. (1957), *Leadership in Administration: A Sociological View*, NY: Harper and Row.

Souder, W. (1987), *Managing New Product Innovations*, Lexington, MA: Lexington Books.

Strauss, A. (1987), *Qualitative Analysis for Social Scientists*, New York: Cambridge University Press.

Tushman, M. and P. Anderson (1986), "Technological Discontinuities and Organizational Environments," *Administrative Science Quarterly*, 31, 439–465.

____ and E. Romanelli (1986), "Organizational Evolution: a Metamorphisis Model of Convergence and Reorientation," in L. L. Cummings and B. Staw (Eds.), *Research in Organizational Behavior*, Greenwich CT: JAI Press, 7, 171–222.

Westley, F. (1990), "The Eye of the Needle; Cultural Transformations in a Traditional Organization," *Human Relations*, 43, 273–293.

Yin, R. (1989), *Case Study Research: Design and Methods* (2nd Ed.), Newbury Park, CA: Sage Publications.

Zirger, B. and M. Maidique (1990), "A Model of New Product Development: An Empirical Test," *Management Science*, 36, 867–883.

Zucker, L. (1977), "The Role of Institutionalization in Cultural Persistence," *American Sociological Review*, 42, 726–743.

____ (Ed.), (1988), *Institutional Patterns and Organizations: Culture and Environment*, Cambridge, MA: Ballinger.

[2]

© *Academy of Management Journal*
1996, Vol. 39, No. 5, 1120–1153.

SUSTAINED PRODUCT INNOVATION IN LARGE, MATURE ORGANIZATIONS: OVERCOMING INNOVATION-TO-ORGANIZATION PROBLEMS

DEBORAH DOUGHERTY
CYNTHIA HARDY
McGill University

We examined problems with sustained product innovation in 15 firms that averaged 96 years of age, 54,000 employees, and $9.4 billion in annual revenues. Findings reveal that the inability to connect new products with organizational resources, processes, and strategy thwarted innovation in these large, mature organizations and that innovators lacked the power to make these connections. We suggest that these organizations must reconfigure their systems of power to become capable of sustained innovation and offer recommendations for practice.

Successful new products and services are critical for many organizations, since product innovation is one important way that organizations can adapt to changes in markets, technology, and competition. There is, accordingly, a large and growing literature on product innovation, at the level of both specific projects (Cooper, 1983; Zirger & Maidique, 1990) and the organization as a whole (Nevens, Summe, & Uttal, 1990; Wheelright & Clark, 1992). Researchers have identified organizational characteristics that relate to successful product innovation, such as organizational configurations (Burns & Stalker, 1961; Mintzberg, 1979a), culture (Kanter, 1983), strategy (Day, 1990), leadership (Quinn, 1985), and various combinations of these (Jelinek & Schoonhoven, 1990; Roberts, 1988; Van de Ven, 1986). Although many details remain to be articulated, this work has produced a good understanding of the innovative organization, at least as an ideal type.

However, many organizations still have difficulty with sustained product innovation, or managing a number of product innovations over time (Arthur D. Little, 1991). Sustained product innovation is particularly difficult for organizations with long histories of stable operations. Hage (1988) argued that long-stable organizations are especially challenged by changes in technology and global competition: they must become more innovative if they are to survive, but to do so they must fundamentally change how they organize.

We would like to acknowledge the Social Sciences and Humanities Research Council of Canada, which helped support this work.

This research seeks to extend theory on organizing for innovation by focusing on (1) sustained product innovation and (2) organizations with histories of stable, noninnovative practices that are struggling to become innovative. We define sustained product innovation as the generation of multiple new products, as strategically necessary over time, with a reasonable rate of commercial success. We define new products as those (1) intended for customers who are unfamiliar to an organization or (2) that require unfamiliar product or process technologies. Most organizations can produce a successful new product occasionally—IBM's PC and General Motors' Saturn are good examples. The question is whether they can sustain or repeat what they did. Peters (1992) described the introduction of a successful new product by a 120-year-old machinery manufacturer but wondered if the organization could replicate that success. Dougherty and Cohen (1995) visited the firm several years later to discover that all subsequent new product efforts had failed, because of a lack of the organization-wide change needed to accommodate multiple product innovation efforts. Many large, mature organizations must become capable of sustained product innovation for competitive reasons. However, most ideas for organizing for innovation come from already innovative firms (e.g., Clark & Fujimoto, 1991; Nevens et al., 1990). Although informative, these insights do not reveal enough about the barriers that noninnovative firms must deal with to become innovative.

To explore the problems with sustained product innovation in large, mature firms, we examined 40 product/service innovations in 15 very large firms. We found that most of these firms were not organized to facilitate innovation: occasionally innovation did occur, but it occurred in spite of the system, not because of it. We also found that product innovation is a fragile and vulnerable activity. We develop new theory to explain why inability to sustain product innovation is so deeply engrained in these large, mature organizations and to identify the organization-wide changes that must be made before they can become consistently innovative over time.

INNOVATION PROBLEMS

Two levels of problems are associated with innovation: those affecting a particular project and those affecting the organizational context. At the level of the particular product, problems include positioning the product strategically in the market, developing production, marketing, and sales, securing expertise, managing external relations (Kazanjian, 1988), understanding new markets (Cooper, 1983; Leonard-Barton, 1991), forming multifunctional teams and sharing knowledge (Ancona & Caldwell, 1990; Dougherty, 1992), and evaluating progress (Griffin & Page, 1993). When project-level problems are resolved across multiple innovations and multiple stages simultaneously, sustained innovation can occur. Such problem solving occurs at the organizational level. According to Sykes, "Successful new ventures usually focus on a single product. Successful mature corporations must learn to manage the complexities of multiple products, [making] older products obsolete" (1986: 74).

The challenge of connecting innovations with routine operations has long been noted (Burns & Stalker, 1961; Kanter, 1983). Structures and strategies in mature organizations reinforce existing practices and, according to Hlavacek and Thompson (1973), are "hostile to creativity" (Burgelman, 1983; Dougherty, 1990; Meyer, 1982). The inertia of current practice can overwhelm concerted efforts to change (Hannan & Freeman, 1984; Johnson, 1988). One solution is to put new products into separate venture units (Hlavacek & Thompson, 1973; Galbraith, 1982). Unfortunately, new products are inextricably bound up with the rest of an organization, so avoiding the connections is not a real solution. Fast (1978) found that new product ventures failed because they no longer fit with a corporation's strategic posture, or their political positions eroded so they were rejected by the existing power structure. In a postmortem of Exxon's venture division, Sykes (1986) also found that the failure to connect internal ventures to mainstream operations was central to the division's demise.

The literature suggests that for a mature organization to develop the capacity for sustained innovation, it must successfully make these innovation-to-organization connections in three key areas: (1) make resources available for new products, (2) provide collaborative structures and processes to solve problems creatively and connect innovations with existing businesses, and (3) incorporate innovation as a meaningful component of the organization's strategy. These three categories are not exhaustive, but they do focus attention on important organization-level problem areas. We briefly describe how these three connections can be made in ideal terms, and then suggest why they remain problematic for mature organizations.

Resources

An organization with both innovation projects and mature businesses ideally will have a resource system that channels money, equipment, expertise, and information to all these activities simultaneously. This resource system should also nurture new ideas and continuously raise and solve problems (Kanter, 1983). These resources should not rely on the availability of slack (extra padding, or a looseness in normal practice; Singh, 1986); rather, they should be deliberately distributed to foster innovation. Pockets of seed money should exist throughout the organization so that ideas have multiple chances for development (Jelinek & Schoonhoven, 1990). Market and customer information should flow throughout (Moorman, 1995), and innovators should be able to access necessary expertise from all functions to resolve design and manufacturing problems and to test ideas against market and operating constraints (Dougherty, 1992; Souder, 1987). Major resource systems like manufacturing facilities and sales channels should be specifically designed so that new products can be included readily (Wheelright & Clark, 1992).

Unfortunately, resources do not always flow smoothly to innovation, particularly where prevailing practice supports established activities (e.g.,

Henderson & Clark, 1990). Many writers have suggested the use of product champions and networks of entrepreneurial roles and relationships to facilitate the flow of resources to innovations (Ancona & Caldwell, 1990; Maidique, 1980; Roberts, 1988; Schon, 1963). However, in large, mature organizations champions may be too busy keeping an idea alive to generate adequate managerial and budgetary support, as Burgelman (1983) found in a case study of innovation in a chemicals firm. A new product project may not connect with supporting assets unless someone with substantial power steps in to strengthen its position, as Day (1994) found in a large survey of established firms.

Collaborative Structures and Processes

Each innovation project also needs administrative structures and processes appropriate to its development stage and access to decision making across the organization. An organization should have structures and processes designed to make decisions continually, to follow through on problems, and to bring new issues to the ongoing agenda (Jelinek & Schoonhoven 1990). Multifunctional teams should be put in place early on for each innovation, and committees and task forces should work through technical problems faced by multiple projects and incorporate all the new products into the organization's structure and processes (Van de Ven, 1986; Wheelwright & Clark, 1992). These collaborative structures and problem-solving processes should connect laterally and vertically, so that people throughout the organization can participate in selecting, defining, and refining innovations across functions, product lines, and divisions (Kanter, 1983, 1988; Quinn, 1985). Regular operations reviews should be held to raise issues, renegotiate targets, and assure disciplined follow-up so that people deliver on promised goals (Brock & Macmillan, 1993; Jelinek & Schoonhoven, 1990).

Unfortunately, structures and processes in mature organizations are often not designed for organization-wide collaboration and problem solving. Instead, a segmentalist orientation exists, leading managers to break tasks down and then assign them to separate units (Hlavacek & Thompson, 1973; Kanter, 1983). The reward system punishes people for stepping out of established work roles, as Quelch, Farris, and Olver (1987) found in a sample of packaged goods firms. Certain departments dominate the innovation process despite the existence of formal multifunctional teams and committees, as Workman (1993) found in a large computer manufacturer. Organizational routines limit interfunctional interaction and inhibit the development of customer understanding, as Dougherty (1990) found in five mature firms.

Strategic Value and Meaning

Finally, innovators must tap into existing competencies and assets if they are to build on know-how, take advantage of unique resources, and create new competencies (Day, 1994; Leonard-Barton, 1992). These assets and their supporting processes should themselves change to accommodate new products so, ideally, innovations and the organization mutually "constitute" one another over time (Leonard-Barton, 1988). Van de Ven (1986) called this connection the parts-whole relation, and Kanter (1988) called it managing institutional relations: ideally, an organization's strategy explicitly values innovation, openly welcomes initiative, and clearly rewards those who successfully resolve problems. The constituent activities of innovation (such as understanding markets and tracking technological change) should be understood as appropriate activities for all organization members (Dougherty, 1992). Senior managers should set the strategic direction but involve people well down in the organizational hierarchy to solve problems and to create assessment criteria (Quinn, 1985). Involvement helps people understand their part in the innovation process and creates a shared responsibility for success (Jelinek & Schoonhoven, 1990). Involvement also legitimates the role of middle managers in setting the strategic agenda, which in turn energizes them (Westley, 1990).

Unfortunately, innovations are often excluded from an organization's strategy and are not part of senior management's agenda (Burgelman, 1983). Studies show a correlation between a lack of strategic connection and innovation failure (e.g., Cooper & Kleinschmidt, 1987). Dougherty and Heller (1994) found that the activities of product innovation were illegitimate in large, mature firms, either violating prevailing norms or falling into a vacuum; no shared understanding existed to make them meaningful. Successful innovators reframed prevailing patterns of thinking and acting to incorporate their new products; however, this reframing only embraced those particular products. Looking at the same data, Frost (1994) argued that reframing needs an atmosphere of trust to allow people to experiment with different ways of seeing things. What was missing in the organizations studied by Dougherty and Heller was, he suggested, the ability to create meaning for new products that enabled others to understand them.

This brief review of organization-level problems with resource acquisition, collaboration, and strategic meaning and value indicates that large, mature organizations often privilege existing businesses over new products, avoid uncertainty in favor of the tried and true, and emphasize control over flexibility and creativity. Although these problems are not new (cf. March & Simon, 1958), our purpose is to understand why organizations that are attempting to become more innovative still fall prey to them. Why can't they connect product innovations with their resources, structures, and strategies effectively? By answering these questions, we can understand why and how these problems persist, and suggest how organizations can resolve them.

METHODS

We used in-depth interviews with 134 innovators in 15 large, mature organizations to explore whether and how resources flowed to innovation projects, whether and how structures connected the innovations to ongoing work in other functions, divisions, and managerial levels, and whether and how innovation projects became embodied in the organizations' strategies. As noted, firms averaged 96 years of age, 54,000 employees, and $9.4 billion (U.S.) in annual revenue: these are very large, very mature organizations. All had dominated at least several niches in their markets for decades but, at the time of the study, faced heightened competition and technological change, which, according to senior managers we interviewed, altered the nature of their businesses and pushed them to rethink the manner in which they worked.

Table 1 summarizes the 15 firms in the study. Four are in different sectors of the chemicals industry, 2 are in consumer packaged goods, and the rest are in various industrial and service industries. The variety of industry types assures that the findings do not relate only to specific industries. The firms were also undergoing different degrees of change when the interviews were held. Some were in the midst of major downsizings or mergers, and others were relatively stable. The firms also varied on their experiences with innovation: some had been trying to be more innovative for several years; others were just beginning. Thirteen were headquartered in the United States, 1 in Canada, and 1 in the United Kingdom. By agreement with the participants, none of the firms can be identified, so Table 1 presents the years since founding and total revenues in multiples of ten. Only 2 organizations had been founded less than 50 years ago, and only 2 generated less than $1 billion in annual revenue. We interviewed six or more people in 12 of the 15 firms and learned about at least two different kinds of product efforts in all but 1 of them.

Within these 15 organizations, we selected 40 cases of new product development[1] for in-depth study. All the new products were intended for unfamiliar markets or used unfamiliar technologies, and all were either still under development or had recently been canceled. All had been officially approved by senior management. To learn about each case, we interviewed people who worked directly on the project. We interviewed participants from different departments in all but 5 of the 40 cases, where we had access to only one participant. (In another 3 cases, only one person was involved in the product.) Interviewees averaged nine years of tenure within their firms and came from the sales, engineering, manufacturing, marketing, and accounting functions.

The interviews focused on people's understandings of a new product's development, including its connection with the organization's resources, structures and processes, and strategy. All the interviews followed a common protocol: we initially asked people to tell the story of the product so that they would not feel constrained by inappropriate or irrelevant questions. As the interviews progressed, we asked more specific questions, asking people to describe what they knew about the market and technology and how they

[1] For the sake of simplicity, we use the term "new products" to refer to all cases, even though some of the products did not get out into the market.

TABLE 1
Summary of Firms in Study

Firms and Principal Products	Industry	Firm Age in Years	Firm Size: Annual Revenue[a]	Number of People Interviewed	Number of Innovation Projects Studied	Status of Projects after 2-Year Follow-Up
FLOWCO Chemicals used in industrial processing	Chemicals	>80	>$5	8	3	2 in development; 1 in market, status unclear
CHEMCO Chemicals from commodities to plastics, and equipment	Chemicals	>120	>$20	16	4	1 success; 2 in market, status unclear; 1 canceled
LUBECO Specialty chemicals for industrial processing	Chemicals	>70	<$1	7	3	2 in development; 1 failed
UTILCO Industrial gases	Chemicals	>90	>$10	7	2	2 in market, status unclear
FOODCO Consumer food products, packaged goods	Packaged goods	>60	>$20	8	2	1 success; 1 in market, status unclear
PACKCO Consumer food products, packaged goods	Packaged goods	>60	>$5	15	2	1 success; 1 canceled
PAPCO Paper products and office supplies	Paper	>90	>$5	10	3	3 in market, status unclear
BUILDCO Building products, supplies for industrial and residential uses	Building products	>80	>$10	6	2	2 in development
MACHCO Industrial machinery and equipment	Machinery	>70	>$10	10	4	1 in market, status unclear; 1 in development; 1 canceled; 1 failed

TABLE 1 (continued)

Firms and Principal Products	Industry	Firm Age in Years	Firm Size: Annual Revenue[a]	Number of People Interviewed	Number of Innovation Projects Studied	Status of Projects after 2-Year Follow-Up
DOCCO						
Office equipment	Office equipment	>30	>$10	4	3	1 success; 2 in development
INFOCO						
Computers	Computers	>100	>$20	2	1	1 in development
OPCO						
Telephone operations	Telephone	>100	>$10	6	2	1 in market, status unclear; 1 canceled
DATCO						
Financial reports, industry summaries	Information service	>80	>$10	4	3	2 in market, status unclear; 1 in development
BANKCO						
Banking services, bonds	Finance	>30	<$2	16	4	1 success; 1 in market, status unclear; 1 in development; 1 failed
CONSCO						
Engineering consulting	Consulting	>50	<$1	11	2	2 in market, status unclear

[a] In billions of U.S. dollars.

TABLE 2
New Product Cases by Current Status and Innovativeness[a]

Innovativeness[b]	Success	In Market, Status Not Clear	In Development	Canceled In Development	Failed
Low					
Unfamiliar in one or two ways	Bond (3) Food item (7) Document system (2)	Bond (8) Information package (2)	Bond (1) Information package (1)		Bond (4)
Medium					
Unfamiliar in three ways	Food item (3) Chemical (4)	Rock crusher (2) Document system (5) Office product (4) Chemical (2) Chemical (3) Information package (1) Food item (5) Chemical (3) Communication system (4) Plastic (6)	Specialty chemical (1) Lubricant (3) Building product (1) Machine (4) Solvent (4) Office machine (1)		Specialty chemical (3)
High					
Unfamiliar in four or five ways		Medical system (2) Expert system (4) Expert system (7) Warehouse system (1)	Medical product (3) Computing system (2) Robot (5) Office machine (1)	Communication system (2) Site management system (2) Waste remediation (4) Food item (10)	Operating system (4)

[a] The numbers in parentheses indicate the number of individuals interviewed for a project. The 5 successful products come from 5 different firms; the 16 in-market products, from 10 different firms; the 12 in-development products, from 8 different firms; the 4 canceled products, from 4 different firms; and the 3 failed products, from 3 different firms. The status of the cases is therefore not a result of firm affiliation.

[b] The five ways in which a product could be innovative were new users, new uses, new product technology, new manufacturing, new distribution.

got the necessary resources, how they worked with other departments and divisions, and whether the firm had helped or hindered the innovation. Eleven people described products that had already been canceled, and 123 described products still in development. To capture insight into changes over time, we conducted 98 follow-up interviews two years after the first round. We used these follow-up interviews to establish the commercial status of the products that had not already failed at the time of the first interview. In the first round, most people presented their innovation as a winner, but two years later we found only five clear successes.

Table 2 gives the number of people interviewed for each product and the product's degree of innovativeness and commercial success at the time of the follow-up. Of the 37 products that did not fail, 5 were commercially successful, 16 were in the market but their fate was uncertain, 12 were still in development, and 4 had been canceled.

The data set is notable for its size and richness. Since our focus was on sustained innovation and large, mature firms, we deliberately developed a theoretical sample (rather than a random one) that includes only firms with long histories of stable practices to gain a rich, in-depth look at this type of organizational context. Even the computer manufacturer in our sample had roots going back more than 100 years, and the rather young banking firm had been in a very regulated portion of that industry for all of its history. The 40 new products also varied so we could compare the experiences of those working on different kinds of innovations.

The data set obviously has limitations. These firms do not represent all large, old firms, or all firms in their industries, and these cases do not represent the population of product innovations. We view the connection between the innovations and the organizations only through the descriptions of those who worked on the innovations and do not have the insights of functional and senior managers. These limits impose constraints on the interpretation of results and suggest interesting topics for subsequent research; both issues are taken up in the Discussion section.

DATA ANALYSIS

Qualitative researchers generally use two approaches to data analysis: an in-depth analysis of data to uncover key themes, and an analysis of how strongly the proposed themes feature in the data (Miles & Huberman, 1984; Sutton & Callahan, 1987). We used both and added an initial overview because our data set was so large.

Overview

We began with a description of the extent to which the innovators we interviewed accessed resources, worked collaboratively across the organization, and developed the strategic meaning of their projects. First we categorized the problems discussed in all 134 interviews into one of those three areas of connection (resources, collaboration, and strategic meaning), and into a level (within-project or project-to-organization). Next, we coded the problems as solved or not solved (see the Appendix for details on codes and coding procedures). Within-project problems concerned issues that could be resolved within or by a product's team, such as working with people from another function (e.g., getting the "guys in the warehouse" to insert extra material) and defining a product to fit the targeted market. Project-to-organization problems involved reaching across major organizational boundaries, such as working with another business unit and determining whether a product fit the company's strategy.

These problems are normal in the sense that they can be expected to arise during most innovations. Previous research suggested that people in all types of innovations described roughly the same number of problems, so the quantity of problems per se did not distinguish success from failure (Dougherty & Heller, 1994). Rather, the key to effectiveness appeared to be problem solution. Figure 1 compares the average proportions of problems solved by the successful innovators and the others.[2] Successful innovators solved an average of 57 percent of their problems, and others solved only 37 percent.[3] We infer that the proportion of problems solved indicates more effective innovation.

Our concern was not with the success or failure of individual cases but with whether organizations could sustain innovation continuously. Thus, we compared the proportion of problems that were solved for all three areas of connection at both the within-project and project-to-organization levels. As Figure 2 indicates, successful innovators solved a much higher proportion of problems at the within-project level than the other innovators: they acquired more resources, more often built effective interfunctional teams, and conceptualized their products more thoroughly. However, successful innovators did not solve more project-to-organization level problems,[4] indi-

[2] Inductive research should use exploratory data analysis techniques such as boxplots, because no hypothesis tests or random data are involved. We used inferential statistics instead, but only as a shorthand way to compare and contrast various groups in our data. The probability that the groups are different provides some, albeit indirect, insight into the variation around the means for the groups.

[3] We excluded the innovators involved with already-failed products from all analyses. These people described very few solved problems, but since they were the only ones in the data set who were looking back, their reports may have been biased. If they were included, the differences in rate of solution between the successful innovators and others would be larger but, we think, inflated. The first bar of Figure 1 excludes the failed innovators. The second bar of Figure 1 excludes innovators working on very innovative products and those in the early stages of development, since the successful category contained no cases with these attributes, and people in both these groups had lower solution rates. Again, we see that the successful innovators still solved more problems (57% vs. 39%), so degree of innovativeness and stage of product development do not account for the difference. The third bar shows the figures from the first line averaged by case first, and they are virtually the same (55 percent solution for successes versus 35 percent for the others).

[4] When we control for innovators working on very innovative projects or those in early stages, the difference in the rate of solution of resource problems at the project level becomes

FIGURE 1
Proportion of Problems Solved by Project Success[a, b]

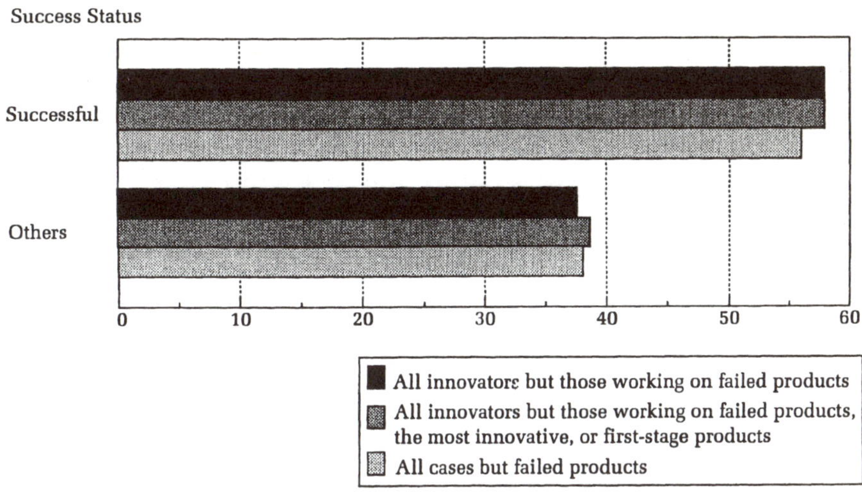

[a] One-tailed tests of the differences between successful cases and others are significant for the first two comparisons (p = .004, .02, and .13, respectively).
[b] For the three comparisons, n = 16 vs. 102, 16 vs. 54, and 5 vs. 32, respectively.

cating that all innovators had considerable difficulty establishing effective working relationships with senior managers, getting cooperation from other divisions, and improving risk-averse climates. Those innovators who had managed to get their new products effectively designed and launched had done so without organizational support.

The successful cases in our data illustrate the effects of limited organizational support on the ability to sustain innovation. In 3 of the 5 firms with successful cases, the special units that housed the new products were eliminated over the subsequent two years. In our follow-up interviews, people at these three firms said that management had shifted its attention to cost containment. For example, the marketing manager of a successful new product commented on FOODCO's shutdown of the new product unit:

> In the process of [a merger with another firm] there was a number of upper management changes which gave conflicting signals in regard to the viability of new products . . . the new regime is much more conservative and less willing to try new things.

---

nonsignificant (the averages are 53 versus 39 percent instead of 32 percent). When we average the results by case first, this difference gets quite small (the other two project-level comparisons are still significantly different, even with case averages). It may be that getting resources at the project level was problematic as well, so this activity requires deeper examination.

FIGURE 2
Proportion of Problems Solved by Problem Level and Project Success

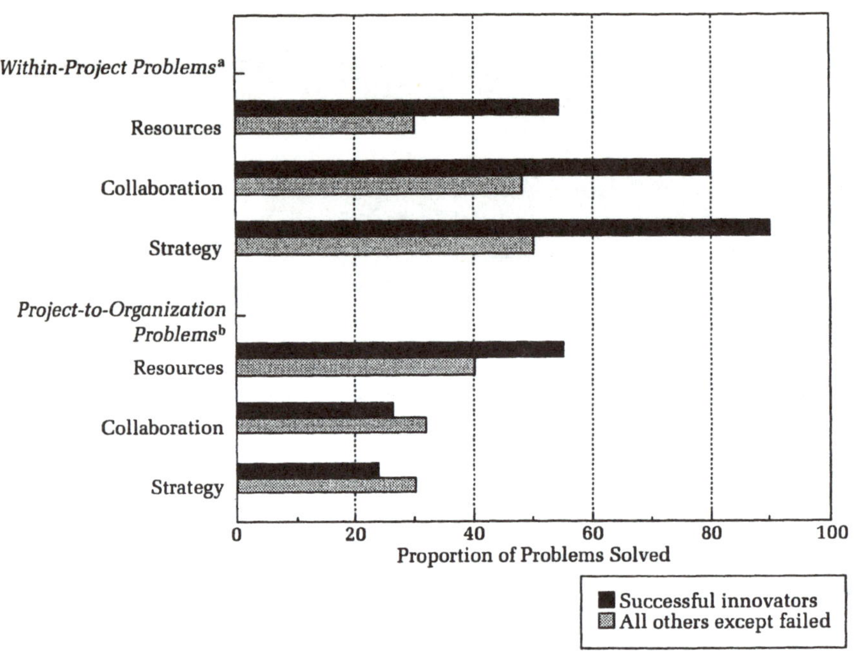

[a] One-tailed *t*-tests of differences in within-project problem solving are significant (*p*'s range from .07 to .02).

[b] One-tailed *t*-tests show no significant differences in project-to-organization problem solving.

> Despite its success, this [multiple new product] process was a one-time-only endeavor.

Similarly, when one of us met the vice president for market research at PRODCO about two years later, he confirmed that the new products group in his firm had been closed as well, in favor of more conservative operations, although he had wanted the group to continue. What happened to the successful products lends support to our inference (developed more fully below) that product innovations occurred in spite of the organizations, not because of them, and were only occasional events rather than part of a sustained process.

In-Depth Analysis

Our next step developed a richer appreciation for why none of the innovation teams in our study readily showed project-to-organization connection problems. Following the methodology described by Bailyn (1977) and by Strauss (1987), we first examined a number of these problem descriptions in detail, to identify the underlying factors that made them so difficult. Mintzberg (1979b) refers to such an analysis as "detective work" designed to trace down patterns and consistencies. We thoroughly scrutinized interviews from several cases, writing out problems and how they were solved, if they were. We then examined problem descriptions from other interviews to revise and elaborate our initial ideas in light of this additional evidence. The interplay between the data and the emerging patterns continued until the patterns were refined into adequate conceptual categories (Bailyn, 1977; Eisenhardt, 1989a.) We do not assume that our findings perfectly match all products in our data set, or that we have considered every possible explanation. Our goal was to identify common themes, so we concentrated on common resource, collaboration, and strategic meaning issues among the cases (Sutton & Callahan, 1987; Van Maanen, 1983). Our themes fit with our data but, as is the case in quantitative research, not all of the variation is explained.

Before presenting illustrations from the product cases, we summarize our findings. First, we found that where individual innovation projects were successful, they depended on the efforts of particular individuals to use their organizational positions (e.g., Brass, 1984) to further and protect innovation efforts: they did not result from an organization-wide commitment to innovation. In the organizations in our study, innovation was not the responsibility of the organization as a whole. Sometimes individuals were able to resolve project-to-organization connection problems successfully by accessing resources, establishing collaborative processes, and creating strategic meaning for their innovation. But connections made in this way were fragile and vulnerable, because they depended on the initiatives of the incumbents of specific positions (usually in middle management) and their particular networks rather than on organization-wide systems. In any event, positions per se did not guarantee connections since they did not carry much weight in other divisions. Individuals also drew on their own networks and reputations, but often networks did not reach far enough to solve specific issues—for instance, a network might not enable an individual to get a particular sales force to carry a new product. Some innovators were either too new or had spent too much time in only one function to have networks in the first place. In fact, the prevailing organizational systems encouraged conformity and stability.

Second, innovators had only piecemeal access to the necessary resources, had limited structures and processes to work with, and faced tenuous strategic connections for innovation across their organizations. These findings are consistent with Fast's (1978). However, rather than conclude that the strategic support and political positions of the ventures eroded over time, as did Fast, we suggest that innovations never had strategic support or power in the first place. Innovation had little positive, strategic meaning in these organizations. Innovators could rarely get people in different functions, divisions, or hierarchical levels to comprehend their role in making innovation happen. People not directly involved with an innovation did not seem to know what they should do to help out, or even that they should help out. Innovation was not simply suppressed, it was unseen; it was ignored and invisible in a wider organizational community that could not understand its role.

Third, we infer that strategic support from senior management was nonexistent or only temporary. Except for one company, we found no attempt to embed innovation into the decision premises, day-to-day web of understandings, and taken-for-granted rules that make activities meaningful (Drazin & Sandelands, 1992; Pettigrew, 1979). In most of the firms, senior managers made other concerns, such as mergers, performance pressures, or downsizing, more meaningful. Innovation was not only cut adrift, it was canceled. Consequently, successful innovation was merely a one-time event, not a sustained, continuous process supported by an organization-wide commitment.

We turned to a more systematic comparison to see if other attributes of the cases or firms explained differences in the proportion of problems solved, comparing two extreme subsets of cases—the 10 with the highest average proportion of project-to-organization problems solved and the 10 with the lowest average proportion of such problems solved. Table 3 shows this comparison. In the 10 cases with the most project-to-organization problems solved, the rate of solution ranges from 100 to 56 percent, and in the bottom 10 it ranges from 17 to 0 percent (8 have 0 percent). The table also lists additional attributes, such as each product's success status, degree of innovativeness, and company. The company may affect the extent of problem solving. Two of the cases in the top 10 are from DOCCO, which, interviews suggested, had developed a more systematic approach to managing innovation and resembled the ideal type. In addition, 3 of the bottom 10 cases come from BANKCO, which had only recently begun innovation attempts. With regard to the other attributes, however, the top and bottom 10 cases in Table 3 do not differ a great deal. On the basis of this comparison, we suggest that the problems described below are fairly well distributed across our data.

ILLUSTRATIONS OF KEY THEMES

In this section, we illustrate the key themes. We show that innovation owed much to the efforts of individuals who used their organizational positions to acquire resources, establish collaborative processes and structures, and create strategic meaning for individual projects. We demonstrate that these innovative efforts were, however, one-time events: they occurred in spite of organizational systems, not because of them, and were, accordingly, fragile and vulnerable rather than parts of a sustained process. Finally, we describe a particular problem in these organizations: the difficulties in creating organization-wide strategic meaning and value for innovation.

TABLE 3
Cases Classified by Proportion of Solved Project-to-Organization Problems

Case Number	Product	Percentage of Problems Solved	Company	Success Status	Degree of Innovativeness	Stage of Development
Top 10—Most project-to-organization problems solved						
1	Chemical	100	LUBCO	In development	Medium	Middle
2	Document system	100	DOCCO	Success	Low	Middle
3	Lubricant	83	FLOWCO	In development	Medium	Middle
4	Engineering plastic	80	CHEMCO	In market, unclear	Medium	Middle
5	Building product	75	BUILDCO	In development	Low	Middle
6	Medical system	68	CHEMCO	In development	High	Middle
7	Engine	67	MACHCO	In market, unclear	Medium	End
8	Office machine	60	DOCCO	In development	Medium	Middle
9	Robot	56	BUILDCO	In development	High	Middle
10	Food item	56	FOODCO	Success	Medium	End
Bottom 10—Fewest project-to-organization problems solved						
31	Office machine	17	DOCCO	In development	High	Middle
32	Waste remediation	3	CHEMCO	Canceled	High	Middle
33	Information package	0	DATCO	In development	Medium	Middle
34	Information package	0	DATCO	In development	Low	End
35	Chemical	0	LUBECO	Failed	Medium	End
36	Lubricant	0	LUBECO	In development	Medium	Middle
37	Computing system	0	INFOCO	In development	High	Middle
38	Bond	0	BANKCO	Successful	Low	Middle
39	Bond	0	BANKCO	In market, unclear	Low	Middle
40	Bond	0	BANKCO	Failed	Low	End

Resources

To understand difficulties in acquiring resources, we looked closely at the problems innovators had working with senior managers and gaining access to resources in other functions or divisions. In the high-problem-solution cases in Table 3, at least some resources were available, but they were not deliberately designated to support innovation, existing more as slack that innovators could only access by working their networks. Innovators called on acquaintances developed during a lifetime with a firm and used position and location (for instance, as head of a lab or of an office at corporate headquarters) to beg, borrow, or steal resources. A corporate planner with more than 25 years of experience at CHEMCO (case 4 in Table 3) described how he provided a young researcher with access to senior managers, who in turn provided support to develop a new engineering plastic material:

> This material has unique properties—it can be molded very easily but the molecules line up tightly in one direction so the material is strong as steel in that direction. So I told the executive vice president that I had a gut feel that we had a success here. I set up a couple of reviews where Jim [the researcher] would come in and talk to the VP. They hit it off very well, and Fred [the VP] thinks Jim is very clever.

The planner then worked his own networks further to keep the project funded:

> Fred and I would meet in the men's room, and I'd drop little hints, like "Gee, we're looking at new breakthroughs," or "Hey, all 21 claims on the patent were approved." Then I worked with the research management at the lab to convince them to fund this.

His descriptions of events show how he used his corporate staff position, reputation, and acquaintances around CHEMCO to nurture this new initiative and to generate support. Later on, the project was officially sanctioned and a project leader was formally appointed. But the new project leader saw most of his resources stripped away almost immediately, as he explained:

> In September I was brought back from London and given the job to bring the product out, and a budget of several million dollars. But then the corporation believed that there would be a recession in the next year, so this project was on the plate to be cut. I was then set up only with R&D in the budget, and everyone else had to commit time on their own.

The new project leader was, however, able to "hustle" resources informally to get around this arbitrary decision from corporate headquarters, as the planner described:

> Jim has done a very good job of convincing people to commit themselves. He was hustling out of the electronics division research, and now almost every division except commodity chemicals and agriculture is involved.

Critical resources were not deliberately provided to assure effective problem resolution. Indeed, even committed funding was removed as the innovation got caught up in routine corporate belt-tightening. Senior managers seemed to expect innovators to survive on their own. Two years later, the project had lost the support of the U.S. marketing group, and the project leader was looking for a new home in Europe.

One might argue that this case demonstrates good championing and boundary spanning (Ancona & Caldwell, 1990; Roberts, 1988) and that these activities are sufficient for successful innovation. However, when we compared the experiences of these savvy old-timers with those of much younger or more marginal innovators working on the hazardous waste remediation project at CHEMCO (case 32 in Table 3), we could see the limits of relying on individuals rather than on organization-wide support. The hazardous waste product was a biology-based approach to toxic waste remediation, and its champion was a young chemical engineer in his late twenties. He had moved from a plant in Alabama to corporate headquarters in the northeastern United States to carry out his plan, so he was willing to take risks. He had received approval to develop the idea from a corporate committee and was told he could have resources from several divisions. However, he could not arrange to get these resources from the divisions in a timely fashion.

Compare his understanding of how things should work with the savvy networking and hustling of his older, wiser CHEMCO colleagues quoted above:

> We presented the plan to the corporate committee in June of last year and got buy-in to build a team as requested. We were given a trial period of two years. All the plans were based on a team being in place by the end of last year, but it's only been in the last three months that I have gotten any people. I am still facing the same deadline, but my 1.5 years has shrunk in half. The past year has been the most frustrating period of my life, trying to get these things off the ground. It turned out that nobody wanted to live up to their commitments. Everyone said: "Gee, we have a manpower shortage. You just wait until the budget is approved." It was the kind of a deal that you feel great when you come out of the room, but all of a sudden the obstacles come up, but only one at a time. You clear one and another comes out. It just wore me out.

He did not know how to acquire resources and was too naive to appreciate the need to do so. Unfortunately, his two team members were equally inexpert: one was new to CHEMCO and the other had worked within corporate R&D only. They also described frustration in not getting resources. Although the organization officially sanctioned these individuals' drawing resources from multiple divisions, it did not provide the means for doing so. The R&D engineer described their difficulties:

> We have zero autonomy over funding and equipment, and no control over the project or who we hire, or even whether we can go on trips. You need to ask two bosses for everything. . . . The basic concept of our being a venture in the first place is to get to market or to a decision point quickly rather than create the normal administrative overhead, but that has not happened. Assume you need a piece of equipment that costs $430,000. I go to the first boss and they all agree that I need it, and they say OK. Then I go to my own manager, and he says that he will only provide money for my salary, not capital expenses. He says,

"Why should we give the other division capital money? We are already doing them a favor by giving them you." Then you go back to the other side and they say "Well, if the project does not work, then the equipment stays with engineering, so why should we buy it?" The decision making is such a lengthy process that has become so complex that it just stops.

During the year following the first interviews, the young champion quit the project, and a year later the project itself was canceled. The product may or may not have been a good idea, but CHEMCO took over five years and made a considerable investment to decide not to proceed. When resources are not systematically available, those without experience or political savvy are at a disadvantage and find it difficult to secure necessary resources. Consequently, their projects suffer regardless of how good they may be.

Even innovators with good networks can encounter difficulties procuring major resources such as assistance from manufacturing. For example, the new engine at MACHCO (case 7 in Table 3) was saved from cancellation by a long-time member of the research staff who used his personal credibility to convince senior managers that the product had merit. He explained

[After the prototype unit fell apart in a demonstration] George White (a VP of the business) called for a total review. There was no question that his plan was to stop it, because MACHCO was losing money at the time and they wanted to cut out anything that did not make sense. I became convinced that we were on the right track but using the wrong mechanism, so I asked George to give us another shot. I promised to have it working in eight weeks, and I did. Then George said he would back us for two years provided we had something ready to sell. We sold the first model in six months.

Although senior managers were willing to support the engineer, he ran into problems because the strong boundaries between the functions at MACHCO prevented the acquisition of manufacturing resources. As the researcher explained,

Manufacturing was not involved with the project because we knew what they would say—no. This product is very difficult to make. I did contact a manufacturing manager and he agreed to meet me out here one Saturday, but that meeting never happened.

Manufacturing was not part of his normal network, so he had no way to procure resources that division controlled. (The manufacturing manager we interviewed about the engine dismissed the project and instead told us about another innovation.) As a result, the engine innovators went to an outside vendor to manufacture a key part. Two years later the follow-up interviews showed that the key part was breaking down in the products already sold and that the project was now in serious jeopardy. The supposed solution to the lack of resources had not worked.

When we examined the bottom 10 cases, we found similar problems with access to resources. For example, 3 of the cases with the lowest number of problem solutions (cases 38–40 in Table 3) come from BANKCO, which was organized in functional departments that had always worked separately and had had no experience with product innovation. Consequently, the resource allocation system had never addressed innovation before. BANKCO formed a new product project management unit and layered it over the very strong functions. However, simply adding a formal structure and giving official notice that all functions should cooperate did not align resources with innovation. To make matters worse, BANKCO was starting to downsize, draining the usual slack from the system. As one employee said

> The biggest obstacle for doing new products is resource constraints. We like to do a hundred things. Right now we are not suffering from an absence of ideas, and bunches of things get on the conveyor belt. You jump on with your product, and there are lots of products right ahead of you. So the obstacles now are selling the idea and making sure that everyone thinks it's a good one.

Comparing the top 10 cases with the bottom 10 cases, we found only differences in the degree of access to resources, not differences in the kind of access; in neither set of cases did the organizations provide access to the necessary resources. Rather, resources were targeted toward established businesses, and individual champions did not have enough power to shift entire systems to solve project-to-organization resource problems. Other individuals were unsuccessful because they were new to the game and lacked adequate networks or had no networks at all. As we examine the question of resources, we see a link to structure and processes: one of the reasons resources were difficult to obtain was that organizational processes also failed to support innovation. Structures and processes nurtured functional fiefdoms and conservative decisions rather than encouraging cross-functional activity and risk taking. The next section examines these processes in more detail.

Collaborative Structures and Processes

We looked for how well structures and processes involved organizational members, both laterally and vertically, in selecting, defining, and refining innovation projects. We found that structures and processes sustained routine work, not innovation. Many of the innovations had teams, but the extensive collaborative processes recommended in the literature were not in evidence. Nor did decision making flow upwards and sideways, nor relate evaluation criteria to innovation.

As we anticipated from the literature, we found that power imbalances played an important role in the lack of collaboration. In some cases, different functions were not equal. Even in DOCCO, the most innovative company in our sample, projects were driven by engineering, and marketing and sales played more marginal roles. Similar technological domination occurred at CHEMCO, even though all the innovations used teams. The salesperson who worked on the engineering plastic (case 4 in Table 3) explained how cross-functional teams were new and still uncomfortable in a firm dominated by science:

> I was assigned to work with these folks even though I am in the sales division. I am an essential member of the team, but this has seldom if ever happened in the past. Me working with these engineers did not come all that easy in a company as hidebound science as we are.

His comment suggests that although collaborative structures existed, they did not really lead to collaborative working processes, because of power imbalances and a lack of commitment to collaboration.

Strong functional boundaries also inhibited innovation. Most of the time, manufacturing people were not included in innovation teams. In the case of the engineering plastic, the hustling project manager had, in fact, angered people at one potential site by attempting to force his way in. The situation was redeemed only because the planner had previous ties to the plant site.

> Jim has the manufacturing people livid. He went in and said: "Don't tell me you can't do it; just tell me what you need and I'll go get it." But the manufacturing guys were all upset that they were not involved earlier. Our manufacturing types like to go by the book, so the problem is still very sensitive. But I know the plant and its culture from my fibers background, so I was able to manipulate around the problem.

So, although cross-functional teams were formed, they were often incomplete and ineffective. And there were no organization-wide mechanisms for weaving new products into ongoing production processes.

Another barrier to effective innovation was a lack of collaborative vertical relationships. Many of the innovators described how their innovations were bumped from agendas and budgets as a matter of course. For example, a chemist at FLOWCO working on a new industrial gas (case 3 in Table 3) explained the lengthy delays in getting his product going as follows:

> I conceived of the need about three years ago. I added an agent to XXX and postulated several possibilities for development. But management is skeptical and they prefer to wait for another budget cycle, or if it is a bad year they turn down a proposal. Last year I transferred over here and made it an objective to get started. Management still held off on buying the equipment, so it took us another three months to buy the furnace. . . . We travel very linearly until we have a winner.

He secured senior management attention and funding only after three years, because FLOWCO did not have a systematic problem-solving process. Innovations often encountered delays and postponements, as day-to-day processes of decision making and budgeting were oriented to routine work, not innovation.

Contrasting these experiences with BANKCO's cases in the bottom 10 in Table 3 again suggests that the primary difference was a matter of degree, not kind. At BANKCO, because innovation was new, processes were aligned with function-based decision making. Not surprisingly, people in the functions did not known how to collaborate when they did start innovating. As one manager explained:

> One problem is the individual functions, which often say that they will not work on a problem until the new products division calls a meeting. There is less interest in new products in some functions, like information systems. They announced in a meeting that the system could not handle the security administration for this product. It is really a matter of personalities, because that department has a single focus. You need power and the ability to push them, but most people don't know how to push them.

In these organizations, then, structures and processes were not designed to channel the kinds of decisions, participation, and problem solving necessary for innovation. Often, there were no workable ways to bring all departments together, to link different levels of hierarchy, or to make meaningful judgments of different projects. "Politics as usual" prevailed because there was no force for change. People often did not know how to collaborate laterally and vertically because collaboration across these boundaries was not part of their day-to-day repertoire of work. Sometimes, individuals in particular positions, with particular expertise and particular networks, could fill this vacuum through their own knowledge of how an organization worked. They were able to bridge departments, engender participation in teams, circumvent restrictive decision criteria, and secure approval from senior levels. Such solutions were, however, highly tenuous because such activity had no meaning for the wider organizational community. So, as our problem of resources led us to examine structures and processes, our discussion of structures and processes leads us to consider strategic connections.

Strategic Value and Meaning

To explore this connection, we examined the fit between the innovations and the firms' strategies, and whether the innovators encountered anti-innovation climates. Our findings show that working out strategic connections was highly problematic, as have the findings of others (Burgelman, 1983; Fast, 1978; Sykes, 1986). Our analysis also suggests why these connections were so difficult: innovation was not valued, so its constituent activities were perceived to be neither legitimate nor part of individuals' responsibilities. Moreover, there were few strategic conversations (cf. Westley, 1990) open to the lower-level people who innovated. Innovation had no permanent or inherent strategic meaning, certainly none that outlived regular changes in senior management. At best, belief in innovation was localized in time or place.

In a number of cases, when senior managers or their attitudes toward innovation changed, support for the projects declined or disappeared entirely. The marketing manager of the new food item at FOODCO (case 10 in Table 3) explained that the team was now spending a good deal of its time reconfirming product specifications and market projections at the behest of senior management, rather than focusing on the market launch and organizing the business:

> The management now are conservative. I think that if this were a year ago, we would not be confronting this conservative concern.

At OPCO, the vice president who sponsored one new project left the firm, and the businesses were restructured into separate market segments. Because of these changes, the project lost its support and was canceled, despite two years of extensive development. The woman in charge of market analyses explained that the new officers involved with the project had no "buy-in" since they were not familiar with all the data that had been developed:

> There has been a change in structure between before and after. The officers of the corporation now had no buy-in. If they had been involved before they would have been living with all the data. The old VP was a supporter. The new VP was not. The official reason for discontinuing the project was that "we have since discovered that customers really do not want [this service]." But that market research never got done.

To be sure, corporate strategies necessarily change, but if the strategic attention span is shorter than the development time of the average innovation, then an organization does not value innovation. In these firms, innovators described open, trusting strategic conversations that suddenly ceased when the management changed. Strategic conversations, when they did occur, were localized events, not part of normal organizational functioning.

In firms in which senior managers did not change so often, people described a risk-averse, short-term focus that clearly did not value innovation. The leader of the new plastic project at CHEMCO explained how this perspective had permeated the shared understanding of the firm's reward system:

> It is difficult for anyone running a big business to get excited about taking money off the bottom line. It is easier for people working here to ride the wave rather than stick their neck out. If

> you do stick your neck out it is either positive or negative. You will either fail or succeed. If you succeed you will not be much better off than if you hadn't done anything, but if you fail, you lose, you are out.

He went on to explain that anyone could take risk at CHEMCO, provided they were willing to take the consequences. Risk was not mediated by the organization.

A project manager at FLOWCO was more pointed about the lack of strategic value for innovation, despite a memo from the president in favor of innovation:

> I am so frustrated with the lack of support from management. A year ago Rick Burns [the president] sent out a memo about being entrepreneurial. So I wrote him back and we had lunch. That gave me an idea on how to talk to management—you have to hold a gun to their heads, and I use his memo to push them to help out.

The project leader for successful document processor at DOCCO (case 2 in Table 3) explained that they had only recently begun to incorporate innovation into their organization systematically. Before, innovation had occurred only occasionally and had not been embedded in the web of everyday meaning, expectation, and conduct:

> Before this project, we would put out a new product every four years. They would appoint a chief engineer (project leader), and he would go around and get people. It would take six months to get a group to coalesce, and a year before they had the team up and running, because you get such in-fighting between the units and divisions. That is the reason that it would take four years to get the product out. So after the project the team would be disbanded, and they would appoint another chief engineer, and he starts all over again.

The project leader described how DOCCO's new system made the practices of innovation meaningful by making them part and parcel of everyone's work:

> Two things have changed. First, we've invested a lot of money in a residency program (with a key foreign division that participates in this product line), so that people can spend time there and learn to work with these people. The team is made up of people with this experience. Second, after we put this team together we will keep it in place. By keeping a constant team in place, I have a lot of talent and a lot of depth. All of my team is seasoned, and the average age is 47, so they know where all the bodies are buried. These people are not fast trackers, but they can do things in a day that takes other people weeks.

BANKCO had never developed strategic conversations of any kind, since senior managers did not work with operations-level people on innovations. Instead, the operations-level people constantly had to negotiate and renegotiate support from a subordinate position. The person managing the new product efforts pointed out that setting up good teams was not enough: senior managers got in the way of innovation because they did not understand or believe in it. Contrasting BANKCO with another company at which she had worked, she suggested that innovation had no meaning for BANKCO's officers:

> The task force members take the product back to their departments for review, but the department officers could reject the product for no good reason. At BANKCO we have officers coming out of the woodwork. The are like a pantheon of gods who sit over here and say no. So you can't just get all the right people on the task force, because making innovation happen is not only a matter of that. At XCO, where I had worked before, things were more understood, it was more understood by everyone what was going to happen, so you could get new projects through. Here at BANKCO, there is no sense that people understand what we are trying to do with innovation, and no personnel policies that support it.

So, although product innovation was officially sanctioned at BANKCO, how and why it fit into the organization was not understood. Senior department heads still decided issues in favor of routine practice. In such a situation, strategic conversations may ostensibly occur between senior and middle managers, but they do not address the fundamental issues. They are either concerned with etiquette and status (i.e., people having to prove their eligibility to participate in the conversation), or they are briefing sessions in which senior managers are brought up to speed on a particular project that they do not really understand. In both cases, innovation has no strategic meaning.

Ideally, innovation should be integrated into an organization's strategy, the rules governing eligibility should be clean, the background information should be well known, and senior managers should take on the responsibility of sponsorship, helping champions to access resources and processes. In that situation, a strategic conversation can address key issues of content. But this was not the case with our sample. New products were excluded from the strategic thinking that was driving restructuring and performance evaluation. Consequently, product innovation took a back seat to other initiatives. Without strategic meaning, product innovation, with all its attendant risks and uncertainty, is particularly tenuous and fragile, and easily rooted out. When meaning is lost, processes and resources unravel as well.

AN ANTI-INNOVATION ORGANIZATIONAL CONFIGURATION

Our findings suggest that even when product innovation did occur, it did so in spite of organizational systems and only because of the unstinting efforts of individuals who bucked the system. Only in one case, DOCCO's document system, were resources really available, collaborative processes in place, and strategic meaning and value attached to innovation, in anything like the ideal organizational configuration recommended in the literature.

The experiences of the four other successful cases add further support for our contention that these organizations were configured against innovation: innovation had to be created and sustained by the innovators themselves, who succeeded only by walling themselves off from the anti-innovation configuration in the rest of the organization, in separate new product units. These units created bubbles of innovation meaning that approached the ideal type, where innovation had legitimacy and value in the eyes of the participants. These bubbles were self-contained, micro configurations in which resources, processes, and meaning were aligned with innovation. For example, the manufacturing manager with the successful product at FOODCO described how his team generated a sense of legitimacy for innovation by working apart:

> I have been involved with a lot of different development projects, because that has been my job. But this project is very different, in that we have much more authority and responsibility, and make more of our own decisions. The team sits as a group to make decisions, which gives us more responsibility. . . . No one is really in our way, because we make our own decisions.

The senior scientist who worked on the successful chemical at CHEMCO also attributed the group's success to its separation from management:

> Our top management should get a lot of the credit for this because they set us up and then left us totally alone.

These bubbles were vulnerable, however. First, most of the top 10 problem-solving cases (Table 3) were managed by old-timers; 3 of the bottom 10 were managed by young people who had only a few years experience with their firms, and 3 were in BANKCO, which, as we have illustrated, was new to innovation. People with more tenure in firms solved more project-to-organization problems than others (the difference was statistically significant) by drawing on their deep familiarity with their organizations. Their expertise and extensive networks of relationships in the firms enabled them to cajole resources, to cross major functional and divisional boundaries, and to gain legitimacy from senior managers. Projects managed by organizational neophytes were particularly vulnerable because they lacked political savvy and credibility and had yet to develop personal networks. Second, 9 of the 10 cases in Table 3 occurred in companies that were stable during the time of the interviews, and 4 of the bottom 10 were in companies undergoing extensive downsizing. Downsizing usually means fewer resources, as innovation is supplanted by cost cutting and reporting relationships and networks are disrupted.

In summary, the anti-innovation configuration of resources, processes, and meaning in these firms made sustained innovation very unlikely, and even separate innovation projects were vulnerable. When things got tough, the power available to innovators (knowledge, networks, contacts, and so forth) was rarely adequate to counter the power embedded in the organizational systems, which were aligned to prevent innovation. To develop the capability for sustained innovation, large, mature organizations cannot focus simply on the management of individual projects. They must also create organization-wide systems that weave together innovations and existing operations.

DISCUSSION: THE POWER OF ORGANIZATIONAL CONFIGURATION

This study has enabled us to move beyond the idea that large, mature organizations have difficulty with sustained innovation and to explain more precisely why this is so. The study is limited and does not take into account all organization-level problems. Nonetheless, we found that large, mature organizations could not achieve sustained innovation because innovators within them could not solve innovation-to-organization problems. The availability of resources, processes, and meaning was piecemeal in most of the organizations, and it depended primarily on individuals rather on the organizational system. Product innovation, when it did occur successfully, was powered by the operational and middle levels of the organizational hierarchies and based largely on the particular networks, connections, and experiences of lower-level managers. But rather than celebrate lone champions and other individual heroes, we suggest, as did Schon (1963), that primary reliance on such personal power is inherently ineffective for sustained innovation. Such power is limited by the reach of individual networks, knowledge, and experience and is easily uprooted by downsizing, restructuring, and changes in senior managerial focus. Moreover, it is unavailable to young people and newcomers who lack experience with an organization, as well as to people in organizations that have no history of building informal systems to get around formal ones.

We do not dispute that power is an integral part of product innovation. Product innovation does not happen spontaneously or magically—power is needed to facilitate, orchestrate, and shape it (Frost & Egri, 1991). According to Kanter, "What it takes to get the innovative organization up and running is essentially the same two things all vehicles need: a person in the driver's seat and a source of power" (1983: 216). But our findings suggest that the conceptualization of power must extend beyond the personal and encompass the organizational. For large, mature organizations to become innovative, they must reconfigure the power embedded in the organizational system—in its resources, processes, and meanings. Unless product innovation has an explicit, organization-wide power basis, there is no generative force, no energy, for developing new products continuously and weaving them into ongoing functioning. We agree with both Burns and Stalker (1961) and

Schon (1963): senior managers must alter their organizational systems of power if their organizations are to become capable of sustained product innovation—that is, capable of more than the occasional success.

Unfortunately, discussions of power in the innovation and management literatures tend to emphasize the personal power of individual managers and, more specifically, the power associated with the control of resources (e.g., Pfeffer, 1981; Pfeffer & Salancik, 1974). Accordingly, studies of power focus on individuals' control of such resources as budgets, information, expertise, sanctions, political access, and credibility (e.g., French & Raven, 1968; Pettigrew, 1973). Even work that adopts a departmental perspective (e.g., Hickson, Hinings, Lee, Schneck, & Pennings, 1971) directs attention toward resources—or contingencies—that allow a particular unit to control uncertainty and render itself immune to substitution.

Such work only scratches the surface of power dynamics (see Clegg, 1989; Hardy, 1994; Hardy & Clegg, 1969; Lukes, 1974). For example, Bachrach and Baratz (1962) pointed out that power is also exercised in "nondecision making," by suppressing opposition, keeping it out of decision-making arenas, and confining agendas to safe questions (Crenson, 1972; Hunter, 1980). In other words, power also lies in processes. Traditionally, research has focused on how such power inhibits change and innovation; more recently, however, work has been undertaken that shows how the power embedded in processes can be mobilized to encourage and stimulate change (e.g., Hardy & Redivo, 1994). In addition, power also lies in the deep structure of meaning whereby activities possess or lack legitimacy (Clegg, 1975; Frost, 1987; Hardy, 1985). By managing meaning (Pettigrew, 1979), managers can create momentum for the activities associated with innovation. So, as researchers incorporate these dimensions of power, they can start to see how power can be grounded in an organization, and not just tenuously held in the hands of an individual or even a department. In this way, the concept of power is deepened from its focus on resources to include processes and meaning and broadened from its focus on the individual to encompass the organization.

A quick fix to innovation problems would be for organizations to build up networks of personal power—by, for instance, training champions and sponsors, retaining old timers with networks, knowledge, and expertise, mentoring youngsters and newcomers to help them learn the political ropes, and separating innovations into self-contained new product units. However, the longevity of such a solution is limited so long as innovation remains a foreign body in a system that values the routine. Such a solution is weak especially when downsizing, mergers, and restructurings disrupt networks of personal power and reduce slack resources. We propose, instead, that organizations take a more lasting approach to developing an organization-wide capability for sustained innovation by changing the underlying configuration of power, from a personal network base to an organizational system base.

Without meaning to support product innovation, resources and processes easily unravel. Thus, the power of the meaning supporting innovation is crucial. If senior managers focus on managing the meaning of innovation and make concomitant changes in processes and resources, it is, we suggest, possible for large, mature organizations to become capable of sustained innovation. We know from theory that deep structures like power are tied to micro structures of everyday action (Drazin & Sandelands, 1992; Morgan, 1986). Our analysis suggests that actively targeting the two missing elements of meaning at the day-to-day level of behavior might spearhead a move toward sustained innovation.

First, managers need to make the activities of product innovation more meaningful to people throughout an organization. Altering everyone's understanding will take time, but managers can begin by making sure that nothing contradictory, such as cost control or not rocking the boat, has greater meaning. This step is an essential symbolic move necessary to counter the deep mistrust we found regarding senior management's commitment to innovation. Cost cutting need not be ignored, but it must be redefined to be consistent with product innovation practice. In addition, managers can build in more systematic approaches to working out the kinds of project-to-organization problems we described above, such as acquiring equipment and funding after an annual budget has been finalized, or moving new products into manufacturing more quickly. These systems need not be redesigned to support only innovation, since resources allocated to product families and technology platforms can combine innovation and routine (Wheelright & Clark, 1992). Jelinek and Schoonhoven (1990) showed how manufacturing can emphasize both cost efficiency and new product introduction if manufacturing managers are rewarded properly and given the resources needed to work out the complex interfaces; for example, they need money to fund pilot lines and enough experienced staff to oversee the connections between new and old products.

Second, we showed that these large, mature organizations had few strategic conversations (Westley, 1990) between senior and middle managers in which both sides participated in enacting product innovation and the strategic context that framed it. By actively and deliberately engaging in open strategic conversations around product innovation, senior managers can initiate the recursive process of changing the deep structure of the power configuration and everyday action. The more people participate in these conversations, the more they feel energized. Consequently, innovators must not only be included but also given the opportunity to frame the conversations and steer the choices that are made (see Westley [1990] for more details; see Fiol [1994] for a related analysis). Eisenhardt's (1989b) description of how to make fast strategic decisions suggests that even in "high-velocity" environments, effective managers broaden the number of people involved in strategic conversations.

These two ways of increasing the strategic meaning of innovation can be reinforced by changes in processes and resources. A number of techniques have been developed to marshal what we would call resource and process power behind product innovation (e.g., Nevens et al., 1990; Wheelright & Clark, 1992). If implemented concurrently with changes in the meaning of innovation, processes can begin to link the right people and emphasize the right criteria, and resources can begin to flow to the right places. We think that a shift from an anti-innovation system to a pro-innovation one is feasible, provided that senior managers are willing to mobilize the power of meaning for innovation.

In conclusion, being capable of sustained innovation is not simply a matter of adding procedures, teams, champions, and visionary leaders, although these factors are important. We argue that sustained innovation requires a fundamental shift in the configuration of power in an organization that, in turn, may mean firing senior managers (e.g., Pfeffer & Salancik, 1978). Indeed, the failure to acknowledge the role of power, both in theory and in practice, may be one big reason why researchers and practitioners do not understand the project-to-organization problems with innovation well enough to do much about them.

Deeper study of both innovative and noninnovative organizations is necessary to develop our model for powering innovation. Process studies of organizations that are attempting to change are especially important, because they examine whether and how reconfiguring power enables organizations to become more innovative. The rationales of senior managers in these organizations should also be assessed. Other kinds of mature organizations should be studied to see if the problems we found in our limited sample exist there, and if other issues also exist. Future research should also address the links between market and technological change and organizations. Finally, we have focused only on product innovation; how to organize for other kinds of innovation, and whether that is the same as organizing for product innovation, are important questions. Broadening the scope of the innovation literature to include sustained product and service innovation in large, mature organizations opens up important new frontiers for research.

REFERENCES

Ancona, D., & Caldwell, D. 1990. Beyond boundary spanning: Managing external development in product development teams. ***High Technology Management Research,*** 1(2): 119–136.

Arthur D. Little 1991. ***Worldwide survey on product innovation.*** ADL, 25 Acorn Drive, Cambridge, MA.

Bachrach, P., & Baratz, M. 1962. The two faces of power. ***American Political Science Review,*** 56: 947–952.

Bailyn, L. 1997. Research as a cognitive process: Implications for data analysis. ***Quality and Quantity,*** 11: 97–117.

Brass, D. J. 1984. Being in the right place: A structural analysis of individual influence in an organization. ***Administrative Science Quarterly,*** 29: 518–539.

Brock, Z., & MacMillan, I. 1993. ***Corporate venturing: Creating new businesses within the firm.*** Boston: Harvard Business School Press.

Burgelman, R. 1983. Corporate entrepreneurship and strategic management: Insights from a process study. ***Management Science,*** 29: 1349–1363.

Burns, T., & Stalker, G. M. 1967. ***The management of innovation.*** London: Tavistock.

Clark, K., & Fujimoto, T. 1991. ***Product development performance: Strategy, organization, and management in the world auto industry.*** Boston: Harvard Business School Press.

Clegg, S. 1975. ***Power, rule, and domination.*** London: Routledge.

Clegg, S. 1989. ***Frameworks of power.*** London: Sage.

Cooper, R. 1983. A process model for industrial new product development. ***IEEE Transactions on Engineering Management,*** 30: 2–11.

Cooper, R., & Kleinschmidt, E. 1987. Success factors in product innovation. ***Industrial Marketing Management,*** 16: 215–233.

Crenson, M. 1972. ***The un-politics of air pollution.*** Baltimore: Johns Hopkins University Press.

Day, D. 1994. Raising radicals: Different processes for championing innovative corporate ventures. ***Organization Science,*** 5: 148–172.

Day, G. 1990. ***Market driven strategy: Processes for creating value.*** New York: Free Press.

Dougherty, D. 1990. Understanding new markets for new products. ***Strategic Management Journal,*** 11: 59–78.

Dougherty, D. 1992. A practice-centered model of organizational renewal through product innovation. ***Strategic Management Journal,*** 13: 77–92.

Dougherty, D., & Cohen, M. 1995. Product innovation in mature firms. In B. Kogut & E. Bowman (Eds.), ***Redesigning the firm:*** 87–115. New York: Oxford.

Dougherty, D., & Heller, T. 1994. The illegitimacy of successful new products in large firms. ***Organization Science,*** 5: 200–218.

Drazin, R., & Sandelands L. 1992. Autogenesis: A perspective on the process of organizing. ***Organization Science,*** 3: 230–249.

Eisenhardt, K. 1989a. Building theories from case study research. ***Academy of Management Review,*** 14: 532–550.

Eisenhardt, K. 1989b. Making fast strategic decisions in high-velocity environments. ***Academy of Management Journal,*** 32: 543–576.

Fast, N. 1978. ***The rise and fall of corporate new venture divisions.*** Ann Arbor, MI: UMI Research Press.

Fiol, C. M. 1994. Consensus, diversity, and learning in organizations. ***Organization Science,*** 5: 403–437

French, J., & Raven, B. 1968. The bases of social power. In D. Cartwright & A. Zander (Eds), ***Group dynamics:*** 259–269. New York: Harper & Row.

Frost, P. 1987. Power, politics and influence. In F. M. Tablin, L. Putnam, K. Roberts, & L. Porter (Eds.), ***Handbook of organizational communications:*** 503–548. London: Sage.

Frost, P. 1994. Leading with innovation in mind. ***Creativity and Innovation Management,*** 3: (2): 79–84.

Frost, P., & Egri, C. 1991. The political process of innovation. In L. L. Cummings & B. M. Staw (Eds.), ***Research in organizational behavior,*** vol. 13: 229–295. Greenwich, CT: JAI Press.

Galbraith, J. 1982. Designing the innovating organization. ***Organizational Dynamics,*** 10(3): 5–25.

Glaser, B., & Strauss, A. 1967. ***The discovery of grounded theory: Strategies for qualitative research.*** Chicago: Aldine.

Griffin, A., & Page, A. 1993. An interim report on measuring product development success and failure. ***Journal of Product Innovation Management,*** 10(4): 291–308.

Hage, J. (Ed.) 1988. ***Futures of organizations.*** Lexington, MA: Lexington Books.

Hannan, M., & Freeman, J. 1984. Structural inertia and organizational change. ***American Sociological Review,*** 49: 149–164.

Hardy, C. 1985. ***Managing organizational closure.*** Aldershot, England: Gower Press.

Hardy, C. 1994. ***Managing strategic action: Mobilizing change.*** London: Sage.

Hardy, C., & Clegg, S. R. 1996. Some dare call it power. In S. R. Clegg, C. Hardy, & W. Nord (Eds.), ***Handbook of organization studies:*** 622–641. London: Sage.

Hardy, C., & Redivo, F. 1994. Power and organizational development: A framework for organizational change. ***Journal of General Management,*** 20(2): 1–13.

Henderson, R., & Clark, K. 1990. Architectural innovation: The reconfiguration of existing product technologies and the failure of established firms. ***Administrative Science Quarterly,*** 35: 9–31.

Hickson, D., Hinings, C., Lee, C., Schneck, R., & Pennings, J. 1971. A strategic contingency theory of intraorganizational power. ***Administrative Science Quarterly,*** 16: 216–229.

Hlavacek, J., & Thompson, V. 1973. Bureaucracy and new product innovation. ***Academy of Management Journal,*** 16: 361–372.

Hunter, D. J. 1980. ***Coping with uncertainty.*** Chichester, England: Research Studies Press.

Jelinek, M., & Schoonhoven, C. 1990. ***The innovation marathon: Lessons from high technology firms.*** Oxford: Basil Blackwell.

Johnson, G. 1988. Rethinking incrementalism. ***Strategic Management Journal,*** 9: 75–91.

Kanter, R. 1983. ***The changemasters.*** New York: Simon & Schuster.

Kanter, R. M. 1988. When a thousand flowers bloom. In B. M. Staw and L. L. Cummings (Eds.), ***Research in organizational behavior,*** vol 10: 169–211. Greenwich, CT: JAI Press.

Kazanjian, R. 1988. Relation of dominant problems to stages of growth in technology-based new ventures. ***Academy of Management Journal,*** 31: 257–279.

Leonard-Barton, D. 1988. Implementation as mutual adaptation of technology and organization. ***Research Policy,*** 17: 251–267.

Leonard-Barton, D. 1991. Inanimate integrators: A block of wood speaks. ***Design Management Journal,*** 2:61–67.

Leonard-Barton, D. 1992. Core capabilities and core rigidities: A paradox in managing new product development. ***Strategic Management Journal,*** 13: 111–126.

Lukes, S. 1974. ***Power: A radical view.*** London: Macmillan.

Maidique, M. 1980. Entrepreneurs, champions, and technological innovation. ***Sloan Management Review,*** 21(winter): 57–76.

March, J., & Simon, H. 1958. ***Organizations.*** New York: Wiley.

Meyer, A. 1982. Adjusting to environmental jolts. ***Administrative Science Quarterly,*** 27: 515–538.

Miles, M., & Huberman, A. 1984. ***Qualitative data analysis.*** Beverly Hills, CA: Sage.

Mintzberg, H. 1979a. ***The structuring of organizations.*** Englewood Cliffs, NJ: Prentice-Hall.

Mintzberg, H. 1979b. An emerging theory for direct research. ***Administrative Science Quarterly,*** 24: 582–589.

Moorman, C. 1995. Organizational market information processes: Cultural antecedents and new product outcomes. ***Journal of Marketing Research,*** 32: 318–335.

Morgan, G. 1986. ***Images of organization.*** Beverly Hills, CA: Sage.

Nevens, T., Summe, G., & Uttal, B. 1990. Commercializing technology: What the best companies do. ***Harvard Business Review,*** 68(3): 154–163.

Peters, T. 1992. ***Liberation management: Necessary disorganization for the nano-second nineties.*** New York: Knopf.

Pettigrew, A. 1973. ***The politics of organizational decision-making.*** London: Tavistock.

Pettigrew, A. 1979. On studying organizational cultures. ***Administrative Science Quarterly,*** 24: 570–581.

Pfeffer, J. 1981. ***Power in organizations.*** Boston: Pitman.

Pfeffer, J., & Salancik, G. 1974. Organizational decision making as a political process. ***Administrative Science Quarterly,*** 19: 135–151.

Pfeffer, J., & Salancik, G. 1978. ***The external control of organizations.*** New York: Harper & Row.

Quelch, J., Farris, P., & Olver, J. 1987. The product management audit: Design and survey findings. ***Journal of Consumer Marketing,*** 4(3): 45–58.

Quinn, J. B. 1985. Managing innovation: Controlled chaos. ***Harvard Business Review,*** 63(3): 78–84.

Roberts, E. 1988. What we've learned: Managing invention and innovation. ***Research-Technology Management,*** 31(1): 11–29.

Schon, D. 1963. Champions for radical new inventions. ***Harvard Business Review,*** 41(2): 77–86.

Singh, J. 1986. Performance, slack, and risk taking in organizational decision making. ***Academy of Management Journal,*** 29: 562–585.

Souder, W. 1987. ***Managing new product innovations.*** Lexington, MA: Lexington Books.

Strauss, A. 1987. ***Qualitative analysis for social scientists.*** New York: Cambridge University Press.

Sutton, R. I., & Callahan, A. L. 1987. The stigma of bankruptcy: Spoiled organizational image and its management. ***Academy of Management Journal,*** 30: 405–436.

Sykes, H. 1986. Lessons from a new ventures program. ***Harvard Business Review,*** 64(3): 69–74.

Van de Ven, A. 1986. Central problems in the management of innovation. ***Management Science,*** 32: 590–607.

Van de Ven, A., & Polley, D. 1992. Learning while innovating. ***Organization Science,*** 3: 92–116.

Van Maanen, J. 1983. Epilogue: Qualitative methods reclaimed. In J. Van Maanen (Ed.), ***Qualitative methodology:*** 247–268. Beverly Hills, CA: Sage.

Westley, F. 1990. Middle managers and strategy: Microdynamics of inclusion. ***Strategic Management Journal,*** 11: 337–351.

Wheelright, S., & Clark, K. 1992. ***Revolutionizing product development.*** New York: Free Press.

Workman, J. 1993. Marketing's limited role in new product development in one computer systems firm. ***Journal of Marketing Research,*** 30: 405–421.

Zirger, B. J., & Maidique, M. 1990. A model of new product development: An empirical test. ***Management Science,*** 36: 867–883.

APPENDIX
Coding for the Data Analysis

Innovation Problems

One of the authors worked with a doctoral student to first identify each problem in each interview and then to categorize the problems into one of eight types. Classifying the problems into eight original types was difficult; in preliminary coding of six cases, the interrater reliability ranged from 68 to 90 percent. These rates suggested too great a variation, so we made further distinctions among the categories of problems and established more decision rules for placing problems. Then each interview was coded again separately by each researcher, and discrepancies were discussed. This process did not produce interrater reliability ratings, but the interactive coding helped to clarify the problem types. For this study, a team of undergraduate research assistants recoded the eight types to separate out within-project and project-to-organization issues. The interrater reliability rates ranged from 80 to 90 percent, which suggested adequate consistency. We then grouped the problems into the resources, collaboration, and strategic meaning categories.

Solutions of Innovation Problems

All the problems were then coded for whether or not they were solved, and if so, how, by the author and the doctoral student. For solution, any indication that the issue was worked out was coded as solved, even if, as we illustrate in the text, some of the solutions seemed temporary or partial. The interrater reliability between the two coders was 84 percent in the first round of coding, indicating adequate stability.

Categories for Cases

Degree of innovativeness. The measure was based on the product manager's judgment of the product's unfamiliarity to the firm on five dimensions: market, application, technology, distribution, and manufacturing. We coded a product as low in innovativeness if it was unfamiliar in one or two ways, as medium if unfamiliar in three ways, and as high if unfamiliar in four or five ways. There are no widely accepted measures of innovativeness. Our measure is consistent with the usual distinction between familiar and new product technology and markets but includes additional dimensions.

Stage of development. The codings were early—an idea still being fleshed out prior to formal approval to proceed; middle—the product had been approved and development was proceeding; and end—the product was almost completed and ready to be launched.

Success status. The only difficult distinction was between the successes and products that were in the market but not yet successful. We based this choice on the degree to which the product was, according to the follow-up interviews, garnering expected revenues. Products that had had no or few sales, despite forecasts that they would, are coded as uncertain. We conducted a sensitivity analysis to see if including cases whose category was not clear with the successes affected the implications regarding the differences; no real effect occurred, although the actual numbers were slightly diminished.

Deborah Dougherty received a Ph.D. degree in management from MIT's Sloan School in 1987. Since 1992 she has taught in the policy group at McGill University, Faculty of Management. Her research considers new product development, problems understanding customer needs, how and why organizational barriers inhibit effective product innovation, and how these underlying barriers can be overcome, especially in large, established organizations.

Cynthia Hardy is a full professor in the policy area at the Faculty of Management at McGill University. She received her Ph.D. degree from Warwick University in the U.K. Her research interests focus on the role of power and politics in organizations, especially with regard to interorganizational collaboration, strategy making in universities, and downsizing. She is currently heading a team of researchers in Canada and Australia that is examining collaboration between business, government, and nongovernment organizations from a critical perspective.

[3]

Strategic Management Journal, Vol. 13, 111–125 (1992)

CORE CAPABILITIES AND CORE RIGIDITIES: A PARADOX IN MANAGING NEW PRODUCT DEVELOPMENT

DOROTHY LEONARD-BARTON
Graduate School of Business Administration, Harvard University, Boston, Massachusetts, U.S.A.

This paper examines the nature of the core capabilities of a firm, focusing in particular on their interaction with new product and process development projects. Two new concepts about core capabilities are explored here. First, while core capabilities are traditionally treated as clusters of distinct technical systems, skills, and managerial systems, these dimensions of capabilities are deeply rooted in values, which constitute an often overlooked but critical fourth dimension. Second, traditional core capabilities have a down side that inhibits innovation, here called core rigidities. Managers of new product and process development projects thus face a paradox: how to take advantage of core capabilities without being hampered by their dysfunctional flip side. Such projects play an important role in emerging strategies by highlighting the need for change and leading the way. Twenty case studies of new product and process development projects in five firms provide illustrative data.

INTRODUCTION

Debate about the nature and strategic importance of firms' distinctive capabilities has been heightened by the recent assertion that Japanese firms understand, nurture and exploit their core competencies better than their U.S.-based competitors (Prahalad and Hamel, 1990). This paper explores the interaction of such capabilities with a critical strategic activity: the development of new products and processes. In responding to environmental and market changes, development projects become the focal point for tension between innovation and the *status quo*—microcosms of the paradoxical organizational struggle to maintain, yet renew or replace core capabilities.

In this paper, I first examine the history of core capabilities, briefly review relevant literature, and describe a field-based study providing illustrative data. The paper then turns to a deeper description of the nature of core capabilities and detailed evidence about their symbiotic relationship with development projects. However, evidence from the field suggests the need to enhance emerging theory by examining the way that capabilities inhibit as well as enable development, and these arguments are next presented. The paper concludes with a discussion of the project/capabilities interaction as a paradox faced by project managers, observed management tactics, and the potential of product/process development projects to stimulate change.

THE HISTORY OF CORE CAPABILITIES

Capabilities are considered *core* if they differentiate a company strategically. The concept is not new. Various authors have called them distinctive

Key words: Core capabilities, innovation, new product development

0143–2095/92/060125–15$12.50

competences (Snow and Hrebiniak, 1980; Hitt and Ireland, 1985), core or organizational competencies (Prahalad and Hamel, 1990; Hayes, Wheelwright and Clark, 1988), firm-specific competence (Pavitt, 1991), resource deployments (Hofer and Schendel, 1978), and invisible assets (Itami, with Roehl, 1987). Their strategic significance has been discussed for decades, stimulated by such research as Rumelt's (1974) discovery that of nine diversification strategies, the two that were built on an existing skill or resource base in the firm were associated with the highest performance. Mitchell's (1989) observation that industry-specific capabilities increased the likelihood a firm could exploit a new technology within that industry, has confirmed the early work. Therefore some authors suggest that effective competition is based less on strategic leaps than on incremental innovation that exploits carefully developed capabilities (Hayes, 1985; Quinn, 1980).

On the other hand, institutionalized capabilities may lead to 'incumbent inertia' (Lieberman and Montgomery, 1988) in the face of environmental changes. Technological discontinuities can enhance or destroy existing competencies within an industry (Tushman and Anderson, 1986). Such shifts in the external environment resonate within the organization, so that even 'seemingly minor' innovations can undermine the usefulness of deeply embedded knowledge (Henderson and Clark, 1990). In fact, all innovation necessarily requires some degree of 'creative destruction' (Schumpeter, 1942).

Thus at any given point in a corporation's history, core capabilities are evolving, and corporate survival depends upon successfully managing that evolution. New product and process development projects are obvious, visible arenas for conflict between the need for innovation and retention of important capabilities. Managers of such projects face a paradox: core capabilities *simultaneously* enhance and inhibit development.[1] Development projects reveal friction between technology strategy and current corporate practices; they also spearhead potential new strategic directions (Burgelman, 1991). However, most studies of industrial innovation focus on the new product project as a self-contained unit of analysis, and address such issues as project staffing or structure (Souder, 1987; Leonard-Barton, 1988a; Clark and Fujimoto, 1991. Chapter 9).[2] Therefore there is little research-based knowledge on managing the interface between the project and the organization, and the interaction between development and capabilities in particular. Observing core capabilities through the lens of the project places under a magnifying glass one aspect of the 'part-whole' problem of innovation management, which Van de Ven singles out as '[p]erhaps the most significant structural problem in managing complex organizations today. . . ' (1986:598).

Recent field research on 20 new product and process development projects provided an opportunity to explore and conceptually model the relationship between development practices and a firm's core capabilities. As described in the Appendix, four extensive case studies in each of five companies (Ford, Chaparral Steel, Hewlett Packard, and two anonymous companies, Electronics and Chemicals) were conducted by joint teams of academics and practitioners.[3] (Table 1). Before describing the interactions observed in the field, I first define core capabilities.

Dimensions of core capabilities

Writers often assume that descriptors of core capabilities such as 'unique,' 'distinctive,' 'difficult to imitate,' or 'superior to competition' render the term self-explanatory, especially if reference is also made to 'resource deployment' or 'skills.' A few authors include activities such as 'collective learning' and explain how competence is and is not cultivated (Prahalad and Hamel, 1990).Teece, Pisano and Shuen provide one of the clearest definitions: 'a set of differentiated skills, complementary assets, and routines that provide the basis for a firm's competitive capacities and sustainable advantage in a particular business' (1990: 28).

[1] According to Quinn and Cameron, '(t)he key characteristic in paradox is the simultaneous presence of contradictory, even mutually exclusive elements' (1988:2.)

[2] Exceptions are historical cases about a developing technical innovation in an industry (see for example, Rosenbloom and Cusumano, 1987.)

[3] Other members of the data-collection team on which I served are: Kent Bowen, Douglas Braithwaite, William Hanson, Gil Preuss and Michael Titelbaum. They contributed to the development of the ideas presented herein through discussion and reactions to early drafts of this paper.

Table 1. Description of projects studied

Company	Product/process description
Ford Motor Company	**FX15** Compressor for automobile air conditioning systems **EN53** New full-sized car built on carryover platform **MN12** All new car platform including a novel supercharged engine **FN9** Luxury automobile built on carryover platform with major suspension system modifications
Chaparral Steel	**Horizontal Caster** New caster used to produce higher grades steel **Pulpit Controls** Furnace control mechanism upgrade from analog to digital **Microtuff 10** New special bar quality alloy steel **Arc Saw** Electric arc saw for squaring ends of steel beams
Hewlett-Packard Company	**Deskjet** Low cost personal computer and office printer using new technology **Hornet** Low cost spectrum analyzer **HP 150** Terminal/PC linked to high-end computer **Logic Analyzer** Digital logic analyzer
Chemicals	Special use camera Large format printer for converting digital input to continuous images New polymer used in film 21st century 'factory of the future'
Electronics	New RISC/UNIX workstation Local area network linking multiple computer networks Software architecture for desktop publishing High-density storage disk drive

In this article, I adopt a knowledge-based view of the firm and define a core capability as the knowledge set that distinguishes and provides a competitive advantage. There are four dimensions to this knowledge set. Its content is embodied in (1) employee *knowledge and skills* and embedded in (2) *technical systems*. The processes of knowledge creation and control are guided by (3) *managerial systems*. The fourth dimension is (4) the *values and norms* associated with the various types of embodied and embedded knowledge and with the processes of knowledge creation and control. In managerial literature, this fourth dimension is usually separated from the others or ignored.[4] However, understanding it is crucial to managing both new product/process development and core capabilities.

[4] Barney (1986) is a partial exception in that it poses organizational culture as a competitive advantage.

The first dimension, knowledge and skills embodied in people, is the one most often associated with core capabilities (Teece *et al.*, 1990) and the one most obviously relevant to new product development. This knowledge/skills dimension encompasses both firm-specific techniques and scientific understanding. The second, knowledge embedded in technical systems, results from years of accumulating, codifying and structuring the tacit knowledge in peoples' heads. Such physical production or information systems represent compilations of knowledge, usually derived from multiple individual sources; therefore the whole technical system is greater than the sum of its parts. This knowledge constitutes both information (e.g. a data base of product tests conducted over decades) and procedures (e.g. proprietary design rules.) The third dimension, managerial systems, represents formal and informal ways of creating knowledge (e.g. through sabbaticals, apprenticeship programs or networks with partners) and of controlling knowledge (e.g. incentive systems and reporting structures).

Infused through these three dimensions is the fourth: the value assigned within the company to the content and structure of knowledge (e.g. chemical engineering vs. marketing expertise; 'open-systems' software vs. proprietary systems), means of collecting knowledge (e.g. formal degrees v. experience) and controlling knowledge (e.g. individual empowerment vs. management hierarchies). Even physical systems embody values. For instance, organizations that have a strong tradition of individual vs. centralized control over information prefer an architecture (software and hardware) that allows much autonomy at each network node. Such 'debatable, overt, espoused values' (Schein, 1984: 4) are one 'manifestation' of the corporate culture (Schein, 1986: 7).[5]

Core capabilities are 'institutionalized' (Zucker, 1977). That is, they are part of the organization's taken-for-granted reality, which is an accretion of decisions made over time and events in corporate history (Kimberly, 1987; Tucker, Singh and Meinhard, 1990; Pettigrew, 1979). The technology embodied in technical systems and skills usually traces its roots back to the firm's first products. Managerial systems evolve over time in response to employees' evolving interpretation of their organizational roles (Giddens, 1984) and to the need to reward particular actions. Values bear the 'imprint' of company founders and early leaders (Kimberly, 1987). All four dimensions of core capabilities reflect accumulated behaviors and beliefs based on early corporate successes. One advantage of core capabilities lies in this unique heritage, which is not easily imitated by would-be competitors.

Thus a core capability is an interrelated, interdependent knowledge system. See Figure 1. The four dimensions may be represented in very different proportions in various capabilities. For instance, the information and procedures embedded in technical systems such as computer programs are relatively more important to credit card companies than to engineering consulting firms, since these latter firms likely rely more on

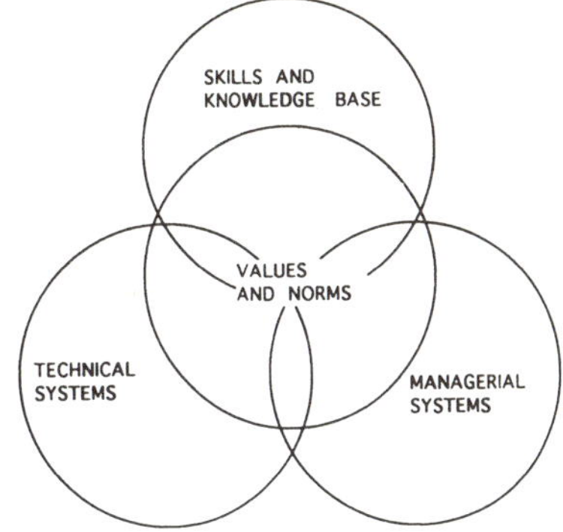

Figure 1. The four dimensions of a core capability.

the knowledge base embodied in individual employees (the skills dimension).[6]

Interaction of development projects and core capabilities: Managing the paradox

The interaction between development projects and capabilities lasts over a period of months or years and differs according to how completely aligned are the values, skills, managerial and technical systems required by the project with those currently prevalent in the firm. (See Figure 2). Companies in the study described above identified a selected, highly traditional and strongly held capability and then one project at each extreme of alignment: highly congruent vs. not at all (Table 2). Degree of congruence does not necessarily reflect project size, or technical or market novelty. Chaparral's horizontal caster and Ford's new luxury car, for instance, were neither incremental enhancements nor small undertakings. Nor did incongruent projects necessarily involve 'radical' innovations, by market or technological measures. Electronic's new workstation used readily available, 'state-of-the-shelf' components. Rather, unaligned projects

[5] Schein distinguishes between these surface values and 'preconscious' and 'invisible' 'basic assumptions' about the nature of reality (1984: 4).

[6] Each core capability draws upon only *some* of a company's skill and knowledge base, systems and values. Not only do some skills, systems and norms lie outside the domain of a particular core capability, but some may lie outside *all* core capabilities, as neither unique nor distinctly advantageous. For instance, although every company has personnel and pay systems, they may not constitute an important dimension of any core capability.

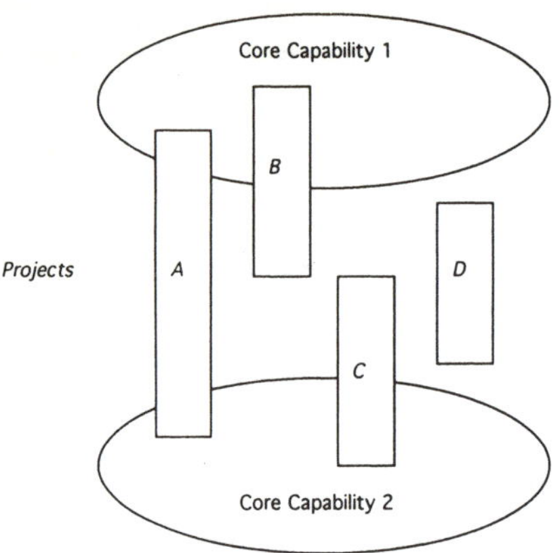

Figure 2. Possible alignments of new product and process development projects with current core capabilities at a point in time.

were nontraditional for the organization along several dimensions of the selected core capability.

For instance, Chemicals' project developing a new polymer used in film drew heavily on traditional values, skills and systems. In this company, film designers represent the top five percent of all engineers. All projects associated with film are high status, and highly proprietary technical systems have evolved to produce it. In contrast, the printer project was nontraditional. The key technical systems, for instance, were hardware rather than chemical or polymer and required mechanical engineering and software skills. Similarly, whereas the spectrum analyzer project at Hewlett Packard built on traditional capabilities in designing measurement equipment, the 150 terminal as a personal computer departed from conventional strengths. The 150 was originally conceived as a terminal for the HP3000, an industrial computer already on the market and as a terminal, was closely aligned with traditional capabilities. The attempt to transform the 150 into a personal computer was not very successful because different technical and marketing capabilities were required. Moreover, the greater system complexity represented by a stand-alone computer (e.g. the need for disk drives) required very untraditional cross-divisional cooperation.

Similar observations could be made about the other projects featured in Table 2. Chaparral's horizontal caster pushed the traditional science of molds to new heights, whereas the arc saw required capabilities that turned out to be

Table 2. Relationship of selected projects with a very traditional core capability in each company studied

		Degree of alignment	
Company name	Traditional core capability	Very high	Very low
Ford Motor Co.	Total Vehicle Architecture	luxury car built on carryover platform (FN9)	compressor for air conditioner system (FX15)
Chaparral Steel	Science of Casting Molds	horizontal caster	electric arc saw
Hewlett Packard	Measurement Technology	low cost spectrum analyzer	150 terminal/ personal computer
Chemicals	Silver Halide Technology	new polymer for film	factory of the future
Electronics	Networking	local area network link	stand-alone workstation

unavailable. The local area networks project at Electronics grew directly out of networking expertise, whereas the new RISC/UNIX workstation challenged dominant and proprietary software/hardware architecture. At Ford, the three car projects derived to varying degrees from traditional strengths—especially the new luxury car. However, the air-conditioner compressor had never been built in-house before. Since all new product development departs somewhat from current capabilities, project misalignment is a matter of degree. However, as discussed later, it is also a matter of kind. That is, the type as well as the number of capability dimensions challenged by a new project determines the intensity of the interaction and the project's potential to stimulate change.

THE UP SIDE: CAPABILITIES ENHANCE DEVELOPMENT

In all projects studied, deep stores of knowledge embodied in people and embedded in technical systems were accessed; all projects were aided by managerial systems that created and controlled knowledge flows, and by prevalent values and norms. That is, whether the projects were aligned or not with the prominent core capability identified by the company, *some* dimensions of that capability favored the project. However, the closer the alignment of project and core knowledge set, the stronger the enabling influence.

In order to understand the dynamic interaction of project with capabilities, it is helpful to tease apart the dimensions of capabilities and put each dimension separately under the microscope. However, we must remember that these dimensions are interrelated; each is supported by the other three. Values in particular permeate the other dimensions of a core capability.

Skills/knowledge dimension

Excellence in the dominant discipline

One of the most necessary elements in a core capability is excellence in the technical and professional skills and knowledge base underlying major products. The professional elite in these companies earn their status by demonstrating remarkable skills. They expect to 'achieve the impossible'—and it is often asked of them. Thus managers of development projects that draw upon core capabilities have rich resources. In numerous cases, seemingly intractable technical problems were solved through engineering excellence. For instance, although engineers working on the thin film media project at Electronics had little or no prior experience with this particular form of storage technology, (because the company had always used ferrite-based media) they were able to *invent* their way out of difficulties. Before this project was over, the geographically dispersed team had invented new media, new heads to read the data off the thin film media, as well as the software and hardware to run a customized assembly and test line for the new storage device.

Pervasive technical literacy

Besides attracting a cadre of superbly qualified people to work in the dominant discipline, time-honored core capabilities create a reservoir of complementary skills and interests outside the projects, composed of technically skilled people who help shape new products with skilled criticism. In the Electronics Software Applications project, the developers enlisted employees through computer networks to field test emerging products. After trying out the software sent them electronically, employees submitted all reactions to a computerized 'Notes' file. This internal field testing thus took advantage of both willing, technically able employees and also a computer system set up for easy world-wide networking. Similarly, Electronics Workstation developers recruited an internal 'wrecking crew' to evaluate their new product. Employees who found the most 'bugs' in the prototype workstations were rewarded by getting to keep them. At Chemicals, developers tested the special purpose camera by loading down an engineer going on a weekend trip with film, so that he could try out various features for them. In these companies, internal testing is so commonplace that it is taken for granted as a logical step in new product/process creation. However, it represents a significant advantage over competitors trying to enter the same market without access to such technically sophisticated personnel. Internal 'field testers' not only typify users but can translate their reactions into technical enhancements; such swift feedback helps development teams hit market windows.

The technical systems dimension

Just as pervasive technical literacy among employees can constitute a corporate resource, so do the systems, procedures and tools that are artifacts left behind by talented individuals, embodying many of their skills in a readily accessible form. Project members tap into this embedded knowledge, which can provide an advantage over competitors in timing, accuracy or amount of available detail. At Ford Motor Company, the capability to model reliability testing derives in part from proprietary software tools that simulate extremely complex interactions. In the full-sized car project, models simulating noise in the car body allowed engineers to identify nonobvious root causes, some originating from interaction among physically separated components. For instance, a noise apparently located in the floor panel could be traced instead to the acoustical interaction of sound waves reverberating between roof and floor. Such simulations cut development time as well as costs. They both build on and enhance the engineers' skills.

The management systems dimension

Managerial systems constitute part of a core capability when they incorporate unusual blends of skills, and/or foster beneficial behaviors not observed in competitive firms. Incentive systems encouraging innovative activities are critical components of some core capabilities, as are unusual educational systems. In Chaparral Steel, all employees are shareholders. This rewards system interacts with development projects in that employees feel that every project is an effort to improve a process they own. 'I feel like this company partly belongs to me,' explains a millwright. Consequently, even operators and maintenance personnel are tenacious innovation champions. The furnace controls upgrade (incorporating a switch from analog to digital) was initiated by a maintenance person, who persevered against opposition from his nominal superiors. Chaparral Steel also has a unique apprenticeship program for the entire production staff, involving both classroom education and on-the-job training. Classes are taught by mill foremen on a rotating basis. The combination of mill-specific information and general education (including such unusual offerings as interpersonal skills for furnace operators) would be difficult to imitate, if only because of the diversity of abilities required of these foremen. They know what to teach from having experienced problems on the floor, and they must live on the factory floor with what they have taught. This managerial system, tightly integrating technical theory and practice, is reflected in every development project undertaken in the company (Leonard-Barton, 1991).

Values dimension

The values assigned to knowledge creation and content, constantly reinforced by corporate leaders and embedded in management practices, affect all the development projects in a line of business. Two subdimensions of values are especially critical: the degree to which project members are empowered and the status assigned various disciplines on the project team.

Empowerment of project members

Empowerment is the belief in the potential of every individual to contribute meaningfully to the task at hand and the relinquishment by organizational authority figures to that individual of responsibility for that contribution. In HP, 'Electronics,' and Chaparral, the assumption is that empowered employees will create multiple potential futures for the corporation and these options will be selected and exercised as needed. The future of the corporation thus rests on the ability of such individuals to create new businesses by championing new products and processes. Since strategy in these companies is 'pattern in action' or 'emergent' rather than 'deliberate' (Mintzberg, 1990), empowerment is an especially important element of their core capabilities, and project members initiating new capabilities were exhilarated by the challenges they had created. The Hewlett Packard printer and the Electronics storage teams actually felt that they had turned the course of their mammoth corporate ship a critical degree or two.

High status for the dominant discipline

A business generally recognized for certain core capabilities attracts, holds, and motivates talented people who value the knowledge base underlying that capability and join up for the challenges, the camaraderie with competent peers, the status associated with the skills of the dominant discipline or function. Each company displays a cultural bias towards the technical base in which the corporation has its historical roots. For Chemicals, that base is chemistry and chemical engineering; for Hewlett Packard and Electronics, it is electronics/computer engineering and operating systems software. A history of high status for the dominant discipline enables the corporation and the projects to attract the very top talent. Top chemical engineers can aspire to become the professional elites constituting the five percent of engineers who design premier film products at Chemicals. At Hewlett Packard and Electronics, design engineers are the professional elite.

A natural outgrowth of the prominence of a particular knowledge base is its influence over the development process. In many firms, a reinforcing cycle of values and managerial systems lends power and authority to the design engineer. That is, design engineers have high status because the new products that are directly evaluated by the market originate in design engineering; in contrast, the expertise of manufacturing engineers is expended on projects less directly tied to the bottom line and more difficult to evaluate. The established, well-paid career path for product designers attracts top engineering talent, who tend to perform well. The success (or failure) of new products is attributed almost entirely to these strong performers, whose high visibility and status constantly reinforce the dominance of their discipline.

As the above discussion suggests, projects derive enormous support from core capabilities. In fact, such capabilities continually spawn new products and processes because so much creative power is focused on identifying new opportunities to apply the accumulated knowledge base. However, these same capabilities can also prove dysfunctional for product and process development.

THE DOWN SIDE: CORE RIGIDITIES INHIBIT DEVELOPMENT

Even in projects that eventually succeed, problems often surface as product launch approaches. In response to gaps between product specifications and market information, or problems in manufacture, project managers face unpalatable choices. They can cycle back to prior phases in the design process (Leonard-Barton, 1988a), revisiting previous decisions higher up the design hierarchy (Clark, 1985), but almost certainly at the cost of schedule slippage. Or they may ship an inadequate product. Some such problems are idiosyncratic to the particular project, unlikely to occur again in the same form and hence not easily predicted. Others, however, occur repeatedly in multiple projects. These recurring shortfalls in the process are often traceable to the gap between current environmental requirements and a corporation's core capabilities. Values, skills, managerial systems, and technical systems that served the company well in the past and may still be wholly appropriate for some projects or parts of projects, are experienced by others as core rigidities—inappropriate sets of knowledge. Core rigidities are the flip side of core capabilities. They are not neutral; these deeply embedded knowledge sets actively create problems. While core rigidities are more problematic for projects that are deliberately designed to create new, nontraditional capabilities, rigidities can affect all projects—even those that are reasonably congruent with current core capabilities.

Skills and knowledge dimension

Less strength in nondominant disciplines

Any corporation's resources are limited. Emphasizing one discipline heavily naturally makes the company somewhat less attractive for top people in a nondominant one. A skilled marketing person knows that she will represent a minority discipline in an engineering-driven firm. Similarly, engineers graduating from top U.S. schools generally regard manufacturing in fabrication industries less attractive than engineering design, (see Hayes *et al.*, 1988) not only because of noncompetitive salaries, but because of a lower level of expertise among potential colleagues.

In each of the nonaligned and hence more difficult projects (Table 2), specific nontraditional types of knowledge were missing. Chaparral Steel's electric arc saw project required understanding electromagnetic fields for a variety of alloys—a very different knowledge set than the usual metallurgical expertise required in casting.

The Hewlett Packard 150 project suffered from a lack of knowledge about personal computer design and manufacture. The company has a long history of successful instrument development based on 'next-bench' design, meaning the engineering designers based their decisions on the needs and skills of their colleagues on the bench next to them. However, such engineers are not representative of personal computer users. Therefore traditional sources of information and design feedback were not applicable for the 150 project. Similarly, the new workstation project of Electronics met with less than optimal market acceptance because the traditional focus on producing a 'hot box,' i.e. excellent hardware, resulted in correspondingly less attention to developing software applications. The knowledge relevant to traditional hardware development flows through well-worn channels, but much less knowledge exists about creating application software. Therefore, the first few working prototypes of the UNIX/RISC workstation were shipped to customers rather than to third-party software developers. While this practice had worked well to stimulate interest in the company's well-established lines of hardware, for which much software is available, it was less appropriate for the new hardware, which could not be used and evaluated without software.

Technical systems dimension

Physical systems can embody rigidities also, since the skills and processes captured in software or hardware become easily outdated. New product designers do not always know how many such systems they are affecting. For example, in the RISC/UNIX workstation project at Electronics, the new software base posed an extreme challenge to manufacturing because hundreds of diagnostic and test systems in the factory were based on the corporate proprietary software. The impact of this incompatibility had been underestimated, given the very tight 8 month product delivery targets.

Management systems dimension

Management systems can grow just as intractable as physical ones—perhaps more so, because one cannot just plug in a new career path when a new project requires strong leadership in a hithertofore underutilized role. Highly skilled people are understandably reluctant to apply their abilities to project tasks that are undervalued, lest that negative assessment of the importance of the task contaminate perceptions of their personal abilities. In several companies, the project manager's role is not a strong one—partly because there is no associated career path. The road to the top lies through individual technical contribution. Thus a hardware engineer in one project considered his contribution as an engineering manager to be much more important than his simultaneous role as project manager, which he said was 'not my real job.' His perception of the relative unimportance of project leadership not only weakened the power of the role in that specific project but reinforced the view held by some that problem-solving in project management requires less intelligence than technical problem-solving.

Values dimension

Core rigidities hampered innovation in the development projects especially along the values dimension. Of course, certain generic types of corporate cultures encourage innovation more than others (Burns and Stalker, 1961; Chakravarthy, 1982). While not disagreeing with that observation, the point here is a different one: the very same values, norms and attitudes that support a core capability and thus enable development can also constrain it.

Empowerment as entitlement

A potential down side to empowerment observed is that individuals construe their empowerment as a psychological contract with the corporation, and yet the boundaries of their responsibility and freedom are not always clear. Because they undertake heroic tasks for the corporation, they expect rewards, recognition and freedom to act. When the contract goes sour, either because they exceed the boundaries of personal freedom that the corporation can tolerate, or their project is technically successful but fails in other ways, or their ideas are rejected, or their self-sacrifice results in too little recognition, they experience the contract as abrogated and often leave the company—sometimes with a deep sense of betrayal.

Engineers in projects that fall towards the 'incongruity' end of the spectrum speak of 'betting their [corporate identification] badges,' on the outcome, and of having 'their backs to the cliff' as ways of expressing their sense of personal risk. One engineering project manager describes 'going into the tunnel,' meaning the development period, from which the team emerges only when the job is done. 'You either do it or you don't. . . You don't have any other life.' Such intrapreneurs seem to enjoy the stress—as long as their psychological contract with the company remains intact. In this case the manager believed her contract included enormous freedom from corporate interference with her management style. When corporate management imposed certain restrictions, she perceived her contract as abrogated, and left the company just 2 months before product launch, depriving the project of continuity in the vision she had articulated for an entire stream of products.

Empowerment as a value and practice greatly aids in projects, therefore, until it conflicts with the greater corporate good. Because development requires enormous initiative and yet great discipline in fulfilling corporate missions, the management challenge is to channel empowered individual energy towards corporate aims—without destroying creativity or losing good people.

Lower status for non-dominant disciplines

When new product development requires developing or drawing upon technical skills traditionally less well respected in the company, history can have an inhibiting effect. Even if multiple subcultures exist, with differing levels of maturity, the older and historically more important ones, as noted above, tend to be more prestigious. For instance, at Chemicals, the culture values the chemical engineers and related scientists as somehow 'more advanced' than mechanical engineers and manufacturing engineers. Therefore, projects involving polymers or film are perceived as more prestigious than equipment projects. The other companies displayed similar, very clear perceptions about what disciplines and what kinds of projects are high status. The lower status of nondominant disciplines was manifested in pervasive but subtle negatively reinforcing cycles that constrained their potential for contributions to new product development and therefore limited the cross-functional integration so necessary to innovation (Pavitt, 1991). Four of these unacknowledged but critical manifestations are: who travels to whom, self-fulfilling expectations, unequal credibility and wrong language.[7]

One seemingly minor yet important indication of status affecting product/process development is that lower status individuals usually travel to the physical location of the higher. Manufacturing engineers were far more likely to go to the engineering design sites than vice versa, whether for one-day visits, or temporary or permanent postings. Not only does such one-way travel reinforce manufacturing's lower status, but it slows critical learning by design engineers, reinforcing their isolation from the factory floor. The exception to the rule, when design engineers traveled to the manufacturing site, aided cross-functional coordination by fostering more effective personal relationships. Such trips also educated the design engineers about some of the rationale behind design for manufacture (Whitney, 1988). A design engineer in one project returned to alter designs after seeing 'what [manufacturing] is up against' when he visited the factory floor.

Expectations about the status of people and roles can be dangerously self-fulfilling. As dozens of controlled experiments manipulating unconscious interpersonal expectations have demonstrated, biases can have a 'pygmalion effect': person A's expectations about the behavior of person B affect B's actual performance—for better or worse (Rosenthal and Rubin, 1978). In the engineering-driven companies studied, the expectation that marketing could not aid product definition was ensured fulfillment by expectations of low quality input, which undermined marketers' confidence. In the Electronics Local Area Network project, the marketing people discovered early on that users would want certain very important features in the LAN. However, they lacked the experience to evaluate that information and self-confidence to push for inclusion of the features. Not until that same information was gathered directly from customers by two experienced consulting engineers who presented it strongly was it acted upon. Precious time was lost as the schedule was slipped

[7] Such cycles, or 'vicious circles' as psychiatry has labeled them, resemble the examples of self-fulfilling prophecies cited by Weick (1979: 159–164).

four months to incorporate the 'new' customer information. Similarly, in the Hewlett Packard printer project, marketing personnel conducted studies in shopping malls to discover potential customers' reactions to prototypes. When marketing reported need for 21 important changes, the product designers enacted only five. In the next mall studies, the design engineers went along. Hearing from the future customers' own lips the same information rejected before, the product developers returned to the bench and made the other 16 changes. The point is certainly not that marketing always has better information than engineering. Rather history has conferred higher expectations and greater credibility upon the dominant function, whereas other disciplines start at a disadvantage in the development process.

Even if nondominant disciplines are granted a hearing in team meetings, their input may be discounted if not presented in the language favored by the dominant function. Customer service representatives in the Electronics LAN project were unable to convince engineering to design the computer boards for field repair as opposed to replacing the whole system in the field with a new box and conducting repairs back at the service center, because they were unable to present their argument in cost-based figures. Engineering assumed that an argument not presented as compelling financial data was useless.

Thus, nondominant roles and disciplines on the development team are kept in their place through a self-reinforcing cycle of norms, attitudes and skill sets. In an engineering-dominated company, the cycle for marketing and manufacturing is: low status on the development team, reinforced by the appointment of either young, less experienced members or else one experienced person, whose time is splintered across far too many teams. Since little money is invested in these roles, little contribution is expected from the people holding them. Such individuals act without confidence, and so do not influence product design much—thus reinforcing their low status on the team.

THE INTERACTION OF PRODUCT/PROCESS DEVELOPMENT PROJECTS WITH CORE RIGIDITIES

The severity of the paradox faced by project managers because of the dual nature of core capabilities depends upon both (1) the number and (2) the types of dimensions comprising a core rigidity. The more dimensions represented, the greater the misalignment potentially experienced between project and capability. For example, the Arc Saw project at Chaparral Steel was misaligned with the core metallurgical capability mostly along two dimensions: technical systems (not originally designed to accommodate an arc saw), and more importantly, the skills and knowledge-base dimension. In contrast, the Factory-of-the-Future project at Chemicals challenged all four dimensions of the traditional core capability. Not only were current proprietary technical systems inadequate, but existing managerial systems did not provide any way to develop the cross-functional skills needed. Moreover, the values placed on potential knowledge creation and control varied wildly among the several sponsoring groups, rendering a common vision unattainable.

The four dimensions vary in ease of change. From technical to managerial systems, skills and then values, the dimensions are increasingly less tangible, less visible and less explicitly codified. The technical systems dimension is relatively easy to alter for many reasons, among them the probability that such systems are local to particular departments. Managerial systems usually have greater organizational scope (Leonard-Barton, 1988b), i.e. reach across more subunits than technical systems, requiring acceptance by more people. The skills and knowledge content dimension is even less amenable to change because skills are built over time and many remain tacit, i.e. uncodified and in employees' heads (see von Hippel, 1990). However, the value embodied in a core capability is the dimension least susceptible to change; values are most closely bound to culture, and culture is hard to alter in the short term (Zucker, 1977), if it can be changed at all (Barney, 1986).

Effects of the paradox on projects

Over time, some core capabilities are replaced because their dysfunctional side has begun to inhibit too many projects. However, that substitution or renewal will not occur within the lifetime of a single project. Therefore, project managers cannot wait for time to resolve the paradox they face (Quinn and Cameron, 1988).

In the projects observed in this study, managers handled the paradox in one of four ways: (1) abandonment; (2) recidivism, i.e. return to core capabilities; (3) reorientation; and (4) isolation. The arc saw and factory-of-the-future projects were abandoned, as the managers found no way to resolve the problems. The HP150 personal computer exemplifies recidivism. The end product was strongly derivative of traditional HP capabilities in that it resembled a terminal and was more successful as one than as a personal computer. The special-use camera project was reoriented. Started in the film division, the stronghold of the firm's most traditional core capability, the project languished. Relocated to the equipment division, where the traditional corporate capability was less strongly ensconced, and other capabilities were valued, the project was well accepted. The tactic of isolation, employed in several projects to varying degrees, has often been invoked in the case of new ventures (Burgelman, 1983). Both the workstation project at Electronics and the HP Deskjet project were separated physically and psychologically from the rest of the corporation, the former without upper management's blessing. These project managers encouraged their teams by promoting the group as hardy pioneers fighting corporate rigidities.

Effects of the paradox on core capabilities

Although capabilities are not usually dramatically altered by a single project, projects do pave the way for organizational change by highlighting core rigidities and introducing new capabilities. Of the companies studied, Chaparral Steel made the most consistent use of development projects as agents of renewal and organization-wide learning. Through activities such as benchmarking against best-in-the-world capabilities, Chaparral managers use projects as occasions for challenging current knowledge and for modeling alternative new capabilities. For instance, personnel from vice presidents to operators spent months in Japan learning about horizontal casting and in the case of the new specialty alloy, the company convened its own academic conference in order to push the bounds of current capabilities.

In other companies, negative cycles reinforcing the lower status of manufacturing or marketing were broken—to the benefit of both project and corporation. In the workstation project at Electronics, the manufacturing engineers on the project team eventually demonstrated so much knowledge that design engineers who had barely listened to 20 percent of their comments at the start of the project, gave a fair hearing to 80 percent, thereby allowing manufacturing to influence design. In the deskjet printer project at Hewlett Packard, managers recognized that inequality between design and manufacturing always created unnecessary delays. The Vancouver division thus sought to raise the status of manufacturing engineering skills by creating a manufacturing engineering group within R&D and then, once it was well established, moving it to manufacturing. A rotation plan between manufacturing and R&D was developed to help neutralize the traditional status differences; engineers who left research to work in manufacturing or vice versa were guaranteed a 'return ticket.' These changes interrupted the negative reinforcing cycle, signalling a change in status for manufacturing and attracting better talent to the position. This same project introduced HP to wholly unfamiliar market research techniques such as getting customer reactions to prototypes in shopping malls.

As these examples indicate, even within their 1–8-year lifetime, the projects studied served as small departures from tradition in organizations providing a 'foundation in experience' to inspire eventual large changes (Kanter, 1983). Such changes can be *precipitated* by the introduction of new capabilities along any of the four dimensions. However, for a capability to become *core*, all four dimensions must be addressed. A core capability is an interconnected set of knowledge collections—a tightly coupled system. This concept is akin to Pfeffer's definition of a paradigm, which he cautions is not just a view of the world but 'embodies procedures for inquiring about the world and categories into which these observations are collected. Thus', he warns, 'paradigms have within them an internal consistency that makes evolutionary change or adaptation nearly impossible' (1982: 228). While he is thinking of the whole organization, the caution might apply as well to core capabilities. Thus, new technical systems provide no inimitable advantage if not accompanied by new skills. New skills atrophy or flee the corporation if the technical systems are inadequate, and/or if the managerial systems such as training are incompatible. New values will not take root if associated behaviors are not rewarded. Therefore, when the development process encounters rigidities, projects can be managed consciously as the 'generative' actions characteristic of learning organizations (Senge, 1990) only if the multidimensional nature of core capabilities is fully appreciated.

CONCLUSION

This paper proposes a new focus of inquiry about technological innovation, enlarging the boundaries of 'middle range' project management theory to include interactions with development of capabilities, and hence with strategy. Because core capabilities are a collection of knowledge sets, they are distributed and are being constantly enhanced from multiple sources. However, at the same time that they enable innovation, they hinder it. Therefore in their interaction with the development process, they cannot be managed as a single good (or bad) entity.[8] They are not easy to change because they include a pervasive dimension of values, and as Weick (1979: 151) points out, 'managers unwittingly collude' to avoid actions that challenge accepted modes of behavior.

Yet technology-based organizations have no choice but to challenge their current paradigms. The swift-moving environment in which they function makes it critical that the 'old fit be consciously disturbed. . . ' (Chakravarthy, 1982: 42). Itami points out that 'The time to search out and develop a new core resource is when the current core is working well,' (1987: 54)—a point that is echoed by Foster (1982). Development projects provide opportunities for creating the 'requisite variety' for innovation (Van de Ven, 1986: 600; Kanter, 1986). As micro-level social systems, they create conflict with the macro system and hence a managerial paradox. Quinn and Cameron argue that recognizing and managing paradox is a powerful lever for change: 'Having multiple frameworks available. . . is probably the single most powerful attribute of self-renewing. . . organizations' (1988: 302).

Thus project managers who constructively 'discredit' (Weick, 1979) the systems, skills or values traditionally revered by companies may cause a complete redefinition of core capabilities or initiate new ones. They can consciously manage projects for continuous organizational renewal. As numerous authors have noted, (Clark and Fujimoto, 1991; Hayes *et al.*, 1988; Pavitt, 1991) the need for this kind of emphasis on organizational learning over immediate output alone is a critical element of competition.

[8] This observation is akin to Gidden's argument that structure is 'always both constraining and enabling' (1984: 25).

ACKNOWLEDGEMENTS

The author is grateful to colleagues Kim Clark, Richard Hackman and Steven Wheelwright as well as members of the research team and two anonymous reviewers for comments on earlier drafts of this paper, to the Division of Research at Harvard Business School for financial support, and to the companies that served as research sites.

A full report on the research on which this paper is based will be available in Kent Bowen, Kim Clark, Chuck Holloway and Steven Wheelwright, *Vision and Capability: High Performance Product Development in the 1990s*, Oxford University Press, New York.

REFERENCES

Barney, J. B. 'Organizational culture: Can it be a source of sustained competitive advantage?, *Academy of Management Review*, **11**(3), 1986, pp. 656–665.

Burgelman, R. 'A process model of internal corporate venturing in the diversified major firms', *Administrative Science Quarterly*, **28**, 1983, pp. 223–244.

Burgelman, R. 'Intraorganizational ecology of strategy making and organizational adaptation: Theory and field research', *Organization Science* **2**(3), 1991, pp. 239–262.

Burns, T. and G. M. Stalker. *The Management of Innovation*, Tavistock, London, 1961.

Chakravarthy, B. S. 'Adaptation: A promising metaphor for strategic management', *Academy of Management Review*, **7**(1), 1982, pp. 35–44.

Clark, K. 'The interaction of design hierarchies and market concepts in technological evolution' *Research Policy*, **14**, 1985, pp. 235–251.

Clark, K. and T. Fujimoto. *Product Development Performance*, Harvard Business School Press, Boston, MA, 1991.

Foster, R. 'A call for vision in managing technology,' *Business Week*, May 24, 1982, pp. 24–33.

Giddens, A. *The Constitution of Society: Outline of the Theory of Structuration*. Polity Press, Cambridge, UK, 1984.

Hayes, R. H. 'Strategic planning—forward in reverse?', *Harvard Business Review*, November–December 1985, pp. 111–119 (Reprint # 85607).

Hayes, R. H., S. C. Wheelwright and K. B. Clark. *Dynamic Manufacturing: Creating the Learning Organization*, Free Press, New York, 1988.

Henderson, R. and K. B. Clark. 'Architectural innovation: The reconfiguration of existing product technologies and the failure of established firms', *Administrative Science Quarterly*, **35**, 1990, pp. 9–30.

Hitt, M. and R. D. Ireland. 'Corporate distinctive competence, strategy, industry and performance', *Strategic Management Journal*, **6**, 1985, pp. 273–293.

Hofer, C. W. and D. Schendel. *Strategy Formulation: Analytical Concepts*. West Publishing, St. Paul, MN, 1978.

Huber, G. and D. J. Power. 'Retrospective reports of strategic-level managers: Guidelines for increasing their accuracy', *Strategic Management Journal*, **6**(2), 1985, pp. 171–180.

Itami, H. with T. Roehl. *Mobilizing Invisible Assets*, Harvard University Press, Cambridge, MA, 1987.

Kanter, R. M. *The Change Masters*. Simon and Schuster, New York, 1983.

Kanter, R. M. 'When a thousand flowers bloom: Structural, collective and social conditions for innovation in organizations', Harvard Business School Working Paper #87–018, 1986.

Kimberly, J. R. 'The study of organization: Toward a biographical perspective'. In J. W. Lorsch (ed.), *Handbook of Organizational Behavior*, Prentice-Hall, Englewood Cliffs, NJ, 1987, pp. 223–237.

Leonard-Barton, D. 'Implementation as mutual adaptation of technology and organization', *Research Policy*, **17**, 1988a, pp. 251–267.

Leonard-Barton, D. 'Implementation characteristics in organizational innovations', *Communication Research*, **15**(5), October 1988b, pp. 603–631.

Leonard-Barton, D. 'The factory as a learning laboratory', Harvard Business School Working Paper # 92–023, 1991.

Lieberman, M. and D. B. Montgomery. 'First-mover advantages', *Strategic Management Journal*, **9**, Summer 1988, pp. 41–58.

Mintzberg, H. 'Strategy formation: Schools of thought'. In J. W. Fredrickson (ed.), *Perspectives on Strategic Management*, Harper & Row, New York, 1990.

Mitchell, W. 'Whether and when? Probability and timing of incumbents' entry into emerging industrial subfields', *Administrative Science Quarterly*, **34**, 1989, pp. 208–230.

Pavitt, K. 'Key characteristics of the large innovating firm', *British Journal of Management*, **2**, 1991, pp. 41–50.

Pettigrew, A. 'On studying organizational cultures', *Administrative Science Quarterly*, **24**, 1979, pp. 570–581.

Pfeffer, J. *Organizations and Organization Theory*, Ballinger Publishing, Cambridge, MA, 1982.

Prahalad, C K. and G. Hamel. 'The core competence of the corporation', *Harvard Business Review*, **68**(3), 1990, pp. 79–91, (Reprint # 90311).

Quinn, J. B. *Strategies for Change: Logical Incrementalism*, Richard D. Irwin, Homewood, IL, 1980.

Quinn, R. and K. Cameron. 'Organizational paradox and transformation'. In R. Quinn and K. Cameron (eds), *Paradox and Transformation*, Cambridge, MA, Ballinger Publishing, 1988.

Rosenbloom, R. and M. Cusumano. 'Technological pioneering and competitive advantage: The birth of the VCR industry', *California Management Review*, **29**(4), 1987, pp. 51–76.

Rosenthal, R. and D. Rubin. 'Interpersonal expectancy effects: The first 345 studies', *The Behavioral and Brain Sciences*, **3**, 1978, pp. 377–415.

Rumelt, R. P. *Strategy, Structure and Economic Performance*, Harvard Business School Classics, Harvard Business School Press, Boston, MA, 1974 and 1986.

Schein, E. 'Coming to a new awareness of organizational culture', *Sloan Management Review*, Winter, 1984, pp. 3–16.

Schein, E. *Organizational Culture and Leadership*, Jossey-Bass, San Francisco, CA, 1986.

Schumpeter, J. *Capitalism, Socialism, and Democracy*, Harper, New York, 1942.

Senge, P.'The leader's new work: Building a learning organization', *Sloan Management Review*, **32**(1), 1990, pp. 7–23, (Reprint # 3211).

Snow, C. C. and L. G. Hrebiniak. 'Strategy, distinctive competence, and organizational performance', *Administrative Science Quarterly*, **25**, 1980, pp. 317–335.

Souder, W. E. *Managing New Product Innovations*, Lexington Books, Lexington, MA, 1987.

Teece, D. J., G. Pisano and A. Shuen. 'Firm capabilities, resources and the concept of strategy', Consortium on Competitiveness and Cooperation Working Paper # 90–9, University of California at Berkeley, Center for Research in Management, Berkeley, CA, 1990.

Tucker, D., J. Singh and A. Meinhard. 'Founding characteristics, imprinting and organizational change'. In J.V. Singh (ed.), *Organizational Evolution: New Directions*, Sage Publications, Newbury Park, CA, 1990.

Tushman, M. L. and P. Anderson. 'Technological discontinuities and organizational environments', *Administrative Science Quarterly*, **31**, 1986, pp. 439–465.

Van de Ven, A. 'Central problems in management of innovations', *Management Science*, **32**(5), 1986, pp. 590–607.

von Hippel, E. 'The impact of 'Sticky Data' on innovation and problem-solving', Sloan Management School, Working Paper # 3147-90-BPS, 1990.

Weick, K. E. 'Theory construction as disciplined imagination', *Academy of Management Review*,

14(4), 1989, pp. 516–531.
Weick, K. E. *The Social Psychology of Organizing*, Random House, New York, 1979.
Whitney, D. 'Manufacturing by design', *Harvard Business Review*, **66**(4), 1988, pp. 83–91.
Zucker, L. G. 'The role of institutionalization in cultural persistence', *American Sociological Review*, **42**, 1977, pp. 726–743.

APPENDIX: METHODOLOGY

Structure of research teams

Four universities (Harvard, M.I.T., Standford and Purdue) participated in the 'Manufacturing Visions' project. Each research team was composed of at least one engineering and one management professor plus one or two designated company employees. The research was organized into a matrix, with each research team having primary responsibility for one company and also one or more specific research 'themes' across sites and companies. Some themes were identified in the research protocol; others (such as the capabilities/project interaction) emerged from initial data analysis. In data collection and analysis, the internal company and outside researchers served as important checks on each other—the company insiders on the generalizability of company observations from four cases and the academics on the generalizability of findings across companies.

Data-gathering

Using a common research protocol, the teams developed case histories by interviewing development team members, including representatives from all functional groups who had taken active part and project staff members. These in-person interviews, conducted at multiple sites across the U.S., each lasted 1–3 hours. Interviewers toured the manufacturing plants and design laboratories and conducted follow-up interview sessions as necessary to ensure comparable information across all cases. The data-gathering procedures thus adhered to those advocated by Huber and Power (1985) to increase reliability of retrospective accounts (e.g. interviews conducted in tandem, motivated informants selected from different organizational levels, all responses probed extensively). In addition, the interviewers' disparate backgrounds guarded against the dominance of one research bias, and much archival evidence was collected. I personally interviewed in 3 of the 5 companies.

Data analysis

Notes compiled by each team were exchanged across a computer network and joint sessions were held every several months to discuss and analyze data. Company-specific and theme-specific reports were circulated, first among team members and then among all research teams to check on accuracy. Team members 'tested' the data against their own notes and observations and reacted by refuting, confirming or refining it. There were four within-team iterations and an additional three iterations with the larger research group. Thus observations were subjected to numerous sets of 'thought trials' (Weick, 1989).

Each team also presented interim reports to the host companies. These presentations offered the opportunity to check data for accuracy, obtain reactions to preliminary conclusions, fill in missing data and determine that observations drawn from a limited number of projects were in fact representative of common practice in the company. The examples of traditional core capabilities presented in Table 2 were provided by the companies as consensus judgments, usually involving others besides the company team members. While the 20 projects vary in the degree of success attributed to them by the companies, only two were clear failures. The others all succeeded in some ways (e.g. met a demanding schedule) but fell short in others (e.g. held market leadership for only a brief period).

[4]

British Journal of Management, Vol. 2, 41–50 (1991)

Key Characteristics of the Large Innovating Firm*

K. Pavitt
Science Policy Research Unit, University of Sussex

SUMMARY **Large innovating firms are a major source of the world's technology, and in the 20th century have shown great resilience in absorbing successive waves of radical innovations. The key characteristics of these firms derive from the properties of their innovative activities. First, given the specific, differentiated and cumulative nature of technological development, the range of possible choices about both product and processed technologies open to the firm depends on its accumulated competence. Second, given functional and professional specialization, the implementation of technological choices requires organization and orchestration across disciplinary, functional and divisional boundaries. Third, given cumulative development and uncertainty, the improvement of these competences requires continuous and collective learning. Fourth, in the light of these characteristics, systems for allocating resources must take into account the benefits of learning by doing, as well as the benefits of outcomes. As a consequence, the technical function in large firms involves not just the implementation of innovations, but also the definition of appropriate divisional objectives and boundaries, the exploration of radical technologies, and the formation of technological expectations about the future.**

1. Introduction

In what follows, I shall propose four key characteristics that typify the large innovating firm. There are a number of reasons for doing this.

The first is that large firms are a major source of technology and innovations. Although formal R&D activities exaggerate the share of firms with more than 10 000 employees, their contribution is at least in proportion to their sales and employment, and some earlier studies have suggested that it is greater and growing (Soete, 1979; Pavitt *et al.*, 1987a). They make particularly big contributions in the chemical, electrical and electronic, aerospace and automobile sectors, where innovative activities in most countries are concentrated in relatively few firms (Patel and Pavitt, 1989a). Strategic decisions by these firms can have a major impact on the sectoral patterns of technological activities, and competitive performance, of whole countries.

The second is that large innovating firms in the 20th century have shown resilience and longevity, in spite of successive waves of radical innovations that have called into question their established skills and procedures (Mowery, 1983a). Such institutional continuity in the face of technological discontinuity cannot be explained simply by the rise and fall of either talented individual entrepreneurs, or of groups with specific technical skills. The continuing ability to absorb and mobilize new skills and opportunities has to be explained in other terms.

The third is that, despite the importance attributed to large innovating firms in the theories of such writers as Schumpeter (1947), Penrose (1959), and Nelson and Winter (1982), very little analytical attention has been directed to identifying the internal characteristics that enable them to survive over long periods, by continuously changing their products, processes, markets and operating procedures.

*This paper is part of the research programme of the ESRC-funded Centre for Science, Technology and Energy Policy at the Science Policy Research Unit. I am grateful to Mike Hobday, Margaret Sharp and an anonymous referee for very helpful comments. The usual disclaimers hold.

* 1045–3172/91/010041–10$05.00

Received 8 September 1989
Revised 10 May 1990

In this paper, I shall argue that these characteristics derive from the properties of innovative activities in large firms. I identify these properties in section 2, and discuss the four key characteristics in sections 3 to 6: firm-specific competences, their organization, their development over time, and methods of allocating resources for them.

2. Key Properties of Innovative Activities in Large Firms

Past empirical research has helped to delineate the following key properties of innovative activities in large firms.

(a) They are largely *firm specific* in nature, and *cumulative* in development over time. Most technological knowledge emerges from the development, testing, production and use of specific products within firms. Actual and desirable performance characteristics of products and production processes are usually multi-dimensional and complex, and cannot easily be reproduced from scratch. Tacit knowledge obtained through experience is therefore of central importance. Although firms can buy in some technology and skills from the outside, what they have been able to do in the past strongly conditions what they can hope to do in the future.

(b) They are highly *differentiated*. The range of feasible choice open to a firm is limited strongly by the extent to which its accumulated technology skills are proximate to other technologies: for example, knowledge of the development of pharmaceutical products may be applicable in developing pesticides, but it is not much use in design and building of automobiles. Technological competences also vary in the volume of technological opportunities. For example, firms in chemicals and electronics have rich possibilities in closely related products and markets, whilst firms in textiles do not.

(c) In large firms, innovative activities involve continuous and intensive collaboration amongst *professionally* and *functionally specialized groups*. Knowledge inputs for any specific innovation normally draw on a wide variety of professional skills within both science and engineering, and within management. In nearly all innovating firms with more than 10 000 employees, these skills are organized into product divisions and functional departments (Pavitt *et al*., 1989).

(d) Contrary to Schumpeter's prediction, innovative activities have remained *highly uncertain* in relation to their commercial outcome (Freeman, 1982). Only about one in ten R&D projects turn out to be a commercial success, and about half industrial R&D firms find no profitable application. In addition, both practitioners and theorists still have great difficulties predicting the rate and direction of radical technical change (see, for example, recent experience of electronic mail compared to FAX; also, the continuing uncertainties about satellite and cable television, and the commercial applications of biotechnology).

In the light of these characteristics, it is plainly misleading to assume – as in standard production theory in economics – that technological strategies in firms consist of easily implemented choices from amongst a large and accessible range of process technologies, on the basis of clear signals about relative factor costs. Given the specific, differentiated and cumulative nature of technological development, the range of possible choices about both product and process technologies open to the firm depends on its accumulated competence (Section 3). Given functional and professional specialization, the implementation of technological choices requires organization and orchestration across disciplinary, functional and divisional boundaries (Section 4). Given cumulative development and uncertainty, the improvement of these competences requires continuous and collective learning (Section 5). And in the light of all these characteristics, appropriate systems are necessary for evaluating progress and allocating resources (Section 6).

3. Firm-specific Competences

Firms gain profitable innovative leads through building up firm-specific competences that take time or are costly to imitate. Innovating firms can discourage imitation through secrecy and patent protection, but their competitive advantage essentially results from the ability to do useful and difficult things better than their competitors. Even if we concentrate only on those related to technology, the nature of these competences, the rate and directions in which they can be developed, and their implications for management, vary greatly according to the firm's size and its core business activities. Table 1 summarizes an attempt to map out this variety.

Small innovating firms are typically specialized in their technological strategies, concentrating on product innovation in specific producers goods, such as machine tools, scientific instruments, specialized chemicals or software. Their key strategic strengths are in the ability to match technology with specific customer requirements The key strategic tasks are finding and maintaining product niches, and benefiting systematically from user experience.

Large innovating firms, on the other hand, are typically broad front in their technological activities, and divisionalized in their organization. The key technological strengths can be based on R&D laboratories (typically in chemicals and electrical-electronic products), or in the design and operation of complex production technology (typically in mass production and continuous process industries), and – increasingly – in the design and operation of complex information processing technology (typically in finance and retailing).

In R&D based technologies, the key strategic opportunities are horizontal diversification into new product markets. The key strategic problems are those of mobilizing complementary assets to enter new product markets (e.g. obtaining marketing knowledge when a pharmaceutical firm moves into pesticides), and continuous organizational redesign to exploit emerging technological opportunities (e.g. personal computers cutting across previous responsibilities in computers, office machinery, and even consumer electronics (see Section 4 below).

In production-based and information-based technologies, the key strategic opportunities are in the progressive integration of radical technological advances into products and production systems, and in diversification vertically upstream into potentially munificent production technologies (e.g. CAD–CAM, robots, and software). The key strategic tasks are ensuring diffusion of best practice technology within the firm, and choices about the degree of appropriation (i.e. internalization) of production technology.

Thus, in reality, firms have constraints on choices about whether or not to be broad front or specialized, or to be product or process oriented. In one sense, the pattern of innovative activities described above can be seen as the result of cumulative and differentiated diffusion amongst firms of four pervasive technological systems, each with its distinctive skills and sources of technological competence: (1) mechanical (design and production engineering); (2) chemical (R&D laboratories); (3) electrical-electronic (R&D laboratories); and (4) software (systems departments). These long-term processes are well described and analysed by US economic and business historians (in particular Mowery, 1983a, 1983b; Rosenberg, 1976, 1985; Mowery and Rosenberg, 1989; Hounshell and Smith, 1989), and for the spread of software in services by Barras (1986). More detailed analyses of the development of competences include the development of videocassette recorders, particularly by Japanese firms (Rosenbloom and Cusumano, 1987), and Canon's strategy in optical recording technology (Doz *et al.*, 1989).

4. Organizing Firm-Specific Competences

The firm-specific competences described above are based on skills and knowledge that are functionally and organizationally specialized. An essential dimension of the large firm's managerial competence is the ability to combine these largely technological competences into effective units for identifying and developing innovations.

Considerable progress has been made in understanding the importance for the successful implementation of innovation of interfunctional integration, stretching back to pioneering work of Burns and Stalker in the early 1960s. Horizontal communications, across-functional boundaries, flexibility in the definition of tasks, links with outside sources of expertise and with users, and the authority and experience of responsible managers, are all factors that influence a successful implementation, in addition to the quality and competence of R&D and related technological activities (Rothwell *et al.*, 1975; Rothwell, 1977; Cooper, 1983; Maidique and Zirger, 1984).

Reviews of our state of understanding have been published by (amongst others) Schrivastava and Souder (1987), and by Burgelman (1985). However, the translation of these research findings into action remains a non-trivial task, especially in large and hierarchical organizations. The recent major reductions in product development times in Japanese automobile industry appear to have resulted from organizational changes entirely consistent with the

Table 1. Basic Technological Trajectories

Definition	Source of Technology	Trajectory	Typical product Groups	Strategic problems for Management
Science-Based	R and D Laboratory	Synergetic New Products. Applications Engineering	– Electronics – Chemicals	– Complementary Assets – Integration to Exploit Synergies – Patient Money
Scale Intensive	Production Engineering and Specialized Suppliers	Efficient and Complex Production and Related Products	– Basic Materials – Durable Consumer Goods	– Balance and Choice in Production Technology Among *Appropriation* (Secrecy and Patients), *Vertical Disintegration* (Co-operation with Supplier), and *Profit Centre* – 'Fusion' with Fast-Moving Technologies
Information Intensive	Software/ Systems Dept and Specialized Suppliers	Efficient (and Complex) Information Processing, and Related Products	– Financial Services – Retailing	– Diffusion of Production Technology Amongst Divisions – Exploiting Product Opportunities – Patient Money
Specialized Suppliers	Small-Firm Design and Large-Scale Users	Improved Specialized Producers Goods (Reliability and Performance)	– Machinery – Instruments – Speciality Chemicals – Software	– Matching Technological Opportunity with User – Absorbing User Experience – Finding Stable or New Product 'Niches'.

result of this earlier academic research (Clark *et al.*, 1987), but automobile firms in other parts of the world apparently have not yet been so successful.

However, whilst considerable progress has been made in our understanding of the problems that the functional form of organization poses for the management of innovation, we know much less about the problems posed by the divisional form of organization, which Chandler (1977) identifies as a key element in the managerial revolution and the emergence of large firms. At first sight, this may appear puzzling given that, as we have seen above, innovative activities – especially in science-based firms – are often a major source of entirely new ranges of products, and consequently of new product divisions. Perhaps this is because theories of the M-form organization (e.g. Williamson, 1975) have been essentially static rather than dynamic, concerned with the efficient management of what exists, rather than with the creation and management of the new. In any event, there are at least three problems that innovative activities pose for the 'pure' M-form organization, and that deserve further research.

The first is the existence of synergies across divisions or, alternatively, of core competences that pervade the technologies of all product divisions. As we can see in Table 1, these are of central importance in all types of large innovating firms. At the very least, they require central (i.e. corporate-wide) coordination, and interdivisional exchanges of personnel and experience (Aoki, 1986). They may also require strong direction from central R&D or production engineering activities. We have little systematic evidence on the nature and determinants of inter-firm and intersectoral differences in this corporate-wide technical function. We would expect it to be strongest in sector and firm with competences in technologies with rich and pervasive opportunities.

Second, the development of technological opportunities and competences do not necessarily fit tidily into established divisional structures. Rigid definition of divisional markets and missions can result in missed opportunities that cut across existing organizational structures: for example, PABX (small telephone exchanges) probably requires competences from divisions in telecommunications, office machinery, computers and components. In addition, existing firm-specific technological competences may not be sufficient to exploit new opportunities, and may require the purchase of what Teece (1986) has called 'co-specific assets': for example, marketing competence for pharmaceutical firms moving into pesticides (Achilladelis *et al.*, 1987), or for computing firms moving into telecommunications.

Thus, the strategic management and deployment of firm-specific technological competences is an intrinsically untidy process, so that rigid divisional structures can stifle or miss opportunities. Together with Robson and Townsend (1989), I have shown elsewhere that a high proportion of significant innovations in the UK between 1945 and 1983 were not developed in designated product divisions. And in their more finely-grained case studies of the corporate development, Doz, Angelmar and Prahalad (1989) conclude that success depends (amongst other things) on not being locked into established organizational forms, and on flexibility and variety in exploring opportunities.

Once again, this organization and deployment of corporate competences requires, at the very least, central coordination of decisions to redefine divisional missions and competences in the light of emerging technological opportunities. It may also require some strong central involvement in technological and managerial activities, based on an established R&D laboratory. Again, we have little systematic evidence on inter-industry and inter-firm differences.

The third organizational problem is the inevitable tension and balance between corporate centralization and decentralization. On the one hand, the strategic exploitation of technology at the corporate level requires a strong technological and managerial input at the centre, in order to exploit synergies and to redesign organizational missions and competences in the light of emerging opportunities (for example, see Reader, 1975, on the emergence of plastics in Imperial Chemicals Industry). On the other hand, we have seen that effective transformation of technology into commercial advantage requires decentralization, with effective horizontal communications and rapid decision taking. Thus, too much centralization is likely to result in ambitious, radical and ill-conceived innovations. Too much decentralization is likely to result in incremental and safe innovations in established businesses, with consequent diminishing returns and decline. However, the continuing debates and changing fashions about the appropriate degree of centralization and decentral-

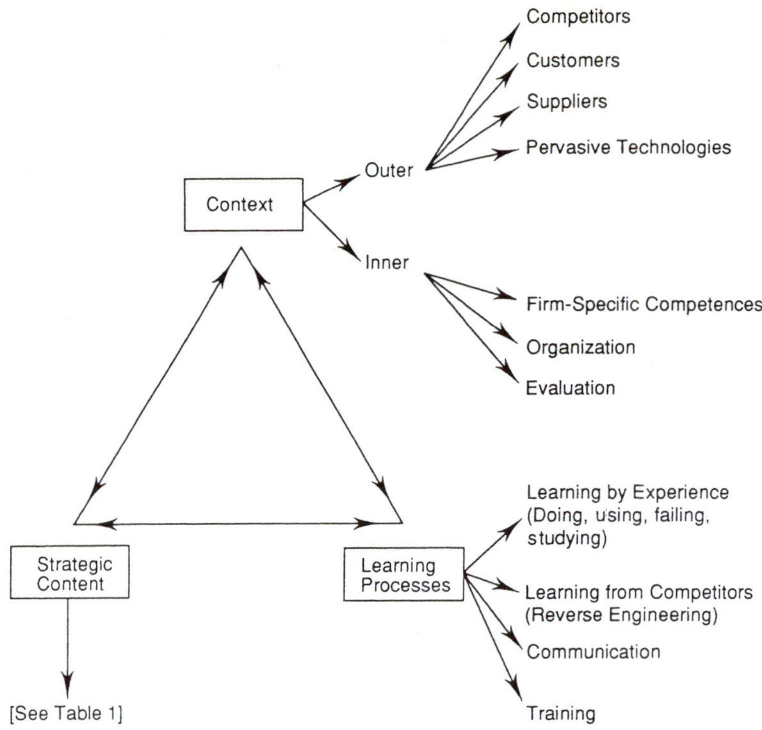

Figure 1. Learning processes in the Innovative Activities of Large Firms.

ization of R&D and related technical activities suggests that what is 'too much' or 'too little' is not easy to define in practice. This is another challenging research problem for the future.

5. Firm-specific Learning

In an activity as complicated and unpredictable as innovation, it is misleading to represent innovative activities in large firms as once-for-all decisions on the content of strategies or policies which, when taken, are easily and predictably implemented. This is well recognized in the 'processual' school of industrial organization, some of whose members even argue that 'strategies' and 'decisions' are no more than resultant or outcomes of political battles amongst functional and professional groups within the firm (Pettigrew, 1985, 1987).

Whilst this element of corporate behaviour is certainly real, it cannot be the whole story. Corporations are purposive organizations. As a result, they develop what Nelson and Winter (1982) call 'routines', or rules of thumb, to help them cope with a murky, messy and every-changing world. In the terminology of this paper, 'routines' embody 'firm-specific competences'; and their adaptation and change in the light of experience and further information is 'learning'. The processes of learning dissolve the sharp distinction between the 'content' and 'process' schools of strategy. As Figure 1 shows, they allow continuing feedback between content of strategy on the one hand, and knowledge of the context outside the firm, together with competences within the firm, on the other. Three other features also emerge from Figure 1.

First, sources of learning are very diverse, and their relative importance will vary according to the nature of the core competences of the firm:

- *Learning by doing* (i.e. by producing) is of greatest importance in production and information intensive firms, coping with complex and interdependent process technologies; it is also likely to involve some 'learning from suppliers';

- *Learning by using* (i.e. by operating production equipment) is of greatest importance to suppliers of capital goods and software, the limitations and further potentialities of whose products emerge from experience in use;
- *Learning by failing* (i.e. by modifying failed product innovations) is important over a wide range of sectors, where market experience enables modifications to products innovations, and where so-called 'robust designs' can be extended in different dimensions to cover a range of market segments (Rothwell and Gardiner, 1988);
- *Learning by studying* (i.e. by experimenting and assessing in R&D laboratories) is important for exploring potential opportunities and uses of pervasive technologies and radical discoveries. Their eventual assimilation into firm-specific competences may involve 'strategic alliances', and eventually require 'learning by hiring' or 'learning by takeover';
- *Learning from competitors* (i.e. evaluating competitor performance) is important for all innovating firms, although the means of doing so will vary. Reverse engineering is the main method of learning from competitors' product technologies. Equipment suppliers and informal exchanges among production engineers are channels for learning about process technologies. A number of firms are now beginning to use bibliometric methods to assess competitors' strategies.

Second, in the large firm, learning is a collective activity requiring frequent communication amongst specialists and functions. Since knowledge accumulated through experience is partly tacit, and the tasks to which such knowledge is applied are complex and loosely structured, personal contact and discussions are the most frequent and effective means of communication and learning. Policies for effective learning therefore go beyond training and organization to include those of geographical location. Tom Allen (1977) and other scholars have shown the importance of physical location in influencing patterns of communication, both within the technical function and between the technical and other functions in the firm. And Howells (1990) has shown that decisions about the location of R&D laboratories by firms in the UK pharmaceutical industry have been strongly influenced by the requirements for effective internal communication with other functional areas.

Third, R&D laboratories and other technical functions in the firm are necessary and centrally important components in nearly all the dimensions of learning described above, and they often have strong linkages with the marketing function. This may help to explain the longevity and capacity for adaptation of the large innovating firms of the 20th century. R&D laboratories have given them the means to learn about, evaluate and – if necessary – assimilate major technological discontinuities: examples include the assimilation of computing and solid state physics into the core competences of electro mechanical firms (like IBM) in the 1950s and 1960s; and the present process of evaluation and assimilation of biotechnology in firms in chemicals, pharmaceuticals and food products (Orsenigo, 1989; Sharp, 1989). In addition, large firms' accumulated knowledge of users' needs gives them a strong advantage in exploiting new technologies; again IBM is a good example.

This institutional continuity of large firms confirms the cumulative and multi-dimensional nature of firm-specific technological competences. In the short term, few technological discontinuities are now 'competence destroying' in that they make completely obsolete the whole range of existing competences in large innovating firms with strong technical functions (Tushman and Anderson, 1986). However, in the long term, cumulative change can completely transform what firms do and how they do it.

6. Allocating Resources

The ultimate purpose of firm-specific competence is to create profitable investment opportunities that improve the present value of the firm. Put another way, the nature and extent of potentially profitable investment opportunities are constrained in a large part by accumulated firm-specific competences. The allocation of resources to create such competences poses unusual and difficult problems, since they involve processes that are both lengthy and uncertain, and whose outcomes (organization-embodied competences) are often intangible and difficult to measure. Given these properties, *ex ante* project assessments turn out to have wide and irreducible errors, and attempts to use purely quantitative 'figures of merit' for projects and programmes can be seen as part of processes of advocacy rather than as attempts to improve rigour and precision in resource allocation. Empirical research has shown that, given these uncertainties, methods of resource allocation tend to be incremental and closely coupled to the learning processes described in section 5, with constant feedback from improved knowledge and experience to evaluation (Freeman, 1982).

Nonetheless, the appropriate criteria and procedure for allocating resources to the creation of firm-specific competences still poses important and unresolved problems for theory and practice. These emerge from the growing debate (particularly in the UK and USA) about the appropriateness of financial performance criteria as guides for the allocation of resources to R&D, or even to the commercialization of innovative products and production processes. Some practitioners argue that this leads to 'short-termism', reflected in under-investment in technological activities and undue concentration on safe and largely incremental modifications (EIRMA, 1986).

As Stewart Myers (1984) has pointed out, these problems result in part from the use of incorrect financial performance criteria. Instead of assessing investments using discounted cash flow (DCF) as the basis of their contribution to the net present value of the firm, emphasis is often given to short payback periods, and to quarterly profit performance, which introduces bias against longer term projects. However, Myers also points out that to DCF is inappropriate when there are strong links between today's investment and tomorrow's opportunities, which is precisely the case for cumulative learning and firm-specific competences. Here, investment projects do not necessarily produce additions to the net present value of the firm now, but have an 'option value' for further investments at some time in the future. Since it cannot deal with option values: 'DCF is no help at all for pure research and development. The value of R&D is almost all option value. Intangible asset's value is usually option value' (Myers, p. 135).

There is also the more complex case when a firm builds on its own firm-specific competences to enter a new product market, or to adopt a radically new production technology. Such investments often combine both contributions to the net present value of the firm, and strong components of learning, with expectations of follow-on investments in the future. They normally take a long time before making a profit. Complete reliance on DCF and neglect of their 'option value' will presumably reduce the long term growth of the net present value of the firm.

As Myers points out, coping with option values is an important challenge to the developments in financial theory. In the meantime, large innovating firms have developed (more or less effective) 'routines' to deal with learning and option values, and these are often observable in the qualitative checklists commonly used by large innovating firms to evaluate R&D related programmes and projects. Again, we would expect characteristics of the technico-economic expertise at the centre of the corporation to be particularly important in the formation of corporate expectations about future developments in technology, and their implications for R&D programmes to open up future investment opportunities. Evidence shows that such expertise is stronger in Japanese firms than those in Western Europe and the United States (Patel and Pavitt, 1987). We also know that expectations can sometimes turn out to be badly wrong: for example, in the 1950s and 1960s, some very competent large electrical firms bet more heavily on nuclear energy than the semi-conductor. Until now, we have little knowledge of the nature and determinants of the formation of technological expectations in large innovating firms, and their impact on the allocation of resources to R&D, and on investment decisions.

7. Conclusions

We have identified and explored in this paper four central characteristics of the large innovative firm:

- differentiated and firm-specific competences that dictate the direction and range of technological opportunities that firms are capable of exploiting;
- organizational forms that reconcile both the decentralization required for effective implementation, and the centralization required for the exploitation of core technologies, and for the continuous re-definition of appropriate divisional boundaries;
- processes of learning that enable firms to augment specific competences as a consequence of experience, monitoring the external environment and assimilation of radical technologies;
- methods of resource allocation that reconcile the requirements for profitable investment oppor-

tunities now, with the creation of profitable investment opportunities in the future.

These four characteristics are proposed as a common basis for the definition of the central tasks of the strategic management of technology, for the building of models at large innovating firms, and for the specification of hypothesis for empirical test. Suffice at this stage to draw two conclusions.

The first concerns the role of R&D and other technical functions within the large firm. Our analysis shows that the technical function should involve more than being a major actor in the implementation of innovations. It also involves contributions to the definition of the appropriate divisional boundaries, to the exploration of radical technologies and other forms of corporate learning, and to the formation of technological expectations that influence the corporate allocation of resources to R&D and to investment opportunities.

Second, although we now have considerable possibilities, through bibliometric techniques, for collecting systematic (if imperfect) evidence on many dimensions of firm-specific technological competences, we still lack systematic knowledge of the organizational forms, learning processes and methods of resource allocation that determine the development and exploitation of these competences.

References

Achilladelis, B., A. Schwarzkopf, and M. Cines (1987). 'A Study of Innovation in the Pesticide Industry: Analysis of the Innovation Record of an Industrial Sector'. *Research Policy*, **16**, 2–4, pp. 175–212.

Allen, T. (1977). *Managing the Flow of Technology*. MIT Press, Cambridge, Mass.

Aoki, M. (1986). 'Horizontal vs. Vertical Information Structure of the Firm'. *American Economic Review*, **76** (December).

Barras, R. (1986). 'Towards a Theory of Innovation in services'. *Research Policy*, **15** (4), pp. 161–173.

Burgelman, R. (1985). 'Managing the New Venture Division: Research Findings and Implications for Strategic Management'. *Strategic Management Journal*, **6**, pp. 39–54.

Burns, T. and G. Stalker (1961). *The Management of Innovation*. Tavistock, London.

Chandler, A. (1977). *The Visible Hand: the Managerial Revolution in American Business*. Harvard University Press, Cambridge, Mass.

Clark, K., W. Chew, and T. Fujimoto (1987). 'Product Development in the World Auto Industry'. *Brookings Papers on Economic Activity*, No. 3.

Cooper, R. (1983). 'A Process Model For Industrial New Product Development' *IEEE Transactions in Engineering Management*, **EM-30**, pp. 2–11.

Doz, Y., C. Prahald and R. Angelmar (1989). 'Managing the Scope of Innovation: a Dilemma for Top Management'. In: R. Rosenbloom, and R. Burgelman (eds), *Research on Technological Innovation Management and Policy*, **4**. JAI Press, Greenwich, Conn.

European Industrial Research Management Association (EIRMA). (1986). *Developing R and D Strategies*, Working Group Report No. 33, Paris.

Freeman, C. (1982). *The Economics of Industrial Innovation*. Francis Pinter. (First edition published by Penguin in 1974.)

Hounshell, D. and J. Smith (1989). *Science and Corporate Strategy*. Cambridge University Press. Cambridge.

Howells, J. (1990). 'The Location and Organization of Research and Development: New Horizons'. *Research Policy*, **19**, 2, pp. 133–146.

Maidique, M. and B. Zirger (1984). 'A Study of Success and Failure in Product Innovation: The Case of the UK Electronics Industry'. *IEEE Transactions on Engineering Management*, **EM-31**, pp. 192–203.

Mowery, D. (1983a). 'Industrial Research and Firm Size, Survival and Growth in American Manufacturing, 1921–1946: An Assessment'. *Journal of Economic History*, **43**, pp. 953–980.

Mowery, D. (1983b). 'The Relationships Between Intra-firm and Contractual Forms of Industrial Research in American Manufacturing'. *Explorations in Economic History*, **20**, pp. 351–374.

Mowery, D. and N. Rosenberg (1989). *Technology and the Pursuit of Economic Growth*. Cambridge University Press, Cambridge.

Myers, S. (1984). 'Finance Theory and Finance Strategy'. *Interfaces*, **14**, 1, pp. 126–137.

Nelson, R. and S. Winter (1982). *An Evolutionary Theory of Economic Change*. Belknap, Cambridge, Mass.

Orsenigo, L. (1989). *The Emergence of Biotechnology*. Pinter, London.

Patel, P. and K. Pavitt (1987). 'Is Western Europe losing the Technological Race?'. *Research Policy*, **16**, pp. 57–85.

Patel, P. and K. Pavitt (1989a), 'A Comparison of Technological Activities in FR Germany and the UK'. *National Westminster Quarterly Review*, May, London.

Pavitt, K., M. Robson and J. Townsend (1987a). 'The Size Distribution of Innovating Firms in the UK: 1945–83'. *The Journal of Industrial Economics*, **XXXV**, 3, pp 297–316.

Pavitt, K., M. Robson and J. Townsend (1989), 'Technological Accumulation, Diversification and Organisation in UK Companies, 1945–1983'. *Management Science*, **35**, 1, pp. 81–99.

Penrose, E. (1959). *The Theory of the Growth of the Firm*. Blackwell, Oxford.

Pettigrew, A. (1985). *The Awakening Giant: Continuity and Change in Imperial Chemical Industries*. Blackwell, Oxford.

Pettigrew, A. (ed) (1987). *The Management of Strategic Change*. Blackwell, Oxford.

Reader, W. (1975). *Imperial Chemical Industries: A History*. Oxford University Press, Oxford.

Rosenberg, N. (1985). 'The Commercial Exploitation of Science by American Industry'. In: K. Clark, R. Hayes and C. Lorenz (eds.), *The Uneasy Alliance: Managing the Productivity/Technology Dilemma*. Harvard Business School, Cambridge, Mass.

Rosenberg, N. (1976). *Perspectives on Technology*. Cambridge University Press, Cambridge.

Rosenbloom, R. and M. Cusumano (1987). 'Technological Pioneering and Competitive Advantage: the Birth of the VCR Industry'. *California Management Review*, **XXIX**, No. 4.

Rothwell, R. (1977). 'The Characteristics of Successful Innovators and Technically Progressive Firms'. *R&D Management*, **7**(3), pp. 191–206.

Rothwell, R., C. Freeman, P. Jervis, A. Robertson and J. Townsend (1975). 'SAPPHO Updated – Project SAPPHO Phase II'. *Research Policy*, **3**, 3, pp. 258–291.

Rothwell, R. and P. Gardiner (1988). 'Re-innovation and Robust Designs: Producer and User Benefits'. *Journal of Marketing Management*, **3**, 3, pp. 372–387.

Schumpeter, J. (1947). *Capitalism, Socialism and Democracy*, Harpers, New York.

Sharp, M. (1987). *Technological Trajectories and Firm Strategies: The Case of Biotechnology*. DRC Working Paper No. 68, Science Policy Research Unit, Un. of Sussex.

Shrivastava, P. and W. Souder (1987). 'The Strategic Management of Technological Innovation: a Review and a Model'. *Journal of Management Studies*, **24**, 1, pp. 25–41.

Soete, L. (1979). 'Firm Size and Inventive Activity: The Evidence Reconsidered'. European Economics Review, **12**, pp. 319–340.

Teece, D. (1986). 'Profiting from Technological Innovation: Implications for Integration, Elaboration, Licensing and Public Policy'. *Research Policy*, **15**(6), pp. 285–305.

Tushman, M. and M. Anderson (1986). 'Technological Discontinuities and Organisation Environments', *Administrative Science Quarterly*, **31**, pp. 439–465.

Williamson, O. (1975). *Markets and Hierarchies: Analysis and Anti-Trust Implications*. Free Press, New York.

[5]

EUROPEAN JOURNAL OF WORK AND ORGANIZATIONAL PSYCHOLOGY, 1996, 5 (3), 351–375

Technological and Organizational Innovation: A Dilemma of Fundamental Change and Participation

Jaap J. Boonstra

Organizational Studies, University of Amsterdam, Amsterdam, The Netherlands

Maurits J. Vink

SANT Management Consultancy, Amsterdam, The Netherlands

This article proposes sociotechnical system theory as a framework for analysing the relationship between technological and organizational innovation and as a tool for managing change as a process of organizational learning. The article focuses on the barriers to change and the way in which the dilemma between expert design and participatory development is approached. The technological and organizational innovation in an automated clearing house for payment transactions has been used as an example. The longitudinal case research focuses on the dynamics of change and illustrates the importance of learning processes during the innovation to realize flexibility and innovative capacity within the organization. The article concludes that sociotechnical system theory provides a basis of knowledge for redesigning organizations as well as developing organizations by learning processes. It indicates six barriers to technological and organizational innovation and offers a perspective on how to integrate design strategies with a participative learning strategy for fundamental change.

INTRODUCTION

An understanding of the development and implementation of technological and organizational innovations is crucial, given the importance of these innovations to the improvement of labour and work processes in organizations. The development and introduction of new information technologies are directly related to changes in business strategy, the flow of information, and the design of business processes. Technological development also creates the potential for new choices in work organization and the quality of working life (Child & Loveridge, 1990; Walton, 1988).

Influenced by technological innovations and higher market demands, organizations strive to enhance their flexibility and ability to innovate and to

Requests for reprints should be addressed to J.J. Boonstra, Organizational Studies, University of Amsterdam, O.Z. Achterburgwal 237, 1012 DL Amsterdam, The Netherlands.

increase their learning capacities. The traditional organizational paradigm of maximal division of labour is increasingly abandoned. Attempts are made to break with the functional structuring of organizations by redesigning business processes on the basis of customers or product flows. Within these flows, self-managing teams are formed. These teams integrate operational tasks with planning, support, and control activities. The teams are to a certain extent autonomous and are expected to improve the execution of assignments while learning (Cherns, 1987; Herbst, 1976).

The realization of technological and organizational innovation is a complex change process and many organizations do not attain the desired outcomes. A possible explanation for these failures can be found in the approach of the change process. Fundamental organizational change tries to create flexible organizations with a high innovative potential, but at the same time most of our organizations lack the learning capacities that are needed for innovation. So, what are the barriers to complete transformation of business and how can traditional organizations learn to become learning and innovative organizations?

A dilemma is that an expert design approach permits a far-reaching break through innovation but it neglects the development of learning capacities, whereas a participatory development approach gives way to learning but the drawback is that it allows participants to fall back to conventional and fragmental solutions in their thoughts and deeds, while innovative and completely new ideas are needed.

This article examines the barriers to technological and organizational innovation and explores the tension between expert design and participative development. In the first section, the relation between technological and organizational innovation will be conceptualized in a system theory of organizations. It will also consider the way in which fundamental change is achieved by business process redesign (BPR) and sociotechnical system theory (STST). The second section presents the results of an in-depth longitudinal case study. The relations between business strategy, information technology, work organization, and the quality of working life will be made clear. The focus of the study is to examine the barriers to change and the way in which the dilemma between expert design and participatory development is approached. In the third section we present some lessons for realizing technological and organizational innovation.

THEORETICAL FRAMEWORK

System Theory of Organizations

For technological and organizational innovation and the integration of change to take place, some unifying framework is needed to guide the process. The open sociotechnical systems theory offers such a framework.

Organizations are viewed as open systems. The production process takes place within socio-economic exchange networks between the organization and its environment. Economic, technological, and social developments form a complex of more or less structured situations that affect the organization and influence its functioning (Emery & Trist, 1965). Interactions take place between the organization and stakeholders within the transactional environment (Ansoff, 1985; Freeman, 1984). In order to survive, an organization has to respond adequately to changes in the environment and the relations with stakeholders. The environment of many organizations is becoming more complex and changes occur at an ever increasing pace, compelling organizations to develop a more flexible and innovative work organization.

The sociotechnical perspective considers every organization to be made up of a social and a technological aspect-system. People working together in an organizational context (the social system) are using information systems, tools, techniques, and knowledge (the technical system) to produce a service or product valued by the environment (the environmental system) (Emery, 1959; Pasmore, 1988; Trist, 1982). The social and technological aspect-systems interact continuously and are inclined towards a dynamic equilibrium in relation to the environment of the organization. Change in one aspect-system directly affects its relation to other aspect-systems (Pava, 1986). The ability of each of the systems to adjust means that the organization forms a flexible system capable of adjusting to environmental changes.

The sociotechnical system theory provides a useful framework for assessing the system-wide implications of information technologies (Shani & Sena, 1994). Compatibility between the technical and environment aspect-systems requires that new information technologies are effective in meeting the needs of the stakeholders. Introducing new technology inevitably requires a redefinition of the relationship between the organization and the environment through adjustment to business strategy. Compatibility between technical and social aspect-systems implies that a balance must be struck between the new information technologies with the social aspect-system to accommodate the requirements of the new information technology (Clark & Staunton, 1989).

Technological and Organizational Innovation

The introduction of new information technology in organizations will involve the development of new ideas about technical and social processes and is related to business strategy and business processes. This perspective contrasts with technological determinism in which technology determines the social aspect-system and organizational choices cannot be made on how to relate the technological and social aspect-systems (Turner & Lawrence, 1965). Swan and Clark (1992) debate that cognitive processes and decision making are important in the process of innovation and the choices to be made. A question is how the existing organizational paradigm influences the decision-making process on technological and organizational innovation. Weick (1990) argues that people design technology and organizations in keeping with their perceptions and explanatory frameworks. This viewpoint is subscribed to by Child and Loveridge (1990). In a study on information technology in European services they concluded that the opportunities offered for organizational innovation by information technology appear to have been realized very frequently; only occasionally had substantial change in organizational design and tasks structure been introduced. This lack of novelty might be attributed to a delayed process of organizational learning in which existing perspectives continue to dominate. There seems to be a process of organizational conservatism that is shaped and bound by forces of a social and political nature in the sense that those involved have a concern to preserve organizational arrangements with which they are comfortable. Traditions that are long-established and have institutionalized into bureaucratic structures, and strong cultures as a means of ensuring predictability, support the prevailing systems of the division of labour.

Realizing strategic, technological, and organizational change is a difficult process and a lot of efforts fail to realize the objectives. Beer (1988) gives reasons why broad change programmes fail. First, programmes seem to be unidimensional and do not change the technical and social aspect system at the same time. In addition, programmes are seldom targeted at behaviour. Second, programmatic changes are often not connected to the most pressing problems experienced by employees. At best, the programmes are a response to a general diagnosis of business problems. This makes it difficult to learn from earlier experiences and to translate the general themes into action. Third, the programmes are often initiated and managed by top management and experts. This top-down and expert character makes it difficult for employees and line management to feel committed. Swan and Clark (1992) indicate that particular problems occur when employees have inadequate knowledge bases and have conflicting ideas about the chosen innovation. Knowledge and cognitions are important in the innovation process. Organizational as well as technological knowledge bases are important to decisions about technological innovation because its appropriation requires a blending of technical systems with organizational procedures and practice.

Design Perspective on Organizational Change

The term business process redesign (BPR) is often used when redesign of strategy, information technology, and organizational processes is concerned (Davenport, 1993; Hammer & Champy, 1993). In essence, BPR is a fundamental rearrangement of business processes enabling information technology to realize reduction of costs, increase of profitability, and enhancement of performance in quality, service, and speed.

The design philosophy of BPR concerns the radical redesign of business processes. Business processes are rearranged on a customer or product basis. In the customer- or product-oriented process design, process segments are placed in a natural sequence. Teams bear the responsibility for the execution of tasks within a segment and are held accountable for measurable results. Frequently, separate teams are formed for innovation, planning and preparation, and execution of tasks. The operational teams are confronted with an elaborately modelled and automated production method. In the application of redesign principles in the service sector, a distinction is often made between a front office for direct interaction with customers and a back office for administrative processing. In the front office the task is to inform the customer quickly and adequately. Information technology enables decision making while the customer is served. In the back office all activities suitable for automation are subsumed. The technological governance of the work process results in a situation in which people have little influence over their own actions and in which they face considerably increased expectations with respect to their work pace and output. Teams are expected to contribute to the enhancement of a more efficient production method.

The organization of the redesign process is primarily a task of the management. Top management contributes to the motivation for change and is responsible for the designation of goals and the allocation of means. Teams of line managers are responsible for the design of sub-processes. A steering committee of managers develop the strategy for the change process and co-ordinate the course of events. Consultants support the entire process with techniques and resources (Harrison & Pratt, 1993). In the design methodology a number of stages are distinguished. Teams of managers analyse business processes and circumscribe performance criteria for the redesign. With the consultant's assistance, a perspective is developed on the organization of business processes. The analyses of the teams are combined into a blueprint for the organization form, the appropriate technological architecture and information systems. The new organization form is implemented by the line management. Communication about the importance of the new design is seen as a success factor for change. Pilot projects and training programmes could illustrate the significance of change. Finally, team-based activities are built into the entire organization in order to replace conventional management methods (Guha, Kettinger, & Teng, 1993; Harrison & Pratt, 1993).

Development Perspective on Organizational Change

The development perspective on organizational change is based on sociotechnical experiences. The sociotechnique was initially preoccupied with the criteria for the design of tasks on an individual or group level. The purpose of this redesign was an improvement of organizational effectiveness, an improvement of the quality of work life, and the levelling of power. In the 1970s and 1980s, the sociotechnical design principles were further developed into an integral redesign of organizations. In this integral redesign, attention is paid to the relation between corporate strategy, organizational form, the nature of the transformation process, the technology, and labour.

The central design principle of the contemporary sociotechnique can be summarized as the formation of complex tasks within simple structures, instead of the performance of simple tasks within complex structures. What is central is the shift from the maximal division of work in classically structured organizations to the minimal division of work as the leading principle of design for flexible and modern organizations. According to sociotechnical views, the team is the smallest unit of organizing. In the organization, groups are always interdependent. It would benefit the flexibility, the effectiveness, and the quality of work life, if groups can regulate their own tasks, can shape their own work organization, have a high measure of control and the ability to solve problems independently (Ashby, 1969; Cherns, 1987; Susman, 1976).

Management of the change process rests on experience in the practice of the classical organization development and is theoretically founded on theories of group dynamics, learning processes, process intervention, and systemic change (Argyris, 1990; Beer & Walton, 1987; Schein, 1969). Practical experience has led to the conclusion that insufficient results are achieved with the sociotechnical designs when a fundamental change process is based exclusively on the sociotechnical design principles. Van Beinum (1990) states that the change process will inevitably result in some form of "social engineering" when organizational redesign is shaped by external experts who, solely on the basis of a sociotechnical system analysis, prescribe how the new organization must be shaped. The members of the organization are then insufficiently involved in fundamental decisions and little opportunity is left for organizational learning and the incorporation and acceptance of the change process. The designing of organizations which is characterized by autonomy, self-regulation, and participation can, according to Van Beinum, only genuinely take place when all members are actively involved in the shaping of their own work situation and are allowed to experience a learning process during the change process that enhances their understanding of their own situation. A participative approach usually employs search conferences, group discussions, workshops, and the experience gained through team-based work to redesign the work organization (Mohrman & Cummings, 1989).

The Dilemma of Technological and Organizational Innovation

In the design perspective the emphasis lies on the application of new technology and the designing of a new organization. The design starts with the designation of abstract objectives. Particular attention is paid to the desired output of the organization, the formal transformation process, and the related information process. The change process is singular and linear, and the number of alternatives is restricted. If the new organization is implemented and a stable final situation is attained, the change process has been concluded. Changes are often initiated, co-ordinated, and controlled by the top of the organization. The decision-making process is highly structured and formalized. There is hardly any opportunity for a discussion of possible differences in opinion. The approach is normally supported by consultants who, as experts, primarily focus on the design of the new information technology and work organization. A problem with the design approach is that it hardly contributes to the enhancement of the ability to change on lower levels in the organization. Cultural and political aspects are easily left outside of consideration. There is a great danger that collective norms and values will not develop, power structures are not influenced, and that, therefore, fundamental change cannot be achieved.

In the development approach, organizational problems and shortcomings are analysed first. The organization's ability to change is enhanced by involving members of the organization in the problem analysis. During the process, attention is given to the organization's culture and capability of the people to solve problems. The decision-making process concentrates on attaining shared objectives by consultation and negotiation. There is a phased and progressive change in which ideas from the basis of the organization play an important role. The change process is characterized by rough planning. Members of the organization are involved in all phases of the process. Participation is very possible, because the starting-point is the existing organization, objectives are established gradually, and deliberation and adjustment are facilitated. By participation of all organizational members, an enhancement of the self-learning ability of all members is attempted. A problem with the development approach is that it is difficult to achieve fundamental changes. Because of the existing social and political nature, the grounded values, norms and traditions, and the existing bureaucratic structures, organizational conservatism supporting the prevailing systems of the division of labour and hindering fundamental organizational change can exist.

From an interventionist perspective, two important questions are raised: (1) What are the barriers to technological and organizational innovation? (2) What are the possibilities of broadening the perspectives of the participants in the decision-making process and overcoming organizational conservatism and simultaneously developing learning capacities?

RESEARCH SITE AND METHODOLOGY

Action research is a method to study dynamic processes and actions that are temporally interconnected and embedded in context. The research is aimed at developing descriptive accounts and explanations through looking at patterns of events to gain knowledge of problems and the solving of problems in social reality (Argyris, 1983).

The research reported in this section sought to address the dynamics of change over a three-year period in a single company faced with the demands of becoming more flexible and integrating strategic, technological, and organizational innovation. The research is based on real-time longitudinal analyses of the change process and a retrospective analysis of the collected data and the acquired experiences and knowledge. The second author of the study served as a consultant in a team of internal and external employees that facilitated the change process. The first author facilitated the action research process during the study. Data collection involved ongoing semi-structured interviews, the keeping of a diary, questionnaires, conferences, workshops, and quarterly process evaluations.

The research has been conducted in the BankGiroCentrale (BGC), an automated clearing house for payment transactions for the commercial banks in the Netherlands. The product of the BGC is operation services of pre-arranged batch payment items submitted on magnetic tape, diskettes, computer-cartridges, cheques, payment documents, and conversion forms. The BGC is also providing data-networks for cash dispensers, point-of-sale terminals, and telegiro. In addition, BGC is processing and exchanging information about payment transactions between banks and is supporting the standardization and the risk management in information technology for payment transactions. The BGC has two processing centres in the Netherlands and 800 people are employed by the organization.

A CASE OF FUNDAMENTAL CHANGE

BGC as an Open System

The market of payment transactions has become rather turbulent during the last years. The costs of payment transactions has to be reduced under the influence of the demands of the commercial banks and their customers. New forms of payment by credit card, debit card, or data communication require low transaction costs, reliable operation, high performance, and security. Deregulation of the financial services by government offers possibilities for merging bank activities with insurance. The pursuit of a European economic and monetary market by the European Commission influences the scaling of the financial market and an increase of international activities and collaboration by banks and insurance companies. Competition between financial conglomerates is rising. This leads to very strong stakeholders that put higher demands on costs and the quality of services that is offered by the BGC. Banks make high demands on swift and timely processing of payments and settlement of payments between banks. Service levels and customer satisfaction are becoming more and more important.

The availability of swifter and better mainframe computers, the developments in information technology and the application of data communication have resulted in significant shifts in the different types of payment order. Transactions are more frequently presented on cartidges, tapes, and data communication than via paper. These shifts require adaptations in work organization and job qualifications. During the past few years, technological developments have generated all sorts of new services and products, such as cash dispensers, point-of-sale terminals, the development of the chip card, and the possibility of giving payment orders via interactive television. This demands an innovative capacity from an organization.

For the management of the BGC, the analysis of the environment formed the basis for a new business strategy. The environment and the changing market demands from the BGC further cost reduction, improvements in quality and customer service, a flexible attitude towards market developments, and an innovative ability to make optimal use of new information technology. The business strategy results in three projects: (1) the development of a new automated payment system including the renewal of system architecture and the technological infrastructure; (2) the realization of a new technological and logistic infrastructure for high-speed imaging of payment documents; (3) the re-engineering of the business processes and the reorganization of the company into an effective and efficient organization that is compatible with the new information technology.

BGC as a Sociotechnical System

Information technology is essential for the functioning of the BGC. All payment orders are processed by means of automated systems. The information on the production is recorded in automated data files or on microfilm. All the BGC products are highly automated. Administrative organization and procedures are important in order to keep track of the transformation process and to reduce susceptibility to fraud. The existing information systems no longer met requirements because of the high cost of maintenance and the limited possibilities of adaptation. Furthermore, the system was insufficiently capable of coping with the growth in financial traffic and it no longer met the requirements of swift and reliable processing. The new information systems were to be flexible and easily maintained. In the new system, a distinction is made between technical management of the hardware control systems and functional management of the application systems.

To realize compatibility between the new technological aspect-system and the social aspect system, the top management installed task groups of line managers to study the effects of the new technology on the organizational structure. This gradually revealed that the line managers were unable fully to consider the operational processes. The task groups reached a deadlock in discussions on the adjustment of the boundaries between the existing departments. There proved to be an organizational conservatism in which line managers proceed from the present division of labour and try to protect their own position within the organization. At the same time, employees are worried about the effect of the technological innovation on the quality of working life. A committee for the quality of working life discussed the perils of technological determinism and the possible negative consequences of the new technology with the top management.

The top management, confronted with the limited capacity to change of the line management and the uncertainty of the employees, asked for assistance from consultants in managing the technological and the organizational innovation.

Facilitating the Change Process

The formulated strategic policy induced the innovation of the technical aspect-system. The strategic policy had been limitedly communicated within the organization and only a few organization members had been involved in the technological innovations. So far, little attention had been paid to the social aspect-system. The advisers suggested a clarification of organizational strategy and a formulation of the points of departure for the changing technological and social aspect-system. A conference model was chosen to elaborate the points of departure (Axelrod, 1992; Weisbord, 1992).

In the work conferences, the top management presented the analysis of the environment and market changes and discussed the strategic goals with the line management and the employees. Three work conferences were held, with about 40 participants per conference. The participants were a cross-section of the organization. Besides discussions on the strategic objectives and the development of information technology, pressure points within the existing organization were analysed and an inventory was made of suggestions for improvement. Additionally, success factors for change were charted. The outcome of the work conferences was the basis of the points of departure for the renewal of the technological and social system and of the way in which the change process was to be dealt with. The points of departure were presented during group meetings and discussed with all employees. During these meetings the feasibility of the change was specifically discussed.

In order to further facilitate the change process, a task force of employees and external advisers was formed. The task of this group was to gather information on pressure points within the organization and to organize work meetings to develop proposals for the new set-up of the organizational processes and to formulate ideas for an appropriate form of organization. The task force consisted of employees who collectively had a clear image of the work processes in the different departments and who were considered capable of guiding group discussions on the future work organization. Top management and the work council were both involved in the change process by means of regular meetings and workshops. Line management was involved in work conferences. Employees were involved in questionnaires and group discussions to diagnose problems in the social aspect-system and in workshops to suggest ideas for problem solving and to develop new designs for business processes, information technology, and work organization.

Problem Diagnosis in the Social System

The points of departure and the reactions to them formed the basis on which a specific form of diagnosis was developed for each unit. Three units are to be distinguished within the production process. (1) *Operations* dealt with the processing of payment traffic. About 450 people, spread over two branches, were active in this unit. The unit had been organized in a linear structure with small processing steps divided over many departments. The processing was to be distinguished into: (a) receipt and unpacking and sorting of tapes, diskettes, and cartridges, (b) control of payment information, (c) input of data, (d) correction and recoding of data, (e) authorization and automated processing, and (f) production and supply of output. Separate service departments in Operations supplied telephonic and written information on the processing. (2) *Commercial Affairs* dealt with the account management of clients and with the product management of payment products. About 50 people were active in this unit. The department also developed specific automated applications for individual banks. (3) *Computer and Network Services* dealt with the technical support of the operations, in particular. About 250 people were active in this unit. The unit supplied computer and network facilities for the processing and took care of the daily control of the applications needed for the processing. Additionally, the unit developed new information systems in accordance with the wishes of the commercial unit.

The diagnosis consisted of interviews, specific questionnaires for all the employees and group discussions to verify and discuss the results of the questionnaire. The questionnaire included such items as contacts with customers, exchange of information and compatibility among departments, pressure points in the work, style of leadership, quality of working life, and barriers to fundamental change. The diagnosis provides a sharp picture of the problems within the various units.

Operations was characterized by a far-reaching division of labour. The number of functional contacts between the departments was very high and a great deal of co-ordination of different tasks is required in order to have the work process run smoothly. The exchange of information and the task co-ordination took a lot of time, proceeded with difficulty, and caused a great deal of attuning problems and mistakes in the operations. The quality of working life was rather low owing to limited tasks with little responsibility. Employees were given limited information on the achievement of results. Owing to their dependence on others they had few opportunities to solve the problems encountered in their own work. There was a very limited learning potential.

Commercial Affairs was differentiated in account managers, product managers, and customer services. Account managers as well as product managers visited customers but the co-ordination between the two departments was very problematic. The customers' questions about operations were answered by customer services as well as by the service desk from operations. The result was that clients did not know which department to turn to and that they were often referred from one department to another. No systematic survey was kept of the problems, questions, and wishes of the clients. Relations between Commercial Affairs and Operations was problematic because Commercial Affairs made promises to clients that Operations was unable to fulfil.

Computer and Network Services consisted of about 20 departments. Half of them dealt with day-to-day hardware operations and the operating of the information systems for the transactions in the unit operations. The activities of this service unit and the unit operations needed a lot of co-ordination. This co-ordination often proceeded with difficulty owing to distances between locations and differences in time between the detection of problems in the execution of the payment traffic and the control of this traffic by means of automated systems. The departments dealing with the development of systems were all responsible for a separate phase within the system development or for a specific technological subject. For the greater part, the co-ordination of these activities within the unit proceeded with difficulty.

The outcomes of the diagnosis have been widely presented within the organization. For this purpose, general information sessions were organized, as well as presentations to smaller groups. The presentations were given by the management. This way they emphasized that the pressure points that had been indicated in the diagnosis by the employees were taken seriously. The presentations were accompanied by written material in which the outlines of the outcomes had been listed systematically. During these presentations, the employees and the managers had the opportunity to respond to the outcomes and, if neccessary, to indicate gaps or mistakes. During the presentations it was also indicated which themes were to be further elaborated. The management had determined these themes on the basis of the outcomes of the diagnosis, in consultation with the heads of the department.

The diagnosis revealed that the high degree of task differentiation within the organization resulted in pressure points in the exchange of information, in the effectiveness of working by making projects, and in customer service. Task differentiation within the business processes resulted in a strong interdependence between departments and groups, which reduced the decisiveness and efficiency of the organization; moreover, it put a heavy burden on communication and co-ordination. The task division also contributed to the fact that responsibilities were not assigned unambiguously. This limited the swiftness of reaction in case of changing circumstances or problems. The division of tasks also resulted in a limited quality of labour. If the present social aspect-system were to be taken as a starting point for further automation, there is a risk that the deficiencies within this system would be embedded in the technology and that the opportunities for innovation of the entire organizational system would not be realized. Simultaneous innovation of the technical and social aspect-system was indicated in order to realize the strategic objectives and to meet the demands made on the organization by the environment.

Barriers to Change

One of the most important reasons why change programmes fail is that they do not deal with fundamental barriers to the development and implementation of organizational and technological innovation (Beer, Eisenstat, & Spector, 1990). Therefore, three questions about the failures of change were included in the questionnaire. (1) Why were change programmes not successful in the past? (2) What are the barriers to the realization of the innovation as presented in the points of departure? (3) What is needed to solve the problems of this organization? The open questions were answered in writing by more than 60% of all employees. A content analysis of the answers was made by the task force and feedback was given to all the organizational members.

The answers revealed three significant reasons why change programmes had not been successful in the past: (1) because the employees had not been sufficiently informed; (2) because employees had not been involved in the changes; (3) because the changes had not been carried through on account of their possible consequences for the managers. Five significant barriers that may hinder the process were mentioned: (1) the quality of leadership and an autocratic style of management; (2) an ineffective top team and inadequate management skills in a bureaucratic structure with an overload of hierarchical levels; (3) the existing boundaries between the departments and the ensuing "realms", in combination with insufficient co-operation between the departments; (4) poor vertical communication and unclear strategic priorities; (5) the existing power configurations of managers who strive to preserve the existing balances and try to secure their interests, objectives, and positions.

The conditions for success reflected the barriers. Many employees stressed the necessity of openness on the objective and the method of the change. Great importance was attached to clear and regular information and there was a great need for truthful feedback of the information from the diagnosis. A significant proportion of the employees suggested that the ideas and opinions existing on all levels should be attentively listened to. Involvement of the employees in the changes and the contribution of practical experience of operating personnel were considered to be essential when searching for solutions to existing problems. The third success factor to be mentioned was that the process needed to be completed and that conclusions were to be drawn from the diagnosis, even if this would have consequences for the position of the top management and the line managers.

As a result of the barriers to change, specific attention was paid to the contribution by employees to the shaping of the social and technological aspect-system. Additionally, a process was started off to enhance management skills and to have the style of leadership fit in with the future form of organization. The communication on the change process was further strengthened and consultation between the top management and the work council was intensified.

Common Ground for Innovation

Employee task forces were set up to analyse the pressure points and to develop new ideas for the work organization. The task forces were guided and co-ordinated by an umbrella task group of employees and external advisers. Everyone could sign up for a task group with a theme related to his or her field of work. Additionally, people were directly invited to take part in these task groups. In total, some 200 employees in 25 task groups have tackled various pressure points and possibilities of improvement. Among other things, these task groups examined which improvements would yield an integration of the tasks. Team-oriented work on a completed production process was particularly considered. Placing the control of the information system and the applications under the unit operation was also considered because this would result in unity of time, place, and action. The task groups also studied how the customer-oriented service and the rendering of services could be enhanced, and how the development of the automated systems could be optimized. Specific task groups dealt with the culture and the desired style of leadership. Task groups with information analysts, information system designers, and employees of customer services and operations studied which demands were to be made by the user upon the new information system and what space was offered by the new information system for an optimal fit between the technological and social aspect-systems. The outcomes and the proposals from the task groups were compiled and translated by the umbrella task group into demands on the technological aspect-system and into proposals for redesigning business processes and the organizational structure. The desired culture has been made concrete in values and norms, and the desired style of leadership has been made operational in specific manners of behaviour and skills. All the proposals have been presented to the management, which, in consultation with the work council, took a final decision on the design of the new organization.

Some of the most important barriers to change were an unclear business strategy, inadequate management skills, and poor teamwork between managers of interdependent departments. A new set of cultural values was needed to encourage co-operation and teamwork. Also, reflection of the existing management style and renewal of leadership was necessary to realize an optimal fit between the organizational structure, the culture, and the style of leadership. To realize these objectives, a series of four conferences was organized for all the supervisors and managers. The number of participants to the conferences ranged from 30 to 60. The purpose of the conferences was to examine issues on strategy, organization, culture, and leadership from a variety of viewpoints, to learn from each other, and to develop common ground for change; in other words: What ideas and values do we share to bring about fundamental organizational change? During the conferences the participants analysed the data from the diagnosis from a variety of perspectives. As a result of the conferences, energy is directed towards resolving the issues at hand. New visions on strategy, culture, and business processes were developed. Introspection on leadership styles led to intense discussions about the hindrances put up by top management to real leadership and delegation of decision making. During the discussions on leadership styles, the criteria, qualifications, and preconditions for new leadership became clear.

The barriers to change indicated that communication was of vital importance to the realization of the change. During the change process, the entire organization was informed on the progress on a regular basis. Written communication took place via an information bulletin and the internal staff magazine. This information was sometimes general, but it was often also aimed at specific groups of employees, departments, or units. Besides written information, verbal communication was a recurrent part of the process. This provided an opportunity for the employees to ask questions. During the meetings, the top management played a clear role; by doing so, they not only indicated that they endorsed the necessity of the change but showed how important the contribution of the employees was to them. This manner of communicating demanded time and effort, but it proved to be an important means towards the progress of the process.

Innovation of Technology and Organization

The innovation of the technological aspect-system had already from the outset been primarily aimed at operating more swiftly to meet market demands and at increasing the efficiency. In the first instance, the technology is not regarded as a means to achieve organizational innovation. Different options regarding the technological as well as the organizational renewal were made debatable at an early stage. This working method had been stimulated by an early dialogue on the points of departure and designing philosophies for information technology and organization. Possible limitations within the technological aspect-system have put only minimal restrictions on the design of the social aspect-system. The information technology has been deployed as much as possible to support the organizational innovation. For instance, a division had been made within the system between the operating of the hardware and the operating of the applications. This division made it possible to assign the control of the payment traffic to the operations and to increase the control capacity of the teams. The new information system also offers possibilities for decentralized control and for the generation of management information. This allows for decision making at lower levels within the organization and a reduction in the number of management levels. Additionally, the new technology permits the teams to receive information on the results of their efforts. This also enables the teams to analyse the effectiveness of their activities and to improve their results while learning.

The innovation of the social aspect-system is based on teams dealing with a completed part of the business process. The teams carry out tasks that are logically linked. Executive tasks as well as steering and controlling tasks have been assigned to these teams. This way the teams have the possibility of taking action in the execution of their own work. In the operational functions, the teams deal with all the recurrent operations concerning the processing of specific information carriers, which had previously been separated. Moreover, the team carries out such tasks as the planning of the work, the monitoring of the schedule for payment processing and the primary maintenance of the equipment and the co-ordination of testing procedures, which permits a higher degree of autonomy than in the past. The on-line and real-time steering of payment processing enables the operation unit to steer and monitor the information and payment processing without interference from the computer department. The renewal of the information systems for payment processing and management information requires new ways of co-operation and project management in the development of information systems. The traditional division in information analyses, the formulation of functional requirements, the system development, the technical testing, and the implementation of new information systems is increasingly integrated and demands a new organizational form. The new department for computer services is composed of capacity teams with specific professional knowledge of information processing, network architecture, and hardware configurations. These teams are responsible for their own professional development and qualifications. The development of informational systems is fulfilled in multidisciplinary teams in which the various professionals and the users of the systems are working together under the supervision of a professional project manager. These teams are responsible for the realization of change in software configurations requested by other departments on a contractual basis with respect to results, cost, and planning. The professional teamwork reduces communication problems and makes demands on multidisciplinary co-operation by the specialists.

In the commercial functions, the information technology is used to improve the service to customers. All information processes to realize the commercial services have been integrated in an information system that supports the commercial functions. This renewal of information technology enables the integration of client-centred tasks. As a result, the clients have one office for all their requests and demands.

The most obvious result of the renewal of the information technology is the integration of tasks in teams and the arrangement of teams on the basis of market groups or processing related tasks. Less transfer of work and exchange of information contributes to a lesser degree of interdependence. Employees within the production and the professional and commercial teams can identify themselves more with the product or the service for which they are responsible. The new organization has three hierarchical levels: team manager, departmental manager, and management team.

For the implementation, conferences were conducted for each of the newly identified organizational departments and for all newly formed teams. During these conferences the tasks of the teams were clarified for all team members and the structure of the department was defined. Each team defined their goals, developed their team structure, identified a set of behaviours and values the team will abide by, and established a line for implementation. The new social aspect-system was implemented ahead of the new information system. This is to conform to the maxim: organize before you automatize. But the reasoning behind this was practical rather than ideological. The new information system was not ready to be implemented. Innovation of the social-aspect seemed to be easier and less expensive than renewal of information technology. At the time of writing this article, the information system has also been implemented.

DISCUSSION

The following conclusions, although roughly based on the case described above, are derived not only from the BGC case, but also on other studies of fundamental change (Boonstra, 1991; Boonstra, Steensma, Demenint, 1996). The conclusions focus on the relevance of the proposed sociotechnical framework, the barriers to change, and the relationship between fundamental change, design methodology, and participation.

Relevance of the Sociotechnical Framework

Sociotechnical system thinking provides a possibility for integration of institutional and transaction cost theories (organizations as open systems), theories about technological and organizational innovation (organizations as sociotechnical systems), and theories of planned change and organizational development (organizations as evolutionary and learning systems). The process of fundamental change in the BGC illustrated some of the integration among the three theoretical views within the sociotechnical framework.

Sociotechnical system theory looks upon organizations as open systems (Emery & Trist, 1965; Trist, 1981). The importance of environment and market demands for the performance and the continuity of the organization was illustrated. The need for businesses to develop a proactive business strategy and to realize flexible and innovative organizations was made clear. Cost reduction and customer satisfaction are no longer sufficient to be competitive. Developments in the environment, technological innovations, and market demands have become strong forces to abandon the classical paradigm of the maximal division of labour and to invest in teamwork that contributes to flexibility and innovation by learning principles of self-organization.

Sociotechnical system theory sees an interrelationship between the technological and social aspect-systems (Emery, 1969; Shani & Sena, 1994). In the BGC case it became clear that information technology can facilitate the transformation of organizations and that the technological aspect-system and the social aspect-system are strongly related. Renewal of information technology provided opportunities for fundamental changes in the social system. Organizational conservatism can be overcome when managers, information technologists, management consultants, and organizational members consciously make a choice for joint optimization of the technological and social systems. Information technology can facilitate the redesign of business processes and the transformation of structure, culture, leadership style, teams, and individuals. In this way it can contribute to the quality of working life.

Sociotechnical system theory emphasizes competence and self-learning capacities of organizations to realize continuous improvement. The theories of change are founded on group dynamics, learning processes, process intervention, and systematic change (Argyris, 1990; Beckhard, 1987; Beer & Walton, 1987; Schein, 1969). According to the sociotechnical change theories, the designing of organizations characterized by self-regulation and innovation can only take place when all members are involved in understanding and shaping their own work situation and are allowed to experience a learning process during the change process. The BGC case showed how concept creation, survey feedback, group discussions, self-designing task forces, and conferences were used to influence the design of the information technology and to realize a transformation of the social aspect-system from the perspective of a self-designing organization (Mohrman & Cummings, 1989).

It can be concluded that the sociotechnical system theory offers a solid framework for technological and organizational innovation. It also offers a strong theoretical alternative for business process redesign (BPR). Against the loose collection of non-theoretically founded ideas and techniques on corporate strategy, information technology, and organizational design of BPR, sociotechnical system theory puts forward a theory and methodology that is underpinned by psychological, sociological, and organizational theories and is anchored in a system theory that through the years has been further developed into concrete tools for fundamental organizational design and development. A further development of the sociotechnical system theory, however, is needed. Although the theory sees organizations as open systems, its concepts and methods for strategic development and implementation have been elaborated only slightly. First steps have been made by Emery (1987), Weisbord (1992), and Axelrod (1992), who suggest search conferences as a method for participative and interactive development of business policy and strategy. What is needed is a more elaborate theoretical foundation of strategic change and case studies on a deep level to analyse the methods and outcomes of strategic search conferences. Also, sociotechnical system theory has paid little attention to organizations as political systems when dealing with the actual transformation of organizations. In cases of fundamental change, several groups will try to influence the process of change towards an outcome that is favourable to them. Studies on power and influence in sociotechnical change projects have been made by Boonstra (1995) and Swan and Clark (1992), but further research into the relationship between the political aspect-system and the other aspect-systems in organizations is required. Case studies with a longitudinal dimension studying the politics of change processes for a period of time can add another layer to the theory of sociotechnical change.

Barriers to Change

Innovation of information technology and organizational structures is a complex process of fundamental change. The BGC case shows us that these innovation processes meet several hindrances that must be overcome.

It is important to realize that none of the organizational members in the BGC case attribute impediments to change to the information technology. It seemed that information technology could even promote a fundamental transformation of the entire organizational system. The impediments to change were not related to information technology but to the social aspect-system.

The existing division of labour and poor interfunctional teamwork is an important barrier to change. The BGC case made clear that the division of labour inhibits the division's and teams' ability to learn, because they do not possess all the information necessary to solve problems. The division of labour makes it difficult to see and analyse the entire problem. As a result, solutions are made on an *ad hoc* basis and are directed at the realization of sub-tasks of a single department. The detailed division of tasks often results in competition, misunderstandings, and conflicts between departments because people in different departments have a limited understanding of what goes on in the organization. Different patterns of behaviour and expectations develop while the specialized and confined operations do not encourage co-operation and interfunctional teamwork.

Behaviour in organizations is closely related to norms and values. The norms and values originate from the socialization process, education, and conventions of the organization. The BGC case shows that norms and values limit people's choice of behavioural alternatives and, hence, people's ability to change. Managers in particular have difficulties with changes in norms and values, because they have come to think of their position and behaviour as suitable. What appears from the BGC case is that cultural aspects and management behaviour are closely related and can yield serious impediments to change. Work conference can support a shift in cultural values and norms and stimulate new styles of leadership.

Resistance to organizational and cultural changes can primarily be expected within the management. The BGC case made clear that managers could be cultural defenders because the existing culture serves as an instrument to give meaning to incidents and events in a way consistent with their conception of the work organization, the work situation, and the people employed. Understanding of environmental changes helped to broaden the perspective. Based on the acquired understanding of the market and the product, the business strategy could be discussed and specified so that a shared value-system could emanate from the organization. The top management's role was to disseminate new norms and values concerning the manners of behaviour, desired and undesired actions, communication, important activities and events, the way operations should be conducted, and the style of management.

Forces in the organization to preserve the existing balance of power can hinder the change process. In the process, different coalitions will direct their attention to securing their interests, objectives, and power positions (Kanter, 1993). It is, therefore, imperative to consider the power processes during change processes (Pfeffer, 1992). At the start of the change process in the BGC case, the top management neglected to translate general objectives into concrete measures. Line management, being uncertain about their new position within the organization, were enabled to pursue their own objectives and hindered concrete changes. In the middle levels of the organization, groups or coalitions were developing which did not contribute to fundamental changes in culture and organization. With respect to the power and political processes, an important prerequisite for a successful change process is that the largest support possible should be generated in the earliest stage possible. Interviews, questionnaires, and work conferences were methods to realize a large support for innovation.

The way decision making is organized contributes to the success of change with respect to organizational innovation. The respondents in the case research attached much value to the participation of the members of the organization in the problem analysis, the designation of the objectives of change, and the choices for innovation. Making a clear and well-informed decision on innovation and the communication thereof is essential. The BGC case shows that facilitating problem analyses and application of ideas of operating personnel and an open consultation about solutions and alternative supports the change process. It is apparent that an in-depth problem analysis will take much time and effort. The question arises whether this investment is really necessary when there is a clear idea of the problems and the possible solutions among the members of a design team. The case shows that participation of all members of the organization in the decision-making process can contribute positively to the change process. By gaining experience with problem solving, change processes, and organizational development, organization members gradually learn to shape changes and react flexibly to changing circumstances on their own.

There is no standard approach for the innovation of information technology and organizational development. Each and every change process has its own characteristics. Therefore, a reflection of the change objectives and the way the change process can be approached is required: managing the process for change. Because change processes often develop unpredictably, it is required to monitor the course of events and to intervene when necessary. In the BGC case the management of change was the responsibility of a co-ordinating team consisting of employees and external consultants, which facilitated the change process. It seemed that proper information flow during the process is essential for a good development of the changes. Resistance to change does not solely stem from the attempt to keep the situation stable and secure, but originates principally from the lack of clarity about the change objectives and the approach to change process (Beer, Eisenstat, & Spector, 1990). Communication with the members of the organization during the change process is of essential importance for the reduction of uncertainty, and the visualization of advancements in the process. It is meaningful to plan the approach to the change process thoroughly in advance, and make an inventory of the possibilities and impediments to the change process. This concerns the existing views on change, interests, power relations, the support for change, and impediments within the organization's structure, culture, and style of management.

The Dilemma of Designing and Developing

Competence and self-learning seem to be critical elements of technological and organizational innovation. A development approach can initiate these learning processes, but, in order to be successful, common values, willingness to co-operate, a clear vision on the business processes, and clarity as to the reasons for changes are needed. The BGC case indicates that organizations with a strong division of labour and predominantly bureaucratic characteristics cannot meet these conditions for learning and development. The BGC organization was unable to follow development and learning processes independently because the learning approach is contrary to the methods that had been used for years to analyse and solve problems.

A dilemma is created by fundamentally changing organizations. The expert-design approach offers possibilities for radically redesigning the organization and drastic and revolutionary change. Business process redesign claims to achieve dramatic performance improvements by using a design approach with linear steering from the top, tasks forces of management, and the contribution of business consultants. At the same time, many projects aimed at redesign of organizations do not yield the desired outcomes. It is estimated that three-quarters of the re-engineering projects fail (Davenport, 1993). With the design approach it becomes difficult to contribute to the realization of self-managing teams and the enhancement of the organizational learning ability. The development approach is preferred in the case of fundamental changes, but is often appears to be difficult to break with traditionally-shaped organizations when only the development strategy is used. The BGC case give some ideas on how to deal with this dilemma between designing and developing organizations. The basic assumptions for innovation and change were formulated in work conferences and discussed between top management and work council. After sanctioning the basic assumptions by top management, the analysis of the organization can be executed by a facilitating team with the co-operation of all members involved. However, the knowledge of an expert is often necessary to ensure an integral diagnosis and to prohibit signalled problems from being immediately solved according to the existing principles, patterns, and procedures. The interpretation of data can take place in a participative learning process, but a contribution of a change agent is necessary to establish procedures, guide meetings, and discussions, and to clarify the relationships in the data. After the diagnosis, it often appears to be difficult to develop a new work organization in co-operation with all the organization members, because there is often a divided culture, distrust, different objectives, and conflicts of interest. The subdivision of labour has alienated the organization's members from their product, the market, and the mission of the organization, and they do not see the entire transformation process. New organizational forms are difficult to envision, and the willingness jointly to develop this understanding is often insufficiently present. Apparently, the prerequisites for employing a development approach in which the organization is shaped from the bottom up in a participative way are not met. The dilemma could be solved by alternating between the formulation of co-ordinating and innovative frameworks and the interpretation of these frameworks from the bottom up. As the process progresses, the emphasis gradually shifts to the development approach in which the organization's members manage the changes themselves.

CONCLUSION

Technological and organizational innovation needs a theoretical framework to understand the relationships between strategy, technology, and organization and to overcome organizational conservatism and guide the change process. The contemporary sociotechnical system theory offers such a framework. The theory provides a base of knowledge for redesigning organizations as well as developing organizations by learning processes. In this respect the theory is more funded, mature, and helpful than the loose collection of insights and methods of business process redesign. However, further development of the sociotechnical system theory is needed, specifically in the field of strategic development and issues concerned with barriers, power, and influence during fundamental change.

Information technologies offer opportunities for organizational innovation and could contribute to the flexibility and innovative capacity of organizations. It also creates the potential for increasing the quality of working life. Impediments to technological and organizational innovation are seldom related to the technological system. Barriers to innovation and reasons for organizational conservatism are to be found in the social system. Case research indicates six barriers in the social system itself: the existing division of labour and poor interfunctional teamwork; the norms and values limiting people's ability to change; top-down leadership and poor vertical communication; inadequate management skills; the existing power configuration; and lastly a linear and formal process of decision making on innovation. Successful innovation needs a process of learning to analyse market demands and organizational problems and to design information systems, business processes, and work organization by self-designing teams and dedicated management of the change process.

Competence and self-learning appear to be crucial elements of technological and organizational innovation. The participative development approach initiates and stimulates these learning processes, but at the same time interferes with the change process because people find it difficult to be objective towards the existing situation and to form an idea of a completely new situation. An expert design approach seems to offer possibilities for radical and revolutionary change. Nevertheless, many design projects fail because fundamental change is not a programme, but a learning process. The dilemma between designing and developing organizations can possibly be solved by alternating between a top-down formulation of goals and coordination of the change process and bottom-up self-designing activities in which organizational members manage the change process themselves.

ACKNOWLEDGEMENTS

The authors would like to thank Rob Leliveld for his support in case research, Interpay-BGC for access to case studies, and SANT for research funds.

REFERENCES

Ansoff, H.I. (1985). *Implanting strategic management*. Englewood Cliffs, NJ: Prentice Hall.

Argyris, C. (1983). Action science and intervention. *Journal of Applied Behavioral Science, 43*(5), 115–140.

Argyris, C. (1990). *Overcoming organizational defenses: Facilitating organizational learning*. Boston, Mass.: Allyn & Bacon.

Ashby, W.R. (1969). Self-regulation and requisite variety. In F.E. Emery (Ed.), *Systems thinking*. London: Penguin Books.

Axelrod, D. (1992). Getting everyone involved: How one organization involved its employees, supervisors, and managers in redesigning the organization. *Journal of Applied Behavioral Science, 28*(4), 499–509.

Beckhard, R. (1987). Strategies for large systems change. In W.A. Pasmore & J.J. Sherwood (Eds.), *Sociotechnical systems: A sourcebook*. San Diego, Calif.: University Associates.

Beer, M. (1988). The critical path for change: Keys to success and failure in six companies. In R.H. Killmann & T.J. Covin (Eds.), *Revitalizing organizations for a competitive world*. San Francisco, Calif.: Jossey-Bass.

Beer, M., Eisenstat, R.A., & Spector, B. (1990). *The critical path to corporate renewal*. Boston, Mass.: Harvard.

Beer, M., & Walton, A.E. (1987). Organization change and development. *Annual Review of Psychology, 38*, 339–367.

Beinum, H.J.J. van. (1990). *Participative democracy*. Leiden, Germany: University Press.

Boonstra, J.J. (1991). *Integrale organisatie-ontwikkeling: Vormgeven aan fundamentele veranderingsprocessen* [Integral organizational development: Managing fundamental change processes in organizations]. Utrecht, The Netherlands: Lemma.

Boonstra, J.J. (1995). The use of power and influence tactics in change processes. In J.J. Boonstra (Ed.), *Power dynamics and organizational changes*. Leuven, Belgium: EAWOP.

Boonstra, J.J., Steensma, H.O., & Demenint, M.I. (1996). *Ontwerden en ontwikkelen van organisaties [Designing and developing organizations]*. Utrecht, The Netherlands: Lemma.

Cherns, A. (1987). The principles of sociotechnical design revisited. *Human Relations, 29*(8), 783–792.

Child, J., & Loveridge, R. (1990). *Information technology in European service: Towards a micro-electronic future*. Oxford: Basil Blackwell.

Clark, P.A., & Staunton, N. (1989). *Innovations in technology and organization*. London: Routledge.

Davenport, T.H. (1993). *Process innovation: Reengineering work through information technology*. Boston, Mass.: Harvard.

Emery, F.E. (1959). *Characteristics of sociotechnical systems*. London: Tavistock.

Emery, F.E. (1969). *Systems thinking*. London: Penguin Books.

Emery, F.E., & Trist, E.L. (1965). The causal texture of organizational environment. *Human Relations, 20*(1), 21–32.

Emery, M. (1987). *The theory and practice of search conferences*. Paper presented at the Einar Thorsrud Memorial Symposium, Oslo.

Freeman, R.E. (1984). *Strategic management: A stakeholder approach*. Boston, Mass.: Pittman.

Guha, S., Kettinger, W.J., & Teng, J.T.C. (1993). Business process redesign: Building a comprehensive methodology. *Information Systems Management, Summer*, 13–22.

Hammer, M., & Champy, J. (1993). *Reengineering the corporation: A manifesto for business revolution*. New York: Harper.

Harrison, B.D., & Pratt, M.D. (1993). Reengineering business processes. *Planning Review, 9*(2), 53–61.

Herbst, P.G. (1976). *Alternatives to hierarchies*. Leiden, Germany: Martinus Nijhoff.

Kanter, R.M. (1993). *The change masters: Corporate entrepreneurs at work* (2nd ed.). London: Routledge.

Mohrman, S.A., & Cummings, T.G. (1989). *Self-designing organizations: Learning how to create high performance*. Reading, Mass.: Addison-Wesley.

Pasmore, W.A. (1988). *Designing effective organizations: Sociotechnical system perspective*. New York: Wiley.

Pava, C.H. (1986). Redesigning sociotechnical system design: Concepts and methods for the 1990s. *Journal of Applied Behavioral Science, 22*(3), 201–221.

Pfeffer, J. (1992). *Managing with power: Politics and influence in organizations*. Boston, Mass.: Harvard.

Schein, E.H. (1969). *Process consultation: Its role in organization development*. Reading, Mass.: Addison-Wesley.

Shani, A.B.R., & Sena, J.A. (1994). Information technology and the integration of change: Sociotechnical system approach. *Journal of Applied Behavioral Science, 30*(2), 247–270.

Susman, G.I. (1976). *Autonomy at work: A sociotechnical analysis of participative management*. New York: Praeger.

Swan, J.A., & Clark, P. (1992). Organizational decision making in the appropriation of technological innovation: Cognitive and political dimensions. *The European Work and Organizational Psychologist, 2*(2), 103–127.

Trist, E.L. (1981). *The evolution of sociotechnical systems: A conceptual framework and an action research program*. Ontario, Canada: The Quality of Working Life Center.

Trist, E.L. (1982). Sociotechnical system perspective. In A.H. van der Ven & W.F. Joyce (Eds.), *Perspectives on organization design and behavior*. New York: Wiley.

Turner, A.N., & Lawrence, P.R. (1965). *Industrial jobs and the worker: An investigation of response to task attributes*. Boston, Mass.: Harvard.

Walton, R.E. (1988). *Up and running: Integrating information technology and the organizations*. Boston, Mass.: Harvard.

Weick, K. (1990). Technology as an equivoque: Sense making in new technologies. In P.S. Goodman & L.S. Sproull (Eds.), *Technology and organizations*. San Francisco, Calif.: Jossey-Bass.

Weisbord, M.R. (1992). *Discovering common ground*. San Francisco, Calif.: Berrett-Koehler.

Part II
Managing Innovation Through Organization and HR Strategies

[6]

© *Academy of Management Review*
1996, Vol. 21, No. 4, 1055–1080.

THE CHALLENGE OF INNOVATION IMPLEMENTATION

KATHERINE J. KLEIN
JOANN SPEER SORRA
University of Maryland at College Park

Implementation is the process of gaining targeted organizational members' appropriate and committed use of an innovation. Our model suggests that implementation effectiveness—the consistency and quality of targeted organizational members' use of an innovation—is a function of (a) the strength of an organization's climate for the implementation of that innovation and (b) the fit of that innovation to targeted users' values. The model specifies a range of implementation outcomes (including resistance, avoidance, compliance, and commitment); highlights the equifinality of an organization's climate for implementation; describes within- and between-organizational differences in innovation-values fit; and suggests new topics and strategies for implementation research.

Innovation implementation within an organization is the process of gaining targeted employees' appropriate and committed use of an innovation. Innovation implementation presupposes innovation adoption, that is, a decision, typically made by senior organizational managers, that employees within the organization will use the innovation in their work. Implementation failure occurs when, despite this decision, employees use the innovation less frequently, less consistently, or less assiduously than required for the potential benefits of the innovation to be realized.

An organization's failure to achieve the intended benefits of an innovation it has adopted may thus reflect either a failure of implementation or a failure of the innovation itself. Increasingly, organizational analysts identify implementation failure, not innovation failure, as the cause of many organizations' inability to achieve the intended benefits of the innovations they adopt. Quality circles, total quality management, statistical process control, and computerized technologies often yield little or no benefit to adopting organizations, not because the innovations are ineffective, analysts suggest, but because their implementation is unsuccessful

We are very grateful to Lori Berman, Amy Buhl, Dov Eden, Marlene Fiol, John Gomperts, Susan Jackson, Steve Kozlowski, Judy Olian, Michelle Paul, Ben Schneider, and the anonymous reviewers for their extremely helpful comments on earlier versions of this article. We also thank Beth Benjamin, Pamela Carter, Elizabeth Clemmer, and Scott Ralls for their help in collecting and analyzing the interview data for the Buildco and Wireco case studies.

(e.g., Bushe, 1988; Hackman & Wageman, 1995; Klein & Ralls, 1995; Reger, Gustafson, DeMarie, & Mullane, 1994).

Innovation scholars have long bemoaned the paucity of research on innovation implementation (Beyer & Trice, 1978; Hage, 1980; Roberts-Gray & Gray, 1983; Tornatzky & Klein, 1982). Although cross-organizational studies of the determinants of innovation adoption are abundant (see Damanpour, 1991; Tornatzky & Klein, 1982, for reviews), cross-organizational studies of innovation implementation (e.g., Nord & Tucker, 1987) are extremely rare. More common are single-site, qualitative case studies of innovation implementation. Each of these studies describes pieces of the implementation story. Largely missing, however, are integrative models that capture and clarify the multidetermined, multilevel phenomenon of innovation implementation.

In this article, we present an integrative model of the determinants of the effectiveness of organizational implementation. The primary premise of the model, depicted in Figure 1, is that implementation effectiveness—the quality and consistency of targeted organizational members' use of an adopted innovation—is a function of (a) an organization's climate for the implementation of a given innovation and (b) targeted organizational members' perceptions of the fit of the innovation to their values.

FIGURE 1

Determinants and Consequences of Implementation Effectiveness

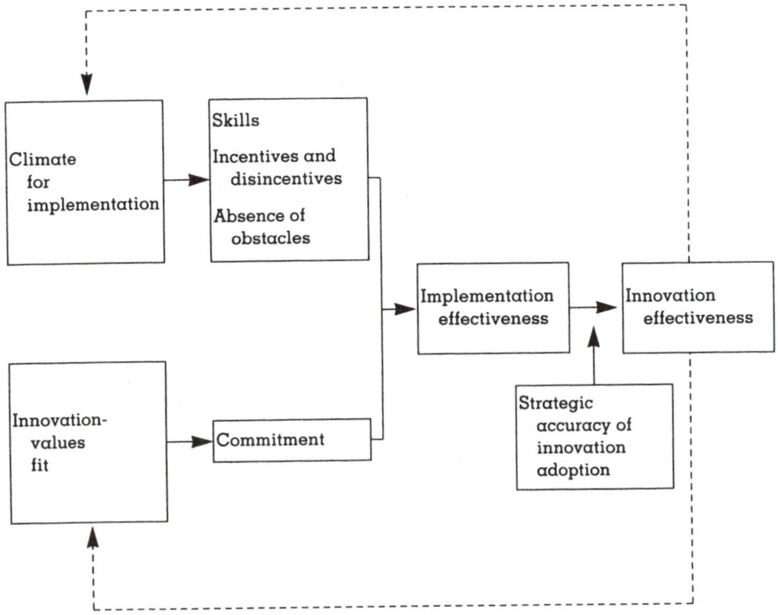

We begin by defining several key terms and outlining our levels of theory. We then present the model. We focus first on the organization as a whole, examining instances, determinants, and consequences of homogeneous innovation use within an organization. We then explore between-group differences, examining instances, determinants, and consequences of varying levels of innovation use by groups within an organization. Next, we consider the feedback processes suggested by the model: the influences of implementation and innovation outcomes on an organization's subsequent climate for implementation and on employees' values. We illustrate the model with examples from our own and others' implementation research, and we conclude with a discussion of the implications that the model may have for implementation researchers.

KEY TERMS

Two types of stage models are commonly used to describe the innovation process. The first, source-based stage models, are based on the perspective of the innovation developer or source. They trace the creation of new products or services from the gestation of the idea to the marketing of the final product (e.g., research, development, testing, manufacturing or packaging, dissemination) (Amabile, 1988; Kanter, 1988; Tornatzky & Fleischer, 1990). Within source-based stage models, an innovation is a new product or service that an organization, developer, or inventor has created for market.

User-based stage models, in contrast, are based on the perspective of the user. They trace the innovation process from the user's awareness of a need or opportunity for change to the incorporation of the innovation in the user's behavioral repertoire (e.g., awareness, selection, adoption, implementation, routinization) (Beyer & Trice, 1978; Nord & Tucker, 1987; Tornatzky & Fleischer, 1990). Within user-based stage models (and within our model), an *innovation* is a technology or a practice "being used for the first time by members of an organization, whether or not other organizations have used it previously" (Nord & Tucker, 1987: 6).

We focus on innovations that require the active and coordinated use of multiple organizational members to benefit the organization. Because innovations of this type by definition affect numerous organizational members, they are typically implemented within an organization only following a formal decision on the part of senior managers to adopt the innovation. Examples of innovations of this kind include total quality management (TQM), statistical process control (SPC), computer-aided design and manufacturing (CAD/CAM), and manufacturing resource planning (MRP).

Implementation is the transition period during which targeted organizational members ideally become increasingly skillful, consistent, and committed in their use of an innovation. Implementation is the critical gateway between the decision to adopt the innovation and the routine use of the innovation within an organization. We conceptualize innovation use as a continuum, ranging from avoidance of the innovation (nonuse) to meager and unenthusiastic use (compliant use) to skilled, enthusiastic, and consistent use (committed use). *Implementation effectiveness* refers to the consistency and quality of targeted organizational members' use of a specific innovation. *Targeted organizational members* (or targeted users) are individuals who are expected either to use the innovation directly (e.g., production workers) or to support the innovation's use (e.g., information technology specialists, production supervisors).

Innovation effectiveness describes the benefits an organization receives as a result of its implementation of a given innovation (e.g., improvements in profitability, productivity, customer service, and employee morale). Implementation effectiveness is a necessary but not sufficient condition for innovation effectiveness: Although an innovation is extremely unlikely to yield significant benefits to an adopting organization unless the innovation is used consistently and well, effective implementation does not guarantee that the innovation will, in fact, prove beneficial for the organization.

LEVELS OF THEORY

Klein, Dansereau, and Hall (1994: 206) urged organizational scholars to specify and explicate the level(s) of their theories and their "attendant assumptions of homogeneity, independence, or heterogeneity." We begin to do so here, weaving further discussion of the levels of the model throughout the article.

The fundamental organizational challenge of innovation implementation is to gain targeted organizational members' use of an innovation: to change individuals' behavior. However, for the innovations on which we focus, the benefits of innovation implementation are dependent on the use of the innovation not by individuals but by all, or a critical group of organizational members (Tornatzky & Fleischer, 1990). Thus, although we acknowledge that innovation use may vary between individuals and between groups within an organization, we conceptualize implementation effectiveness as an organization-level construct, describing the overall, pooled or aggregate consistency and quality of targeted organizational members' innovation use. An organization in which all targeted employees use a given innovation consistently and well is more effective in its implementation effort than is an organization in which only some of the targeted employees use the innovation consistently and well. Futher, because the benefits of innovation implementation depend (again, in the case of the innovations we describe) on the integrated and coordinated use of the innovation, an organization in which all or most targeted employees' innovation use is moderate in consistency and quality shows greater implementation effectiveness than an organization in which some targeted members use the innovation consistently and well while others use it inconsistently and poorly. Thus, to use Klein and colleagues' (1994) terminology, implementation effectiveness is a homogeneous construct, describing the quality and consistency of the use of a specific innovation within an organization as a whole.

Implementation effectiveness results, we argue in the following section, from the dual influence of an organization's climate for the implementation of a given innovation and the perceived fit of that innovation to targeted users' values. We posit that implementation climate, too, is a homogeneous construct, describing a facet of targeted users' collective, perceived work environment. Innovation-values fit, in contrast, may vary between individuals, between groups, or between organizations. We focus on between-organization and between-group differences in innovation-values fit, thus conceptualizing innovation-values fit primarily as a homogeneous construct that may characterize the shared values of either an organization's targeted users as a whole or distinct groups of targeted users within an organization.

CLIMATE FOR IMPLEMENTATION

The empirical literature on the implementation of workplace innovations is dominated, as we noted previously, by qualitative, single-site studies (e.g., Markus, 1987; Roitman, Liker, & Roskies, 1988; Sproull & Hofmeister, 1986). In rich detail, the authors of these studies have described a variety of innovation, implementation, organizational, and managerial policies, practices, and characteristics that may influence innovation use. These include training in innovation use (Fleischer, Liker, & Arnsdorf, 1988), user support services (Rousseau, 1989), time to experiment with the innovation (Zuboff, 1988), praise from supervisors for innovation use (Klein, Hall, & Laliberte, 1990), financial incentives for innovation use (Lawler & Mohrman, 1991), job reassignment or job elimination for those who do not learn to use the innovation (Klein et al., 1990), budgetary constraints on implementation expenses (Nord & Tucker, 1987), and the user-friendliness of the innovation (Rivard, 1987). (We will use the shorthand phrase "implementation policies and practices" to refer to the array of innovation, implementation, organizational, and managerial policies, practices, and characteristics that may influence innovation use.)

Because each implementation case study highlights a different subset of one or more implementation policies and practices, the determinants of implementation effectiveness may appear to be a blur, a hodge-podge lacking organization and parsimony. If multiple authors, studying multiple organizations, identify differing sources of implementation failure and success, what overarching conclusion is a reader to reach? The implementation literature offers, unfortunately, little guidance. To highlight the collective influence of an organization's multiple implementation policies and practices, we introduce the construct of an organization's climate for the implementation of an innovation.

Our discussion of this construct builds on Schneider's conceptualization of climate (e.g., Schneider, 1975, 1990). Schneider (1990: 384) defined *climate* as employees' "perceptions of the events, practices, and procedures and the kinds of behaviors that are rewarded, supported, and expected in a setting." Three distinctive features of Schneider's conceptualization of climate bear note here. First, Schneider's conceptualization highlights employees' perceptions—not their evaluations—of their work environment. Second, Schneider's conceptualization draws attention to employees' shared perceptions, not employees' individual and idiosyncratic views. And, third, Schneider's conceptualization focuses on employees' shared perceptions of the extent to which work unit practices, procedures, and rewards promote behaviors consistent with a specific strategic outcome of interest. Schneider's conceptualization does not focus on employees' perceptions of generic work unit characteristics—such as socioemotional supportiveness (e.g., Kopelman, Brief, & Guzzo, 1990)—that are generalizable to any work unit.

An organization's *climate for the implementation of a given innovation* refers to targeted employees' shared summary perceptions of the extent to which their use of a specific innovation is rewarded, supported, and expected within their organization. Employees' perceptions of their organization's climate for the implementation of a given innovation are the result of employees' shared experiences and observations of, and their information and discussions about, their organization's implementation policies and practices. Climate for implementation, we emphasize, does not refer to employees' satisfaction with the innovation, the organization, or their jobs; it also does not refer to employees' perceptions of their organization's openness to change or general innovativeness.

The Influence of Climate for Implementation

The more comprehensively and consistently implementation policies and practices are perceived by targeted employees to encourage, cultivate, and reward their use of a given innovation, the stronger the climate for implementation of that innovation. A strong implementation climate fosters innovation use by (a) ensuring employee skill in innovation use, (b) providing incentives for innovation use and disincentives for innovation avoidance, and (c) removing obstacles to innovation use. An organization has a strong climate for the implementation of a given innovation if, for example, training regarding innovation use is readily and broadly available to targeted employees (ensuring skill); additional assistance in innovation use is available to employees following training (ensuring skill); ample time is given to employees so they can both learn about the innovation and use it on an ongoing basis (ensuring skill, removing obstacles); employees' concerns and complaints regarding innovation use are responded to by those in charge of the innovation implementation (removing obstacles); the innovation itself can be easily accessed by the employees (e.g., TQM meetings scheduled at convenient times, user-friendly computerized technology) (removing obstacles); and employees' use of the innovation is monitored and praised by managers and supervisors (providing incentives for use and disincentives for innovation avoidance).

Research on climates for specific strategic outcomes reveals the influence that an organization's climate for a specific outcome has on employees' behaviors regarding that outcome. Researchers have found, for example, that climate for safety is related to factory safety (Zohar, 1980), that climate for innovation in R&D subsystems is related to technological breakthroughs (Abbey & Dickson, 1983), that climate for technical updating is related to engineers' performance (Kozlowski & Hults, 1987), and that climate for service is related to customers' perceptions of the quality of service received (Schneider & Bowen, 1985; Schneider, Parkington, & Buxton, 1980). Thus, we posit that the stronger an organization's climate for the implementation of a given innovation, the greater will be the employees' use of that innovation, provided employees are committed to innovation use.

The Limits of Climate for Implementation

Our caveat—"provided employees are committed to innovation use"—indicates the limits of climate. Psychological theories and research on conformity and commitment (Kelman, 1961; O'Reilly & Chatman, 1986; Sussman & Vecchio, 1991) have been used to distinguish between *compliance,* "the acceptance of influence in order to gain specific rewards and to avoid punishments," and *internalization,* "the acceptance of influence because it is congruent with a worker's values" (Sussman & Vecchio, 1991: 214).[1] Applied to innovation implementation, these works suggest that employees who perceive innovation use to be congruent with their values are likely to be internalized—committed and enthusiastic—in their innovation use, whereas individuals who perceive innovation use merely as a means to obtain and avoid punishments are likely to be compliant—pro forma and uninvested—in their innovation use.

Because a strong implementation climate provides incentives and disincentives for innovation use, it may, in and of itself, foster compliant innovation use. Climate for implementation does not, however, ensure either the congruence of an innovation to targeted users' values or internalized and committed innovation use. Skillful, internalized, and commited innovation use takes more: a strong climate for the implementation of an innovation *and* a good fit of the innovation to targeted users' values.

We discuss the combined effects of implementation climate and innovation-values fit in greater detail in a subsequent section, but an

[1] Also mentioned in these theories is *identification,* the acceptance of influence "in order to engage in a satisfying role-relationship with another person or group" (Sussman & Vecchio, 1991: 214). Identification seemed to us to have relatively little relevance to innovation implementation.

example—close to many readers' academic homes—may be helpful here. Imagine a university that has historically valued, rewarded, and supported teaching far more than research. If the university adopts a new emphasis on research, the university can surely create—through its policies and practices—a strong climate for research. But how will professors, drawn to the university for its teaching emphasis, respond to such a change? Will they not simultaneously recognize the new climate for research and resist it because it is incongruent with their values?

An Example of Climate for Implementation: Buildco, Inc.

Buildco, Inc. (a pseudonym) is a large engineering and construction company that experienced great difficulty in implementing three-dimensional computer-aided design and drafting (3-D CADD), a sophisticated computer graphics program used to design and test computerized representations of products (in this case, buildings and plants). Buildco's senior managers complained of "employee resistance to change," yet researchers (Klein, 1986; Klein et al., 1990) found, in their interviews with 26 targeted users and their supervisors, that targeted users were, in fact, very enthusiastic about 3-D CADD, per se. For example, one employee raved, "I think CADD is the greatest thing since sliced bread. I like the whole concept, the speed, the accuracy, [and] the uniformity of the drawings."

Targeted users complained vociferously, however, about many aspects of the implementation process. Targeted users were satisfied with the content of the company's 60-hour 3-D CADD training program, but often they had little opportunity to use their 3-D CADD training on the job. As a result, employee skill in 3-D CADD often decayed sharply following training. Targeted users complained, too, that managers and supervisors offered few rewards for 3-D CADD use: "Supervisors fall short of letting people know when they're doing a good job," one employee commented. "From what I hear, CADD's made a lot of money for the company, but how many people who use CADD know it?" In addition, users complained about a variety of obstacles to their use of 3-D CADD: "The system is designed to handle 6 or 7 terminals at once, but now there are 17 terminals. . . . It takes a long time for the computer to do a simple placement, and this disrupts your train of thought and creativity. It kills your efficiency."

Despite users' appreciation of 3-D CADD and the appropriateness of the content of the company's training program, the overall climate for the implementation of 3-D CADD at Buildco was weak: Targeted users' CADD skills often grew rusty, rewards for using CADD were slim, and obstacles to using CADD were many.

INNOVATION-VALUES FIT

Building on psychological theories of conformity, we posit that employees' commitment to the use of an innovation is a function of the perceived fit of the innovation to employees' values. *Values* are "generalized, enduring beliefs about the personal and social desirability of modes of conduct or 'end-states' of existence" (Kabanoff, Waldersee, & Cohen, 1995: 1076). Individuals have values, as do groups, organizations, societies, and national cultures (Kabanoff et al., 1995).

We focus on organizational and group values in our analysis of innovation-values fit. Organizational values are implicit or explicit views, shared to a considerable extent by organizational members, about both the external adaptation of the organization (i.e., how the organization should relate to external customers, constituencies, and competitors) and the internal integration of the organization (i.e., how members of the organization should relate to and work with one another) (Schein, 1992). Organizational members come to share values as a result of their common experiences and personal characteristics (Holland, 1985; Schein, 1992; Schneider, 1987). Organizational values are stable, but not fixed, and may evolve in response to changing organizational and environmental events and circumstances. Organizational values vary in intensity. High-intensity organizational values encapsulate strong, fervent views and sharp strictures regarding desirable and undersirable actions on the part of the organization and its members. Low-intensity organizational values describe matters of relatively little importance and passion for organizational members.

Group values are implicit or explicit views, shared to a considerable extent by the members of a group within an organization, about the external adaptation and internal integration of the organization and of the group itself. Group values vary among groups in an organization, and they often reflect the self-interests of the group (cf. Guth & MacMillan, 1986). Functional and hierarchical groups (e.g., senior managers, supervisors, technicians) are likely to differ in their values as a function of (a) their roles in the organization (Dougherty, 1992), (b) their common interactions and experiences (Rentsch, 1990), and (c) their distinctive backgrounds and traits (Holland, 1985). Like organizational values, group values vary in their intensity and may evolve over time.

We highlight the fit of innovations to organizational and group values, rather than individual values, because our aim is to explain organizational implementation effectiveness, not individual differences in innovation use. A poor fit between an innovation and organizational or group values affects relatively large numbers of organizational members, and it is thus more likely to derail innovation implementation than is a poor fit between an innovation and any one organizational member's values.

Innovation-values fit describes the extent to which targeted users perceive that use of the innovation will foster (or, conversely, inhibit) the fulfillment of their values. Targeted users assess the objective characteristics of an innovation and its socially constructed meaning (e.g., Barley, 1986; Goodman & Griffith, 1991; Hattrup & Kozlowski, 1993; Zuboff, 1988) to judge the fit of the innovation to their values. Because senior managers adopt innovations to alter production, service, or management, innovations often represent an imperfect fit with organizational members' values. Innovation-values fit is *good* when targeted innovation users regard the innovation as highly congruent with their high-intensity values. Innovation-values fit is *poor* when targeted users regard the innovation as highly incongruent with their high-intensity values. Innovation-values fit is *neutral* when targeted users regard the innovation as either moderately congruent or moderately incongruent with their low-intensity values.

Innovation-Values Fit: Some Examples of Poor Fit

Innovation-values fit has not, to our knowledge, been the object of researchers' explicit attention. However, several scholars have commented implicitly on the topic. In a case study of the implementation of statistical process control in a manufacturing plant, for example, Bushe (1988: 25) suggested that because members of manufacturing plants value performance (i.e., production) more than change and learning, "both the implementation of SPC and the nature of the technique are countercultural, in that learning must be as highly valued as performing for SPC to be used successfully." In a similar vein, Schein (1992: 140) has commented,

> One of the major dilemmas that leaders encounter when they attempt to change the way organizations function is how to get something going that is basically countercultural. . . . For example, the use of quality circles, self-managed teams, autonomous work teams, and other kinds of organizational devices that rely heavily on commitment to groups may be so countercultural in the typical U.S. individualistic competitive organization as to be virtually impossible to make work unless they are presented pragmatically as the only way to get something done.

Further, Schein (1992) and others (e.g., March & Sproull, 1990) documented the poor fit between top managers' and information technology (IT) specialists' values. For example, top managers' assumption that "hierarchy is intrinsic to organizations and necessary for coordination" (Schein, 1992: 291) clashes with the IT specialists' assumptions that "a flatter organization will be a better one" and "a more fully connected organization with open channels in every direction will be a better one" (Schein, 1992: 286).

A last example of poor innovation-values fit comes from a case study of the implementation of a computerized inventory control system in a wire manufacturing company with the pseudonym Wireco (Klein, Ralls, & Carter, 1989). (The conclusions we make are based on interviews with 37 employees: managers, supervisors, and targeted users.) When the decision to adopt the computerized inventory control system was mandated by corporate headquarters, Wireco's manufacturing procedures were unstructured, fluid, and disorganized. If Customer A placed a rush order for one kind of wire, preliminary work on Customer B's order for a different kind of wire was either put aside (and often lost) or transformed and used to meet Customer A's order. Employees at Wireco believed that customers were well served by the flexibility of their production procedures. The new computerized inventory control system, however, required employees (a) to track each customer's order throughout the production process and (b) to maintain accurate inventory records. Employees could no longer use preliminary work on one customer's order to complete a different customer's order. The inventory control system represented a poor fit with the employees' values supporting flexible, if disorganized, production procedures.

THE EFFECTS OF IMPLEMENTATION CLIMATE AND INNOVATION-VALUES FIT ON INNOVATION USE: WHEN FIT IS HOMOGENEOUS

To predict innovation use, we consider the combined influence of implementation climate and innovation-values fit. We first describe the implications of a strong or weak climate for implementation and good, neutral, or poor innovation-values fit, when innovation-values fit is homogeneous (i.e., when there are few within-organization, between-group differences in innovation-values fit).

The six cells in Table 1 summarize the predicted influence of varying levels of implementation climate and innovation-values fit on employees' affective responses and innovation use. When innovation-values fit is good and the organization's implementation climate is strong, employees are skilled in innovation use, incentives for innovation use and disincentives for innovation avoidance are ample, obstacles to innovation use are few, and employees are likely to be highly committed to their innovation use. This is the ideal scenario for innovation implementation. Employees are enthusiastic about the innovation, and they are skilled, consistent, and committed in their innovation use.

When innovation-values fit is good, yet the organization's implementation climate is weak, targeted users are committed to innovation use, but they lack skills in and experience few incentives for and many obstacles to innovation use. Thus, employees' use of the innovation is likely to be sporadic and inadequate. Committed to the idea of innovation use, users are likely to be disappointed and frustrated by their organization's weak implementation climate and by their own and their fellow employees' poor use of the innovation. Good innovation-values fit, in the absence of a strong implementation climate, is not sufficient to produce skillful and consistent innovation use.

When innovation-values fit is poor, yet the organization's implementation climate is strong, employee resistance is likely. A strong implementation climate creates an imperative for employees to use an innovation that, given poor innovation-values fit, employees oppose. If innovation-values fit is very poor, targeted innovation users may opt to leave the organization if they can find alternative employment. Those who cannot

TABLE 1
Implementation Climate and Innovation-Values Fit: Effects on Employees' Affective Responses and Innovation Use

	Innovation-Values Fit		
	Poor	**Neutral**	**Good**
Strong implementation climate	Employee opposition and resistance Compliant innovation use, at best	Employee indifference Adequate innovation use	Employee enthusiasm Committed, consistent, and creative innovation use
Weak implementation climate	Employee relief Essentially no innovation use	Employee disregard Essentially no innovation use	Employee frustration and disappointment Sporadic and inadequate innovation use

leave the organization are likely to engage in compliant innovation use, at best.

When innovation-values fit is poor and implementation climate is weak, targeted innovation users are likely to regard their organization's weak implementation climate—its anemic and erratic implementation policies and practices—with some relief. Targeted users are likely to be pleased to face little pressure to use the innovation. Unskilled, unmotivated, and opposed to innovation use, targeted users are unlikely to use the innovation at all.

Between these extremes of enthusiasm and frustration (when innovation-values fit is good) and resistance and relief (when innovation-values fit is poor) lies a middle group defined by neutral innovation-values fit. In this middle ground are innovations that are perceived to be neither highly congruent nor highly incongruent with organizational values that are of low intensity. When fit is neutral and the implementation climate is strong, targeted users are indifferent to the prospect of innovation implementation, and they face a strong imperative in favor of innovation use. In this case, we predict adequate innovation use—more than compliant innovation use but less than committed use. When fit is neutral and the implementation climate is weak, employees are not likely to use the innovation at all.

We note that employee resistance to innovation implementation is predicted in only one of the six cases that are depicted in Table 1, that is, when an organization's implementation climate is strong and innovation-values fit is poor. The term *resistance* connotes protest and defiance against an opposing pressure or force. A strong implementation climate is such a force. However, when an organization's implementation climate is weak, employees need not "resist" innovation use; there is, by definition, little pressure on employees to use the innovation. In sum, when an organization's climate for innovation implementation is weak, the organization's failure to create an imperative for innovation use, not employee resistance, is the likely cause of employees' lackluster innovation use.

Implementation Climate and Innovation-Values Fit: Two Examples

Buildco represents a case of a weak implementation climate and good innovation-values fit. Targeted users complained about many aspects of the implementation process, but they liked 3-D CADD. They valued their own and their company's technical expertise and use of cutting-edge technologies. They strived to create economical, creative, and fail-safe designs, and these users believed that 3-D CADD enhanced their efforts. As suggested in Table 1, targeted users were frustrated and disappointed by their company's weak implementation policies and practices (its weak implementation climate) and by employees' resultant inability to use 3-D CADD as much or as well as they would have liked to use it.

Markus's (1987) case study of one company's attempted implementation of a computerized financial information system (FIS) provides an example of a strong climate for innovation implementation and poor innovation-values fit.[2] Championed by corporate headquarters, FIS allowed corporate accountants new access to divisional performance data. Corporate headquarters fostered a strong climate for the implementation of FIS in the divisions of the corporation by (a) ensuring divisional accountants knew how to use the system, (b) fixing technical problems regarding FIS, and (c) instituting policies that virtually necessitated the divisions' use of FIS. Nevertheless, divisional accountants actively resisted using FIS. They valued their financial authority and autonomy and perceived FIS to be an affront and a threat to these values.

THE EFFECTS OF IMPLEMENTATION CLIMATE AND INNOVATION-VALUES FIT ON INNOVATION USE: WHEN FIT DIFFERS BETWEEN GROUPS

In an organization characterized by between-group differences in high-intensity values, the same innovation may be regarded by the members of one group as highly congruent with their values (good fit) and by the members of a second group as highly incongruent with their values (poor fit). Such a situation is, of course, ripe for conflict if the effective implementation of the innovation requires innovation use (or at least support for innovation use) across both groups. Next, we explore the consequences of between-group differences in innovation-values fit: (a) when neither of the opposing groups has formal power over the other (horizontal groups) and (b) when one of the opposing groups does have formal power over the other (vertical groups).

Horizontal Groups

When innovation-values fit is good for one group within an organization and poor for another group, and when neither of the groups has power over the other, the strength of the organization's implementation climate determines the "winner" of the conflict over innovation use. If the organization's climate for implementation is strong, the group in favor of innovation implementation (whose members find the innovation congruent with their group's values) is likely to win for two reasons. First, a strong implementation climate creates an imperative for innovation use for all targeted users. Second, a strong implementation climate indicates to targeted innovation users that managers, who are senior to both groups, support implementation, thus throwing the weight of management behind the group favoring implementation. Ultimately, all targeted users are likely to use the innovation. Conflict may be drawn out, however, and implementation may be slow, as those opposed to innovation implementation actively or passively resist using the innovation.

---

[2] Because we did not conduct this case study, our knowledge of it is more limited than our knowledge of the Buildco and Wireco case studies.

Conversely, if the climate is weak, those opposed to implementation are likely to win, for the same reasons. A weak implementation climate discourages innovation use and indicates managers' ambivalence or antipathy toward implementation (and thus their tacit support of those who oppose innovation). Under these circumstances, employees' use of the innovation is likely to be limited at best, after a period of perhaps high but then declining use of the innovation by those who support innovation implementation.

An Example of Horizontal Groups: Production Operators and IT Specialists

We have described Wireco as an example of poor innovation-values fit. Although the fit of the computerized inventory control system to production operators' values *was* poor, the fit of the system to the company's IT specialists was good. Wireco's IT specialists valued the computerized system, believing it to be modern, efficient, organized, and beneficial. (Recall Schein's, 1992, description of IT values.) Further, the IT specialists saw in the prospective implementation of the system an opportunity to increase their own influence and status in the company.

Wireco's managers and supervisors, however, tacitly supported production operators' views of the system. As a result, the company's resulting implementation climate was very weak. For example, operators experienced few rewards for using the system and few punishments for neglecting it. One operator commented, "Are there any rewards or recognition for effective use of the system? No. I pet my dog at home more than I get petted here, and I don't pet my dog very often."

Given the poor fit of the inventory control system to production operators' values and the weak implementation climate, implementation of the system was not successful. Operators' and their managers' and supervisors' use of and support for the system declined, and Wireco's IT specialists lost the battle for implementation.

Vertical Groups

When innovation-values fit is good for one group within an organization and poor for another group and when one group does have power over the other, the strength of the organization's implementation climate again determines the "winner" of conflict over innovation use, yet the dynamic is a little different than the one just described. If innovation-values fit is good for the higher authority group and poor for the lower authority group, then the higher authority group (e.g., supervisors) will strengthen and augment the organization's climate for the implementation of the innovation. For example, the higher authority group may establish additional incentives or training for innovation use. Under these circumstances, lower authority group members—experiencing a strong implementation climate and poor innovation-values fit—will resist innovation use and/or engage in compliant innovation use.

Conversely, if innovation-values fit is poor for the higher authority group and good for the lower authority group, then the higher authority group is likely to undermine the organization's implementation climate. Higher authority group members may diminish or constrain lower authority group members' innovation use by, for example, minimizing the time available to use the innovation. Under such circumstances, lower authority group members—experiencing good-innovation values fit and a weak implementation climate—feel frustrated and disappointed, and they engage in only sporadic and inadequate innovation use.

Examples of Vertical Groups: Supervisors and Their Subordinates

In a study of employee-involvement programs in eight manufacturing plants, Klein (1984) found that employees generally welcomed opportunities for greater involvement in plant decision making (good fit). Supervisors, however, often resisted the implementation of employee-involvement programs, believing that these programs limited their authority and threatened their job security (bad fit). For example, in one plant (Klein, 1984: 88),

> the foremen saw [team meetings among employees] as a threat to their control and authority, which they tried to regain by bad-mouthing the program. This bad-mouthing, in turn, discouraged many of their subordinates from participating. In the end, the whole effort just faded away for lack of interest.

In sum, supervisors created impediments to workers' involvement, weakening the climate for implementation that their subordinates experienced and thereby undermining innovation implementation.

THE OUTCOMES OF INNOVATION IMPLEMENTATION: EXPLORING CONSEQUENCES FOR IMPLEMENTATION CLIMATE AND VALUES

Prior to the 1980s, most researchers who studied the determinants of innovation adoption did not study its aftermath: implementation (Tornatzky & Klein, 1982). Although research on implementation is now more prevalent, research on *its* aftermath is, to our knowledge, nonexistent. In this section, we consider briefly the aftermath of implementation: the effects (depicted by dashed lines in Figure 1) of varying implementation outcomes on an organization's subsequent implementation climate and values.

Innovation implementation may result in one of three outcomes: (a) implementation is effective, and use of the innovation enhances the organization's performance; (b) implementation is effective, but use of the innovation does not enhance the organization's performance; and (c) implementation fails. Each of these three outcomes may influence an organization's subsequent implementation climate and organizational members' values.

When Implementation Is Effective and Innovation Use Enhances Performance

When innovation implementation succeeds and enhances an organization's performance, the organization's implementation climate is strengthened. Managers' and supervisors' support for innovation implementation increases, yielding likely improvements in implementation policies and practices (e.g., innovation training for additional employees, more praise for targeted employees' innovation use). Further, when innovation implementation enhances an organization's performance, organizational values may be affected. If the innovation is largely congruent with the organizational members' homogeneous values, these values are reinforced and organizational members' confidence in the fit of the innovation to their values is strengthened. If the innovation is incongruent with organizational members' homogeneous values, members' values may shift. Organizational members' confidence in new values congruent with use of the innovation increases, as does the perceived efficacy of innovation adoption and implementation in general. As a result of such changes in organizational members' values, the fit of future innovations to organizational values is improved. If the innovation fits well with the values of one group of targeted users and it fits poorly with the values of a second group of targeted users', the "good-fit" group that encouraged innovation implementation is vindicated. Support for this group and its values may grow, whereas support for the "poor-fit" group and its values declines.

When Implementation Is Effective But Innovation Use Does Not Enhance Performance

When implementation succeeds but does not enhance an organization's performance, the organization's climate for implementation is weakened. Managers' and supervisors' support for implementation declines. If innovation-values fit is homogeneous within the organization and poor, preexisting organizational values are reinforced (e.g., "We should have known computerization would never work for us."). If innovation-values fit is homogeneous and good, existing organizational values are challenged. At the same time, however, the perceived value of innovation adoption and implementation in general may be questioned, potentially leading to pessimism regarding the organization's implementation of future innovations. Finally, if innovation-values fit varies between groups, support for the group that advocated innovation use lessens.

When Implementation Is Not Effective

When implementation fails, an implementation climate, which has in all likelihood always been weak, weakens further unless—in response to initial signs of implementation failure—managers demonstrably increase their support for innovation implementation by changing the organization's implementation policies and practices to better support implementation. If the innovation was largely congruent with organizational members' homogeneous values, organizational members may question not just the merits of change, but the very possibility of change. If the innovation was largely incongruent with organizational members' homogeneous values, organizational members may feel empowered by their thwarting of the innovation's implementation. Finally, if innovation-values fit varies between groups, the influence within the organization of the group that advocated innovation implementation is reduced.

The Outcomes of Innovation Implementation: Two Examples

Buildco provides an interesting example of implementation and innovation outcomes over time. The company's initial climate for the implementation of 3-D CADD was weak, and innovation use was, accordingly, sporadic. However, Buildco's managers stepped in to strengthen the company's climate for implementation. The early organizational benefits of 3-D CADD use further strengthened Buildco's implementation climate. Given an ultimately strong climate for implementation and good fit between 3-D CADD and organizational values, use of 3-D CADD is now routine at Buildco, and the values for computerization appear even stronger than they were prior to the company's adoption of 3-D CADD.

In contrast, Wireco did not succeed in implementing its computerized inventory control system. Respect within Wireco for the company's IT specialists declined. The company has not, in the years since its foiled implementation of the inventory control system, adopted any other computerized technology that would diminish the flexibility of, or change in any other significant way, the company's production procedures.

RESEARCH IMPLICATIONS OF THE MODEL

The subject of relatively little research, implementation is the neglected member of the innovation family. Even the *Academy of Management Review*'s Call for Papers on the Management of Innovation (1994: 617–618) had a distinct, if implicit, focus on the development and adoption—not the implementation—of innovations. Our model brings new attention to implementation and invites new research on the topic. In this section, we underscore key constructs of the model, note additional research topics suggested by the model, and highlight research methods most useful for the study of implementation.

Key Constructs

Climate for implementation. We have proposed that implementation effectiveness is in part a function of the strength of an organization's climate for implementation. The climate construct subsumes and integrates many of the findings of past implementation research. However, the contributions of the construct go beyond parsimony. The construct suggests that an organization's implementation policies and practices should be conceptualized and evaluated as a comprehensive, interdependent whole that together determines the strength of the organization's climate for implementation. Further, the construct highlights the equifinality of implementation climate. Implementation climates of equal strength may ensue from quite different sets of policies and practices. For example, an organization may ensure employee innovation skill by training employees, by motivating employees through the reward system, by selecting employees skilled in innovation use for hire or promotion, or by shaping the innovation to match employees' existing skills.

The climate for implementation construct thus pushes researchers away from the search for *the* critical determinants of implementation effectiveness—training or rewards or user friendliness—to the documentation of the cumulative influence of all of these on innovation use. Further, the climate construct facilitates the comparison of implementation effectiveness across organizations. The specific implementation policies and practices that facilitate innovation use may vary tremendously from organization to organization. Training may be critical in one organization, rewards in a second organization, and so on. Thus, specific implementation policies and practices may show little consistent relationship to innovation use across organizations. Climate, however, is cumulative and thus, in concert with innovation-values fit, predictive of innovation use across organizations.

Innovation-values fit. The construct of innovation-values fit indicates the limits of implementation climate. In the face of poor innovation-values fit, a strong implementation climate results in only compliant innovation use and/or resistance. Further, innovation-values fit may vary across the groups of an organization, engendering intraorganizational conflict and lessening implementation effectiveness. The construct of innovation-values fit thus directs researchers to look beyond an organization's global (or homogeneous) implementation policies and practices and to consider the extent to which a given innovation is perceived by targeted users to clash or coincide with their organizational and group values.

Implementation effectiveness and innovation effectiveness. The construct of implementation effectiveness helps to focus researchers' attention on the aggregate behavioral phenomenon of innovation use. The construct of innovation effectiveness, in contrast, directs researchers' attention to the benefits that may accrue to an organization as a result of successful innovation implementation. These two distinct constructs, too often blurred in prior innovation research and theory, are critical for implementation research and theory. The first underscores the difficulty of innovation implementation; targeted organizational members' consistent and appropriate innovation use is not guaranteed. The second underscores the varying effects of innovation implementation; even when the implementation of an innovation is effective, the innovation may fail to yield intended organizational benefits.

Additional Topics for Research

The model invites research not only on the effects of implementation climate and innovation-values fit on implementation and innovation effectiveness, but it also suggests several questions only hinted at in this article, given space limitations. We consider four.

Managers and the creation of a strong implementation climate. The organizational change and innovation literatures (e.g., Angle & Van de Ven, 1989; Beer, 1988; Leonard-Barton & Krauss, 1985; Nadler & Tushman, 1989; Nutt, 1986) suggest that the primary antecedent of an organization's climate for implementation is managers' support for implementation of the innovation. If this is true, why do managers fail to support the implementation of many of the innovations adopted in their organizations? The available literature, although limited, suggests at least two possible answers. First, innovation adoption decisions are often made by executives at corporate headquarters without the participation or input of local, lower level managers (Guth & MacMillan, 1986; Klein, 1984). Left out of this decision-making process, local managers may not be inspired to create a strong climate for innovation implementation. Second, managers may support innovation implementation, but they may lack an in-depth understanding of the innovation. Managers who know little about an innovation are likely to delegate implementation management to subordinates who are more knowledgeable but who lack the authority and resources to create a strong climate for implementation. Although plausible, these explanations for managers' failure to support innovation implementation are tentative and preliminary. The topic warrants further empirical and conceptual analysis.

"Upward implementation" of innovations. The preceding paragraph, and much of our model, highlights the roles that managers play in creating a strong implementation climate among targeted users. Are nonmanagers powerless to affect their organization's implementation climate? We know of no research explicitly designed to answer this question. We suspect, however, that in all but the most participative, flat organizations, nonmanagers have relatively little influence in creating a strong implementation climate. Even though nonmanagers can advocate, or champion, their managers' adoption of a given innovation (Dean, 1987; Howell & Higgins, 1990), they lack the authority and resources to institute the policies and practices that yield a strong implementation climate. Yet as organizations strive to become both more innovative and flatter, the role of nonmanagers in fostering implementation becomes an increasingly important topic for research.

Implementing multiple innovations. Can an organization successfully and simultaneously implement multiple innovations? If an organization's multiple innovations necessitate diverse, new, time-consuming, and difficult-to-learn behaviors of a common group of targeted users, the likelihood of successful simultaneous implementation of the innovations is slim. An organization's climate for the implementation of one such innovation may compete with and undermine its climate for the implementation of another innovation. For example, rewards for the use of one innovation may impose obstacles to the use of the second innovation. More likely to be successful are organizational efforts to implement innovations that require complementary changes in the behavior of distinct groups of users. In such a case, the climate for the implementation of one innovation may indeed enhance the climate for the implementation of a second innovation. However, additional research is needed because relatively little is known about the success or failure of organizations' attempts to implement multiple innovations.

Fostering innovation-values fit. The actions an organization might take to strengthen its climate for the implementation of an innovation are relatively clear, but what can an organization do to foster good innovation-values fit? The available literature suggests three possible strategies. First, an organization may provide opportunities for employees to participate in the decision to adopt the innovation (Kotter & Schlesinger, 1979). Employees' participation in the adoption decision increases the likelihood that the chosen innovation fits their preexisting values. Employees' participation in the adoption decision also may change employees' values, rendering their new values congruent with the adopted innovation. Second, an organization may foster good innovation-values fit by educating employees about the need for (value of) the innovation for organizational performance. Although senior executives may recognize the need for an innovation that is discrepant with organizational members' preexisting values, lower level employees may not understand this (Floyd & Wooldridge, 1992; Guth & MacMillan, 1986; Klein, 1984). Third, employees' values may shift over time, and innovation-values fit may increase if an organization's implementation of an innovation that represents a poor fit with employees' preexisting values yields clear and widely recognized benefits for the organization. This, however, is a risky strategy; employees' use of an innovation that represents a poor fit with their values is likely to be compliant at best, and compliant innovation use is unlikely to yield great benefits to the adopting organization. Given the predicted importance of innovation-values fit in fostering innovation use, the determinants of innovation-values fit warrant focused research attention.

Methods for the Study of Implementation

Multiorganizational research. As we have noted, single-site, qualitative case studies dominate the implementation literature. To verify the sources of between-organization differences in implementation effectiveness proposed in the model, however, researchers must move beyond single-site research to analyze innovation implementation across organizations. The topic is sufficiently complex to warrant studying the implementation of a single innovation (e.g., a specific computer program), rather than the implementation of diverse innovations, across organizational sites. Ultimately, such studies may provide the groundwork for studies that are used to compare the implementation of different types of innovations across organizations.

Multilevel research. Although designed to capture between-organizational differences in innovation implementation, our model is expressly multilevel. Implementation effectiveness summarizes the innovation use of multiple individuals. Implementation climate describes the shared perceptions of multiple individuals. And innovation-values fit may vary not only between organizations but also between groups and even between individuals. Accordingly, we advocate the collection of data from multiple individuals across multiple groups, if present, within each organization in a multiorganizational sample.

Longitudinal data. Implementation is a process that occurs over time. Ideally, implementation research begins prior to implementation, with analysis and documentation of the decision to adopt an innovation. Research then continues over time to capture increases and decreases in the strength of implementation climate, in the fit of the innovation to employee values, and in innovation use and innovation effectiveness.

Qualitative and quantitative data. To gather data from multiple individuals across multiple groups in multiple organizations over multiple periods, researchers will surely need to use quantitative survey measures. The use of qualitative methods across such a sample would be far too labor intensive, far too time consuming. Further, the use of quantitative measures will allow researchers to conduct needed statistical tests of within- and between-group and within- and between-organization variability in implementation climate, innovation-values fit, innovation use, and innovation effectiveness.

However, qualitative research on implementation is still valuable. Preliminary qualitative research is likely to be essential for a researcher to gain an in-depth understanding of a given innovation and its implementation across organizations. Qualitative research may foster further development of our constructs and may provide the groundwork for the creation of survey instruments that are focused on a specific innovation. Finally, qualitative methods may be used to gather in-depth information about specific organizations that were revealed in surveys to be particularly interesting and important (e.g., organizations characterized by strong implementation climates and poor innovation-values fit).

Few researchers are likely, of course, to collect multiorganizational, multilevel, longitudinal, quantitative and qualitative data within a single study. Yet, studies that follow even two of the four research design recommendations proposed in this section will represent a step in the right direction—a step toward a deeper, more thorough understanding of innovation implementation.

CONCLUSION

When organizations adopt innovations, they do so with high expectations, anticipating improvements in organizational productivity and performance. However, the adoption of an innovation does not ensure its implementation; adopted policies may never be put into action, and adopted technologies may sit in unopened crates on the factory floor. The organizational challenge is to create the conditions for innovation use: a strong climate for innovation implementation and good innovation-values fit. Only then is an organization likely—but, unfortunately, by no means certain—to achieve the intended benefits of the innovation.

REFERENCES

Abbey, A., & Dickson, J. W. 1983. R&D work climate and innovation in semi-conductors. ***Academy of Management Journal,*** 26: 362–368.

Amabile, T. 1988. A model of creativity and innovation in organizations. In B. M. Staw & L. L. Cummings (Eds.), ***Research in organizational behavior, vol. 10***: 123–167. Greenwich, CT: JAI Press.

Angle, H., & Van de Ven, A. 1989. Suggestions for managing the innovation journey. In A. Van de Ven, H. Angle, & M. S. Poole (Eds.), ***Research on the management of innovations: The Minnesota studies:*** 663–697. New York: Harper & Row.

Barley, S. R. 1986. Technology as an occasion for structuring: Evidence from observations of CT scanners and the social order of radiology departments. ***Administrative Science Quarterly,*** 31: 78–108.

Beer, M. 1988. The critical path for change: Keys to success and failure in six companies. In R. H. Kilmann & T. J. Covin (Eds.), ***Corporate transformation:*** 17–45. San Francisco: Jossey-Bass.

Beyer, J. M., & Trice, H. M. 1978. ***Implementing change.*** New York: Free Press.

Bushe, G. R. 1988. Cultural contradictions of statistical process control in American manufacturing organizations. ***Journal of Management,*** 14: 19–31.

Damanpour, F. 1991. Organizational innovation: A meta-analysis of effects of determinants and moderators. ***Academy of Management Journal,*** 34: 555–590.

Dean, J. W., Jr. 1987. ***Deciding to innovate.*** Cambridge, MA: Ballinger.

Dougherty, D. 1992. Interpretive barriers to successful product innovation in large firms. ***Organizational Science,*** 3: 179–203.

Fleischer, M., Liker, J., & Arnsdorf, D. 1988. ***Effective use of computer-aided design and computer-aided engineering in manufacturing.*** Ann Arbor, MI: Industrial Technology Institute.

Floyd, S. W., & Wooldridge, B. 1992. Managing strategic consensus: The foundation of effective implementation. ***Academy of Management Executive,*** 6(4): 27–39.

Goodman, P. S., & Griffith, T. L. 1991. A process approach to the implementation of new technology. ***Journal of Engineering Technology and Management,*** 8: 261–285.

Guth, W. D., & MacMillan, I. C. 1986. Strategy implementation versus middle management self-interest. ***Strategic Mangagement Journal,*** 7: 313–327.

Hackman, J. R., & Wageman, R. 1995. Total quality management: Empirical, conceptual and practical issues. **Administrative Science Quarterly,** 40: 309–342.

Hage, J. 1980. **Theories of organizations.** New York: Wiley.

Hattrup, K., & Kozlowski, S. W. J. 1993. An across-organization analysis of the implementation of advanced manufacturing technologies. **Journal of High Technology Management Research,** 4: 175–196.

Holland, J. L. 1985. **Making vocational choices: A theory of careers.** Englewood Cliffs, NJ: Prentice Hall.

Howell, J., & Higgins, C. 1990. Champions of technological innovation. **Administrative Science Quarterly,** 35: 317–341.

Kabanoff, B., Waldersee, R., & Cohen, M. 1995. Espoused values and organizational change themes. **Academy of Management Journal,** 38: 1075–1104.

Kanter, R. M. 1988. When a thousand flowers bloom: Structural, collective, and social conditions for innovation in organization. In B. M. Staw & L. L. Cummings (Eds.), **Research in organizational behavior,** vol. 10: 169–211. Greenwich, CT: JAI Press.

Kelman, H. C. 1961. Processes of opinion change. **Public Opinion Quarterly,** 25: 57–78.

Klein, J. A. 1984. Why supervisors resist employee involvement. **Harvard Business Review,** 84(5): 87–95.

Klein, K. J. 1986. **Using 3D CADD: The human side.** Technical report. College Park: University of Maryland, Department of Psychology.

Klein, K. J., Dansereau, F., & Hall, R. J. 1994. Levels issues in theory development, data collection, and analysis. **Academy of Management Review,** 19: 195–229.

Klein, K. J., Hall, R. J., & Laliberte, M. 1990. Training and the organizational consequences of technological change: A case study of computer-aided design and drafting. In U. E. Gattiker & L. Larwood (Eds.), **Technological innovation and human resources: End-user training:** 7–36. New York: de Gruyter.

Klein, K. J., & Ralls, R. S. 1995. The organizational dynamics of computerized technology implementation: A review of the empirical literature. In L. R. Gomez-Mejia & M. W. Lawless (Eds.), **Implementation management of high technology:** 31–79. Greenwich, CT: JAI Press.

Klein, K. J., Ralls, R. S., & Carter, P. O. 1989. **The implementation of a computerized inventory control system.** Technical report. College Park: University of Maryland, Department of Psychology.

Kopelman, R. E., Brief, A. P., & Guzzo, R. A. 1990. The role of climate and culture in productivity. In B. Schneider (Ed.), **Organizational climate and culture:** 282–318. San Francisco: Jossey-Bass.

Kotter, J. P., & Schlesinger, L. A. 1979. Choosing strategies for change. **Harvard Business Review,** 57(2): 106–114.

Kozlowski, S. W. J., & Hults, B. M. 1987. An exploration of climates for technical updating and performance. **Personnel Psychology,** 40: 539–563.

Lawler, E. E., & Mohrman, S. A. 1991. Quality circles: After the honeymoon. In B. M. Staw (Ed.), **Psychological dimensions of organizational behavior:** 523–533. New York: Macmillan.

Leonard-Barton, D., & Krauss, W. A. 1985. Implementing new technology. **Harvard Business Review,** 63(6): 102–110.

March, J. G., & Sproull, L. S. 1990. Technology, management, and competitive advantage. In P. S. Goodman & L. S. Sproull (Eds.), **Technology and organizations:** 144–173. San Francisco: Jossey-Bass.

Markus, M. L. 1987. Power, politics, and MIS implementation. In R. M. Becker & W. A. S. Buxton (Eds.), ***Readings in human-computer interaction: A multidisciplinary approach:*** 68–82. Los Angeles: Morgan Kaufmann.

Nadler, D. A., & Tushman, M. L. 1989. Leadership for organizational change. In A. M. Mohrman, Jr., S. A. Mohrman, G. E. Ledford, Jr., T. G. Cummings, & E. E. Lawler (Eds.), ***Large-scale organizational change:*** 100–119. San Francisco: Jossey-Bass.

Nord, W. R., & Tucker, S. 1987. ***Implementing routine and radical innovations.*** Lexington, MA: Lexington Books.

Nutt, P. C. 1986. Tactics of implementation. ***Academy of Management Journal,*** 29: 230–261.

O'Reilly, C., & Chatman, J. 1986. Organizational commitment and psychological attachment: The effects of compliance, identification, and internalization on prosocial behavior. ***Journal of Applied Psychology,*** 71: 492–499.

Reger, R. K., Gustafson, L. T., DeMarie, S. M., & Mullane, J. V. 1994. Reframing the organization: Why implementing total quality is easier said than done. ***Academy of Management Review,*** 19: 565–584.

Rentsch, J. R. 1990. Climate and culture: Interaction and qualitative difference in organizational meanings. ***Journal of Applied Psychology,*** 75: 668–681.

Rivard, S. 1987. Successful implementation of end-user computing. *Interfaces,* 17(3): 25–33.

Roberts-Gray, C., & Gray, T. 1983. The evaluation of text editors: Methodology and empirical results. ***Communications of the ACM,*** 26: 265–283.

Roitman, D. B., Liker, J. K., & Roskies, E. 1988. Birthing a factory of the future: When is "all at once" too much? In R. H. Kilmann & T. J. Covin (Eds.), ***Corporate transformation:*** 205–246. San Francisco: Jossey-Bass.

Rousseau, D. M. 1989. Managing the change to an automated office: Lessons from five case studies. ***Office: Technology & People,*** 4: 31–52.

Schein, E. H. 1992. ***Organizational culture and leadership.*** San Francisco: Jossey-Bass.

Schneider, B. 1975. Organizational climates: An essay. ***Personnel Psychology,*** 28: 447–479.

Schneider, B. 1987. The people make the place. ***Personnel Psychology,*** 40: 437–453.

Schneider, B. 1990. The climate for service: An application of the climate construct. In B. Schneider (Ed.), ***Organizational climate and culture:*** 383–412. San Francisco: Jossey-Bass.

Schneider, B., & Bowen, D. E. 1985. Employee and customer perceptions of service in banks: Replication and extension. ***Journal of Applied Psychology,*** 70: 423–433.

Schneider, B., Parkington, J. J., & Buxton, V. M. 1980. Employee and customer perceptions of service in bands. ***Administrative Science Quarterly,*** 25: 252–267.

Sproull, L. S., & Hofmeister, K. R. 1986. Thinking about implementation. ***Journal of Management,*** 12: 43–60.

Sussman M., & Vecchio, R. P. 1991. A social influence interpretation of worker motivation. In R. M. Steers & L. W. Porter (Eds.), ***Motivation and work behavior:*** 218–220. New York: McGraw-Hill.

Tornatzky, L. G., & Fleischer, M. 1990. ***The process of technological innovation: Reviewing the literature.*** Washington, DC: National Science Foundation.

Tornatzky, L. G., & Klein, K. J. 1982. Innovation characteristics and innovation adoption-implementation: A meta-analysis of findings. ***IEEE Transactions on Engineering Management,*** 29: 28–45.

Zohar, D. 1980. Safety climate in industrial organizations: Theoretical and applied implications. ***Journal of Applied Psychology,*** 65: 96–102.

Zuboff, S. 1988. ***In the age of the smart machine: The future of work and power.*** New York: Basic Books.

Joann Speer Sorra received her master's degree from Michigan State University and is currently a doctoral candidate in industrial and organizational psychology at the University of Maryland. Her research interests include training, technical updating, organizational climate and culture, and organizational change.

Katherine J. Klein received her Ph.D. from the University of Texas. She is an associate professor of psychology at the University of Maryland. Her current research interests include innovation implementation and organizational change, level-of-analysis issues, and part-time work.

[7]

ELSEVIER

OOOO

The Breakfast of Champions: Associations Between Champions and Product Development Environments, Practices and Performance

Stephen K. Markham and Abbie Griffin

According to conventional wisdom, if an innovative new product development (NPD) effort is to stand any chance for success, the project must have a champion. The role of the champion has taken on almost mythic proportions, through oft-told tales of the development of such disparate products as instant cameras, automobiles, and microprocessors. Notwithstanding the purportedly essential role that champions play, however, we have only anecdotal evidence of the manner in which effective champions operate and the benefits that they offer.

Stephen K. Markham and Abbie Griffin suggest that before we can explore questions about how champions affect product development performance, we must address an even more fundamental issue: whether champions actually influence performance. Using data from the 1995 PDMA study of best practices in product development, they test various widely held assumptions about champions and NDP performance. Specifically, they investigate the association between championing and the following variables: NPD performance at the program, firm, and project levels; industry characteristics; and project- and firm-related NPD characteristics.

In several respects, the results of their study run counter to current beliefs about product development champions. For example, the study suggests that champions are just as likely to be found in large firms as they are in small firms. Similarly, the results indicate that the likelihood of finding a champion does not differ significantly between technology-driven firms and marketing-driven firms. For the firms in this study, champions are no more likely to support radical innovations than they are to back incremental innovations or product line extensions.

The results of the study suggest that champions do not directly affect firm-level NPD performance. Instead, the results of this study associate increased championing with higher levels of NPD program performance, which positively affects firm-level performance. The results of this study also do not support the notion that a champion can directly improve the market success of a particular project. © 1998 Elsevier Science Inc.

Address correspondence to Stephen K. Markham, Associate Professor of Management, North Carolina State University, College of Management, Box 7229, Raleigh, NC 27695. E-mail: Stephen_Markham@ncsu.edu

J PROD INNOV MANAG 1998;15:436–454

655 Avenue of the Americas, New York, NY 10010

0737-6782/98/$19.00
PII S0737-6782(98)00010-1

J PROD INNOV MANAG 1998;15:436–454

Introduction and Background

The role of the champion in new product development has been a topic of discussion since 1963 [46]. Champions have long been thought to have a profound positive impact on new product development (NPD) [4,7,10,11,13,14,19,21,22,25,28, 41–43,46–48], yet quantitative data are surprisingly rare. Consequently, we do not know much more now in what to expect from champions than we did decades ago. The concept of the champion also has been clouded by the sometimes mythical accounts of their behavior. For example, Lee Ioccoca, Edwin Land, and Ken West have each received recognition as champions for their role in commercializing various products. Nevertheless, the successes they achieved are not necessarily representative of the rates of success achieved across all champions, or in firms developing something other than durable goods.

There has long been a positive bias toward the anecdotal effect of champions [6,7,11,12,19]. Many people suspect, and some even have what they consider to be irrefutable evidence of, the effects of champions on NPD outcomes based on individual cases [13]. These presumed effects include improving project performance, reducing cycle time, and overcoming obstacles in the NPD process. Little published empirical evidence has supported or refuted any of these claims. In truth, we have neither stable theories nor accurate information on which to form formal hypotheses about the extent to which, or the situations in which, champions impact success.

Championing understanding generally arises from post hoc stories of successes rather than real-time processes. This has resulted in long-running misperceptions about champions. The evidence from which we generally draw our knowledge about champions is biased by past successes. Observers naturally associate visible (successful) outcomes with the champions involved, but may not be able to for invisible (failed) outcomes. Project supporters tend to distance themselves from failed projects, and it is more difficult to assign responsibilities for unsuccessful projects. Failed champions rarely seek attention, thus are less noticed. Fewer people see them or their effect (or lack thereof). Selective retention of championing stories help reinforce the statistically unsubstantiated belief that champions positively impact NPD. In this article, a number of these beliefs are empirically tested.

The *PDMA Handbook of Product Development* defines a champion as [45, p. 519]: "A person who takes an inordinate interest in seeing that a particular process or product is fully developed and marketed. The role varies from situations calling for little more than stimulating awareness of the opportunity to extreme cases where the champion tries to force a project past the strongly entrenched internal resistance of company policy or that of objecting parties." As this definition indicates, there is great latitude in the breadth of behavior of product development champions. Howell and Higgins [19] concluded that champions are informal transformational leaders. They found that champions generally work outside official roles, using visionary statements, concern for others, and stimulating ideas to influence others' actions. Champions contribute to NPD through asserting some level of project leadership. However, champions work more through informal influence to lead a part of the overall effort than through a formal leadership or power assignment from management.

The organizational literature has yet to establish how people influence each other. "There is more conceptual confusion about influence processes than any other facet of leadership" [49, p. 193]. In addition, the general dependency of formal leadership capabilities on the influence process is also a poorly understood area [2,24]. The cognitive task of assigning leadership attributes such as capability to influence others to formally appointed and formally recognized managers is difficult [15]. Misattribution routinely occurs. Making influence attributions for a champion, who is most likely operating outside an official leadership role, must be even more difficult. Misattribution in formal leadership is so widespread that it has led to different leadership attribution theories [15,26,27]. So little is known about the informal influence process that no

BIOGRAPHICAL SKETCHES

Stephen Markham is an associate professor of management at North Carolina State University. He received his Ph.D. in Organizational Behavior from Purdue University, M.B.A. from University California Irvine, and M.S. and B.S. in Psychology from Brigham Young University. He is the co-director of the Technology, Education, and Commercialization Program, which specializes in commercializing high technology.

Abbie Griffin is Professor of Marketing at the University of Illinois at Urbana-Champaign. She received her Ph.D. in Management from the Massachusetts Institute of Technology, M.B.A. from Harvard University, and B.S. in Chemical Engineering from Purdue University. Her research investigates methods for measuring and improving new product development. In addition, she is an avid scuba diver and quilter.

theories have been developed for, or extended to, champion activities. Because we cannot routinely correctly attribute characteristics such as leadership capability or influencing other individuals, linking those leadership characteristics to performance outcomes is not likely to provide usable empirical results in an area we do not yet understand, such as championing.

Although Markham [30] has linked championing to the power and influence literature by finding that champions act politically, the power and influence literature does not incorporate the concept of the champion into theory. Pfeffer [39] has written extensively about power and influence yet does not include the champion role in any models. Porter et al's [40] frequently cited model of upward influence similarly does not mention the champion role. Given the unsettled nature of these literatures, it seems unlikely that a concept as specific as champion influence processes can become better understood than the general body of influence knowledge of which the concept is one aspect.

Forcing undeveloped behavioral theory onto an untested set of assumptions about champion performance seems premature. That neither the power and influence nor leadership literatures have dealt explicitly with the champion concept suggests that the field could benefit from a more fundamental understanding about the link between champion presence and performance prior to developing specific leadership hypotheses about champion influence mechanisms. We need to answer the questions surrounding *whether* champions impact performance before answering ones about *how* they make their impact. In situations such as this, Yukl [49, p. 18] suggests, "the best way to see how variables are interrelated is to find points of convergence among different approaches." The purpose of this research is to examine some of the existence and performance assumptions about champions (the whether) so that we then may begin to use other theoretical bases, such as power and leadership, to understand champion operation better (the how).

To better understand championing prevalence and effects, this article uses data from the 1995 Product Development & Management Association's (PDMA's) best practices in product development survey to address empirically a number of the assumptions about champions [16,20]. The Best Practices study contains unique data that can be used to empirically test several of the common assumptions outlined above about champions. Unfortunately, these data cannot provide behavioral insight about how successful champions operate or which provide clues as to what differentiates between successful and unsuccessful champions.

As we answer fundamental questions about champions using these data, we find that they provide few direct statistical links between champions and performance. These findings conflict with many anecdotal data, and thus may disappoint those who firmly believe in the efficacy of champions. Although there are limitations in the operationalizations of some of the constructs, these findings, in conjunction with other research findings, suggest that we do not yet understand the basic championing phenomena well enough to justify relying upon them for NPD success.

Research Issues and Associated Literature

This article examines three major championing practice and performance issues in the aggregate. These questions empirically investigate championing's association with:

1. NPD program, firm-level and project-level performance
2. Industry characteristics, and
3. Project- and firm-related NPD characteristics.

The dearth of existing theory and empirical analyses in this area means that formal hypotheses have not been developed or tested by previous researchers. We review the relationships for these associations, which are believed to exist or have been promoted or postulated in the literature. We then use the data and exploratory analyses to portray a more accurate depiction of champion effects and relationships.

Since Schon [46] introduced the concept of the product champion in 1963, they have been thought to have a large positive impact on NPD performance [13,14]. The existence and nature of this impact, however, has remained veiled in anecdotal and sometimes mythical accounts of individual champions [4,12]. Discussions on championing often focus on exceptional occurrences rather than the general phenomenon [13,21,38]. Empirical data have not existed that could be tested statistically to relate champion use to performance. We do not really know what general impact champions have on the firm or even on the projects they promote [12,29]. Therefore, we first examine aggregate championing impact on NPD programs and on the firm as a whole. We investigate the extent to which championing within a firm is related to NPD program success, overall firm success, firm profits, the

 J PROD INNOV MANAG 1998;15:436–454

number of new products commercialized over the last 5 years, and changes in NPD cycle times over the last 5 years.

Anecdotal stories of champions often portray champions in high-technology, innovative companies, such as Andy Grove of Intel [7,43]. No empirical evidence has existed to support or refute this general depiction of where champions are most likely to operate to support NPD. We do not know in which environments champions are most likely to arise [12]. Thus, we next examine industry conditions relating to increased levels of championing.

Finally, we look at champions and a number of project- and firm-specific characteristics. Champions are associated anecdotally with high-risk projects [8,28,44,46]. Conventional wisdom suggests that the more radical the project, the more champions are attracted to providing support to it. Again, no empirical evidence has existed to corroborate or refute this conjecture. Therefore, we examine the relationship between championing and project newness.

Numerous product development improvement tools have been devised since the concept of the champion was introduced, including both organizational and procedural methods [10]. To date no research has examined how champions and these new methods interact with each other. For example, venture teams [36] were not conceived of when the concept of championing was first identified. Therefore, we examine if the level of championing is enhanced or reduced by particular NPD processes and organizational structures.

The champion issues introduced above have long-established common knowledge associated with them. True to the concept of the champion, many individuals hold these beliefs passionately, even if they are not supported by empirical evidence. Yet, empirical research has not existed to substantially answer whether this "knowledge" is biased or not. After empirically examining these questions, we conclude with managerial implications and further research directions.

Research Methods

The first PDMA study of best practices in product development was in 1990. The first research project identified norms describing product development practices [36] and several best practices found in high-impact NPD [37]. The second PDMA survey on product development best practices, upon which this article is based, was fielded in the summer of 1995. One of the objectives of this research was to investigate the change in the status of implementation of various product development tools and determine which of them differentiates successful product development. This article uses a subset of these data to address the role champions seem to play in NPD.

Survey Development

A number of product development practices surveys have been developed and reported on recently. In developing the PDMA research, surveys and results were gathered from multiple sources [3,5,32,36]. A multiplicity of sources were used because this research was to cover a broader set of issues than any one of these previous surveys. Potential survey questions were identified, formatted, and circulated to three academics and three practitioners who had previously been involved in best practices research. Changes were made to increase clarity, and several issues and questions were eliminated based on their suggestions. Another draft of the survey was developed and pretested with 12 knowledgeable product development practitioners. Additional rewordings of the survey were made based on their suggestions.

The final survey consisted of nine pages of questions and a one-page cover letter. Questions covered issues surrounding the product development process, organizing for product development, tools supporting product development, measuring product development, product development outcomes, and background information on the firms.

The survey was a pre-addressed self-mailer. Respondents folded the finished survey in half, taped or stapled it shut, placed a stamp in the corner, and dropped it in the mail. Reminder postcards were mailed to all potential respondents 2 weeks after the initial survey was sent out. No incentives were provided to participants for filling out this rather long survey. However, if they stapled a business card to the form, we promised to send them working papers derived from the research as they became available.

Sample

The survey was sent out to over 14,500 potential respondents obtained from three separate sources as outlined in Table 1. Random samples of mailing lists were purchased from the American Marketing Association (AMA) and CorpTech. The mailing lists were chosen to maximize the sample diversity. Previous

Table 1. Sample and Response Rates

	PDMA Members	American Marketing Association	CorpTech List	Total
No. mailed out	1,601	6,650	6,500	14,751
No. undelivered	0	225	57	252
No. usable returns	159	86	138	383
Response rate	9.9%	1.3%	2.1%	2.7%

studies had shown that PDMA members are primarily goods producers in the business-to-business market, from somewhat larger firms. Because the goal was to get a broader understanding of NPD practices, lists were sought that would provide more consumer, service-providing, and smaller-firm respondents. Table 2 shows that the diversity of the sample was increased statistically significantly across four demographic variables by using the AMA and CorpTech lists in addition to surveying PDMA members. The sample is still more goods-oriented (80.6%) than service-oriented and predominantly sells into the business-to-business market rather than directly to consumers. The CorpTech list helped increase the numbers of smaller firms in the sample.

Variable Operationalization

Dependent variables. The survey included four project-level measures of NPD cycle times and nine measures of overall performance. Factor analysis of eight overall performance measures revealed three factors (Program Performance, Firm-Level Success Rates, and Firm-Level Sales and Profitability) with eigen values over one (Table 3). All variables loaded over .50 on the indicated factors and there were no ambiguous loadings [23]. The ninth overall measure (number of new products introduced) is statistically unrelated to any other measure and is thus treated separately.

Project-level performance: NPD cycle times. Respondents provided estimates of the percentage that cycle times had changed in the last 5 years at their firm for four categories of projects: new-to-the-world projects, new product lines, major revisions of current products, and incremental improvements to current products. Chronbach's α ($\alpha = .82$) suggests that the four items can be used reliably as a single measure [35].

Program performance. The program performance factor consists of three items: (1) Our new product program meets performance objectives; (2) Overall, our new product program is a success; and (3) Our new product program is important to my organization's sales and profits. Together, these items, which have been used extensively in previous research [9], form a scale that measures how well the product development process is performing. All items were measured on a 1 (completely disagree) to 9 (completely) agree scale (5 = neither agree nor disagree). All items loaded on the factor at or above .58 [23]. Chron-

Table 2. Demographics by Source of the Sample

		PDMA		AMA Sample		CorpTech		Total Sample	
		No.	%	No.	%	No.	% CorpTech	No.	% Total
Technology	High tech	43	27.7%	18	22.2%	67	49.3%	128	34.4%
	Mixed	64	41.3%	41	50.6%	48	35.3%	153	41.1%
Dependency[a]	Low tech	48	31.0%	22	27.2%	21	15.4%	91	24.5%
	Consumer	39	25.0%	20	24.7%	7	5.2%	66	17.8%
	Mixed	28	17.9%	14	17.3%	22	16.4%	64	17.3%
Market[b]	Business	89	57.1%	47	58.0%	105	78.4%	241	65.0%
Product	Goods	142	91.0%	39	48.8%	119	87.5%	300	80.6%
type[c]	Services	14	9.0%	41	51.3%	17	12.5%	72	19.4%
	<$10 M	6	4.0%	12	15.3%	44	33.6%	62	17.0%
	$10–$24 M	6	4.0%	7	9.0%	28	20.7%	41	11.2%
	$25–$99 M	18	11.8%	19	24.4%	43	31.9%	80	21.9%
	$100–$499 M	63	41.4%	22	28.2%	16	11.9%	101	27.7%
	$500–$999 M	18	11.8%	6	7.7%	2	1.5%	26	7.1%
Sales[d]	= $1,000 M	41	27.0%	12	15.4%	2	1.5%	55	15.1%

ANOVA test: $^{a}F = 11.1, p < .01, df = 371$; $^{b}F = 12.4, p < .01, df = 370$; $^{c}F = 40.5, p < .01, df = 371$; $^{d}F = 79.1, p < .01, df = 364$.

bach's α (α = .72) also suggests that the three items can be used reliably as a single measure [35].

Firm-level success rates. Three items are included in the factor that measures NPD success rates at the firm level: (1) Based on your firm's definition of success, what percent of all new products introduced into the market during the last 5 years were successful?; (2) What percent were successful in terms of profitability?; and (3) What percent of the products commercialized over the last 5 years are still on the market? Success rates have been recommended in previous research as useful measures for firms following moderately innovative technology strategies [18]. All items loaded higher than .76 on this factor. Chronbach's α (α = .79) suggests that the three items can be used reliably as a single measure [35].

Firm-level sales and profitability. The third factor measures the growth contribution of the new product program for the firm with two items: (1) New product sales as a percent of total sales in the past 5 years; and (2) New product profits as a percent of total profits, both of which have been recommended in prior research as useful firm-level measures for firms with more innovative technology strategies [18]. Both items loaded at .90 on this factor. Chronbach's α (α = .83) also suggests that the three items can be used reliably as a single measure [35].

Firm-level performance: Number of new products introduced. The number of new items introduced consists of a single item: number of new products commercialized by your firm in the past 5 years. Although not found to be a recommended measure of overall success [18], these figures have been repeatedly tracked and reported over the years as indicators of the importance of new products to ongoing firm competitiveness [5,32].

Table 4 provides summary statistics for each item in each factor as well as the means and standard deviations across the items for each factor. Strong variations exist across the data. The percentages of sales and profits contributed by new products, numbers of new products, and cycle time reductions especially are highly variable across respondents, with high coefficients of variation (.82, 2.65, and 1.51, respectively). This is a necessary condition to determining whether championing has any effects.

Table 5 gives the correlation matrix for the five dependent variables. The number of new products introduced by a firm is uncorrelated with any other measure of NPD success. Just because a firm introduces many new products does not mean that their firm is successful at product development, or that they have decreased NPD cycle time. Program performance, overall success rates, and sales and profitability statistically are correlated in the data. Decreasing product development cycle times also are associated with higher levels of program success. However, the

Table 3. Factor Loading for New Product Performance Measures

	Factor 1	Factor 2	Factor 3
Program success			
Met project objectives	.24	**.83**	.03
Met success goals	.33	**.86**	.02
Met project sales goals	−.08	**.58**	.32
Firm success rate			
% success	**.76**	.38	.27
% profitable	**.78**	.30	.28
% still on the market	**.81**	−.01	−.06
NPD sales and profitability			
New product sales as % of total revenue	.09	.08	**.90**
New product profits as a % of total profit	.16	.09	**.90**
Eigen values	3.42	1.49	1.06
Percent variability	42.8%	18.6%	13.2%

Table 4. Summary Statistics for Dependent Variables

	Mean	Standard Deviation
Program success[a]	6.3	1.5
Program met objectives	5.4	2.0
Overall, program is a success	5.6	2.1
Program is important to the firm	7.9	1.6
Firm success rates	64.0%	22.5%
% commercially successful	59.1%	26.7%
% of projects financially	54.7%	27.8%
% of products still on market	78.2%	25.7%
NPD sales and profitability	31.8%	26.1%
% of sales from last 5 years NPs	32.3%	27.8%
% of profits from last 5 years NPs	30.6%	28.1%
Number of New Products Introduced	37	98
Cycle time changes (%)	−17.4%	26.2%
New-to-the-world	−14.2%	31.4%
New product lines	−17.8%	36.6%
Major revisions	−19.2%	27.9%
Incremental improvements	−16.6%	32.7%

[a] Scale for this factor's items: 1 = completely disagree, 5 = neither agree nor disagree, 9 = completely agree.

Table 5. Correlation Matrix for Dependent Variables

	Program Success	Firm Success Rate	NPD Sales and Profitability	No. of New Products Introduced
Firm success rate	**.43**[a,b]	—	—	—
NPD sales and profitability	**.23**[b]	**.32**[b]	—	—
No. of new products introduced	.02	−.02	−.01	—
Cycle time changes	**−.32**[b]	−.05	−.03	−.11

[a]In this and subsequent tables, number in bold indicate a significant relationship.
[b]Correlation is significant at the .01 level.

magnitudes of the correlations, although statistically significant, are all less than .5.[1]

Independent variables. Data were collected for two measures of championing, two control variables, innovation strategy and process implementation, and a number of other independent variables that provide information on company and project characteristics.

Champion leadership. Respondents first indicated who leads the more innovative projects at their firms: champions, process owners, project managers, leaderless structures, or someone else. Of the 381 respondents, 151 (40%) indicated that their firm uses champions to lead projects. Factor analyzing the leadership options revealed that respondents see champion leaders differently than other types of NPD leaders, such as process owners and project managers, because each loads on separate factors. Although projects may have multiple leaders, whether a champion leads a new product project is independent of whether the project is also led by a project manager or process owner. The champion thus is a role separate from other leadership mechanisms. This result resolves a potential problem with whether the role of the champion can be distinguished from other roles, particularly the project manager.

Champion support. The second champion measure asked respondents to identify the extent to which their more innovative NPD projects use champions to support the product development effort (1 = never, 2 = ¼ of the time 3 = ½ of the time, 4 = ¾ of the time, 5 = virtually always). A large percentage of the sample (293 [77%]) responded that they used champions at least to some extent to support NPD efforts at their firm. Thus, whereas only 40% of the respondents use champions to lead their more innovative projects, another 37% use them to support NPD efforts in some way, but not to lead the projects. Of the respondents, 16.3% (57) use champions "virtually always" in their more innovative NPD projects, with 41 of those (72%) also using champions to lead their projects, not just support the efforts.

As one might expect, the two championing measures are correlated significantly ($\rho = .45, p < .01$). It is unlikely that respondents would report champions leading a project if there are no champions supporting projects in the first place. However, the two measures allow us to test issues from different perspectives. The first measure allows us to test differences across populations when project leadership is by champion or not. The second measure of championing is used in statistical correlations and regressions, because it provides a linear firm-level measure of the extent of championing support in more innovative projects.

Champion saturation/champion free. A third, more highly contrasting test of champion impact is obtained by combining the two measures and comparing effects for two smaller subsets of responses: champion-free firms, in which champions do not lead or ever support any projects (54 responses, 15.4% of the total) and champion-saturated firms, in which champions lead projects and are associated with all innovative projects undertaken (41, or 11.7% of the total).

Innovation strategy. Strategy was a four-level measure corresponding to the typology of Miles and Snows [34]. Respondents indicated which of the types they thought their organization was from a descriptive paragraph. Each response was coded as follows: Prospectors = 4, Analyzers = 3, Defenders = 2, Reactors = 1. Thus, we have a strategy inovativeness scale from least (1) to most (4) innovative.

NPD process implementation. The level of NPD process implementation assesses formal NPD process use at firms. Respondents chose the level of imple-

[1]While previous research had demonstrated that project-level measures differ significantly from overall success measures, a confirmatory factor analysis (CFA) was run, which included the eight correlated overall measures of success and the four project-level measures to determine whether the project-level variables should be analyzed separately from the overall measures in this research. The factor analysis produced four factors with eigen values over 1.0 and accounting for at least 10% of the variation in the data. The first three factors were identical to the eight-variable, three-factor solution with one exception. The item "our new product program is important to my organization's sales and profits" no longer loaded unambiguously on any factor. Based on this structure, this item would be eliminated from the analysis. The fourth factor consisted of the four cycle time items, each of which loaded over .50. From this CFA, we conclude that the cycle time measure should be included as a separate item. We also retain the eighth overall measure in the analysis because it loads unambiguously on the program factors when only the overall measures are included in the factor analysis.

J PROD INNOV MANAG 1998;15:436–454

mentation present in their organization: no standard approach to NPD (1), no formal approach but we have a clearly understood path (2), formally documented functional approach (3), formally documented cross-functional approach (4), formally documented approach that involves a process owner facilitating a project through stages with management review (5), or formally documented process with overlapping, fluid stages or conditional stage decisions (6). This provides a scale of the level of NPD process implementation in the organization. As with strategy, process implementation level was used as a covariate in some analyses.

Company characteristics. Respondents provided information on four company characteristics that previously had been thought to correlate with champion use: size, in terms of sales per year, whether the firm produces manufactured goods or services, technology level (high tech, low tech, or mixed), and whether they sell into the consumer or business-to-business markets.

Project characteristics. Four project characteristics that had been thought to correlate with champion use also were captured in the data. First, respondents indicated the percentage of the projects their organization had undertaken in the last 5 years across each of seven different categories [5]: new-to-the world goods/services, new product lines, additions to existing product lines, major revisions, minor revisions, repositionings, and cost reductions. Thus, we have a weighted-average project radicalness scale ranging from 1 (most radical) to 7 (least radical). Second, process complexity is provided by the number of steps in the NPD process followed. Third, respondents indicated in which of six organizational structures their NPD projects resided. Fourth, respondents indicated the extent to which multifunctional teams were used in projects.

Results and Discussion

This section examines the PDMA best practices data for empirical evidence for each of the issues introduced above. We first examine the direct and indirect effects of championing on NPD project, program, and firm-level results. We then examine the association between championing and other known predictors of NPD success, namely, whether the firm's strategy supports innovation and whether the firm has a well-developed NPD process in place. As will be seen in each section, significant biases appear in the common knowledge associated with champions. Empirical results consistently are at some odds with anecdotal information.

Champions and NPD Performance

Direct relationships between champions and performance. Although there is widespread belief that champions have large positive effects on projects, data have yet to show this effect. In fact, Markham et al. found that although champions do use a variety of influence tactics [31], engage in political activity [30], and have an impact on project management practices [29], these do not in turn impact firm performance. Because this is a controversial finding, we seek to replicate it here.

In the Best Practices data, few direct associations were found between champions and performance. Highlights of the performance results detailed below are summarized in Exhibit 1. Direct relationships are presented in Tables 6, 7, and 8. The ANOVA tests in Table 6 show that there are no performance differences on any dimension between champion-free and champion-saturated firms. Champion leaders are associated significantly with decreasing cycle time, although they are not associated with any differences in program or firm-level performance. Table 7 shows that using champions as leaders produces larger decreases in cycle time across each of the four different types of NPD projects, with the differences statistically significant for the less innovative major-improvement and incremental-improvement projects. Table 8 shows that higher percentages of champion support in more innovative projects is correlated significantly with higher program success, but not with either firm-level success or faster cycle times.

Although champion support is correlated with program performance, the impact is much smaller than commonly expected anecdotally and in the literature. Regressing program success on level of champion support produces a statistically significant regression equation ($F = 9.8$, $p < .01$), with the coefficient for the level of champion support also significant ($t = 3.1$, $p < .01$). However, the regression equation only accounts for 2.8% of the total variation in the data and the coefficient for level of champion support is .19. Level of champion support ranges from 1 (0% support) to 5 (100% support). Average program performance in the sample is 6.3 on a 1 to 9 scale. Thus, if a firm moves from no champion support for projects to support for 100% of their projects, program performance will increase by $(5 - 1 = 4) * .19 = .76$. An

Exhibit 1.

Champions and Performance

The relationship between champions and performance has never been clear. These results show that the effect of championing on firm success rates is mediated by program-level performance, innovation strategy, and use of NPD processes.

- Champions are not related to firm success rates or sales.
- Champions are related to the product development program performance, innovation strategy, and use of product development processes.
- The product development program, innovation strategy, and use of product development processes are related to firm success rates and sales.
- Therefore, champions have an indirect, rather than direct, effect on firm success rate.

Mediated Relationship Between Champions and Firm Success Rate

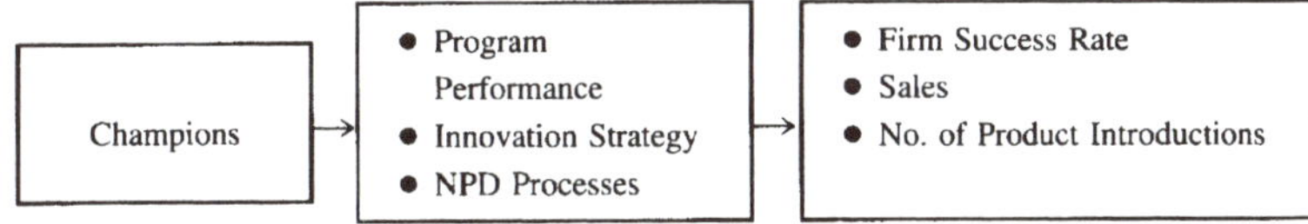

average firm that moves from no to complete champion support could only expect to improve program performance by 12%. Thus, large program performance improvements cannot be produced through just implementing champions as project support mechanisms.

The direct analyses support the findings of Markham et al [29]. Champions slightly improve project and program performance. However, champions do not produce directly any discernible overall effects on NPD performance at the firm level. Because we are examining championing at the firm level, individual champion contribution may be confounded with other factors. Therefore, lack of strong results is not surprising.

Champions, strategy, and process. If champions are not related to firm-level success, are they related to other variables that in turn impact a firm's performance? Specifically, what is the relationship between champion and a firm's innovation strategy and use of modern NPD processes? High-performance (best practice) new-product firms are more likely to use formal development processes than other firms [16]. They are also more likely to have more innovative strategies, being Prospectors or Analyzers, than lower-performing firms, which are more likely to follow Defender or Reactor strategies [16]. If championing is related to either following processes or implementing strategies, then we may be able to detect indirect influences of championing on firm performance, even though we have not found that championing directly influences firm performance.

Table 9 shows how champion leadership varies by formal process use. The relationship is nearly statisti-

Table 6. NPD Performance by Champion Population

	Program Success	Firm Success Rate	NPD Sales and Profits	No. of New Products	Cycle Time Changes
Sample ave.	6.3	64.0%	31.8%	36.9	−17.4%
Champions lead	6.4	62.7%	31.6%	45.4	**−23.3%**[a]
Others Lead	6.3	64.9%	31.9%	30.4	**−13.7%**[a]
Champion-saturated	6.6	69.3	33.9%	37.2	−32.8%
Champion-free	6.1	66.0%	32.4%	20.0	−25.1%

[a]ANOVA test: $F = 3.9$, $p = .05$, $df = 118$.

Table 7. Percentage Decreases in Cycle Time by Project Leadership Last 5 Years

	New-to-the-World	New Product Lines	Major Improvements	Minor Improvements
Sample Ave.	−14.2%	−17.8%	−19.2%	−16.6%
Champions Lead	−17.5%	−23.6%	**−25.9%**[a]	**−24.6%**[b]
Others Lead	−12.0%	−14.1%	−15.0%	−11.7%

ANOVA test: [a]$F = 4.9$, $p = .03$, $df = 130$; [b]$F = 5.1$, $p = .03$, $df = 132$.

cally significant ($\chi^2 = 3.03, p = .08, n = 362, df = 1$). This table can be interpreted in two ways. Comparing the columns vertically, if a champion leads projects, the firm is less likely to use a formal process. Reading the rows, if a firm does not use a formal process for NPD, projects are equally likely to be led by champions or by others. If a firm uses a formal NPD process, however, champions lead only 40% of the projects. Sixty percent of the firms with formal processes use someone other than a champion to lead projects. Because championing is an older concept [46] than NPD current processes [17], process influx into NPD may have reduced champion leadership of NPD projects. Like other substitutes for leadership [48], these processes may act as a surrogate, at least to some degree, for needing a champion leader to enable a project to move through the firm's infrastructure. As more firms increasingly adopt NPD processes, we expect champion leadership to decline over time.

Champion support for projects, however, is unrelated to whether or not formal NPD processes are used. Champions support projects about 50% of the time, whether or not a formal process is used at a firm. Whether a firm is champion-free or champion-saturated is also unrelated to formal use of NPD processes. Although champions may not be directly leading as many teams in firms with formal NPD processes in place, their level of support activity remains the same. This indicates the role of champions may be changing to supporters of processes with embedded projects rather than projects themselves.

Table 9. Champion Leadership and Formal NPD Process Use

	Champion Leads	Others Lead	Total
No NPD Process	70 (49%)	72 (51%)	142
Formal NPD Process	88 (40%)	132 (60%)	220
Total	204	158	362

For strategy, the variables involved in the relationship change. Here, project leadership is unrelated to strategy. Champion support of projects, however, differs across the four innovation strategies (ANOVA test: $F = 4.6$, $p < .01$, $df = 343$). Champions provide support for only about 25% of the innovative projects in Reactor firms. For Defenders, Analyzers, and Prospectors, champions support over 50% of the projects. In addition, Reactor firms are most likely to be champion-free. Only 8% of all Reactor firms are champion-saturated. Prospectors are equally likely to be champion-free or champion-saturated. Defenders and Analyzers are slightly more likely to be champion-saturated. These differences are nearly statistically significant ($\chi^2 = 7.35$, $p = .06$, $n = 95$, $df = 3$). Champions do not appear to flourish in firms that are not innovative.

Indirect champion effects on firm performance. Championing support of projects statistically significantly improves program success and occurs with more innovative strategies, which in turn differs in likelihood across higher- and lower-performance firms. Champion leadership is slightly less likely to exist where firms use formal NPD processes, which also in turn differs across performance-related populations. The next step in the analysis is to determine whether we can statistically find that program performance, strategy innovation level, and process implementation level impact firm-level success, and which of these are impacted by championing.

The level of champion support simultaneously was regressed on program success, firm-level performance, innovation strategy, and level of process implementa-

Table 8. Correlations Between Level of Champion Support and Performance

	Program Success	Firm Success Rate	NPD Sales and Profits	No. of New Products	Cycle Time Changes
Correlation (ρ)	**.17**	.08	.07	.05	−.09
p (significance)	**< .01**	.17	.26	.39	.36

tion using multivariate regression. Multivariate regression controls for the correlation between multiple dependent variables when testing their relationships with independent variables. This approach minimizes false indications of univariate impact by controlling for interactions with all other variables while testing the effects of championing on each dependent variable, resulting in a conservative test of the hypothesis. Because we found statistically significant correlations between our dependent variables, multivariate regression is more appropriate than univariate regression.

The multivariate test, presented in Table 10, was significant and indicates that higher levels of champion support correlate with higher levels of program success, as we had seen previously in the univariate tests (Table 8). Process implementation and strategy innovativeness are also somewhat related to champion support. Whereas the previous univariate analyses had also shown the champion support-strategy relationship, this regression indicates that the level of process implementation relates to champion support when the two are tested simultaneously, even though whether or not a formal process is used was not related to champion support level in the univariate tests. As found before in the univariate tests, however, champion support does not directly impact firm success. Although champion support impacts on the internal workings of NPD and the firm's overall assessment of the NPD program's success, its effects are not quantifiable in firm-level outcomes.

We repeated this analysis using the champion leadership variable rather than the champion support variable. Because the leadership variable is an indicator variable rather than a continuously scaled variable, the test used in the analysis becomes a multivariate one-way ANOVA. The test is not significant ($F = 1.04$, $p = .39$), which means that there is no discernible multivariate relationship between champion leadership and program success, firm-level success, strategy innovativeness, or even process implementation. Even though there is some univariate evidence that formal processes are linked to less champion leadership, this relationship becomes insignificant in the more conservative test that controls for correlation between multiple dependent variables.

We next investigate both the direct effects of champion support on NPD and, because champions are associated with process implementation and strategy innovativeness, the indirect effects championing may have by operating through these two variables using multivariate multiple regression. Because there are statistically significant correlations between the three firm-level measures of success (Table 5), multivariate regression, which controls for the multicollinearity between the dependent variables, is more appropriate than performing three separate multiple regressions, one for each dependent variable. This is a more conservative test of the question.

As seen in Table 11, firm success rate and sales and profits are predicted by program success. Strategy innovativeness also predicts new product sales and profits at the firm level, whereas process implementation predicts the number of new products a firm commercializes. Thus, even though there are *no* direct effects between the level of champion support and firm-level performance measures, positive champion effects are manifested through these mediating variables. More champion support is associated with higher program success, even though the total impact is not large. Higher levels of NPD program success are related to higher levels of overall firm success. Addi-

Table 10. Champion Support and NPD Performance, Strategy, and Process Use (Multivariate Regression)

	Champion Support (Independent Variable)	
Dependent Variables	Beta	t
Strategy innovativeness	.09	1.8[a]
Process implementation	.09	1.8[a]
Program success	**.14**	**2.8**[c]
Firm-level performance		
Firm success rates	.07	1.4
Profitability and sales	.08	1.5
No. of new products	.07	0.9

Wilkes lambda ($\lambda = .97$, $F = 1.84$, $p = .09$, $df = 1.36$).
[a]$p < .10$; [b]$p < .05$; [c]$p < .01$.

Table 11. Firm-Level New Product Performance and Champion Support (Multivariate Multiple Regression)

	Firm-Level Success Factors (Dependent Variables)		
Independent Variables	Firm Success Rates	NPD Sales and Profits	No. of New Products
Level of championing	.01	.04	.04
Program success	**.41**[c]	**.16**[c]	−.06
Strategy innovativeness	.02	**.11**[b]	.03
Process implementation	−.02	.00	**.19**[c]

Wilkes Lambda = .77 ($F = 7.8$, $df = 4{,}358$, $p < .01$).
[a]$p < .10$; [b]$p < .05$; [c]$p < .01$.

tionally, both strategy and process integration are significantly related to some measures of firm-level success. Because champion support has an impact on program success, strategy, and process (Tables 8 and 10), the effect of championing on firm performance is indirect.

Summary: Champions and performance. These results present a more complicated picture of champion influence on NPD performance than previously thought. Mediating variables for champion activity previously have not been introduced in the literature. For the first time variables have been identified and measured that mediate champion influences on firm-level performance. The impact of champion support for projects appears to be indirect through program success, innovation strategy, and the degree of NPD process implementation, as depicted in Figure 1. Champions do have a direct association with innovation strategy, process implementation, and program success, which can be uncovered through both univariate and multivariate analyses. All these variables, except champion support, have in turn a direct impact on firm-level performance.

Champion leadership produces a much weaker impact on NPD performance. Although directly linked to shortening product development cycle times, and thus capable of improving NPD at the project level, using champion project leaders does not impact NPD product development at either the program or firm level. They are not even shown to impact NPD performance at the firm level indirectly, as occurs with champion support.

One might conclude, looking only at the results from Table 6, that if champion leaders divert resources to particular projects that we cannot show directly benefit the firm, then we perhaps should try to limit championing. This, however, misses the impact champion support has on NPD. Although champions may not be able reliably to promote only winning projects, they do get products to market. It may be too much to ask champions to both shepherd a project through the firm and guarantee its market success.

Looking for the effect of champion support in just the bottom line of firm-level performance also may result in discounting their overall effect. We may underestimate the value of championing unless we examine all of the effects of championing. In fact, champions appear to make a larger part of their contribution in the intermediate steps of development. That championing is not related directly to measures of market success should not be used as an argument against championing any more than one can argue that R&D should be eliminated because it is an expense and does not produce revenue directly. R&D gets something done that is needed to make a profit. Similarly, champions get something done that is necessary to get products into the market, but does not produce profits directly.

Champion Association with Company Characteristics

If championing has the effects found above, under what circumstances does championing behavior produce these types of results? Specifically, is champion leadership or support more prevalent in companies with particular characteristics? In testing these questions (see Table 12 for results), we find that champions do not seem to be attracted to any particular corporate situation, with two exceptions. Champion support is more likely for services than for manufactured goods, and, as already indicated, Reactors are less likely to use champion support than firms following any other innovation strategy. Champion leadership is not associated with any particular kind of firm characteristics. Highlights of the findings detailed below are summarized in Exhibit 2.

The findings in Table 12 contradict much of the "common" knowledge about champions. Although one typically thinks of champions in large, corporate R&D structures [8,44], they appear in the same ratios in small- and medium-sized firms. Champions are sometimes believed to be attracted to certain industries thought to have high-prestige, high-technology occupations. ANOVA of our data reveals that champions are equally likely to appear in any industry and in either a high- or low-technology environment (although there is a slight trend toward high technology). Similarly, we often think of champions in manufactured goods firms, yet they are slightly more likely in services development. Champions are not predominately associated with high-technology firms, they do not just work in large companies or just develop manufactured goods, they are endemic. From an analytical point of view, these findings simplify the analyses of champion relationship to performance. Because there are no statistical differences in these descriptive variables, we do not need to split the sample for analyses.

The perception of champions as creatures of large, high-technology, goods-oriented firms is a common, biased characterization of champions. Although cham-

Table 12. Company Characteristics and Champions

	No. of Firms	Average Level of Championing[a,b]	% Champion Leaders[a]	% Champion Saturated[c]
Total sample	381	3.04	42.9%	43.5%
Sales				
Less than $1 million	6	3.44	12.5%	25.0%
$1 to $9 million	48	3.08	42.6%	41.2%
$10 to $24 million	39	2.97	46.3%	25.0%
$25 to $99 million	74	2.93	42.5%	47.6%
$100 to $499 million	96	2.95	43.6%	44.0%
$500 to $999 million	26	3.38	50.0%	71.4%
Greater than $1 billion	53	3.06	40.7%	50.0%
		F = .62 (1)	χ^2 = 3.88 (2)	χ^2 = 4.74 (2)
df		6, 364	6, 364	6, 92
p (significance)		NS	NS	NS
Primary deliverable				
Services	66	**3.32**	50.0%	60.0%
Manufactured goods	282	**2.95**	40.7%	37.7%
		F = 7.32	χ^2 = 2.07	χ^2 = 16.78
df		1, 346	1, 372	1, 94
p (significance)		.04	NS	.054
Level of technology				
High technology	122	3.15	40.6%	48.6%
Some of both	141	3.04	41.8%	35.3%
Low technology	85	2.82	45.1%	48.0%
		F = 2.64	χ^2 = .44	χ^2 = 1.50
df		2, 345	2, 372	2, 94
p (significance)		NS	NS	NS
Market				
Consumer market	62	3.05	48.5%	50.0%
Mixed market	62	2.89	37.5%	35.7%
Business-to-business	223	3.06	41.5%	43.5%
		F = .44	χ^2 = 1.70	χ^2 = .65
df		2, 344	2, 371	2, 94
p (significance)		NS	NS	NS

[a]Champion support: 1 = never; 2 = 25% of the time; 3 = 50% of the time; 4 = 75% of the time; 5 = virtually always.
[b]ANOVA tests of means.
[c]Chi-squared tests of cross-tabulations.

pions have been found to occur in similar proportions across different lines of business and in different functional areas [29], none of the studies in the literature have examined boundary conditions for where champions exist or do not exist. The results we found suggest that championing behavior is a personal choice made by individuals independent of situation rather than a reaction to particular industry characteristics, with one exception. Champions are more likely to be found in service-delivering firms. It should be noted, however, that services are far less likely to use formal NPD processes [16]. Over 55% of service firms do not use formal NPD processes, whereas only 35% of goods manufacturers do not use formal processes. As we found in Table 9, formal NPD processes seem

Exhibit 2.

Champions and Company Characteristics

Champions are related to company characteristics in unexpected ways.

- Championing occurs in equal quantities in organizations of all sizes.
- Championing occurs in equal quantities in high-, medium-, and low-technology companies.
- Companies with formal processes have less championing.
- There is more championing in service organizations.
- Service organizations typically have fewer formal processes.

to substitute for champions. Thus, services, with less process use, are a natural place to find more championing.

It appears that the championing phenomenon is robust and will likely be found in most industries. Recognizing this, managers should prepare to manage champions as they arise.

Champion Associations with Project Characteristics

Project radicalness. The literature associates champions with project characteristics, such as radicalness and complexity. It is unclear, however, what relationships exist between champions and NPD structures and teams. From the inception of the concept, champions were thought to be promoters of radically new products. In fact, Schon [46] argued that radical projects must either find a champion or die. Since then, others have also suggested that champions seek to promote radical projects [28,44]. To the contrary, Markham et al. [29] found that champions are not inclined to promote radical projects more than other projects. The idea that champions are associated with radical types of projects is so firmly rooted in the champion concept that we examine this question separately. The relationships we found are summarized in Exhibit 3.

These data show that champions are just as likely to support radical projects as they are incremental projects. New to the world (10% of the projects), new product line (20%), additions to existing product line (23%), major revisions (21%), minor revisions (15%), repositioning (5%), and cost reductions (9%) were all championed at about the same level (R^2 = .01, F = .24, df = 7,98, p = NS). Neither correlation nor regression indicates that championing is associated with more radical types of product development.

Champions are equally likely to support NPD projects independent of innovation level. Champions emerge for all types of projects, rather than just the high-risk projects. This finding may suggest a different mindset of champions than previously assumed. Rather than being technological mavens, they may promote projects for many reasons other than just exciting technology. Managers should expect people to champion projects with varying degrees of risk. This can be a source of useful energy if recognized and channeled.

Exhibit 3.

Champions and Project Characteristics

The traditional relationships between champions and projects are not supported.

- More championing is not related to more radical projects.
- Championing is related to significant cycle time reductions for both major and minor improvements.
- Championing is related to modest cycle time reductions for new-to-the-world and new product lines.
- The level of championing is unaffected by NPD structures such as venture teams, NP departments, committees, and divisions.
- When NPD is dominated by marketing there is less championing.

NPD process complexity. NPD research has examined what social roles are necessary for successful NPD, ignoring the impact of process [1]. Similarly, research focused on NPD processes often ignores the roles individuals play [10]. Initiating formal NPD processes can be seen as a substitute for championing activities, as the results in Table 9 suggest. Further, as more elaborate processes are included in NPD, the less a champion may have to do to support a project, the less they are needed. A pervasive approach to NPD is the use of stages and gates. Best practice firms in this sample use 6.2 of 9 possible process stages, whereas lower-performing firms use only 4.7 stages [16]. The more stages in the process, the more elaborate is the process. Thus, if process substitutes for championing, the more stages there are in a NPD process, the less championing we should observe. However, multiple regression analysis did not find that more NPD process components are associated with less championing (R^2 = .12, F = .46, df = 10,324, p = NS). Championing appears to be insensitive to the structure of the firm's formal NPD process. Using a process may reduce the use of champions, but more complex processes do not reduce champion use further.

NPD organizational structures. How firms organize themselves for NPD is a major topic of discussion, with many organizational configurations possible. Championing behavior, however, is not often found in official job descriptions or on organizational charts. NPD programs and structures do not usually specify championing as part of the official organization. Champions, however, do work with other people in organizations and within established procedures. How people and activities are organized and directed

450 J PROD INNOV MANAG 1998;15:436–454

thus may stimulate or retard the level of championing. Present champion research does not examine championing with respect to recent organizational innovations such as new product committees, departments, or distributed NPD. Although not dealt with in the literature, perhaps the level of championing is related to how NPD is managed. We now investigate this question with our data.

The top portion of Table 13 examines the relationship between championing and NPD organizational structures. ANOVA did not show championing support, leadership, or saturation to vary across any of the different types of NPD structures used by firms. Because most firms use two organizational approaches to NPD [33], two additional analyses were conducted. First, two-way interactions between organizational types were examined. Testing interactions indicates whether the use of two organizational structures simultaneously affected championing firms. No interactions were significant ($F = .97$, $df = 21{,}328$, $p =$ NS). The second analysis examined the total number of organizational structures used by a firm and the level of championing. Again, no correlation was found ($r = .06$, $p =$ NS). Championing does not appear to be related to how a firm organizes its NPD activities.

The bottom section of Table 13 examines championing when a particular functional area dominates the NPD process. When the product development function reports to the marketing function, projects are less likely to be led by champions than by other types of project leaders. Neither champion support nor champion saturation differs depending upon the function into which NPD reports. Champion leaders are no more or less likely to be found if the project reports into any function other than marketing. Marketing, however, does not appear to foster championing.

Championing and multifunctional teams. Another organizational innovation commonly used in NPD is the multifunctional team. Multifunctional teams are organizational hybrids that combine inputs from various functional disciplines and combine formal structure with informal roles. Like many other product development tools, multifunctional teams were initiated after the idea of the champion was established. Because champions are reported to build support for projects from around the company [28], they should interact well with multifunctional teams. Results from the most conservative test of this question, multiple regression, do not indicate that the level of championing is predicted by the use of multifunctional teams. Nevertheless, correlation analysis, a less conservative test, reveals that the extent of championing is associated with multifunctional teams for each kind of product development project (Table 14). This suggests some relationship exists between multifunctional teams and championing.

Summary of Results and Discussion

The effect champions have on NPD outcomes are more complex than previous literature indicates. Examining business unit and company level data, champion impact on firm-level performance seems to be indirect rather than direct. Champions improve NPD

Table 13. Product Development Organization and Champions

	No. of Firms	Level of Championing[a,b]	% Champion Leaders[c]	% Champion Saturated[c]
Total sample	381	3.04	42.9%	43.5%
NPD organizational structures				
NP department	125	3.06	45.1%	48.2%
NP division or venture group	36	3.11	46.2%	33.3%
NP committee	111	3.11	47.8%	47.8%
Business unit general manager	122	3.02	40.9%	51.9%
Functional responsibility	133	2.85	38.2%	33.3%
NP process owner	122	3.16	47.2%	53.3%
Functional dominance of NPD				
Research and development	47	3.14	50.0%	57.1%
Engineering department	43	2.81	31.9%	22.2%
Marketing department	48	2.85	**29.4%**[d]	31.6%

[a]Champion support: 1 = never; 2 = 25% of the time; 3 = 50% of the time; 4 = 75% of the time; 5 = virtually always.
[b]ANOVA tests of means.
[c]Chi-squared tests of cross-tabulations.
[d]Significance $p < .05$.

J PROD INNOV MANAG 1998;15:436–454

Table 14. Championing and Multifunctional Teams (Correlation Between Team Use and Championing)

	Pearson Correlation (ρ)
Champions and the use of multifunctional teams with	
New-to-the-world products	.07[a]
New to your organization	**.12**[b]
Major revision of current product	**.13**[b]
Minor revision/incremental improvement	**.13**[b]
Product repositioning	**.14**[b]
Cost reduction	**.12**[b]

[a] $p < .10$; [b] $p < .05$.

program performance and operate in concert with processes and strategies, all of which in turn lead to improved firm-level performance. This finding challenges basic assumptions commonly held about champions and their effects. Although many anecdotal stories abound according the success of a particular project to a particular champion, this research does not demonstrate that champion project leadership or higher levels of champion support lead to generally more successful NPD.

This is also the first study to systematically examine relationships between championing and industry, company, and project contexts. Company, project type, and NPD structure do not impact the level of champion support or champion leadership. Formal NPD processes may substitute for the contributions of champions, but more sophisticated processes do not reduce their use more. Service-providing firms are the only subsample of the data in which higher champion support is more likely to be found. The higher incidence of champion support in service firms may be linked to their lack of formal NPD process use [16]. These data question assumptions about the conditions that give rise to champions.

Although general industry and firm-level characteristics are not related to championing, perhaps it is a firm's hostility (or conduciveness) to innovation that brings champions forth [12]. On the one hand, one can argue champions may be most likely to arise when organizations actively support innovativeness. This may release the talents of individuals to be creative and champions may arise in response to the innovative environment [11]. On the other hand, one can argue that champions could arise in environments that make it difficult to innovate. Seeing a great need, individuals in these situations rise up to fight against the system to innovate. Both Badawy [4] and Fischer et al [12] assert that champions arise out of conditions that are unfavorable to innovation.

As seen in Table 10, higher levels of champion support are moderately related to strategy innovativeness and process implementation. The more institutionalized the NPD process and the more innovative the company strategy, the higher the level of champion support. Championing thus appears to be more prevalent in more positive environments (e.g., firms with strategies that emphasize innovativeness and have implemented NPD processes, demonstrating their support for NPD). Champions appear to respond favorably to companies that have more complete commitments to innovation. Although this may be an intriguing interpretation of the findings, support in the data is only moderate. A great deal of championing activity is not accounted for in the data.

Taken together, these results identify a system of relationships that informs us about how champions affect firms at the aggregate level. What we have learned from these analyses include the following. First, champion support is associated with program success but not firm-level success. Second, champion support is associated with strategy and NPD process use, whereas NPD process implementation substitutes for champion leadership. Third, strategy, process, and program success are positively related to firm-level success. Thus, these findings reveal that champions have indirect effects on firm performance, rather than direct effects, as depicted graphically in Figure 1. Figure 1 recognizes strategy innovativeness and the use of NPD processes as mediators of champion impact. The figure also does not include variables previ-

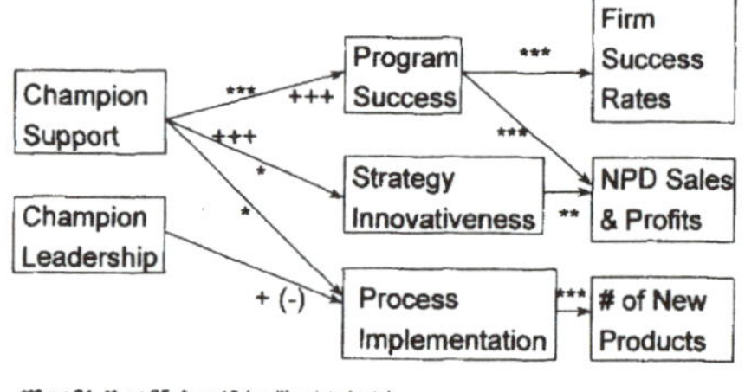

Figure 1. Champion effects on performance. ***p < .01, **p < .05, *p < .10 (multivariate tests), +++p < 01, ++p < 05, +p < .10 (univariate tests).

ously thought to influence the championing process such as project radicalness. These data reveal a modified set of variables associated with championing than exists in the anecdotal literature about champions. Recognizing that different variables active in championing both research and managerial questions are raised.

Managerial Implications

Managerial implications are highlighted in Exhibit 4. From a managerial standpoint, understanding that championing indirectly effects firm-level outcomes is significant. It suggests that championing has limits. Despite well-known anecdotal accounts, champions do not always produce winning products or assure market or financial success. This suggests that management should monitor championed projects and actively support or discourage the project champion on the basis of other indicators of eventual project success [9,10]. Projects with champion support or leaders must still meet all relevant evaluation criteria at each project stage. There is anecdotal evidence of champions holding too long onto projects that ultimately fail. Again, our biased impressions of champions may cloud how much champions actually contribute.

Even though champions do not ensure marketplace success for a particular project, this does not suggest that one should disregard or discourage champions.

Exhibit 4.

Managerial Implications

A new understanding about champions based on data rather than anecdotal information calls for a new approach to managing champions.

- Indirect effects. Measures of champion performance needs to be at the NPD program level or below, not at the firm level.
- Championing has its limits. You cannot expect champions to do everything.
- Traditional issues such as project radicalness, complexity, technology, goods or service do not matter.
- Management can foster champions with a commitment to innovation.
- Champions can help reduce cycle time, particularly for product improvements.
- Role of champions shifts from project leaders to sponsors as new processes are adopted.

Just the opposite is probably true. Champions still play a vital role in NPD, and there may be spillover effects from the manner in which they operate. For example, because champions have the project as their focus, they naturally have a multidisciplinary perspective [31]. Thus, they are willing to try to integrate different areas of the firm. This can have positive effects on other business processes. For example, if a champion brings marketing and production people together to work on a new product, these same people will have a basis for communication on other issues.

Understanding what helps champions can also be used to decrease championing activity, when appropriate. In a stable, profitable situation, management may not want champions to divert funds to a new, risky project. Successful champions might also divert resources from strategic initiatives set by management. These findings can be equally helpful to managers who want to curtail championing by engineering an environment not conducive to championing.

The idea of cycle time reduction was not articulated until long after champions were identified. Nevertheless, champions have a substantial impact on reducing cycle time and are associated with more products reaching the market. Supporting champions may have the effect of getting more products to market faster. This may or may not be what management wants done. Depending on whether the firms wants more or less new products, management can decide whether or not to encourage champions.

NPD managers frequently have an active role in setting NPD strategy and implementing processes. Recognizing the relationship between innovative conditions and championing will enhance management's ability to increase or decrease the level and effectiveness of championing. One may argue that the champion role is redundant with well-established processes, yet we see champions operating in more innovative and process-oriented firms. We also see that their contribution is valued in these firms. This suggests that as helpful as our NPD processes are, they are not complete. There may be significant variations in the process that require advocates to keep the project on tract.

Champions appear to shift to NPD program support role instead of leading individual projects in firms with formal NPD process managers. Champions may be partly responsible for companies adopting NPD processes. This may explain champions relationship with high levels of process implementation. Management may find champions play an important role in initiating new processes for NPD, not just leading teams.

Because champions do not seem to respond to company or project conditions, we might interpret championing as a private, individual decision. It appears that firms can do little operationally to promote championing. Champions seem immune to managerial intervention. But they do seem to be associated with the mission, vision, and direction of the company. If the firm really is committed to innovation there is more championing. However, if management does not support NPD in general, and if innovation is not sought, those with the potential to become champions may not choose to try to overcome the lack of NPD support. Even champions must have a reasonable resource base from which to work. If champions feel the firm has ceased to support innovation they may reduce their level of championing, or go elsewhere.

Future Research Directions

These results inform and deepen our understanding about whether champions impact performance to the point where we can begin to ask additional interesting questions and develop new research propositions. Additional research first must assess whether the mediating variables found here are the right list of mediators or if other variables have stronger relationships with performance. Furthermore, although these results also open up a whole new line of research examining how champions affect these mediating variables, this research has not investigated how champions operate. We do not know how champions actually influence other people to support their projects. This will require gathering longitudinal data about specific influence tactics. These data may also be used to understand how the champion role might change over time during the project. For example, the fuzzy front end role of champions may be to help sell the idea to enlist team members. Later champions may "find" critical resources for the project.

Future research also could address how champions interact with management and multifunctional teams. Although champions are more likely to be associated with multifunctional teams, we do not know the nature of this relationship. Champions might be integral parts of the team, sideline supporters, or they could be antagonistic to the development team. As an individual level construct, how can championing and team work be reconciled?

The marketing department's negative relationship with championing is interesting. The nature of projects in marketing may be more focused on customer needs and not require the care and support a raw technology project would require. Previous research found champions occur most often in R&D and very often in marketing [29]. The motivation and incentive structures for people to champion is likely to vary between departments.

Finally, these data are aggregate level. This restricts us from examining important issues associated with how champions actually support projects. Research needs to identify tactics and practices champions use and which are more successful. A clear understanding of champion impact must include examination of project level data.

Although this empirical research moves our knowledge of champions forward, much additional research remains to be done.

References

1. Ancona, D. G. and Caldwell, D. F. Beyond boundary spanning: Managing external dependence in product development teams. *Journal of High Technology Management Research* 1:119–135 (1990).
2. Ashforth, B. E. and Saks, A. M. Socialization tactics: Longitudinal effects on newcomer adjustment. *Academy of Management Journal* 39:149–178 (1996).
3. Little, Arthur D. *The Arthur D. Little Survey on the Product Development Process*. Arthur D. Little: Cambridge, MA, 1991.
4. Badawy, M. K. What we've learned: Managing human resources. *Research Technology Management* 31:19–35 (1988).
5. *New Products Management for the 1980's*. New York: Booz, Allen, and Hamilton, 1979.
6. Burgelman, R. A. Design for corporate entrepreneurship in established firms. *California Management Review* 26:154–166 (1984).
7. Chakrabarti, A. The role of champion in product innovation. *California Management Review* 17:58–62 (1974).
8. Chakrabarti, A. and Hauschildt, J. The division of labor in innovation management. *R&D Management* 19:161–171 (1989).
9. Cooper, R. B. *New Products: The Key Factors in Success*. Chicago: American Marketing Association, 1990.
10. Cooper, R. G. and Kleinschmidt, E. J. New products: What separates winners from losers? *Journal of Product Innovation Management* 4 (1987).
11. Day, D. L. Raising radicals: Different processes for championing innovative corporate ventures. *Organization Science* 5:148–172 (1994).
12. Fischer, W. A., Hamilton, W., McLaughlin, C. and Zmud, R. W. The elusive product champion. *Research Management* May-June:13–16 (1986).
13. Frey, D. Learning the ropes: My life as a product champion. *Harvard Business Review* September-October (1991), pp. 46–56.
14. Frost, P. J. and Egri, C. P. Influence of political action on innovation, Part II. *Leadership and Organization Development Journal* 11:4–12 (1991).
15. Green, S. G. and Mitchell, T. R. Attributional processes of leaders in leader-member interactions. *Organizational Behavior and Human Performance* 23:429–458 (1979).
16. Griffin, A. PDMA research on new product development practices:

Updating trends and benchmarking best practices. *Journal of Product Innovation Management* 14 (1997).

17. Griffin, A. The effect of project and process characteristics on product development cycle time. *Journal of Marketing Research* XXXIV: 24–35 (1997).
18. Griffin, A. and Page, A. L. PDMA success measurement project: Recommended measures for product development success and failure. *Journal of Product Innovation Management* 13:478–496 (1996).
19. Howell, J. M. and Higgins, C. A. Champions of technological innovation. *Administrative Science Quarterly* 35:317–341 (1990).
20. Hustad, T. P. Reviewing current practices in innovation management and a summary of selected best practices. In: *The PDMA Handbook of New Product Development*. M. D. Rosenau, et al. (eds.) New York: John Wiley & Sons, 1996, pp. 489–511.
21. Kanter, R. M. *Change Masters*. New York: Simon and Schuster, 1983, pp. 342–355.
22. Kanter, R. M. When a thousand flowers bloom: Structural, collective, and social conditions innovation in organization. *Research in Organizational Behavior* 10:169–211 (1988).
23. Kim, J. and Mueller, C. W. *Introduction to Factor Analysis*. Beverly Hills, CA: Sage Publications, 1978.
24. Korsgaard, M. A., Schweiger, D. M., and Sapienza, H. J. Build commitment, attachment, and trust in strategic decision-making teams: The role of procedural justice. *Academy of Management Journal* 38:60–84 (1995).
25. Lawless, M. W. and Price, L. L. An agency perspective on new technology champions. *Organization Science* 3 (1992).
26. Lord, R. G. An information processing approach to social perceptions, leadership, and behavioral measurement in organizations. *Research in Organizational Behavior* 7:87–128 (1985).
27. Lord, R. G., DeVader, C. L., and Alliger, G. M. A meta-analysis of the relation between personality traits and leadership perceptions: An application of validity generalization procedures. *Journal of Applied Psychology* 71:402–410 (1986).
28. Madique, M. Entrepreneurs, champions and technological innovation. *Sloan Management Review* Winter:59–76 (1980).
29. Markham, S. K., Green, S. G. and Basu, R. Champions and antagonists: Relationships with R&D project characteristics and management. *Journal of Engineering and Technology Management* 8:217–242 (1991).
30. Markham, S. K. Championing and antagonism as forms of political behavior: An R&D perspective. *Organization Science* (1998) In press.
31. Markham, S. K. A longitudinal examination of how champions influence others to support their projects. *Journal of Product Innovation Management* (1998) In press.
32. *High Performance New Product Development: Practices that Set Leaders Apart*. Boston: Mercer Management Consulting, Inc., 1994.
33. McDonough III, E. F. and Griffin, A. J. *Matching The Right Organizational Practices to a Firm's Innovation Strategy: Findings from the PDMA's Best Practices Research*. Working paper. Northeastern University, 304 Hayden Hall, Boston, MA 02115.
34. Miles, R. E. and Snow, C. C. *Organizational Strategy, Structure and Process*. New York: McGraw Hill, 1978.
35. Nunnally, J. *Psychometric Theory*. New York: McGraw Hill, 1978.
36. Page, A. L. Assessing new product development practices and performance: Establishing crucial norms. *Journal of Product Innovation Management* 10 (1993).
37. Page, A. L. *Results from PDMA's Best Practices Study: The Best Practices of High Impact New Product Programs*. The EEI/PDMA Conference on New Product Innovation. June 1994.
38. Peters, T. J. and Waterman, R. H. *In Search of Excellence*. New York: Warner Books, Inc., 1980.
39. Pfeffer, J. *Power in Organizations*. Boston: Pitman, 1981.
40. Porter, L. W., Allen, R. W., and Angle, H. L. The politics of upward influence in organizations. In: *Research in Organizational Behavior*. B. M. Staw & L. L. Cummings (eds.) Greenwich, CT: JAI Press, 1981, pp. 109–149.
41. Pinto, J. K. and Slevin, D. P. Critical factors in successful project implementation. *IEEE Transactions on Engineering Management* 34: 22–27 (1987).
42. Roberts, E. B. New venture for corporate growth. *Harvard Business Review* 58 (1980).
43. Roberts, E. B. What we've learned: Managing invention and innovation. *Research Technology Management* January-February (1988).
44. Roberts, E. B. and Fusfeld, A. C. Critical function: Needed roles in the innovation process. In: *Career Issues in Human Resource Management*. R. Katz (ed.). Englewood Cliffs, NJ: Prentice-Hall, Inc., 1981, pp. 182–207.
45. Rosenau, M. C., Griffin, A. J., Anscheutz, N. and Castellion, G. (eds.). *PDMA Handbook on New Product Development*. New York: John Wiley and Sons, 1996.
46. Schon, D. A. Champions for radical new inventions. *Harvard Business Review* March-April:77–86 (1963).
47. Shane, S. A., Venkataraman, S. and MacMillan, I. C. The effects of cultural differences on new technology championing behavior within firms. *Journal of High Technology Management Research* Fall (1995).
48. Van de Ven, A. H. and Grazman, D. N. Technical innovation, learning, and leadership. In: *Technological Oversights and Foresight*. Garud, R., Nayyar, P. and Shapira, Z. (eds.). New York: Cambridge University Press, 1995.
49. Yukl, G. *Leadership in Organizations* 3rd Edition. Englewood Cliffs, NJ: Prentice Hall, 1994.

[8]

MANAGING CREATIVE PEOPLE: STRATEGIES AND TACTICS FOR INNOVATION

Michael D. Mumford

The University of Oklahoma, Norman, OK, USA

With rapid changes in technology, and global competition, the success of many organizations has become progressively more dependent on their ability to bring innovative products to market. Ultimately, however, innovation depends on the generation of creative, new ideas. Accordingly, the literature bearing on the nature of creativity is reviewed to identify the conditions that influence innovation. Observations about the nature of creativity are used to draw conclusions about the kind of human resource management strategies that might enhance creativity. It is argued that organizations should consider multiple interventions that take into account the individual, the group, the organization, and the strategic environment when selecting interventions intended to enhance creativity.

With ever more rapid technical change, and increasing global competition, it has become clear that the ability of organizations to develop and field innovative new products and services is a crucial influence on long-term performance (Hitt, Hoskisson, & Kim, 1997; Porter, 1990). Organizational innovations come in many forms (Damanpour, 1998; Tushman & O'Reilly, 1997). For example, in service organizations, the adoption of new business practices represents a particularly important influence on performance (Mone, McKinley, & Baker, 1998). In other organizations, however, technical innovations—those involving the development of new products or new technologies—may represent a more important influence on performance. Although a number of strategies, including acquisitions, imitation, and research consortium, can be used to acquire innovations, quite frequently organizations must develop new ideas "in house" (Bolton, 1993; Cohen & Levinthal, 1990; Pavitt, 1990). These conditions place a premium on effective management of people in developing new ideas.

The need for innovation has sparked a new cottage industry proffering advice and "How To" manuals on management practices that should be applied

Direct all correspondence to: Michael D. Mumford, Department of Psychology, The University of Oklahoma, Room 705, 455 W. Lindsey Street, Norman, OK 73019-2007, USA.

Human Resource Management Review,
Volume 10, Number 3, 2000, pages 313–351

ISSN: 1053–4822

to encourage creativity. Unfortunately, as Montouri (1992) points out, few of these efforts consider available research examining the nature of creativity. With this point in mind, the present article examines what is known about creative thought and innovation, particularly the working strategies applied in developing creative new ideas. Implications of this research for the kind of management practices likely to promote creativity and innovation are then considered with respect to specific human resources practices, drawing a series of propositions that might be used to guide further research. In this regard, I will argue that to manage creativity and innovation, effective human resource practices must consider the individual, the group, the organization, and the strategic environment confronting the organization.

CREATIVITY

The Creative Process

While management practices can enhance the likelihood of innovation, ultimately, it is the individual who is the source of a new idea. Thus, to identify effective human resource practices, we must have some understanding of the requirements for creative thought as well as the characteristic work styles of creative people. Recent work on creative thought stresses the importance of three key considerations—knowledge, process, and work styles.

Knowledge

Creativity involves the production of useful new ideas, or ideas that can be implemented to solve some significant novel problem (Ghiselin, 1963; Mumford & Gustafson, 1998). Viable solutions to novel problems do not arise in a vacuum. Thus, it is not surprising that knowledge, or expertise, has been found to influence creative problem solving. Simonton (1988), for example, has shown that scientific productivity is related to experience or time working in a field. Other works by Baer (1998), Erickson and Charness (1994), Kulkarni and Simon (1990), Qin and Simon (1990), Redmond, Mumford, and Teach (1993), and Weisburg (1986) indicate that expertise, or knowledge acquired with experience, influences peoples' ability to generate viable, original solutions to novel problems.

Expertise, however, should not be seen as a simple accumulation of discrete facts. Instead, expertise involves a principal-based organization of information that incorporates prototypic exemplars in a systematic structure (Chi, Bassock, Lewis, Reitman, & Glaser, 1989; Holyoak & Thagard, 1997). As a result, expertise may have a number of complex effects on peoples' creative problem solving, by promoting (a) the more rapid acquisition of new knowledge (Chi et al., 1989), (b) use of systematic, as opposed to trial and error, solutions in solving novel problems (Kaizer & Shore, 1995), and (c) application of the principles, relationships, and prototypic cases in transferring extant knowledge to new problems through the use of analogical reasoning mechanisms. (Finke, Ward, & Smith, 1992; Mumford & Gustafson, in press; Ward, Byrnes, & Overton, 1990).

Formal domain expertise, however, is not the only form of knowledge that plays a role in creativity. Zuckerman and Cole (1994) interviewed eminent and more "run-of-the-mill" scientists drawn from a variety of disciplines. They found, in an examination of work methods, that eminent, innovative scientists differed from their more "run-of-the-mill" counterparts with regard to procedural knowledge. More specifically, eminent scientists tended to focus on strategic research methods and strategic sites. A case in point may be found in genetic engineering where the development of gene splicing techniques was contingent on identifying bacteria that could live at high temperatures. Along related lines, Nickels (1994) has argued that innovation not only depends on knowledge about methods but also the skills needed to apply these methods. Thus, when developing new initiatives, we often seek to hire people who have acquired these implementation skills in their past work.

Process

Of course, if we only had existing knowledge, it would be impossible to create something new. As a result, a substantial body of work has examined the processes by which people acquire and manipulate information to generate new ideas. Creative problems tend to be ill-defined or poorly structured, indeed, one must often must define what the problem is in the first place (Fredericksen, 1984; Getzels & Csikszentmihalyi, 1976). In fact, Rostan (1994) found that successful scientists differed from their less successful counterparts in that they spent more time defining and structuring problems before starting work. Problem definition, or problem construction, is a complex process. However, it appears that this process is based on the systematic screening and manipulation of applicable representations to identify relevant goals, procedures, key information, and restrictions (Mumford, Reiter-Palmon, & Redmond, 1994). Problem definitions—by virtue of their linkage to experience, goals, and motives—evidence an affective dispositional aspect with problem construction efforts being more successful when people are working in domains consistent with their broader life history (Jausovec, 1997; Reiter-Palmon, Mumford, & Threlfall, 1998). Typically, however, problem definitions that focus on procedures and restrictions appear more effective than those that focus on externally defined goals or specific pieces of information (Mumford, Baughman, Threlfall, Supinski, & Costanza, 1996b).

In some cases, a redefinition or restructuring of a problem may permit sudden insight where the solution is apparent once the problem has been defined correctly (Davidson, 1995; Finke et al., 1992). Although cases of insight do occur, more often than not creative thought calls for information acquisition and the selection of appropriate concepts for understanding this information. Creative problem solutions are most likely to arise when (a) people actively search for key relevant facts, (b) seek to identify anomalies or inconsistent observations, and (c) examine a variety of different concepts particularly concepts relevant to long-term goals that might be used to organize this information (Davidson & Steinberg, 1984; Mumford, Baughman, Supinski, & Maher, 1996a).

The key to creative thought, however, appears to be the combination and reorganization of information and concepts to advance new understandings or new conceptual systems. Rothenberg (1996), in his study of Nobel laureates, found that these new combinations often provide a basis advances in science and technology. Along similar lines, Owens (1969) and Mumford, Baughman, Maher, Costanza, and Supinski (1997) found that skill in combining and reorganizing concepts is one of the best predictors of creative achievement, in such fields as mechanical engineering and advertising. In conceptual combination, analogical reasoning mechanisms are used to abstract key features of concepts, and these features, and their hypothesized linkages, are used to generate new explanatory systems. (Cheng, 1996; Miller, 1992, 1996). Subsequently, this new system is tested through elaboration to assess whether it can account for various relevant phenomena in an integrated coherent system. Within this process, creative ideas are most likely to arise through the use of diverse concepts, multiple features, and multiple strategies for linking features as well as elaborative exercises focusing on the ability of new concepts to account for anomalies within a broader pattern of observations (Baughman & Mumford, 1995). In fact, given the importance of conceptual combination to creative thought, simply selecting people for skill in combining concepts may prove one of the simplest and most effective human resources strategies for enhancing innovation.

These new understandings and new conceptual systems, however, must subsequently be used to generate potentially useful new ideas. Thus, combination and reorganization, a relatively unconstrained activity, is followed by idea generation, or exploration of the implications and applications of a new understanding (Finke et al., 1992). Idea generation begins as a free-flowing activity where applications, implications, and consequences are identified and then shaped through refinement into a new idea or set of ideas. The evaluation of these ideas occurs after ideation or idea generation (Basadur, 1995, 1997). What is important to remember here, however, is that evaluation is a complex process which considers multiple factors, including usefulness, impact, originality, others' likely reactions, and the source of the idea, among other considerations (Brophy, 1998; Kasoff, 1997; Runco, 1997; Runco & Chand, 1994). Of course, generating an idea, regardless of its merits, is not the same thing as putting an idea into practice. Thus, there is a need for implementation planning. By virtue of their novelty, creative ideas make implementation planning a difficult task, one that must often proceed opportunistically and incrementally (Mumford, Mobley, Uhlman, Reiter-Palmon, & Doares, 1991). Accordingly, plans that specify key steps, contingencies, and revision points are more likely to be successful than plans adhering to a lock-step schedule. When this approach is applied, ongoing monitoring and progressive refinement of ideas—through learning from both failures and successes—appears critical to creative work. This point is nicely illustrated in Wentroff's (1992) development of synthetic diamonds where a long series of studies were used to enhance the efficiency of the synthesis process.

As Basadur (1997), Brophy (1998), Kirton (1987), and Martinsen (1993) note, different problems emphasize different processes and impose different requirements. Thus, one may see different types of creative problems and different creative problem solving styles. The most commonly observed stylistic difference appears to be innovation versus adaptation with (a) innovation stressing initial creation of new understandings and new ideas, and (b) adaptation stressing the progressive extension and refinement of existing ideas (Mumford & Gustafson, in press). Thus, some people may make a greater contribution to the earlier phases of creative problem solving efforts where new ideas must be generated, while other people may be more effective in later phases, where new ideas and understandings must be implemented and refined (Puccio, Treffinger, & Talbot, 1995).

Work Styles

Implicit in these comments about creative problem solving are a number of observations bearing on the nature of creative work and the characteristics of people likely to do this work. Given the fact that creative people must deal with novel, ambiguous, ill-defined problems, it is not surprising that they tend to evidence strong achievement motives, substantial self-confidence, tolerate ambiguity, display an interest in learning, and show substantial openness and flexibility (Barron & Harrington, 1981; Brophy, 1998; Walberg & Stariha, 1992). Moreover, they tend to be independent—following their own ideas and their own interests without being overly concerned about socially imposed expectations for certain kinds of behavior or how others will view them (Dudeck & Hall, 1991; Gruber, 1996).

Many of these characteristics are consistent with our stereotypes of the creative person. However, recent research has revealed other characteristics that are, perhaps, a bit less stereotypic. Mills and Cameron (1993) found that curiosity and persistent interest are two of the best markers of creative potential, while Dudeck and Hall (1991) found that focused interests, persistence, and self-discipline all appear to play an important role in creative work. Given the need to devote substantial resources to problem solving over a long period of time, as well as the need to acquire sufficient knowledge, it is not surprising that this disciplined, persistent focus is often a key influence on creative achievement (Wild, 1992).

In addition to this disciplined focus, creative people appear skilled at integrating a variety of activities and interests around their work (Root-Berstein, Berstein & Garnier, 1995; Sheldon, 1995). This integration of multiple activities, in fact, seems to be an endemic characteristic of highly creative individuals who organize their lives around networks of related enterprises (Gruber, 1989, 1996).

These networks of interrelated activities appear to contribute to creative work in a number of different ways providing a source of identity and a set of diverse but related concepts for use in problem solving, while allowing people to shift their focus to other related projects when they encounter an impasse. In fact, Root-Bernstein, Bernstein, and Garnier (1993) found that successful scientists tended to shift fields periodically over the course of their careers as a way of maintaining creativity. Typically, however, a broad overall life theme is used to integrate and guide the selection of these diverse activities.

This focus on diversity has another somewhat more subtle effect. These experiences provide creative people with a diverse store of tacit knowledge and associational relationships. As Policastro (1995) and Tweney (1996) point out, these implicit associational connections—threads of experience—are used by creative people in their work allowing an intuitive identification of relevant materials and likely outcomes. In fact, the ready arousal and breadth of attention characteristic of introversion, and often found in creative people, may promote such activities when accompanied by periods of withdrawal, and removal from distractions, to maintain focus and permit the articulation of these threads of experience, vis-a-vis the problem at hand. Thus, Gick and Lockhart (1995) and Zuckerman and Cole (1994) found that creative people planned time away to think and allow ideas to percolate.

MANAGING THE INDIVIDUAL

Time and Information

My foregoing observations with regard to work styles brings us to the first point that should be considered in managing creative people. Specifically, one must provide staff with the time needed to think. This point is illustrated in a study by Redmond et al. (1993) concerning the influence of managerial behavior or subordinate creativity. In that study, marketing interns were asked to generate advertising campaigns for a new product—the 3D holographic television. It was found that higher quality, more original advertising campaigns were obtained when supervisors asked interns to provide a list of alternative problem definitions before they actually began work on the problem as compared to a control condition where interns were allowed to go right to work. Thus, one way managers can encourage creativity is by encouraging people to stop and think before they begin work. This advice may seem straightforward, but in a world of ever-increasing production pressures, it may prove difficult to follow. Some human resource strategies that could be used to promote requisite thinking time might include implementing flexible work schedules, providing time management strategies that recognize the need for thinking time, and accounting for personnel costs based on the work being done rather than product output.

Time, of course, is a precious resource. As Nohari and Gulati (1996) point out, unlimited resources, including unlimited time, may not always prove beneficial since time contributes to creativity only up to a point. This kind of inverted relationship is not especially surprising when it is recognized that creative efforts are cumulative involving pursuit of a number of requisite activities. Moreover, in creative efforts, which are inherently ambiguous, there is always the possibility that unlimited time may lead people to spend too much effort pursuing what are essentially unprofitable, ineffective approaches to the problem (Fiest, 1997). This observation, in turn, suggests that the amount of time allocated to creating and the flexibility provided in time management should be guided by the nature and complexity of the task with more time and greater flexibility being called on tasks where people must work with a number of sources of information—where a number of considerations must be synthesized in generating new ideas, and when a number of restrictions are imposed on idea generation and implementation.

These observations about providing time for thought are closely related to another issue. As I pointed out earlier, creative people typically have a broad attention span. This broad span of attention, however, implies that effective, focused creative thought may be disrupted by the presence of an undue number of organizational distractions. Moreover, as Amabile (1983) notes, extraneous events—particularly events inducing external performance pressure—may reduce the intrinsic motivation and curiosity needed for creative work. As a result, the use of strategies intended to buffer people from extraneous demands may prove useful, particularly when they are being asked to generate new ideas. From a human resources perspective, this buffering may range from providing extra administrative support to providing space where individuals can work without undue disruption. In fact, the need for buffering may in part account for Dougherty and Bowman's (1995) findings that downsizing and reorganization often disrupt innovation. In this regard, however, it should be recognized that buffering may prove less important after initial idea generation, when implementation plans, production plans, and testing must occur, and integration with other organizational units is at a premium (Pierce & Delbecq, 1977).

Time and freedom from distractions, of course, represent only one type of resource that must be available to support creative work. Creative work also depends on the availability of relevant information along with access to strategic sites and strategic materials (Qin & Simon, 1990; Zuckerman & Cole, 1994). One implication of this observation is that fundamental new methodologies, techniques, or procedures must be monitored on an ongoing basis. Managers must insure that the staff has the opportunity to familiarize themselves with these methodologies either through strategic hiring or developmental interventions such as sabbaticals, external collaborative work, and subcontracting assignments. Further, access to strategic research sites should be provided through travel, professional collaborations, internet use, best practices reviews, etc. Effective use of interventions of this sort, however, will often require convincing staff and senior management that they must avoid falling prey to the "not invented here" syndrome, recognizing that useful techniques and information can be obtained from a variety of sources including sources outside the organization—an approach that builds knowledge, organizational learning, and innovative capability (Cohen & Levinthal, 1990).

Clearly, to leverage strategic materials and strategic sites, efforts must be made to keep staff up to date on advances in their field. Thus, incentives must be provided for ongoing professional development. Innovation, however, is not simply a matter of acquiring available information, often the information needed to formulate new ideas and assess their implications must be obtained on site. Information generation, however, can be, and often is, a costly time-consuming activity (Campbell, 1992). Thus, information generation efforts, data searches, field observations, etc., must be targeted, focusing on the key facts needed to proceed with the work. Information generation efforts, moreover, should be carefully planned being structured to provide a high yield with relatively low investment.

By the same token, it should be recognized that creative work is often associated with the identification of anomalies. (Katz, 1994; Kuhn, 1970). This observation implies that even as we seek efficiency in information generation, we must remain flexible, seeking out and pursuing the implications of unexpected anomalous observations. One strategy that might prove useful in this regard is to encourage peer review and an open discussion concerning the substantive, as well as the practical, implications of various findings.

Knowledge acquired from external and internal sources must be combined and reorganized to generate new understandings and new ideas. The creation of new understandings, however, is a difficult, time-consuming, rather halting process, where patterns are identified and progressively refined through observation (Mobley, Doares, & Mumford, 1992). From a management perspective, the observation has a number of implications. First, key questions pertaining to a new concept must be identified. Second, the nature and necessary amount of elaborative work must be carefully delineated taking into account the effects of diminishing returns. Third, premature closure must be avoided by providing adequate time for elaboration. Fourth, pressure for immediate results should be minimized—recognizing the demanding nature of the process, the need to learn from mistakes, and the fact that application will be contingent on successful model development.

New concepts, or rearrangements of existing concepts, provide a basis for idea generation and application development. As Finke et al. (1992) point out, exploration of multiple applications and different application development strategies must be encouraged if viable new ideas are to be developed. Thus, idea generation and development may require a period of extended exploration and testing. Further, because new ideas are necessarily fuzzy and implementation procedures unclear, one cannot expect requirements and implementation strategies to be clearly defined. Thus, progressive, adaptive refinements will be required with implementation plans being formulated in such a way as to permit progressive refinement through testing and evaluation. Here, however, it may be important to evaluate implementation attempts in terms of revision guides as well as overall success (Filipczak, 1997). These observations about the role of time and information in creative work lead to five propositions about the kind of human resources interventions likely to contribute to innovation.

Proposition 1. *Select for breadth and depth of expertise and skill in working with expertise.* Because creative thought is based on information, innovation is more likely when individuals are recruited and selected based on demonstration of relevant expertise. Innovation, however, is more likely to occur when expertise is evident across a number of relevant areas and when individuals selected bring certain value-added expertise bearing on strategic materials and strategic sites of interest. Of course, selection for expertise is most likely to prove successful if peoples' skills in working with this expertise in conceptual combination, problem definition, and idea generation is also assessed.

Proposition 2. *Provide incentives for ongoing knowledge development.* Knowledge is not static. Thus, human resources interventions that promote ongoing development of requisite expertise across a range of relevant fields should contribute to innovation. These interventions should take a variety of forms appropriate to the work at hand including self-study programs, conference attendance, visits to other sites, external courses, and sponsored technical mentoring as well as traditional classroom training. Additionally, development plans describing expertise to be acquired, how it is to be acquired, and how it would be applied should be considered as part of yearly career development sessions.

Proposition 3. *Define job expectations in terms of broad core duties.* Because creative efforts require a focus on the work and freedom from distractions as well as allowing the individual to reallocate effort based on changing requirements and emerging opportunities, jobs should be defined in terms of broad core creative production activities (e.g., develop advertising campaigns) rather than administrative requirements (e.g., manage account budgets) or financial objectives (bill 80% of time). Along related lines, core duties should be defined broadly to allow people to pursue emerging opportunities.

Proposition 4. *Allow discretion in structuring work activities.* The outcomes of creative efforts are uncertain and people need time to explore options. Creative people, furthermore, are typically motivated and autonomous. As a result, people working on creative efforts should be allowed substantial discretion in how they allocate time to core duties. Human resources practices that promote discretion such as flexible work schedules, telecommunicating, and self-defined work plans are, therefore, likely to contribute to innovation.

Proposition 5. *Periodically review work progress.* Because creative work involves exploration and changes in approach, a single yearly performance appraisal is unlikely to provide adequate guidance and feedback. Instead, local procedures for periodic technical evaluations based on peer feedback should be developed and used in conjunction with more traditional evaluation strategies. These technical evaluations should consider problems encountered, key outcomes, and plans for subsequent work focusing on progress and opportunities rather than production expectations.

Goals and Rewards

These comments about progress in idea generation and implementation point to a broader issue that must be considered in managing innovation. Traditionally, management theorists have argued that work should be directed with specific, concrete objectives in mind (Locke, Shaw, Saari, & Latham, 1981). An undue reliance on predefined objectives, however, may limit innovation. In keeping with this proposition, Mehr and Schaver (1996) found that specific performance objectives were unlikely to prove useful in settings where creativity and innovation were needed. Along similar lines, Scott (1995) has argued that creative work is better managed by directing process and approach rather than specifying a single desired outcome.

A number of studies have examined the effects of goals on creativity. In an initial set of investigations along these lines, Amabile (1997) found that the imposition of external evaluative goals may reduce intrinsic motivation and thereby inhibit creativity. Using an in-basket task where creativity was evaluated with respect to the solutions provided to novel personnel problems, Shalley (1991) found that creativity goals contributed to performance while production goals and low discretion lead to limited innovation. Along similar lines, Zhou (1998) used an in-basket task manipulating feedback variance, feedback style, and autonomy to assess their effects on creativity. He found that positive, informative feedback provided under conditions of high autonomy resulted in greater creativity.

These observations about the direction provided by goals and feedback have a number of implications for managing creative people. First, goals and objectives should be defined in broad terms, focusing on creativity rather than production, framed in such a way to allow people to pursue a number of different approaches and products (Tesluk, Farr, & Klein, 1997). For example, the goal of DuPont's synthetic fiber laboratory was simply to develop polymers that mimicked the characteristics of natural fibers (Hounshell, 1992). Second, rather than focusing on outcomes, managers should focus on how people are approaching the work and the strategies being used, providing coaching to overcome problems and clarify approach (Zhou, 1998). Thus, Zuckerman (1979) found that successful scientists typically had mentors—more senior scientists—who not only imparted knowledge but also strategies and methods for approaching problems. Third, and finally, direction of the work should rely on collaborative peer review, when requisite expertise and motivation are present.

Broadly speaking, these observations suggest that goals in creative work should be used as an informative, directional mechanism rather than a fixed evaluative standard. Use of goals as an informational directive mechanism may prove particularly important because creative work is often ambiguous and this ambiguity, as well as evaluative pressure, may induce stress. As Amabile (1983) and Backer (1992) point out, management of stress, ambiguity, and conflict is necessary to insure creative thought and requisite intrinsic motivation. However, it should be noted that the clarity and complexity of feedback information provided to manage creative work should vary with the capabilities of the individual. Thus, James (1995) found that conflict among task goals can lead to enhanced creativity, but only when the individuals involved have sufficient expertise to manage the conflict.

When an organization invests in the development of new ideas, some evaluation must occur along the way. Creative efforts are commonly appraised in terms of quality, originality, and overall productivity with expert judgment and more objective indices (e.g., patents) showing a high degree of agreement (Huber, 1998; Mumford & Gustafson, 1998; Simonton, 1988). What we often forget, however, is that there is not one absolute standard for evaluating creative work and, different evaluation standards may be needed for different types of work at different points in the development cycle (Brophy, 1998). For example, early in the development cycle, perceived impact, conceptual elegance, and the potential for developing useful applications may be appropriate evaluation criteria. Later in cycle, however, product refinement, production design, and cost control may be more appropriate considerations. Thus, human resources should allow some flexibility on the part of staff, and managers, in selecting the dimensions to be used in appraising different types of creative work.

Due to the ambiguity of creative work and the existence of multiple standards, it can prove difficult to evaluate creative efforts, particularly when information about objective outcomes is not available. As a result, evaluations of creative work are often subject to social biasing processes such as past history and stereotypes about creative individuals (Kasoff, 1995). Moreover, evaluations of creativity often imply risk, resulting in a tendency of evaluations to be overly critical. This criticism may effectively inhibit creative work while demotivating creative people (Amabile, 1982; Sternberg, O'Hara, & Lubart, 1997). These findings suggest that systematic appraisal procedures expressly designed to provide feedback about the approach and outcomes of the work being done may prove valuable (Carson & Carson, 1993). Unfortunately, in their review of the performance appraisal procedures commonly used by companies in evaluating creative work, Mullin and Sherman (1993) found that most evaluations focused more on general organizational requirements (e.g., administration) as opposed to the outcomes and activities involved in creative work. A similar problem appears in many career progression systems where creative achievement receives less recognition than management activities, a problem that has led many organizations to develop two-track progression systems.

Performance evaluations are commonly used as a basis for rewarding creative work. A series of studies by Amabile and her colleagues (Amabile, 1983; Amabile, Hennessey, & Grossman, 1986; Hennessey & Amabile, 1998) have examined the influence of extrinsic and intrinsic rewards on motivation and creative achievement. Her findings indicate that extrinsic rewards—concrete tangible rewards such as bonuses, pay increases, awards, and promotions—are detrimental to creativity. Baer (1997) and Eisenberger and Cameron (1996), however, have provided evidence that material rewards can encourage creative thought. Of course, extrinsic rewards provide information about performance while signaling organizational worth. Thus, as Amabile (1997) points out, what may be needed is an optimal mix of both extrinsic and intrinsic rewards. Because creative work is linked to curiosity and independence, providing time to pursue topics of personal professional interest, or reducing administrative burdens, may prove useful reward strategies particularly when accompanied by pay incentives, bonuses, and patent rights.

These observations about goals and rewards have a number of implications for human resources practices. Although one might draw a number of conclusions from this research, three central propositions emerge.

> **Proposition 1.** *Tailor performance objectives to creative elements of the work.* Because expectations for creativity can contribute to innovation, performance objectives should stress the creative aspects of the job rather than routine administrative functions. In developing performance objectives, however, it should be recognized that autonomy contributes to creativity and that the unique work being done by different people presents different issues. Thus, objectives should be defined collaboratively in relation to the work being done with the person doing the work having significant input into the identification of key objectives.
>
> **Proposition 2.** *Evaluate progress in work not outcomes.* Fixed, externally imposed production goals can inhibit creativity. Thus, performance evaluations should be based on progress made in reaching objectives serving to provide informative feedback rather than critical evaluations of outcomes. Because objectives for a person are tied to the unique work being done, evaluations of progress should be made with respect to the objectives of the work rather than global, administrative issues.
>
> **Proposition 3.** *Provide a mix of rewards based on progress towards objectives.* Creative work calls for both intrinsic and extrinsic motivation operating in a synergistic fashion. Thus, a mix of rewards should be provided that capitalize on both intrinsic (e.g., greater autonomy, additional developmental opportunities, etc.) and extrinsic motives (e.g., pay increases, promotions, etc.). Rewards should also recognize progress made with regard to objectives as well as outcomes using a mix of intrinsic and extrinsic rewards. Thus, an individual might be promoted for successfully completing project objectives even if a marketable product did not result from the effort. Contributions tc the "bottom-line" can be recognized through other mechanisms linked to product success such as profit sharing, bonuses, stock options, or sharing patent rights.

People and Context

Although the preceding discussion has stressed information, work strategies, and rewards, one must remember that creative work often depends on the quality of the people involved. Zuckerman (1979), for example, found that the creative scientists sought out and were more likely to work with other creative scientists. These findings suggest that the careful recruitment and selection of talented people may play a key role in creating the conditions needed for innovation. As a result, it is not surprising that successful firms establish recruiting networks, systematically seek out new talent, and create coherent developmental programs for this talent. Frequently, development is accomplished through assignments intended to capitalize on existing interests that build core skills within a discipline, encourage the acquisition of new skills, and develop a knowledge of the organization as a whole. Hammerschmidt's, (1996) findings with regard to the allocation of people to creative tasks, moreover, suggests that better performance is observed when people are assigned to projects consistent with their interests and work styles. These findings suggest that allowing people to self-select or bid for projects that are particularly interesting to them may contribute to creativity by capitalizing on extant skills and intrinsic motivation (Zuckerman, Porac, Lathum, Smith, & Deci, 1978).

The attraction and development of people to intrinsically interesting projects can create a kind of hot house effect under certain conditions that builds a continual cycle of innovation. A group of scientists and engineers who share diverse but related backgrounds develop more threads of ideas and bring a broader range of experience to bear on a problem, both trends that contribute to creative thought (Guastello, 1998; Mumford & Connelly, 1993). Moreover, recent studies by Cummings and Oldham (1997) and Shalley and Oldham (1997) indicate that competition, at least among groups of confident skilled workers, can also enhance creativity and innovation. Along similar lines, Zuckerman and Cole (1994) have found that the self-confidence of successful scientists often allows them to profit from competition particularly competition with other laboratories and other organizations. Thus, the day-to-day interactions among talented scientists and engineers may serve to stimulate creativity.

The findings of Oldham and his colleagues are of interest, in part, because they point to the importance of work context in shaping creativity. In one study along these lines, Oldham and Cummings (1996) examined the influence of job characteristics, autonomy, skill variety, task identity, task feedback, and task significance, on creativity in two manufacturing facilities using supervisory ratings, patent disclosures, and suggestions as measures of creativity. They found that a composite index of these job characteristics was an effective predictor of creativity for supervisory ratings and patents noting that job characteristics not only provide the information needed to guide creative thought but also the independence needed to pursue new alternatives. Other works by Amabile and Gryskiewicz (1987), Greenberg (1992), and Witt and

Beorkem (1989) also indicate that job characteristics promoting autonomy and task identity contribute to creativity. Taken as a whole, these findings suggest that it might be possible to restructure jobs and job requirements to enhance technical innovation.

The Witt and Beorkem (1989) study makes a noteworthy point in this regard. Perceptions of these contextual factors may be as important as their objective presence, an observation that, in turn, suggests interpersonal appraisal processes and desired amounts of these work characteristics may moderate the effects of contextual manipulations. This observation is of some importance because it suggests that contextual manipulations selected to be consistent with the preferred work styles may represent particularly powerful interventions. Thus, redesign effects that allow greater autonomy in pursuing substantive interests, permit greater freedom to schedule time and activities, and provide recognition for completed work may prove especially useful in enhancing technical innovation.

With regard to human resource practices, these observations about people and context suggest four propositions.

> **Proposition 1.** *Collaboratively define work context.* Work context can have an impact on creativity. However, desired amounts of these characteristics vary as a fraction of peoples' work styles and the nature of the work. Thus groups should be allowed to define optimal context to facilitate innovation and managers should actively work with group members in defining appropriate content.

> **Proposition 2.** *Provide training in defining work context.* Individuals, groups, and managers will have different perceptions of desirable context or working conditions. Further, the organization and the work may impose a variety of constraints or how context is defined. Thus, human resources should provide training as to how to go about identifying and changing context, managing group dynamics, and conducting work context and process reviews.

> **Proposition 3.** *Establish procedures that maximize self-selection.* Creative work depends on interest, curiosity, and intrinsic motivation. This observation in turn implies that creativity is more likely to be observed after people are granted the maximum possible autonomy in selecting the work they will pursue and the conditions under which they will pursue this work. Thus, open assignments policies may prove useful in enhancing creativity. Further, in pursuing these assignments individuals should be provided with the opportunity to meet with coworkers, and realistic description of the nature of the work should be provided to help insure an informed decision and an accurate appraisal of likely collegial interactions.

> **Proposition 4.** *Provide coherent developmental programs.* Effective creative work requires progressive acquisition of skills and expertise. Thus, human resources should provide necessary training in core skills. Additionally, human resources should provide guidance in establishing

career paths, identifying assignments likely to promote the growth of requisite skills, and in establishing and managing effective mentoring relationships for new employees.

MANAGING THE GROUP

Leadership

Traditionally, studies of creativity have focused primarily on the individual and tend to assume that creative people work alone. The reality of most current creative efforts, however, is that they occur in a team setting. This phenomenon is hardly surprising when one considers the complex nature of most current development efforts and the need to bring a variety of resources to bear in solving significant problems. One aspect of the group that appears to have a marked impact on creative work is the nature of the leader.

As noted above, creative work is ambiguous, risky, and subject to criticism. As a result, it can be expected that supportive supervision will facilitate creativity while more controlling critical supervision will tend to inhibit creativity (Amabile & Gryskiewicz, 1987; West & Farr, 1989). In one study along these lines, Oldham and Cummings (1996) examined the impact of supportive supervisory styles on creativity and found that support was related to innovation. Other works by Redmond et al. (1993) and Vosberg (1998) have shown that supervisory behavior intended to build feelings of self-esteem contributed to creative work as does the positive affect associated with self-confidence.

Providing support and building feelings of confidence, are only two ways in which leaders can influence creativity. Leaders, by nature of the influence they exercise and the opportunities they provide, can effect who will be creative and in what types of projects their creativity is likely to be evidenced. Scott and Bruce (1994) have, in fact, shown that both leader role expectations and leader–member relationships influence innovation in research and development settings. The downside of these findings is that innovation and creativity may sometimes be contingent on the relationship between people and their supervisors.

Another way leader behavior may influence creative work is through the vision provided. Vision, the positive alternative images of the future provided by charismatic or transformational leaders, serves both to direct and motivate subordinates. Because creative people display a high degree of autonomy, vision may prove to be a particularly powerful influence on technical innovation—a phenomenon evident in many anecdotal studies of successful research and development laboratories (Hounshell, 1992). Although strong empirical evidence demonstrating the effects of charismatic or transformational leadership is not available, one recent study by Sosik, Kahai, and Avolio (1998) has shown that transformational leadership can result in enhanced creativity on a computer-based brainstorming task.

Leaders, of course, must not only set direction but they must also acquire and allocate resources to projects. Typically, we all tend to assume that more resources are better whenever we are trying to get work done. As noted earlier, Nohari and Gulati (1996) found that there may be an invented u-shaped relationship between resources and innovation with the positive effects of resources diminishing when an overabundance of resources results in unfocused work and the pursuit of trivial, low-impact projects. These findings suggest that leaders of research and development groups need to identify the projects that should be invested in, allocate resources to projects in accordance with technical needs, and maintain the focus of project teams on the work at hand.

These observations about the influence of leader behavior on creativity suggest that by improving the effectiveness of leadership and management, human resources' interventions can make an indirect, but potentially significant contribution to innovation. In this regard, three interventions appear especially useful.

> **Proposition 1.** *Select leaders based on management skills as well as technical expertise.* Clearly, groups working on the kind of complex novel problems that call for creativity need some job-relevant expertise. The most creative individuals, however, may not have, or wish to develop, the kind of managerial skills needed to ensure effective group performance. Thus, managers should be selected not only on the basis of expertise and prior performance but also on the basis of requisite management and leadership skills, particularly their ability to communicate a vision of the work.

> **Proposition 2.** *Provide managers with training in managing creative enterprises.* It is often assumed that managers who know the work can manage creative people. Frequently, however, requisite management skills are lacking and must be developed. Thus, training and career development experiences should be provided that focus on leadership, communication, employee relations, and resource management. These training and development interventions are most likely to prove effective if they take into account the unique characteristics of creative workers such as the need for autonomy, achievement concerns, stress, and competitiveness among other variables.

> **Proposition 3.** *Provide multiple career tracks for advancement.* Promotion and development of some individuals based on the need for management and leadership skills can foster the perception that creativity does not let one get ahead. To minimize these perceptions and capitalize on expertise, attempts should be made to develop a two-track progression system that provides for advancement in pay and status for creative contributions per se without acquiring extensive management responsibilities. Moreover, training or coaching might be provided to help senior experts and managers work as a team in structuring group activities.

Group Structure

Relatively few studies have examined how groups should structure themselves to maximize creativity and innovation. A notable exception to this general trend may be found in Dunbar's (1995) study of microbiology laboratories. He used participant observation techniques to follow the progress of a number of projects—focusing on developmental biology and pathogens—in four laboratories. His findings indicate that more successful laboratories evidenced a mix of high- and low-risk projects. Additionally, more productive laboratories typically drew staff from a variety of relevant backgrounds, a strategy that apparently increased the diversity of available knowledge, and encouraged active collaboration among staff members when working on these projects.

These observations lead Mumford (1998) to propose a general structure for managing project teams interested to enhance innovation. This model was based, in part, on prior work by Damanpour (1991) and Pierce and Delbecq (1977), indicating that differentiation, integration, professionalism, and communication represent important structural influences on innovation. In part, however, this model draws from prior work by Gruber (1996) and Root-Bernstein et al. (1993), indicating that successful creative endeavors are characterized by capitalization on a network of enterprise providing a diverse background with respect to relevant knowledge and experience. The basic proposition of Mumford's (1998) model is that an overall vision, or identification of a major issue, is used to identify a limited set of two to five work themes intended to address significant problems bearing on this issue. Within each work theme, three to seven different project teams are established. Both themes and projects may differ with respect to the degree of risk evident in a project, its time frame, and the number of individuals involved. It is assumed, however, that exploratory high-risk projects will typically involve fewer people and less resources than more advanced projects working their way to implementation.

This work theme approach to structuring the activities of creative enterprises evidences a number of advantageous characteristics. First, it explicitly seeks to build diverse professional expertise by pursuing a number of themes. Second, the size of project teams, or thematic groups, need not become so large that it prohibits effective communication. Third, expertise developed on one project can be shared with closely related projects, and projects can be structured that promote integration of themes and the movement across the teams over time, thereby providing a basis for both integration and differentiation. Fourth, the array of available projects allows different individuals to pursue different interests thereby enhancing motivation. Fifth, individuals who are more concerned with exploration have the opportunity to work on smaller high-risk, exploratory projects while individuals who are more concerned with adaptation and refinement are provided with the opportunity to work on larger, late-stage development projects. Sixth, risk is minimized by distributing effort across multiple related themes. Seventh, exploratory projects within a theme provide a basis for ongoing learning, development of new ideas proposed by staff, and progressive development of staff skills and expertise.

Although group structure and the nature of the projects being pursued is typically seen primarily as a prerogative of management, certain actions taken by human resources can facilitate effective implementation of this kind of group structure. The four most useful actions would appear to be the following.

> **Proposition 1.** *Orient work group planning around project and project development.* A number of models can be applied in career planning. For creative workers, however, who are focused on the work being done or projects being pursued, it may prove most useful to focus career plans on projects or types of projects they would like to work on. These kind of project planning exercises are likely to prove especially useful if people are asked to identify both what they would bring to certain projects and what would be gained by others, and other projects, from their efforts.

> **Proposition 2.** *Allow individuals to develop and maintain a mix of projects.* Frequently, individuals are assigned to work on a single project for a relatively long period of time. Although this assignment strategy may sometimes prove necessary, it may not provide optimal results. Thus, human resources should encourage the distribution of time across a limited number of related efforts allowing individuals to shift time allocations, and projects, on a periodic basis as indicated by the needs of their work or the requirements of other project teams.

> **Proposition 3.** *Use smaller exploratory projects as a basis for development.* Creativity requires ongoing skill development and risk taking. Frequently, small-scale exploratory projects may be used to allow people to acquire needed new skills at low cost and with little risk. Thus, human resources should establish policies, as part of career development programs, that show people how to develop on "Bid for" exploratory work while encouraging managers to use these projects as developmental tools.

> **Proposition 4.** *Encourage diversity in project assignments.* Successful innovative work depends on bringing many perspectives to bear on a problem. Groups that include a moderate degree of diversity in interests and background are more likely to produce creative ideas and usable products than highly homogenous groups. Accordingly, an attempt should be made to staff projects in such a way as to insure a mix of skills and diversity of perspective.

Group Climate

Although this thematic model provides an attractive framework for managing innovation, it assumes that creative people will be working in collaborative groups. Groups have not always been seen as contributing to creative work.

The tendency to minimize the value of collaboration may be traced to early brainstorming studies, which found that groups did not outperform an individual working alone in terms of the number and quality of the ideas generated. These effects, however, may be attributed to group process variables that mitigate against creativity including social loafing, group think, inability to process cues on line, deficiencies in communication, constraints imposed by power structures, and use of simple, non-involving tasks. When these social inhibiting effects are controlled through the use of electronic brainstorming tasks, groups can exhibit higher creativity (Guastello, 1998; Siau, 1995; Sosik et al., 1998).

These findings, however, indicate that the climate prevailing in a group may have a marked impact on technical innovation (Richards, Aldrige, & Gaston, 1988). One implication of this observation pertains to the nature and structure of collaboration. As Abra (1994) points out, collaboration within groups working on creative efforts may occur in a variety of ways differing in terms of time frame (how long the collaboration lasts), and hierarchy (power differences between partners). Typically, successful creative efforts in group settings structure the kind of collaboration that occurs in relation to the demands of the task and the nature of the people involved. When tasks must be planned, implementation issues emerge quickly, and time frames are short—conditions characteristic of late cycle development efforts—then more intimate, hierarchically-driven collaborative efforts are likely to be required. On the other hand, when creative efforts focus on initial definition of the problem and generation of new understandings and new ideas, less intimate but longer term collaborations may be required.

The nature of collaborative work, however, is only one of a number of considerations that should be taken into account in managing technical innovation. Clearly, managers must take actions and formulate policies needed to encourage effective collaborations. For example, managers should explicitly recognize both group and individual achievement. Rewards should be provided for taking time out to help colleagues. People should be encouraged to develop and pursue new ideas in dynamic partnerships. In other words, the climate should convey the message that what is important are viable new ideas that bring people together in their development (Basadur & Hausdorf, 1996; Tesluk et al., 1997).

It should also be recognized that effective collaborations, whatever form they take, require an open exchange of ideas and debate focusing on the work. Thus, managers, and senior investigators should encourage productive questioning of ideas and approach, extensions of ideas, and a willingness to accept errors as a way of learning (Mumford, 1998). Under these conditions, direction of group activities should be delegated as much as possible to collaborating project teams, and reliance on tradition and power—as a way of directing others—should be minimized. Team members, moreover, should be encouraged to take risks pursuing the implications of surprising findings or new ideas particularly as they pertain to new markets and new opportunities. Thus, what seems to be called for is an open, intellectually challenging environment where entrepreneurial behavior on the part of collaborating teams is actively encouraged (Abbey & Dickson, 1983; Engle, Mah, & Sardi, 1997).

The importance of this dynamic, intellectually open climate in fostering technical innovation is illustrated in a study by Nystrom (1990). He examined innovation across four divisions of a chemical manufacturing firm. In the more successful divisions, the climate was found to emphasize risk taking, challenge and intrinsic enjoyment of the work, change, and competitiveness. In less successful divisions, profit, survival, and efficiency were seen as most important. Although there is reason to suspect that an entrepreneurial, intellectually challenging climate contributes to innovation, it should be recognized that specific climate characteristics called for may vary somewhat with the nature of the work. Moreover, the feasibility of developing a climate of this sort and encouraging entrepreneurial behavior may depend, in part, on the characteristics of the broader organizational environment surrounding the enterprise.

Because climate is a pervasive rather complex organizational phenomenon, it may appear, at least at first glance, that human resources interventions are unlikely to have much influence on the climate needed for innovation. It does appear, however, that human resources, particularly by providing requisite information and training, can influence climate. In this regard, four propositions about the kind of interventions likely to influence creativity seem called for.

Proposition 1. *Conduct climate surveys examining the climate for creativity.* Climate surveys specifically designed to capture perceptions relevant to innovation may prove helpful. Use of this approach is especially likely to prove effective if it is targeted on groups where innovation is a crucial aspect of performance and feedback sessions are conducted that expressly try to find strategies for ameliorating problematic perceptions.

Proposition 2. *Provide training in the nature and management of innovation.* Socialization and established patterns of organizational behavior often create the perception that creativity and innovation are not valued. Creativity training programs, however, may be used to change these perceptions providing people with guidelines for the kind of behaviors and strategies that might prove useful in enhancing innovation; this kind of training has also proven effective in changing both attitudes and behavior. Again, training programs of this sort are most likely to prove effective if focused on groups where innovation is at a premium.

Proposition 3. *Provide team training focused on collaboration and innovation.* Creative work often occurs in a team setting where collaboration is required. Creative people, by virtue of their autonomy, often have difficulty working with others. Thus, team training, especially team training focusing on effective collaboration strategies, may prove useful.

Proposition 4. *Insure that awards and recognition are consistent with climate and collaboration requirements.* Although many organizations provide awards for innovation, these awards may not always prove effective if they are not consistent with the climate required for innovation. Awards and recognition are, therefore, more likely to prove effective if they recognize team effort, intellectual achievement, risk taking, and entrepreneurial activity.

MANAGING THE ORGANIZATION

Support and Integration

Creative people, by their nature, are rather insular. They share a common background, a common language, and a tendency to focus on the work at hand that makes it easy, often far too easy, to lose sight of the broader organization that surrounds their enterprise. Creative efforts, however, depend on obtaining support from the broader organization for successful implementation of new products and new ideas. Thus, in the long run, management of interactions with the broader organization may prove just as important as effective management of a highly creative work group.

One key influence on the success of any creative enterprise is the acquisition of requisite resources particularly necessary financial support (Damanpour, 1991; Scott & Bruce, 1994). New efforts, however, are inherently a risky enterprise where the rewards of investments will not appear for some time, if, indeed, they ever appear at all. Thus, it is not surprising that Hitt and his colleagues (Hitt, Hoskisson, & Ireland, 1994; Hitt, Hoskisson, Johnson, & Moesel, 1996) found that a strong financial focus tended to inhibit the development of new products. On the other hand, firms that focused on control through strategic, as opposed to financial, mechanisms were more likely to produce innovative products. These findings imply that creative efforts are most likely to be successful when managers insure that the projects being pursued are likely to produce products consistent with the organizations strategic objectives, current markets, and projected markets. Thus, it is important to make a strategic as well as a financial case for research and development proposals stressing markets, market development, capability acquisition, and competitive positioning as well as the costs and requirements of development (Pavitt, 1990; Prahalad & Hamel, 1990).

Because innovation involves broader strategic decisions and ambiguity surrounds any new idea, it can be expected that in the early phases any creative effort will be fraught with and surrounded by politics. New ideas do not sell themselves. Indeed, successful, creative people are often gifted at sales efforts (Dudeck & Hall, 1991). In organizations, however, a number of factors appear to influence the likelihood that an investment will be made in new ideas. One of the most important factors in this regard, is the need for top management support (Collins, Hage, & Hull, 1988; Hage & Dewar, 1973; Jelnek & Schoonhoven, 1990). For example, Dougherty and Hardy (1996), in a qualitative study of 40 product introductions, found that management support was often a crucial factor influencing the success of a product. Moreover, as Jelnek and Schoonhoven (1990) point out, this support is most likely to be obtained when senior managers were knowledgeable about the technology and involved in the technology development process. This observation, in turn, suggests that effort devoted to senior management "sales" should begin early in the development cycle and should continue as the work progresses.

Early involvement of senior management, however, may not prove sufficient to guarantee acceptance of a new idea. Acceptance appears to involve at least two other considerations. First, managers who have connections to, and credibility with, various key constituencies should be brought aboard. These managers may serve as project champions garnering support from various constituencies, and, potentially, laying the social, technical, and intellectual groundwork needed for successful implementation of new products, or new ideas (Dougherty & Bowman, 1995; Howell & Higgins, 1988). Second, alliances must be established with influential groups who have a stake in the implementation process (e.g., sales and marketing, to accrue their support). The need for alliances and product champions, however, has a noteworthy, albeit neglected implication. To build this support, those involved in the innovative effort must have connections with relevant constituencies. Although these connections may be built over time—through techniques such as rotations, on-sight consulting, and committee work—it may prove difficult to convince creative people to engage in these activities due to their preoccupation with requisite technical work. One way of handling the problem might be to provide incentives (e.g., opportunities to pursue preferred projects) for these "off-line" activities.

Coalition building and the development of a network of organizational connections may help alleviate another problem that plagues creative efforts. When ambiguities exist about the value of new ideas, or new products, social appraisal processes are often used as a way to reduce ambiguity. (Anderson, 1992; Kasoff, 1995). In a study of managerial attitudes towards creativity, Basadur and Hausdorf (1996) identified three factors: (1) the value placed on new ideas, (2) negative stereotypes of creative individuals, and (3) the attitude that I am too busy for new ideas. Negative stereotypes and immediate work demands can lead to a premature rejection of potentially valuable new ideas. Familiarity with people involved in developing an idea along with prior collaborative work, however, represent two strategies for minimizing the impact of these negative attributions. However, a track record of success is certainly just as important as familiarity.

Studies of innovation indicate that the integration of various functions may represent a particularly important influence on the successful implementation of new ideas (Damanpour, 1991; Miller, Droge, & Toulouse, 1988). Dougherty and Hardy (1996), for example, in their study of product introductions, found that failure was more likely to occur in organizations that lacked the structures needed to encourage different departments to collaborate in producing new products and technologies. Along similar lines, Bahrimi and Evans (1987) found that successful high technology firms tended to use teams and task forces, along with extensive interpersonal communication, as structural mechanisms to support integration while rapidly rotating people through different roles and assignments to build connections among the staff.

As noted earlier, creative people may need buffering during certain phases of their work. In other phases, however, there is less need for buffering. By integrating the people generating new ideas into different aspects of the organization during these non-buffering phases, it is possible that managers might make a particularly significant contribution to the likely success of creative efforts. The intent of creative efforts is to provide *useful* new ideas. Useful new ideas, however, are more likely to emerge when people have acquired substantial familiarity with the organization, its current products and production processes, and the market for these products. Not only will this exposure allow people to find or construct problems in such a way that they are consistent with organizational needs, it will also allow them to identify and incorporate relevant organizational constraints as they generate ideas and formulate plans for implementation.

It should also be recognized that implementation of new ideas will typically involve a number of groups who, at best, have had limited involvement in the initial work underlying development of these ideas. The people who worked on the initial development effort will often have the most knowledge about new products and technologies as well as the technical issues that must be taken into account as they are brought to market. Thus, those developing new ideas can, and should, serve as a learning resource for other relevant constituencies in the organization. Because implementation of a new idea often requires a more structured directed approach, creative people evidencing an adaptive orientation—who are concerned with development and enhancement of existing ideas—may be more appropriate for filling these technology transfer roles than explorers concerned with the generation of new ideas.

These observations about the need for organizational support and integration suggest a number of actions that might be taken by human resources to promote innovation. Of these actions, four appear to be especially likely to prove effective.

> **Proposition 1.** *Develop rotational assignment programs.* Contact with and knowledge of the broader organization appears crucial to identification and successful implementation of new ideas. Thus, human resources should design rotational programs that bring staff working on new ideas or new products into contact with other groups who must support or implement these ideas. These rotational assignments are most likely to prove useful if they focus on groups that play a key role in supporting or implementing new ideas and are used as a basis for developing requisite leadership skills.

> **Proposition 2.** *Help prepare staff to support development and implementation.* A key aspect of successful idea development is the use of group expertise gained in developing an idea to help in managing its implementation. Unfortunately, however, not all individuals who are

effective in generating ideas are skilled at implementation. Moreover, they may lack the skills needed to train others with respect to implementation issues. As a result, programs intended to help identify individuals with requisite skills, and provide training needed to develop coaching and consulting skills, may prove useful.

Proposition 3. *Provide group interaction consulting.* When groups with different goals and objectives must work together on developing and implementing ideas, friction and conflict may arise. Thus, innovation is more likely to occur if procedures are provided for managing and resolving this conflict either through training or by providing consulting services.

Proposition 4. *Provide training in strategic sales briefings.* Senior management support appears to be necessary for innovation. Unfortunately, by virtue of their focus on the work and their expertise, creative people often have difficulty in communicating with people outside their area. Moreover, they are not always skilled at selling their ideas. Thus, development of programs intended to provide sales skills and briefing skills may prove useful. Such efforts are likely to prove especially useful if training provides guidelines for identifying, evaluating, and communicating the contribution of new ideas, or products, with regard to strategic objectives of the organization.

Culture and Structure

Although integration appears to be a particularly important influence on innovation, it is not the only organizational variable that influences the likelihood of innovation. For example, organizations differ in the degree of structure imposed upon work, the complexity of this structure, and the degree of interdependency among different people doing specialized work. As Arad, Hanson, and Schneider (1997) point out, when organizations evidence these characteristics, they typically place relatively little value on innovation—perhaps because it is difficult to introduce changes into a highly differentiated organization where process control is likely to be a paramount concern. Along similar lines, Burns and Stalker (1964) and Damanpour (1991) found that the formalization and centralization—characteristic of mechanistic structures—appear to inhibit innovation. In mechanistic organizations, particularly when there is a large investment in the current production process, it may be necessary to look for incremental innovations to be introduced into the production process slowly over a period of time. When more radical ideas are being developed, in this kind of organization, it may be useful to consider some of the alternative strategies for pursuing new ideas suggested by Burgleman (1983) and Strebel (1987) such as creating new divisions, spinning off part of the company, or licensing the technology to another company.

Even when an organization's structure evidences the flexibility needed to support the implementation of new ideas, the organization's culture may influence the likelihood of a new idea being generated and implemented. Some effects of culture may be quite direct. For example, Mone et al. (1998) note that ideas consistent with the organization's current mission and core values are far more likely to garner support and be successfully implemented: a tendency which may make if difficult for creative people to pursue certain ideas. Organizational cultures that stress the value of innovation, autonomy, human resources, and collaboration appear more likely to produce innovative products (Arad et al., 1997; Mumford & Simonton, 1997). What should be recognized, however, is that these cultural values—which are also likely to attract capable, creative people to the organization—encourage investment in their development, and promote acceptance of and support for their work. Thus, culture can, like structure, create a subtle and pervasive effect on the organization's willingness and capability for pursuing new ideas by shaping staffs' capabilities and organizational learning.

Traditionally, it has been assumed that human resources practices have little impact on structure and culture. However, as Arad et al. (1997) point out, human resources policies may be one of the more visible and directly manageable aspects of organizational structure and culture. As a result, human resources policies may have a significant impact on creativity and innovation. These observations in turn suggest the following propositions.

Proposition 1. *Implement policies that emphasize professional growth and development.* Research of the nature of creativity indicates that opportunities to acquire, and apply, expertise and programs that emphasize active ongoing skill development help develop a climate likely to foster creativity. Thus, one might expect innovation to be more likely to occur if human resources institutes policies and programs that emphasize training, external education, and professional involvement by providing support for training conference attendance, best practices seminars, etc.

Proposition 2. *Promote high performance work place policies.* Many of the characteristics of high performance work places—for example, autonomy, collaborative goal setting, team work, and ongoing learning—are also interventions that contribute to innovation. As a result, efforts by human resources to promote and support the implementation of these kind of policies may contribute to innovation.

Proposition 3. *Develop recruitment policies that emphasize growth and innovation.* Creative people actively seek out environments that provide opportunities for acquiring expertise and developing new ideas. Further, the kind of people recruited over time can have a marked impact on culture. Thus, human resources should develop recruitment programs that emphasize these opportunities.

Proposition 4. *Conduct innovation audits.* Both characteristics of the people and characteristics of the organization influence the need for and likely success of implementing new ideas. Accordingly, human resources staff should play an active role in appraising whether the skills, practices, and structure are in place to support the implementation of new ideas. These audits should be conducted prior to attempts to implement new ideas. Human resources should also play an active role in suggesting strategies that might overcome perceived blockages including activities such as training to provide requisite new skills, identification of changes in personnel management policies, and assessment of new skill sets that need to be acquired.

MANAGING THE ENVIRONMENT

Innovation Monitoring

Monitoring and managing the strategic environment is commonly considered a prerogative of senior management. Creative people, to the extent they influence these kinds of decisions, are seen as staff who bring valuable expertise but lack the broader understanding of the organization and its operating environment needed to make informed strategic decisions. As the pace of technological change accelerates and technology becomes ever more complex, it is difficult to see how executive teams that lack adequate expertise in the relevant aspects of new practices, technologies, and ideas can make informed decisions about where they should take the organization. Thus, there is a significant, yet unfortunately often unfilled role, for creative people in helping the organization manage certain aspects of the strategic environment.

Tushman (1997) and Tushman and Anderson (1986) have shown that periodically organizations go through periods of catastrophic change, and sometimes rebirth, as a function of radical changes in technology that affect the fundamental characteristics of production processes and markets. Even less radical, more incremental changes, can result in the loss of initial competitive advantage. These effects suggest that organizations must monitor changes or advances in process, markets, and technology. This scouting role is one more area that creative people are well suited to, in part, as a result of their diverse interests and background, and, in part, because their expertise and intuition make them the best people able to identify the implications of new technologies. Accordingly, Cohen and Levinthal (1990) have argued that the development and maintenance of this strategic scouting functioning is one of the best reasons for investing in research and development efforts.

On the other hand, it is open to question how successful organizations have been in performing this scouting function. One problem here is that, once a company has fixed on a particular technology, idea development often becomes become unduly focused on adaptations and enhancements of existing systems (Henderson & Clark, 1990). Another problem is that it can prove difficult to attract creative, cutting edge explorers to environments focused exclusively on the adaptation of existing technologies (Zuckerman, 1979). These phenomenon suggest that firms dependent on technology should try to maintain at least some basic development capacity even in relatively stable times. Moreover, as Jelnek and Schoonhoven (1990) point out, it may be useful to provide more innovative people with both opportunities to explore new developments and "dotted-line" relationships that allow them to feedback this information to senior managers in a timely fashion.

Innovation Strategy

It is not enough simply to identify the implications of new ideas and new technologies, organizations must make decisions about which ideas to explore and which they should try to exploit. In selecting ideas to pursue, it is generally advisable to "stick to the knitting," partly because work in areas of a current concern to the organization is more likely to be consistent with the strategic focus of the company, and, partly because the requisite knowledge and strategic material will be available to pursue cutting edge work at a relatively low cost. However, in selecting ideas and technologies to pursue, it is important to bear two points in mind. First, a mistake made by some firms is rejecting potentially valuable ideas because they are inconsistent with current market needs. The consequences of this error are nicely illustrated in IBM's failure to join the micro computing revolution, and indicate that in evaluating new technologies or new ideas, organizations—particularly their people—must continually ask the question "What if it works?" Second, it should be recognized that viable idea development requires a healthy mix of projects to maintain innovative capacity. Thus, some projects might be selected to build new staff capabilities and explore potential synergies even when immediate, direct applications are not apparent (Wise, 1992).

By virtue of their training and interests, creative people typically want to be the ones who develop new ideas. Investments in the development of fundamentally new ideas, however, may not always be in a firm's best interest, particularly if it is already successful at what it is doing (Bolton, 1993). Instead, it may be advantageous for firms to let other organizations accrue initial development costs bringing out related products later (Pavitt, 1990). As Cohen and Levinthal (1990) note, however, this approach is less likely to prove successful when (a) technological change is rapid, (b) public sources do not provide the information needed for product development, and (c) large marginal competitive advantage is associated with innovation. These observations, in turn, suggest that organizations must carefully weigh the strategic value of "in-house" development efforts. In making these evaluations, one should consider the need to build the knowledge and capacity that would permit rapid integration of new technologies, even those developed elsewhere. Thus, people in organizations must come to see their work not only as a matter of generating new ideas but also as a key adaptive capacity of the organization where the progressive generation and refinement of new ideas and new products serves to prepare the organization for the future.

These observations about the strategic environment may, at first glance, seem to be of little relevance to human resources. However, a number of activities can be taken by human resources that will help the organization monitor and respond to changes in the strategic environment. Many of those activities involve assessing human resources and their implications for the organization's ability to identify and respond to change. Accordingly, the following propositions might be proposed.

> **Proposition 1.** *Assess the implications of strategic changes for expertise requirements.* Changes in technology, markets, and competition, typically imply shifts in the expertise mix of the organization needed to implement new practices and adapt to change. Accordingly, human resources should identify likely changes occurring in the business area and identify the expertise that needs to be developed or acquired to cope with these changes.

> **Proposition 2.** *Monitor work force capabilities and expertise.* Capabilities for responding to or adapting to change depend partly on the expertise and skills currently available in the organization. Thus, human resources should inventory and monitor the expertise and skills currently available in the work force in relation to emerging trends or new initiatives. Analysis of gaps between current expertise and skills and those required by emerging changes in markets, technologies, and practices would be used to identify strategies for remediating these deficiencies either by developing "in house" staff, acquiring new staff, or some mix of these approaches.

> **Proposition 3.** *Actively pursue strategic hires.* Frequently, change in the strategic environment will require organizations to acquire "in house" expertise capable of monitoring and appraising the implications of change who bring with them available knowledge obtained from working at strategic sites with strategic materials. Thus, human resources should consult with internal and external experts in various areas using their observations to identify strategic hires who might be used to bring requisite expertise aboard. These strategic hires might then be used as seed points for monitoring and guiding responses to changing strategic conditions.

CONCLUSIONS

Before turning to the broader implications flowing from this review, an important limitation should be noted. In this article, I have examined the research on creativity and its implications for human resources management, with respect to general requirements for idea generation and implementation. Indeed, the nature of creative thought and innovation allow one to formulate some propositions about the kind of human resource practices that are likely to influence the likelihood of innovation. One must remember, however, that these practices do not, and cannot, *insure* innovation. Instead, they make innovation more *likely*. It should be recognized moreover, that innovation in organizations comes in many forms ranging from the generation of fundamentally new ideas to the introduction of practices already applied in other settings (Abrahamson, 1991; Damanpour, 1991). As a result, it is quite possible that some of these recommendations about human resources practices will prove more useful in some settings than others. Further, as Mumford, Whetzel, and Reiter-Palmon (1997) point out, not all jobs call for substantial creativity, nor do all organizations depend on innovation. Thus, these recommendations and potential human resources practices are most appropriately applied, and most likely to prove successful, when applied in organizations where innovation is a key aspect of corporate success, and when they focus on those jobs where innovation is an important element of performance.

Even bearing those caveats in mind, the present effort does lead to a number of conclusions with respect to requisite human resources practices. In fact, in the present article, I have presented a number of propositions about the kind of human resources practices likely to enhance innovation. For example, human resources specialists should search for depth and breadth of expertise. Jobs and job descriptions, should be structured to maximize autonomy and discretion. Organizations should seek people who will bring knowledge of strategic methods to the problems that must be addressed. The people selected, moreover, must be provided with time to think and requisite resources. Table 1 summarizes these propositions.

When one examines those propositions, they lead to three general conclusions. First, some traditional human resource practices must be adjusted, or fundamentally changed, if we wish to promote innovation. It is open to question, for example, whether our traditional procedures for defining jobs, appraising performance, and allocating awards are really useful. In fact, there is reason to suspect that some traditional practices (e.g., narrow job definitions, outcome evaluation and individualized incentives) may actually inhibit creativity. Second, we must provide the kind of training and career development systems that promote skill development and provide requisite expertise bearing on both the work at hand and the nature of people's creative efforts. Third, we should encourage diversity in both people and their work allowing creative people the autonomy needed to express their potential.

These interventions, and a number of the other human resources propositions provided in the foregoing discussion, indeed seem to reflect the conventional wisdom about managing people to maximize the potential for innovation (Pelz & Andrews 1996). One key implication of the present review, however, is that to successfully manage people to bring about innovation, the organization must go beyond the kind of conventional wisdom illustrated in some of these propositions. For example, management practices and effective leadership appear to have a marked impact on innovation. In developing strategies to enhance innovation, however, we frequently ignore the impact managers and management practices have on innovation. This apparently straightforward observation suggests that effective human resources interventions may often call for a more indirect approach focusing on development of the leadership skills needed to manage creative people. In fact, one might argue that this kind of management development intervention may represent a necessary precon-

TABLE 1
Summary of Human Resource Propositions

The individual	*The group*
1. Select for breadth and depth of expertise and skill in working with expertise.	1. Select leaders based on management skills as well as expertise.
2. Provide incentives for ongoing knowledge development.	2. Provide managers with training in managing creative enterprises.
3. Define job expectations in teams of broad core duties.	3. Provide multiple career tracks for advancement.
4. Allow discretion in structuring work activities.	4. Orient work group planning around projects and project development.
5. Periodically review work progress.	5. Allow individuals to develop and maintain a mix of projects.
6. Tailor performance objectives to creative elements of the work.	6. Use smaller explanatory projects as a basis for development.
7. Evaluate progress in work, not work outcomes.	7. Encourage diversity in project assignments.
8. Provide a mix of rewards based on progress towards objectives.	8. Conduct climate surveys examining this climate for creativity.
9. Collaboratively define work context.	9. Provide training in the nature and management of innovation.
10. Provide training in defining work context.	10. Provide team training focus on collaboration and innovation.
11. Establish procedures that maximize self-selection.	11. Insure awards and recognition are consistent with climate and collaboration requirements.
12. Provide coherent developmental programs.	
The organization	*The environment*
1. Develop rotational assignment programs.	1. Assess the implications of strategic changes for expertise requirements.
2. Help prepare staff to support development and implementation.	2. Monitor work force capabilities and expertise.
3. Provide group interaction consulting.	3. Actively pursue strategic hires.
4. Provide training in strategic sales briefings.	
5. Implement policies that emphasize professional growth and development.	
6. Promote high performance workplace policies.	
7. Develop recruitment policies that emphasize growth and innovation.	
8. Conduct innovation audits.	

dition for more traditional, or more conventional, human resources interventions. Thus, by influencing the context surrounding innovation, human resources practices may influence creativity as much as they do by focusing on the individuals doing the work.

Attempts to enhance innovation through human resources practices have traditionally focused on the people doing the work. Typically, attempts to influence individual workers have been based on one of two general strategies: management of outcomes and management of people. In outcome management, an attempt is made to provide incentives for creative work using rewards, performance appraisals, and profit sharing, among other techniques, to encourage innovation. The present review, of course, suggests that many of these strategies may, indeed, prove useful in enhancing creativity. By the same token, however, a careful examination of the literature on creativity suggests a number of other possible interventions. One might capitalize on intrinsic motives and the need for exploration by using opportunities to pursue personal interests as a reward. Alternatively, given the curiosity and openness of innovative people, opportunities for ongoing skill development might provide an effective incentive. Thus, the literature on creativity and innovation suggests a wider array of incentives should be applied in our attempts to encourage creativity.

The available evidence also suggests that interventions focusing on management of peoples' work can prove useful. For example, the acquisition of requisite expertise about the organization and its business areas clearly contributes to the capacity for creative thought. This principal, in turn, implies that rotations may prove useful in building the conditions needed for innovation. Rotations, however, may not prove especially useful unless they provide people with the kind of knowledge likely to make a real contribution to the work being done. Thus, rotations must be carefully selected and carefully timed to bring to bear relevant knowledge. This observation, of course, points to an important conclusion flowing from this review, specifically, human resources interventions must be based on the nature of the creative work being done by the individual, building the capabilities needed to do this work.

Although the present review indicates that we can influence innovation by focusing on the people doing the work, the findings obtained and propositions presented indicate that we must also take a broader view in designing interventions. Creative people must have effective leadership. This leadership must be able to obtain requisite resources. The work of creative people must be integrated into the organization and its broader strategic objectives. At first glance, it may appear that human resources can have little, if any, influence on these broader organizational practices. However, the propositions presented in the present effort suggest a number of strategies human resources might use to develop the infrastructure needed to support creative work. For example, managers might be provided with the training needed to acquire resources. Given the importance of collaboration, human resources might provide team training focusing on the skills needed to work with others. Alternatively, human resources might restructure career planning to focus on projects and project development encouraging people and programs to maintain a mix of projects. Application of these, and a number of other strategies mentioned above, represent non-traditional, albeit potentially successful, human resources strategies for influencing innovation at a systems level.

The potential value of these systems interventions, however, suggests the need to reconsider how human resources approaches the problem of innovation. Traditionally, in managing for innovation, human resources have operated as a support function. The observations made in the course of the present review, however, suggest that human resources practices intended to enhance innovation should include a directive, strategic element. These strategic practices include analysis of, and adjustment in relevant management practices through the use of climate surveys, innovation audits, and performance policies. Moreover, human resources should seek to identify emerging expertise requirements and guide strategic hiring decisions. The need for these strategic interventions in turn, suggests that human resources must play a key role in developing innovation plans taking an active part in formulating strategy by analyzing the needs of the organization in relation to the nature of creative people and creative work. In fact, it is only by considering the strategic environment, the organization, the nature of the group, and the characteristics of the people doing the work that human resources can identify the policies and approaches most likely to make a real contribution to innovation.

ACKNOWLEDGEMENTS

I would like to thank Shane Connelly, Roni Reiter-Palmon, and Sol Pelavin for various comments that have contributed to my thoughts on these issues. Parts of this effort were supported by a series of grants and contracts from the United States Department of Defense, Michael D. Mumford, principal investigator.

REFERENCES

Abbey, A., & Dickson, J. W. (1983). R & D work climate and innovation in semi-conductors. *Academy of Management Journal, 26*, 362–368.

Abra, J. (1994). Collaboration in creative work: An initiative for investigation. *Creativity Research Journal, 8*, 205–218.

Abrahamson, E. (1991). Managerial fads and fashions: The diffusion and retention of innovations. *Academy of Management Review, 16*, 586–612.

Amabile, T. M. (1982). Children's artistic creativity: Detrimental efforts as competition in a field setting. *Personality and Social Psychology Bulletin, 8*, 573–578.

Amabile, T. M. (1983). *The social psychology of creativity*. New York: Springer-Verlag.

Amabile, T. M. (1997). Entrepreneurial creativity through motivational synergy. *Journal of Creative Behavior, 31*, 18–26.

Amabile, T. M., & Gryskiewicz, S. S. (1987). *Creativity in the R & D laboratory*. Greensboro, NC: Center for Creative Leadership (Tech Rep #30).

Amabile, T. M., Hennessey, B. A., & Grossman, B. S. (1986). Social influences on creativity: The effects of contracted-for-reward. *Journal of Personality and Social Psychology, 50,* 14–23.

Anderson, J. R. (1992). Problem solving and learning. *American Psychologist, 48,* 35–44.

Arad, S., Hanson, M. A., & Schneider, R. J. (1997). A framework for the study of relationships between organizational characteristics and innovation. *Journal of Creative Behavior, 31,* 42–58.

Backer, T. E. (1992). On work place creativity: Psychological, environmental, and organizational strategies. *Creativity Research Journal, 5,* 439–441.

Baer, J. (1997). Gender differences in the effects of anticipated evaluation on creativity. *Creativity Research Journal, 10,* 25–32.

Baer, J. (1998). The case for domain specificity of creativity. *Creativity Research Journal, 11,* 173–178.

Bahrimi, H., & Evans, S. (1987). Stratocracy in high-technology firms. *California Management Review, 30,* 51–66.

Barron, F., & Harrington, D. M. (1981). Creativity, intelligence, and personality. *Annual Reviews of Psychology, 32,* 439–476.

Basadur, M. (1995). Optimum ideation–evaluation ratios. *Creativity Research Journal, 8,* 63–75.

Basadur, M. (1997). Organization development interventions for enhancing creativity in the work place. *Journal of Creative Behavior, 31,* 54–73.

Basadur, M., & Hausdorf, P. A. (1996). Measuring divergent thinking attitudes related to creative problem solving and innovation management. *Creativity Research Journal, 9,* 21–32.

Baughman, W. A., & Mumford, M. D. (1995). Process-analytic models of creative capacities: Operations influencing the combination and reorganization process. *Creativity Research Journal, 8,* 37–62.

Bolton, M. K. (1993). Organizational innovations and substandard performance: Often is necessity the mother of invention? *Organizational Science, 4,* 57–75.

Brophy, D. R. (1998). Understanding, measuring, and enhancing individual creative problem solving efforts. *Creativity Research Journal, 11,* 123–150.

Burgleman, R. A. (1983). A process model of internal corporate venturing in the diversified major firm. *Administrative Science Quarterly, 28,* 223–244.

Burns, T., & Stalker, G. (1964). *The management of innovation.* London: Tavistock.

Campbell, W. C. (1992). The genesis of the antipalasitic drug Invermetcin. In R. R. J. Weber & D. N. Perkins (Eds.), *Inventive minds: Creativity in technology* (pp. 194–216). New York: Oxford University Press.

Carson, P. O., & Carson, E. D. (1993). Managing creativity enhancement through goal-setting and feedback. *Journal of Applied Psychology, 27,* 36–45.

Cheng, P. C. H. (1996). Scientific discovery with law encoding diagrams. *Creativity Research Journal, 9,* 145–162.

Chi, M. T. H., Bassock, M., Lewis, M. U., Reitman, P., & Glaser, R. (1989). Self-explanations: How students study and use examples in learning to solve problems. *Cognitive Science, 13,* 145–182.

Cohen, W. M., & Levinthal, D. A. (1990). Absorptive capacity: A new perspective on learning and innovation. *Administrative Science Quarterly, 35,* 128–152.

Collins, P. D., Hage, J., & Hull, F. M. (1988). Organizational and technological predictors of change in automaticity. *Academy of Management Journal, 31,* 512–543.

Cummings, A., & Oldham, G. R. (1997). Enhancing creativity: Managing work contexts for the high potential employee. *California Management Review, 40,* 22–39.

Damanpour, F. (1991). Organizational innovation: A meta-analysis of effects of determinants and moderators. *Academy of Management Journal, 34*, 555–590.

Damanpour, F. (1998). Innovation type, radicalness, and the adoption process. *Communication Research, 15*, 545–567.

Davidson, J. E. (1995). The suddenness of insight. In R. G. Sternberg & J. E. Davidson (Eds.), *The nature of insight* (pp. 125–156). Cambridge, MA: MIT Press.

Davidson, J. E., & Steinberg, R. J. (1984). The role of insight in intellectual giftedness. *Gifted Child Quarterly, 28*, 58–64.

Dougherty, D., & Bowman, E. H. (1995). The effects of organizational downsizing on product innovation. *California Management Review, 37*, 28–43.

Dougherty, D., & Hardy, B. F. (1996). Sustained innovation production in large mature organizations: Overcoming innovation to organization problems. *Academy of Management Journal, 39*, 826–851.

Dunbar, K. (1995). How do scientists really reason: scientific reasoning in real world laboratories. In R. J. Sternberg & J. E. Davidson (Eds.), *The nature of insight* (pp. 365–396). Cambridge, MA: MIT Press.

Dudeck, S. Z., & Hall, W. B. (1991). Personality consistency: Eminent architects 25 years later. *Creativity Research Journal, 4*, 213–232.

Eisenberger, R., & Cameron, J. (1996). Detrimental effects of reward: Reality of myth? *American Psychologist, 51*, 1153–1166.

Engle, D. E., Mah, J. J., & Sardi, G. (1997). An empirical comparison F.O. entrepreneurs and employees: Implications for innovation. *Creativity Research Journal, 10*, 45–49.

Erickson, K. A., & Charness, W. (1994). Expert performance: Its structure and acquisition. *American Psychologist, 49*, 725–747.

Fiest, G. J. (1997). Quantity, quality, and depth of research as influences on scientific eminence: Is quantity most important? *Creativity Research Journal, 10*, 325–336.

Filipczak, B. (1997). It takes all kinds: Creativity in the work force. *Training, 34*, 32–40.

Finke, R. A., Ward, T. B., & Smith, S. M. (1992). *Creative cognition: Theory, research and applications*. Cambridge, MA: MIT Press.

Frederiksen, R. (1984). Implications of cognitive theory for instruction in problem solving. *Review of Educational Research, 43*, 363–407.

Getzels, J. W., & Csikszentmihalyi, M. (1976). *The creative vision: A longitudinal study of problem finding in art*. New York: Wiley.

Ghiselin, B. (1963). Ultimate criteria for two levels of creativity. In C. W. Taylor & F. Barron *Scientific creativity: Its recognition and development* (pp. 30–43). New York: Wiley.

Gick, M. C., & Lockhart, R. S. (1995). Cognitive and affective components of insight. In R. J. Davidson Davidson & J. E. Davidson (Eds.), *The nature of insight* (pp. 197–228). Cambridge, MA: MIT Press.

Greenberg, E. (1992). Creativity, autonomy, and the evaluation of creative work: Artistic worriers in organizations. *Journal of Creative Behavior, 26*, 75–80.

Gruber, H. E. (1989). The evolving systems approach to creative work. *Creativity Research Journal, 1*, 27–51.

Gruber, H. E. (1996). The life space of a scientist: The visionary function and other aspects of Jean Piaget's thinking. *Creativity Research Journal, 9*, 251–265.

Guastello, S. J. (1998). Creative problem solving groups at the edge of chaos. *Journal of Creative Behavior, 32*, 38–57.

Hage, J., & Dewar, R. (1973). Elite values versus organizational structure in predicting innovation. *Administrative Science Quarterly, 18*, 279–290.

Hammerschmidt, P. K. (1996). The Kirton adaption innovation inventory and group problem solving success rates. *Journal of Creative Behavior, 30*, 61–74.

Henderson, R. M., & Clark, K. B. (1990). Architectural innovation: The reconfiguration of existing product technologies and failure of established firms. *Administrative Science Quarterly, 35*, 9–30.

Hennessey, B. A., & Amabile, T. M. (1998). Reward, intrinsic motivation, and creativity. *American Psychologist, 53*, 674–675.

Hitt, M. A., Hoskisson, R. E., & Ireland, R. D. (1994). A mid-range theory of the interactive effects of international and product diversification on innovation and performance. *Journal of Management, 20*, 297–326.

Hitt, M. A., Hoskisson, R. E., Johnson, R. A., & Moesel, D. D. (1996). The market for corporate control and firm innovation. *Academy of Management Journal, 39*, 1084–1196.

Hitt, M. H., Hoskisson, R. E., & Kim, H. (1997). International diversification effects on innovation and firm performance in product diversified firms. *Academy of Management Journal, 40*, 767–798.

Holyoak, K. J., & Thagard, P. (1997). The analogical mind. *American Psychologist, 52*, 35–44.

Hounshell, E. A. (1992). Invention in the industrial research laboratory: Individual act or collective process. In R. J. Weber & D. N. Perkins (Eds.), *Inventive minds: Creativity in technology* (pp. 273–291). New York: Oxford Univ. Press.

Howell, J. M., & Higgins, C. A. (1988). Champions of technological innovation. *Administrative Science Quarterly, 35*, 317–341.

Huber, J. C. (1998). Invention and inventivity as a special kind of creativity, with implications for general creativity. *Journal of Creative Behavior, 32*, 58–72.

James, K. (1995). Goal conflict and originality of thinking. *Creativity Research Journal, 8*, 270–285.

Jausovec, N. (1997). Differences in EEG activity during the solution of closed and open problems. *Creativity Research Journal, 10*, 317–324.

Jelnek, M., & Schoonhoven, C. B. (1990). *The innovation marathon: Lessons learned from high technology firms*. Oxford, England: Blackwell.

Kaizer, C., & Shore, B.M. (1995). Strategy flexibility in more and less competent students on mathematical norm problems. *Creativity Research Journal, 8*, 77–82.

Kasoff, J. (1995). Explaining creativity: The attributional perspective. *Creativity Research Journal, 8*, 311–366.

Kasoff, J. (1997). Creativity and breadth of attention. *Creativity Research Journal, 10*, 303–316.

Katz, B. M. (1994). Planning and following the unexplored in scientific research. *Creativity Research Journal, 7*, 225–238.

Kirton, M. (1987). Adaptations and innovations: Cognitive style and personality. In S. G. Isaksen (Ed.), *Frontiers of creativity research: Beyond the basics* (pp. 282–304). Buffalo, NY: Bearly.

Kuhn, T. S. (1970). *The structure of scientific revolutions*. Chicago, IL: Univ. of Chicago Press.

Kulkarni, D., & Simon, H. (1990). The process of scientific discovery: The strategy of experimentation. *Cognitive Science, 12*, 129–175.

Locke, E. A., Shaw, K. N., Saari, L. M., & Latham, G. P. (1981). Goal setting and performances: 1969–1980. *Psychological Bulletin, 90*, 125–150.

Martinsen, O. (1993). Insight problems revisited: The influence of cognitive styles and experiences of creative problem solving. *Creative Research Journal, 6*, 435–448.

Mehr, D. G., & Shaver, P. R. (1996). Goal structures in creating motivation. *Journal of Creative Behavior, 30*, 77–104.

Miller, A. I. (1992). Scientific creativity: A comparative study of Henri Poincare and Albert Einstein. *Creativity Research Journal, 5*, 385–418.

Miller, A. I. (1996). Metaphors in creative scientific thought. *Creativity Research Journal, 9*, 113–130.

Miller, D., Droge, C., & Toulouse, J. (1988). Strategic process and content as moderators between organizational content and structure. *Academy of Management Journal, 31*, 544 – 569.

Mills, J. A., & Cameron, R. B. (1993). Creativity and biologists. *Creativity Research Journal, 6*, 319–328.

Mobley, M. I., Doares, L. M., & Mumford, M. D. (1992). Process analytic models of creative capacities: Evidence for the combination and interorganization process. *Creativity Research Journal, 5*, 125 – 155.

Mone, M. A., McKinley, W., & Baker, V. C. (1998). Organization decline and innovation: A contingency framework. *Academy of Management Review, 23*, 113 –115.

Montouri, A. (1992). Two books on creativity. *Creativity Research Journal, 5*, 199 – 203.

Mullin, R. F., & Sherman, R. (1993). Creativity and performance appraisal: Shall never the twain meet. *Creativity Research Journal, 6*, 425 – 434.

Mumford, M. D. (1998). Managing the creative process: Techniques and approaches in scientific organizations. In D. Sessa (Ed.), *Paradigm for the successful utilization of renewable resources* (pp. 1–16). Champaign, IL: AOCS Press.

Mumford, M. D., Baughman, W. A., & Reiter-Palmon, R. (1997). Thinking creativity at work: Organizational influence on creative problem solving. *Journal of Creative Behavior, 31*, 7 – 17.

Mumford, M. D., Baughman, W. A., Suppinski, E. P., & Maher, M. A. (1996). Process based on measures of creative problem solving skills: II. Information encoding. *Creativity Research Journal, 9*, 77 – 88.

Mumford, M. D., Baughman, W. A., Threlfall, K. V., Supinski, E. P., & Costanza, D. P. (1996). Process based measures of creative problem solving skills: I. Problem construction. *Creativity Research Journal, 9*, 62 – 76.

Mumford, M. D., & Connelly, M. S. (1993). Cases of invention. *Contemporary Psychology, 38*, 1210 –1212.

Mumford, M. D., & Gustafson, S. B. (1998). Creativity syndrome: Integration, application, and innovation. *Psychological Bulletin, 103*, 27 – 43.

Mumford, M. D., Gustafson, S. B. (in press). Cognitive thought: Cognition and problem solving in dynamic systems. In M. A. Runco (Ed.), *Creativity research handbook*. Cresskill, NJ: Hampton.

Mumford, M. D., Mobley, M. I., Uhlman, C. E., Reiter-Palmon, R., & Doares, L. M. (1991). Process analytic models of creative capacities. *Creativity Research Journal, 4*, 91–122.

Mumford, M. D., Reiter-Palmon, R., & Redmond, M. R. (1994). Problem construction and cognition: Applying problem representations in ill-defined domains. In M. A. Runco *Problem finding, problem solving, and creativity* (pp. 3 – 39).

Mumford, M. D., & Simonton, D. K. (1997). Creativity in the work place: People, problems, and structures. *Journal of Creative Behavior, 31*, 1–7.

Mumford, M. D., Baughman, W. A., Maiter, M. A., Costanza, D. P., & Supinski, E. P. (1997). Process-based measures of creativity problem-solving skills: IV. Category combination. *Creative Research Journal, 10*, 69 – 76.

Nickels, T. (1994). Enlightenment versus romantic models of creativity in science and beyond. *Sociological Inquiry, 48*, 65 – 95.

Nohari, K., & Gulati, S. (1996). Is slack good or bad for innovation. *Academy of Management Journal, 39*, 799 – 825.

Nystrom, H. (1990). Organizational innovation. In M. S. West & J. L. Farr (Eds.), *Innovation and creativity at work: Psychological and organizational strategies* (pp. 143 – 162). New York: Wiley.

Oldham, G. R., & Cummings, N. (1996). Employee creativity: Personal and contextual factors at work. *Academy of Management Journal, 39*, 607–628.

Owens, W. A. (1969). Cognitive, non-cognitive, and environmental correlates of mechanical ingenuity. *Journal of Applied Psychology, 53*, 199–208.

Pavitt, K. (1990). What we know about strategic management of technology. *California Management Review, 33*, 17–126.

Pelz, D. C., & Andrews, F. M. (1996). *Scientists in organizations: Productive climates for research and development.* New York: Wiley.

Pierce, J. L., & Delbecq, A. C. (1977). Organizational structure, individual attitudes and innovation. *Academy of Management Review, 2*, 26–37.

Policastro, E. (1990). Creative intuition: An integrative review. *Creativity Research Journal, 8*, 99–113.

Porter, M. E. (1990). *The competitive advantage of nations.* New York: Free Press.

Prahalad, C. K., & Hamel, G. (1990). The core competencies of the corporation. *Harvard Business Review, 68*, 79–91.

Puccio, G. J., Treffinger, D. J., & Talbot, R. J. (1995). Explanatory examination of the relationship between creative styles and creative products. *Creative Research Journal, 8*, 157–172.

Qin, Y., & Simon, H. A. (1990). Laboratory replication of scientific discovery processes. *Cognitive Sciences, 14*, 281–312.

Redmond, M. R., Mumford, M. D., & Teach, R. J. (1993). Putting creativity to work: Leader influences on subordinate creativity. *Organizational behavior and human decision processes, 55*, 120–151.

Reiter-Palmon, R., Mumford, M. D., & Threlfall, K. V. (1998). Solving everyday problems creatively: The role of problem construction and personality type. *Creativity Research Journal, 11*, 187–198.

Richards, T., Aldridge, S., & Gaston, K. (1988). Factors affecting brainstorming: Towards the development of diagnostic tools for assessing creative performance. *R & D Management, 18*, 309–320.

Root-Bernstein, R. S., Bernstein, M., & Garnier, H. (1993). Identification of scientists making long-term, high impact contributions, with notes on their methods of working. *Creativity Research Journal, 6*, 329–344.

Root-Bernstein, R. S., Bernstein, M., & Garnier, H. (1995). Correlations between avocations, scientific style, work habits, and professional impact of scientists. *Creativity Research Journal, 8*, 115–137.

Rostan, S. M. (1994). Problem finding, problem solving, and cognitive controls: An empirical investigation of critically acclaimed productivity. *Creativity Research Journal, 7*, 97–110.

Rothenberg, A. (1996). The Janusian process in scientific discovery. *Creativity Research Journal, 9*, 207–232.

Runco, M. A. (1997). Introduction. In M. A. Runco (Ed.), *The Creativity Research Handbook: Volume One* (pp. ix–xiv). Cresskill, NJ: Hampton Press.

Runco, M. A., & Chand, I. (1994). Problem finding, evaluation thinking, and creativity. In M. A. Runco (Ed.), *Problem finding, problem solving, and creativity* (pp. 40–76). Norwood, NJ: Ablex.

Scott, R. K. (1995). Creative employees: A challenge to managers. *Journal of Creative Behavior, 29*, 64–71.

Scott, S. G., & Bruce, R. A. (1994). Determinants of innovative behavior: A path model of individual innovation in the work place. *Academy of Management Journal, 37*, 580–607.

Shalley, C. E. (1991). Effects of productivity goals, creativity goals, and personal discretion on individual creativity. *Journal of Applied Psychology, 76*, 179–185.

Shalley, C. E., & Oldham, G. R. (1997). Competition and creative performance: Effects of competition, presence, and visibility. *Creativity Research Journal, 10*, 337–346.

Sheldon, K. M. (1995). Creativity and goal conflict. *Creativity Research Journal, 8*, 299–306.

Siau, K. L. (1995). Group creativity and technology. *Journal of Creative Behavior, 29*, 201–216.

Simonton, D. K. (1988). Age and outstanding achievement: What do we know after a century of research. *Psychological Bulletin, 104*, 251–267.

Sosik, J. J., Avolio, B. J., & Kahai, S. S. (1997). Effects of leadership style and anonymity on group potency and effectiveness in a group decision support system environment. *Journal of Applied Psychology, 82*, 89–103.

Sternberg, R. J., O'Hara, L. A., & LuBart, T. I. (1997). Creativity as investment. *California Management Review, 40*, 8–32.

Strebel, P. (1987). Organizing for innovation over an industry cycle. *Strategic Management Journal, 8*, 117–124.

Tesluk, P. E., Farr, J. L., & Klein, S. R. (1997). Influences of organizational culture and climate on individual creativity. *Journal of Creative Behavior, 31*, 27–41.

Tushman, M. L. (1997). Winning through innovation. *Strategy and Leadership, 25*, 14–20.

Tushman, M. C., & Anderson, P. (1986). Technological discontinuities and organizational environments. *Administrative Science Quarterly, 31*, 439–465.

Tushman, M. L., & O'Reilly, C. A. (1997). *Winning through innovation: A practical guide to leading organizational change and renewal.* Boston, MA: Harvard Business School Press.

Tweney, R. D. (1996). Pre-symbolic processes in scientific discovery. *Creativity Research Journal, 9*, 163–172.

Vosberg, S .K. (1998). The effects of positive and negative affect on divergent thinking performance. *Creativity Research Journal, 11*, 165–172.

Ward, S. C., Byrnes, J. P., & Overton, W. F. (1990). Organization of knowledge and conditional reasoning. *Journal of Educational Psychology, 82*, 849–855.

Weisburg, R. W. (1986). *Creativity: Genius and other myths.* New York: Freeman.

Wentroff, R. H. (1992). The synthesis of diamonds. In R. J. Weber & D. N. Perkins (Eds.), *Inventive minds: Creativity in technology* (pp. 154–165). New York: Oxford University Press.

West, M. A., & Farr, J. L. (1989). Innovation at work: Psychological perspectives. *Social Behavior, 3*, 31–57.

Wild, J. J. (1992). The origin of soft tissue ultrasonic echoing and early instrumental application to clinical medicine. In R. J. Weber & D. N. Perkins (Eds.), *Inventive minds: Creativity in technology* (pp. 115–141). New York: Oxford Univ. Press.

Wise, G. (1992). Inventors and corporations in the maturing electrical industry. In R. J. Weber & D. N. Perkins (Eds.), *Inventive minds: Creativity in technology* (pp. 291–310). New York: Oxford Univ. Press.

Witt, L. A., & Beorkem, M. N. (1989). Climate for creative productivity as a organization. *Creativity Research Journal, 2*, 30–40.

Zhou, J. (1998). Feedback balance, feedback style, task autonomy, and achievement origination: Interactive effects on creative performance. *Journal of Applied Psychology, 83*, 261–276.

Zuckerman, H. (1979). Theory choice and problem choice in science. *Sociological Inquiry, 48*, 65–95.

Zuckerman, H., & Cole, J. R. (1994). Research strategies in science: A preliminary inquiry. *Creativity Research Journal, 7*, 391–406.

Zuckerman, M., Porac, J., Lathin, D., Smith, R., & Deci, E. L. (1978). On the importance of self-determination and intrinsically motivated behavior. *Personality and Social Psychology Bulletin, 4*, 443–446.

[9]

Fostering and Facilitating Entrepreneurship in Organizations: Implications for Organization Structure and Human Resource Management Practices*

Randall S. Schuler

Two particularly important factors involved in successful corporate entrepreneurship are organization structure and human resource management practices. By selecting and implementing the appropriate structure and practices, human resource professionals can systematically foster and facilitate innovation and entrepreneurship within their organizations. The more that new and different entrepreneurial activities are needed, the more that complete structural arrangements as well as policy and procedure flexibility are needed. In this article, structural practices appropriate for different degrees of entrepreneurial activity are described. But because appropriate structural practices alone are not sufficient for effectiveness, necessary human resource management practices are also described in detail. Throughout, implications for structural and human resource management practices in advancing entrepreneurship are considered.

What distinguishes entrepreneurial from nonentrepreneurial firms is the rate of new product introduction (innovation). This is not to say that firms are *either* entrepreneurial or nonentrepreneurial, but that the greater the *rate* of new product innovation, the more entrepreneurial the firm (Kanter, 1985; Drucker, 1985). Other things being equal, the greater the rate of product innovation, the greater the level of effectiveness, particularly higher profitability and growth as well as enhanced ability to survive and be competitive. Consequently, organizations today consider entrepreneurship, or being more entrepreneurial, a desired state of affairs. The question then looms, "how to become more entrepreneurial?" This article breaks

*Support for this paper was provided by the NYU Center for Entrepreneurial Studies and the Human Resource Planning Society. The author wishes to thank Ian MacMillan and Susan Jackson for helpful comments and Joe Martocchio in the preparation of an earlier draft of the manuscript.

Human Resource Management, Winter 1986, Vol. 25, Number 4, Pp. 607–629

CCC 0090-4848/86/040607-23$04.00

the answer into two major components: organization structure and human resource management practices. While both are under the purview of human resource management professionals in a growing number of organizations (Fombrun et al., 1984), because there has been less discussion regarding the nature of HR practices that foster and facilitate entrepreneurship, *they* are the primary focus of this article and their complementary association with organization structural practices is highlighted. To provide a basis for understanding this association and the organization structure and HRM practices suggestions, it is appropriate to first review what is known about entrepreneurship and entrepreneurism.

ENTREPRENEURISM

Block (1985), defines entrepreneurism as:

> . . . the study of the processes or stages, activities and characteristics involved in the creation or innovation of new products or services that identify and fulfill opportunities within existing businesses or that create and build products or services forming new businesses.

While entrepreneurism is "the study of," entrepreneurship is

> . . . the practice of creating or innovating new products or services within existing businesses or within newly forming businesses or as Kanter suggests it means the creation of new combinations (1985).

So entrepreneurship is the practice or activity of creating, of innovating (Drucker, 1985). Not creating or innovating is nonentrepreneurship or administrativeship. The process of innovation is central to entrepreneurship, or as Drucker (1985) states: "Innovation is the tool of the entrepreneur." The innovation process is distinguished by:

Uncertainty—". . . progress on a new innovation comes in spurts among unforeseen delays and setbacks. . . in the essential chaos of development" (Quinn, 1979). Consequently, ROIs are unpredictable and success is problematic.

Knowledge-Intensity—". . . the innovation process is knowledge-intensive, relying on individual human intelligence and creativity. New experiences are accumulated at a rapid pace, the learning curve is steep" (Kanter, 1985). Under these conditions, processes and procedures are difficult to codify and employee turnover can spell disaster.

Competition with alternatives—New ideas and inventions often pose a threat to existing conditions; thus, innovation often prompts resistance and undermining political efforts (Fast, 1976). Within this scenario, being and doing different things requires courage and commitment, if not outright protection, by a significant other.

Boundary Crossing—Innovative requires the crossing of boundaries, the combining of two or more ideas, thoughts, products, etc. Consequently, conditions must exist to facilitate the flow of people and ideas across separate entities.

Central to administrativeship is the process of maintaining the *status quo,* of predictability and routinization. This process is essentially distinguished by conditions opposite to the four of innovation outlined above. Thus, administrativeship and entrepreneurship are at odds with each other (Kanter, 1985). One demands managing the old and the same, and the other, managing the new and the different. Conflict and tension are typical byproducts; ineffectiveness may be as well, but is not a necessary consequence. In fact, recognizing and effectively dealing with entrepreneurship and administrativeship in the same organization is essential to success in most firms:

> To be a successful enterprise, we have to do two apparently contradictory things quite well: We have to stay innovative and creative, but at the same time we have to be tightly controlled about certain aspects of our corporate behavior. But I think that what you have to do about paradox is embrace it. So we have the kind of company where certain things are very loose and other things are very tight. The whole art of management is sorting things into the loose pile or the tight pile and then watching them carefully (Mitchell Kapor, CEO, Lotus Development Corporation; *Boston Globe,* 1/27/85).

Perhaps easier said than done. Achieving this balanced loose–tight mix constitutes the essential challenge, and meeting it successfully is aided by an understanding of the structural and human resource management practices required to foster and facilitate entrepreneurship. Although the practices necessary for realizing administrativeship are generally well known to most readers, they are discussed by implication in our consideration of those practices that encourage entrepreneurship.

STRUCTURAL PRACTICES FOR ENTREPRENEURSHIP

In describing structural practices for entrepreneurship, it is essential to keep in mind that:

> Entrepreneurial activity can be depicted as falling into two broad categories: (1) *Identifying and fulfilling opportunities within existing activities*—the development of new products and processes, improving existing operations, developing new marketing methods—basically innovating effectively within the existing product markets of the firm. (2) *Creating and building new businesses*—those which differ significantly in products, technology, markets, and even in financial characteristics (capital intensity, cost element distribution, inherent balance sheet differences, margins), from the existing businesses of the company (Block, 1985).

These distinctions are critical because of their implications for structural practices. Essentially, the more new and different the nature of the entrepreneurial activity (i.e., the more it is typical of creating and building new businesses distinctively different from existing businesses), the more complete the structure arrangements have to be and the more flexibility is needed in policies and procedures. The more an entrepreneurial activity is new and different, the more there will be uncertainty, knowledge-intensity, and competition with alternatives, and there will be greater need for boundary crossing. Accordingly, varying the degrees of entrepreneurial activity will moderate the extent of structural arrangements and policy and practice flexibility necessary for effectiveness.

Structural Arrangements

At the heart of structural arrangements to promote entrepreneurship is the granting of some degrees of freedom and support to an individual or group of individuals in the organization. Typically, the more different the entrepreneurial activity, the more unique the products developed or produced, and the more unique the industry characteristics compared to the parent organization, the more structural autonomy is necessary. Campbell Soup Company recognized that the soup business is far different than the gourmet food business. Because the lion's share of revenue growth was coming from gourmet foods, Campbell Soup determined that it had to have new structural arrangements:

> Convinced that Campbell was missing the action in the food business, McGovern began looking for inspiration, not from within his own 116-year-old company, but from entrepreneurs like Murray Lender of Lender's Bagel Bakery and Mo Siegel of Celestial Seasonings Inc. "Both those guys taught me a lot," he says. "They had the right feedback systems. They were quick to act. It takes us too long to get things through management."
>
> To overcome that weakness, McGovern broke Campbell into some 50 independent business units–averaging $50 million in sales–and gave each a charter to develop its own products. Each business unit has its own general manager who, as effective chief executive officer, has under him a marketing director, controller, and product development staff.
>
> "McGovern lets the managers play on their own until he hears the glass break," observes one company insider. "Everyone goes out, comes up with ideas, and competes for resources. Each unit is run like an independent company except that McGovern plays the banker" (Kotkin, 1985).

The result of creating highly autonomous but functionally complete business groups has been more innovation:

> In 1984 alone, the company introduced 92 new products, bringing its five-year total to 334–far more than such larger competitors as Beatrice, Nestle, and General Foods. And although not all the new products have been clear successes (some, such as Pepperidge Farm's Star Wars cookies, were notable failures), others have reaped spectacular rewards. Two new products introduced in 1983, Prego Spaghetti Sauce and Le Menu Frozen Dinners, already contribute a combined $450 million a year to Campbell's coffers (Kotkin, 1985).

But companies need not provide structural autonomy to all units of the organization. IBM was successful in forwarding entrepreneurship by creating a single autonomous group in Boca Raton, Florida to develop the PC. Apple Computer did the same with its MacIntosh. Similarly, new units do not necessarily need to be created. Rather, the present structure can be left intact and temporary task forces or a parallel organization can be created (Kanter, 1985).

Although the Campbell Soup and IBM structural arrangements are different from the creation of task forces or parallel organizations in the degree of structural autonomy given to foster and facilitate entrepreneurship, they are similar in the fact they represent official action of top management to *systematically* create innovation. But as Kanter (1985) suggests:

> Innovation and new venture development may originate as a deliberate and official decision of the highest levels of management or they may be the more-or-less "spontaneous" creation of mid-level people who take the initiative to solve a problem in new ways or to develop a proposal for change. Of course, highly successful companies allow both, and even official top management decisions to undertake a development effort benefit from the spontaneous creativity of those below.

Representing a less systematic though not necessarily less successful effort to create innovation is 3M's informal doctrine of employees bootlegging 15% of their time to work on their own projects (Peters and Waterman, 1982). An even less systematic effort is to encourage all employees in the organization to look at their work in new ways, offer suggestions for new and improved ways or products, etc.

The point is that there are many structural arrangements that can be used to further the establishment of entrepreneurship. Moreover, these arrangements vary in the extent to which they foster and facilitate systematic innovation (entrepreneurship). As depicted in Exhibit 1, the more significant and complete the structural arrangement (and granting of autonomy), the more innovation is systematically advanced. While not necessarily always producing more of the new and different, it substantially increases the likelihood of this occurring. Innovation may occur under more modest structural arrangements, but it is apt to occur less frequently and at a less predictable rate. In other words, innovation under more modest structural arrangements is less systematic.

Thus, as the structural arrangements go from more modest to more significant and complete, innovation becomes more likely and represents a higher level of entrepreneurial activity. That is, more of the new and different results as structural arrangements go from modest to complete.

Use of an inappropriate structural arrangement for the extent of entrepreneurial activity required is apt to be unnecessary and inefficient. When Levi Strauss' 1984 profits dropped 74% from the preceding year, management knew that it had to get into the faster growing, more entrepreneurial (requiring more innovation) fashion clothes market. The company also knew that it had to view the fashion business much differently. Trouble began, however, with the structural arrangement Levi selected to accommodate its new entrepreneurial business:

> The company soon realized that it needed to view the fashion business differently. "We need to be like commandos, special forces, and SWAT teams, and that's

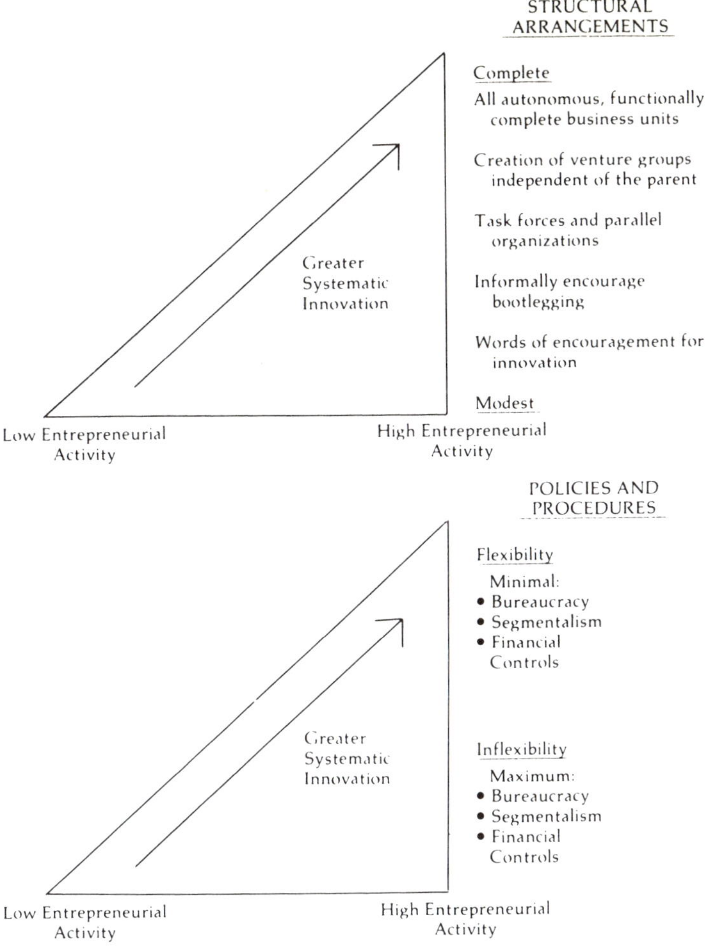

Exhibit 1. Structural practices to foster and facilitate entrepreneurship.

different from being the Third Army sweeping across Europe," says Leo Isotalo, who oversees all of Levi's business units.

The company partly blamed its plush campus for lulling managers and designers into complacency. So its new approach to fashion called for shuttling some top managers to the decrepit building, where the group devised marketing, merchandising, and distribution strategies for its fashion lines. Traces of the parent were erased from clothes tags and shipping cartons. "They didn't have to

> worry about thinking or looking like the division next door," explains Thomas Kasten, an executive vice-president.
>
> But Levi's strategy had faulty seams. The idea that an atmosphere of small cubicles and bare fluorescent light bulbs would stimulate creativity was just that—atmospherics. "They put the people in a dump and just scared them" says one observer. "You can't scare people into creativity."
>
> The company also failed to bring in fresh talent. Employees who understood the jeans market still had no feel for the fast-paced fashion world. And they were far from Manhattan, the nation's fashion capital. As a result, the unit's two lines have been troubled, one so badly that it was pulled off the market for a season (Hyatt, 1985).

In other words, Levi's structural arrangements were too modest. The businesses weren't really given sufficient autonomy and independence from the parent. However:

> The lessons haven't been lost on Levi. It recently reached outside to hire fashion designers. And its new unit is based in New York, with few employees drawn from Levi's ranks.

According to Drucker, something similar happened at General Electric:

> One is to believe that you can truly innovate within the existing operating unit. I myself made this mistake 30 years ago when I was a consultant on the first major organizational change in American industry, the General Electric reorganization of the early 1950s. I advised top management, and they accepted it, that the general managers would be responsible for current operations as well as for making tomorrow. At the same time, we worked out one of the first systematic compensation plans, and the whole idea of paying people on the basis of their performance in the preceding year came out of that.
>
> The result of it was that for ten years General Electric totally lost its capacity to innovate, simply because tomorrow produces costs for ten years and no return. So, the general manager—not only out of concern for himself, but also out of concern for his group—postponed spending any money for innovation. It was only when the company dropped this compensation plan and at the same time organized the search for the truly new, not just for improvement outside the existing business that

> G.E. recovered its innovative capacity, and brilliantly. Many companies go after the new and slight today and soon find they have neither (Rutigliano, 1986).

But as shown in Exhibit 1, more is needed to foster and facilitate entrepreneurship than new structural arrangements. Policies and procedures must also be considered, and more specifically, they must become more flexible if systematic innovation is to be realized.

Policy and Procedure Flexibility

More new and different entrepreneurial activity is fostered and facilitated by increased flexibility in a firm's policies and procedures. The policies and procedures particularly relevant to entrepreneurship are those with bureaucracy, segmentalism, and financial processes (Kanter, 1985; Drucker, 1985; Brandt, 1986).

Bureaucracy describes the preciseness and tightness of department arrangements, reporting practices, the chain of command, and rules and procedures as to who does things and how they are to be done. Systematic innovation is strengthened to the extent that the bureaucracy is minimized. Less precise and looser departmental boundaries facilitate the flow of information and ideas so critical to forming new combinations. Less necessity to adhere to the chain of command also facilitates interaction and knowledge exchange. And, less reliance on rules and procedures recognizes the dynamics of knowledge-intense activities so characteristic of innovation.

Closely associated with increasing flexibility by reducing bureaucracy, is reducing segmentalism. Reducing segmentalism and increasing integration across groups, teams, departments, and divisions fosters and facilitates idea, information, and product exchanges (Kanter, 1983a, b; 1985). Reduction of segmentalism occurs as a matter of both top management support and company culture reflecting teamwork and cooperation. It is facilitated by alternations in structural rearrangements from more modest to complete.

Financial processes also need to become more flexible if systematic innovation is to be fostered and facilitated:

> Following the lead of 3M, and now several other major organizations such as Eastman Kodak, an increasing number of companies are setting up special "innovation banks" to fund new ventures or innovations outside of operating budgets. This not only permits a large new venture to be supported inside the company as a separate business, but it also permits many small development activities to be undertaken that would otherwise find no place in a line manager's budget (with its usual

> requirement for immediate profitability). Efforts that are more experimental, or may take more time to bring returns, or do not fit neatly within existing areas, can still find a home. This is useful not only for those innovations in products or technology that might normally fall within the scope of an R&D operation, but also for numerous other special projects in marketing or information systems or personnel or dealer relations that can themselves net considerable payoffs. A large computer manufacturer has funded innovative organizational improvement projects out of a corporate innovation council (Kanter, 1985).

Other forms of flexibility include allocating portions of budgets to uncommitted projects or uses. This budget slack, provided either with direct funds or employee time, facilitates employee innovation and entrepreneurship. Another form of increased financial flexibility is top management sponsoring as many small and diverse entrepreneurial projects as possible rather than just a few big ones.

In spite of all the structural practices in place for innovation and entrepreneurship, success is not guaranteed even though the cost of implementing these practices could be enormous. In fact, according to Drucker, a big mistake

> . . . is believing that money can be used in lieu of good people. It's very common when it comes to the question of how do you staff, that people will say, "We can't spare Joe for the new. What he's doing is so important, we can't take him off it." The result is that companies staff with people they can spare. And whenever I hear, "All we can spare is Joe," I say, "You are staffing by proven incompetence." Unfortunately, that is the most common staffing principle. Organizations then try to make up for this by giving new money. That is the quickest way to kill something—the combination of poor people and generous budget. It's a guarantee of failure. It is the biggest mistake of all large organizations from the Pentagon on down (Rutigliano, 1986).

Thus, there is a charge to attend to staffing issues in fostering and facilitating entrepreneurship. But as is becoming more apparent than ever, when it comes to managing people, one human resource practice such as staffing cannot be examined in isolation. Human resource management practices have to be executed in an integrated fashion in order to systematically stimulate and reinforce needed characteristics and behaviors from employees. Not systematically approaching and designing human resource management practices to fit what the organization needs from its employees is likely to result in ineffective employee behavior (Schuler, 1987). Accordingly, it is useful to examine human resource management practices and determine the ones required to further entrepreneurship.

HUMAN RESOURCE MANAGEMENT PRACTICES FOR ENTREPRENEURSHIP

Human resource management practices in any organization articulate its true culture (Lawler, 1984; Fombrun et al., 1984). The extent to which a company is concerned for the development of its people is reflected in the amount of money it spends on training and development and the extensiveness of its socialization process. Thus, while stating a culture of concern for employees is important to foster and facilitate entrepreneurship, there must be support from human resource practices consistent with that particular culture and consistent with what's needed from the employees. Key is determining what's needed from employees to be effective at entrepreneurship. Once this is determined, the specific HRM practices that organizations need to utilize to achieve entrepreneurship can be described.

To be effective, organizations need their employees to express particular characteristics. These are essentially general behaviors and attitudes, ways of doing and thinking about things. They are at a level more general than the specific skills, knowledge, and abilities required to perform specific jobs (Schneider, 1985). General employee characteristics that have been identified as important in strategy execution are shown in Exhibit 2.

What determines these characteristics is the strategy or general thrust being pursued by the organization (Gerstein and Reisman, 1983). Different strategies require different employee characteristics. As described by Kanter (1985), what's required from employees in firms striving to be entrepreneurial is quite different from what firms require when pursuing a nonentrepreneurial posture. This results from the inherent needs and qualities that are at the root of these strategies. As indicated earlier, the essence of effective performance under the entrepreneurial strategy is based on employees' ability to manage uncertainty, knowledge-intensity, competition with alternatives, and boundary-crossing.

In Exhibit 2, employee characteristics critical for strategy execution are depicted using descriptions of behavior at either end of a continuum. Consequently, organizations can choose to foster and facilitate highly creative, innovative behavior or highly repetitive, predictable behavior. This is true for all the employee characteristics shown in Exhibit 2; however, not all characteristics are equally relevant in executing of all strategies (Schuler et al., 1985). The characteristics most relevant in the successful execution of an entrepre-

	GENERAL EMPLOYEE CHARACTERISTICS FOR STRATEGY EXECUTION		
1.	Highly Repetitive, Predicatable Behavior	________	Highly Creative Innovative Behavior
2.	Very Short Term Focus	________	Very Long Term Focus
3.	Highly Cooperative, Interdependent Behavior	________	Highly Independent Automonous Behavior
4.	Very Low Concern for Quality	________	Very High Concern for Quality
5.	Very Low Concern for Quantity	________	Very High Concern for Quantity
6.	Very Low Risk Taking	________	Very High Risk Taking
7.	Very High Concern for Process	________	Very High Concern for Results
8.	High Preference to Avoid Responsibility	________	High Preference to Assume Responsibility
9.	Very inflelxible to Change	________	Very Flexible to Change
10.	Very Comfortable with Stability	________	Very Tolerant of Ambiguity and Unpredictability
11.	Very Low Task Orientation	________	Very High Task Orientation
12.	Very Low Organizational	________	Very High Organizational Identification
13.	Primary Focus on Efficiency	________	Primary Focus on Effectiveness

Exhibit 2

neurial strategy have been identified and described in some detail, [e.g., Brandt (1986); Kanter (1985); Drucker (1985); Pinchot (1984); Brocknaus (1980); Hornaday and Aboud (1971); Miller (1983); Burgelman (1983); Roberts (1980); Peterson (1981); and Maidique (1980)]. These characteristics include:

- Creative, innovative behavior
- Long term focus
- Cooperative, interdependent behavior
- Risk taking
- High concern for results
- Preference to assume responsibility
- Flexibility to change
- Tolerance of ambiguity
- Task orientation
- Focus on effectiveness

Just as the level of entrepreneurial activity varies, so do the needed levels of these characteristics for entrepreneurial strategy execution.

The greater the level of entrepreneurial activity, i.e., the more of the new and different that is desired, the more that extreme levels of the above characteristics are needed. With the entrepreneurial strategy, the thrust is idea creation, innovation, and new product development. In firms that are noted for their innovation and new product development, such as 3M and Hewlett-Packard, these comprise the mandatory employee characteristics (Drucker, 1985; Peters and Waterman, 1982; Kanter, 1985; Mortiz, 1984).

Accordingly, to increase the likelihood of systematic innovation, thereby fostering and facilitating entrepreneurship, organizations need to stimulate and reinforce these characteristics via human resource management practices. These are the primary employee characteristics. Based upon them, the HRM practices needed to nurture entrepreneurship can be described and their rationale explained (Schuler, 1987).

Human Resource Management Practice Choices

Central to the notion that human resource management practices can systematically foster and facilitate an organization's strategy are: a) the existence of a menu of choices for each practice, and b) the ability of different choices to stimulate and reinforce different employee characteristics (Schuler, 1987; Schuler et al. 1985).

The menu of choices for the HR practices of planning (including strategic planning and job analysis), staffing, appraising, compensating, and training and development are shown in Exhibit 3. The choices to be selected for promoting entrepreneurship and an entrepreneurial strategy are many. A description of the choices to be made in each practice will illustrate this.

Planning. Entrepreneurial strategy is fostered and facilitated to the extent that planning practices are formal, long term, tight, implicit, broad, integrative, and encourage high employee participation. These planning practices stimulate innovation, willingness to work well and cooperate with others, and get employees to assume responsibility (Angle et al. 1985; Burgelman, 1983; Kanter 1983b; Milkovich et al., 1983; Schuler, 1984). Additionally, calculated risk taking may be facilitated through the use of more broadly written job descriptions that focus more on results than process. Unstructured tasks not easily bound by rigid policies necessitate that employees work by general job descriptions. Objectives and milestone accomplishments (results criteria) should serve as the content of job descriptions. Results criteria as a basis for job analysis force employees to work toward implementing ideas and systems. Oftentimes, their work is unprecedented. In such cases, the establishment of process-centered guidelines is not practical where refinements realized through experience have not yet happened.

HUMAN RESOURCE MANAGEMENT
PRACTICE MENUS

Planning Choices

Informal------------------Formal
Loose------------------Tight
Short term------------------Long term
Explicit Analysis------------------Implicit Analysis
Narrow Jobs------------------Broad Jobs
Segmental Design------------------Integrative Design
Low Employee Involvement------------------High Employee Involvement

Staffing Choices

Internal Sources------------------External Sources
Narrow Paths------------------Broad Paths
Single Ladder------------------Multiple Ladders
Explicit Criteria------------------Implicit Criteria
Limited Socialization------------------Extensive Socialization
Closed Procedures------------------Open Procedures

Appraising Choices

Loose, Incomplete Integration------------------Tight, Complete Integration
Behavioral Criteria------------------Results Criteria
Purposes: Development Remedial Maintenance
Low Employee Participation------------------High Employee Participation
Short-term Criteria------------------Long-Term Criteria
Individual Criteria------------------Group Criteria

Compensating Choices

Los Base Salaries------------------High Base Salaries
Internal Equity------------------External Equity
Few Perks------------------Many Perks
Standard, Fixed Package------------------Flexible Package
Low Participation------------------High Participation
No Incentives------------------Many Incentives
Short-term Incentives------------------Long-term Incentives
No Employment Security------------------High Employment Security
Hierarchical------------------Egalitarian

Training and Development

Short Term------------------Long Term
Narrow Application------------------Broad Application
Spontaneous, Unplanned, Unsystematic---------------Planned, Systematic
Individual Orientation------------------Group Orientation
Low Participation------------------High Participation
Extensive Organizational Structure------------------Minimal Organizational Structure

Adapted from R.S. Schuler, Human resource management practice choices. In R.S. Schuler and S.A. Youngblood (Eds.), Readings in personnel and human resource management, 3e. St. Paul: West Publishing, 1987.

Exhibit 3

Organizations also need to engage in more formal long range human resource planning. A result of more formal planning is Hewlett-Packard's willingness and ability to state and support its human resource policy of "not to be a hire and fire company" (Peters and Waterman, 1982). An advantage of this type of formalized planning is that it enables a company to provide employees employment security, a facet of human resource management critical for stimulating a long term orientation and moderate risk taking behavior (Peters and Waterman, 1982; Dyer and Heyer, 1984).

Staffing. Entrepreneurial strategy is fostered and facilitated to the extent that staffing practices offer individuals broad paths and multiple ladders, have implicit criteria and open procedures, use external sources, and allow extensive socialization. These staffing practices stimulate employee innovation, cooperation, and longer term focus in the organization (Burgelman, 1983; Cummings, 1984; London and Stumpf, 1982; Maidique and Hayes, 1984; Peters and Waterman, 1982).

An entrepreneurial strategy also requires that employees be flexible and tolerant of ambiguity. Tolerating uncertainty means feeling comfortable with change and unpredictable situations. It implies being adaptable.

Consequently, organizations recruit and select individuals most likely to tolerate ambiguity. Organizations also engage in open staffing procedures to enable individuals to select themselves into more entrepreneurial positions. Individuals cannot simply be selected to manage and lead an organization's venture activity based on previous performance in any functional area, or because there simply is no other person readily available with the requisite skills and knowledge. Peters stresses that an entrepreneur "... cannot be 'assigned' or 'appointed'. He must possess the characteristics of an entrepreneur, be a doer – not a thinker or talker – have a clear vision of what he wants to 'create' and volunteer ..." (de Chambeau and Shays, 1984).

Note that these staffing practices, in part, are the same characteristics stimulated by the planning practices. Essential here is that there be a consistency attained across HRM practices within a strategy type. A consequence of this is that different HRM practices unavoidably stimulate some of the same characteristics. Similarly, different practices stimulate the opposite characteristics. Therefore, these HRM menu choices need to be made cautiously and systematically.

Appraising. Entrepreneurial strategy is fostered and facilitated to the extent that appraising practices emphasize results criteria, use longer-term criteria, encourage high employee participation, and recognize the accomplishments of groups of individuals. These appraising practices stimulate risk taking, a willingness to assume responsibility, and a longer term orientation (Carroll and Schneier, 1982; Cummings, 1984; George and MacMillan, 1984; Giles and

Landauer, 1984; Kanter, 1983a; Roberts and Fusfeld, 1981; Timmons, 1979). At 3M, division managers are appraised on their division's contribution to total profits, not on the merits of individual plans and the processes employed to achieve them (*Business Week*, 1984a). Creating more functionally complete and independent business units also provides the opportunity for managers to assume more responsibility.

The 3M example indicates that while division results serve as the basis of appraising, each division is comprised of functional specialists who have contributed to the division's overall performance. Oftentimes, it is impossible to separate and quantify particular individual contributions. Essentially, an overall contribution cannot easily be divided up into the contributions of each individual. As a consequence, group level performance criteria are appropriate.

Group level criteria as a basis for performance appraisal and compensation are instrumental in creating synergies of corporate entrepreneurs such as are practiced within TRW's venture groups. These HRM practices set the stage for Kanter's proverbial right places: "The right places are the integrative environments that support innovation, encourage the building of coalitions and teams to support and implement visions" (Kanter, 1983a).

Consistent with the idea of performance appraisal based on results, it is useful that a significant portion of compensation be a function of results. Yet, there needs to be an acceptable amount of failure allowed to achieve results. Here there are two major considerations. First, as Frank de Chambeau and E. Michael Shays (1984) believe, "Mistakes, even one big one, are not necessarily reason to cancel a project or dismiss an intrapreneur (corporate entrepreneur). People in new situations make mistakes. The question is whether they learn from them. If they do, they're more valuable to the firm." Second, inherently risky factors generally make it impossible for the entrepreneur to have total control of outcomes. In a report on senior management responsibilities in corporate venturing, Rain Hill Group's Robin George and New York University's Ian MacMillan (1984), imply that results criteria facilitate entrepreneurship since they prompt managers to focus on the distinction ". . . between a situation where the venturer made a poor decision and a situation where the venturer made a good decision with all the limited information available at the time of the decision, but the outcome was poor because the 'ball bounced the wrong way'."

Many of the fruits of entrepreneurial effort may not ripen in the short term (i.e., less than 12 months). A performance appraisal policy based on a predetermined, fixed interval may not be effective. A long-term appraisal policy tailored to the particular situation may be appropriate. For example, with regard to Cheesebrough-Ponds' "Polishing Pen," the results of its entrepreneurial efforts were not expected to be realized until the end of 1985 even though the project began in 1983 (*Business Week*, 1984b).

Compensating. Entrepreneurial strategy is fostered and facilitated to the extent that compensating practices emphasize external equity, are flexible, contain many long-term incentives, encourage high employee participation, offer some employment security, and are administered in a more egalitarian fashion. These compensation practices reinforce the appraising practices quite nicely. Accordingly, they shoud stimulate and reinforce risk taking, or willingness to assume responsibility and a longer term orientation (Bentson and Schuster, 1983; Hutton, 1985; Lawler, 1984).

Related to a sense of responsibility is the enjoyment of significant rewards resulting from high performance. Jeffrey Timmons, professor of entrepreneurial studies at Babson College, indicates that many corporate entrepreneurs are given profit and loss responsibility for their ventures. To further foster and facilitate a sense of responsibility, companies can provide many compensation benefits such as stock option plans, perquisites, and bonus plans that strengthen commitment to entrepreneurship. In a recent study, McKinsey and Company has found that, "In addition to such extensive stock ownership, financial motivation in the winner companies is stimulated by tying incentives to company performance" (Albertine and Levitt, 1983).

Consistent with a significant period before results may be realized, organizations need to establish long-term financial arrangements to compensate entrepreneurial employees. Employee stock ownership plans and profit sharing plans ensure that employees will be compensated in accordance with the performance of the product or service over its life. Entrepreneurship is also fostered and facilitated by providing choices in compensation. Accordingly, companies need to have flexibility and employee participation in their compensation practices.

Training and Development. Entrepreneurial strategy is advanced to the extent that training and development practices are characterized by broad applications, emphasize quality of work life, encourage high employee participation, and rely upon minimal organizational structure. These training and development practices should stimulate a willingness to assume responsibility, be innovative, promote a willingness to work with others, and be flexible. These practices also help retain key employees (Beer, 1981; Madique and Hayes, 1984; de Chambeau and Shays, 1984).

Training programs that enable individuals to keep up with changing technologies and job demands help keep people flexible and willing to tolerate changes. This is aided greatly by some degree of employment security. Thus, individuals who tolerate uncertainty can be brought into the organization and helped to stay. Meanwhile those currently in the organization can be made to feel more comfortable with change and ambiguity.

The entrepreneurial process is an ever changing one requiring continuous data gathering and rapid decision making. Policies and procedures specifying action plans for entrepreneurial conditions cannot be prescribed in advance; to do so would only hinder a correct response. Similarly, requiring several levels of management approval would only hinder a timely response. Consequently, human resource practices fostering spontaneity include more implicit and loosely written job descriptions, a more results oriented performance appraisal system, and some employment security. Structurally, the organization should reflect minimal levels of management and approval. In order to enhance progress at Unimation, Westinghouse has slashed the number of management layers that direct operations. It has discarded rules requiring approval by corporate committees for many major expenditures. "If we need to buy something, we can just go and do it," states Ira Pence, Unimation's research director. As a result, Unimation scientists recently purchased software only a few weeks after the need was realized. Normally, it would have taken a year to receive approval (Levin, 1984).

A summary of all these human resource management practice menu selections to foster and facilitate entrepreneurship, are shown in Exhibit 4.

SUMMARY AND IMPLICATIONS

This discussion of HRM practices and structural practices that foster and facilitate entrepreneurship suggests that entrepreneurship is becoming a more dominant force in society, comprising a significant slice of all business activity (Kanter, 1983a,b). We have seen it thrive outside existing organizational structures, yet many major corporations have initiated action to keep entrepreneurial activity within the organization for two major reasons: 1) To maintain a strong foothold in order to remain competitive; 2) To enhance organizational profitability, survival, growth, and competitiveness by extending use of existing product lines, diversifying into markets and lines of business in which its efforts are not currently directed, and being pioneers in the development of needed products and services for which no markets previously existed (Pinchot, 1984). The question for corporations then is not whether they should or should not engage in entrepreneurial activity, but rather what can be done to encourage establishment of entrepreneurship.

In addressing the question of what structural practices can be used to foster and facilitate entrepreneurship, it was suggested that organizations need to first consider the desired level of entrepreneurial

HUMAN RESOURCE MANAGEMENT PRACTICES
TO FOSTER AND FACILITATE ENTREPRENEURSHIP

PLANNING

Formal
Tight
Long-term
Implicit
Integrative
High Involvement

STAFFING

External Sources
Broad Paths
Multiple Ladders
Implicit Criteria
Extensive Socialization
Open Procedures

APPRAISING

Results Criteria
High Participation
Long-term Criteria
Group/Individual Determined Criteria

COMPENSATING

External Equity
Flexible Benefits Package
Many Incentives
Some Employment Security
Highly Egalitarian

TRAINING & DEVELOPMENT

Broad Application
Quality of Work Life Emphasis
Group Orientation
High Participation
Minimal Organizational Structure

Exhibit 4

activity. That is, organizations need to determine exactly how much of the new and different is desired or necessary. The more that is desired, the more organizations need to choose structural practices that are more complete and policies and procedures that are highly flexible.

In addressing the question of what HRM practices can be systematically used to further entrepreneurship, several suggestions relevant to each HRM function and activity were suggested. Implied by these suggestions may be the thought that there is a "one best set of structural and HRM practices for entrepreneurship." To the contrary, there are likely to be several different sets of HRM practices for entrepreneurship with the appropriateness of each set dependent upon the level of entrepreneurial activity or the stage of the activity. This is the same with the structural practices. Nevertheless, while these different sets of practices may vary somewhat, they are likely to be rather similar since the requisite employee characteristics for any level or stage of entrepreneurial activity is likely to vary in degree but not in kind (Burgelman, 1983). Consequently, if corporations have several entrepreneurial groups going on simultaneously but in different levels and states of activity, there are likely to be several sets of HRM practices fostering and facilitating entrepreneurship. Companies such as GE, Equitable Life Assurance Society, and

Manufacturer's Hanover Trust, with many satelite venture groups have already begun to experience this.

The existence of concomitant sets of HRM practices is also expected to occur in corporations with just one venture or entrepreneurial group. This is because the behaviors and attitudes of employees in the parent organization are likely to be more nonentrepreneurial than those in the venture group. As a result, companies wanting to foster and facilitate just one entrepreneurial group will end up utilizing at least two sets of HRM practices, challenging the HR practitioner with designing, implementing, and managing both. Because of the existence of two or more sets of HRM practices, the HR practitioner will have to manage the likely perceptions of inequity that typically arise when two different sets of practices are employed. As at Manufacturer's Hanover Trust, the personnel group has to work that much harder to explain to employees the differences in practices. A change in their perceptions may not be immediate, but implementing dual practices will convey that the HRM department understands the situation.

The HR practitioner is also likely to face a much larger challenge in the near future. As Kanter suggests, ". . . sooner or later all U.S. corporations will be forced to develop innovative entrepreneurial structures in order to survive." If interpreted to mean that all corporations as a whole will have to become more entrepreneurial, human resource practitioners will have to begin changing the HRM practices of their parent organizations in the direction of the entrepreneurial groups' needs. Conceived as such, practitioners are in for a future in which HRM practices are constantly being altered and fine tuned to simultaneously stimulate and reinforce a variety of employee behaviors and attitudes, especially those necessary for some degree of entrepreneurship. Without a willingness and ability to do this, the very survival, not to mention profitability and competitiveness, of corporations is at stake.

Dr. Randall S. Schuler is Visiting Associate Professor at The University of Michigan Business School on leave from the Graduate School of Business, New York University. Dr. Schuler's interests are stress management, organizational uncertainty, personnel and human resource management, entrepreneurship, and the interface of business strategy and human resource management. He has authored and edited a dozen books including Personnel and Human Resource Management *2e.,* Case Problems in Management *3e.,* Effective Personnel Management, Book of Readings in Personnel and Human Resource Management *2e.,* Human Resources Management in the 1980s, *and* Managing Job Stress. *In addition, he has contributed fourteen chapters to reading books and has published over seventy articles in professional journals and academic proceedings. Currently, he is serving on the Board of the Eastern Academy of Management and is on the editorial board of* Academy of Management Executive, Human Resource Management, Journal of Management, Group Organizational Studies, *and is the new editor of* Human Resource Planning.

REFERENCES

"3M's Aggressive New Consumer Drive," *Business Week,* July 16, 1984a, pp. 114, 116, 118, 122.

"How Cheesebrough-Ponds Put Nail Polish in a Pen," *Business Week,* October 8, 1984b, pp. 196, 200.

Albertine, J. and Levitt Jr., A. "The Successful Entrepreneur: A Personality Profile," *The Wall Street Journal,* August 29, 1983, p. 12.

Angle, H. L., Manz, C. C., and Van de Ven, A. H. Integrating human resource management and corporate strategy: A preview of the 3M story. *Human Resource Management Journal,* Spring 1985, 51-68.

Beer, M. Performance Appraisal: Dilemmas and Possibilities, *Organizational Dynamics,* Winter 1981, 25-33.

Bentson, M. A., and Schuster, J. R. Executive compensation and employee benefits, In S. J. Carroll and R. S. Schuler (Eds.), *Human resources management in the 1980s.* Washington, D.C.: The Bureau of National Affairs, 1983, pp. 6-1-6-31.

Block, Z. Concepts for corporate entrepreneurs, *The Texas A&M Business Forum,* January 1985.

Brockhaus, R. H. Risk taking propensity of entrepreneurs, *Academy of Management,* September 1980, 509-520.

Brandt, S. C. *Entrepreneuring in established companies.* Homewood, IL: Dow Jones-Irwin, 1986.

Burgelman, R. A. Corporate entrepreneurship and strategic management: Insights from a process study, *Management Science,* December 1983, 1349-1364.

Carroll, Jr., S. J., and Schneier, C. E. *Performance appraisal and review systems.* Glenview, IL.: Scott, Foresman and Company, 1982.

Cummings, L. L. Compensation, culture, and motivation: A systems perspective, *Organizational Dynamics,* Winter 1984, 33-43.

de Chambeau, F., and Shays, E. M. Harnessing entrepreneurial energy within the corporation, *Management Review,* September 1984, 17-20.

Drucker, P. F. *Innovation and entrepreneurship.* New York: Harper & Row, 1985.

Dyer, L., and Heyer, N. D. Human resource planning at IBM, *Human Resource Planning,* VII(3), 1984.

Fast, N. D. The future of industrial new venture departments. *Industrial Marketing Management,* November 1976, 264-273.

Feinberg, A. Inside the entrepreneur, *Venture,* May 1984, 86, 80-83.

Fombrun, C., Tichy, N. M., and Devanna, M. A. *Strategic human resource management.* New York: John Wiley & Sons, 1984.

George, R. and MacMillan, I. C. Corporate Venturing/Senior Management Responsibilities, (working paper, Center for Entrepreneurial Studies, New York University, 1984).

Gerstein, M., and Reisman, H. Strategic selection: Matching executives to business conditions. *Sloan Management Review,* Winter 1983, 33–49.
Giles, R., and Landauer, C. Setting specific standards for appraising creative staffs. *Personnel Administrator,* 1984, **29,** 35–47.
Greenwald, J. Earning more than equity. *Venture,* September 1983, 60, 62.
Hornaday, J. A., and Aboud, J. Characteristics of successful entrepreneurs. *Personnel Psychology,* Summer 1971, 141-153.
Hutton, T. J. Recruiting the entrepreneurial executive. *Personnel Administrator,* January 1985, 35-36, 38, 40–41.
Hyatt, J. Levi Strauss learns a fitting lesson. *Inc.,* August 1975, 17.
Kanter, R. M. Supporting innovation and venture development in established companies. *Journal of Business Venturing,* Winter 1985, 47-60.
Kanter, R. M. Change masters and the intricate architecture of corporate culture change. *Management Review,* October 1983a, 18–28.
Kanter, R. M. Superstars and lone rangers rescue dull enterprises. *The Wall Street Journal,* January 23, 1984, 22.
Kanter, R. M. *The change masters.* New York: Simon and Schuster, 1983b.
Kotkin, J. The revenge of the Fortune 500. *Inc.,* August 1985. 39-44.
Lawler III, E. E. The strategic design of reward systems. In R. S. Schuler and S. A. Youngblood (Eds.), *Readings in personnel and human resource management.* 2nd edition, St. Paul: West Publishing, 1984, 253-269.
Levin, D. P. Westinghouse move into robotics shows pitfalls of high-tech field. *The Wall Street Journal,* May 14, 1984, 29.
London, M., and Stumpf, S. A. *Managing careers.* Reading, MA: Addison-Wesley Publishing Company, 1982.
Maidique, M. A. Entrepreneurs, champions, and technological innovation. *Sloan Management Review,* Winter 1980, 559-576.
Maidique, M. A., and Hayes, R. H. The art of high-technology management. *Sloan Management Review,* Winter 1984, 17-31.
Milkovich, G. T., Dyer, L., and Mahoney, T. A. HRM planning. In S. J. Carroll and R. S. Schuler (Eds.), *Human resources management in the 1980's.* Washington, D.C.: The Bureau of National Affairs, 1983, pp. 2-1–2-28.
Miller, D. The correlates of entrepreneurship in three types of firms. *Management Science,* July 1983, 770–790.
Moritz, M. *The little kingdom.* New York: William Morrow and Company, Inc., 1984
Peters, T. A., and Waterman, Jr., R. H. *In search of excellence.* New York: Warner Books, 1982.
Peterson, R. A. Entrepreneurship and organization. In P. Nystrom and W. Starbuck (Eds.), *Handbook of organizational design.* New York: Oxford University Press, 1981, 65–83.
Pinchot III, G. Intrapreneurship: How to top corporate creative energies. *The Mainstream,* 1984, **I**(2).
Quinn, J. B. Technological innovation, entrepreneurship, and strategy. *Sloan Management Review,* Spring 1979, 20–30.
Roberts, E. B. New ventures for corporate growth. *Harvard Business Review,* July-August 1980, 134-142.
Roberts, E. B., and Fusfeld, A. R. Staffing the innovative technology-based organization. *Sloan Management Review,* Spring 1981, 19-34.
Rutigliano, A. J. Managing the new: An interview with Peter Drucker. *Management Review,* January 1986, 38–41.
Schneider, B. Organizational behavior. *Annual Review of Psychology,* 1985, **36,** 573-611.

Schuler, R. S. *Personnel and human resource management,* 2nd edition. St. Paul: West Publishing, 1984.

Schuler, R. S. Human resource management practice choices. In R. S. Schuler and S. A. Youngblood (Eds.), *Readings in personnel and human resource management,* 3rd edition. St. Paul: West Publishing, 1987.

Schuler, R. S., MacMillan, I. C., and Martocchio, J. J. Key strategic questions for human resource management. In W. D. Guth (Ed.), *Handbook of business strategy 1985/1986 yearbook.* Boston: Warren, Gorham and Lamont, 1985.

Timmons, J. A. Careful self-analysis and team assessment can aid entrepreneurs. *Harvard Business Review,* November/December 1979, 198–200, 202, 206.

International Journal of Innovation Management
Vol. 4, No. 3 (September 2000) pp. 347–369

THE MANAGEMENT OF INNOVATION PROBLEM

JOHN STOREY
The Open University Business School,
The Open University, Walton Hall,
Milton Keynes, MK6 7AA,
United Kingdom

Received 1 February 2000
Revised 10 April 2000
Accepted 17 April 2000

The vital importance of innovation in today's competitive climate has been widely canvassed. But while the *need* for more innovation is intensively proclaimed, the response for some time now has been widely regarded as falling well short of what is required. In other words, there is and has long been a perceived "innovation problem" in the UK and of course in many other countries. There is a large literature exploring the barriers to innovation and this has identified a whole array of factors ranging from the macro-level (such as a tendency towards short-termism) to the micro-level (including personality traits and team characteristics). This article reports the results from a new extensive study which addresses the "problem" by attending to the perceptions, assumptions, interpretations and cognitions of managers — i.e. those actors who determine organisational priorities and who make crucial resource allocation decisions. These managerial ways of seeing have vital consequences for organisational innovation. This article reports on the marked variety of managerial interpretations of innovation; it presents new ways of classifying these and it describes the practical implications of these insights.

Keywords: innovation, management, problems

Introduction

"Innovate or die" is one of the mantras of today's economy. It is widely proclaimed by governments, economists, consultants, business spokespersons and academics. The message has been pressed in varying degrees for over a century at least but, in the context of the new "knowledge economy", it has perhaps rarely been urged so insistently as now. The UK government, for example, in its *Competitiveness White Paper* constructed its analysis around the concept of an economy based on knowledge, intellectual capital and the need for innovation (DTI, 1998). The idea has international currency and a statement by Tushman typifies the mood: "In today's business environment, there is no executive task more vital and demanding than the sustained management of innovation and change... to compete in the new environment, companies must create new products, services and processes... they must adopt innovation as a way of corporate life" (Tushman & Nadler, 1986:74). Such statements — especially when supported by official bodies, tend to create a climate of concern about the "problem" of innovation.

And yet, despite this (or perhaps because of this in the sense of adverse comparison between action and rhetoric), the actual response appears to be lacklustre and insufficient — particularly so in the UK where the DTI's innovation index based on R&D investment reveals poor participation by UK firms. Firms are more than happy to use the concept of innovation in their advertising and corporate PR, but sustained behaviour in practice seems to present managers with a difficulty. On the face of it, at least, there seems to be a mismatch between exhortation and action. To put this another way, there is apparently a fundamental "problem" with the management of innovation.

This gap between proclamation and practice deserves some exploration. The problem of innovation is of long-standing and the sources of the problem have been investigated at many levels and from diverse perspectives. For example, at the macro-level, issues of financing and short-termism have been highlighted; some have focused on organisational structures and cultures, while others have addressed issues of team dynamics and individual personality traits. The innovation problem would seem to be deep-seated and enduring. This suggests that it is not likely to be amenable to superficial remedies today any more so than it has been in the past.

Some observers have even suggested that there is a problem with the overall body of research on innovation management. For example, Tidd (1997:1) notes that it is "highly fragmented... much of the research has been conducted within three separate disciplines with relatively little overlap or interaction". Other reviews of the literature have come to a not dissimilar conclusion (Dougherty, 1996; Wolfe, 1994). For example, Wolfe (1994:405) observes that, "Our understanding of innovative behaviour in organisations remains relatively underdeveloped". The results of organisational innovation research, he suggests, have been "inconclusive, inconsistent and characterised by low levels of explanation". Two natural responses to this state of affairs have occurred: the first is to seek a new integrative framework and the second is to intensify the search for the critical variable or combination of variables which might better explain how innovation can be managed to the most effect.

While not denying the worth of either of these suggestions, nor in any way denying the value of much of the previous other modes of work to date, this article reports on a research project which took a rather different approach. Instead of searching for another key "variable" or seeking a new conceptual framework, we set out to examine the issue of innovation management by viewing it through the eyes of the participants most critical to the process — i.e. managers themselves, the people who establish priorities, devise strategies, allocate or withhold resources, control rewards and manage performance. Managers often declare publicly that their organisations "ought" to innovate and even that they want to innovate, and yet despite this, they too recognise a shortfall in actual performance.

The aim of the article is draw upon managers' accounts in order to gain a richer insight into the sources of the apparent problem with innovation. In particular, the aim is to examine how managers themselves understand the meaning and priority of innovation, and the ways in which they explain the factors which facilitate or conversely inhibit innovation. Such an approach is of course not entirely new, other studies have pioneered the way (for example, Bandura, 1986; Coopey *et al.*, 1997; Dougherty, 1992; Lefebvre *et al.*, 1997; Watson, 1994; Weick, 1979a; Weick, 1979b; Weick, 1995). But the systematic application of this approach to the understanding of the barriers to innovation remains relatively undeveloped.

The article is organised into three sections. The first section draws on the existing literature in order to identify what, and how much, is currently known about the problem of the management of innovation. The second section reports on a recent study of over 300 managers in order to explore what can be revealed through paying careful attention to the insights of these key players, and the third section analyses the implications of the findings.

The Management of Innovation Problem

Innovation in context

The very meaning of the term "innovation" has been contentious and problematical. It is often used loosely and interchangeably with terms such as creativity, invention and change. This in fact is the first problem. The concept is often deployed with such imprecision and variation that it can seem to mean almost anything. However, some commentators have wanted at least to distinguish between "invention" and "innovation". The Department of Trade and Industry (DTI) has defined innovation as "the successful exploitation of new ideas". In a similar vein, some seek to restrict its meaning to instances where firms have been "first to commercialise a new product or process in the market" (Teece, 1987:185). Others are content to include instances where the product or process is new to the "system" in which it is introduced. Whichever relative degree of novelty is involved, such an activity requires a whole series of management processes ranging from environmental scanning, an understanding of threats and opportunities, an assessment of internal capabilities, the acquisition and mobilisation of resources and capabilities, and the deployment and management of those resources and capabilities in pursuit of the chosen end. In sum, part of the literature recognises that innovation is closely intertwined with business strategy (Ettlie, 1984; Markides, 1997; Quinn, 1979; Saren, 1987; Starkey & McKinlay, 1988).

Given the vast literature on the subject of innovation, one might imagine that the explanation of the persisting problem of achieving it would come easily to hand. As we noted above, innovation has been tackled from various perspectives, at various levels and with various units of analysis in mind — ranging from the individual to "national innovation systems" and at multiple levels in between. Prescriptions exist for enhancing individual creativity (Farr, 1990), forming innovative groups and teams (Anderson *et al.*, 1992; Katz, 1994), promoting organisational innovation (Rosenfeld & Servo, 1990), and using inter-firm partnerships, alliances and networks for innovation (Hargaon & Sutton, 1997; Quinn, 1992). But, despite this degree of attention, "organisations continue to have problems innovating effectively" (Dougherty, 1996). It has been noted that "what the literature prescribes and what most firms do are miles apart" (Cooper & Kleinschmidt, 1986:73). One possible source of this gap, we suggest, can be traced to, and revealed by, the way key actors — i.e. managers — see and interpret the issue. Thus, we suggest it will be fruitful to pay close attention to managers' own perceptions of the nature and meaning of the innovation process.

Managers and innovation

The crucial importance of managers' perceptions and (literally) "sense-making" with regard to innovation has been noted by a number of researchers (Kim, 1997; Lefebvre *et al.*, 1997; Rickards, 1999; Sutcliffe & Huber 1998; Weick, 1995). There is a close association between the issue of managerial perspectives on and understanding of innovation and that segment of the strategy literature which deals with the problem of "strategic persistence" in mature firms (Lant & Milliken, 1992). Persistence with a known strategy has been recognised as a function of managerial interpretations (Milliken & Lant, 1991). This strand of the strategy literature could in turn be seen as associated with the literature on organisational learning (Senge, 1990).

A crucial point which emerged from our research was the sheer *extent* of the differences and divisions between managers concerning just about every dimension of innovation — for example, its meaning, its priority, the kind of innovations required, the expected consequences, how it should be achieved, what the consequences are likely to be, and so on. These express the tensions, conflicts and dilemmas residing at the heart of innovation in practice. With a few notable exceptions (see, for example, Dougherty, 1996; Milliken & Lant, 1991; Sharma, 1999), this important point has been under-explored.

Some progress in this direction has been made by Coopey *et al.* (1997; 1998) who focus on the social construction of innovation in organisations. Their focus is on the innovation process from the point of view of individual actors. While we share Coopey and coworkers' interest in individual perceptions, our approach differs from theirs in that we pay greater regard to the organisational contexts in which individual accounts are constructed.

Such a perspective also draws upon the sociology of the management of innovation. This literature helps to illuminate the influence of power, the differing rationalities, and the relations between management and development engineers (Webb, 1992). The potential this approach offers for new insights has been shown by West and Anderson (1996) who, in a study of top teams in 27 hospitals, revealed that group processes best predicted the extent of team innovation. Moreover, they noted that "arguably the most influential group in an organisation in implementing or preventing innovation is the top management team charged with determining strategy and ensuring organisational effectiveness" (1996:680). Group processes included factors such as participation, task orientation, commitment to objectives, and support for innovation. Likewise, other previous research had suggested the importance of the top team role in innovation (see, for example, Cummings, 1965; Hage & Dewar, 1973; Kimberley, 1981).

From this body of literature, it can be hypothesised that an important set of clues to the problem of the management of innovation will be located in the domains of managerial perceptions of *the need for change*, managerial perceptions of *the opportunity to change* and the perceptions about *the way to change*. Perceptions, beliefs and assumptions are thus vital aspects to be understood.

It was this realisation of the need to pay attention to issues of perception and cognition which led us to emphasise two major themes in our research: the first concerns what has been termed the "illegitimacy" of innovation in established firms (Dougherty, 1994) and the second concerns the strategic issue of an organisation's capability and preparedness to innovate and to change.

The legitimacy and illegitimacy of innovation in established organisations

It has been observed that "despite all the lip service paid to it, innovation is often not legitimate within the organisation" (Dougherty, 1996:430). Surveys have revealed that middle managers judge that their senior managers are not fully committed to innovation (Gupta & Wileman, 1990). While most of the contemporary rhetoric about innovation appears to cast the innovator as heroic and someone to be admired, in practice, organisational members in established organisations are well aware that to "be innovative" can all too readily invite resistance and reprisal. Established organisations operate through routines and standard operating procedures. Power and status systems reinforce these routines (Buchanan & Badham, 1999; Pettigrew, 1973). To be innovative is, in effect, to challenge this established order. This aspect of innovation would seem to merit much more investigation than it has so far achieved.

In addition, while the positivist literature tends to treat innovation as an accepted and undisputed good thing, organisation members who are not only potential innovators and change-makers but also recipients of innovative change are likely to be more questioning about its value. In part, this may not only reflect their awareness of fads and fashions but also their awareness that innovation is risky and can carry significant costs, and further, that even those innovations which are successful in yielding some gain for the "organisation" can at the same time incur costs for individuals and groups.

Thus, we are suggesting an exploration from an interpretist stance. In the main, the literature to date has tended to pursue separate tracks with a perceptual/cognitive focus on the one hand (Amabile, 1983; 1997; Amabile & Gryskiewicz, 1988; Kirton, 1976; 1994) and a socio-political focus on the other (Buchanan & Badham, 1999; Dougherty, 1994; Pettigrew, 1973). We sought to draw upon both these traditions (as has for example, Nicholson 1990) by exploring managers' accounts while being sensitive to their sense-making in context.

Innovation, strategy and change

What are — and should be — an organisation's distinctive advantages? What core capabilities does it have and to what extent are these still relevant to the changing environment? These questions go to the heart of what organisations are and how they operate. For some, innovation will not be a peripheral option, indeed, for a minority at least, it seems likely that innovation will go beyond what the organisation *does* and take in what the organisation *is* — or needs to be.

On the one hand, there is Schumpeter's analysis which suggested that in the modern age, significant innovations would be the preserve of the large corporations with their centralised R&D labs (Schumpeter, 1934; 1942). On the other hand, there is a widespread view that small firms are the fount of creativity and innovation. The conventional view appears to be that large firms need to emulate many of the characteristics of small entrepreneurial firms (Kanter, 1983).

The main arena where the critical problems in the management of innovation has been addressed is to be found in the discussion of "established firms". To a large extent, much of this literature rehearses the familiar attack on the supposedly deadening effect of bureaucracy (for example, Kanter, 1983; Peters, 1997). There are, however, some further lessons in the work of Sharma (1999) and Van de Ven (1986). For example, Sharma (1999) presents an analysis which suggests that there are a number of central dilemmas which large firms must negotiate if they are to be successful innovators. Sharma's analysis, however, tends to treat firms as singular entities and thus it misses the social dynamics which are at play and which are vital to understand. In part, this is addressed by Van de Ven (1986) who identifies four fundamental problems of innovation faced by established firms. First, the human problem of focusing organisational members' attention on the desired innovation; second, the process problem of realising value from the new idea; third, the structural problem of "part–whole" relationships; and fourth, the strategic problem of institutional leadership.

Each of these contains the potential for considerable disputation. Innovation in organisations — especially in established organisations — entails, by definition, some measure of disturbance to the status quo. As a result, routines will be threatened and established interests and distributions of status at least rendered uncertain. Innovation involves a game with uncertainty; many key players in large organisations see their role as minimising uncertainty. In consequence, innovation involves a socio-political process (Kanter, 1982; 1983; Pettigrew, 1973). Internal acceptance of, let alone commitment or buy-in to, organisational innovation is not a one-off decision. On the contrary, it typically requires a whole series of repeated decisions (Cool, 1997). Even when an innovation has been secured in one part or unit of a large organisation, the intraorganisational diffusion may be highly problematic.

One classic problem is how to negotiate the dilemma of managing for today while building for the future. Thus, as noted by Tushman and Nadler (1986:81), successful firms become "trapped by their own success". When faced with a technological threat, "dominant firms often respond with even greater reliance on old technology". A "paradoxical result of long periods of success may be increased organisational complacency and a stunted ability to learn" (Tushman & Nadler, 1986:81). One dimension of this problem is the role of strategic leadership in establishing a favourable climate for innovation — a point emphasised by Nystrom (1990). This point reinforces the idea that central importance needs to be accorded to the way CEOs perceive the environment and the place of their organisations within it (Lefebvre *et al.*, 1997). However, this whole business of strategic leadership, the setting of new directions and the balancing of the needs of sustaining today's business and income stream while planning for actions which may well erode its viability, is fraught with dilemmas and is the source of potential conflict. As Schein has observed, organisations have cultures which often fail to align and this can be a source of a failure of organisational learning and innovation. Learning, innovation and change, as Schein (1996) points out, are closely interrelated.

In summary, the literature offers some clues as to the possible sources and the nature of the "management of innovation problem". We can expect these tensions to be revealed rather acutely in those settings where mainstream organisations enjoy some of the benefits of established firms but which at the same time contain some members who perceive environmental changes to be requiring of innovative responses. This is precisely the set of circumstances which we seek to illuminate in this article. The key identified features suggested by the literature have been: the stifling effects of "bureaucracy" in established organisations (i.e. mindsets which elevate rules, routine and hierarchy over responsiveness, agility and empowerment); a learned incapacity in previously successful organisations; the effects of organisational politics; failings in institutional leadership, and doubts about leader priorities and commitment. At the heart of each of these we suggest, and crucial to the way they are actually played-out in practice, is the way in which organisational actors — especially managers — perceive and interpret their nature and importance.

Despite some attention to managerial cognitions, the vast bulk of the research on the subject of innovation has tended to under-explore the perceptions, insights, assumptions and understandings of managers themselves. This is unfortunate because if there is a problem of insufficient innovation (as the many government-sponsored campaigns in many countries suggests there is) then the clues to the source of this may be located in the way managers themselves interpret the issue. Thus, it is worthwhile to spend some time examining managerial perceptions in this domain. This is what we set out to do and, in the next section we describe how we went about this task.

Research Methods

There have been numerous surveys (both postal- and telephone-based) which have sought to track the incidence of innovation. Our research objectives required rather different methods. We needed to gain close access to the perceptions and cognitions of a whole array of managers. Also, we needed to put these perceptions and insights into context. These dual requirements suggested a case study approach. But, at the same time, we wanted to get beyond the limitations of understanding the detail as found in only one or two cases. Thus, we aimed to conduct qualitative research but in an unusually large number of different organisations — 20 in all. The study was designed to allow 20 interviews per case for large organisations though rather less than this in small and medium-sized enterprises. This number was chosen in order to allow access to a sufficient number of senior level managers from a range of functions while also leaving sufficient scope for us to interview a sample of managers and other key participants from various operational levels.

Conscious of the likely importance of context, we also wanted to make comparisons between organisations within and across industry sectors. We targeted certain sectors and sought out at least two cases per sector. The sectors were: banking and finance; manufacturing; the media; pharmaceuticals; telecommunications; and the voluntary sector. The case studies included the BBC, GEC, Marconi/GPT, Hewlett-Packard, NatWest Bank, Nortel, Psion, Oxfam and Zeneca. The logic in selecting a number of sectors and indeed these in particular was that, from the literature, one might expect certain sector-specific influences on the way managers would report the way in which innovation was treated in their context. If this was indeed the case, then it would be important for us to be able to take such sector variations into account.

For example, it could be hypothesised that managers in pharmaceutical companies would be familiar with and possibly take for granted the routinised methods of laboratory research, and the well-established routines and roles of R&D in their sector. In contrast, managers in banking and finance could be expected to be much more uncertain of how their organisations should respond to the pace of change in the environment of banking and finance with new players entering their markets and offering new forms of services. Manufacturing companies could be expected to vary depending on the extent to which they had placed a priority on innovation both internally and with regard to inter-firm collaborations. Telecommunications equipment manufacturers and infrastructure service providers can be seen as a special sub-category where the degree of innovation in the sector is especially intense at this time. The voluntary sector was included for a special reason. It is sometimes argued that, in general, these organisations are inherently "innovative" in that they have grown to exploit opportunities missed by public and private sector organisations.

In addition, as the research progressed, it became clear that managers in these large organisations often suggested that small and medium-sized companies would have some advantages in innovation. Thus, we sought out a sample of SMEs. This sample was selected in collaboration with a Chamber of Commerce and Business Link. We asked their innovation counsellors to agree on the top six innovative companies in the locality.

With regard to the large organisations, our main line of inquiry was the broad swathe of organisations which, to some degree and in at least some quarters, had taken the innovation message seriously. Indeed, a guiding logic in our selection of cases was that, to some extent, they had adopted the innovation message. In the current climate, this was not too stringent a test — we only decided against two organisations which appeared to have firmly and decisively chosen a follower strategy. It should be made clear that for the larger organisations (i.e. those outside the local SME sub-sample), the main criterion for selection was not that they were necessarily the international or even national leaders on some objective measure of innovativeness but rather that there was some evidence that top management (or at least some segment of top management) had made it known that "innovation" was now, if not before, a goal to be taken seriously if not indeed a high priority. The vast majority of the case organisations had recently embraced (at least officially) a high-level policy to "be more innovative". In effect, these companies had issued *injunctions* (either formally or informally) to managers and staff at all levels that innovation was to be a strategic objective. Many of the organisations studied had even gone so far as to declare innovation to be an adopted "core value". To an extent therefore, we entered these organisations at a time when managers at all levels were confronted with the formal requirement to "do something" about innovation. It seems likely that we benefited greatly from catching this moment because our access to companies (and just as important, access within companies) to discuss these themes was greatly enhanced as the managers concerned were eager to examine and *debate the meaning* and implications of this (in some cases) newly discovered "priority". Our method of selection and access was essentially to discuss with expert informants which major organisations within the pre-selected sectors were taking at least some steps to deal with innovation. We then approached these organisations at a very senior level and entered into discussions about our aims and objectives. The logic and practical relevance of the study were usually easily appreciated by these managers and in virtually all cases, we gained access and high-level sponsorship for the research.

Each interview lasted on average somewhere between one and a half and two hours All interviews were tape-recorded and professionally transcribed. The transcripts were analysed by members of the research team. The content and format of the interviews was as follows. We asked about the interviewees' role within the organisation, their work history, their understanding of the idea of innovation, what innovations they had been part of or had observed, what innovations they believed were still required, what pathways innovations typically followed, what blockages there were within the organisation to innovation and which factors enabled innovation. An important component of the method was the space we allowed for narrative approach. We encouraged each interviewee to tell the story of an attempted innovation in their organisation (whether eventually judged a success or not) — how it started, by whom, why it gained credence, how it was received by various players, what impact it had and so on.

Before considering the results, the scope and limitations of this study should be noted. The organisations discussed here are not necessarily representative of all organisations operating in the UK. Some of the cases are well-known internationally-leading companies (such as Nortel and Hewlett-Packard). The others, as explained, had at least in part declared some aspiration to be "more innovative". Thus, in total, the sample is unlikely to reflect the long tail of non-innovating organisations. In broad terms, the sample was designed to reflect the middle band of major organisations operating in the UK which in reality continue to struggle with what being "more innovative" might entail for them (classic examples were NatWest Bank, the BBC and GEC). At the top end, the Nortels and Hewlett-Packards were included as comparative benchmarks of what best practice was thought to be.

Another limitation should be noted. This article reports on work-in-progress. A great deal of this extensive and rich data-set has yet to be fully analysed. Related to this is the point that the scope of this article does not run into an inclusive coverage of the various themes which the full research project addressed — for example, we do not report here on the SME sample, nor does it consider examples of apparent "best practice". Rather, the intent of this particular article is to focus on that middle band of organisations which, while broadly successful in conventional terms, are now seen to require a shift in behaviour in order to meet the innovation challenge. Their previous success, to some extent, inhibits them from innovating too radically and at the same time, they are faced with competing models of how to proceed. We believe that many other organisations are broadly locatable within this categorisation and that in consequence the insights, struggles and tribulations of this sample is likely to have relevance to a wider community.

Results

As discussed in the introduction to this paper, we sought through this project on the understanding of managers' meanings of innovation to reveal some clues as to why British industry seems to have a persistent *problem* with innovation.

This discussion of results here focuses on that issue. Analysis of the interview transcripts reveals two sets of clues. The first set relates to the explicit explanations which managers were able to offer of the problem of innovation as they saw it. The second set of clues derives from what remained unsaid or only partially said and from an uncovering of "hidden" sources of problems — including, for example, the major discrepancies revealed between managers in the same organisation about priorities, objectives and means.

Explicit explanations and managers' theories

We asked managers for their personal explanations and accounts of the "barriers" to innovation in their organisation. There were organisations which had gone to explicit lengths to audit the "creativity" of their managers and staff by using the services of external consultants and trainers. But even here, where creative individuals were deemed to exist in abundance, there was a persisting perceived problem of innovation. The managers in our research produced a wealth of explanations for this phenomenon, including: lack of resources (time and money); short-termism; people confined to (and indeed sometimes preferring) their narrow "boxes"; and fear of failure as it was safer to ply the routine rather than to take risks. These were the surface explanations. We were able to additionally reveal problems which lay at a deeper level: these we term "implicit explanations".

Implicit explanations

The literature has pointed, as we noted earlier, to the idea of the "illegitimacy of innovation". It is perhaps not surprising then that a number of our respondents expressed rather firmly the point that innovators required senior sponsorship and protection. In one organisation, this notion was graphically described as the need for "air cover". Innovation was clearly viewed as a contested terrain. It was understood to be the source of tension and even conflict about a range of important issues — about the allocation of resources (including the deployment of some of the best staff), about product and service offerings, and about, in consequence, the operating procedures and infrastructure of the organisation which would be needed to support the new activities. In sum, innovation was recognised as involving a debate about the very nature of these businesses.

The most notable result across the interviews as a whole was the extent to which managers had such diverse and often conflicting understandings about what innovation actually means. In most organisations, we found there was no consensus about the place or importance of innovation. Even among senior managers, there were typically significant differences of opinion about whether to innovate, follow fast or pursue some other strategy. In practice, there are important and far-reaching differences between managers in the same organisation concerning just about every aspect of innovation — including its meaning, its significance, its priority, its relevance, the means of its implementation and the appropriate areas for its application.

To reveal some of the more significant patterns, it is worthwhile to begin with the broad comparisons between sectors. One could hypothesise that there would be differences between sectors with regard to the significance and place of innovation. After all, the classic analysis by Burns and Stalker (1968) has famously shown the link between environment and firm behaviour. Our first set of findings, uncontroversially, confirmed this hypothesis. There was a variation in emphasis given by managers from the different sectors. These patterns were not a matter of surprise and the managers involved were broadly reflecting the dominant cultural understandings in such companies. Thus, for example, managers in pharmaceutical companies tended to talk about product innovations and the problems involved in achieving breakthroughs in this regard. Issues relating to patents and to regulative regimes tended to figure large in their discourses. In engineering companies on the other hand, managers were more likely to discuss process innovations.

There was however an interesting phenomenon at play here. Certain companies, such as Zeneca, whose very business was the large-scale and routinised innovation of drugs had a shared and reasonably stable repertoire of ways to deliver on this objective. They represented one end of a spectrum. At the other end were enterprises in software and advertising whose approach to innovation was much more individualised and self-consciously "creative". They tried to draw upon creativity-promoting devices and artifices such as fun-days, artists-in-residence and they punctuated the work day with "surprises".

However, we were especially interested in the broad band of organisations which were located between these two extremes of the spectrum. Here, we found that the main group of organisations had neither routinised innovation nor adopted the more bizarre array of creativity events. This group is of special interest for a number of reasons. First, because they represent, we believe, the main bulk of organisations in the UK. Second, because they were under pressure in varying degrees to be "more innovative" in order to cope with what they were told was — and sometimes experienced as — a fast-changing environment. Third, because faced with the conflicting examples from companies at both extreme ends of the spectrum, managers in the mainstream produced some fascinating *competing prescriptions* for innovation in their own organisations. Managers returning from conferences featuring advertising agencies and software houses would be enthused with the idea of promoting innovation through the adoption of fun-inducing triggers allied with individual reward systems. Conversely, those introduced to the routines of the large-scale innovators in pharmaceuticals and engineering urged a different recipe based on planning, monitoring and phased-evaluation reviews.

We found extensive differences between managers in the same company — even among managers in the same top level teams — about the actual meaning of the injunction to be innovative, the priority that should be accorded to it, the ways in which the organisation would have to behave in order to facilitate this objective, and the kinds of innovation which were deemed to be required. There were also some commonalties, of course, and we will discuss these below, but here we want to emphasise the importance of differences because these seemed to give important clues to the problem of organisational innovation.

Such differences between managers in the same "team" meant that attempts to "successfully exploit new ideas" had to run a gauntlet of competing expectations, strategies and rationales — not to mention entrenched routines and inertia. Many of the key differences hinged upon the extent to which innovation was regarded as a result of individual initiative (sometimes referred to as the "hero innovator") or was seen as the outcome of social cooperation. Another dimension was the degree of emphasis given to looking inwards to the organisation's internal resources and capabilities or external to collaborators in other organisations. By cross-cutting these two dimensions, we can classify some of the key differences as shown in Fig. 1.

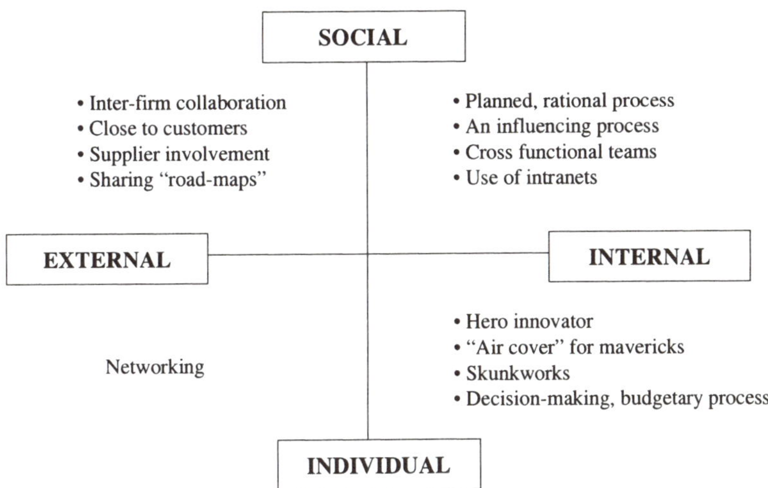

Fig. 1. Competing theories of innovation.

Starting with the top right quadrant here, we see the idea of innovation as a **planned, rational process** represented. This meant that managing it entailed a series of stages with each culminating in a phase or stage review. These review points enabled formal managerial assessment and a decision opportunity to proceed with further investment or project curtailment. Typical phases were: idea conception, specification of product, planning the project, prototyping and so on, through to final review. This type of understanding of the process of innovation and its management is closely allied to the idea of product life cycles.

Such understandings of innovation were more typical in the contexts of telecommunications equipment manufacturers and pharmaceuticals where large investments were periodically required in new products or new versions of established products. But, even in these settings, we found managers who were critical of this approach. For example, one telecoms manager observed: "I think the stage review approach is a serious constraint. It's a good system for killing off creative ideas". The problem as reported by the technology managers was that directors would often use the review procedure as a way to protect their turf and thus they argued it was inherently conservative and tended towards low tolerance of risk.

Also in the top right quadrant but operating under a different conception of the nature of the process is the view that innovation is essentially **an influencing process**. These managers argued that there is a need to build a degree of enthusiasm among colleagues in order to enable a new idea to be accepted. The term "influence" is rather too mild for some of the instances of change that were being discussed. Innovation for some managers was seen as a **fight for resources**. It involves competition between projects and even between change and the status quo. This kind of approach was prevalent in sectors where product innovation was accepted as the norm — for example, in pharmaceuticals and computers, and also in some engineering companies.

In yet other circumstances, the perception was even more forthright than this. Innovation in organisations that were perceived as conservative and resistant to change was analysed by those who wished to change them as requiring **"disruptive interventions"**. This is the politics of change. For example, one of the inner band of innovators at the BBC, an executive closely allied to the then Director General, Sir John Birt, observed:

> *I think you do need to be a bit like Trotsky. There has to be a permanent revolution. I mean, funnily enough, the revolutionaries of yesterday inevitably have turned into the conservatives of today.*

Alternative perspectives in this quadrant were that innovation occurred through informal groups and **cross-functional teams** sparking ideas off each other and, by extension, that innovation could be facilitated if virtual teams could be established through the use of intranet technology.

Another important set of perceptions located in this quadrant were those which regarded innovation as a **corporate capability** or competence — the capability of the organisation to reinvent itself. These managers argued that sustainable innovativeness can only be ensured if the capacity to produce serial innovations is embedded in the wider system. Such conceptualisations are in tune, of course, with current academic theory on knowledge management (Prusack, 1997), the resource-based view of the firm (Barney, 1991), and the concept of core competence (Hamel & Prahalad, 1994).

In the lower right quadrant are located those perceptions which, while continuing to emphasise an internal focus, switch emphasis towards the role of individuals in delivering innovation. Tom Peters has celebrated the idea of "skunkworks" — that is, officially-tolerated experimentation by individuals. This was an idea that was widespread in Hewlett-Packard. A cultural symbol of it was the tale of Bill Hewlett using bolt cutters to remove the lock from a steel cabinet so that any engineer could access components and tools in order to experiment — even if this meant playing around at home building toys for the children.

A related popular managerial conception was the idea of the individual **hero innovator**. Indeed, in one of the financial institutions, the majority of managers interviewed made reference to one specific individual and told stories about this individual in order to illustrate the point about innovation in that organisation. This suggested the general absence of a systematic process for innovation and it elevated the notion of an exceptional individual in challenging the system. Closely related to this was the idea that he and the people working under his aegis would require special protection from powerful board directors. A number of informants used the metaphor of these innovators requiring "air cover" for their activities. They were seen as vulnerable should that cover be removed.

Also in this quadrant can be placed those accounts which perceived innovation as part of the normal **budgetary and decision-making** process. Here, a key individual, the managing director, would subject a range of alternative proposals to critical scrutiny and decide what resources should be allocated or withheld. One such managing director emphasised the need "to avoid individuals being 'let loose' to pursue their 'pet intellectual challenges'". He continued:

> *My management philosophy is that authority should go with accountability, that generally, an organisation benefits more from people having a real ownership of a particular part of the business and being given the tools to control that ownership and then deliver on it and be accountable. I am a strong believer in always having that choice made by people who*

have commercial accountability for a bottom line. I think you can waste an awful lot of time, effort and money pursuing ideas for the sake of the intellectual challenge and enjoyment. In an organisation like ours, a lot of money can be consumed that way.

Another belief about innovation that belongs to this quadrant was that it occurred through **creative individuals** (by implication, the priority is to find them and keep them). One manager in the BBC argued:

Innovation comes first and foremost from the ideas of individuals and from the way in which the ideas are captured. So the ownership of ideas and the development of ideas are absolutely critically, and this is what's interesting about the negotiations that have gone on between production (the creative supplier side) and broadcast (the purchaser). It is now accepted that the ownership and exploitation of the ideas have been recognised as belonging to production.

Here, we can see that perceptions of innovation are closely aligned with arguments about the strategic future of firms. Thus, this manager continued:

There was a time when the BBC made this split when people predicted that the BBC would become a commissioning organisation like Channel 4. What I think we've won is the battle which says the creative content is king and that actually the BBC is dead without it.

The importance of this struggle is made further evident by the post-Birt developments in the BBC with the new Director General, Greg Dyke, seeking to reverse many of the innovations of his predecessor.

Those managerial perceptions which emphasised an individual focus allied to an external perspective are located in the bottom left quadrant. Most important here were those views which stressed the need for certain **individuals to network widely** through company visits, attendance at conferences and trade exhibitions. For example, a technology manager in a high-tech company manufacturing modems and mobile phone interconnections observed:

The most important thing is to meet the customer and discuss with them what they need to develop their business in terms of mobile telecommunications capability. So, last week I was at Ford in Detroit and at Marks & Spencer in London, next week I am at Shell in Belgium, then back to the US to see Deloitte-Touche.

Significantly, he went on to say, "We maintain friendly competition with our rivals in the marketplace, I know most of my equivalent post-holders in other companies personally very well indeed and we discuss technology and product developments on a regular basis".

The fourth quadrant locates those managerial perceptions which emphasised an external-facing posture and a view of innovation as a social phenomenon. Thus, many managers emphasised the importance of **inter-firm collaboration.** This appeared to be an increasing phenomenon as product life-cycles shorten and new products and technologies require complementary capabilities. In the companies associated in varying ways with telecommunications in particular, a whole gamut of types of inter-firm collaborations was evident. These ranged from information-sharing on an informal and formal basis; co-marketing and co-promotion; technology licensing and co-branding; sharing "road maps", cross-licensing and engaging in the co-development of future products. For example, one British ICT company was sharing information with Cisco and Bay, they were also in a licensing agreement with Nokia, Motorola and Ericsson. To varying degrees, managers judged that they had access to the "developmental road maps" of these companies as a result of these collaborations. This gives crucial advantages:

> *For example, when Nokia brought out the 6110 model, we had a compatible product available from day one for people to buy. The timing has to be right, there's no point in us having a compatible product three months later.*

Reflecting on these types of collaborations, another manager from this company observed that the social relationships were critical:

> *In the end, it's about interpersonal relations and personalities. Trust is vital but also, there is a role for key individuals. Innovation is associated with individuals, in my experience, you need a charismatic figure in there somewhere.*

Instances of the growing importance of inter-firm collaborations were cited by respondents across most case companies. These included closer relations with suppliers (this sometimes entailed having representatives of suppliers on-site and occasionally, this meant housing supplier activities including manufacturing and sub-assembly on-site); closer relations with "competitors" as exemplified above; closer relations with complementary producers who were neither direct competitors, suppliers nor customers; and closer relations with customers.

A key part of the collaboration that was often emphasised was with customers. When asked to identify a current focus of innovation, one manager in a telecoms company replied "the front-line issue for us is undoubtedly customer intimacy, it's about sitting down with them as we develop new products and services together". This was echoed in other companies, though the meaning of being "customer-focused" was open to different interpretations. Some meant only designing new products and modifications to existing products where there was evidence of clear customer demand. This was an attempt to reduce or even avoid risk. Others were more adventurous and were trying to anticipate future demands — sometimes, as in telecoms, those of the customers of their immediate customers.

Implications and Applications

Where management teams acknowledge and make transparent these competing beliefs, perceptions and expectations concerning innovation, they can put the findings to practical use. Managers can compare their expectations and make more explicit strategic choices. The different perceptions of what innovation means and the different perceptions concerning how it happens are likely to be important in influencing behaviour. There are numerous implications and applications but some of the more important can be summarised as follows.

If the individual creative hero is perceived to be the solution, then organisations may allow considerable freedom to particular individuals. Conversely, the rational, planned perspective results in the orderly linear approach to research and development. A third belief system results in an attempt to create a culture of experimentation and "play".

Crucially, it can be hypothesised that the largest proportion of managers across the country is likely to be located in organisations which do not have a track record of significant and sustained innovation. Our findings suggest that if and when managers in these settings do become attracted to the idea of innovation (or are instructed to embrace it), they will tend to champion one or other of the models to which they happen to have been exposed. Thus, within mainstream organisations with a new top–down edict to "be innovative", one finds managers variously urging or assuming that this implies the establishment of an R&D unit or alternatively a liberal culture. The middle band is thus caught between competing models of innovation. Our recommendation is that those senior managers seeking, with serious intent, for greater organisational innovation need to attend not only to the idea of "creativity" but they also need to surface and examine the *different* kinds of ways through which "innovation" can occur, and to hold healthy, open and informed debate about which approach is to be preferred in a given situation.

Perceptions and beliefs about innovation influence the allocation of resources. They influence the organisation of innovative activity — including, for example, the extent to which innovation is allocated to a select few or is regarded as a diffused responsibility. There are implications too for the way R&D is organised — indeed whether there will actually be any R&D and if so on what scale. Competing perceptions affect whether information and forward plans are kept secret or are shared across organisational boundaries and thus they influence the degree of collaboration with suppliers, customers and competitors.

Clarification of understandings about the nature of innovation in a particular setting (e.g. in a particular organisation) can help in the strategy formulation process. Managers can debate their current compared with their desired exposure to new markets, new customers and new technologies, and the varied risks and competency requirements associated with these. Innovation ultimately results from managerial perceptions of the need for change, the perception of the opportunity to change and the perceptions about the way to change. Perceptions, beliefs and assumptions are thus vital aspects to be understood. The overall conclusion is that organisations can benefit if perceptions and beliefs about innovation are clarified, made explicit and made subject to debate and challenge.

References

Amabile, T.M. (1983) *The Social Psychology of Creativity*. New York: Springer-Verlag

_________ (1997) Motivating creativity in organisations. *California Management Review*, **40**(1), 39–58

Amabile, T.M. & Gryskiewicz, S. (1988) Creative human resources in the R&D laboratory: how environment and personality affect innovation. In *Handbook for Creative and Innovative Managers*, ed. R.L. Kuhu. New York: McGraw-Hill

Anderson, N., Hardy, G. & West, M. (1992) Management team innovation. *Management Decision*, **30**(2), 17–21

Bandura, A. (1986) *Social Foundations of Thought and Action: A Social Cognitive Theory*. Englewood-Cliffs, NJ: Prentice-Hall

Barney, J. (1991) Firm resources and sustained competitive advantage. *Journal of Management*, **17**(1), 99–120

Buchanan, D. & Badham, R. (1999) *Power, Politics and Organisational Change*. London: Sage

Burns, T. & Stalker, G.M. (1968) *The Management of Innovation*. London: Tavistock

Cool, K.O. (1997) Diffusion of innovations within organisations: electronic switching in the Bell System, 1971–1982. *Organisation Science*, **8**(5), 543–559

Cooper, R. & Kleinschmidt, E. (1986) An investigation into the new product process: steps, deficiencies and impact. *Journal of Product Innovation Management*, **3**, 71–85

Coopey, J., Keegan, O. & Emler, N. (1997) Managers' innovations as "sense-making". *British Journal of Management*, **8**, 301–315

Coopey, J., & Keegan, O. (1998) Managers' innovations and the structuration of organisations. *Journal of Management Studies*, **35**(3), 263–284

Cummings, L. (1965) Organisational climates for creativity. *Academy of Management Journal*, **8**, 220–227

Dougherty, D. (1992) Interpretive barriers to successful product innovation in large firms. *Organisation Science*, **3**, 179–202

________ (1994) The illegitimacy of successful product innovation in established firms. *Organisation Science*, **5**, 200–218

________ (1996) Organizing for innovation. In *Handbook of Organisation Studies*. ed. S. Clegg, C. Hardy & W.R. Nord, pp. 424–439. London: Sage

DTI, (1998) *The Competitiveness White Paper*. London: Department of Trade and Industry

Ettlie, J.E. (1984) Organisational strategy and structural differences for radical versus incremental innovation. *Management Science*, **30**, 682–695

Farr, J. (1990) Facilitating individual role innovation. In *Innovation and Creativity at Work*. ed. M. West & J. Farr. London: Wiley

Gupta, A. & Wileman, D. (1990) Accelerating the development of technologically based new products. *California Management Review*, **33**, 24–44

Hage, J & Dewar, R (1973) Elite values verus organisational structure in predicting innovation. *Administrative Science Quarterly*, **18**, 279–290

Hamel, G. & Prahalad, C.K. (1994) *Competing for the Future*. Boston: Harvard Business School Press

Hargaon, A. & Sutton, R. (1997) Technology brokering and innovation in a product development firm. *Administrative Science Quarterly*, **42**, 716–749

Kanter, R.M. (1982) The middle manager as innovator. *Harvard Business Review*, **61** (July–August), 95–105

________ (1983) *The Changemasters: Corporate Entrepreneurs at Work*. New York: Routledge

Katz, R. (1994) Managing high-performance R&D teams. *European Management Journal*, **12**(3), 243–253

Kim, W.C. (1997) Value innovation: the strategic logic of high growth. *Harvard Business Review*, **Jan–Feb**, 103–111

Kimberley, J.R. (1981) Managerial innovations. In *Handbook of Organisational Design*, ed. P.C. Nystrom & W.A. Starbuck. New York: Oxford University Press

Kirton, M. (1976) Adaption and innovation: a description and a measure. *Journal of Applied Psychology*, **61**(October), 622–629

________ (1994) *Adapters and Innovators: Styles of Creativity and Problem Solving*. London: Routledge

Lant, T.K. & Milliken, F.J. (1992) The role of managerial learning and interpretation in strategic persistence and reorientation: an empirical exploration. *Strategic Management Journal*, **13**(8), 585–608

Lefebvre, L., Mason, R., *et al.* (1997) The influence prism in SMEs: the power of CEOs' perceptions of technology policy and its organisational impacts. *Management Science*, **43**(6), 856–878

Markides, C. (1997) Strategic innovation. *Sloan Management Review*, **Spring**, 9–23

Milliken, F.J. & Lant, T.K. (1991) The effect of an organisation's recent performance history on strategic persistence and change: the role of managerial interpretations. In *Advances in Strategic Management* Vol. 7, ed. P. Shrivastava. Greenwich, CT: JAI Press

Nicholson, N. (1990) Organisational innovation in context: culture, interpretation and application. In *Innovation and Creativity at Work: Psychological and Organisational Strategies*, ed. M. West & J.L. Farr. Chichester: Wiley

Nystrom, H. (1990) Organisational innovation. In *Innovation and Creativity at Work: Psychological and Organisational Strategies*, ed. M. West & J. Farr. Chichester, Wiley

Nystrom, H. (1990) *Technological and Market Innovation: Strategies for Product and Company Development*. Chichester: John Wiley

Peters, T. (1997) *The Circle of Innovation*. London: Hodder and Stoughton

Pettigrew, A.M. (1973) *The Politics of Organisational Decision Making*. London: Tavistock

Prusack, L., Ed. (1997) *Knowledge in Organisations*. Boston: Butterworth-Heinemann

Quinn, J.B. (1979) Technological innovation, entrepreneurship and strategy. *Sloan Management Review*, **21**, 19–30

_________ (1992). The intelligent enterprise: a new paradigm. *The Academy of Management Executive*, **6**(4), 48–64

Rickards, T. (1999) *Creativity and the Management of Change*. Oxford: Blackwell

Rosenfeld, R. & Servo, J. (1990) Facilitating innovation in large organisations. In *Innovation and Creativity at Work: Psychological and Organisational Strategies*, ed. M. West & J. Farr. London: Wiley

Saren, M. (1987) The role of strategy in technological innovation: a reassessment. In *Organisation Analysis and Development*, ed. I.L. Mangham. Chichester: Wiley

Schein, E. (1996) Three cultures of management: the key to organisational learning. *Sloan Management Review*, **Fall**, 9–20

Schumpeter, J. (1934) *The Theory of Economic Development*. Cambridge, MA: Harvard

_________ (1942). *Capitalism, Socialism and Democracy*. New York: Harper & Row

Senge, P. (1990) *The Fifth Discipline*. New York: Doubleday

Sharma, A. (1999) Central dilemmas of managing innovation in large firms. *California Management Review*, **41**(3), 146–164

Starkey, K. & McKinlay, A. (1988) *Organisational Innovation, Competitive Strategy and Management of Change in Four Companies*. Aldershot: Avebury

Sutcliffe, K.M. & Huber, G.P. (1998) Firm and industry as determinants of executive perspectives of the environment. *Strategic Management Journal*, **19**, 793–807

Teece, D.J. (1987) Profiting from technological innovation: implications for integration, collaboration, licensing and public policy. In *The Competitive Challenge: Strategies for Industrial Innovation and Renewal*, ed. D.J. Teece, pp. 159–185. Cambridge, MA: Ballinger

Tidd, J. (1997) Complexity, networks and learning: integrative themes for research on innovation management. *International Journal of Innovation Management*, **1**(1), 1–21

Tushman, M. & Nadler, D. (1986) Organising for innovation. *California Management Review*, **28**(3), 74–88

Van de Ven, A. (1986) Central problems in the management of innovation. *Management Science*, **32**, 591–607

Watson, T. (1994) *In Search of Management*. London: Routledge

Webb, J. (1992) The mismanagement of innovation. *Sociology*, **26**(3), 471–492

Weick, K. (1979a) Cognitive processes in organisations. In *Research in Organisational Behavior*, ed. B.M. Staw, pp. 41–74. Greenwich: JAI Press

________ (1979b). *The Social Psychology of Organizing*. Reading, MA: Addison-Wesley

________ (1995) *Sensemaking in Organisations*. Newbury Park, CA: Sage

West, M. & Anderson, N. (1996). Innovation in top management teams. *Journal of Applied Psychology*, **81**(6), 680–693

Wolfe, R.A. (1994) Organisational innovation: review, critique and suggested research directions. *Journal of Management Studies*, **31**(3), 405–431

Part III
The Role of Managers in Innovation

Journal of Management Studies 35:3 May 1998
0022-2380

MANAGERS' INNOVATIONS AND THE STRUCTURATION OF ORGANIZATIONS*

JOHN COOPEY

University of Lancaster

ORLA KEEGAN

Royal College of Surgeons, Ireland

NICK EMLER

University of Oxford

ABSTRACT

Drawing on interview data from managers in three organizations a theoretical framework based on structuration theory is offered for understanding the social construction of innovation in a way that overcomes the duality of individual and structural perspectives that fragments the literature on innovation and other related domains. Three case studies, one from each organization, illustrate and help link the elements of an argument that focuses first on how an organization's openness to its external environment allows for conflicting interpretations of necessary action. Individual agents exploit the ambiguity, making choices which help sustain or develop their self-identities, drawing on experience to shape innovations that promise to reconcile the constraints of the personal and organizational domains. Their capacity to transform circumstances in the desired direction depends on the extent to which they can deploy personal and organizational resources to negotiate appropriate meanings through social and political relationships with relevant others. The socio-political process and the substance of the innovation have reciprocal effects, yielding the possibility of agreement on a 'working innovation' which, once institutionalized, modifies the existing system and structures in ways that constrain, in new modes, the behaviours of all of those involved.

INTRODUCTION

In this paper we offer a theoretical framework for understanding processes of innovation in organizations. This framework is developed by integrating various research perspectives within an envelope of 'structuration theory' (Giddens, 1984). We focus deliberately on the actions and self-perceived innovations of individual

Address for reprints: John Coopey, 24 Kendal Green, Kendal, Cumbria LA9 5PN, UK.

managers, an approach which contrasts both with most of the studies reviewed by King (1990) which favour an organizational level of analysis, and much of the creativity literature, which has emphasized personality traits and the products of creative behaviour (e.g. Barron and Harrington, 1981). Ours is an attempt, therefore, to respond to the need defined by West and Farr (1990) for more research into the everyday ways in which people express themselves creatively in the workplace, rather than to the research agenda suggested by Wolfe (1994), which makes almost no reference to personal agency.

Our objectives are to make sense of the innovation process from the point of view of different individual actors, to amalgamate their various stories and to relate the key themes to the proposed theoretical framework. The data used stem largely from narratives derived from interviews with managers drawn from a university (Uni), an IT manufacturer (ITC), and the social work department of a regional council (SWD). The diversity of organizations and of managers within them – and hence the diversity of types of innovation reported by them – is consistent with principles set out by Campbell and Fiske (1959) in defining validity, reflected in Patton's (1987) term 'maximum variation sampling'. He argues that when similar patterns emerge from diverse contexts they are more likely to be of value in capturing 'core phenomena', providing in the present case a potentially robust basis for theorizing the relationship between modes of innovative behaviour, social relationships and organizational context.

RESEARCH SAMPLE

Interviewees were recruited following a survey in which 50 managers in each of the three organizations were invited to 'give an example of a recent innovation of yours'. For the purposes of the survey a manager was defined as:

> a person in a formal position involving some responsibility for the work of other people and for other resources, especially financial.

Innovation was defined as:

> a particular form of change characterized by the introduction of something new. This 'something' may relate to a product, service or a technology or it may involve the introduction of new managerial or administrative practices or changes in other elements of the organization. Innovations may vary in magnitude from those which affect only the manager's own role to others which have major implications for the whole organization. Ultimately innovations bring about beneficial change.

The term 'beneficial' is typically part of definitions of creativity used in psychology. It was included in this definition to encourage the reporting of only innovations that had been or were likely to be implemented and, hence, could more probably be verbalized. In a second stage of the survey respondents provided information on their perceptions of their innovations and the organizational setting. From this stage we selected for interview ten respondents in each organization who had described an innovation, seeking to ensure that we sampled all hierarchical levels and functions and a wide range of experience, while maintaining the gender balance. Despite the difficulties involved in relying on volunteers, this sub-sample did not differ in age or years in present position from the total group reporting innovations.

In open-ended, tape-recorded interviews lasting about an hour managers were encouraged to give freely their account of the innovation project. The 'attributes' of their innovations differ considerably, for example in terms of Wolfe's (1994) dimensions of centrality, complexity, magnitude, focus (i.e. technological, managerial or administrative) and radicalness (see appendix 1).

Each interviewee was asked to nominate for interview two individuals crucial to the progress of the innovation. Not all were able to do so and it was not possible to interview all of those nominated. But except in one case at least one such 'collaborator' was interviewed. In all, 44 collaborators' narratives were generated and analysed in addition to those of the 30 innovators.

EMERGENT THEMES AND THEIR INTERPRETATION

In using a qualitative methodology we acknowledge our active involvement in choosing the organizations, defining the terms 'innovation' and 'manager' against which accounts of innovations were elicited, and in shaping 'a causal description' of underlying individual and social processes. The research process moved from level to level of 'analytical abstraction' in three broad steps: (a) the creation of texts and the categorization of the data therein, (b) the drawing out of themes and of relationships between them, and (c) the synthesis of those themes and supporting data into an explanatory framework (Miles and Huberman, 1994).

The interviews were framed by our definitions and shaped by our invitation to talk 'about your experience of imagining, developing and implementing the innovation', and by various follow-up prompts. Like Watson (1994a, b), therefore, we are likely to have influenced those who took part in the research.

Narratives were analysed using some of the procedures of a grounded theory approach (Glaser and Strauss, 1967; Strauss and Corbin, 1990), a cumulative, iterative procedure for defining categories that capture overlapping accounts of specific contexts, people or events. An initial analysis of 15 innovator narratives yielded over 80 separate categories of data, of which the 14 most 'saturated' (i.e. those to which a high proportion of the separate narratives contributed) provided a framework for analysing the remaining data.

'Fragmenting' narratives can cause the text segments to become 'decontextualized' such that narrative and its implicit process of change are lost (Dey, 1995). To avoid this we returned regularly to original texts and to case summaries of how the process seemed to have evolved, using collaborators' narratives to complement those of innovators. Hence, we are more confident that linkages created between the categories reflect explicit and implicit connections within the flow of the narratives.

We did not, as suggested by Glaser and Strauss, expect theory to 'emerge' from the data unprompted. Instead, we were actively involved in an 'interplay' between the narratives and their interpretation. By employing practical strategies for close, detached qualitative analysis provided by grounded theory we were able to adopt the perspective in the research process of 'an outsider within', creating the possibility of seeing 'what is ordinarily invisible from within a dominant order' (Henwood and Pidgeon, 1994, p. 17).

The insights of the 44 collaborators helped, and since 27 of them did not meet our definition of 'manager' they were, presumably, less likely to share closely in any managerial discourse. Additional data was provided by our principal contacts in each of the three organizations, including documentary evidence – on policies, planning frameworks, etc. – supplementing that received from many respondents. Further data arose from feedback meetings with participants at which preliminary findings were discussed. Finally, vital contextual knowledge was gleaned from our own involvement in the university, from site visits and from published accounts of extensive external pressures to which, from our data, the three organizations appeared to be subject (e.g. Cowen, 1991; Storey, 1992; Wilson and Game, 1994).

Hence, by applying grounded theory approaches, supplemented by these other sources of data, we were enabled – like other researchers such as Currie (1988) – to address questions of structure and process despite the personalized, subject-centred interview mode. This is consistent with Silverman's (1993) view that interview data can give access both to 'cultural particulars related to the patterns of social organization' as well as 'displays of members' artful practices in assembling these particulars' during interviews. Thus we have been able to shape, from the analytical categories and the connections between them, a 'generic cultural and social account' of the initiation and development of an innovative idea from origins through to implementation and eventual institutionalization (see figure 1).

A Generic Account

This account is structured within a framework of 'levels' of phenomena in one dimension and an implicit timescale in the other, running from the past (as 'memories drawn from experience'), to the origination of the innovation and then through its development to implementation and institutionalization. The levels start with the self in social interaction with others throughout the timescale. To a greater or lesser degree, the participants in the interactions perceive themselves as subject to various internal, systemic influences at the next level. Possibly moderated by higher levels of management engaged within the innovation process, these include pressures to work within ever tighter resource constraints, to increase flexibility, to improve control, to import new ideas and so on. Some pressures are perceived to emanate directly or indirectly from more distal sources within the environment external to the organization, such as legislation, the market and technology. In some cases innovators, collaborators and other organizational members involved in the process deal directly with representatives of external organizations, such as the parent company, charitable foundations and government agencies.

The process that connects these levels along the time axis derives first from feelings experienced by one or more of the various actors, especially the self-nominated innovator – of dissatisfaction, anxiety, anticipation and so on – prompted by perceptions of a problem to be resolved or an opportunity to be grasped. Those perceptions and the associated feelings are usually related in some way via memory to experience.

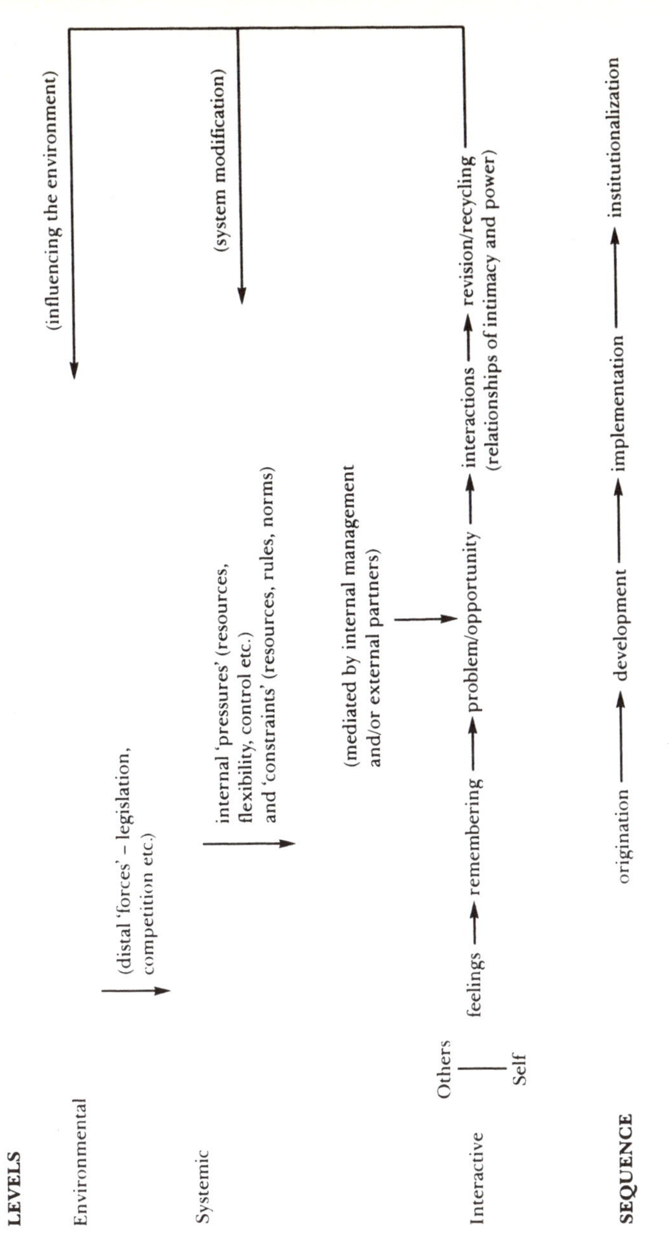

Figure 1. A generic account

The innovation is carried forward through various social interactions, especially between the innovator and other actors, in relationships subject to structural constraints of resource allocation and rules, procedures and norms which regulate resource use. Actors benefit from the intimacy of relationships but have the potential to exploit positional power within social networks, dependent on their capacity to mobilize appropriate social and political skills.

Once an innovation is implemented and, in time, becomes institutionalized, the cycle of reciprocal influence between individual and system is closed. The revised pattern of resource allocation and of the controlling rules and norms brought about by the innovation become embedded at the level of the system, now experienced as constraint or opportunity by various members of the organization in their everyday or innovative activities.

Our main purpose in this paper is to suggest an integrative theoretical framework within which these cyclical processes can be better interpreted. Unfortunately, much of the literature on psychological and social theory is not yet up to this task, leaving unresolved the dualism of collective and individual perspectives. This is true in two branches of literature most relevant to our particular focus: that on innovation research, described in Wolfe's (1994) review as yielding 'a relatively undeveloped' and 'fragmented' understanding of innovative behaviour, and the decision-making literature, a source of only partial frameworks (Zey, 1992).

Taking Wolfe's advice to build on 'extant research and theory', we use Giddens' theories of structuration (1984) and of the self (1991) to reconcile the continuity and potential for transformation that stem both from individual actors and the social system of which they are members.

Crucial to structuration theory is the proposition that the very rules and resources on which actors draw in producing and reproducing social action are at the same time the basis for reproducing the social system within which those actors relate to each other. Hence the theory promises a flexible approach to integrating the behaviour of individual agents and the social relationships and institutional structures that constitute organizational forms, an integration that is implicit in the narratives, made more explicit in the 'generic account' of the innovation process represented in figure 1.

For the purposes of this paper we extend and elaborate Giddens' theory in a number of ways. The concept of self-efficacy is introduced to account for the confidence with which innovators launch their projects and the persistence they show in carrying them through. More explicitly than Giddens we include the discursive, rhetorical process within social relations through which the ambiguities of complex organizational life are exploited. Account is also taken of the quality of intimacy that characterizes social relationships to varying degrees and is a vital influence on people's behaviour. Finally, we focus on the reciprocal, generative development of both social relationships and of the substance of the innovation.

THREE CASE STUDIES

Discussion of the narrative data within this framework is developed using three case studies, one from each organization. They illustrate and focus the discussion, providing lines of reference along which to structure its flow and connections. Each case is not the most radical from its organization and its effects are not likely to be the most far-reaching. Together they encompass all of the analytical categories, provide much of the attribute variety referred to earlier, and illustrate some less usual aspects of the total set. Where relevant, references to other cases will be made.

Ian's 'Umbrella Management' within ITC

ITC, part of a large US multinational corporation, manufactures computer-based products. The research was conducted at its main location where about 1,500 people are employed.

Following a row with the CEO of his previous company Ian joined ITC, where he set up and managed a new plant separate from the main location. On taking up his present post managing a key assembly department Ian concluded that it had been subject to considerable interference. Resolved to change the managerial style, he confronted a director to stop him interfering, an intervention that provided an 'umbrella' under which reorganization could proceed.

Ulrich and Managerial Accounting in Uni

Uni is a small university with approximately 5,000 students and 1,500 staff. Its form is conventional: academic departments within faculties and a tiered policy-making committee system.

Ulrich, an academic department head, was keen to prepare for delegation to departments of greater responsibility for resource management. He wanted to relate departmental accounts more transparently to the complex resource flows within the department, to reduce sub-discipline compartmentalization, and to resolve several 'moral' issues including the responsibilities and rights of tenure compared to temporary staff.

Ulrich developed a spreadsheet accounting format as a vehicle to persuade colleagues to accept a new approach to departmental management that would resolve these various difficulties. In parallel he tried to persuade the finance department to adapt to his format the monthly data they provided.

Susan and the Sex Offenders Programme in SWD

The region's dispersed population is served by SWD's 3,000 staff. Most managers moved into their positions as a natural progression within a social work career.

Susan, a division manager, reported the creation of a three-member team to run a sex-offenders treatment programme but, unlike Ian and Ulrich, did not lay claim to the original idea. The innovation process started when divisional staff became interested in the new approach and received Susan's agreement to attend an outside training course. Afterwards, with her encouragement, they set up a 'self-help' group, supporting each other in the difficult task of dealing with offenders. About a year before our interview the group had appreciated the great demands the new approach made on staff and proposed that a special team be set up to take a lead in the offender programme.

INTERPRETATION AND THEORETICAL CONNECTIONS

We now turn to our interpretations of the data and links made between those interpretations and relevant theoretical formulations. First we consider the context of the three organizations and their internal 'logics of action' (Whittington, 1992), related in the second section to the origins of the innovations in the sense of identity and personal agency of those most closely involved in the process. From that point on the discussion focuses on social and political processes: the rhetorical process through which arguments are developed to a state where they can serve as the basis for action; how the development of the innovation is mediated by social and political relationships in which intimate mutual knowledge is important; the reciprocal effects of the innovation's social and substantive strands and, lastly, the institutionalization of the innovation.

Organizational Flux and Competing 'Logics of Action'

In considering organizational settings we employ Giddens' (1984) notion that a 'social system' is constituted by the patterning of social relations. System integration depends on reciprocal interrelationships between individuals or collectivities. Its maintenance depends on the use made of sets of rules that guide action and resources that empower action – rules and resources which also constitute the organization's structure. Actors draw on rules and resources in their social relationships, generally with the effect of maintaining the order and continuity of the system. In times when that order is disrupted they draw on the same rules and resources to re-establish that order or – consistent with the main focus of our research – they attempt to transform it.

In each of the organizations managers had experienced a considerable degree of disruption to the ordering of the social systems within which they were positioned. Any sense of continuity experienced earlier had been giving way progressively to one of change. The management of ITC, for example, had embraced a wide range of modern techniques designed to reduce costs, maintain quality, enhance flexibility and bring new products to market rapidly. References were made by our respondents to approaches which litter the management literature such as just-in-time, total quality management, process re-engineering and project management control systems.

Most ITC narratives refer to a closely choreographed, top-down culture change programme such as Peters and Waterman (1982) popularized; British examples have been reviewed by Williams et al. (1989). Innovation was a key value, supported at the research site by various programmes. In parallel, ITC's long-standing interest in human resource management – consistent again with the literature (e.g. Legge, 1995; Storey, 1992) – had prompted a playing-down of managers' authoritative role, emphasizing teamworking instead. Managers were called 'coaches', symbolizing their new role in facilitating improved employee performance.

In common with most UK higher education institutions, Uni had for many years been responding to a government strategy since 1979 to disrupt academic values and practices which, it was alleged, had reinforced national cultural patterns based on social status which were inimical to the needs of the modern economy. The goal of such initiatives is the 'entrepreneurial university', strongly linked to business and more accountable to its clients (Cowen, 1991).

To some extent Uni's management systems had been adapted to conform more closely to models proposed by the likes of Jarratt (CVCP, 1985) and Sizer (e.g. 1987, 1988). A strategic and resource planning process had been introduced, greater resource management responsibility was being delegated to departments, more formal systems existed for evaluating performance, and a body of specialists had been recruited to assist decision making.

In this context it was not surprising that many respondents perceived themselves as coping with pressures caused by reduced government funding, increased competition for students and research grants, and the audit of academic output. Key issues were raising revenue, improving research and teaching ratings, and enhancing management quality, all areas subject to frequent changes in government policy.

In SWD managers were also caught up in a dynamic created during the 1980s and 1990s when, under legislative and other pressures, innovation became endemic in local government. By the time our research project started SWD seemed to have undergone most of the transformations experienced in local authorities across the UK (Leach et al., 1994; Wilson and Game, 1994).

Like other local authorities, SWD had been expected to become a purchaser as well as a provider of services, and to tighten up its policies and practices following widely publicized major social work debacles throughout the UK. Most recently, in anticipation of the NHS and Community Care Act, SWD had been reorganized radically. The directorate's role had been modified to enable it to deal better with strategic issues, central policy units had been strengthened, and structures had been 'flattened' by removing layers of management and delegating more responsibility to field units. Attempts had also been made to transform SWD's culture to correspond with this new reality. Narratives of those nearer the apex do make reference to changes in values, policies and styles that may have facilitated some of the innovations, whereas others, organizationally and/or geographically further from the directorate, tell of the burdens of new rules.

In such fluid contexts, organizations are probably less 'monolithic and determined' than they have ever been, becoming ever more open to external influences. Hence strategic efforts to influence the way in which the social system is reproduced or modified are unlikely to be complete, leaving the organization vulnerable to transformation through deliberate action by people within and outside its boundaries (Whittington, 1992).

ITC illustrates well the ambiguities of 'the large, diversified and managerially controlled firm ... [that] have fragmented the simplicity of the profit-maximizing rule into a plethora of competing managerial "logics of action"' (Whittington, 1992, p. 705). Meanwhile, in the flux of externally prompted change, organizations traditionally not measured against profit, such as Uni and SWD, have become ever more difficult to model and manage. Their logics of action proliferate, providing an ambiguous field of information out of which innovations emerge through the deliberate choices of individual agents.

For example, in Uni there were several different rationales for the management of a university ranging from a traditional 'logic' – a form of 'collegiality' that enabled academics to 'do their own thing' – through to an 'enterprise culture' logic that universities should be subject to a form of 'executive management'. Ironically, in ITC, top-down control stemming from the executive management model competed with something nearer a 'collegial' model based on notions of 'delegation', 'empowerment' and 'autonomous work groups'. In SWD, pressures for devolved forms, giving managers more scope to take initiatives, conflicted with a bureaucratic tightening up of service accountability.

Changes external to an organization – whether attributed to government, competition or technology – become operative internally only when the basis for such change exists there. Similarly, internal change, as with the development within ITC of a less autocratic style of management and Uni's greater delegation to departments, prompts 'knock-on' change only if, again, the basis for further change exists or can be created. At both levels nothing happens if individuals who can choose freely, such as Ian, Ulrich and Susan, do not feel cause within themselves for wishing to create the change. If a person has no choice about undertaking a project, as was the case in a small minority of the innovations reported, we hypothesize that its success will depend on how much of that individual's self is invested in the project. In either situation the essential element is personal agency, a theme to which we now turn.

The Basis of Innovation in Personal Agency

Self-identity. A key concept in our interpretation and attempt to build theory is 'self-identity', used in a sense similar to that employed by other researchers using qualitative methods – e.g. Maclure (1993) and Watson (1994a) for whom identity serves as an organizing principle in understanding, respectively, the jobs of teachers and managers. Self-identity is concerned with being 'an individual to and for oneself', and how that individuality is presented in the sense-making process through which people position themselves within discursive practices (Harré and Gillett, 1994). To have and to be able to present this uniqueness of self requires a sense of spatial location that yields a 'point of view', of existing at a moment in time along one's life trajectory, of being a responsible agent within a network of mutual obligations and commitments, and of being socially situated according to criteria such as status, age and reputation.

The continuity of an individual's self-identity is safeguarded by his or her feeling of *ontological security*, established early in life as part of mechanisms to control anxiety (Giddens, 1984). Security of being is maintained through the predictability of routine discursive practices such as tactful behaviours which sustain mutual trust. Even while acting as an agent of transformation, as in our cases, an individual behaves in ways that both sustain 'continuity of the personality' as he or she 'moves along the paths of daily activities' (Giddens, 1984, p. 60) and reproduce the structures to which he or she is subject.

Central to our theme, however, is how individuals transform those structures by repositioning themselves discursively in attempts to make sense of some disruption to everyday routines or, spontaneously, to promote some innovative idea. Engaged as they are in the flux of organizational activity, those individuals are able to tap into its 'flows of social and psychological information about possible ways of life'. In attempting to make sense of and influence that flux in innovative ways they are faced with the question 'How shall I live?' (Giddens, 1991, p. 14). An organization's members can address this question by drawing on experience, not just from the work context but as social beings in various other domains. Through membership of other bodies managers may be able to import into their imaginings and actions alien values, rules and resources (Whittington, 1992).

References to seemingly key aspects of identity are common in the narratives. Ulrich's innovation was motivated by an overall concern for his academic discipline, probably a more important contributor to his sense of self than his managerial role. However, from his positioning in that role Ulrich realized that Uni could survive without his discipline, especially as the department was subject to high levels of uncertainty and therefore difficult to manage. So he accepted responsibility for initiating steps to secure an improvement.

Ulrich also revealed strong security needs in admitting that what had sustained him through 18 difficult months was 'the avoidance of chaos and the need for a tidy world ... a degree of anxiety sometimes, fear about things being out of control...'. But an academic collaborator, in describing how Ulrich took risks as a mountain climber under severe conditions, and in challenging authority within the university, provided evidence that Ulrich could quell his anxiety in critical situations. Moral issues also seemed important to Ulrich, illustrated by his hope that, whether or not colleagues agreed with him, they would say he 'was fair and treated them properly, with respect...'.

Ian exhibited a great need for personal autonomy, reacting strongly when its security was threatened by the unreasonable exercise of authority by superiors. His identity as a manager, especially after his new plant experience, hinged on a capability to enable others to exercise their personal agency with greater independence. These values were rationalized and made potent in ITC's setting by his attachment, as a professional manager, to the ideas of various gurus (e.g. Peters and Waterman, 1982). While it may be that company policies on greater empowerment were consistent with guru literature, perhaps ITC directors might not have wished to move as quickly or as far as Ian did.

Susan's sense of self was buttressed by very strong convictions about good social work practice that may not have been consonant with what was managerially efficient as defined by civil servants responsible for her division's funding, but which were probably shared by colleagues in the judiciary, the police and the prison service. Reputation seemed important, too. A collaborator noted that Susan 'is quite a career person' and the project would be 'something for her to be seen doing' – reflected perhaps in her own comment, 'another first for the Region'.

Drawing on the evidence that these case studies illustrate, as framed by the context of organization and external environment discussed earlier, we hypothesize that our respondents, in making the various interventions recounted to us, were exhibiting what Giddens (1979) calls 'transformative capacity'. This is concerned with the capability of agents to achieve certain outcomes, a function of their freedom to choose between alternative ways of behaving, expressing how they are 'willing to exist as particular subjects'; their deployment of knowledge and other resources; and their self-efficacy.

Within the structuration framework we are proposing, a person's self-identity is shaped and confirmed by adherence to routines that ensure organizational continuity. Conversely, in attempting to forge his or her own work-based identity, the same individual contributes to re-shaping the organization, exerting social influences which, potentially, have wide consequences. Innovative initiatives can thus be conceived as having reciprocal effects, through personal agency, on both the organization and the agent's sense of self. This seems to mirror how Watson

(1994b) interprets the stories told by his sample of managers; in attempts to shape their organizations they 'shape themselves as individual human beings ... continually having to realize themselves and make sense of their place in a potentially chaotic world' (p. 82).

Drawing on experience. The 'trajectory' of life's experiences along which identity is formed is also a source of the knowledge and understanding that managers can mobilize in developing their innovation. Some had long-standing interests which endowed them with expertise. For example, Susan's work with sex-offenders had made her aware of the severe problems of recidivism associated with traditional modes of treatment. Even Ulrich's limited interest in spreadsheets was of practical and symbolic value.

Experience had sensitized some individuals to current problems, as when an SWD manager recognized that an organization he had inherited was likely to be a particular 'hot spot' of trouble with NHS consultants. More specific still, some imported the basic idea of an innovation directly from their experience, as with Ian's creation of a flat departmental structure and radical 'ethos', building on his achievement at another ITC plant.

Crucial, too, is what Giddens (1984) calls 'discursive penetration', referring here to the depth of managers' understanding of, and degree of fluency with, key discourses which shape their own and other organizations. Such understanding and fluency enables managers to direct their energies and to form their arguments effectively. The three case managers had deep discursive penetration of their own organizations, while Susan, out of painful experience of dealing with a government department and its civil servants, used her understanding of that context to good effect in the negotiation of funding.

Experience also provided for many the foundation of self-beliefs which yielded a sense of confidence that they would achieve successful outcomes, examples of what Bandura (1986) calls 'self-efficacy', based on the person's judgement of their 'capabilities to organize and execute courses of action required to attain designated types of performances' (p. 391). Hence, 'the successful, the innovative, the sociable, the non-despondent, and the social reformers take an optimistic view of their personal efficacy to exercise influence over events that affect their lives' (Bandura, 1989, p. 418). Moreover, in critical situations, as Ulrich showed strongly, when the security of everyday routines is disrupted, such people are able to think ahead and risk choosing from alternative courses of action rather than suffer a collapse of the will.

There is evidence in our data that some managers were not entirely reliant on their own capacity to recall from experience. Instead, they and their collaborators drew on 'community memory', a coping strategy similar to that of photocopier technicians who collaborated to solve seemingly intractable problems (Orr, 1990). Like the technicians, our respondents – such as Susan and her colleagues wrestling with issues related to sex offenders, university managers attempting to establish a leading-edge research centre, and the ITC team charged with introducing new micro-chip technology – seemed to have been involved in 'the reflective manipulation of a set of resources accumulated through experience ... piecing together an understanding from bits of experience, their own and others, in the absence of definite information' (Orr, 1990, pp. 184–5).

Freedom of action and command over resources. Narratives also provided evidence that most managers had some choice as to where and how they channelled their energies, an essential element of 'agency'. They seemed to be on a relatively light rein, with scope to manipulate their roles (cf. Fondas and Stewart, 1994; Katz and Kahn, [1966] 1978). Our three cases provide clear examples, and in other narratives even quite junior managers claimed that, provided they got the 'bread and butter work' done, their own superiors let them get on with local innovations.

Capacity to transform social situations is also a function of resources of two forms: 'allocative', which facilitate command over raw materials, production methods and products, and 'authoritative', yielding command over persons (Giddens, 1984). But it is neither necessary nor sufficient to have formal authority. The narratives revealed that only about six of the 30 innovators interviewed were able to implement the innovation within the sphere of their own authority. The remainder seemed to feel constrained to consult and negotiate with some set of peers, bosses and external agencies. Even those who had direct authority to command resources consulted or negotiated with those over whom they had nominal command. This behaviour may have been part of an 'education strategy' intended to overcome resistance (Kimberly, 1981). It is also consistent with two other arguments: that the managerial role can be legitimized only through co-operation (Hales, 1993; Kaplan, 1984), or that followers can make a contribution to effective leadership (Hollander and Offermann, 1990). In general our data suggests a greater incidence of co-operation and joint contribution strategies.

Even so, command over resources – which, for example, gave Susan scope to rebalance social work teams without agreement from bosses – is seen as a useful asset in furthering an innovative initiative. But the evidence from the narratives places the mobilization of that advantage clearly within the constraints of social and political relationships, to which we now turn.

Furthering Innovation through Social and Political Relationships

The narratives are replete with stories of a great variety of social interactions within which the focal managers and others used their intrinsic and acquired capability to transform situations. Many refer to *meetings*, regular and irregular, formal and informal, including those related to the procedures managers had to follow in order for their project to be sanctioned by others. For example, internal departmental meetings and those with the finance department were particularly crucial to the success of Ulrich's project.

One-to-one exchanges feature frequently, being used to persuade someone to join an alliance; to 'chat up' people before a key meeting; and to deal discreetly with some difficulty, as when Ian told his director to stop interfering. Some managers are revealed as good networkers, facilitating access to unusual sources of information and other forms of support, enhancing their discursive penetration of different settings, and enriching the range of exotic perspectives and arguments they are able to import into the workplace.

Anchored relations. West (1990) hypothesizes that 'innovation is more likely in situations of high psychological safety' (p. 312). This notion implies a degree of interpersonal intimacy consistent with what Goffman (1971, 1983) called 'anchored relations', anchored in mutual knowledge which comes from regular face-to-face interactions, along a continuum from mere 'acquaintanceship' through degrees of increasing intimacy.

Anchored relations, as the source of non-sexual friendship bonds, provide the 'preconditions for something crucial: the sustained intimate co-ordination of action, whether in support of closely collaborative acts or as a means of accommodating closely adjacent ones' (Goffman, 1983, p. 3). It is through such relations that 'intersubjective meanings' emerge, a level of social reality created when 'individual thoughts, feelings, and intentions are merged or synthesized into conversations during which the self gets transformed from "I" into "we"' (Weick, 1995, p. 71).

How well we are known by others can be crucial in many senses as revealed in narrative examples. One SWD manager, new in his role, felt that his boss did not know him well enough to trust him to progress an innovative idea without taking it 'up the line' into the bureaucracy. So he went ahead with his project without consulting his boss in advance. Conversely, close and trusting relationships were revealed which, while implicitly providing 'a traffic' of relatively unthinking, routine actions that maintain order and integrate existing social systems (Goffman, 1983), are drawn on by those involved in developing an innovative project. Ulrich made clear that he traded on his good working relationship with the finance officer. Ian and his senior supervisor, Tom, built up a degree of trust that served them well in the arm's-length nature of their formal relationship under 'umbrella management'. Susan's assistant manager, involved with her in all stages of the offender project, claims that: 'We get on well professionally and that makes a whole lot of things possible ... we can go together to these meetings [with civil servants] in the knowledge that we will cover each other ... because we trust each other.'

Within the narratives anchored relations seem to facilitate easy acceptance of each other's ideas and plans. But there is evidence to the contrary, as when Ulrich and the finance officer, and Ian and his supervisor, Tom, disagreed strongly on issues central to their innovations. Probably more important then is the development of trust within the relationship so that each person can believe 'that relinquishing some degree of control over a situation to one or more others will not lead to personal loss or harm' (Moingeon and Edmondson, 1996, p. 2).

Each example of anchored relations referred to above corresponds to what Goffman (1971) calls a 'two-person', formed by friends for various kinds of social participation. There is a suggestion in the narratives that, adapting the term used by Bandura (1986, 1989), the reciprocal effect of the partnership is one of 'mutual self-efficacy'. From their shared experience of each other's support they derive beliefs that bolster their own sense of self-efficacy.

The importance of anchored relations as the source of 'structure building entities' – as reflected in our data – tends to have been ignored by Giddens in his structuration theory (Cohen, 1987). We argue, therefore, that the theory needs to be extended to include the structural potential of such relations if it is to be used as a framework for interpretation of innovation in organizations.

A rhetorical process. Though friends and other close acquaintances share the goals to which change is directed, they may still need to be persuaded of the wisdom of the action proposed, engaging rhetorically in a form of social dialectic through which arguments can be refined and agreed on as a basis for action (Billig, 1989).

The novelty of an argument seems to depend on two creative streams, one more cognitive and reflective, the other social and interactive. Creative insights help us to reframe circumstances that constrain into ones that enable and facilitate opportunities to transform social systems (cf. Giddens, 1984; Shotter, 1993). The products of those insights are processed in the social challenge of argumentation, through which differences are revealed and conflicts resolved, potentially generating sufficient creative energy to sustain action. In practice, as the narratives reveal, it is difficult to separate these two creative activities.

The individual actor reflects on his or her perceptions of contextual ambiguities. Strongly motivated to resolve any inherent problems, or to translate them into opportunities, he or she draws on 'domain relevant knowledge and skills' which are cognitively processed (Amabile, 1983). Yet thought, like talk, is subject to strong social influences – constrained by the thinker's reliance on culturally derived discursive practices and the need to justify memories and ideas as the basis for future action in a social setting where other people's attitudes and expectations are crucial (Middleton and Edwards, 1990).

The three case managers talk of their perceptions of such constraints: of colleagues whose meanings cause them to compartmentalize their academic lives, or to await instructions from outsiders before acting, or to consider it more important to provide services to the victims of crime than to deal with the perpetrators. These constraints operate within, and sometimes flow from, the ambiguities of competing 'logics of action' at higher levels of the organization.

In shaping arguments intended to change existing meanings in such constrained contexts, those with sufficient cognitive flexibility, sense of self-efficacy and knowledge of their audience may be in a position to exploit the very ambiguities that cause the confusion, especially if they are able to import values and cultural props from other domains as Ian and other respondents did. Ulrich, more than the others, provides indirect access to an internal dialogue in which 'the same arguments which we use in persuading others when we speak in public, we employ also when we deliberate in our thoughts' (Billig, 1989, p. 110). Ulrich reveals how he rehearsed, in an internal dialogue facilitated by the symbolism of the spreadsheet, a narrative to present to his colleagues that he knew would be questioned. He realized that only if his arguments were perceived by others as authoritative would they be acceptable, capable of turning the audience to new meanings (Shotter, 1990). A more vivid example is the boast of an SWD manager, confirmed spontaneously by a collaborator, that when 'I know the person that I am going to speak to ... [I am] able to change and adapt and communicate in a way that person ... feels at ease with'.

Finally, although the narratives are not a rich source of actual 'talk' within the innovation process, there is evidence of the creative use of rhetoric to win key people over. Susan and one of her collaborators, for example, tell from their different perspectives how members of SWD's top policy-making committee were persuaded to sanction, despite strong reservations, the use of scarce resources to help the perpetrators rather than the victims of abuse. It was argued that perpetrators would go on behaving in the same way and creating yet more victims unless they could be persuaded to behave differently. So, in the long run local politicians' constituents would lose out. Meanwhile, Susan and her collaborator put reciprocal pressures on civil servants and area managers. The former were told, if you want to spread the costs of our service this project is the route and a lot hangs on it in the region; on the other side managers were pressed to yield one member each from their teams to service the project because it was argued, if they didn't, government would insist on savings anyway and they might well lose people without compensating support from a project team.

Of Ulrich's crucial meeting with the finance department he said: 'Not only was I able to convey the importance I attached to this in the long term, but also to understand one or two of the things that had been getting in the way . . . interfaces with their systems that hadn't been explained to me in a way that I could see as anything other than inertia.' It was a sort of 'translation of the context to each other' without which 'energy is lost in the friction between central services and departments'.

Reciprocal, generative effects of the social and substantive. This extract exemplifies parallel series of changes that take place, each implicated in the other. As the meaning evolves through the dialectic, the relationship moves on; and the developing relationship assists in freeing up the dialectic. Arguments that flow from the 'old logic' are kept in dialogue with the 'new logic' long enough for some resolution to be achieved, so that 'the innovation process enacts and is enacted by the relational patterns which commit the different parties as they deal with the diversity, difference and ambiguity which surround them' (Steyaert et al., 1996, p. 83). Exchanges of feeling within the relationship provide a release of tension that eventually help the partners rethink their personal values and interpretive frames.

Many of the narratives illustrate the interweaving of social process and the construction of the substantive elements of the innovation, and the importance of expressions of feeling to that development. This is particularly well portrayed in reports by Ulrich and a collaborator of how departmental colleagues presented serious challenges to Ulrich's reasoning, both technical and moral. Tensions were released as some of them indulged in vituperative outbursts, spilling over into the wider university. It was claimed that this led to a show of support from others, securing a movement towards Ulrich's position. On another level both Ulrich and his other collaborator spoke of how the relationship between his department's administrative assistant and finance department staff 'began to oil the wheels between the two parts of the system', bringing substantive progress.

Synergy between relational events and the substance of the innovation was also evident in Ian's case. Only by challenging early the authority of the director, he believed, could he begin to help the supervisors change the meanings that constrained them. This act ensured that he did not get caught up in the earlier meanings and practices; it also symbolized new meanings in a very dramatic way, modelling how he wished the supervisors to behave. As Tom, the senior supervisor reported, Ian provoked them to start doing things their own way. There were frictions and disputes and those who could not accept the transformed meaning of what it was to be a supervisor dropped out of the team, their need for security threatened by the lack of assurance from external authority and internal structure. Within the team that survived, strong relationships developed based on a robust openness that could tolerate difference and argument. At this stage Ian was able to trust the team more fully, allowing him to achieve another susbtantive end, greater autonomy for himself.

In the case of the sex offender project the substantive proposal to set up a special team arose only after the relations between members of the ad hoc mutual support group had matured. Susan spoke of how the support group, having collected data about departmental attitudes to the new approach to treating offenders, put their interpretation to her, proposing the creation of a mechanism for supporting those involved in dealing directly with offenders. In partnership with her assistant manager, a collaborator, Susan was then able to develop existing relationships with directorate colleagues, elected members and civil servants to the position where they were willing to endorse the proposal for a special team.

Conclusion: Institutionalization of the Innovation

At such a stage an innovative proposal can be converted into a 'working innovation', becoming institutionalized, overlapping with and integrated into the existing social system and related structures of the organization (Steyaert et al., 1996). In Susan's case she and her collaborators report on steps taken to rebalance resources by transferring staff from the area teams to the project team, and to define the team's role and to establish rules which would sustain that role in practice.

Formal implementation is only one, if a key, stage of institutionalization, a process that evolves, as paths of the innovation's development converge on and link into ongoing operational routines (Steyaert et al., 1996). In the sex offender project we assume, for example, based on our interpretation of the data, that the proposals put to the policy-making committee would have been screened to ensure that the resource implications and any new rules envisaged for controlling the proposed service meshed with existing arrangements.

Similarly, Ulrich and a collaborator reported how, prior to final implementation of the management accounting system, agreement had already been reached with the finance department to change their monthly reporting practices. But this was possible only after Ulrich's original proposal had been modified to take account of constraints within which the finance department operated. Convergence had been assured by a willingness of each party to accommodate to the other's objectives and practices.

In Ian's case it was necessary to ensure that any changes in practice proposed by the supervisory team were consistent with the company's normal operating procedures. In the extended period during which the innovation was consolidated and built upon – for example, in achieving ISO 9001 status for the quality of the department's operations – it is likely, according to our interpretation, that the substantive changes were also linked more closely to the institutions of both the company and external agencies.

In Giddens' (1984) terms, for these three and all the other cases researched, steps taken to implement the innovation had the effect of reconstituting the established systems of social relations and the structure of rules and resources that are implicated in the reproduction of those systems. Collaborators spoke of how members of area teams in Susan's division had to build up new sets of social relations with the new project team, the members of which had similarly to create relationships with other parties such as offenders, police officers and members of the judiciary. The data also suggests that Susan herself controlled the use of resources that had previously been subject to the direct authority of area team leaders. We also assume that all of the participants in the offender programme were constrained by rules published as part of the innovation and any norms which evolved as the revised programme was implemented. All those affected by the innovation were, in effect, re-positioned to some degree within the discursive practices which evolved in the development and implementation of the innovative idea and in the subsequent operation of the 'live' programme.

We have come full circle as envisaged in the crucial relationship between individual agency on the one hand and the organization's social system and structure that sustains it on the other (Giddens, 1984). Our interpretation of the data, consistent with the methodology discussed in the early part of the paper, is that, through the innovative project agents spontaneously used their capacity to transform circumstances, producing definite outcomes by influencing the actions of others in ways that disrupted everyday routines. To achieve this outcome they drew on knowledge, social skills and access to resources they already had or could acquire. In mobilizing and expressing power in this way their actions had an effect on both the social system and structure on the one hand and their own identity on the other. But, once implemented and operational, the new arrangements constrained, admittedly in new modes, the behaviours of all of those affected, including the agents involved in the creation of the innovative product. The 'reality' of the changed arrangements was now part and parcel of the context which these organizational members would monitor in their attempts to sustain control reflexively over their everyday conduct. And through the mutual deployment of skilful behaviour as they collaborate with others to maintain both the routine order of daily life and the continuity of their own personality, they continually reconstitute the organization's newly modified system of social relations and its sustaining structure of rules and resources.

So, in effect, our conclusions emphasize the duality of the shaping process referred to by Watson (1994b). Yes, managers in shaping the organization also 'shape themselves as human beings' in the process. But in doing so they also create new structures which, in turn, serve to constitute – no less directly but in more subtle ways – the identities of the organization's members, including the innovators.

APPENDIX

Interviewees' Innovations, Listed by Organization

The number in brackets at the end of each line indicates the number of analytical categories that are referred to in the narrative. The hash sign (#) indicates one of the three cases described in the paper.

University

U1. Structures to improve functioning of a department's academic board (11)

U2. Postgraduate diploma course for language teachers in region's secondary schools (14)

U3. Restructuring of departmental accounting format to facilitate better use of resources (13) #

U4. Establishment of new research centre funded by major medical charity (14)
U5. Masters' course in surgery based on self-directed learning (12)
U6. Neurosurgical programme for treating chronic mental disorders (12)
U7. Devolved department management as part of strategy for improving teaching and research performance (12)
U8. 'Well-being' programme for staff and students with potential for raising revenue from public (12)
U9. New budget system for academic departments (13)
U10. Management system for halls of residence to deal with over-spending and vandalism (11)

IT company

IT1. New management style and structure introduced by manager of core production department (13) #
IT2. Visible work in progress system introduced into a production department (11)
IT3. Team of recently recruited graduate engineers formed to conceive, propose and implement an innovative project (11)
IT4. Incorporation of new 'application specific integrated circuit' into major product range (12)
IT5. Training programme for customers' help-desk personnel to optimize use of new generation of hardware (11)
IT6. Delegation of performance appraisals to project leaders in conjunction with peer input into the process (8)
IT7. Formal system to evaluate and screen projects for process improvement (12)
IT8. A new generation desk-top publishing system in a department controlling product information (13)
IT9. Computerized system for employee records (10)
IT10. Market research for, and specification of, equipment to deal with various types of 'smart card' (14)

SWD

S1. Specialized service in support of field workers charged with dealing with sex offenders (13) #
S2. Flexible scheme for the care of children of parents affected by HIV/AIDS developed in partnership with a national charity (12)
S3. Policies, roles and systems for consultation with carers and agencies involved in community care (14)
S4. Restructuring of care roles to support elderly clients in hospital (12)
S5. Restructured roles and rules for the work of a duty social work team responding to initial client contacts from an extensive city area (13)
S6. Criteria introduced to facilitate parental attendance at case conferences concerning their children (14)
S7. System of group supervision for a set of social workers new to a team (12)
S8. Mission and rules of community centre revised so that parents whose children no longer attended could continue to receive support at the centre without eroding its principal service to families (13)

S9. A team of social workers were transformed into care managers able to deliver services consistent with community care legislation (13)
S10. A newsletter designed for all women in SWD (12)

NOTE

*The authors acknowledge the support of the ESRC, through grant no. R000221143, for the conduct of the research on which this paper draws. They also wish to thank the *JMS* referees for the many positive criticisms and suggestions which served to prompt considerable improvements in the paper.

REFERENCES

AMABILE, T. M. (1983). The Social Psychology of Creativity. New York: Springer-Verlag.

BANDURA, A. (1986). *Social Foundations of Thought and Action.* Englewood Cliffs, New Jersey: Prentice-Hall.

BANDURA, A. (1989). 'Perceived self-efficacy in the exercise of personal agency'. *The Psychologist*, **2**, 10, 411–24.

BARRON, F. and HARRINGTON, D. (1981). 'Creativity, intelligence and personality'. *Annual Review of Psychology*, **32**, 439–76.

BILLIG, M. (1989). *Arguing and Thinking: A Rhetorical Approach to Social Psychology.* Cambridge: Cambridge University Press.

CAMPBELL, D. T. and FISKE, D. W. (1959). 'Convergent and discriminant validation by the multitrait-multimethod matrix'. *Psychological Bulletin*, **56**, 81–105.

COHEN, I. J. (1987). 'Structuration theory and social *praxis*'. In Giddens, A. and Turner, J. H. (Eds), *Social Theory Today.* Cambridge: Polity, 273–308.

COWEN, R. (1991). 'The management and evaluation of the entrepreneurial university: the case of England'. *Higher Education Policy*, **4**, 3, 9–13.

CURRIE, D. (1988). 'Re-thinking what we do and how we do it: a study of reproductive decisions'. *Canadian Review of Sociology and Anthropology*, **25**, 2, 231–53.

CVCP (1985). *Report of the Steering Committee for Efficiency Studies in Universities* (Chairman: Sir Alex Jarratt). London: CVCP.

DEY, I. (1995). 'Reducing fragmentation in qualitative research'. In Kelle, U. (Ed.), *Computer-aided Qualitative Analysis.* London: Sage, 69–79.

FONDAS, N. and STEWART, R. (1994). 'Enactment in managerial jobs: a role analysis'. *Journal of Management Studies*, **31**, 1, 84–103.

GIDDENS, A. (1979). *Central Problems in Social Theory: Action, Structure and Contradiction in Social Analysis.* London: Macmillan.

GIDDENS, A. (1984). *The Constitution of Society.* Cambridge: Polity.

GIDDENS, A. (1991). *Modernity and Self-Identity.* Cambridge, Polity.

GLASER, B. G. and STRAUSS, A. L. (1967). *The Discovery of Grounded Theory: Strategies for Qualitative Research.* New York: Aldine.

GOFFMAN, E. (1971). *Relations in Public.* New York: Basic Books.

GOFFMAN, E. (1983). 'The interaction order'. *American Sociological Review*, **48**, 1–17.

HALES, C. (1993). *Managing Through Organization.* London: Routledge.

HARRÉ, R. and GILLETT, G. (1994). *The Discursive Mind.* Thousand Oaks, CA: Sage.

HENWOOD, K. and PIDGEON, N. (1994). 'Grounded theory: a resource for reflexive and deconstructive analysis?'. Submitted to a Special Issue of *The Journal of Community and Applied Social Psychology*, February 1994.

Hollander, E. P. and Offermann, L. R. (1990). 'Power and leadership in organizations: relationships in transition'. *American Psychologist*, February, 179–89.

Kaplan, R. E. (1984). 'Trade routes: the manager's network of relationships'. *Organizational Dynamics*, **12**, 37–52.

Katz, D. and Kahn, R. L. ([1966] 1978). *The Social Psychology of Organizations*, 2nd edn. New York: Wiley.

Kimberly, J. R. (1981). 'Managerial innovation'. In Nystrom, P. C. and Starbuck, W. (Eds), *Handbook of Organizational Design*. New York: Oxford University Press, 84–104.

King, N. (1990). 'Innovation at work: the research literature'. In West, M. A. and Farr, J. L. (Eds), *Innovation and Creativity at Work: Psychological and Organizational Strategies*. Chichester: Wiley, 15–59.

Leach, S., Stewart, J. and Walsh, K. (1994). *The Changing Organization and Management of Local Government*. London: Macmillan.

Legge, K. (1995). *Human Resource Management: Rhetorics and Realities*. London: Macmillan.

Maclure, M. (1993). 'Arguing for your self: identity as an organizing principle in teachers' jobs and lives'. *British Educational Research Journal*, **19**, 4, 311–22.

Middleton, D. and Edwards, D. (1990). 'Conversational remembering: a social psychological approach'. In Middleton, D. and Edwards, D. (Eds), *Collective Remembering*. London: Sage, 23–45.

Miles, M. B. and Huberman, A. M. (1994). *Qualitative Data Analysis*. Thousand Oaks, CA: Sage.

Moingeon, B. and Edmondson, A. (1996). 'Trust and organizational learning'. Paper presented at a Symposium on Organizational Learning and the Learning Organization. Lancaster University, 1–3 September 1996.

Orr, J. E. (1990). 'Sharing knowledge, celebrating identity: community memory in a service culture'. In Middleton, D. and Edwards, D. (Eds), *Collective Remembering*. London: Sage, 169–89.

Patton, M. Q. (1987). *How to use Qualitative Methods in Evaluation*. Newbury Park, CA: Sage.

Peters, T. J. and Waterman, R. H. (1982). *In Search of Excellence*. New York: Harper & Row.

Shotter, J. (1990). 'The social construction of remembering and forgetting'. In Middleton, D. and Edwards, D. (Eds), *Collective Remembering*. London: Sage, 120–38.

Shotter, J. (1993). *Conversational Realities*. London: Sage.

Silverman, D. (1993). *Interpreting Qualitative Data: Methods for Analysing Talk, Text and Interaction*. London: Sage.

Sizer, J. (1987). 'Universities in hard times: some policy implications and guidelines'. *Higher Education Quarterly*, **41**, 4, 354–72.

Sizer, J. (1988). 'In search of excellence – performance assessment in the United Kingdom'. *Higher Education Quarterly*, **42**, 2, 152–61.

Steyaert, C., Bouwen, R. and Van Looy, B. (1996). 'Conversational construction of new meaning configurations in organizational innovation: a generative approach'. *European Journal of Work and Occupational Psychology*, **5**, 1, 67–89.

Storey, J. (1992). *Developments in the Management of Human Resources: An Analytical Review*. Oxford: Blackwell.

Strauss, A. L. and Corbin, J. (1990). *Basics of Qualitative Research: Grounded Theory Procedures and Techniques*. Newbury Park, CA: Sage.

Watson, T. J. (1994a). *In Search of Management: Culture, Chaos & Control in Managerial Work*. London: Routledge.

Watson, T. J. (1994b). 'Managing crafting and research: words, skill and imagination in shaping management research'. *British Journal of Management*, **5**, Special Issue, 77–87.

WEICK, K. E. (1995). *Sensemaking in Organizations*. Thousand Oaks, CA: Sage.

WEST, M. A. (1990). 'The social psychology of innovation in groups'. In West, M. A. and Farr, J. L. (Eds), *Innovation and Creativity at Work: Psychological and Organizational Strategies*. Chichester: Wiley, 309–33.

WEST, M. A. and FARR, J. L. (1990). 'Innovation at work'. In West, M. A. and Farr, J. L. (Eds), *Innovation and Creativity at Work*. Chichester: Wiley, 3–13.

WHITTINGTON, R. (1992). 'Putting Giddens into action: social systems and managerial agency'. *Journal of Management Studies*, **29**, 6, 693–713.

WILLIAMS, A., DOBSON, P. and WALTERS, M. (1989). *Changing Culture*. London: Institute of Personnel Management.

WILSON, D. and GAME, C. (1994). *Local Government in the United Kingdom*. London: Macmillan.

WOLFE, R. A. (1994). 'Organizational innovation: review, critique and suggested research directions'. *Journal of Management Studies*, **31**, 3, 405–31.

ZEY, M. (1992). 'Criticisms of rational choice models'. In Zey, M. (Ed.), *Decision Making*. Newbury Park, CA: Sage, 9–31.

[12]

Commitment to innovation: the impact of top management team characteristics

Urs S. Daellenbach,[1] Anne M. McCarthy[2] and Timothy S. Schoenecker[3]

[1] School of Business and Public Management, Victoria University of Wellington, P.O. Box 600, Wellington, New Zealand, 64.4.495.5233 (v), 64.4.495.5253 (f)
[2] Department of Management, Colorado State University, Fort Collins, CO 80523–1275, 970.491.6876 (v), 970.491.3522 (f)
[3] Department of Management, Southern Illinois University at Edwardsville, Edwardsville, IL 62026–1100, 618.692.2707 (v), 618.692.3979 (f)
Alphabetical order of authorship reflects equal contribution.

Many organizational and environmental factors influence a firm's commitment to innovation. Among the organizational factors, the perceptual lens of the top management team and the team's dynamics are posited to have a significant direct impact on the firm's commitment to innovation. This study revisits the classic arguments of Hayes and Abernathy and empirically examines several of their propositions. The results clearly indicate a positive relationship between the technical orientation of the TMT/CEO and above-average R&D intensity. This effect remains even after controlling for the impact of performance in prior periods and firm diversification. Overall, these results suggest that establishing a high level of commitment to innovation will be promoted or impeded in many organizations because of the predispositions of the CEO and top management team.

Innovation is the lifeblood of change; it destroys and recreates markets and firms (Schumpeter, 1950), circumvents entry barriers and raises barriers where none existed before (Porter, 1985), and is a source of sustainable competitive advantage. In a world filled with rapid change, investing in innovation is the equivalent of holding options for the future. Yet, such authors as Hayes and Abernathy (1980) and Porter (1990) argue that firms risk losing their competitive advantage due to a lack of commitment to investing in research and development. This paper explores a range of factors affecting top management team (TMT) commitment to innovation.

Innovation has been the focus of many recent studies in strategic management and economics. Kortum (1993) found a strong relationship between research and development (R&D) expenditures and patents. Similarly, Ito and Pucik (1993) reported that export sales for Japanese manufacturing firms are positively associated with R&D expenditures as well as the overall R&D intensity of the industry. Franko (1989) demonstrated that a strong association exists between investments in R&D and subsequent market share gains in global industries. In a multi-industry study using COMPUSTAT data, Morbey and Reithner (1990) noted a strong correlation between R&D expenditures per employee and future profit margins and sales, but no direct relationship between R&D intensity and performance.

Given this evidence for both the value and lack of R&D expenditures, an examination of the factors that impact the amount spent on R&D seems warranted.

R&D investment decisions typically involve the top management team considering a range of external and internal factors. In considering these external and internal factors, senior managers act as filtering mechanisms, interpreting the data through their own cognitive base and values. Thus, a manager's education and work experiences are significant, because these demographic characteristics have been proposed as the primary determinants of each individual's cognitive base, values and biases (Hambrick and Mason, 1984).

The central question then becomes: how might a manager's education, work experience, and background affect his/her decision-making with respect to commitment to innovation? Over a decade ago, Hayes and Abernathy (1980) started a debate centering on this question. They argued that firms are headed for long-term decline if they rely predominantly upon financial control, corporate portfolio management, and excessively market-driven behavior. Moreover, they reasoned that this over-reliance is associated with a change in career paths for top managers – marketing, financial and legal executives have been and will continue to be favored for promotion over production and engineering executives. This, in turn, leads to a dependence on management systems that select projects with clear, quantifiable net present value benefits which assign a lower valuation to innovative, but higher risk, projects. A decade later, Michael Porter (1990) echoed these same arguments, stating that managerial leaders with scientific or technical backgrounds were more likely to make investments in R&D.

Both of these articles, though, were based on case studies. A more detailed empirical study that systematically examines these relationships has yet to be conducted. This research addresses this gap by developing and testing a series of hypotheses indicating how TMT characteristics affect a firm's commitment to innovation.

Literature review

What factors influence a firm's commitment to innovation? Top managers factor in numerous information sources as they consider R&D investment decisions, including organizational factors and environmental factors. External factors include competitors' commitment to R&D, environmental munificence and uncertainty. Internal factors include the organization's ability to undertake technology initiatives given its current resources, the skill and capability levels within the organization, previous commitments made to R&D, firm performance, and diversification. The evaluation of these external and internal factors by top managers will be based on individual managerial perceptions of these factors, and these perceptions are the result of filtering the available information through each manager's cognitive base and values (Hambrick and Mason, 1984). A restricted amount of information is considered largely because each manager's environmental scanning, storage and processing capabilities/activities are limited (Lord and Maher, 1990). In turn, this restricted assessment of environmental and organizational factors in strategic decision making will be framed by each manager's work experiences and education (Hambrick and Mason, 1984) and is likely to focus on those aspects that hold the greatest salience for each manager (Fiske and Taylor, 1991).

Anecdotal support for the impact of top managers' experiences is given by Hayes and Abernathy (1980), Hayes *et al.* (1988), and Porter (1990). Some of these arguments have been formalized by Hambrick and Mason (1984), but none have been tested. The evidence from these studies suggests a variety of factors related to top management team experience and composition that impact an organization's decision to commit resources to innovation. These include the levels of industry and company experience in the TMT, the proportion of top managers with technical backgrounds versus those with support staff backgrounds, diversity in functional backgrounds, educational background, and the chief executive officer's (CEO) openness to innovation. Each of these will be addressed in turn.

Industry and company experience

Hayes and Abernathy (1980 : 77) state that 'companies are increasingly choosing to fill new management posts from outside their own ranks' and that 'senior managers who are less informed about their own industry and its confederation of parts suppliers, equipment suppliers, workers, and customers [...] *are likely to exhibit a noninnovative bias in their choices*' (emphasis added). Thus, longer careers in a particular company or industry should enhance a manager's knowledge of the technological trends in the industry and make him/her more open to investments in innovation that are necessary to capitalize on these changes. In contrast, Hambrick and Mason (1984) suggest that executives who have spent their entire careers primarily in one organization are more likely to focus on current products and markets rather than new terrain. Substantial same-company experience in the TMT would then be associated with limited information search and a reliance on a restricted knowledge base biased toward the status quo (Bantel and Jackson, 1989).

Although these studies propose opposite relationships between company/industry experience and openness to innovation, consideration of innovation type and environmental state may help to reconcile these conflicting perspectives. First, while top managers with the majority of their work experience in one company or industry are more likely to have a bias toward the current strategic direction, this does not necessarily mean that they will be biased against all types of innovation. Innovations that fit well with the current strategy and are developed through the induced strategy-making process would be more likely to receive support than initiatives that emerge autonomously outside the scope of the current strategy (Burgelman, 1991). Similarly, Tushman and Anderson (1986) found that 'competence enhancing' innovations are usually introduced by industry incumbents, while 'competence destroying' innovations are typically developed by firms from outside the industry.

Second, in proposing a negative relationship between innovation and the amount of industry and company experience in the TMT, Hambrick and Mason (1984, p. 200) were focusing primarily on situations where 'an organization [was] facing a severe environmental discontinuity' which would require a revolution or reorientation in the organization's strategy, which is a relatively infrequent event.

Overall, we will test Hayes and Abernathy's argument and hypothesize that:

> *Hypothesis 1a*: The average years of work experience within the firm's industry by members of its TMT will be positively related to the firm's commitment to innovation.
>
> *Hypothesis 1b*: The average years of work experience within the current firm by members of its TMT will be positively related to the firm's commitment to innovation.

Hambrick and Mason (1984) also suggest that firms with older managers are less inclined to pursue risky strategies. They based this proposition on the negative relationship between age and corporate growth found in earlier studies (Child, 1974; Hart and Mellons, 1970). However, since a more recent study by Bantel and Jackson (1989) found no significant relationships between age and innovation, a proposition relating top manager age to commitment to innovation is not included.

Functional area background

There are two issues pertaining to the impact of functional area background on TMT decisions: the functional experience of the individual TMT member and the diversity of functional backgrounds found within the TMT.

Functional experience of the TMT member. The functional area in which a member of the TMT has the most experience has consistently been proposed as a major influence on the strategic choices that the executive makes (Song, 1982; Finkelstein, 1992; Michel and Hambrick, 1992). Dearborn and Simon (1958) reported that executives, when presented with the same decision-making situation, tended to define the issues, goals, and actions primarily in terms of their own functional track. With respect to commitment to innovation, researchers have primarily investigated the impact of the functional area experience in finance, law, production, engineering, and marketing/sales.

Finance and law vs. technical backgrounds. Hayes and Abernathy (1980) point to the substantial increase in senior managers whose background and expertise lie in the financial and legal areas as a major determinant of the decreased commitment to innovation. They suggest that these managers attempt to assess technological issues using financial methodologies, distilling investments in innovation into quantifiable terms in communicating them across levels of the managerial hierarchy. Conversely, top managers with experience primarily in production, engineering, or R&D are more likely to focus on and comprehend the technical, operational, and financial implications that proposed investments in product innovation and process technology would have (Hayes and Abernathy, 1980; Porter, 1990). Additional evidence comes from Rothwell's (1977) review of innovation studies conducted in the 1960s, in which he notes that in four of the nine studies successful innovators were characterized by the CEO or senior staff being scientists or technologists.

Marketing/sales vs. technical backgrounds. Hambrick and Mason (1984, p. 199) theorize that managers from 'output functions – marketing, sales, and product R&D – emphasize growth and the search for new domain opportunities.' In contrast, managers from 'throughput functions (production, process engineering, accounting)' are hypothesized to emphasize increased efficiency (e.g. automation, plant and equipment newness) and backward integration. Thus, one might expect that marketing/sales executives would be more open to product innovation than executives with technical backgrounds.

However, growth and new domain opportunities can result from product extension as well as product innovation. This is the argument made by Hayes and Abernathy (1980, p. 71) when they state that executives with a marketing/sales orientation will emphasize a 'market-driven strategy', in which formal market surveys favor imitative extensions of existing products and serve to delay and dominate allocating resources to innovative product development. This, they argue, leads to choosing customer satisfaction and lower risk in the short run at the expense of superior products in the future 'as well as a lagging commitment to new technology with new capital equipment'. Thus, we categorize marketing/sales executive with other non-technical executives from support areas.

Miller (1987) provides tentative empirical support for Hayes and Abernathy (1980). Miller found significant correlations between the product innovation strategy and the influence and power of 'technocrats' (professional scientists, engineers) as well as the extensiveness of technical support staff. However, Miller also found a significant correlation between a product innovation strategy and the power of support staff, which included marketing, accounting, and product design personnel, lending some support to Hambrick and Mason. Unfortunately, Miller's categories do not allow the relationships between individual functional tracks and commitment to innovation to be disentangled. Thus, following the reasoning set forth by Hayes and Abernathy (1980), we hypothesize that:

> *Hypothesis 2*: The proportion of top managers with work experience in technical areas (engineering, production/operations, R&D) will be positively related to the firm's commitment to innovation.

Heterogeneity or diversity of the TMT. While heterogeneity in the TMT may increase the level of conflict within the team (McNeil and Thompson, 1971; Priem, 1990), the variety of values, biases and perceptions that result from functional background diversity should lead to a more comprehensive consideration of the investment alternatives. Furthermore, diversity in perspectives can help to reduce uncertainty and resolve ambiguity (Daft and Lengel, 1986). Therefore, heterogeneity in management backgrounds should increase the top team's openness to innovation. Consequently, we hypothesize that:

> *Hypothesis 3*: Heterogeneity in functional area background of the TMT will be positively related to the firm's commitment to innovation.

Educational background

A manager's formal educational background has been utilized extensively as an indicator of that person's values and cognitive preferences, particularly with respect to openness to innovation. Reviewing previous studies, Hambrick and Mason (1984, p. 200) state 'the consistent finding is that level of education (either of the CEO or other central actors) is positively related to receptivity to innovation (Becker, 1970; Hambrick and Mason 1984; Kimberly and Evanisko, 1981; Rogers and Shoemaker, 1971)'. Bantel and Jackson (1989) also supported this finding in their study of TMTs in the banking industry. Thus, we hypothesize that:

> *Hypothesis 4*: The amount of formal education will be positively related to the firm's commitment to innovation.

CEO openness to innovation

Numerous studies have emphasized the importance of the chief executive officer as a central actor in strategic decision making (e.g., Goodstein and Boeker, 1991). The CEO is also perceived to play the most significant role in designing the composition of the top management team (Zahra and Pearce, 1989). These individuals may exhibit added loyalty to the CEO that diminishes consideration of alternative viewpoints and reduces comprehensiveness in strategic decision making. As a result, the CEO's openness to innovation may dominate the effects of the TMT characteristics discussed above. That is, a TMT that would be more open to innovation based on their demographic characteristics may not approve budgets supporting a commitment to innovation if the CEO does not favor this orientation. Following this reasoning, we hypothesize that:

> *Hypothesis 5*: The firm's commitment to innovation will be positively related to the CEO's openness to innovation, as measured by company and industry experience, functional experience and educational background.

Data and methods

Sample characteristics

The primary metals industry (defined as three-digit SIC codes 331–335) and the semiconductor industry (SIC code 3674) in the United States form the empirical setting for the study. Initially, all firms whose primary line of business was listed as one of the above SIC codes by COMPUSTAT were included in the sample. That totaled 145 firms in primary metals and 99 firms in semiconductors. Of these 244 firms, only 57 could be included in the final sample (31 in primary metals and 26 in semiconductors). Firms were excluded if they failed to report data on R&D spending or if TMT demographic data were unavailable.[1]

Variables included in the analysis

Dependent variable. Commitment to innovation, the dependent variable in the subsequent regression analysis, is measured by R&D intensity (R&D expenditures/sales). It is a common proxy for innovativeness (Levin *et al.*, 1985). To reduce the possibility of an extraordinary value (high or low) for R&D intensity in one particular year biasing our results, a three-year average (1991–93) was used. This three-year average was highly correlated with and slightly higher than the average in the preceding three years (1988–90) for both industries. The industry average during the study period was subtracted from each firm's three-year average so that the resulting value indicates the extent to which the firm allocated an above or below average amount to R&D compared to the industry.

We utilized this operationalization for commitment to innovation because a firm's research and development budget is under the direct control of top management. While details of individual items in the R&D budget may not come under their review, each firm's TMT will be involved in setting and approving the corporation's R&D budget (Bower, 1970; Green, 1995; Leet, 1991). R&D expenditures, net sales, and employee data were collected from the COMPUSTAT database.

TMT characteristics. The level of analysis in this study is the firm. Therefore, an aggregate score was calculated for each TMT for each of the background characteristics (tenure, functional and educational background). The top management team is defined as all managers at or above the vice president level (Michel and Hambrick, 1992; Hambrick and D'Aveni, 1992; Virany *et al.*, 1992), which is typically equivalent to the top two layers of an organization's hierarchy. We considered using a narrower definition for the TMT, limiting membership to only corporate officers who were also board members (Hambrick and Finkelstein, 1987). While this narrower definition has some advantages, we chose not to use it because it would have limited TMT membership to one or two members for many firms. Most data on TMT characteristics were collected from Dun and Bradstreet's *Reference Book of Corporate Managements* (1993). Companies either not listed in the Dun and Bradstreet publication or with incomplete information were contacted directly for TMT data. As with R&D intensity, the industry average was subtracted for all variables to remove potential biases due to industry differences.

Industry and company experience. Tenure was measured as the number of years that each member of the TMT had worked within the industry. Company experience was measured as the number of years that managers had been spent with their current firms. The TMT industry or company experience variables are the average levels across the team (including the CEO).

Functional area background. Each manager's dominant functional track was defined as the area in which the manager had the most experience, measured by the number of years spent in any one of the following functional tracks: 1) production-operations, 2) research & development (including engineering), 3) finance, 4) accounting, 5) law, 6) administration, 7) general management, 8) marketing-sales, and 9) personnel and labor relations (Michel and Hambrick, 1992). Categories 1) and 2) were defined as technical staff areas, while categories 3) through 9) were defined as support staff areas. The percentage of TMT members categorized as technical versus support staff will be used to test hypothesis two.

Heterogeneity in TMT background. A version of the Herfindahl index is used to assess diversity across the TMT (see Bantel and Jackson, 1989). Thus, heterogeneity (H) is defined as:

$$H = 1 - \sum_{i \in F} p_i^2$$

where F is the set of functional area categories and p_i is the proportion of the TMT in each category i. H will vary between 0 and 1, where values close to 1 indicate higher diversity in functional area backgrounds and low values indicate that one functional area dominates the TMT. Michel and Hambrick (1992) used this type of measure to assess homogeneity across the nine functional categories.

Educational background. A manager's educational background is typically measured by creating an interval scale covering the possible education levels. We coded educational background into one of four levels: 1) high school, 2) bachelors degree, 3) masters degree, and 4) doctoral degree.

CEO openness to innovation. The CEO's openness to innovation was measured using the CEO's data for industry and company experience, dominant functional track, and educational background.

Control variables

While it is expected that demographic characteristics of the TMT will help to explain a firm's commitment to innovation, other organizational and environmental factors also need to be considered.

Organizational factors. First, an organization will have less discretion to invest heavily in R&D if it has not been performing well (Knight, 1967). R&D expenditures are often among the first to be cut when the organization's financial performance needs to be improved, especially in the short term. Thus, when an organization is experiencing poor financial performance relative to competitors in its industry, it is likely that its commitment to investments in R&D will be reduced. For this study, firm performance is measured using a three-year average of return on assets (ROA) between 1988 and 1990. Again, the industry average ROA was subtracted from each firm's ROA in order to adjust for the performance of the industry as a whole.

The second organizational factor included in the analysis is the firm's level of diversification. Baysinger and Hoskisson (1990) and Hoskisson and Hitt (1988) found that increased diversification was negatively related to R&D intensity. Therefore, we have included each firm's level of diversification as measured by the Herfindahl index.

Urs S. Daellenbach, Anne M. McCarthy and Timothy S. Schoenecker

Table 1. Sample industry characteristics*.

	Industry	
	Primary Metals	Semiconductor
Average R&D intensity (91–93)	1.0%	11.4%
Average ROA (88–90)	5.3%	1.0%
Average firm diversification**	0.134	0.053
Average size/range (Sales $ billions)	$2.1B $0.045–9.5B	$0.954B $0.022–7.4B
Average industry tenure	21.3 years	25.3 years
Average company tenure	17.5 years	14.8 years
Average technical orientation	0.20	0.32
Average educational level	2.65	2.65
Average functional diversity	0.62	0.67

* Statistics presented in this table were derived using the firms in our sample.
** Calculated using the Herfindahl Index.

Environmental factors. To allow assessment of differences associated with industry, our sample consists of firms from two distinct industries. The primary metals industry has fairly low levels of R&D intensity, relatively stable demand, and lower technological uncertainty. On the other hand, the semiconductor industry is research intensive, has experienced much higher growth, and has a more uncertain future in terms of demand and technology. Table 1 compares these two industries along several dimensions.

Results

Table 2 presents the means, standard deviations, and intercorrelations for all variables. As expected, CEOs tended to have slightly longer industry and company tenure, but, on average, did not differ substantially from their TMTs on any characteristics. Table 3 provides the results of the ordinary least squares regression analyses, which were used to test the hypotheses.

Two models are shown in Table 3. The first model utilized aggregated data for the entire top management team;[2] the second model focused solely on the characteristics of the CEO. Thus, model 1 includes a coefficient for functional diversity, while there is no corresponding independent variable for the CEO-only model. Because of the differences between these two industries, it was necessary to test the legitimacy of pooling data from these industries. Chow tests for equality of the regression coefficients across the two samples indicated no significant differences at a 5% level. Therefore, we felt confident that we could combine the data from the two samples. Similarly, the estimates did not appear to be affected by multicollinearity with variance inflation factors all below 2.0.

Both regression models provide clear support for hypothesis 2. A higher level of research and development spending is related to the presence of more technically oriented TMTs and CEOs. Conversely, the results do not lend support for the other hypotheses regarding TMT characteristics and a firm's commitment to innovation. In both models, the control variables are significantly related to R&D intensity. Poor profitability and increased levels of diversification led firms to reduce expenditures on R&D.

Discussion and conclusions

The empirical results support Hayes and Abernathy's (1980) contention that increased technical experience leads to greater support for technology initiatives (see Table 4). The direction of the predicted relationships held for both the TMT and CEO models and across both industries, indicating that the findings may be generalized to other industries and R&D contexts. As a result, an analyst attempting to assess a firm's future strategic direction may wish to study the functional background of (and changes in) that firm's top management team. Turnover in a firm's TMT that leads to the addition of technically oriented members may indicate that the firm's competitive strategy may increasingly emphasize innovation.

Alternatively, Hayes and Abernathy's other proposition, our first hypothesis, on industry/company tenure and commitment to innovation was not empirically supported. In part, this may reflect the conflicting proposed relationship concerning these variables (e.g. Hambrick and Mason, 1984). An interaction term representing type of innovation supported by R&D spending and environmental state might assist future research on industry/company tenure and commitment to innovation. It could be the case that industry incumbents in our sample were supportive of competence enhancing investments, while industry newcomers were supportive of competence destroying investments (Tushman and Anderson, 1986), thus canceling each other out at the aggregate level. Without information on which senior managers support the specific individual research programs included in the firm's R&D budget, it will be difficult to confirm if any relationships between tenure and commitment to innovation exist and if these relationships offset each other.

Another possible explanation is that, while the proposed effects of limited tenure (industry or com-

Table 2. Correlations and descriptive statistics for the sample.

Variables	Average*	Std. Dev.	RDI	ROA	Div	IndTen	CoTen	Tech	Ed
1. RDI (91–93)	0.056	0.072							
2. ROA (88–90)	0.034	0.071	−0.004						
3. Diversification	0.097	0.198	−0.268	0.186					
TMT Characteristics									
4a. Industry tenure	23.098	6.618	0.104	−0.112	−0.142				
5a. Company tenure	16.238	7.263	−0.265	0.020	0.063	0.543			
6a. Technical orientation	0.257	0.193	0.437	−0.120	−0.119	0.221	0.037		
7a. Education level	2.647	0.411	0.047	0.086	0.023	−0.029	0.044	0.164	
8. Functional diversity	0.642	0.177	0.159	0.108	−0.110	0.218	0.297	0.420	0.331
CEO Characteristics						IndTen	CoTen	Tech	
4b. Industry tenure	27.089	11.169	0.130	−0.233	−0.141				
5b. Company tenure	18.375	12.208	−0.144	0.074	−0.038	0.541			
6b. Technical orientation	0.250	0.437	0.425	0.035	0.052	0.327	−0.062		
7b. Education level	2.627	0.774	0.265	−0.075	−0.111	−0.086	−0.186	0.012	

Average values are reported before subtracting the industry average.

Table 3. Results of regression analysis. Dependent variable: R&D intensity.

Regression results	Model 1 TMT characteristics		Model 2 CEO characteristics	
Intercept	0.0013	(0.006)	0.0022	(0.006)
ROA(88–90)	0.2692	(0.094)***	0.2775	(0.110)***
Diversification	−0.0557	(0.032)**	−0.0673	(0.032)**
Industry tenure	−0.0011	(0.001)	−0.0001	(0.001)
Company tenure	−0.0007	(0.001)	−0.0009	(0.001)
Technical orientation	0.1016	(0.037)***	0.0342	(0.018)**
Education level	0.0002	(0.016)	0.0047	(0.009)
Team functional diversity	−0.0215	(0.043)		
R^2	0.2758	$p = 0.012$	0.2848	$p = 0.016$

Significance levels *$p < 0.10$ **$p < 0.05$ ***$p < 0.01$

Table 4. Summary of predicted relationships and results.

	Model used to test hypothesis	Predicted relationship with dependent variable – firm's commitment to innovation	Finding
Independent variables			
Hypothesis 1a: Average years of industry experience	1	(+)	not significant (n.s.)
Hypothesis 1b: Average years of company experience	1	(+)	n.s.
Hypothesis 2: Proportion of technical managers	1	(+)	(+)***
Hypothesis 3: Heterogeneity in functional backgrounds	1	(+)	n.s.
Hypothesis 4: Amount of formal education	1	(+)	n.s.
Hypothesis 5: CEO openness to innovation (measured by company/industry experience, functional background, and formal education)	2	(+)	(+) technical orientation **
Control variables			
Firm performance		(+)	(+)***
Firm's level of diversification		(−)	(−)**

Significance levels *$p < 0.10$ **$p < 0.05$ ***$p < 0.01$

pany) occur at low levels, experience accumulates rapidly and has limited impact after some threshold – five or ten years. For the CEOs in our sample, only 11% had less than ten years experience in the industry. Only 4% of the top management team members had less than ten years experience. Perhaps threshold effects exist, similar to those found by Gimeno *et al.* (1997) for entrepreneurial firm performance.

The other TMT characteristics that were examined (education level and functional heterogeneity) did not exhibit significant relationships to commitment to innovation. In the case of the latter, the explanation may be related to the measure. By definition, a functionally diverse TMT has members from several of the nine different categories, and so has a decreased proportion of technically oriented members. Thus, any positive effect that functional diversity may have on commitment to innovation would be offset by the reduced technical orientation of the team. For education level, the aggregate nature of the interval scale may mask the impact of higher levels of education.

The positive association between firm profitability (as measured by ROA) and commitment to innovation lends support for earlier work that cited the need for slack resources and innovation. The results indicate that firms performing below the industry average also invest in R&D at rates below their rivals. However, the results do not allow us to identify the causal nature of this relationship, that is, does poor performance restrict future R&D investments or was it caused by historically low R&D expenditures. Finally, the results confirm the negative relationship between the level of a firm's diversification activity and its commitment to R&D thereby replicating Baysinger and Hoskisson (1990) and Hoskisson and Hitt (1988). Firms involved in more diverse lines of business tend to invest less than their peers in R&D. This reinforces the widely held view that managers have two options to choose from when determining how to pursue growth. One option is the acquisition/diversification route, while the other involves internal investment in areas such as R&D.

The results lead us to make several recommendations to managers. Firstly, firms wanting to strengthen their innovation strategy should promote or recruit managers with technical experience to the TMT. Similarly, a firm that has chosen to emphasize R&D and product development in its competitive strategy should look toward technical managers to fill vacancies that appear on the top management team. Secondly, management development paths should provide for technical exposure for managers with non-technical backgrounds. Lastly, managers should consider whether R&D budgets are based, at least in part, on the strategic value-added potential of the current proposals or whether they are primarily determined historically as a percentage of sales. Whereas the first approach brings technical and strategic information to the top managers for consideration, the latter reinforces financial evaluation in choosing between competing proposals.

While the regression analysis provided some supportive results, two caveats must be stated. First, there are limitations associated with any analysis based on a small sample. However, given the small sample size, that any of the coefficients were significant is a cause for optimism and an incentive for further study. Additionally, since the relationship between technical orientation and commitment to innovation holds across two industries with very different levels of R&D spending, this may indicate that the relationship can be generalized to a number of different industry settings.

Second, as Pfeffer (1983) originally stated, demographic measures of TMTs are at best proxies for underlying managerial processes and biases. As such, they are not perfect measures of how individual managers (or teams) assess technological, or any other, projects. However, the advantages associated with using these measures (observability, availability, etc.) are significant enough to warrant their use in that they serve as a guide for future research.

Suggestions for future research

The results of this paper suggest several possible avenues for future research. One area would be in the area of TMT characteristics and control systems. Hoskisson and Hitt (1988) and Hoskisson *et al.* (1993) found significant relationships between the types of controls and rewards and commitment to innovation in their study of large multiproduct firms. Goold and Campbell (1987) also note the significance of including strategic controls. While these control and reward systems may directly affect a firm's commitment to innovation, it may be the case that these systems were instituted by a TMT dominated by managers from support staff areas. Linking TMT characteristics to process issues such as characteristics of management systems would be a significant step forward for this area of research.

A second area would be to refine the relationship suggested by Hayes and Abernathy (1980) between tenure and technical background. It may be the case that an interaction between the two variables would have an impact on technological initiatives. That is, TMTs with a high proportion of long tenured members with technical backgrounds may be the most likely to have strong commitments to innovation, while new CEOs and senior managers may see higher profitability as more important during their initial years at a new company. A larger sample with more degrees of freedom would be a more appropriate setting to estimate the effect of this proposed interaction on commitment to innovation.

Third, a future study could investigate cross-country differences. US firms could be compared to firms in the EU and Japan to see if the same relationship exists between technical background of the TMT and commitment to innovation. Such a study may show that the proportion of technical TMT members accounts for differences in R&D investments across international firms. Finally, this study assumes from prior research that increased R&D spending leads to more innovations. While that relationship is undoubtedly true in an aggregate sense, it is also likely that some R&D spending is unproductive and not in the best interest of the firm.

This leads to two potentially fruitful research avenues, both of which could extend the present study in clarifying the R&D investment process. The first is how to measure R&D effectiveness/potential; a problem that is made difficult by the delays between investment (commitments to the R&D budget) and results as well as the uncertainty inherent at all stages in the process. Second, once this tricky measurement question is answered, a study that links TMT characteristics with R&D effectiveness would be of great interest to managers and researchers. The relationship between TMTs with technical backgrounds and R&D effectiveness may prove to be stronger than the one found in this research. One might suppose this is likely given that managers with technical backgrounds would not only be committed to R&D investment, but also would be able to maximize the benefits of R&D spending.

References

Bantel, K. and Jackson, S. (1989) Top management and innovations in banking: does the composition of the top team make a difference. *Strategic Management Journal*, **10**, Summer, 107–124.

Baysinger, B. and Hoskisson, R. (1990) The composition of boards of directors and strategic control: effects on corporate strategy. *Academy of Management Review*, **15**, 1, 72–87.

Becker, M. (1970) Sociometric location and innovativeness: reformulation and extension of the diffusion model. *American Sociological Review*, **35**, 2, 267–304.

Bower, J. (1970) *Managing the Resource Allocation Process: A Study of Corporate Planning and Investment*. Boston: Harvard University.

Burgelman, R. (1991) Intraorganizational ecology of strategy making and organizational adaptation: theory and field research. *Organization Science*, **2**, 2, 239–262.

Child, J. (1974) Managerial and organizational factors associated with company performance. *Journal of Management*, **11**, 1, 13–27.

Daft, R. and Lengel, R. (1986) Organizational information requirements, media richness, and structural design. *Management Science*, **32**, 5, 554–571.

Dearborn, D. and Simon, H. (1958) Selective perceptions: a note on the departmental identification of executives. *Sociometry*, **21**, 2, 140–144.

Dun & Bradstreet (1993) *Reference Book of Corporate Managements*. New York: Dun & Bradstreet.

Finkelstein, S. (1992) Power in top management teams: dimensions, measurement, and validation. *Academy of Management Journal*, **35**, 3 505–538.

Fiske, S. and Taylor, S. (1991) *Social Cognition, 2nd ed.* New York: McGraw-Hill.

Franko, L. (1989) Global corporate competition: who's winning, who's losing, and the R&D factor as one reason why. *Strategic Management Journal*, **10**, 5, 449–474.

Gimeno, J., Folta, T., Cooper, A. and Woo, C. (1997) Survival of the fittest? Entrepreneurial human capital and the persistence of underperforming firms. *Administrative Science Quarterly*, **42**, 4, 750–783.

Goodstein, J. and Boeker, W. (1991) Turbulence at the top: a new perspective on governance structure changes and strategic change. *Academy of Management Journal*, **34**, 2, 306–330.

Goold, M. and Campbell, A. (1987) *Strategies and Styles: The Role of the Centre in Managing Diversified Corporations*. Oxford: Blackwell Business.

Green, S. (1995) Top management support of R&D projects: a strategic leadership perspective. *IEEE Transactions on Engineering Management*, **42**, 3, 223–234.

Hambrick, D. and Mason, P. (1984) Upper echelons: the organization as a reflection of its top managers. *Academy of Management Review*, **9**, 2, 193–206.

Hambrick, D. and D'Aveni, R. (1992) Top team deterioration as part of the downward spiral of large corporate bankruptcies. *Management Science*, **38**, 10, 1445–1466.

Hambrick, D. and Finkelstein, S. (1987) Managerial discretion: a bridge between the polar views on organizations. In Cummings, L. and Staw, B. (eds), *Research in Organizational Behavior* vol. 9. Greenwich, CT: JAI Press, pp 369–406.

Hart, P. and Mellons, J. (1970) Management youth and company growth: a correlation? *Management Decision*, **4**, 1, 50–53.

Hayes, R. and Abernathy, W. (1980) Managing our way to economic decline. *Harvard Business Review*, **57**, 4, 11–25.

Hayes, R., Wheelwright, S. and Clark, K. (1988) *Dynamic Manufacturing: Creating the Learning Organization*. New York: Free Press.

Hoskisson, R. and Hitt, M. (1988) Strategic control systems and relative R&D investment in large multiproduct firms. *Strategic Management Journal*, **9**, 6, 605–621.

Hoskisson, R., Hitt, M. and Hill, C.W. (1993) Managerial incentives and investment in R&D in large multiproduct firms. *Organization Science*, **4**, 2, 325–341.

Ito, K. and Pucik, V. (1993) R&D spending, domestic competition, and export performance of Japanese manufacturing firms. *Strategic Management Journal*, **14**, 1, 61–75.

Kimberly, J. and Evanisko, M. (1981) Organizational innovation: the individual, organizational and contextual factors on hospital adoption of technological and administrative innovations. *Academy of Management Journal*, **24**, 4, 689–713.

Knight, K. (1967) A descriptive model of the intra-firm innovation process. *Journal of Business*, **40**, 4, 478–496.

Kortum, S. (1993) Equilibrium R&D and the patent-R&D ratio: U.S. evidence. *American Economic Review*, **83**, 2, 450–457.

Leet, R. (1991) How top management sees R&D. *Research-Technology Management*, **34**, 1, 15–17.

Levin, R., Cohen, W. and Mowery, D. (1985) R&D appropriability, opportunity and market structure: new evidence on some Schumpeterian hypotheses. *American Economic Review*, **75**, 2, 20–24.

Lord, R. and Maher, K. (1990) Alternative information-processing models and their implications for theory, research, and practice. *Academy of Management Review*, **15**, 1, 9–28.

McNeil, K. and Thompson, J. (1971) The regeneration of social organizations. *American Sociological Review*, **36**, 4, 624–637.

Michel, J. and Hambrick, D. (1992) Diversification posture and top management team characteristics. *Academy of Management Journal*, **35**, 1, 9–37.

Miller, D. (1987) The structural and environmental correlates of business strategy. *Strategic Management Journal*, **8**, 1, 55–76.

Morbey, G. and Reithner, R. (1990) How R&D affects sales growth, productivity and profitability. *Research-Technology Management*, **33**, 3, 11–14.

Pfeffer, J. (1983) Organizational demography. In Cummings, L. and Staw, B. (eds), *Research in Organizational Behavior* vol. 5. Greenwich, CT: JAI Press, pp. 299–357.

Porter, M. (1985) *Competitive Advantage: Creating and Sustaining Superior Performance*. New York: Free Press.

Porter, M. (1990) Have we lost faith in competition? *Across the Board*, September, 37–46.

Priem, R. (1990) Top management team group factors, consensus, and firm performance. *Strategic Management Journal*, **11**, 6, 469–478.

Rogers, E. and Shoemaker, F. (1971) *Communication of Innovations*. New York: Free Press.

Rothwell, R. (1977) The characteristics of successful innovators and technically progressive firms. *R&D Management*, **7**, 3, 191–206.

Schumpeter, J. (1950) *Capitalism, Socialism, and Democracy*. New York: Harper & Bros.

Song, J. (1982) Diversification strategies and the experience of top executives of large firms. *Strategic Management Journal*, **3**, 4, 377–380.

Tushman, M. and Anderson, P. (1986) Technological discontinuities and organizational environments. *Administrative Science Quarterly*, **31**, 3, 439–465.

Virany, B., Tushman, M. and Romanelli, E. (1992) Executive succession and organization outcomes in turbulent environments: an organizational learning approach. *Organization Science*, **3**, 1, 72–91.

Zahra, S. and Pearce, J. (1989) Board of directors and corporate financial performance: a review and integrative model. *Journal of Management*, **15**, 2, 291–334.

Notes

1. We analyzed these 57 firms to see if they differed from the excluded firms along the following dimensions: size (sales and number of employees), R&D intensity, and performance. The only significant difference occurred in the semiconductor sample where the included firms tended to be larger than their excluded counterparts. However, they did not differ in R&D intensity or performance. Results of this analysis are available from the third author.
2. We also analyzed a modified version of model 1 where the demographic characteristics of each team member were weighted by his/her relative structural power. That is, characteristics of managers with more power (higher official title, more titles, and membership on board of directors) were given more weight than their counterparts when calculating the TMT average. These measures of structural power were based in part from the work of Finkelstein (1992). The results using these power-weighted variables were nearly identical to the unweighted results and so are not reported here.

Champions of Technological Innovation

Jane M. Howell
Christopher A. Higgins
The University of Western Ontario

This study investigated the personality characteristics, leadership behaviors, and influence tactics of champions of technological innovations. Analyses of questionnaires and interview transcripts of twenty-five matched pairs of champions and nonchampions revealed that champions reported using transformational leader behaviors to a significantly greater extent than did nonchampions. Champions exhibited higher risk taking and innovativeness, initiated more influence attempts, and used a greater variety of influence tactics than nonchampions. Regression analysis of a model of champion emergence, relating personality characteristics, transformational leader behaviors, and influence tactics, showed that champions were significantly higher than nonchampions on all paths in the model.•

The increased turbulence, complexity, and competitiveness of organizational environments have made the identification, evaluation, and adoption of technological innovations a critical determinant of organizational productivity, competition, and survival (Zaltman, Duncan, and Holbeck, 1973; Bigoness and Perreault, 1981; Morgan, 1988). As a result, a major research effort has focused on variables that facilitate or hinder the adoption of technological innovations (e.g., Rogers and Shoemaker, 1971; Kelly and Kranzberg, 1978; Kimberly and Evanisko, 1981; Pennings and Buitendam, 1987).

One variable that has been strongly linked to the success of technological innovations is the presence of a champion. This is an individual who informally emerges in an organization (Schön, 1963; Tushman and Nadler, 1986) and makes "a decisive contribution to the innovation by actively and enthusiastically promoting its progress through the critical [organizational] stages" (Achilladelis, Jervis, and Robertson, 1971: 14). Twenty-six years ago, in a seminal article on radical military innovations, Schön (1963) identified the role of a champion. He contended that in order to overcome the indifference and resistance that major technological change provokes, a champion is required to identify the idea as his or her own, to promote the idea actively and vigorously through informal networks, and to risk his or her position and prestige to ensure the innovation's success. According to Schön (1963: 84), "the new idea either finds a champion or dies."

A multitude of field and case studies have found strong support for Schön's contention that innovation success is closely linked with the presence of a champion (e.g., Roberts, 1968; Achilladelis, Jervis, and Robertson, 1971; Rothwell et al., 1974; Burgelman, 1983; Ettlie, Bridges, and O'Keefe, 1984). Yet, despite the important contribution attributed to champions in the innovation process, rigorous empirical investigation of these individuals is lacking. Prior studies examining champions are plagued by several conceptual and methodological problems, thereby casting doubt on the validity and interpretability of their findings.

Four problems with previous research on champions are evident. First, prior research has paid little attention to the systematic measurement of individual attributes of champions such as personality and leadership. Most of what is reported about champions is anecdotal, reflecting the researcher's im-

0001-8392/90/3502-0317/$1.00.

•

Funding for this study was supplied by Social Sciences and Humanities Research Council of Canada Grant 494-85-0018 and by the Plan for Excellence, The University of Western Ontario. The authors are indebted to Hugh Arnold, Bruce Avolio, Bernard Bass, Deborah Compeau, Martin Evans, Peter Frost, David Waldman, and three anonymous reviewers for their insightful comments. This paper was originally submitted for the *ASQ* special issue on Technology, Organizations, and Innovation (March 1990). Editorial work was begun by Richard R. Nelson and Michael N. Tushman and was completed by John H. Freeman.

pressions, rather than reliable and valid measurement using well-accepted instruments (e.g., Schön, 1963; Fernelius and Waldo, 1980; Delbecq and Mills, 1985; Dean, 1987). A second, related issue is that comparison groups for champions are not identified in any study. Therefore, it is unclear to what extent champions actually differ from the population of managers in general.

A third problem is that previous studies suffer from methodological flaws in the identification of champions, which makes their results questionable. To illustrate, Table 1 summarizes the methods used to identify champions in fifteen prior studies. Most authors do not even discuss how champions are identified. Other authors use individual responses, uncorroborated by others, to identify the project champion. This latter method, where single individuals are polled as to the presence or absence of champions, is problematic, since bias may be introduced due to the tendency to report oneself as the champion, a socially desirable label.

A final problem in the reliable identification of champions is the lack of specification of the various roles played by individuals in the innovation process. Several authors have identified a number of different roles associated with innovation (e.g., Roberts, 1968; Achilladelis, Jervis, and Robertson, 1971; Maidique, 1980; Curley and Gremillion, 1983; Katz and Tushman, 1983). For example, gatekeepers acquire, translate, and distribute external technological knowledge and advancements to their colleagues (Allen, 1977; Tushman and Scanlan, 1981; Katz and Tushman, 1983). Project champions, the focus of the present study, distill creative ideas from information sources and then enthusiastically promote them within the organization (Achilladelis, Jervis, and Robertson, 1971). Business innovators provide support, access to resources, and protection from organizational interference as innovations emerge (Achilladelis, Jervis, and Robertson, 1971). Technical innovators design and/or develop the innovation, while user champions implement the innovation by training and providing assistance to the users (Achilladelis, Jervis, and Robertson, 1971; Rothwell et al., 1974; Curley and Gremillion, 1983). In order to identify project champions reliably, different types of innovator roles need to be distinguished. To illustrate, while both project champions and gatekeepers are involved in communication and information-processing activities, gatekeepers gather and disseminate external information to project groups while champions seek out creative ideas from information sources and then enthusiastically sell them. Thus, many studies reportedly investigating champions may not be studying champions at all if they have been inappropriately identified.

The conceptual and methodological problems of previous research call into question the adequacy of our current knowledge about champions. Accordingly, the purpose of the present study was to conduct a rigorous, empirical investigation of champions of technological innovations, focusing on three variables that influence the emergence of champions in organizations: personality characteristics, leadership behaviors, and influence tactics. Personality characteristics are the qualities that predispose individuals to engage in champion activities. Leadership and influence are also important,

Champions of Innovation

Table 1

Identification of Champions in Previous Studies

Source	Organizations	Innovation type	Methodology	Identification of champions
Achilladelis, Jervis, and Robertson (1971)*	58 firms in scientific instruments and chemical industries	Various product and process innovations	Case studies and comparative analysis	Not discussed
Burgelman (1983)	6 divisions of a single firm	Various product innovations	Case studies	Not discussed
Chakrabarti (1974)	45 NASA innovations	Various product innovations	Case studies	Investigators' judgment based on interviews, letters, sales brochures, and company memoranda
Dean (1987)	5 manufacturing organizations	Advanced manufacturing technology innovations	Interviews, both retrospective and real-time	Not discussed
Delbecq and Mills (1985)	Several hundred managers in high-technology firms and health-services organizations	Various	Interviews, comparing successes and failures	Not discussed
Ettlie (1983); Ettlie, Bridges, and O'Keefe (1984)	192 firms in meat, canning, and fish industries	Consumer Retort Pouch technology	Surveys, field interviews in 56 firms	Single question: Is there a person in your firm who is currently advocating consumer retortable pouch technology?
Fernelius and Waldo (1980)	78 member firms of the Industrial Research Institute	Unclear from paper	Case histories submitted by organizations	Not discussed
Frohman (1978)	90 Research and Development managers	Not defined	Survey	Self-reports of the amount of time spent in "championing activities"
Galbraith (1982)	Single electronics firm	New electronics product	Case history	Not discussed
Maidique (1980)	9 organizations at different stages of development	Mostly product innovations	Case studies	Not discussed
Roberts (1968)	1 division of an integrated electronics manufacturer	New business ventures	Case studies	Person who headed the new venture
Rothwell et al. (1974)*	86 firms in the chemical and scientific instruments industries	Various product and process innovations	Case studies	Not discussed
Schön (1963)	25 military inventions	Product innovations	Case studies	Not discussed
Souder (1981)	100 projects in 17 member firms of the Industrial Research Institute	Product innovations	Interviews, case studies	Not discussed

* Two phases of the same investigation.

since innovation adoption is largely a process of influence (Burgelman, 1983; Dean, 1987), both with subordinates, as indicated by leadership behavior, and with peers and superiors, as indicated by influence tactics.

While the capacity of champions to influence others has been widely discussed, there has been no attempt to integrate findings with the theoretical and empirical literature concerning social influence processes in organizations. Moreover, researchers have not systematically measured the frequency and variety of influence attempts used by champions or explored whether champions differ from other managers in the amount and quality of their influence.

Although personality characteristics, leadership behaviors, and influence tactics are frequently discussed in the champion literature (e.g., Schön, 1963; Burgelman, 1983; Dean, 1987; Van de Ven, 1986), for the most part, results of different studies have been poorly integrated. In addition, little empirical evidence exists with respect to the contribution of these variables to champion emergence. What appears to be needed is the development and testing of a model that integrates the factors influencing how individuals emerge to assume the champion role.

The relationships posited in the model used here were developed inductively from literature in the areas of entrepreneurship, leadership, and influence. We used the entrepreneurship literature to identify the important dimensions of the champion personality, since several authors have drawn parallels between champions (or intrapreneurs) and entrepreneurs (e.g., Collins and Moore, 1970; Maidique, 1980; Pinchot, 1985). Transformational leadership theory was examined, because champions serve as informal leaders, inspiring others with their vision of an innovation's potential (Van de Ven, 1986). Research on influence was reviewed, because champions act as influence agents to promote their ideas (Burgelman, 1983; Dean, 1987).

BACKGROUND AND HYPOTHESES

Leadership Behavior

The literature on champions and innovation highlights the capacity of champions to inspire and enthuse others with their vision of the potential of an innovation, to persist in promoting their vision despite strong opposition, to show extraordinary confidence in themselves and their mission, and to gain the commitment of others to support the innovation (Maidique, 1980; Burgelman, 1983; Dean, 1987). In Schön's words (1963: 84), "it is characteristic of champions . . . that they identify with the idea as their own, and with its promotion as a cause, to a degree that goes far beyond the requirements of their job." These champion behaviors are similar to the qualities of transformational leaders, leaders who inspire their followers to transcend their own self-interests for a higher collective purpose (Burns, 1978). Drawing on Burns's (1978) analysis of political leadership, Bass (1985) developed a theory of transformational leadership in organizational settings. Based on both qualitative and quantitative procedures, he identified four transformational leadership factors:

Champions of Innovation

charisma, inspiration, intellectual stimulation, and individualized consideration.[1]

Charisma refers to the leader's ability to articulate a captivating vision, to inspire and encourage higher-order effort on the part of followers, and to instill respect, faith, loyalty, and trust in the leader. Inspiration involves the leader's use of emotional appeals, communication of vivid, persuasive images, and provision of examples to enhance followers' confidence and motivation to pursue elevated goals. Intellectual stimulation represents the leader's ability to suggest creative, novel ideas that challenge and refocus followers' conceptualization, comprehension, and discernment of the nature of problems and their solutions. Individualized consideration refers to the leader's developmental and individualistic orientation toward followers. The leader provides examples and assigns tasks to followers on an individual basis to help them significantly alter their abilities and motivation.

Several writers have conceptually linked transformational leadership to the innovation process (Oberg, 1972; House, 1977; Bass, 1985; Conger and Kanungo, 1987). Oberg (1972) discussed the change-agent function of the transformational leader. He contended that the transformational leader brings about radical change by espousing beliefs and values that are different from the established order. According to Bass (1985), who offered a consistent profile of the transformational leader as active innovator, transformational leaders use intellectual stimulation to enhance followers' capacities to think on their own, to develop new ideas, and to question the operating rules and systems that no longer serve the organization's purpose or mission. By using individualized consideration and intellectual stimulation, transformational leaders enhance followers' confidence and skills to devise and implement innovative responses to current problems facing their organization. Thus, in order to promote innovation in organizations, it is likely that champions exhibit transformational leadership behaviors:

Hypothesis 1: Champions will exhibit transformational leader behaviors, that is, charisma, inspiration, intellectual stimulation, and individualized consideration to a greater extent than nonchampions.

Personality Characteristics

The innovation literature describes champions as risk takers (Schön, 1963; Cox, 1976), socially independent (Cox, 1976), and politically astute (Schön, 1963; Burgelman, 1983; Dean, 1987). Moreover, champions are said to display persistence and dedication even in the face of frequent obstacles and imminent failures (Schön, 1963; Frohman, 1978). While these descriptors provide a useful starting point for understanding the champion's personality, they cannot be taken as conclusive, since they tend to be based on the researchers' impressions of the individuals rather than on scores obtained on validated personality tests. Furthermore, the observations are made in the absence of an explicit comparison group, and it is therefore unclear if champions actually differ from managers in general.

While the personality characteristics of champions have not been systematically explored in the innovation literature, research focusing on the entrepreneurial personality offers

1
Bass's (1985) descriptive statements about transformational and transactional leadership were derived from a survey of senior executives and from the leadership literature. These statements were sorted by raters into transformational and transactional categories. Items that raters could reliably assign to each category were retained and placed in a survey administered to senior army officers, who rated their superiors in terms of how frequently they exhibited each leadership characteristic. Principal components factor analysis of the final items resulted in the four transformational leadership factors.

some insights into potentially important dimensions. In a seminal study of the entrepreneurial personality, McClelland (1967), using Thematic Apperception Tests (TATs), discovered that entrepreneurs scored high on need for achievement. He also found that entrepreneurs desired to take personal responsibility for decisions, preferred decisions involving a moderate degree of risk, were interested in concrete knowledge of the results of decisions, and disliked routine work.

Consistent results have been reported by other authors with respect to various personality dimensions of entrepreneurs. Roberts (1968) and Wainer and Rubin (1969), who investigated the relationship between successful research and development (R&D) entrepreneurs and company performance, found that the highest performing companies were led by entrepreneurs with high need for achievement and moderate need for power, as measured by projective TAT tests. Similarly, Hornaday and Aboud (1971), using objective personality measures, reported that entrepreneurs scored significantly higher on achievement and independence than the population in general.

Based on interviews with 40 entrepreneurs and life-history analysis of 30 entrepreneurs, Kets de Vries (1977) observed that entrepreneurs are innovative, doing things not generally done in the ordinary course of business routine. Furthermore, he reported that they exhibit resilience in the face of setbacks and have the ability to start over again when disappointments occur. These findings are consistent with the general literature on innovators, which indicates that they are less conforming, value creativity, have more confidence in their abilities, and want opportunities to test their ideas (Stein, 1968; Maddi, 1976). Thus, we hypothesize:

Hypothesis 2: Champions will exhibit higher achievement, persistence, innovativeness, persuasiveness, and risk taking than nonchampions.

The requisite personality characteristics of entrepreneurs are also common to transformational or charismatic leaders. From biographies, case studies, and theoretical statements a pattern of transformational personality characteristics can be discerned, including innovation, risk taking, achievement, persuasiveness, and endurance. Bass (1985: 176) contended that transformational leaders are high in social boldness, need for achievement, creativity, originality, and self-determination. Other theorists argue that transformational or charismatic leaders, through their passionate advocacy for change, create and take great personal risks, devise novel and unconventional plans for action, and engage in artful persuasion (Conger and Kanungo, 1987; Sashkin, 1988). From this, we hypothesize:

Hypothesis 3: There will be a more positive relationship between personality dimensions and transformational leader behaviors for champions than for nonchampions.

Influence Tactics

The use of influence by champions to promote their ideas has been documented in case studies of innovation (Schön, 1963, Burgelman, 1983; Dean, 1987). According to Schön (1963: 84), champions are "capable of using any and every means of informal sales and pressure in order to succeed." The results

Champions of Innovation

of Burgelman's (1983) investigation of the internal corporate venturing process revealed that astute organizational champions actively influenced the dispositions of top managers toward a new corporate venture and made them see the strategic importance of it. Dean's (1987) study of the decision processes surrounding the adoption of advanced manufacturing technology demonstrated that champions relied on a variety of influence tactics, including rational justification, repeated informal expression of enthusiasm and confidence about the innovation, and sharing of information with potential coalition members.

The social influence literature contends that the decision to engage in influence is a function of several factors, including self-characteristics (e.g., risk-seeking propensity, persuasiveness, need for achievement), characteristics of the influence target (e.g., perceived relative power), and situational factors (e.g., reason for exercising influence) (Mowday, 1979; Porter, Allen, and Angle, 1981). When he examined the personal characteristics of the influence agent, Mowday (1979) found that need for achievement and need for power are positively related to the propensity to engage in influence and to the methods of influence used in organizational decision situations (persuasive argument and manipulation). We thus hypothesize:

Hypothesis 4: There will be a more positive relationship between personality dimensions and influence tactics for champions than nonchampions.

Theoretically, charismatic and transformational leaders are characterized as exercising "diffuse and intensive influence over the normative [ideological] orientations of other actors" (Etzioni, 1961: 203). Imbued with self-confidence in their own capabilities, convinced in the rightness of their beliefs and ideals, and strong in the need for power, these leaders are highly motivated to influence their followers (House, 1977; Bass, 1985). By engaging in impression management to bolster their image of competence and success, by vividly portraying for followers an attractive vision of the outcomes of their efforts, and by relating the mission to strongly held values and ideals shared by members of the organization's culture, charismatic and transformational leaders mobilize their followers with moral inspiration and purpose to accomplish great feats (House, 1977; Bass, 1985). Substantial empirical evidence collected in a wide array of settings with diverse methodologies has confirmed that charismatic and transformational leaders have a profound impact on follower performance, satisfaction, and effectiveness (Yukl and Van Fleet, 1982; Avolio, Waldman, and Einstein, 1988; Hater and Bass, 1988; Howell and Frost, 1989). Thus, we hypothesize:

Hypothesis 5: Transformational leader behaviors will be more positively related to influence tactics for champions than nonchampions.

Characteristics of the influence target, particularly his or her relative power, play a role in determining the choice of influence strategies (Mowday, 1979; Kipnis, Schmidt, and Wilkinson, 1980). Different influence strategies are needed when the target is a superior, peer, or subordinate. Rational presentation of ideas and informal exchange (ingratiation) are associated with upward influence, while assertiveness and sanctions are typical of downward-influence tactics (Kipnis, Schmidt, and Wilkinson, 1980; Schilit and Locke, 1982).

Finally, situational factors also determine the choice of influence tactic. Kipnis, Schmidt, and Wilkinson (1980), in their study of intraorganizational influence tactics, reported that individuals rely on different influence strategies when they are seeking personal assistance, assigning work, attempting to improve others' performance, obtaining benefits, or initiating change. In particular, they found that when individuals try to convince others to accept new ideas, they use a variety of influence tactics, including rationality, assertiveness, ingratiation, coalition, and exchange. In terms of the champion role, where multiple stakeholders must be convinced of the champion's vision, this literature suggests that frequent influence attempts and a variety of influence tactics will be required:

Hypothesis 6: Champions will attempt to influence others more frequently and will use a wider variety of influence tactics than nonchampions.

A GENERAL MODEL OF CHAMPION EMERGENCE

The above theoretical arguments and supporting empirical evidence were combined into a single model of champion emergence, shown in Figure 1. According to this model, champion emergence is a function of personality characteristics, transformational leadership behaviors, and frequency and variety of influence tactics. Particular personality characteristics predispose individuals to engage in transformational leadership behaviors and influence tactics directed toward instigating innovations within organizations. Specifically, personality characteristics, including achievement, innovativeness, persistence, persuasiveness, and risk taking are associated with individuals' propensities to display transformational leadership behavior and to engage in frequent and varied influence tactics. As specified in the entrepreneurial literature, personality characteristics may also directly affect champion emergence, independent of leadership behavior. Finally, transformational leadership is related to the frequency and variety of influence tactics. As Bass (1985)

Figure 1. A general model of champion personality characteristics, transformational leadership, and influence tactics.

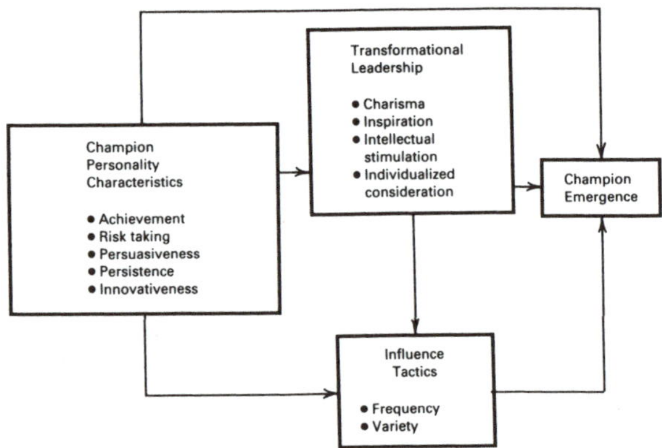

theorized, a fundamental quality of transformational leaders is their ability to influence persuasively the needs and orientations of others.

The relationship between transformational leadership and influence tactics may be reciprocal. Although we expected that transformational leadership behaviors would lead one to engage in many and varied influence tactics, the reverse relationship might prevail. It is conceivable that an individual who exerts maximum influence over other group members may be perceived as a leader. However, the exercise of influence does not automatically result in the attribution of transformational leadership. It could, for example, produce the attribution of transactional leadership in instances in which an individual exerts influence by controlling organizational resources. Thus, given the uncertainty about whether influence tactics lead to transformational leadership, this relationship was excluded from the model.

The model was tested with a study of information-technology innovations in 25 large Canadian companies. A matched sample of champions and nonchampions were interviewed and completed a questionnaire measuring their personality characteristics and leadership behaviors. Content analysis of the interview transcripts was conducted for the presence of themes related to leader behavior and influence tactics.

METHOD

Description of Innovations

For the purpose of this study, an innovation was defined as the adoption of a new product or process that reflected the application of information technology (Pennings, 1987). Information-technology innovations that required hands-on interaction with a computer-based system through a computer keyboard were examined in this study. Three criteria for selecting these innovations were established in light of the importance of clearly specifying the type of innovation to be sampled, in order to overcome the empirical instability and theoretical confusion arising from research on innovation in complex organizations (Downs and Mohr, 1976; Bigoness and Perreault, 1981).

The first criterion was that the technological innovations had to have been designed for use by managers and/or professionals. At management levels, adoption of information technology is typically voluntary rather than mandatory. Consequently, champions may be needed to promote the introduction and implementation of these technologies. To ensure more accurate recall of the innovation process by participants, the second criterion was that the innovation had to have been implemented within the 18 months prior to the study. The third criterion was that the innovation had to have represented a significant financial investment to the company. This criterion ensured that the innovation was visible in the organization and had a potentially important impact on managerial work.

Sample

Eighty-eight organizations that had recently implemented a technological innovation were identified through a survey of

350 chief executive officers (CEOs) of Canadian firms listed on the *Financial Post 500,* an annual enumeration of the largest Canadian companies (in terms of sales). Based on the survey responses, 56 innovations appeared to meet the three selection criteria for inclusion in the study. Preliminary interviews, either in person or by telephone, were conducted with executives from these companies. During these interviews, the investigators explained to the executives the background and general purpose of the study and obtained from them an in-depth description of the innovation. Based on these interviews, 28 information-technology innovations were identified that clearly met our established criteria. All 28 organizations agreed to participate in the study.

Procedure

Individuals who played a major role in the adoption of the innovation were identified by a two-stage process. First, a company executive identified the central individuals involved in the introduction and implementation of the innovation. Interviews with these key individuals often revealed others who played an important role in the innovation. These individuals were then also interviewed, creating a snowball sample (Rogers and Kincaid, 1981). For each innovation, an average of five key individuals were interviewed. In total, 153 interviews were conducted and tape recorded. On average, the interviews took one and one-half hours.

The interviews with key individuals were conducted using a structured protocol. The first part of the interview, described below, was used to identify champions and nonchampions. The remainder of the interview focused on (a) the key individual's personal involvement in the innovation; (b) the initial receptiveness and commitment of targeted users of the innovation; (c) the methods of influence used by the individual to initiate and implement the innovation; (d) the resistance encountered and methods used by the individual to overcome it; (e) the motivation of the individual to participate in the innovation and the recognition received; (f) the risk, both personal and organizational, associated with the innovation; (g) the individual's perception of his or her effectiveness in the process; (h) the identification of factors contributing to the success or failure of the innovation; and (i) the career history of the individual. Transcripts of the interviews were content-analyzed for leadership behaviors and influence tactics used by champions and nonchampions.

After the interview, all key individuals were requested to complete a questionnaire and return it to the investigators. The questionnaire contained measures, described below, of personality characteristics and leadership behaviors. The response rate for this questionnaire was 88 percent.

Identification of Champions and Nonchampions

The first part of the interview identified champions and nonchampions through peer nomination, which has been shown to be a highly reliable and valid technique (Kane and Lawler, 1978; Love, 1981). Initially, via an open-ended question, the respondent was asked to identify the key people associated with the innovation and to describe the roles each of them played. The respondent was subsequently given a set of five role definitions derived from the innovation literature. Four of

Champions of Innovation

these roles—project champion, technical innovator, business innovator, chief executive—were drawn from Achilladelis, Jervis, and Robertson (1971). The fifth role, user champion, was derived from the information-systems literature (Curley and Gremillion, 1983). Each key individual then identified the person or persons who clearly fit each of these roles. The respondents were allowed to name anyone associated with the innovation and were told to leave it blank if no one fit the role.

Several steps were taken to minimize attributional bias in identifying champions. First, respondents were informed that the purpose of the study was to examine factors influencing the introduction of technological innovations. Thus, the explicit purpose of the study was disguised. Second, the role descriptions derived from the innovation literature were not identified as representing different champion roles. Thus, respondents were given a description of activities associated with various roles, but the actual roles were not labelled as "project champion," "technical innovator," and so on. Third, key individuals were not told who had been nominated to the various innovation roles.

The criterion for accurately identifying project champions was complete (100 percent) agreement among the key individuals as to the person who played a particular role in championing the project. Using this criterion, 25 project champions were identified. We dropped from the analysis three projects in which there was disagreement about who was the project champion. To further verify that the 25 identified project champions actually played this role, we examined key individuals' responses to the open-ended question regarding the roles played by people associated with the innovation. In all cases, there was complete agreement between these two methods of identifying champions.

In order to test the hypotheses of the present study, we used four criteria to establish a comparison group, labelled "nonchampions." First, nonchampions and champions had to have been involved in the same innovation within the same organization. Pairing a champion and a nonchampion for each innovation therefore controlled for the cost, type, importance, success, or complexity of the innovations, company size, and industry. Moreover, since champions and nonchampions were involved in the same innovations, the fact that the innovations were judged to be relatively successful by the users should have caused both to receive the same "success bias," as reflected in the interviews and self-report measures. Second, both nonchampions and champions had to have played active, informal roles in the promotion of the innovation. However, in comparison to champions, nonchampions could not have been consensually identified as playing a specific role in the innovation (i.e., project champion, technical innovator, business innovator, chief executive, user champion) in the peer-nomination procedure. This criterion ensured that the champions and nonchampions were highly comparable in technical knowledge (since champions and nonchampions were not identified as the technical innovator) and position power (since champions and nonchampions were not identified as the business innovator, chief executive, or user champion). Third, champions and nonchampions had to be peers at the same organizational level. That is, there was no formal reporting relationship between them. Finally, champions and nonchampions had to have been self-appointed to the project. It was not within their job mandate to seek out and promote new technological innovations. Thus, differences between champions and nonchampions could not be attributed to role requirements of assigned positions, such as project leader.

To confirm that champions and nonchampions were similar on specific demographic variables, paired *t*-tests were conducted. The assumption underlying a paired *t*-test is that the sample of differences is normally distributed. This assumption was tested using the nonparametric Kolmogorov-Smirnov test. The assumption held for both age and salary data. The results indicated that champions and nonchampions were not significantly different with regard to age [$t(24) = .61$; $p > .05$] and salary [$t(24) = .62$; $p > .05$]. In addition, chi-squared tests of significance revealed that champions and nonchampions were not significantly different in job level [$\chi^2(3) = 2.39$; $p = .49$], functional area [$\chi^2(3) = 3.84$; $p = .28$] and educational level [$\chi^2(1) = 1.09$; $p = .29$]. Thus, any differences found between the two groups could not be attributed to differences in these demographic characteristics.

The final sample consisted of 25 pairs of champions and nonchampions. The 50 participants, all of whom were male, had an average age of 45 years and were at executive (52 percent) or middle management (48 percent) levels across a variety of functional areas, including accounting, engineering, finance, general management, information systems, and marketing.

Content Analysis

The transcripts of the champion and nonchampion interviews were content-analyzed for the presence of themes relating to leadership behavior and influence tactics, using the same procedure as House, Woycke, and Fodor (1988). Descriptions of leadership behaviors were developed using charismatic and transformational leadership theories as a guide (Bass, 1985; Conger and Kanungo, 1987; House, Woycke, and Fodor, 1988). Descriptions of influence tactics were adopted from Kipnis and Schmidt (1982).

Transcripts separate from those to be used in the study were selected to clarify the operationalization of the leadership behaviors and influence tactics. Three individuals independently coded these practice passages, discussed their ratings, and then clarified the descriptions where necessary. Five iterations of rating and discussion were completed before we felt that there was an unambiguous operationalization of each leadership behavior and influence tactic. The final coding of these practice passages became the key on which the coders were trained and eventually tested (House, Woycke, and Fodor, 1988).

University students were recruited to code the interview transcripts. They were given a test to ensure that their reading comprehension was adequate for the material they would have to code. Of twelve students who took the reading test, seven passed. Ultimately, six of these seven students were hired to code the transcripts. They were randomly assigned to code either leader behaviors or influence tactics. Using precoded practice material and a description of leader and influence behaviors, the students were trained so that they understood and were able to code the interviews accurately. The six students trained to code leader behaviors or influence tactics met the established criterion of 75 percent agreement with the key. In total, the training required 12 hours. The identification of champions and nonchampions was disguised so that coders could not determine the identity of the people to which the transcripts applied. In addition, coders were unaware of the hypotheses of the study. In total, over 1000 pages of transcripts were analyzed. No significant differences in the lengths of champion and nonchampion interview transcripts were found.

Measures

Personality characteristics. Five scales in the questionnaire assessed the personality characteristics of champions and nonchampions. Three scales from the Jackson Personality Inventory (Jackson, 1976) were used: risk taking, innovation, and social adroitness. In addition, we used two scales from the Personality Research Form E (Jackson, 1967): achievement and endurance. For these personality measures a true-false response format was used. Extensive empirical evaluation of these measures revealed high internal consistency and test-retest reliabilities, minimal acquiescence and social desirability response biases, and adequate convergent and discriminant validity (Jackson, 1967, 1976, 1977).

The number of items per scale, reliabilities (Cronbach's alpha), and the conceptual definition for each scale are as follows: *risk taking* (17 items, $\alpha = .84$): enjoys taking chances; *innovation* (17 items, $\alpha = .84$): develops novel solutions to problems; *social adroitness* (11 items, $\alpha = .63$): persuades others to achieve a particular goal; *achievement* (12 items, $\alpha = .73$): aspires to accomplish difficult tasks; and *endurance* (11 items, $\alpha = .68$): perseveres even in the face of great difficulty.

Leadership behavior. Leadership behavior was assessed in two ways. First, Bass's (1985) Multifactor Leadership Questionnaire (Form 5-Self) was administered to the key individuals. This 34-item questionnaire tapped the four leadership scales of relevance to the present study: charisma, inspiration, intellectual stimulation, and individualized consideration. Key individuals were asked to judge how frequently they engaged in different leadership behaviors measured by the questionnaire. Each behavior was rated on a 5-point frequency scale ranging from 0 = not at all, to 4 = frequently, if not always.

Supportive reliability and validity data for the Multifactor Leadership Questionnaire are presented by Bass and Avolio (1989). Specifically, based on samples of military and industrial leaders, three separate factor analyses of the questionnaire have produced the four factors that constitute the behaviors associated with transformational leadership. The number of items per scale, reliabilities (Cronbach's alpha), and the conceptual definition for each scale are as follows: *charisma* (10 items, $\alpha = .74$): expresses an exciting vision and communicates confidence in followers' abilities to meet high performance expectations; *inspiration* (9 items, $\alpha = .75$): gets others to excel by, for example, giving pep talks; *intel-*

lectual stimulation (9 items, α = .71): questions the tried and true ways and solves problems creatively; and *individualized consideration* (6 items, α = .70): provides encouragement, support, and developmental opportunities for followers.

The second measure of leadership behavior involved content analysis of the interview transcripts to determine if, in comparison to nonchampions, champions engaged more frequently in behaviors that differentiated transformational from nontransformational leaders theoretically. Each passage of the interview was coded separately for the presence or absence of the individual's display of self-confidence; strong conviction about ideological goals; communication of individualized consideration for others (i.e., superiors, peers, subordinates); expression of high expectations for others; communication of confidence in others' ability to accomplish tasks; demonstration of unconventional, innovative, or countercultural behavior; and assessment of environmental resources and constraints for bringing about change (Bass, 1985; Conger and Kanungo, 1987; House, Woycke, and Fodor, 1988).

Influence tactics. The frequency and variety of influence tactics used by champions and nonchampions were assessed using the same content-analysis technique described earlier. Passages describing strategies were coded based on Kipnis and Schmidt's (1982) description of eight different influence tactics, including building coalitions, appealing to higher authority, bargaining, acting in a clandestine manner, presenting rational arguments, applying sanctions, using friendliness and ingratiation, and being assertive. Variety of influence was calculated by determining how many of the eight different influence tactics were used. Frequency of influence was the total count of the number of influence attempts. Both variety and frequency of influence were measured in order to distinguish individuals who used only one influence tactic repeatedly from individuals who used a wide range of influence tactics with differing frequencies.

Intercorrelations of Measures

Pearson correlation coefficients among the measurement scales are presented in Table 2. Many correlations were significant ($p < .05$). The measures of personality characteristics

Table 2

Intercorrelations for Personality, Leadership, and Influence Measures

Variable	1	2	3	4	5	6	7	8	9	10
1. Achievement	–									
2. Risk taking	.26•	–								
3. Endurance	.44••	.21	–							
4. Innovativeness	.32••	.37••	.59••	–						
5. Social adroitness	.26•	.38••	.21	.04	–					
6. Charisma	.05	.29•	−.04	.02	.07	–				
7. Inspiration	.13	.32••	.15	.31••	.14	.60••	–			
8. Intellectual stimulation	.08	.21	.14	.18	.01	.55••	.58••	–		
9. Individualized consideration	.29•	.13	.42••	.44••	.08	.34••	.42••	.29•	–	
10. Frequency of influence tactics	−.03	.39••	.04	.22	.12	.27•	.37••	.33••	.25•	–
11. Variety of influence tactics	.08	.40••	.01	.28•	.14	.26•	.39••	.41••	.29•	.85••

•$p < .05$; ••$p < .01$.

Champions of Innovation

were highly intercorrelated, as were the measures for transformational leadership and influence. The relationships between constructs showed that the measures of transformational leadership and influence were highly correlated, whereas the measures of personality characteristics (with the exception of innovation and risk taking) tended to be weakly correlated with the other measures.

Data Analysis

Hypotheses 1, 2, and 6 postulated differences between champions and nonchampions on several personality, leadership, and influence variables. To test these hypotheses, a sample of differences was calculated by subtracting nonchampion scores from champion scores. Thus, a positive score indicated that the champion in a matched pair scored higher than a nonchampion on a particular variable, For each hypothesis, Hotelling's one-sample multivariate T^2 statistic was used. This test, which is the simplest form of MANOVA, allows for the simultaneous testing of the hypothesis that several population means do not differ from a specified set of constants. Prior to conducting the test, we checked each sample of differences for normality (the primary assumption underlying Hotelling's T^2) using a Kolmogorov-Smirnov test. All samples of differences met the assumption of normality. Individual *F*-tests were then used to identify which of the variables significantly differentiated between champions and nonchampions. Since the probability of committing Type I errors increases as the number of statistical tests increases, the significance level used to evaluate the comparisons was divided evenly among the comparisons actually being made (Kirk, 1982).

Hypotheses 3, 4, and 5 postulated that the strength of the relationships between personality characteristics, leadership behaviors, and influence tactics would be significantly greater for champions in comparison to nonchampions. Regression analysis was used to test these hypotheses. This analysis assumes that the residuals are normally distributed and that variance of the residuals is constant. For each of the three regressions, the normality of the residuals was checked using a Kolmogorov-Smirnov test. Constant variance was assessed by examining plots of the residuals. These assumptions were met.

In the regression analysis, indices were formed on each of the three constructs. Conceptually, the four scales of transformational leadership were viewed as tapping the same higher-order construct (i.e., transformational leadership) and were combined into a single index. In addition, the five scales measuring personality characteristics theoretically represented the higher-order construct "champion personality." Accordingly, these scales were formed into a single index. An index was also computed for influence, given the high intercorrelation between frequency and variety of influence tactics.

Indices were calculated using a procedure recommended by Hotelling (1933), in which weights are obtained from the unrotated factor matrix of a principal components factor analysis. The weights produced can be considered an indicator of each scale's contribution to the higher-order construct. For example, to compute the index for transformational leadership the following formula was used:

Transformational Leadership Index = $A \times Wa + B \times Wb + C \times Wc + D \times Wd$,

where *A, B, C,* and *D* represent the standardized scale scores for charisma, inspiration, intellectual stimulation, and individualized consideration, and *Wa, Wb, Wc,* and *Wd* are their respective weights. Indices for personality characteristics and influence tactics were computed similarly.

Once the indices were computed, regression analysis was conducted on the three paths in the model of champion emergence. This analysis used a dummy variable coded to reflect the champion and nonchampion groups. A significant *t*-value on the dummy variable would indicate that champions and nonchampions are significantly different with respect to the path being tested.

Two supplemental analyses were also conducted. First, in order to understand more fully the interrelationships among constructs in the model of champion emergence, we used Partial Least Squares (PLS) analysis. PLS simultaneously estimates relationships between measures and constructs, as well as paths between constructs. Accordingly, it provides additional information regarding the relationships between personality characteristics, leadership behaviors, and influence tactics of champions.

PLS is an extremely powerful multivariate analysis technique that is ideal for testing structural models with latent variables (see Wold, 1985, for a comprehensive description). It has its roots in regression, path analysis, and principal components factor analysis. Sample sizes can be small and assumptions of normality are not necessary (Fornell, 1982), making the technique ideal in the early stages of theory building and testing. Because PLS requires that the data be analyzed within a theoretical model (Fornell, 1982), it was appropriate to test the model of champion emergence only with the sample of champions. Since relationships in the model are not hypothesized to hold for nonchampions, PLS analysis would be inappropriate for that sample.

The path coefficients from a PLS analysis are standardized regression coefficients. The loadings of the items on the constructs are factor loadings. Thus, the results can easily be interpreted by considering them in the context of regression and factor analysis.

The second supplemental analysis used discriminant analysis in order to determine if champions and nonchampions could be distinguished using our hypothesized personality characteristics and leadership behaviors as discriminating variables. Discriminant analysis requires that the discriminating variables be drawn from a population with a multivariate normal distribution and that the covariance matrices of the two groups not be significantly different (Klecka, 1980). For each discriminant analysis, Kolmogorov-Smirnov tests indicated that the normality criterion was satisfied. Box's *M* test confirmed that the covariance matrices were equal.

Champions of Innovation

RESULTS

Hypothesis 1 posited that champions would score higher than nonchampions on measures of transformational leadership. Two sources of data were used to analyze this hypothesis: the self-ratings of transformational leadership from the Multifactor Leadership Questionnaire and the frequency of transformational themes in the interview transcripts. Table 3 presents the results of the Hotelling's T^2 test for the Multifactor Leadership Questionnaire. The Hotelling's T^2 statistic was significant, indicating that champions and nonchampions can be distinguished on the basis of transformational leadership behaviors. Univariate F-tests, also summarized in Table 3, indicate that inspiration and intellectual stimulation significantly differentiated between champions and nonchampions. Charisma ($p < .02$) just failed to meet the conservative significance levels ($p < .0125$) adopted for these tests. Individualized consideration did not significantly distinguish between champions and nonchampions ($p > .05$).

Content analysis was used to determine the frequency of transformational behaviors exhibited by champions and nonchampions. The results of a paired t-test comparing differences across the two samples revealed that champions reported transformational leadership behaviors to a significantly greater extent than nonchampions [$t(24) = 4.12$; $p < .001$]. Consistent with the analysis of the questionnaire measures, this finding lends further support to Hypothesis 1.

Hypothesis 2 stated that champions would display greater achievement, risk taking, persistence, innovativeness, and persuasiveness than nonchampions. To test this hypothesis, Hotelling's T^2 statistic was calculated on the sample of differences between champion and nonchampion pairs. As shown in Table 3, there was a significant difference between champions and nonchampions for personality characteristics. To

Table 3

Hotelling's T^2 Test for the Personality Characteristics, Leadership Behaviors, and Influence Tactics of Champions and Nonchampions

Variable	Champion Mean	Nonchampion Mean	d.f.	F
Personality characteristics				
Risk taking	.71	.53	1,24	13.13•••
Achievement	.91	.82	1,24	4.42•
Innovativeness	.84	.75	1,24	3.39•
Social adroitness	.50	.43	1,24	2.66
Endurance	.74	.72	1,24	.22
Hotelling's $T^2 = .72$, $F(5,20) = 2.88$, $p < .05$				
Leadership behavior				
Inspiration	2.66	2.19	1,24	18.34•••
Intellectual stimulation	3.19	2.92	1,24	9.39••
Charisma	3.05	2.78	1,24	4.88•
Individualized consideration	3.09	2.89	1,24	2.23
Hotelling's $T^2 = .85$, $F(4,21) = 4.48$, $p < .01$				
Influence tactics				
Frequency	9.16	4.64	1,24	17.92•••
Variety	2.95	1.79	1,24	15.29•••
Hotelling's $T^2 = .78$, $F(2,23) = 8.99$, $p < .001$				

• $p < .05$; •• $p < .01$; ••• $p < .001$.

determine which of the personality characteristics distinguished between champions and nonchampions, univariate F-tests were computed. Using a conservative p-value of .01 (.05 divided by 5, the number of tests), risk taking was the only statistically significant variable. Achievement and innovativeness approached significance. Social adroitness and endurance, however, did not significantly differentiate between champions and nonchampions ($p > .05$).

Hypothesis 3 stated that there would be a more positive relationship between personality characteristics and leadership behaviors for champions than for nonchampions. Hypothesis 4 postulated that there would be a more positive relationship between personality characteristics and influence tactics for champions in comparison to nonchampions. Hypothesis 5 posited that there would be a more positive relationship between transformational leadership behaviors and influence tactics for champions than for nonchampions. For hypothesis 3, the dummy variable distinguishing between champions and nonchampions was significant [$t(47) = 3.81$; $p < .001$; $R^2 = .29$]. Similarly, for hypothesis 4 [$t(47) = 3.96$; $p < .001$; $R^2 = .26$], and hypothesis 5 [$t(47) = 2.87$; $p < .01$; $R^2 = .29$], the dummy variables were significant. These results lend support to hypotheses 3, 4, and 5.

Hypothesis 6, which postulated that champions would initiate more influence attempts and would use a greater variety of influence tactics than would nonchampions, was supported. The Hotelling's T^2 value reached statistical significance and the univariate F-tests showed that both frequency and variety of influence attempts were significantly different across the champion and nonchampion pairs (see Table 3). It should be noted that given the high intercorrelation between frequency and variety of influence tactics, the univariate F-tests are essentially testing the same variable.

Supplemental Analyses

The results of the PLS analysis are shown in Table 4. Factor loadings greater than .7 are generally considered meaningful, since this implies that the construct explains more than 50 percent of the variance in the measure. An examination of the factor loadings clearly indicates that two variables drive the personality construct within the theoretical context of our model. They are risk taking and innovativeness, with loadings of .68 and .75, respectively. Since constructs obtain their meaning from the theoretical relationships in which they are imbedded (Fornell, 1982), these results imply that risk taking and innovativeness are the predominant personality characteristics of champions. The transformational leadership construct is derived mainly from charisma, inspiration, and intellectual stimulation. Individualized consideration is related to the construct but has a much lower loading than the other three items. These results provide partial support for Bass's (1985) conceptualization of transformational leadership. Finally, influence is jointly, and almost equally, defined in terms of frequency and variety of attempts.

As shown in Table 4, the path coefficient between personality and leadership behaviors was large and significant. Similarly, significant relationships were found between transformational leadership and influence and between personality character-

Champions of Innovation

Table 4

Partial Least Squares Analysis of Champion-Emergence Model

Path	Path coefficient
Personality → Leadership	.58***
Personality → Influence	.19**
Leadership → Influence	.27**
Construct	**Factor loading**
Personality characteristics	
Achievement	−.33
Risk taking	.68
Endurance	.01
Innovativeness	.75
Social adroitness	.01
Leadership behavior	
Charisma	.80
Inspiration	.86
Intellectual stimulation	.75
Individualized consideration	.38
Influence tactics	
Frequency	.84
Variety	.99

** $p < .01$; *** $p < .001$.

istics and influence. The model was able to explain 34 percent of the variation in transformational leadership and 17 percent of the variance in influence tactics.

Table 5 presents the results of the discriminant analysis using personality and leadership variables. The discriminant function was significant [$\chi^2(9) = 22.96$; $p < .001$] and the overall classification rate was 84 percent. The structure coefficients, which are the simple bivariate correlations between each variable and the discriminant function, can be used to deter-

Table 5

Discriminant Analysis for the Personality Characteristics and Leadership Behaviors of Champions and Nonchampions

Classification Matrix

Group	Predicted group membership Champion	Nonchampion
Champion	84%	16%
Nonchampion	16%	84%
Percent correctly classified = 84%		

Structure Coefficients

Variable	Loading
Inspiration	.77
Risk taking	.61
Charisma	.48
Intellectual stimulation	.36
Achievement	.35
Individualized consideration	.27
Innovativeness	.23
Social adroitness	.22
Endurance	.09

mine the relative importance of the individual variables (Klecka, 1980). Variables with correlations greater than .3 were, in order of importance: inspiration, risk taking, charisma, intellectual stimulation, and achievement.

DISCUSSION AND CONCLUSIONS

A major substantive contribution of this study is the inductive development and rigorous testing of a model of champion emergence derived from empirical studies and theoretical statements in the domains of entrepreneurship, transformational leadership, and influence. The results of the present study inform the entrepreneurship and transformational leadership literature. In addition, organizational implications for the detection, selection, and development of champions can be drawn.

Our analyses indicate that champions manifest the personality characteristics of risk-taking propensity and innovativeness, which are empirically related to entrepreneurship and theoretically associated with transformational leadership (e.g., McClelland, 1967; Kets de Vries, 1977; Bass, 1985). This suggests that particular personality traits predispose some individuals to emerge informally as champions and thereby enhance the promotion of innovation in organizations. Thus, contrary to Davis-Blake and Pfeffer's (1989) thesis that dispositional effects are less important than situational effects in influencing people's attitudes in organizational settings, our results suggest that by ignoring individual differences, one neglects major variables relevant to an important organizational human resource.

The study's findings further inform transformational leadership theory. The results demonstrated that transformational leadership can be empirically linked to the promotion of innovation in organizations. This link has not been made to date. More specifically, the findings suggest that fundamental components of a champion's capacity to introduce innovations successfully are the articulation of a compelling vision of the innovation's potential for the organization, the expression of confidence in others to participate effectively in the initiative, and the display of innovative actions to achieve goals.

Van de Ven (1986: 594) pointed out that one of the key issues in managing innovation is how to trigger the action thresholds of individuals to appreciate and pay attention to new ideas, needs, and opportunities. The results of the present study suggest that by appealing to larger principles or unassailable values about the potential of the innovation for fulfilling the organization's dream of what it can be, champions capture the attention of others. Moreover, by providing emotional meaning and energy to the idea, champions induce the commitment of others to the innovation.

The present study provides additional information about the transformational behaviors of informal leaders. Previous studies of transformational leaders have focused on elected leaders in the political arena (House, Woycke, and Fodor, 1988) and formally appointed leaders in the military (Yukl and Van Fleet, 1982), in complex organizations (Hater and Bass, 1988), in management simulation games (Avolio, Waldman, and Einstein, 1988), and in the laboratory (Howell and Frost,

1989). In contrast, this study dealt with informal leaders, those who spontaneously emerge to promote innovation. This is the first time that it has been demonstrated that champions are informal transformational leaders. Thus, based on the findings of the present study, transformational leadership theory can be extended to include both formally appointed leaders and emergent informal leaders. This theoretical extension is important, because in order to understand fully the nature and process of innovation, the behaviors of informal leaders, as well as formal leaders, need to be studied.

Limitations

One limitation of this study is that the findings are based on same-source data: champions and nonchampions provided the interview and questionnaire data. It could, therefore, be argued that the sources of information reflect a common-source bias. This argument is considerably weakened by two observations. The first observation concerns the use of peer-nomination, whereby key individuals, unaware of the explicit purpose and hypotheses of the study, independently and unanimously nominated the champion. Second, coders unaware of the hypotheses of the study conducted the content analysis of the interview transcripts. Content analysis showed that champions engaged in transformational behaviors and influence tactics significantly more frequently than nonchampions. These findings strongly support the statistical analyses of the self-report data, thereby corroborating their validity.

Another limitation of the study is the use of cross-sectional, retrospective data. Accordingly, causal interpretations of the results are precluded. With respect to the use of retrospective data, Nisbett and Wilson (1977) concluded that in salient situations individuals' recall of events was likely to reflect the actual events. Since the technological innovations studied in this research represented major changes within the organization, these situations appeared highly salient to organizational members. Hence, it is a reasonable assumption that the events reported by the key individuals were representative of the actual situation.

The sample size of 25 champions and 25 nonchampions was a further limitation of the present study. However, the highly statistically significant differences between champions and nonchampions on the questionnaire measures and the replication of these differences in the content analysis suggest that the findings are robust. In addition, since the champions were closely matched with nonchampions on a variety of demographic characteristics, the present study represents a conservative test of the hypotheses. Even greater differences between champions and nonchampions might be found if a random sample of managers served as the control group for champions.

Implications

It is interesting to speculate about the interaction between contextual variables and champions' individual predispositions to engage in innovation. According to social learning theory (Mischel, 1973), individual differences are most predictive of behavior when environmental conditions are unstructured or weak. Under conditions of significant environmental or technological change, more behavioral options are available to organizational members. In these circumstances, personality characteristics are expressed more strongly and make a greater difference in behavior. Therefore, when organizational and technological constraints are weak, individuals with predispositions associated with championship are more likely to emerge as champions than when organizational and technological constraints are strong and provide cues and guidance for individual behavior.

The above line of reasoning implies that organizational settings are likely to differ with respect to the likelihood of champion emergence. In his discussion of the distribution and exercise of power in different organizational forms, House (1991) argues that organic organizations represent weak psychological situations, since the low degree of social stratification and decentralization of decision-making authority serve to enhance the expression of individual behavior. Mechanistic organizations, in contrast, are strong psychological situations, since their selection and socialization practices produce less variance in the motives and attitudes of members and hence suppress the effects of individual differences. Based on this argument, it is expected that there will be a greater likelihood of champion emergence in organic than in mechanistic organizations.

An interesting question is whether organizations can formally appoint individuals to champion a project. It is possible that formalization of the champion role could lead to its disappearance. Empirical tests of cognitive evaluation theory (Deci, 1975) indicate that external incentives and behavioral monitoring, conditions characteristic of formal roles, can reduce a task's potential to impart feelings of competence or self-determination, which, in turn, may diminish intrinsic motivation (Deci, 1975; Lepper and Greene, 1975). Kiesler (1971), in a series of studies on psychological commitment, reported that the greater the external pressure or inducement for individuals performing acts consistent with their beliefs, the less committed they are to the act. Similarly, Salancik (1977) argued that when the instrumental basis for work is salient, it will reduce a person's felt responsibility. Collectively, these studies suggest that formally appointing individuals to a project-champion role may undermine their intrinsic motivation and commitment and hence jeopardize the innovation's ultimate success.

Our findings further suggest that it is likely that individuals who have champion potential can be identified through the use of psychological tests. Combining both personality characteristics and leadership behavior in the same discriminant function resulted in a successful classification rate of 84 percent. If individuals who are likely to emerge as champions can be identified, then managers could provide them with an appropriate environment and organizational experiences conducive to innovation.

The present study also has implications for training selected individuals to emerge as champions. Bass and his colleagues (1987) reported a falling dominoes or cascading leadership effect, whereby followers of transformational leaders engaged

Champions of Innovation

in behaviors similar to that of their leader. In addition, in their laboratory test of House's (1977) theory of charismatic leadership, Howell and Frost (1989) showed that selected individuals could be trained to exhibit charismatic leader behaviors. The results of these studies suggest that individuals with the requisite personality characteristics and social skills could acquire championing behaviors through transformational leadership training.

Technological innovation is critical to organizational productivity, competition, and survival. The globalization of the world's economies is opening new markets, spawning different industries, and intensifying the competition in existing markets. Firm survival will continue to depend on a stream of creative, technological advances such as those nurtured by champions in our study. Accordingly, in-depth knowledge of champions is vital to understanding the innovation process fully. The findings of the present study take us a step in that direction.

REFERENCES

Achilladelis, B., P. Jervis, and A. Robertson
1971 A Study of Success and Failure in Industrial Innovation. Sussex, England: University of Sussex Press.

Allen, Thomas J.
1977 Managing the Flow of Technology. Cambridge, MA: MIT Press.

Avolio, Bruce J., David A. Waldman, and Walter O. Einstein
1988 "Transformational leadership in a management simulation game." Group and Organization Studies, 13: 59–80.

Bass, Bernard M.
1985 Leadership and Performance beyond Expectations. New York: Free Press.

Bass, Bernard M., and Bruce J. Avolio
1989 Manual for the Multifactor Leadership Questionnaire Profile. Palo Alto, CA: Consulting Psychologists Press.

Bass, Bernard M., David A. Waldman, Bruce J. Avolio, and Michael Bebb
1987 "Transformational leadership: The falling dominoes effect." Group and Organization Studies, 12: 73–87.

Bigoness, William J., and William D. Perreault
1981 "A conceptual paradigm and approach for the study of innovators." Academy of Management Journal, 24: 68–82.

Burgelman, Robert A.
1983 "A process model of internal corporate venturing in the diversified major firm." Administrative Science Quarterly, 28: 223–244.

Burns, James MacGregor
1978 Leadership. New York: Harper & Row.

Chakrabarti, Alok K.
1974 "The role of champion in product innovation." California Management Review, 17(2): 58–62.

Collins, O., and D. G. Moore
1970 The Organization Makers. New York: Appleton-Century-Croft.

Conger, Jay A., and Rabindra N. Kanungo
1987 "Toward a behavioral theory of charismatic leadership in organizational settings." Academy of Management Review, 12: 637–647.

Cox, Lionel A.
1976 "Industrial innovation: The role of people and cost factors." Research Management, 19: 29–32.

Curley, Kathleen F., and Lee L. Gremillion
1983 "The role of the champion in DSS implementation." Information and Management, 6: 203–209.

Davis-Blake, Alison, and Jeffrey Pfeffer
1989 "Just a mirage: The search for dispositional effects in organizational research." Academy of Management Review, 14: 385–400.

Dean, James W.
1987 "Building the future: The justification process for new technology." In Johannes M. Pennings and Arend Buitendam (eds.), New Technology as Organizational Innovation: 35–58. Cambridge, MA: Ballinger.

Deci, Edward L.
1975 Intrinsic Motivation. New York: Plenum.

Delbecq, André L., and Peter K. Mills
1985 "Managerial practices that enhance innovation." Organizational Dynamics, 14(Summer): 24–34.

Downs, George W., and Lawrence B. Mohr
1976 "Conceptual issues in the study of innovation." Administrative Science Quarterly, 21: 700–714.

Ettlie, John E.
1983 "A note on the relationship between managerial change values, innovative intentions and innovative technology outcomes in food sector firms." R & D Management, 13: 231–244.

Ettlie, John E., William P. Bridges, and Robert D. O'Keefe
1984 "Organization strategy and structural differences for radical versus incremental innovation." Management Science, 30: 682–695.

Etzioni, Amitai
1961 A Comparative Analysis of Complex Organizations. New York: Free Press.

Fernelius, W. Conrad, and Willis H. Waldo
1980 "Role of basic research in industrial innovation." Research Management, 23: 36–40.

Fornell, Claes
1982 A Second Generation of Multivariate Analysis Methods. New York: Praeger.

Frohman, Alan L.
1978 "The performance of innovation: Managerial roles." California Management Review, 20(3): 5–12.

Galbraith, Jay R.
1982 "Designing the innovating organization." Organizational Dynamics, 10(Winter): 5–25.

Hater, John J., and Bernard M. Bass
1988 "Supervisors' evaluations and subordinates' perceptions of transformational leadership." Journal of Applied Psychology, 73: 695–702.

Hornaday, John A., and John Aboud
1971 "Characteristics of successful entrepreneurs." Personnel Psychology, 24: 141–153.

Hotelling, Harold
1933 "Analysis of a complex of statistical variables into principle components." Journal of Educational Psychology, 24: 417–441, 498–520.

House, Robert J.
1977 "A 1976 theory of charismatic leadership." In James Gerald Hunt and Lars L. Larson (eds.), Leadership: The Cutting Edge: 189–207. Carbondale, IL: Southern Illinois University Press.
1991 "The distribution and exercise of power in mechanistic and organic organizations." In Henry L. Tosi (ed.), Organizational Structures, Individual Differences and Management Processes. Greenwich, CT: JAI Press (forthcoming).

House, Robert J., James Woycke, and Eugene M. Fodor
1988 "Charismatic and non-charismatic leaders: Differences in behavior and effectiveness." In Jay A. Conger and Rabindra N. Kanungo (eds.), Charismatic Leadership: 98–121. San Francisco: Jossey-Bass.

Howell, Jane M., and Peter J. Frost
1989 "A laboratory study of charismatic leadership." Organizational Behavior and Human Decision Processes, 43(2): 243–269.

Jackson, Douglas N.
1967 Personality Research Form Manual. Goshen, NY: Research Psychologists Press.
1976 Jackson Personality Inventory Manual. Goshen, NY: Research Psychologists Press.
1977 "Reliability of the Jackson Personality Inventory." Psychological Reports, 40: 613–614.

Kane, Jeffrey S., and Edward E. Lawler
1978 "Methods of peer assessment." Psychological Bulletin, 35: 555–586.

Katz, Ralph, and Michael L. Tushman
1983 "A longitudinal study of the effects of boundary spanning supervision on turnover and promotion in research and development." Academy of Management Journal, 26: 437–456.

Kelly, Patrick, and Melvin Kranzberg
1978 "Technological innovations: A critical review of current knowledge." San Francisco: San Francisco University Press.

Kets de Vries, M. F. R.
1977 "The entrepreneurial personality: A person at the crossroads." Journal of Management Studies, 14: 34–37.

Kiesler, Charles A.
1971 The Psychology of Commitment. New York: Academic Press.

Kimberly, John R., and Michael J. Evanisko
1981 "Organizational innovation: The influence of individual, organizational, and contextual factors on hospital adoption of technological and administrative innovations." Academy of Management Journal, 24: 689–713.

Kipnis, David, and Stuart M. Schmidt
1982 Profiles of Organizational Influence Strategies. Toronto: University Associates.

Kipnis, David, Stuart M. Schmidt, and Ian Wilkinson
1980 "Intraorganizational influence tactics: Exploration in getting one's way." Journal of Applied Psychology, 65: 440–452.

Kirk, Roger E.
1982 Experimental Design. Belmont, CA: Wadsworth.

Klecka, William R.
1980 Discriminant Analysis. Beverly Hills, CA: Sage.

Lepper, Mark R., and David Greene
1975 "Turning play into work: Effects of adult surveillance and extrinsic rewards on children's intrinsic motivation." Journal of Personality and Social Psychology, 31: 479–486.

Love, Kevin G.
1981 "Comparison of peer assessment methods: Reliability, validity, friendship bias, and user reaction." Journal of Applied Psychology, 66: 451–457.

Maddi, S. R.
1976 Personality Theories: A Comparative Analysis, 3rd ed. Homewood, IL: Dorsey.

Maidique, Modesto A.
1980 "Entrepreneurs, champions, and technological innovation." Sloan Management Review, 21(2): 59–76.

McClelland, David C.
1967 The Achieving Society. New York: Free Press.

Mischel, W.
1973 "Toward a cognitive social learning reconceptualization of personality." Psychological Review, 80: 252–283.

Morgan, Gareth
1988 Riding the Waves of Change. San Francisco: Jossey-Bass.

Mowday, Richard T.
1979 "Leader characteristics, self-confidence, and methods of upward influence in organizational decision situations." Academy of Management Journal, 22: 709–725.

Nisbett, Richard E., and Timothy DeCamp Wilson
1977 "Telling more than we can know: Verbal reports on mental processes." Psychological Review, 814: 231–259.

Oberg, William
1972 "Charisma, commitment, and contemporary organization theory." M.S.U. Business Topics, 20: 18–32.

Pennings, Johannes M.
1987 "On the nature of new technology as organizational innovation." In Johannes M. Pennings and Arend Buitendam (eds.), New Technology as Organizational Innovation: 3–12. Cambridge, MA: Ballinger.

Pennings, Johannes M., and Arend Buitendam (eds.)
1987 New Technology as Organizational Innovation. Cambridge, MA: Ballinger.

Pinchot, Gifford, III
1985 Intrapreneuring: Why You Don't Have to Leave the Corporation to Become an Entrepreneur. New York: Harper & Row.

Porter, Lyman W., Robert W. Allen, and Harold L. Angle
1981 "The politics of upward influence in organizations." In Barry M. Staw and Larry L. Cummings (eds.), Research in Organizational Behavior, 3: 109–149. Greenwich, CT: JAI Press.

Roberts, Edward B.
1968 "A basic study of innovators: How to keep and capitalize on their talents." Research Management, 11: 249–266.

Rogers, Everett M., and D. Lawrence Kincaid
1981 Communication Networks. New York: Free Press.

Rogers, Everett M., and F. Floyd Shoemaker
1971 Communication of Innovations: A Cross-cultural Approach. New York: Free Press.

Rothwell, R., C. Freeman, A. Horlsey, V. T. P. Jervis, A. B. Robertson, and J. Townsend
1974 "SAPPHO updated—Project SAPPHO phase II." Research Policy, 3: 258–291.

Champions of Innovation

Salancik, Gerald R.
1977 "Commitment and the control of organizational behavior and belief." In Barry M. Staw and Gerald R. Salancik (eds.), New Directions in Organizational Behavior: 1–54. Chicago: St. Clair.

Sashkin, Marshall
1988 "The visionary leader." In Jay A. Conger and Rabindra N. Kanungo (eds.), Charismatic Leadership: 122–160. San Francisco: Jossey-Bass.

Schilit, Warren K., and Edwin A. Locke
1982 "A study of upward influence in organizations." Administrative Science Quarterly, 27: 304–316.

Schön, Donald A.
1963 "Champions for radical new inventions." Harvard Business Review, 41(March–April): 77–86.

Souder, William E.
1981 "Encouraging entrepreneurship in the large corporations." Research Management, 24: 18–22.

Stein, M. I.
1968 "Creativity." In Edgar F. Borgatta and William W. Lambert (eds.), Handbook of Personality Theory and Research: 900–942. Chicago: Rand McNally.

Tushman, Michael, and David Nadler
1986 "Organizing for innovation." California Management Review, 28(3): 74–92.

Tushman, Michael L., and Thomas J. Scanlan
1981 "Boundary spanning individuals: Their role in information transfer and their antecedents." Academy of Management Journal, 24: 289–305.

Van de Ven, Andrew H.
1986 "Central problems in the management of innovation." Management Science, 32: 590–607.

Wainer, Herbert A., and Irwin A. Rubin
1969 "Motivation of research and development entrepreneurs: Determinants of company success." Journal of Applied Psychology, 53: 178–184.

Wold, Herman
1985 "Systems analysis by partial least squares." In P. Nijkamp, H. Leitner, and N. Wrigley (eds.), Measuring the Unmeasurable: 221–252. Dordrecht: Martinus Nijhoff.

Yukl, Gary A., and David D. Van Fleet
1982 "Cross-situational, multimethod research on military leader effectiveness." Organizational Behavior and Human Performance, 30: 87–108.

Zaltman, Gerald, Robert Duncan, and Jonny Holbeck
1973 Innovations and Organizations New York: Wiley.

Human Relations
[0018-7267(200205)55:5]
Volume 55(5): 505–536: 023426

SAGE Publications
London, Thousand Oaks CA,
New Delhi

'Waiting for dead men's shoes': Towards a cultural understanding of management innovation

Darren McCabe

ABSTRACT Managers are often represented as exercising power over others through different discourses such as strategy, total quality management and reengineering. This article seeks to add to our understanding of innovation by considering how managers are also constituted through power relations such that their subjectivity becomes embedded within a particular cultural context that in turn imbues the innovations they adopt. A case study of an insurance company is drawn upon so as to explore how managers may resist new discourses that seem to threaten established ways of thinking and acting. It is argued that innovations reflect and reproduce the past, while simultaneously reshaping it, in ways that are intended and unintended.

KEYWORDS culture ▪ innovation ▪ qualitative ▪ quality ▪ reengineering ▪ technology

Introduction

> We've got like a static promotion . . . *dead man's shoes* . . . basically static. You've asked someone how can you do things better, unless you've redressed what they said the first time they are not going to be able to come up with something new.
>
> (Assistant Manager, AB Insurance; emphasis added)

Accounts which reveal the limited success of innovations and the tendency for one fad to replace another are now commonplace (Ramsey, 1977, 1985, 1991; Ackers et al., 1992; Barley & Kunda, 1992; Gill & Whittle, 1992; Huczynski, 1993; Marchington et al., 1993; Watson, 1994). Few commentators, however, have considered how innovations tend to reproduce, while reshaping, established ways of managing organizations as is considered here (see also McCabe, 1999, 2000). The above epigraph implies that a lack of career progression and hierarchical power relations have militated against innovation at AB Insurance (pseudonym). The Assistant Manager commented that the organization lacks a dynamic for change because levels of management have to 'die off' before anybody with new ideas can replace them. In doing so, he provided a title for this article by summing up the culture at AB Insurance, and its approach towards innovation, as one of 'waiting for dead men's shoes'. This is not to suggest that there has been no change but rather it is to recognize that innovation is mediated through particular ways of life.

The article examines how individuals engage in processes of negotiating and navigating meaning in their everyday lives: how 'intersubjective realities might spawn and maintain organisational action' (Barley et al., 1988: 32). It is also concerned, however, to locate managers within a context of power and inequality, so as to explore how their subjectivity is embedded within and constituted through power relations. The case study considers how management innovations reflect and reshape a given context in ways that are both intended and unintended; it also examines how managers may resist new discourses that threaten established ways of thinking and acting. Through identifying the impact of contextual relations upon the present some insight is provided into how innovations are rarely as radical in practice as management gurus contend. Indeed, the article illuminates how innovations, that are designed to move away from bureaucracy and hierarchy, may generate precisely these conditions (see Barker, 1993; Tuckman, 1995). In doing so, the article provides a more general insight that can be applied to a host of recent innovations including total quality management (TQM) and business process reengineering (BPR).

The article is organized as follows: the next two sections review some of the innovation literature in order to elaborate the position adopted here; it considers the role and representation of managers and their innovations. The literature review provides a theoretical insight into how the case study was interpreted and made sense of and this in turn informs how the narrative is constructed and shaped. The case study findings are then presented and by way of a discussion and conclusion some overall observations will be drawn out regarding management innovation.

Accounting for innovation

The following account of management innovation seeks to avoid both determinism and voluntarism; in terms of the first of these, the concern is to move away from accounts that represent innovation as driven exclusively by external forces or what Slappendel (1996) refers to as a 'structuralist' approach. Such explanations understand innovation to be a direct function of external stimuli that leaves little or no space for managers as thinking beings. So, for instance, McLoughlin and Harris have highlighted how the whole debate around Fordist or Post-Fordist models retains 'a strong flavour of change within organisations as essentially adaptive activity dictated by broader economic and technological factors' (1997: 9). This approach is apparent in Barley and Kunda's (1992) account of surges of 'rational' and 'normative' ideologies of control including scientific management and human relations as these are attributed to 50-year 'Kondratieff' cycles or 'economic longwaves' (see also Abrahamson, 1997). Clearly economic factors have a significant influence upon managers and their propensity to innovate but it is a gross simplification to conflate the two. Any notion of management agency dissolves in the face of economic forces that determine their behaviour and we are left with an image of managers simply responding, as automatons, to external stimuli.

For others, 'technology' is deemed to be the crucial motor in understanding innovation (Dosi et al., 1988). For some time, determinism has featured heavily in discussions of technology (Blauner, 1964) and it is often assumed that technology is introduced simply to secure an economic advantage. Thus 'technology' is understood as an 'independent factor'; 'technical change *causes* social change' and 'is in some sense *autonomous*, "outside of society" ' (Mackenzie & Wajcman, 1985: 4–5, emphasis in original). Technological determinism has been widely criticized (see Wilkinson, 1983; Knights & Murray, 1994; McLoughlin & Clark, 1994; Grint & Woolgar, 1997) not least because managers play a major part in deciding which technologies are adopted and the same technology can have different effects in different situations (Mackenzie & Wajcman, 1985). Nonetheless, technological determinism is resilient as Drucker's (1988) prediction of 'new' information-based organizations reveals:

> Businesses, especially large ones, have little choice but to become information-based. Demographics for one demands the shift. . . . Economics also dictates change, especially the need for large businesses to innovate and to be entrepreneurs. But above all, information technology demands the shift.
>
> (Drucker, 1988: 45)

More recently technological determinism has re-emerged in the guise of BPR, and Hammer and Champy have suggested that organizational change follows technological developments as night follows day:

> Advanced technologies, the disappearance of boundaries between national markets, and the altered expectations of customers who now have more choices than ever before have combined to make the goals, methods and basic organising principles of the classical American corporation sadly obsolete.
>
> (1993: 11)

Major political, economic, social and technological upheavals have occurred during the 1980s and 1990s that have undoubtedly impinged upon financial services (Morgan & Sturdy, 2000). There is a danger, however, in assuming a direct causal relationship between the environment and the innovations that result. For this implies that innovation is inevitable and neutral and suggests that there are no opportunities for resistance or choices to be made. It eliminates agency *as if* innovation can be understood outside of the social relations that constitute its form and content. All of which renders both the environment and innovation artificially concrete and discrete. To suggest that innovations follow on from external stimuli removes a vast degree of uncertainty about organizational life and casts management in the role of 'messengers – of a technical and economic system' (Wilkinson, 1983: 19). Such a representation renders management both passive and homogeneous which is unsustainable in the face of much empirical investigation (see Knights & Murray, 1994; Watson, 1994; Parker, 1995). By contrast, what is proposed here is to question and explore why managers innovate, what innovations they adopt, how they seek to enrol support for innovation, whether they are able to introduce a particular innovation and to consider the outcomes of such innovation.

Not all commentators focus on external explanations for innovation. Many have concentrated upon the labour process which is, of course, intimately related to the wider economic structure (see Braverman, 1974). Innovation cannot, however, be understood as being driven 'purely' or necessarily 'consciously' by a managerial preoccupation with control as is the wont of some labour process commentators (Ramsey, 1991; Delbridge et al., 1992; Parker & Slaughter, 1993). To assume that innovation is purely about control is equally deterministic and reflects both a Marxist tendency to represent management as the agents of capital (Braverman, 1974) and indeed to neglect subjectivity. Hence, for Marx, managers are identified as 'special wage labourers' hired for the purposes of 'supervision' (Marx, 1976 [1867];

quoted in Willmott, 1997: 1333) and are 'the personification of economic categories, the bearers of particular class-relations and interests' (p. 1334). Innovation from this approach is simply the expression of managers as the agents of capital seeking to extract surplus value (Marglin, 1974). Hence, for Braverman, the emergence of job enlargement, enrichment, or rotation, work groups or teams, consultation or worker participation is a response by management to social antagonism in the workplace. Such innovation, as Braverman saw it, is concerned with 'costs and controls, not [in] the humanization of work' (1974: 36).

The insight provided by such commentators is important because it focuses our attention upon the persistent inequalities, power relations and conflict within society that is intimately bound up with the context and content of innovation, nonetheless, it has its limitations. For example, Noble (1985) locates his explanation for the design of Automatically Controlled Machine tools in the 'not always altogether rational', 'ideology of engineers' linked to the wider 'politico/economic system':

> the ideology of control emerges most clearly as a motivating force, an ideology in which the distrust of human agency is paramount. . . . But this ideology is itself a reflection of something else: the reality of the capitalist mode of production. The distrust of human beings by engineers is a manifestation of capital's distrust of labour.
>
> (Noble, 1985: 116)

This, and similar accounts of innovation, contain a number of problematic assumptions. First, although innovation cannot be regarded as distinct from the wider relations of power and inequality within society, it cannot be attributed 'directly' to wider societal influences. That is to say, although managers confront pressures to maintain control or increase profits this pressure is mediated through human interpretations and designs, the outcomes of which, are uncertain. Second, it is a mistake to assume that engineers or managers are a unified body. Thus, it is necessary to recognize that managers are individuals with their own personal and functional interests, subjective experiences and interpretations, which will in turn influence their actions in particular social contexts. Noble's approach is inadequate for just as 'economic explanations are not the whole story' (1985: 116) neither is a universal 'ideology of control' in conjunction with the 'economic' adequate to the task. Instead what is required is an understanding of innovation as part of a far more complex social process: interrelated to the way in which individuals interpret, act and ascribe meaning to their world.

Some theorists have taken account of managers as agents rather than personifications of economic categories (Ackers et al., 1992; Marchington et al., 1993; Watson, 1994; Parker, 1995). These accounts are more pluralistic in orientation and identify competing interest groups that in turn impinge upon and constitute innovation. Hence, Marchington et al. (1993) attribute waves of interest in what they refer to as employee involvement (e.g. TQM, teamworking) to management careerism or impression management. Thus managers seek to gain visibility through innovating: 'The introduction of EI techniques is motivated by a number of forces, but one of the most important is a desire by managers to be noticed, to engage in impression management; via the creation of new schemes' (Marchington et al., 1993: 553). Here, managers 'as sellers of labour' seem 'less concerned with the demands of capital per se than with the security of their employment and their career prospects' (Willmott, 1997: 1338). In a sophisticated account, Watson describes the 'double-control problem faced by all managers: the problem of managing their personal identities, careers and understandings at the same time as contributing to the overall control of the organisation in which they are managers' (1994: 893). Watson is far from unaware of power and inequality, as his work elsewhere reveals (Watson, 1995), nonetheless, his representation of managers in *In search of management* tends to emphasize the former rather than the latter. That is to say, more attention is given to managers' localized interactions and interpretations to the relative neglect of the structural inequalities that their actions serve to reproduce.

Some commentators have focused almost exclusively upon managerial psychodynamics in accounting for innovation. Jackson (1995), for example, considers how the reengineering gurus play on the fears of managers so as to sell their panaceas, while Huczynski (1993) explains a succession of management fads, in terms of 'managers-as-consumers' and 'consultants-as-suppliers' of new ideas. Thus managers may be panicked into adopting a new technique due to falling profits and consultants accommodate this through providing readily available well-packaged ideas. Gill and Whittle (1992) go further and argue that innovations appeal to the neurotic anxieties of managers. The danger in these latter approaches is one of moving towards voluntarism or what Slappendel (1996) has referred to as adopting an 'individualistic' perspective. Thus, it 'seeks to explain innovative behaviour in terms of the characteristics and actions of organisational participants' (Slappendel, 1996: 113). Innovation is not the 'neutral' phenomenon that this individualistic perspective tends to imply and managers cannot be divorced from the structures of power and inequality in which they are situated, and that their innovations serve to reproduce, albeit in ways that are often uncertain (Morgan & Sturdy, 2000). Innovation needs to be embedded, therefore, within social structures but its processes, effects and dynamics need to be explored rather than simply read-off or dismissed as management control. For as with culture, innovation 'is not a form of control created and manipulated by management, but a process in which management, workers and the community at large participates alike' (Meek, 1988: 462). Of course, some actors are in a better position to exercise power than others but this does not mean that innovation can simply be interpreted as a means of securing management's control over labour. Slappendel (1996) proposes an alternative 'interactive process perspective' that is concerned to explore how action and structure interrelate and this reflects the concerns of this article.

Towards a cultural understanding of management innovation

Although management innovation needs to be located within a wider context of power and inequality we have to understand how particular organizational traditions and conditions serve to shape and constitute innovation (see Knights & Willmott, 1987; Meek, 1988). This requires us to focus upon 'the ways of thinking and behaviour that continue to "live on" in, and mould and shape, the present – in other words, culture' (Bate, 1997: 1155) of an organization. In this sense, culture is seen as something an organization *is* rather than what an organization *has* (Smircich, 1983). It follows in the anthropological tradition of 'a process embedded in context' rather than 'an objectified tool of management control' (Wright, 1994: 4). Thus it is distinct from managerial perspectives that prescribe culture as a solution to organizational ills (Deal & Kennedy, 1982; Peters & Waterman, 1982) and it is also different from critical perspectives that describe cultural initiatives as an insidious form of management control (Ray, 1986) or nascent totalitarianism (Willmott, 1993). Instead, culture, as it is used here, is a site wherein the production and reproduction of meaning occurs through subjective interpretations in a context of political machinations, power relations and inequality. It is the socially constituted mask of normality that often conceals antagonism, disorder, resistance and oppression. Thus culture is seen as the very fabric of organizational life and as such innovations are understood as arising through culture to sustain, reproduce, modify and even transform it. The concern in this article then is 'to emphasise description, and concentrate on accessing meaning, both shared and unshared, unearthing conflict and paradox and observing how this is dealt with and accounted for by organisational members' (Linstead, 1997: 88). In particular, the focus is upon managers and how they secure their identities through innovation and work, while operating in a context of, and reproducing, relations of power and inequality (Knights & Murray, 1994; Willmott, 1997).

This 'cultural' approach towards innovation is loosely informed by an understanding of the way in which 'innovation' is 'socially shaped' (see McLoughlin & Harris, 1997). The concern is to explore how a social 'context' is 'inscribed in, rather than merely informing' (Grint & Woolgar, 1997: 114) innovation. Although the social shaping perspective 'immediately draws our attention to contingencies and the uniqueness of the user organisation' (Williams, 1997: 174); it is also necessary to locate and understand the social shaping of innovation in terms of a wider context, wherein the production and reproduction of power and inequality occurs. Rather than unilinear, the concern is to illustrate how innovation is a product of the way in which particular individuals and social groups think, interpret, act and interact. Drawing upon such a perspective is not to slip into 'social determinism' (see Gallie, 1978); for it is recognized that managers already act within and are constituted through a field of power relations that limit the choices available and influence the decisions taken (see Knights & Murray, 1994). Moreover, it is necessary to remember that 'the reproduction and transformation of social and technological relations' often occurs 'not as the direct outcome of the interests of individuals or groups, however constituted, but as their unintended consequence' (Knights & Murray, 1994: 25).

The approach seeks to highlight 'that the relevance of . . . [innovation] . . . lies in actors' interpretative activities rather than in any objective account of its capacities or effects' (Grint & Woolgar, 1997: 178). This means avoiding 'the impression that either the technical or the social has a discrete impact' (Grint & Woolgar, 1997: 25). Thus culture is deployed as a means to describe how innovation 'embodies social aspects' not as 'a stable and determinate object . . . but an unstable and indeterminate artefact whose precise significance is negotiated but never settled' (Grint, 1998: 282). Culture is not seen as 'something to which social events, behaviours, institutions, or processes can be causally attributed; it is a context, something within which they can be intelligibly – that is, thickly, described' (Geertz, 1993: 14).

In order to understand or come to terms with the cultural context, attention will be given to the discourses used by managers. Discourse is understood to be 'the production of knowledge through language and representation and the way that knowledge is institutionalised, shaping social practices and setting new practices into play' (du Gay, 1996: 43; quoted in Morgan & Sturdy, 2000: 31). In the following analysis, it is recognized that there are 'a multiplicity of discursive elements that can come into play in various strategies' (Foucault, 1979: 100) and attention will be given to the tensions between rival discourses (see Watson, 1994). The case is unusual perhaps because managers opposed 'new' discourses as expounded by 'knowledge entrepreneurs' (Abrahamson & Fairchild, 1999: 708) such as management consultants and gurus. Instead they preferred to innovate using an 'older' discourse. In view of this, it will become apparent that 'discourse can be both an instrument and an effect of power, but also a hindrance, a stumbling-block, a point of resistance' (Foucault, 1979: 101).

The case study

Inevitably, in order to say anything, one has to be selective (Gouldner, 1954), and, therefore, 'a process of abstraction and simplification is necessary' (Golding, 1980: 763). Given the constraint of space that an article-length ethnography affords, the focus here is upon middle- to senior-level managers. The concern is to understand how innovation 'emerges as sets of meanings constructed and imputed to organisational events by various groups and interests in pursuit of their aims' (Young, 1989: 190). The interpretation aims to provide some understanding of the emerging processes of innovation rather than how individuals lower down the organization experienced or interpreted such innovations. The account is inevitably 'paritial' (Clifford, 1986) because 'culture exists' in AB Insurance whereas 'anthropology exists' in the academic arena (Geertz, 1993). Of course, the managers represented in this case study cannot be described as unified nor as a group characterized by consensus (see Willmott, 1984; Knights & Murray, 1994; Watson, 1994). Indeed, numerous antagonisms are apparent for 'management was unified and yet it was divided, a self defined collective with widely divergent and often contradictory views' (Parker, 1995: 540). The distinctive insight provided here, however, is how this 'self defined collective' characterized by 'factions' (re)produced the organizational culture, while simultaneously reshaping it, through innovation.

The bulk of the empirical research was conducted over a period of six months during 1994–5. There have been follow-up visits in each subsequent year up to, and including, 1998, so as to keep abreast of recent developments. The case study provides 'analytical' rather than 'statistical' insights into the nature of innovation (Yin, 1989). It involved semi-structured interviews, observational research during service circle meetings and documentary investigation (Silverman, 1986). Taking a vertical slice through the organization, over 50 different grade staff, eight assistant supervisors, 10 supervisors, four assistant managers, four deputy managers, two departmental managers and the training, IT and personnel managers were interviewed. These interviews enabled a coming to terms with 'a multiplicity of complex conceptual structures, many of them superimposed upon or knotted into one another, which are at once strange, irregular, and inexplicit, and which . . .

[one] . . . must contrive somehow to first grasp and then to render' (Geertz, 1993: 10). It needs to be noted, however, that what follows is a constructed representation that cannot be regarded as somehow mirroring reality.

The financial services provides the context in which AB Insurance operates and traditionally this sector has been paternalistic in its outlook towards competitors and employees. By paternalism what is meant is a management style that is gentlemanly and caring (Knights & Willmott, 1993). Hence, AB offers secure employment through a no compulsory redundancies agreement and offers policies that could be described as promoting a community of interests. These include a free staff restaurant, free coffee and drink machines and sports and recreation facilities. Nonetheless, such paternalism presides over a situation where management adopts a largely authoritarian stance which embodies 'a moral legitimation of class domination through the paternalist ethic' (Joyce, 1980: 16). AB is both 'hierarchical' and 'bureaucratic' and has been slow to change. Consequently, adopting 'a paternalistic role helps legitimate managerial prerogative both in the eyes of those who are "protected" from the harsh reality of decision-making, and the decision makers themselves' (Kerfoot & Knights, 1993: 665). Consistent with maintaining the image of a 'respectable institution' managers seem to make 'a virtue of stability, security and moderation' (Morgan & Sturdy, 2000: 64). These virtues form the core of an older discourse to which managers at AB continue to cling. As we shall see, the new continues to be filtered through this triad that appears to be bound up with the managers' sense of self. Since the late 1980s, the sector has become an arena of intense competition following financial deregulation and re-regulation through the Financial Services Act 1986 (Morgan, 1992). The combination of technological and legislative change, consumer demands for improved service quality (Lewis, 1989) and new market entrants has provided an impetus for change from which AB Insurance has not been exempt.

It is possible, however, to identify an organizational world which has, as yet, avoided much of the fragmentation and disruption that has characterized organizational life elsewhere in the sector (see Morgan & Sturdy, 2000). AB has not engaged in large-scale 'downsizing' or 'outsourcing'. In this sense, while a range of interpretations and meanings are apparent, it is possible to identify a 'relative' coherence, that may not be present in those companies that have been fractured by redundancy or major programmes of restructuring. One explanation for this is that AB has avoided the merger mania that has characterized the wider industry and it has refrained from floating on the stock exchange. Thus AB has evaded the intense competitive pressures that are exacted on public limited companies (Morgan & Sturdy, 2000). Nonetheless, as we shall see, despite a 'relative' stability, its 'norms and values have as much potential for creating conflict . . . as they do for creating social cohesion' (Meek, 1988: 458). In terms of management, 'unity and division' exist 'in tandem' (Young, 1989: 188) and a whole set of hierarchical and functional groupings are apparent each competing for power and control over various aspects of organizational life (see Parker, 1995).

AB Insurance is a highly centralized major provider of personal life and non-life insurance. It sells insurance through sales agents and handles claims through regional offices. Apart from these functions all operations are conducted at its Head Office (HO) where policies are processed, issued, designed and marketed. The company has over 100 district offices around the country to which sales personnel report. During the 1980s, a number of environmental and internal developments combined to simultaneously press for, and open up, opportunities for change and questions were raised concerning the company's traditional management approach. These developments included the increased use of direct debit by customers, which reduces customer contact with sales agents, who collect insurance premiums locally. This threatened to undermine existing levels of business and the cross-selling of new products. Second, deregulation of the market place, which enabled AB to move into new markets through the provision of mortgage lending, pensions and investments. Third, AB's computer resources. The Admin Life Manager asserted that 'though creaking' the IT system had worked largely without complaint until the launch of a personal pension product in the early 1990s. Administration staff, at that time, were 'having their ears bent' (Training Manager) by the sales force for the poor quality of back-up services. This included errors on policies; failing to issue policies; or requesting premiums after they had been paid.

An additional impetus for change was the bereavement of the Administration General Manager in the late 1980s. His vacant position ('shoes') led to the appointment of a more innovative general manager who sought consultant advice as to how to improve service quality and efficiency. The consultants were employed to identify areas for improvement and to make recommendations. As 'knowledge entrepreneurs' their role has been minimal and this may explain why there has been a limited 'diffusion' (Abrahamson & Fairchild, 1999: 708) of discourses such as TQM, Culture Change or BPR. Subsequently, the Administration department was restructured into separate life and non-life insurance areas. Previously there had been four insurance sections including industrial life, ordinary life, fire and accident and motor. Nonetheless, this restructuring has reinforced the traditional political tensions and divisions between the IT, administration and sales departments. We can see then, that a number of factors both internal and external to the organization combined during the 1980s to generate a drive for innovation in the 1990s. Nonetheless, the type of changes adopted, the approach followed and the discourse used, are inseparable from, and are only rendered accessible through, a consideration of the organizational culture.

Setting the scene

As one enters the tower block that is AB's HO there is a feeling of not being in a 1990s or even a 1980s organization. The building was built in the 1960s and the decor has retained something of that period. While being refurbished there is something a little worn and a little dated about the PVC black seats in the reception area (which are splitting from use). One could almost be in an original James Bond movie set and about to meet Goldfinger (since the research began in 1994 the seats have been replaced). While waiting for the interview to begin, a receptionist, in a colourful and stretched cardigan (not the usual standardized company uniform) responds to your query 'what's it like to work here?':

> it's terrible on the sections cos it's all women – they're bitchy . . . Everyone wants to get out. . . . It's alright, it's not a bad job. You can come and go as you like, so long as you get the job done . . . there's a no redundancy agreement, even if you're off sick all of the time – so everyone's always sick.

This admission to a complete stranger speaks volumes and that 'everyone wants to get out', and yet remains, underlines the sense in which people are 'waiting for dead men's shoes' even, that is, if these shoes turn out to be their own. Going up in the lift, after having been greeted by a casually dressed member of staff, confirms the sensation of time past. Not least because she has not uttered a word to you, and simply indicated, with a nod of her head, to follow. Once out of the lift and entering the partly partitioned offices, one senses that there is something of a muddle about the place, a confused 'White Heat' of technology, and as you meet the interviewee, your observations are confirmed by everything that is said. Indeed he, the Training Manager, takes great pride in saying 'we are different here. We do things our own way . . . we're very much agin flavour of the month. You know, anything that's theme of the year, we're against it'. It seems that 'Caution' is a defining feature of AB Insurance and this appeared to stem from previous experiences of innovation:

> It's an evolution rather than a revolution. We once burnt our fingers in this organization. . . . We were one of the leaders in using computer technology going back 30 years. . . . We agreed that we would be the 1st to deal with a brand new system . . . but it threw us into turmoil because the damn thing didn't work . . . we were brought to a halt and that was because we wanted to make certain changes which were not evolving . . . so there's been a reluctance to be a leader, to forge ahead.
>
> (Personnel Manager)

Here, behind the apparently age-old sense of caution that underpins AB's culture lies a 'relatively' recent organizational experience that seems to have seeped into the corporate managerial consciousness. It supports the view that thought is 'nothing more and nothing less than a historically locatable set of practices' (Rabinow, 1986: 239; quoted in Linstead, 1997: 90). Thus radical change is apparently taboo and managers seem to be concerned that the company should not be a 'leader' or especially innovative. The lesson was all the more poignant given its 'structural' implications; namely, radical change is deemed to be a threat to corporate profitability, stability and security. It appears then that the culture of caution has suppressed alternative ways of organizing while reinforcing and reproducing others. Hence, IT staff were being recruited in the mid-1990s so as to develop a new mainframe system, at a time when the rest of the UK economy was in recession. This reflects the wary approach towards change in that IT difficulties had to reach a crisis before change was enacted. Moreover, that managers prefer to develop a system in-house, rather than approach consultants, underlines the antipathy towards 'knowledge entrepreneurs' (Abrahamson & Fairchild, 1999) and illustrates the concern to proceed with caution.

Linked to this 'caution' is a rejection of 'novelty'. The training manager explained that the company has a clear fixed vision as to where it wants to be and has corporate objectives that are 'age old'. These are implicit rather than being part of an explicit new 'mission' statement:

> *We don't like words like mission and vision.* I think our Chief Executive [CEO] naturally gets very uncomfortable with words like that, he says it reminds him of his Scottish Methodist upbringing. But we have a statement, we call it our corporate objectives and strategy . . . it's a bit long winded but in effect it is our mission statement.
>
> (Training Manager; emphasis added)

That the CEO does not 'like words like mission and vision' contrasts with the popular yen for fads and fashions across the industry (see McCabe et al., 1997). Rather than instigating a corporate culture change programme as popular accounts extol, it seems that the 'Chief' Executive', as with his anthropological counterpart, 'is as much a part of a local culture as are his tribal or clan compatriots' (Meek, 1988: 459). Hence, the CEO rejects symbols such as mission statements in favour of a not so modern 'objectives and strategy' statement. It seems then that power relations 'shape the coding possibilities and evocational fields which enable, constrain and prefer particular meanings without limiting them' (Linstead & Grafton-Small, 1992: 340). Hence the Training Manager continues to work within the norms of AB and also uses the older discourse. These managers seem to be far removed from 'the new type of manager recruited from outside the industry or trained in business schools' (Morgan & Sturdy, 2000: 36) who are responsible, in part, for spreading new discourses. By contrast, many managers at AB appear to want to remain paternalistic participants 'in an ostensibly genteel, respectable and stable institution' (Morgan & Sturdy, 2000: 37). Thus new discourses are not so easily induced, and resistance to them here, seems to be at least partly bound up with managerial identity concerns, such as one's 'Scottish Methodist upbringing'.

Of course, to discuss a particular approach towards innovation in terms of culture does not mean that there is a uniformity of management styles across the organization. According to the Training Manager, there are a wide variety of management styles, ranging from 'powerful autocratic management towards much more participative types'. Notwithstanding this, the Assistant Manager for claims remarked that the company is 'rather regimented'. AB is a classical bureaucracy and yet, as we shall see, bureaucracy as administration by office and rule is a 'living, changing and diverse set of practices' (Thompson & McHugh, 1995: 195). The company is hierarchical but responsibility for day-to-day operations is delegated to departmental managers, who in turn, delegate to 'officials' or assistant managers and so on.

Another distinguishing feature of AB is an emphasis upon 'cost control' as can be seen in the Admin Life Manager's comments regarding the traditional way in which the company has been managed:

> at the very beginning of the 1960s. . . . We were essentially a paper production line using manual resource. . . . Two things needed doing mechanization and ways to cut staff down as our major expense . . . therefore we started to look at individual work measurement . . . it worked remarkably well. Not particularly liked by many of the people. . . . We've continued that to the present day.

In the 1960s, management found a way of keeping staffing levels low and costs under control using work-study. This approach has continued into the 1990s:

> Historically the company has been managed in a very mechanistic fashion . . . things like . . . [work study and job evaluation] . . . which I would describe as an *old-fashioned language*, a rather mechanistic approach, but it is still very basic management, if you control the head count in a labour intensive industry, then you are controlling costs.
>
> (Non-Life Admin Manager; emphasis added)

This manager distinguished between an 'old' and a 'new' discourse but as a creature of AB he supported the established ways of managing. The importance of controlling costs through work-study and measurement has achieved an almost 'mythical' status among management. This reflects an experience that was frequently reiterated concerning the General Manager's use of work-study to reduce the workforce:

> Initially we reduced by 25 percent or something like that . . . it was a big change because then you've got people having to work to time . . . it was a new concept for clerical staff. They had never had this 'That work's got to be done in an hour and a half'. . . . We were told 'Oh people will never get used to times' but they do. New people . . . just accept it.
>
> (Assistant Manager, Admin Life)

Work-study was supported by all of the managers interviewed. The general manager, the life and non-life managers and a number of assistant managers were promoted from the team that first introduced work-study in the 1960s. This, in part, reflects the profile of these 'Organization and Methods' (O&M) managers who had reduced the workforce so substantially. Thus prestige is conferred upon individuals who increase profitability or cut costs. It is interesting that this emphasis on 'cost control' appears to have been in place since the 1960s because this is a central plank of a 'new' strategic discourse within financial services according to a number of authors (Kerfoot & Knights, 1993; Morgan & Sturdy, 2000). It suggests that there are continuities between the 'old' and 'new'. As elsewhere (Knights & Willmott, 1993), however, the concern to control costs has gained a new immediacy and momentum during the 1990s. The next section explores how, despite awareness among some managers of AB's 'old-fashioned' approach, traditional ways of doing things have continued to impinge upon and define innovation.

Innovation in action

> it certainly wasn't the CEO sitting up there and saying 'We want a quality focus'. . . . You hear examples of the CEO waking up one morning and saying 'Right, I've seen the light, this is the way we go guys'. . . . I'm not criticizing it, it might be right for them, but it wouldn't be right for us. . . . It works in some companies but it wouldn't work for us. Things are more likely to happen bottom up and as a reaction to something. We don't go around looking for trouble but if there's a pain, a pressure point somewhere, we'd say 'Well what's the answer to it?'.
>
> (Training Manager)

In contrast to Lawler and Mohram's (1985) research into quality circles and Hammer and Champy's (1993) exhortations for BPR, these comments suggest that innovation arises bottom up rather than top down in AB. Thus it stems from the need to address existing problems, rather than from a concern to be proactive or strategic. It would seem that there is a willingness to 'wait' for problems as much as there is a concern to 'wait' for promotion or retirement. The Non-Life Admin Manager elaborated upon the corporate approach:

> We're a very pragmatic sort of organization. We don't usually go in for, you know, 'Darra dara TQM'. This is it for 12 months, and we print until the machines melt, and posters all over the place. . . . We will do things in a more measured way, so I think quality will be something which will grow . . . with a set of priorities that reflect what our business objectives are about in that area, and we will come to terms with it in that way. *I don't think the constituent managers . . . are ready for some sort of traumatic thing*, I think we've got to feel our way into it . . . and keep a sense of proportion.
>
> (emphasis added)

This more 'measured' approach is consistent with the tradition of caution and the remarks that 'constituent managers' are not ready for 'traumatic' change reveals a gentlemanly or paternalistic concern with the welfare of others. It is a far cry from the ruthless 'downsizing' of the 1980s and 1990s apparent elsewhere (Morgan & Sturdy, 2000).

One explanation for the approach, that seems to fit with the comments of a number of managers, might be that just as constituent managers would not be ready for 'traumatic' change, likewise, managers at both the executive and departmental level, are unwilling to change:

> To achieve change in this organization you've got to have a very powerful argument. The fact that we've been doing it this way for a number of years is always an argument against change. There's almost a view that because it's always been done like that then it's the right way. 'Prove to me that your way's better'.
>
> (Training Manager)

One manager, who could almost be said to embody this staid way of being as encapsulated in the title 'Waiting for Dead Men's Shoes', remarked:

> You can't change everything in every week. Especially if you are in an area that's loath to change. You can't change things a lot anyway. I mean even if they [staff] had an idea, if it worked, I'd implement it. You see, we have evolved our systems over years and if the systems weren't any good in the first place they wouldn't have worked, you see?
>
> (Admin Life Assistant Manager, claims)

This manager appears to be immersed in the more traditional discourse of 'stability, security and moderation' (Morgan & Sturdy, 2000: 64). It is linked both to how he interprets and acts upon the world, but importantly, it also reflects the community of managers of which he is a part, and also that he is embroiled in the production and reproduction of power relations. Change, it seems, is possible providing that it does not disturb the existing ways of doing things (too much):

> You realize that the way to achieve change is to talk to the top managers separately. You work with who you can work with. That's the CEO's view as well, you see? 'You are responsible for non-life. I expect you to make decisions in that area'. He obviously expects to be consulted but that's the way he works. . . . So one of them decides on Quality Improvement Teams, the other one thinks it's not right for them.
>
> (Training Manager)

The above extract is an example of the politicking that is necessary to secure change and it supports the view that 'culture consists of whatever it is one has to know or believe in order to operate in a manner acceptable to its members' (Goodenough; quoted in Meek, 1988: 467). The next section explores the attempts made to improve service quality during the 1990s in the Administration Life department. In particular, it considers the introduction of a new mainframe system for life products, which could be equated with BPR.

Administration Life

The Administration Life department was created out of the industrial and ordinary life areas and it has 430 staff. There are three key operating divisions each with an assistant manager including: (1) 'life new business' which has five sections – new business, underwriting, endorsements, a postal filing unit and a typing unit; (2) a 'life claims' division which has four sections including death claims, maturity claims, cash surrender claims and quotations; and (3) a personal pensions section which includes new business, endorsements and claims. A new departmental manager was internally promoted in 1989, who had previously been in the Organization and Methods (O&M) department. He identified three main problems facing the department including poor management control, out-dated technology and underdeveloped human resources. This manager recalled that his concern had been to win support for change, even at the supervisory level, rather than to impose it. Change was initiated through holding regular Business Review Meetings (BRMs) with his three assistant managers to discuss business performance:

> It wasn't a matter of saying 'Right lads from now on we're going to change everything and we're going to have a totally new approach' . . . We want people to learn and develop styles *that are appropriate to them rather than something which is forced on them from above.*
>
> (emphasis added)

The departmental manager explained that in 'many areas' of the department 'there just isn't communication'. This was attributed to 'some' supervisors (described as 'old school') who were promoted on the basis of their 'technical' knowledge of insurance, rather than on the basis of their 'people' management abilities. In terms of communication, it was said that some supervisors 'don't like doing it'. Interestingly the Departmental Manager was also concerned that supervisors should not pass on too much information: 'don't over do it' he remarked. This is indicative of the continued hierarchical thinking that seems to militate against communication at AB. Hence, as elsewhere, information is restricted that 'superiors' 'deem' that those lower down the hierarchy 'do not need to know' (Parker, 1995: 538). Though not using the discourse, management espoused the rhetoric of empowerment (i.e. 'we want people to learn and develop styles that are appropriate to them'), paradoxically, however, this does not extend to sharing information to any great degree.

Over the 1990s a number of innovations have been initiated in the Admin Life department including quality circles but the focus here will be upon those that are IT related. A belief has traditionally existed in the company that 'service quality' is what AB has always provided (see the Assistant Manager for claims's comments on p. 17). The Admin Life Manager was concerned to 'challenge' this attitude by providing comprehensive information regarding work performance in each section and initially there was resistance to this: 'when we started to look at those issues, they [supervisors, staff] tended to mask quite a lot' (Admin Life Manager). A weekly service report was introduced which recorded workflow information. A three-month backlog was quite common in the early 1990s and by the mid-1990s this had been reduced to almost zero:

> The first thing was 'God here he is, he's come in as a new guy. He's an O&M man'. . . . I was imposing a new discipline. So initially, it was 'God here we are, it's more add-on, more paper work he's generating . . . that culture that we had before was broken. . . . They said 'Well we can't get it down cos we've got a problem in this area'. We said 'Well what's the problem?' They said 'Staffing'. So we got more staff in. . . . We could clearly see that we had a staffing problem and if it was one *that I had to have an argument with someone over* then I could go and make a bona fide case. To show that this guy needs additional staff.
>
> (Admin Life Manager; emphasis added)

People frequently spoke in a way that implied that resistance was pervasive, not only did the whole department resist the imposition of tighter work controls, but in turn, the Departmental Manager was resisted when additional staff were required. Each section now has a service-level guarantee and has to account for work performance in each area on a weekly basis. The emphasis on work-study is an expression of the existing 'cost control' tradition, however, this tradition was reinforced and extended especially with the introduction of a PC-based work tracking system. The Life Manager's concern to develop such a system initially met with resistance from the IT department:

> They didn't want us doing it . . . they wanted to look after their own empire. They were envious of the fact that we were starting to look at something. . . . So yes, we had to fight a battle. . . . The manager of that department came along and said basically 'This is not your job. Your job is to deal with manual systems . . . if this needs doing, it needs a mainframe system, and it can go in the queue for as, and when, we can deliver'.
>
> (Admin Life Manager)

This manager's account of the situation neglects to mention that introducing PCs is also bound up with 'his' own empire building, career and identity concerns. Hence his status and profile would be elevated through introducing a new PC-based work tracking system. Moreover, it needs to be noted that 'the structure of the relationship between managers and workers conditions managerial perceptions and informs their practical reasoning' (Willmott, 1997: 1352). Hence, the use of PCs to track work more effectively is bound up with a concern to maintain and increase control over work and, of course, employees. Despite resistance, the lead time for the IT department to develop a new 'mainframe' system was such that the Executive approved the Life Manager's request. Here we can see sub-cultures within AB presenting a 'source of conflict' as competition arises for 'scarce resources and prestige' (Meek, 1988: 461).

Administration Life redesign (ALR)

Between 1993 and 1998, a more flexible mainframe system was developed, to cope with new life insurance products and to provide greater capacity for future products. Rather than sales agents passing policy documents to first line underwriters, ALR allows sales agents directly to input sales data into the mainframe system via lap top computers. In view of this, it was anticipated that ALR would remove the need for first line underwriting. ALR has significant implications for business processes and yet the term reengineering was not used:

> Reengineering tends to be a buzz word and that tends to switch an awful lot of people off because it just happens to be flavour of the month and what we're really about is 'Look what do we need from the business point of view?'. . . . If I go to my colleagues and talk about reengineering the way they actually process the work through their departments they'll switch off before I finish the sentence.
>
> (Systems Manager)

The unwillingness to define ALR as reengineering seems to reflect an unwillingness to embrace a 'new' discourse among some managers. One explanation for this might be the threat that such discourses pose to traditional power relations and identities; not least because most managers have not been schooled in discourses such as reengineering. It would appear then that the 'definition' of innovation is 'contingent' upon local contexts. In 1994, the Head of IT contrasted his approach towards redesigning the life system with BPR:

> My understanding of reengineering is that you look at the way the organization is doing things and you say, first of all, could we do these things in a different way?. . . . And if there are any advantages, what is the cost of moving to get there? Now if you are a company that operates reasonably successfully . . . it seems to me, that there is little point in turning the world upside down just for the sake of it because there are many things that can go wrong en route. . . . Now I don't see that we have to, *we're not forced into reorganizing the way we do things.*
>
> (Head of IT; emphasis added)

This manager did not associate ALR with reengineering because for him it is not a break with the past in the sense of 'turning the world upside down'. Yet even the reengineering gurus have begun to question whether a clean slate approach to reengineering is feasible (see Davenport & Stoddard, 1994; Hammer & Stanton, 1995). Nonetheless, the older discourse of 'stability, security and moderation' (Morgan & Sturdy, 2000) appears to have prevailed. This is apparent in the Head of IT's belief that because of 'reasonable' success and the danger that 'things can go wrong', 'there is little point' in embracing more radical change. It is interesting that in contrast to deterministic accounts of innovation this manager does not feel 'forced into reorganizing'. Nonetheless, rejecting reengineering could be interpreted as an attempt to secure and sustain his identity as a competent and knowledgeable manager. Hence in 1994, reengineering was relatively new, and usually involved employing consultants, and so BPR may have been perceived as a threat to his position and status. Here 'the securing of self-importance is accomplished through the negation of [reengineering as] . . . the other' (Willmott, 1997: 1353). Administration Life redesign (ALR) was designed on the basis of controlling costs and this is in keeping with AB's organizational traditions: '*We started off from the viewpoint what does the business need which is the driving force* and the case is *cost effective*' (Systems Manager; emphasis added).

The designers of ALR emphasized breaking tasks down so as to simplify work processes in the belief that this would enable them to control costs. This has led some managers to lament the loss of the more 'interesting' aspects of work:

> We've tried to take as much of the human element out as possible . . . in the old days it was said that *the computer would perform the drudgery work but here we're doing it the other way round* with computers doing the interesting work.
>
> (Training Manager; emphasis added)

Others commented in a matter-of-fact way that ALR will lead to simplified and standardized work processes:

> You will basically be inputting data on the system and it doesn't matter whether you are putting in a proposal for new business or putting in a claim. *The intelligence will be built into the system to do the difficult bit of the job.*
>
> (Systems Officer; emphasis added)

The concern to control costs through IT reinforces past traditions. In this way 'pre-existing models of work organisation, with visions of how these might be transformed, become embedded in information and communication technology (ICT) applications' (Williams, 1997: 177) or to put it another way 'antecedent circumstances are inscribed in, rather than merely informing design' (Grint & Woolgar, 1997: 114).

The anticipated benefits of ALR are the intangible future savings associated with enhanced systems capacity and flexibility. The more tangible benefit is an expected reduction in staffing, which, as of 1998, had not materialized. It needs to be remembered, however, that this expectation reflects an 'interpretation of the technology' (Grint & Woolgar, 1997: 128). So, for instance, it was assumed that a new slicker system would reduce processing time and therefore reduce the number of people employed. It was not foreseen that while new products are being put on to the new system, existing products still have to be processed and maintained on the old system. It was also not anticipated that due to the long life span of insurance products, savings would only be generated as policies pass through the system, which may take many years.

There was an expectation that ALR would reduce the number of clerks needed to underwrite policies. In the past, new products had been processed by an underwriting section, whereby junior clerks examined completed insurance forms, to ensure that they were correctly filled in. Forms that were incorrectly completed would be returned to customers, while those deemed to be problematic, would be passed on to more senior underwriters. The ALR system allows sales agents to input insurance policy details directly into the mainframe system. Therefore, it was thought that checks in the system would remove the need for first line underwriting. Such a transition has been far from seamless, however, because the system rejects policies if data is input incorrectly:

> All these systems are fallible because of the sales people's keying in performance on his lap top. They hit the wrong button or miss out a

> box . . . all those are kicked out . . . I don't think we'll ever get over that . . . you give people as near as perfect technology but they'll still make a hash of it.
>
> (Training Manager)

These comments reveal an interesting paradox. It is assumed that technology can be designed by humans in such a way as to render it 'perfect'. However, post-implementation, it is the intervention of humans that renders it fallible. It is, as if, in the process of designing and building technology it becomes 'objective' and 'infallible' whereas in operation it once more incorporates the 'subjective' and the 'fallible'.

Due to the above interpretations and expectations of ALR, prior to its launch, management reduced staffing in the underwriting section through natural wastage and the use of temporary staff. This act of running down the underwriting section was based upon an interpretation of the technology leading to a particular outcome. The interpretation encompassed a belief about the ability of sales people inputting data correctly. Yet it seems that the salesperson's role, which involves interacting with customers, does not lend itself to error-free work. Sales representatives might be 'balancing a cup of tea in one hand'; 'fighting the dog off with the other' (Training Manager), and at the same time, trying to sell the company, themselves and the products. Consequently, errors continue to be made and first line underwriting is still needed to remedy them.

It was also thought that ALR would reduce staffing because direct inputting via sales agents would become the sole channel of business. Much of AB's business, however, continues to be generated through mail applications and so junior underwriters are still required to input policy information: 'As it turns out, we've had to go out and have a huge bloody recruitment campaign' (Training Manager). Rather than reflecting post-design problems, these uncertainties are a reflection of the assumptions and interpretations of both the designers of ALR and those of Personnel. Following ALR's implementation other problems have emerged due to the highly repetitive and monotonous type of working that has resulted. This outcome confounded the Personnel Manager's expectations of ALR:

> You would expect that you've got fewer jobs at a slightly higher level of complexity. In other words, you try to design more interesting jobs. In reality the way it's happening is that you have fewer jobs but you still have . . . mundane, routine jobs. Mundane, routine jobs I'm afraid, are responsible for our quality . . . so we've got to learn the lessons of that.

The attention given to cost control and simplifying work processes has resulted in repetitive and boring working conditions for administration staff. This has led to low levels of morale among clerks and it seems that this was not anticipated, or thought to be important, by the designers of ALR. Moreover, the negative impact that this has had upon the quality of work processing was also not foreseen. It has fallen upon the Personnel department to motivate staff in the post-implementation malaise:

> We didn't, if you like, build technology around people, we had to build people around technology, but we decided the best way to do it is to emphasize teamworking a lot more. . . . We said 'How do we keep people motivation?' Well let's have teams, let's give them more responsibility for the way they organize their work.
>
> (Training Manager)

Believing that task simplicity would enhance control over the administration of insurance, the designers of ALR prioritized task specialization. Yet ALR has undermined management's ability to motivate (control) employees and this in turn has impacted upon the quality of work processing. Thus ALR in operation has forced management to reinterpret the way in which work is organized. It seems then that the outcomes of such innovation are far from 'settled' let alone 'closed' even after implementation (see Grint & Woolgar, 1997: 85).

The cultural 'context' of AB rather than simply the 'ideology' (Noble, 1985) of IT managers is inscribed in ALR. Yet, this context is not static because it is mediated through power relations that may change in the future. This is apparent in the comments of the Training Manager speaking in December 1998:

> I was talking to the second in command in the IT department on Friday and I accused him basically of taking the interesting work away from people and giving it to the computer and he said 'Oh yes, well that was our objective'.

The above encounter suggests that ALR could have been handled differently. Although from the above quotation, it may seem that deskilling through ALR was intended by the IT managers, this was not necessarily the case. Indeed, it reflects the outcomes of ALR and the interpretations of the Training Manager and the Personnel Manager who were forced to deal with the post-implementation consequences of ALR. By contrast, the concerns of the designers of ALR, whether realized or not, were to meet the needs of the business and to improve cost control. From interviews conducted with the IT managers, it seemed that the implications for people's working lives had simply not been thought through. The above head-to-head between the Training and IT Managers, needs to be understood, in terms of the Training Manager's offensive attempt, to secure his status and identity, as the champion of employment concerns. But also the IT Manager's defensive concern to maintain his sense of competence in the face of a threat to his identity and power due to the failures of ALR. Such existential struggles reproduce, while reshaping, the context of inequality. Nonetheless, the context is far from closed. This is apparent in that the experience of ALR in operation has underlined the need to involve Personnel in the redesign of a new IT system for non-life products. Thus the above encounter could be interpreted as an attempt by the Training Manager to flex his new-found muscles.

Discussion and conclusion

In a number of ways the above innovations reflected and reproduced the existing relations of power and inequality at AB and yet the outcome was never certain. Innovation, while clearly stimulated by external factors, cannot be understood outside of the social context in which it is embedded. The company's 'cautious' approach impinged upon and imbued management assumptions and beliefs regarding both the type of innovations to introduce and the process of innovating. The discourse of fads, fashions and novelty was avoided even though ALR involved quite radical changes that might elsewhere be described as BPR. The intention albeit not the outcome, of introducing ALR was entirely consistent with AB's cost control traditions. It is interesting, however, that the paternalistic concern for others did not extend to protecting either the quantity or the quality of jobs. Nonetheless, the numbers of jobs have been protected, as an unintended, rather than an intended outcome, of ALR.

It is interesting that despite being a native of AB, as an 'O&M man', the Admin Life Manager felt himself to be an outsider within the Administration department. Thus 'unity and division existed in tandem' (Young, 1989: 188). AB's bureaucratic structures remain intact and it is precisely this that enables one to tear away some of the mystification that often surrounds innovation. Innovation involved the past and present merging so as to constitute the future (Pettigrew, 1979) in ways that were uncertain. The past lives on in the present and the past is continually invoked in the exercise of power. This is apparent in the almost 'mythical' status attributed to work-study. Despite current problems, the Training Manager remarked that it is 'heresy' to criticize those responsible for instigating ALR. This partly reflects the perceived power of the IT department but also that in order to achieve change at AB one needs friends. Therefore, to point fingers and apportion blame is inconsistent with generating support for a different approach in the future. Politics then, intervenes to mask the effects of innovation and so its impact cannot be understood outside of the social relations that constitute it.

The managers that were interviewed tended to reproduce and cling to the traditional discourse of 'stability, security and moderation' (Morgan & Sturdy, 2000: 64) that once characterized financial services. Nonetheless, the managers were adaptive in doing so. The culture emerged out of a self-reflexive process rather than one of 'passive reception' (Linstead & Grafton-Small, 1992). Hence, many managers were aware that AB is 'old-fashioned' and they sought to achieve change from the inside through politicking. In this sense, meaning was by no means 'fixed and unidimensional' (Linstead & Grafton-Small, 1992) and yet many managers were seemingly unaware of their place within the reproduction of the culture.

The gentlemanly attributes of paternalism were abundantly apparent in the concern not to upset anyone, unless, that is, business demands require otherwise. Managers, while seeking change, sought to innovate through a process of negotiation and persuasion with other managers. Anything 'too' radical was deemed alien within a culture that appeared to be characterized by caution and resistance to change. Yet change, dressed up as continuity, is taking place, and care for others seemed to be hierarchically distributed with employees at the bottom. Change is seen as essential to economic survival and so some managers were embroiled in a process of modifying while reproducing the culture. The case illustrates how many managers at AB 'are immersed in this unselfconscious negotiation and emergence of their own identity within and without the corporation' (Linstead & Grafton-Small, 1992: 344).

To describe ALR as being driven by a single group of IT specialists is clearly inadequate. Instead of reflecting a particular 'ideology' (Noble, 1985) ALR is infused with meaning drawn from the wider organization. The IT managers designed the new system with a view to controlling costs and it is significant that they failed to achieve this aim in terms of reducing the number of staff employed. Nonetheless, it is also important to remember that ALR need not have been designed in this way. Due to the deleterious impact of ALR upon staff morale and processing quality and its ineffectiveness in reducing staffing, questions are now being asked about how to design a more people friendly pensions system. Thus 'specific conditions of possibility' have served to 'both constrain and open up choices' (Knights & Murray, 1994: 29). It is at the design stage that interventions by trade unionists, personnel managers or academics may have a significant impact upon the design of jobs and people's lives. Such interventions cannot, however, ensure 'that design determines subsequent deployment' (Grint & Woolgar, 1997: 18). This is apparent in the series of unintended consequences that accompanied the implementation of ALR. Nonetheless, intervention for the purposes of producing more meaningful work, may at least set in train different conditions of possibility, that could lead to outcomes that entail less 'drudgery' where, in the Training Manager's words 'computers' are doing 'the interesting work'.

The case allows us to identify the importance of the consumption of technological artefacts for the social organization of work. Employees could have been left individually to input data but instead they were organized into teams. This engendered increased discretion and responsibility about how to perform the work: the same technology but a different relation to the social. Grint and Woolgar argue that 'users', in this case the Training and Personnel Managers and staff, 'are free to make what they will of the machine' (1997: 93). Hence, they can work as individuals or in teams but they can only do so 'within an interpretative context'. The conditions of possibility are limited because the 'context does not exist in isolation from the machine, it is instead defined by the social relations which make up the machine' (1997: 93). Social relations at AB, as we have seen, embody a preoccupation with cost control and this has been inscribed in ALR and has both limited and limits the scope for change.

A shared managerial sense that the company is 'different' may have militated against the introduction of a new discourse. Hence, Abrahamson and Fairchild found that discourses spread 'by reinforcing the belief that organisations are similar in ways that would cause them to benefit equally from adopting a management technique' (1999: 732). Yet if managers are convinced of their distinctiveness then this might prove to be an obstacle to change. There were some signs of a new discourse beginning to emerge as in the importance being given to 'service quality', 'technology', 'sales' and the revitalized interest in 'control' over work processes. It is apparent, however, that new discourses do 'not occur automatically' (Morgan & Sturdy, 2000: 129). It could be argued that the limited use of management consultants and the absence of a new managerial elite are important factors that inhibited the emergence of a new discourse. But perhaps most significant of all is the lack of shareholders or public owners demanding that AB 'has a strategy' (Morgan & Sturdy, 2000: 129). However, despite the absence of discourses such as TQM and BPR, the renewed emphasis on control, IT and quality can be understood as providing 'a way of translating the broad objectives of being "strategic" into a meaningful vocabulary of action' (Morgan & Sturdy, 2000:

133). Thus a new discourse may be beginning to emerge through concerns that are seen as 'operational' (Morgan & Sturdy, 2000: 133).

Innovation is not simply determined by 'economic' or 'technological' considerations, for as the Head of IT remarked 'we're not forced into reorganizing the way we do things'. Therefore innovation also needs to be understood in terms of how managers shape, while deriving meaning and security from participating in, the discursive practices of innovation. Hence, while managers sought to become more competitive through innovating they continued to cling to an older discourse of 'stability, security and moderation' (Morgan & Sturdy, 2000: 64). Thus managers are 'embedded in, rather than enveloped or determined by, these social contexts' (Morgan & Sturdy, 2000: 257). From a number of comments, it seemed that some managers resisted newer discourses perhaps reflecting the threat that such discourses pose to their sense of competence, authority and control. In terms of BPR, this could be the concern of the Head of IT but it may also be apparent in the Non-Life Administration Manager's antipathy towards TQM.

Innovation cannot be dismissed as either reflecting a preoccupation with profit maximization or control. For this oversimplifies the processes, uncertainties and subjectivities involved. The IT managers designed ALR in such a way that resulted in drudgery for staff yet this was not necessarily the intention. These managers seemed to think in terms of a system that would be 'cost effective' and good for 'business' rather than its implications for people's lives. Yet ALR was ineffective in controlling costs, employee morale or the quality of work output. One also needs to note the tensions between managers; hence the Training Manager lamented the way in which ALR was designed. Managers then, cannot be understood as simply the agents of capital remorselessly devising ways in which to dominate, subordinate and exploit employees. Nonetheless, we cannot ignore the context of inequality in which managers operate. Thus ALR reproduced while reshaping this context and one could argue that it is precisely the context of inequality that allows managers to take 'interesting work away from people' so as to 'give it to the computer'. Moreover, even if the Training Manager had successfully intervened at the design stage to humanize ALR, this theory 'Y' approach, is still bound up with control (Willmott, 1993). The Training and Personnel Managers did not question the intended 'ends' (i.e. cost cutting, profitability) of ALR but only the 'means' to attain this 'end'. The revelations, disclosures and stance of these managers have much to do with their beliefs, career and power-based positions. Thus identifying the importance of 'people' issues elevates them and corresponds with how they think things should be done. It offers no guarantee, however, that intervention for the purposes of reduced drudgery will have the desired effect. It is necessary therefore to analyse innovation 'as a product of the organization and the dynamics of the structure of social relations, and not simply as an expression of the choice or will of particular individuals' (Willmott, 1997: 1332). However, despite the limitations of intervention, in that it may serve to reproduce the wider relations of power and inequality, the possibility that ALR could have been designed in ways that may not have led to drudgery, means that such interventions should at least be attempted and encouraged.

To conclude, innovation cannot be separated from the context in which is arises and it reveals a tendency to mirror while reshaping organizational conditions. This is not simply to argue the case for continuity because unintended consequences abound and these in turn shape new conditions of possibility. As has been demonstrated detailed research is needed to tease out quite what has changed and what is reproduced. Critically, it has been suggested that because managers and their innovations are not determined by economics or technology, it is possible to intervene for the purposes of generating more interesting, stimulating and rewarding work, preferably before, but even after, the design and introduction of innovations. Further research is needed to explore the ways in which older structures, cultures and identities are challenged or reinforced through innovation and how intended and unintended consequences can open up new conditions of possibility.

Acknowledgement

The author wishes to thank Mihaela Kelemen for her comments on an earlier draft of this article and those of the anonymous reviewers.

References

Abrahamson, E. The emergence and prevalence of employee management rhetorics: The effects of long waves, labour unions, and turnover, 1875 to 1992. *Academy of Management Journal*, 1997, *40*(3), 491–533.

Abrahamson, E. & Fairchild, G. Management fashion: Lifecycles, triggers and collective learning processes. *Administrative Science Quarterly*, 1999, *44*, 708–40.

Ackers, P., Marchington, M., Wilkinson, A. & Goodman, J. The use of cycles? Explaining employee involvement in the 1990s. *Industrial Relations Journal*, 1992, *23*(4), 268–83.

Barker, J. Tightening the iron cage: Concertive control in self-managing teams. *Administrative Science Quarterly*, 1993, *37*, 363–99.

Barley, S.R. & Kunda, G. Design and devotion: Surges of rational and normative ideologies of control in managerial discourse. *Administrative Science Quarterly*, 1992, *37*, 363–99.

Barley, S.R., Meyer, G.W. & Gash, D.C. Cultures of culture: Academics, practitioners and the pragmatics of normative control. *Administrative Science Quarterly*, 1988, *33*, 24–60.

Bate, S.P. Whatever happened to organizational anthropology? A review of the field of organizational ethnography and anthropological studies. *Human Relations*, 1997, *50*(9), 1147–75.

Blauner, R. *Alienation and freedom*. Chicago, IL: University of Chicago Press, 1964.

Braverman, H. *Labour and monopoly capital: The degradation of work in the twentieth century*. London: Monthly Review Press, 1974.

Clifford, J. Introduction: Partial truths. In J. Clifford & G.E. Marcus (Eds), *Writing culture*. London: University of California Press, 1986.

Davenport, T.H. & Stoddard, D. Reengineering: Business change of mythic proportions? *MIS Quarterly*, 1994, *18*(2), 121–7.

Deal, T. & Kennedy, A. *Corporate cultures: The rites and rituals of corporate life*. Harmondsworth: Penguin, 1982.

Delbridge, R., Turnbull, P. & Wilkinson, B. Pushing back the frontiers: Management control and work intensification under JIT/TQM factory regimes. *New Technology, Work and Employment*, 1992, *7*(2), 97–106.

Dosi, G., Feeman, C., Nelson, R., Silverberg, G. & Soete, C. (Eds) *Technical change and economic theory*. London: Pinter, 1988.

Drucker, P.F. The coming of the new organization. *Harvard Business Review*, 1988, Jan–Feb, 45–53.

du Gay, P. & Salaman, G. The cult[ure] of the customer. *Journal of Management Studies*, 1992, *29*(5), 615–33.

Foucault, M. *The history of sexuality*. London: Penguin, 1979.

Gallie, D. *In search of the new working class*. Cambridge: Cambridge University Press, 1978.

Geertz, C. *The interpretation of cultures*. London: Fontana Press, 1993.

Gill, J. & Whittle, S. Management by panacea: Accounting for transcience. *Journal of Management Studies*, 1992, *30*(2), 281–95.

Golding, D. Establishing blissful clarity in organizational life: Managers. *Sociological Review*, 1980, *28*(4), 763–82.

Gouldner, A.W. *Wildcat strike*. New York: Antioch Press, 1954.

Grint, K. *The sociology of work*, 2nd edn. Cambridge: Polity Press, 1998.

Grint, K. & Woolgar, S. *The machine at work*. Cambridge: Polity Press, 1997.

Hammer, M. & Champy, J. *Reengineering the corporation. A manifesto for business revolution*. London: Nicholas Brealey, 1993.

Hammer, M. & Stanton, S.A. *The reengineering revolution handbook*. London: HarperCollins, 1995.

Huczynski, A. Explaining the succession of management fads. *The International Journal of Human Resource Management*, 1993, *4*(2), 443–63.

Jackson, B.G. Re-engineering the sense of self: The manager and the management guru. *Journal of Management Studies*, 1995, *33*(5), 571–90.

Joyce, P. *Work, sociology and politics: The culture of the factory in late Victorian England*. Brighton: Harvester, 1980.

Kerfoot, D. & Knights, D. Management, masculinity and manipulation: From paternalism to corporate strategy in financial services in Britain. *Journal of Management Studies*, 1993, *30*(4), 659–77.

Knights, D. & Murray, F. *Managers divided*. London: Wiley, 1994.

Knights, D. & Willmott, H. Organisational culture as management strategy: A critique and illustration from the financial services industry. *International Studies of Management and Organisation*, 1987, *17*(3), 40–63.

Knights, D. & Willmott, H. 'It's a very foreign discipline': The genesis of expenses control in a mutual life insurance company. *British Journal of Management*, 1993, 4, 1–18.

Lawler, E. & Mohram, S. Quality circles after the fad. *Harvard Business Review*, 1985, 63 (Jan–Feb), 65–71.

Lewis, B.R. Quality in the service industry: A review. *International Journal of Bank Marketing*, 1989, *17*(5), 4–12.

Linstead, S. The social anthropology of management. *British Journal of Management*, 1997, *8*(1), 85–98.

Linstead, S. & Grafton-Small, R. On reading organizational culture. *Organization Studies*, 1992, *13*(3), 331–55.

McCabe, D., Knights, D. & Wilkinson, A. Financial services: 'Every which way but quality'. *Journal of General Management*, 1997, *22*(3), 53–73.

McCabe, D. Total Quality Management: Anti-union trojan horse or management albatross? *Work, Employment and Society*, 1999, *13*(4): 665–91.

McCabe, D. The swings and roundabouts of innovating for quality in UK financial services. *The Service Industries Journal*, 2000, *20*(4): 1–20.

Mackenzie, D. & Wajcman, J. (Eds) Introduction. In *The social shaping of technology*. Milton Keynes: Open University, 1985.

McLoughlin, I. & Clark, J. *Technological change at work*, 2nd edn. Milton Keynes: Open University Press, 1994.

McLoughlin, I. & Harris, M. (Eds) Introduction. In *Organisational change and technology*. London: International Thomson Business Press, 1997.

Marchington, M., Wilkinson, A., Ackers, P. & Goodman, J. The influence of managerial relations on waves of employee involvement. *British Journal of Industrial Relations*, 1993, *31*(4), 553–76.

Marglin, S.A. 'What do bosses do?': The origins and functions of hierarchy in capitalist production. In A. Gorz (Ed.), *The division of labour: The labour process and class struggle in modern capitalism*. Brighton: Harvester Press, 1974.

Meek, V.L. Organizational culture: Origins and weaknesses. *Organization Studies*, 1988, *9*(4), 453–73.

Morgan, G. Strategic issues in personal financial services. Financial Services Research Centre, Manchester School of Management, UMIST, September 1992.

Morgan, G. & Sturdy, A. *Beyond organizational change*. London: Macmillan, 2000.

Noble, D.F. Social choice in machine design: The use of automatically controlled machine tools. In D. Mackenzie & J. Wajcman (Eds), *The social shaping of technology*. Milton Keynes: Open University, 1985.

Parker, M. Working together, working apart: Management culture in a manufacturing firm. *Sociological Review*, 1995, *43*, 519–47.

Parker, M. & Slaughter, J. Should the labour movement buy TQM? *Journal of Organizational Change Management*, 1993, *6*(4), 43–56.

Peters, T.J. & Waterman, R.H. *In search of excellence: Lessons from America's best-run companies*. New York: Harper & Row, 1982.

Pettigrew, A.M. On studying organizational cultures. *Administrative Science Quarterly*, 1979, *24*, 570–81.

Ramsey, H. What is participation for? A critical evaluation of 'labour process' analysis of job reform. In D. Knights & D. Collinson (Eds), *Job redesign*. London: Routledge, 1985.

Ramsey, H. Reinventing the wheel? A review of the development and performance of employee involvement. *Human Resource Management Journal*, 1991, *1*(4), 1–22.

Ramsey, H. Cycles of control: Worker participation in sociological and historical perspective. *Sociology*, 1977, *11*(3), 481–506.

Ray, C.A. Corporate culture: The last frontier of control. *Journal of Management Studies*, 1986, *23*(3), 287–97.

Silverman, D. *Qualitative methodology: Describing the social world*. Aldershot: Gower, 1986.

Slappendel, C. Perspectives on innovation in organizations. *Organization*, 1996, *17*(1), 107–29.

Smircich, L. Concepts of culture and organizational analysis. *Administrative Science Quarterly*, 1983, *28*(3): 339–58.

Thompson, P. & McHugh, D. *Work organization*, 2nd edn. London: Macmillan Press, 1995.
Tuckman, A. Ideology, quality and TQM. In A. Wilkinson & H. Willmott (Eds), *Making quality critical*. London: Routledge, 1995.
Watson, T.J. *In search of management*. London: Routledge, 1994.
Watson, T.J. *Sociology, work and industry*, 3rd edn. London: Routledge, 1995.
Wilkinson, B. *The shopfloor politics of new technology*. London: Heinemann, 1983.
Williams, R. Universal solutions or local contingencies? Tensions and contradictions in the mutual shaping of technology and work organisation. In I. McGloughlin & M. Harris (Eds), *Organisational change and technology*. London: International Thomson Business Press, 1997.
Willmott, H.C. Images and ideals of management work: A critical examination of conceptual and empirical accounts. *Journal of Management Studies*, 1984, *21*(3), 349–68.
Willmott, H.C. Strength is ignorance: Slavery is freedom: Managing culture in modern organisations. *Journal of Management Studies*, 1993, *30*(5), 515–52.
Willmott, H.C. Rethinking management and managerial work: Capitalism, control and subjectivity. *Human Relations*, 1997, *50*(11), 1329–59.
Wright, S. (Ed.) Introduction. In *Anthropology of organizations*. London: Routledge, 1994.
Yin, R.K. *Case study research design and methods. Applied social research series 5*. London: Sage, 1989.
Young, E. On the naming of the rose: Interests and multiple meanings as elements of organizational culture. *Organization Studies*, 1989, *10*(2), 187–206.

Darren McCabe is a Senior Lecturer in the Department of Management, Keele University. His research has focused upon a variety of innovations in both the manufacturing and financial services sectors including TQM, BPR and Teamworking. His most recent publications include 'The team dream: The meaning and experience of teamworking for employees in an automobile manufacturing company' in S. Proctor and F. Mueller (Eds) *Teamworking: Issues, concepts and problems* (Macmillan, 2000) and 'Factory innovations and management machinations: The productive and repressive relations of power' in *Journal of Management Studies*, 37(7), 2000, 931–51.
[E-mail: mna19@mngt.keele.ac.uk]

Journal of Management Studies 39:2 March 2002
0022-2380

MANAGERS' THEORIES ABOUT THE PROCESS OF INNOVATION

Graeme Salaman

John Storey

The Open University

ABSTRACT

Despite the widely-recognized importance of innovation to organizational competitiveness and national economic well-being, and despite the extensive commentary on the topic, the managerial processes which contribute to innovativeness and the factors and processes inhibiting its achievement remain underexplicated. This article contributes to an understanding of the management of innovation by approaching the innovation problem from an analysis of the accounts, interpretations and theories of the actors closely engaged with the process. Focusing on a large telecommunications equipment manufacturer, this article reveals how managerial discourse may hold the key to understanding the nature of the barriers to effective innovation.

INTRODUCTION

Judging by academic and managerial discourse, innovation is currently considered to be critical for organizational competitiveness and survival. There has been a mushrooming of conferences, courses, publications and even whole journals dedicated to the unpacking of the sources of innovativeness and creativity at work. But, according to one well-known wide-ranging review of the literature, 'Our understanding of innovative behaviour in organizations remains relatively underdeveloped' (Wolfe, 1994, p. 405). Similarly, Tidd (1997, p. 1) in another attempt to review the literature, concluded that it is 'highly fragmented . . . much of the research has been conducted within separate disciplines with relatively little overlap or interaction'. These gloomy summations are the point of departure for the research reported in this paper. We too are interested in the management of innovation. But we wish to approach the issue from a different direction.

Wolfe argues that the solution to the inconsistency of research results is to improve the process of systematic comparison of research findings. And when he talks of 'theories of innovation' he is referring to the theories of scholars and researchers. However, academics are not the only people with an interest in understanding the varying levels of innovation; it is also a focal interest for many prac-

Address for reprints: Professor Graeme Salaman, Open University Business School, The Open University, Milton Keynes, MK6 7AA, UK (j.g.salaman@open.ac.uk).

tising managers. But if managers want to encourage innovation within their organizations, how do they try to do this? What theories do *they* draw upon and use? And how do these theories relate to their wider organizational experiences? These are the questions addressed by our research.

We suggest that these questions are important because innovation has been recognized as a long-standing and intractable problem and it can be suggested that the way in which managers and other influential players in organizations perceive and understand the issue will be a crucial factor. Thus, our response to the inconsistency of conventional research findings is not to attempt to improve the conventional research methodology (although we do not deny that this is a legitimate activity for others) but rather to come at the problem from a different angle. This article reports on the results from one of the case studies researched in depth during a three year study of the management of innovation. The objective of this article (and the wider study) is to allow a different understanding of how innovation occurs, or fails to occur, in organizations by attending closely to the accounts of key actors. We explore how our respondents talked about and understood the nature and production of innovation in organizations. We describe and analyse their theories and understandings about what 'innovation' means in their organizational context, in what areas it has been pursued and the areas where it has not. In addition, we explore the types of innovations which have occurred and the kinds of innovation which are now required, and, not least, *their* analyses of the factors which drive or discourage innovation. Thus, our purpose is to identify, analyse and theorize, managers' accounts of innovation within organizations.

THE THEORETICAL BACKDROP

Max Weber set out the parameters of the approach which we used in this project. He observed that an adequate causal analysis of any human (or organizational) action or artefact required 'adequacy on the level of meaning'. If this was lacking, 'then no matter how high the degree of uniformity and how precisely its probability can be numerically determined, it is still an incomprehensible statistical probability' (Weber, 1968, p. 231). By implication, the 'objective' factors and variables identified by researchers can only be relevant in terms of *the sense that is attached to them by those involved* in terms of their purposes. As Silverman (1970, p. 37) has put it, 'people act in terms of their own and not the observer's definition of the situation'. As our first research objective therefore, we set out to access and analyse the cognitive structures which give rise to, and are expressed in, actors' own accounts of innovation. This means more than mere description. As Silverman (1993, p. 185) puts it, the aim is not to *replicate* common sense but to *explicate* it.

Moreover, this paper does not simply address the nature of participants' meanings. It has a more focused objective: we are interested in how they make sense of the innovation activities and processes within their organization. There is increasing interest in processes of organizational cognition which some commentators see as representing a significant change in the development in the study of organizations. Recent analysis of organizational cognition stems from a number of different directions, some clearly arising from the long established interest in processes of organizational decision-making. These analyses draw on, and are realized in, a number of sometimes separate and sometimes overlapping debates. Notably relevant are those concerned with the examination of discourse in organizational contexts, organizational cultures, organizational processes of cognition, organizational and individual learning, and organizational change. We will now briefly indicate key contributions in these areas and show how they informed our study. We will also reveal how key themes recur in these apparently 'different' literatures.

Examinations of discourse in organizational analysis have revealed the ways in which programmes and strategies of change within organizations require the constitution – or re-constitution – of the person. One tradition within this problematic focuses on the ways in which the nature and character of the employee are known and understood within different organizational regimes (for example, du Gay, 1996a, 1996b; Hollway, 1991; Miller and Rose, 1993; Rose, 1995; Townley, 1992, 1993, 1995). Another tradition addresses the origins and implications of organizational discourses – ways of 'imagining' the organization (Coopey et al., 1998; du Gay and Salaman, 1992). Studies in this tradition usually centre on the notion of 'enterprise'. Enterprise is significant because it acts as a central relay device between employee and organization, organization and the market, the market and forces of globalization.

There are connections between our interest in the ways in which organizational innovators 'make sense of' the processes and structures of innovation and innovations within their organization, and what Potter (1997) describes as 'interpretative repertoires'. However the research reported here is not an analysis of discourse *per se*. We deploy the concept of 'discourse' not in the technical sense of a research methodology based on 'discourse analysis' but in a rather different way. Potter (1997) has usefully clarified the various ways in which the idea of 'discourse' can be used. We use it to refer to the way in which one can reach an understanding of an issue by attending to the way participants talk about it. Thus, discourse in this paper is seen as supplying a way of knowing a defined and constituted object. It also refers to 'how ideas are put into practice and used to regulate the conduct of others' (Hall, 1997, p. 44). A critical implication of discourse in the manner used in this paper is that, as Stuart Hall notes, it 'rules out, limits and restricts other ways of talking and of conducting ourselves in relation to the topic' (Hall, 1997, p. 44). This is the sense in which we employed this concept in this research project. Our concern is to be sensitive to discourse in order to gain extra insights into the way key actors interpret the nature of innovation and the factors which impede or allow it.

We explore the ways in which managers' theories of innovation exist within, and reflect, a wider discourse which defines the relationship between environment, organization and organizational processes. Specifically, we are interested in the extent to which managers' theories of innovation reflect, or are constrained by, a dominant conviction of the necessary centrality of market forms of organization and organizational relationships. We also explore the ways in which managers' theories of innovation articulate structures of power within the organization and, more specifically, reflect the nature and dominance of wider discourses which articulate particular and distinctive ways of understanding and designing or changing organizations and their key processes. We are concerned with participants' attribution of authority to competing theories of innovation, recognizing, as du Gay (1996a) has noted, that authority – as defined by our informants – is a result not of objective truth but of the dominance of the view of the world from which it is derived. Managers' theories of innovation demonstrate not only that knowledge is a form of power but that power is inherent in the dominance of forms of knowledge from which managers find it difficult to distance themselves (Hall, 1997, p. 48).

Our study is also informed by the organizational culture literature. In part we are concerned here to reveal the interconnections with the issues of cognitions, learning and discourse. Like Meyerson and Martin (1987) we regard organizations not simply as 'having' cultures but as *being* cultures – where culture is a manifestation of, and a constraint on, organizational cognition, values and action (Meyerson and Martin, 1987, p. 624). Relevant literature within this area addresses the issues of organizational culture as shared cognition, and organizational culture as systems of shared values that impact on processes of decision-making and learning. Morgan notes that 'Shared meaning, shared understanding and shared sense-making are different ways of describing culture. In talking about culture we are really talking about a process of reality construction that allows people to see and understand particular events, actions, objects, utterances or situations in distinctive ways' (Morgan, 1986, p. 24). This sense of organizational culture as a system of shared cognition is directly relevant to our concerns in this paper.

This sensitivity to shared cognition involves paying attention to 'collective sense-making'. This perspective on organizations has been usefully explored by Sackmann (1992) who conceptualizes organizational culture in these terms. Sackmann reveals how cultural cognitions consist of four elements. The first, 'dictionary knowledge', consists of shared definitions and labels. The second, 'directory knowledge', defines how things work: it is descriptive and refers to common practices. The third, 'recipe knowledge', is more theoretical and prescriptive in character; it suggests how things could be improved. And fourth, there is 'axiomatic knowledge', which draws on deep-seated assumptions and underlying premises (1992, p. 142). The research which we report here draws upon and illustrates these four types of culturally-available cognition.

In addition to types of knowledge there is also an important normative dimension to be taken into account. For example, Smircich (1983, p. 344) points out how organizational cultures can be seen as a 'social or normative glue that holds the organization together' through shared values and symbols. This normative element of organizational cultures plays a vital part in our research. Shared values concerning authority, uncertainty and risk, for example, impact on employees' willingness to engage in radical, innovative or challenging review of innovative processes which they regarded as problematical.

Likewise, the literature on organizational cognitive processes attends to the ways in which organizations consist of 'underlying cognitive boundaries that managers use to make sense of their world' (Sparrow, 1994, p. 151). One example is the study of the factors which influence managers' understanding of their business environments (see Calori et al., 1992; Daniels et al., 1992). In our research we seek to explore these 'cognitive boundaries' in order to reveal some needed insights into internal innovatory processes. Weick argues that a concern with interpretative processes within organizations is critical if organizational analysis is to move beyond a view of organizations as 'static frameworks or mechanical systems' (Weick, 2001, p. 242). He suggests that 'organizations have cognitive systems and memories . . . [they] preserve knowledge, behaviours, mental maps, norms, and values over time' (Weick, 2001, p. 243). This observation forms a crucial part of the cluster of perspectives underpinning the research project reported here.

It has been argued that organizations *per se* involve a shared social construction of organizational reality (Gioia, 1986; Gioia and Poole, 1984). But we go further than this. Our interest is in the specific cognitive models and theories which are available to managers and which they share and use when trying to achieve (or explain failure at) innovation within their organization. Our research is informed by the point made by Isabella (1990): that organizational members actively create or enact their organizational reality; that individual interpretative frames of reference are shared; and that the views of key managers are particularly critical (Isabella, 1990, pp. 9–10). Also at play here are processes of individual and organizational learning (Antonacopoulou, 1998; Nooteboom, 2000). Antonacopoulou's (1998) research, for example, shows how managers' perceptions of, and commitment to, learning is shaped extensively by the organizational contexts which they inhabit. Thus, even in relation to their own learning, managers, she found, tended to choose 'safe' options. It might be expected therefore that managers' perceptions of organizational priorities would be even more critical with regard to the willingness to initiate significant innovations in processes and products.

These literatures (discourse, organizational cultures, cognitive processes and learning) guided the way in which we designed the research methods for our study of innovation. We now turn to a description of those methods.

THE RESEARCH METHODOLOGY AND SETTING

The underlying theoretical and epistemological stance described in the previous section which underpins this research directly influenced the choice of research methodology. Our interest in identifying the nature of managers' theories of innovation led us to a qualitative methodology which would enable us to access and describe managers' cognitive structures. This methodology – semi-structured interviews with a selection of key managers – enabled us, we believe, to gain a richer and deeper analysis of the complexity and subtleties of managers' theories than the variable-based analysis of quantitative studies. Besides, at the beginning of the study we did not know what the key subjective variables would be: we are aware of no other similar study of managers' theories of innovation.

Semi-structured interviews were conducted with virtually all the senior managers in the organization and with a number of key players at middle management level. The latter were, in the main, creative, highly qualified, engineers who had a crucial grasp of, and were leaders in, the core technologies and products. They were identified as a result of discussion between the research team and the main business directors. A total of 20 interviews were conducted. All major management functions were covered. This group included directors and other senior managers. The interviews which lasted on average between one and a half and two hours, were tape recorded and then professionally transcribed. The transcripts were analysed in terms of frequently occurring themes with respect to the three areas covered, first independently by the two principal researchers and then the notes were compared.

The research – and the research interviews – was structured around three broad issues. First, how do managers see the importance and role of innovation within their organization – what is its actual or necessary strategic role? How is innovation defined within their organization? What place does it occupy or fail to occupy within the list of organizational priorities? Secondly, how is innovation encouraged or managed within the organization and what views do our respondents have of the sense and adequacy of these arrangements? And thirdly, how do they explain the levels of innovation within their organization – and specifically how do they see the role of existing structures and forces within the organization in the encouragement of innovation? Insights on each and all of these topics reflect respondents' theories of innovation, since, by articulating their analyses of the organizational features which impact on innovation they reveal their understanding (i.e. their explanatory models) of how innovation is occasioned (or blocked). An additional element of the interviews was a request to the respondents for a number of narrative accounts of concrete instances of attempts to innovate which they had witnessed either as direct participants or as close observers.

The research took place over a 12 month period between 1997 and 1998 in the head office and across multiple sites of the 'Teleco' organization (a pseudonym to protect the confidentiality of the case organization). Teleco is a large designer and manufacturer of telecommunications infrastructure equipment. It is part of a large, multinational conglomerate. To a considerable extent, Teleco was in competition for investment resources with other major businesses in the portfolio of the parent company. Teleco had all the hallmarks of a traditional British engineering company. It had a long and relatively distinguished history with some important past product innovations to its credit. In recent years it had found a need to respond to a rapidly and substantially changing environment. It had enjoyed a close and reliable relationship with its main customer – an arrangement which in the past amounted to a cost-plus pricing policy. At that time too, the major customer had been party to the planning of future technological and product developments. Following deregulation, privatization and rapid technological change most of these erstwhile comfort zones had been removed.

In 1998 the company had a number of main divisions, each offering different products and services. It remained a very big player with a large workforce, substantial revenues and healthy profits. But there were major uncertainties about the future. Aggressive, international competitors were entering its traditional markets and the rapid growth in mobile telephony, innovations such as telephone services via cable as well as the potential for telephony over the internet – let alone new developments in switching technology across all capacity levels from rural to metropolitan and international – all represented major disturbances. It was against this backdrop that our key informants sought to reflect upon and make sense of the place, priority, nature, opportunities and obstacles to innovation.

We readily acknowledge that there are limitations inherent in this kind of study. Our decision to focus in an open-ended way on a limited number of key informants risks a sacrifice, as Silverman puts it, of reliability for authenticity (Silverman, 1995, p. 10). Our concern was to obtain a rich understanding of how managers made sense of the innovative practices in their organization. We initiated this project with no *a priori* expectations of what these might be like. The only expectations we held were that managers would have views – probably shared collective views – on the three areas explored in the semi-structured interview. Therefore our concern was to be able to describe, in as great a detail as possible, managers' theories of innovation. This led us to focus not on a representative sample of managers but on those managers who were key decision makers in their organizations and those with a particular interest in innovation. We cannot claim that the views described below were common within the organization as a whole. But we can say that the managers whom we interviewed, who constituted the group most concerned with the encouragement of innovation within the case organization, held these views. The theories described here may not be representative of the organization as a whole but we are confident that we accurately represent the managers' theories.

RESULTS

Respondents' interpretations of the meanings and significances of innovation were characterized by a number of features. They held strong views about innovation. Innovation, for the respondents, was a real concern; it was a naturally-occurring source of interest and speculation. Most respondents were in no doubt about the importance of innovation for their business. As one respondent observed:

> If you are not a company that innovates you have got no chance of winning or even continuing to exist. I think that we're actually trying to address the way Teleco approaches the future. It's no good just having one or two products that stand out; you need to be able to provide the customer with the complete solution. It's about seeing the connections.

Virtually all informants in this organization agreed with the proposition that innovation was critical for the continued survival of the company. Given the context of a telecommunications equipment designer and manufacturer at this period in time this consensus was perhaps hardly surprising. Rather less expected was the high proportion of respondents who, using a limited number of variants of language, argued that the way forward for the company was to progress from merely supplying 'boxes' of technology, to supplying 'complete solutions'. By this they meant engaging more closely with customers (i.e. various telecom operating companies) in order to identify their market strategies and then, on the back of this, proffer hardware and software packages which would meet their needs.

This corporate narrative, namely that the future demanded a shift towards software in place of the previous reliance on hardware had won remarkable acceptance, at least at the level of espoused theory. Managers from a whole variety of functions and divisions articulated this same analysis. Innovation was absolutely necessary and the nature of that innovation was an integrated mix of hardware and software which gave value-added opportunities for the company and rescued it from the fate of a commodity supplier.

However, while there was a near total consensus on this analysis there was less conviction that the organization was truly committed to, or perhaps even capable of, the delivery of this new approach. As one manager observed, 'There is a strong recognition of the need for change in these areas but [corporate level managers] don't seem to realize that this will require a management response – that we will have to *do* things differently rather than simply react differently.'

A common complaint was that the implications of the corporate narrative were not being realized in practice. It was noted that despite the compelling logic of the corporate line on innovation, the day to day priorities continued to emphasize traditional attitudes and ways of doing. For example, one manager pointed out that the routine practices for authorizing innovations remained focused on careful scrutiny of the technology involved. He protested that:

> Innovation is far more than simply technical innovation. It covers all aspects of the business. Actually there's a risk that by stressing the technical stuff we downplay the other sorts of innovation. Innovation is about seeing new ways of doing things, including new ways of working with clients, new ways of putting together packages of existing technologies, and new ways of working with partners to develop common areas of interest.

Many managers recognized that the 'complete solutions' strategy, if it was to be acted upon in a serious manner, carried wide-ranging implications for the way the organization was managed. For example, one of them expressed the point as follows:

> We have to design innovative technical solutions for our clients; we have to innovate internally to improve our operating practices; we have to innovate in the way we manage and lead our staff and we need to innovate by seeking new market opportunities for our core competences so that they can be deployed in new markets.

This kind of interpretation suggested the need for change, not only to the products and services offered but also to the whole range of management actions, including the ways staff are managed. It was on this point that the apparent consensus about the way forward, the 'total solutions' approach began to break down. Differences in prioritization of different types of innovation began to emerge. By prioritizing different types of innovation they were suggesting a causal connection between innovation and organizational structure and strategy. Some respondents argued that technical innovation was, in practice, still being over-emphasized and that this was resulting in a lack of concern for clients' needs. One informant suggested that 'the whole of this business so far has been driven by anoraks and technology, and they haven't really been looking at customers at all.' This view implicitly argues that technical expertise, and innovation is – or should be – subordinate to marketing or customer demand.

One significant tranche of Teleco managers contended that innovation should be 'customer-facing'. One respondent noted that historically 'our innovation is to do with product and many of our customers don't necessarily attach a great deal of value to technical sophistication – they want something that works and someone to be responsible for making sure it works.'

As we have emphasized, coming to terms with innovation for these managers entailed taking stances about the preferred business strategy. For example, one manager argued:

> What we should be doing is moving up above [the commodity-supplier chain], which is why we might rightly end up, in some instances, going to the full extent of being, in effect, an operator. The bottom end is changing but it is always in danger of making us just a commodity-supplier. You don't want to be in that so we move up as well – to more value-added areas.

Interviewees thus displayed expansive and creative views about innovation. While they recognized the nature and importance of technological innovation, they also recognized the limits to this form of innovation and the possible dangers of an excessive focus on it. They argued that features of the organization tended to encourage technologically driven, product-focused, incremental, innovation, at the expense of more customer-focused solutions which could exploit radical innovative developments.

Respondents worried that the important form of innovation – the big leap – was being neglected: 'I think the Telecoms world is changing so much, particularly with the advent of the internet and I think the opportunities are going to be where the incremental approach won't be sufficient.' There was a tension between sustaining current product portfolios and the activity needed to displace these with new products. Our respondents articulated this: 'This product [their main staple cash-cow product] has now got to the stage where it is cumbersome and it's taking a huge amount of resource – we are just adding to it and it's not going anywhere.'

There were various aspects to this insistence that the company was not following an appropriate strategy of innovation investment: issues of leadership and strategy, concerns about the long term growth of the business and concerns about the way the organization managed and encouraged innovation. Managers worried that the investment strategy (of the parent group) revealed a lack of strategic foresight, a failure of nerve and an unhelpful concern with short term profit making that did not bode well for the long term health of the company. One manager commented:

> We should be spending money to get the best kit in the world. We should be trying it, seeing how good it is and trying things out. We have to be aware that there is a real risk that some developments will mean that there are vendors not in our business who will cross the tracks and come and eat our lunch. Why can't we do the same? We need to make sure that we have a role in this new business. But it will take business courage. This is not a matter of technology. It's a question of business leadership.

Again here one can see the frustration expressed by the senior managers in this business with regard to the constraints imposed by the owning group – and by extension, by their fellow directors. Our informants also questioned whether a concern for incremental, evolutionary improvement actually made sense in terms of the long term growth of the business, and worried that it revealed a lack of corporate vision which would lead to (and had led to) missed business opportunities. As one remarked: 'the danger in a company of our sort is that we expend all our resources on extrapolating and sustaining our current portfolio and not nearly enough on new initiatives. The result is that tomorrow is neglected to sustain today'.

There were also additional worries. One concerned the key objectives that underpinned the way the organization was structured. As one manager asked:

> What are we, in essence, organized to achieve? Now you might say that the way we're organized reinforces the reactive element (to innovation) in the sense that new product development tends to be given to the existing product divisions

whose main interests are of course maintaining their revenue stream because that's how they are judged. So that raises the question: are we really organized for innovation? Should we not find new ways of doing things such as spin-offs or spin outs – where we identify new markets and ring fence them to incentivize the management so they are like entrepreneurs?

Informants often attempted to offer a comprehensive analysis of the various forces that helped or hindered innovation. One important point stressed by many managers was that innovation is bred through necessity, 'You have to have a need which overcomes your reluctance to be innovative because being innovative requires a risk. It requires you to take a chance because you have to say, if there's no security in standing still then it is less risky to move forward.' Despite this awareness, these managers perceived that current market conditions were just sufficiently comfortable to impede this kind of disturbance and risk. At the same time they feared for the future and wondered whether the parent corporation was taking this sufficiently into account given its preferred ways of accounting and control.

It will be recalled that Teleco was a wholly owned subsidiary of a larger engineering conglomerate. Our informants were conscious of the implications:

> Our parent organization is at a mature stage of the product life cycle; they have plateaued. They have a completely different approach to innovation from ours. We are in a young market that will grow. Yet all [the parent company] asks about are quarterly financial returns.

Respondents noted that organizational structures rapidly assumed political significance which then influenced decisions about the encouragement or funding of innovation. Existing businesses focused on innovations that supported their business ends. But the main complaint was simply that the structural emphasis on production and the location of innovation within product units tipped the balance against radical innovation and encouraged an antipathy towards investment in longer term innovation by starving such projects of resources. A respondent argued: 'We are developing our own operating system but we have been directly obstructed in the development of this key component by [the PLC] which has been diverting funds and has stopped us employing the necessary engineers, so there is a risk we will miss the market.'

Not only are tightly-focused product businesses likely to look askance at expensive innovation projects, but the more successful these businesses are, the less likely they might be to see the need for them to support such research. The dilemma is not simply operational activity versus radical research, or certainty versus speculation, but also success versus risk-taking. Businesses have products in different stages of their life cycles and so, according to some respondents at least, someone had to take a broad view which extends beyond the concerns of any product champion. It was suggested that it was necessary 'to start new ventures, ideally sprinkled with individuals who are prepared to take risks and innovate in pursuit of their belief in a new market opportunity. You may have to do both in parallel which is actually quite hard to do in many organizations because the product barons don't give up their positions very easily.' In summary, these managers saw an inappropriate balance between radical and incremental innovation and they interpreted this as reflecting a strategic error or confusion on the part of the organization as a whole.

Teleco had devised a number of formal innovation procedures. The key one was a strategic planning process which tried to take a long term view of the business and which is rolled forward every year. This tries to identify product enhancement and new product projects. It is informed by a Central Marketing function which provides marketing intelligence. In addition there is a 'Phase Review Process' which evaluates in a systematic way new product proposals.

Respondents recognized the need for an organizational process that encouraged innovation. Their concern was not about the concept of phased planning and review but with its features and practical operation. However, while recognizing the deficiencies of the current system, respondents were less clear on how it should be changed. One concern was that the state of mind necessary for developing technical innovation and ensuring its reliability and safety might, paradoxically, be unsuitable for innovation management more widely conceived. Thus, as one said:

> The phase review process is a filter not a catalyst. The pre-ordained product business structure is crucial: new products raise questions of how and where they will fit. We need people to think outside of what their brief says.

Overall, respondents argued that the process enshrined an inappropriate attitude to risk by applying to product development old-fashioned engineering attitudes to risk. 'The strategic planning process is a heavyweight research evaluation process to ensure that we never have a failure. It applies excessive engineering logics (testing and demanding reassurances) to the development of innovation'.

Some saw the phase review process as inherently paradoxical, particularly when the need for certainty and reassurance became excessive: 'In dealing with innovation, by definition, you are dealing with things you do not fully understand. Therefore, pressing for detail is foolish. You are killing it. The watchword should be: "Try It!"' By demanding reassuring information, the process stifled projects. This happens especially when the product is slightly unusual and when the trajectories of the market place are less well known and understood. 'You need people with courage, there seems to be something wrong with how we do it. We lose heart, pull out, focus too much on early sales and lose future ones.' A number of respondents were keen to experiment and were urging a greater preparedness to take risks. Some seemed to be awaiting official sanction to do so while others were seemingly prepared to go beyond the bounds of official sanction.

Respondents identified structural obstacles to innovation. They argued that the officially-sanctioned innovation processes were excessively dominated by bureaucratic priorities rather than by client or market imperative. In this respect their preferences were clear: they wanted the innovation process to be externally, not internally, focused and answerable. They were also critical of the way existing structures (the product businesses) operated. Innovation had to be answerable to the businesses. Managers recognized that this regime could – and did – obstruct long term investment in radical and speculative forms of innovation. They recognized that the dependence of innovation on existing product-based businesses encouraged incremental innovation while discouraging radical innovation; they were clear that short term business targets could stifle longer term opportunities.

Respondents were clear that the vision must be more than financial – it was about the direction of the market – and indeed of several markets – and the place of the organization in relation to these. It also required, they suggested to us, a view of future technologies, and of future relationships with clients, competitors and suppliers.

> Do people at the top [again here they meant both the corporate level and their own colleagues on the business board] have the necessary courage and vision? The overall attitude is a focus on year-on-year returns; it's all about ROI. In contrast, we don't think enough at the highest level of what we want [Teleco] to be and where we want it to be in the next few years. This is not a financial matter: it is a matter of what competencies will it have, what business will it be in, will growth be acquisitive or organic and so on. What is it that we want this thing to be and how are we going to get there?

As is evident then, 'top management' were seen as crucial. They were held responsible for dis-enabling leadership at the business level. The financial control regime was seen as responsible for the failure to identify a sufficiently clear vision; this in turn meant an incomplete business strategy. In consequence, would-be innovators (the undoubtedly talented engineers) were caught in an ambiguous situation which led to massive uncertainty about the kind of products and services thought to be required.

Respondents explained the problem of corporate leadership in terms of the executives' backgrounds and orientations. We uncovered a fascinating divergence here. Approximately half the managers interviewed traced the problem to 'financiers and financial controllers' while the other half traced the problem to the 'engineering' mindsets of organizational power holders.

The first group interpreted the problem as stemming both from the corporate level and from the top team in the Teleco business as well: 'They haven't made the big shift in attitude that is required; they are still paying lip service. They are unwilling to make the big change to a new way of thinking about business risk and investment.'

The second identified the dominance of 'engineering values' as the source of the problem. They saw these as resulting in an excessive concern for technological-driven innovation at the expense of market-driven. Also, it resulted in an emphasis on product innovation at the expense of channel or process innovations. It meant an attention to detail and discipline instead of a more intuitive and far-sighted approach. But the main complaint was in the attitude towards risk inherent within an engineering culture which, with its understandable concern with risk elimination and reliability of performance, was seen to breed an approach to risk which is seriously antithetical to the encouragement of innovation. Innovation by its very nature was seen to involve risk and risk was seen as dangerous; failure was a possibility. But an attitude towards risk that attempted to reduce it (however understandable at one level) could result in a fatal hesitation. Caution not only resulted in a half-hearted approach, it also led to delay: 'That's where we are now – we are starting on a new switch but it's late. We always identify the problem and the opportunity but we are not brave enough, not prepared to take risks.'

The final criticism was possibly the most serious: that senior management – 'they' – were responsible not only for poor innovation but lacked the will or the means to envision and implement an alternative form of organization. This account was given by some middle managers who seemed to have their own senior business managers in mind. Yet, at the same time, it was also an account offered by these same senior business managers when they talked about the corporate level. At each level therefore, managers accounted for the 'problem of innovation' as emerging from the constraints imposed by, and the lack of imagination of, the management tier(s) above. What this amounted to was an articulation of the felt competing priorities – meeting deadlines, keeping within budgets etc. – and, as such, these accounts give a clear indication of the relatively inferior place in the pecking order which product and service innovation was seen to hold.

The main points which our respondents made about the management of innovation may be summarized as follows:

- Innovation is vital for this business.
- Innovation can no longer be regarded in the way it was in the past: it is not enough to think about new technology and new products, the company must gain added value and escape commoditization by developing 'complete solutions' with clients, involving both software and hardware.
- Innovation, if it is to be done properly, requires courage and entails risks.
- The organization at present does not display enough of the necessary courage.
- Current structures (product-based business units) are inimical to the kinds of innovations required.
- Innovation of the kind required will mean that fundamental questions have to be asked about the strategy of the organization including quite literally, what business it is in.

ANALYSIS

Our interpretations of these research findings are fourfold.

First, managers' theories of innovation were characterized by a series of dilemmas. These are explored below. Sharma (1999) makes the point that the problem with defining innovation in terms of dilemmas, is not that one set of polarities is correct and the other wrong, but that thinking in terms of polarities may itself be the problem. Polarities encourage oppositional, either/or thinking; they preclude the existence of the identification of other possible options and they particularly exclude the possibility of thinking beyond both opposed options or finding underlying common ground for both sides of the dilemma. In fact the ways in which the Teleco managers defined the relationship between positive and negative forces is important in itself, and is explored below.

Second, Teleco managers believed that their organizational structures, cognitive systems and organizational priorities obstructed the achievement of innovation. In their view, their organization was systemically reluctant to explore new opportunities because of what Sharma has termed 'faith in the known and fear of the unknown' (Sharma, 1999). In consequence, most Teleco managers chose to follow the path of Antonacopoulou's (1998) bank managers and 'play it safe'.

Third, the research reveals that managers had trouble in imagining the nature of innovative organizations. Possibly because their thinking was polarized, but also possibly because of the dominance of a powerful current view of how organizations should be structured and organized. Although managers in this research organization were vigorous in their analysis of the systemic limitations to innovation, they seemed to draw back from advocating an alternative. Teleco managers were unwilling to speculate in any detail what an alternative, innovative, organization might be like. We explain this in terms of the power of the current discourse of market forms of organization which limit the managers' capacity to describe or imagine an organization capable of generating innovation. We regard this absence created by the perceived truth of the discourse of market forms as a major impediment to innovation.

Fourth, if the development of innovation was hampered by managers' unwillingness to think about, or develop a view of, how organizations could encourage innovation it was also discouraged by their apparent unwillingness to take responsibility for confronting systemic sources of obstruction. The managers in this organization were prepared to identify blockages for the researchers but they were less prepared to tackle these obstructions.

Our analysis of the research findings can usefully be organized in terms of a number of contradictions or tensions. Managers' thinking about innovation displayed a bi-polarity. This in itself is not surprising. After all, a key element of the structure of the interview was the analysis of the managers' views of the forces that obstructed and facilitated innovation. It was natural therefore for managers to organize their answers in terms of supportive and obstructive features of the organization. But the managers did much more than this: first they offered a particular conception of the relationship between the positive and negative forces. Secondly they offered their own interpretations of the positive and negative forces at work in Teleco.

The manner in which people define how positive and negative forces relate to each other varies, as Westenholz has usefully argued (1993, p. 41). Dilemmas, paradoxes, polarities, dialectics, tensions, contradictions, are all different ways in which the relationship between positive and negative forces can be defined. Paradox is at the heart of innovation in organizations. The pressing need for survival in the short-term requires efficient exploitation of current competences and 'requires coherence, coordination and stability'; whereas exploration/innovation requires the discovery and development of new competences and this requires the loosening and replacement of these erstwhile virtues (Nooteboom, 2000). Notebloom states that this tension is the central problem for organizations and their learning. Teleco managers offered some useful insights on this central problem. As will be seen from the analysis below, they offered a subtle understanding of the complexities and paradoxes surrounding the management of innovation.

THINKING FRAMES FOR INNOVATION

Teleco managers shared 'dictionary knowledge' (Sackmann, 1992) of innovation within Teleco. They saw innovation in terms of a series of tensions or paradoxes. Central to this collective view of innovation was a paradox: the features of the organization that made it effective in some areas (operations) made it ineffective in others. Innovation was defined as requiring different supports than the organization's traditional operational strengths and values: business-focused, reliable, technically able and with engineering strength.

Recent interest in organizations as sources of shared cognitive schema show how these schema influence perceptions, values, and beliefs. Much recent research has described the ways in which managers' shared cognitive constructs of the external world (markets, competition and industrial structure) are influenced by entrenched schemas (Calori et al., 1992; Reger, 1990; Sparrow, 1994). Much of this research supports the conclusion that managers learn to focus and to minimize data processing time in order to achieve *efficiencies*, but that these routines may become counter-productive under new circumstances (Stubbart and Ramaprasand, 1990). The outcome has been described by Starbuck (1993): systems of organizational learning may lead to the application of shared cognitive routines and assumptions which are historically based but irrelevant for future success. Likewise, as Van de Ven (1986, p. 596) observes, 'the older, larger, and more successful organizations become, the more likely they are to have a large repertoire of structures and systems which discourage innovation while encouraging tinkering'.

Teleco managers' accounts reflect these assessments. The managers recognized that historically established and culturally valued modes of thinking and decision-making which contributed to organizational success at the operational level were dysfunctional when applied to innovation. The managers' interpretations and recommendations amounted to the view that 'organizing' and 'innovating' were in tension. But they were not able to see a way out of this paradox. Organizing meant applying established cognitive schema and values based on engineering logics, achieving predictability, and making events routine. Innovation meant to disorganize: to seek and embrace variety and unpredictability. For example, technical engineering excellence was accepted as a necessary element in innovation but it was also recognized by many as insufficient and even a drawback if engineering logics were allowed to govern the attitude towards risk. Respondents suggested that innovation was driven by two different – and once again – opposed principles: technology and market. Technology or engineering driven innovation was generated by technical insight and inspiration – and competence. Market-driven innovation was informed by an understanding and anticipation of clients' needs. This latter would require an organization that was able not only to develop in-house innovation but also to identify and develop innovation outside the organization when necessary – a strategy which had to be part of a broader strategy of business development.

Managers argued that engineering standards of quality and risk calculation may not make sense when applied to non-engineering innovations. For example, the new predominant emphasis on software products meant acceptance of much faster development times and of occasional failures. These meant that colleagues' expectations had to be more relaxed than had previously been the case with engineered telecommunications hardware, which everyone expected to be robust and fail-safe.

However, although innovation was viewed as requiring a set of factors which are defined as *different* from prevailing features in the existing organizational structures and processes, managers were reluctant to describe an alternative form of organization. Their *thinking frames for innovation*, their ability to imagine an alternative form of organization, were overwhelmed by the current dominance of a powerful but limited discourse of organization. Current ways of thinking and theorizing *about* organization (those that stress the primacy of market relations, with all support functions accountable to the business units and the business units accountable for levels of short term contribution) have implications for managers' capacity to imagine or describe an organization capable of generating innovation. Managers argued that organizational structures and systems constrained innovation but, in addition, *discourses of organization* also constrain their ability, and even their willingness to think about alternative organizational forms.

THE ROLE OF ORGANIZATIONAL CULTURES: HELPING AND HINDERING

Managers' theories of innovation were intertwined with power relations. This was seen most readily in managers' attribution of *responsibility* for those organizational processes and priorities which are regarded as obstructing innovation. Our data and analysis shed light on the role and implications of managers' conception of their personal responsibility for, and ability to change, aspects of the organization that they see as inimical to the generation of innovation. It is one thing for managers to identify aspects of organizational decision-making and thinking which limit innovation. It is another, and arguably more significant matter, when managers in effect *concede that they are unwilling or unable to tackle these obstacles*. This unwillingness was so widespread as to reflect the organizational culture where Teleco managers learn not to accept responsibility for the persistence of a situation they find unsatisfactory.

Although Teleco managers were convinced that many features of Teleco's organizational structure and systems obstructed innovation, they would not take responsibility for questioning the authority of those responsible for designing and maintaining anti-innovation structures. They saw innovation as something they can do when they are allowed to; but they do not see themselves as able or even willing to confront the obstacles they described so vividly. It is noteworthy that many of the respondents were themselves members of the senior management team: in levelling this criticism they were in effect suggesting a collective paralysis. A number of writers on organizational culture (Bate, 1992; Hofstede, 1980; Sackmann, 1992) offer useful insights here. They have noted the factors which impact on managers willingness to take responsibility for confronting those aspects of organization which they perceive as dysfunctional. These factors include beliefs and values relating to authority and hierarchy.

Blockages to innovation within this company lie not only in the features of the organization that are perceived as anti-innovative, but also in the ways in which managers attribute responsibility for confronting and challenging these organizational obstacles and in their inability to conceive of a pro-innovation form of organization. Managers in Teleco shared 'directory knowledge' of innovation within the organization. They described how innovation was managed, and found these procedures wanting in terms of their shared 'recipe knowledge'. Directory knowledge did not make available shared prescriptions for 'repair and improvement strategies' (Sackmann, 1992, p. 142). Innovation was organized and managed in a coherent manner; it articulated a key principle: namely, that innovation must be encouraged but more importantly, it should simultaneously be *disciplined* by locating responsibility for innovation within the product businesses. Implicit in this approach was the view that innovation was potentially dangerous and therefore it needed to be closely controlled.

The Teleco managers were individually committed to innovation and they were located in an organization that was itself apparently strategically committed to innovation. This was not merely an espoused commitment (Argyris and Schon, 1978) – although espousal alone was certainly often found in other organizations which we researched. In Teleco the commitment was serious; but nonetheless it was, according to our respondents, not sufficiently converted into achieved innovation. The managers explained their organization's poor innovation performance by using a model of innovation in organizations in which many of the normal – and normally effective – features of their organization were seen to hamper innovation. Their views echoed Starbuck's argument that organizational cognition and action becomes trapped within previous ways of thinking and established routines. In other words, 'behaviour programmes' become embedded in standard operating procedures (Starbuck, 1993). We additionally suggest that these established patterns also inhibit the achievement of innovation in two other ways. First, organizational members are encultured into these patterns of thought but, as we have seen, this did not prevent many of them privately critiquing these routines and thought patterns; what the established routines did prevent was open public critique. Second, the critics were, in effect, resigned to living with these impediments to innovation. They recognized the importance of innovation, they were also able to identify major barriers to it; what they were not able (or willing) to do was mount the necessary challenge required in order to confront these barriers. Willingness to act with respect to innovation is a function of not just individual commitment and insight but also of organizational (often virtually equivalent to top management) priorities as perceived by these managers. This reflects the willingness, or unwillingness, to engage in active learning as found by Antonacopoulou (1998).

This state of affairs reflects what Argyris (1990) terms a 'second-order error' – that is, one which is not accidental but *systemic*. Here, the organizational features which discourage effectiveness are also the same ones which lead to the persistence of these features. The key factor in the Teleco case is managers' culturally-based unwillingness to be prepared to actively challenge and confront features of the organization which they themselves identified as fundamentally damaging. Teleco's culture is thus, in Westenholz's (1993) terms, essentially 'paradoxical'. The case reveals the co-existence of a series of mutually contradictory values and cognitions: innovation is regarded by virtually all informants as critically important; most go on to say that it is blocked by aspects of their own organization; finally, and somewhat frustratingly, they also go on to say that this situation cannot be challenged or changed – unless those 'at the top' over-turn the accumulated pattern of priorities, values and procedures and thus legitimate the required actions.

The key to these paradoxes and contradictions stems from the fact that these managers are both producers as well as products of the corporate culture and, as a consequence, ambiguity, consensus and disagreements all co-exist (Meyerson and Martin, 1987). The managers were apparently unable to challenge the dominant regime of truth or, as Foucault (1980, p. 131) would have it, the 'general politics of truth'. The problem of innovation management has been recognized as intractable and persistent. These features of managers' accounts of innovation which we have described and analysed would seem to offer important clues to the sources of these problems. Future researchers might usefully build upon, and probe, these insights more deeply.

REFERENCES

ANTONACOPOULOU, E. P. (1998). 'Developing learning managers within learning organizations'. In Easterby-Smith, M., Araujo, L. and Burgoyne, J. (Eds), *Organizational Learning and the Learning Organization*. London: Sage, 217–42.

ARGYRIS, C. (1990). *Overcoming Organizational Defenses*. Needham Heights, MA: Allyn and Bacon.

ARGYRIS, C. and SCHÖN, D. (1978). *Organizational Learning: A Theory of Action Perspective*. Reading, MA: Addison-Wesley.

BATE, P. (1992). 'The impact of organizational culture on approaches to organizational problem-solving'. In Salaman, G. (Ed.), *Human Resource Strategies*. London: Sage, 213–36.

CALORI, R., JOHNSON, G. and SARNIN, P. (1992). 'French and British top managers' understanding of the structures and dynamics of their industries: a cognitive analysis'. *British Journal of Management*, **3**, 2, 61–78.

COOPEY, J., KEEGAN, O. and EMLER, N. (1998). 'Managers' innovations and the structuration of organizations'. *Journal of Management Studies*, **35**, 3, 263–84.

DANIELS, K., DE CHERNATONY, L. and JOHNSON, G. (1992). 'Theoretical and Methodological Issues Concerning Managers Mental Models of Competitive Industry Structures'. 6th Annual Conference of The British Academy of Management, University of Bradford, 14–16 September.

DERRIDA, J. (1984). *Positions*. Chicago, IL: Univeristy of Chicago Press.

DU GAY, P. (1991). 'Enterprise culture and the ideology of excellence'. *New Formations*, **13**, 45–62.

DU GAY, P. (1996a). *Consumption and Identity at Work*. London: Sage.

DU GAY, P. (1996b). 'Making up managers: enterprise and the ethos of bureaucracy'. In Clegg, S. and Palmer, G. (Eds), *The Politics of Management Knowledge*. London: Sage, 19–35.

DU GAY, P. and SALAMAN, G. (1992) 'The cult(ure) of the customer'. *Journal of Management Studies*, **29**, 5, 615–33.

DU GAY, P., SALAMAN, G. and REES, B. (1996). 'The conduct of management and the management of conduct: contemporary managerial discourse and the constitution of the "competent" manager'. *Journal of Management Studies*, **33**, 263–82.

FOUCAULT, M. (1980). *Power/Knowledge*. Brighton: Harvester.

GIOIA, D. A. (1986). 'Symbols, scripts, and sensemaking: creating meaning in the organizational experience'. In Sims, H. P. and Gioia, D. A. (Eds), *The Thinking Organization*. San Francisco, CA: Jossey-Bass, 49–74.

GIOIA, D. A. and POOLE, P. P. (1984). 'Scripts in organizational behavior'. *Academy of Management Review*, **10**, 527–39.

HALL, S. (1997). 'The work of representation'. In Hall, S. (Ed.), *Representation: Cultural Representations and Signifying Practices*. London: Sage, 13–74.

HOFSTEDE, G. (1980). *Culture's Consequences: International Differences in Work-Related Values*. London: Sage.

HOLLWAY, W. (1991). *Work Psychology and Organizational Behaviour*. London: Sage.

ISABELLA, L. (1990). 'Evolving interpretations as change unfolds: how managers construe key organizational events'. *Academy of Management Journal*, **33**, 1, 7–41.

MEYERSON, D. and MARTIN, J. (1987). 'Cultural change: an integration of three different views'. *Journal of Management Studies*, **24**, 6, 623–47.

MILLER, P. and ROSE, N. (1993). 'Governing economic life'. In Gane, M. and Johnson, T. (Eds), *Foucault's New Domains*. London: Routledge, 75–105.

MORGAN, G. (1986). *Images of Organization*. Beverley Hills, CA: Sage.

NOOTEBOOM, B. (2000). *Learning and Innovation in Organizations and Economies*. Oxford: Oxford University Press.

POTTER, J. (1997). 'Discourse analysis as a way of analysing naturally occurring talk'. In Silverman, D. (Ed.), *Qualitative Research: Theory, Method and Practice*. London: Sage, 144–61.

REGER, R. K. (1990). 'Managerial thought structures and competitive positioning'. In Huff, A. S. (Ed.), *Mapping Strategic Thought*. London: Wiley.

ROSE, N. (1995). 'Identity, genealogy, and history'. In Hall, S. and du Gay, P. (Eds), *Questions of Cultural Identity*. London: Sage.

SACKMANN, S. (1992). 'Culture and subcultures: an analysis of organizational knowledge'. *Administrative Science Quarterly*, **37**, 140–61.

SHARMA, A. (1999). 'Central dilemmas of managing innovation in large firms'. *California Management Review*, **41**, 3, 146–64.

SILVERMAN, D. (1970). *The Theory of Organizations*. London: Heinemann.

SILVERMAN, D. (1993). *Interpreting Qualitative Data*. London: Sage.

SMIRCICH, L. (1983). 'Concepts of culture and organizational analysis'. *Administrative Science Quarterly*, **28**, 339–58.

SPARROW, P. (1994). 'The psychology of strategic management: emerging themes of diversity and cognition'. In Cooper, C. and Robertson, I. (Eds), *The International Review of Industrial and Organizational Psychology*, Volume 9. Chichester: Wiley, 147–81.

STARBUCK, W. (1993). 'Organizations as action generators'. *American Sociological Review*, **48**, 91–102.

STUBBART, C. I. and REMAPRASAND, A. (1990). 'Comments on the empirical articles and recommendations for future research'. In Huff, A. S. (Ed.), *Mapping Strategic Thought*. London: Wiley.

TIDD, J. (1997). 'Complexity, networks and learning: integrative themes for research on innovation management'. *International Journal of Innovation Management*, **1**, 1, 1–21.

TOWNLEY, B. (1992). 'In the eye of the gaze: the constitutive role of performance appraisal'. In Barrar, P. and Cooper, G. (Eds), *Managing Organizations in 1992*. London: Routledge.

TOWNLEY, B. (1993). 'Performance appraisal and the emergence of management'. *Journal of Management Studies*, **30**, 221–38.

TOWNLEY, B. (1995). '"Know thyself": self awareness, self formation and managing'. *Organization*, **2**, 271–89.

VAN DE VEN, A. (1986). 'Central problems in the management of innovation'. *Management Science*, **32**, 5, 590–607.

WEBER, M. (1968). *Economy and Society*. New York: Bedminster Press.

WEICK, K. (2001). *Making Sense of the Organization*. Oxford: Blackwell.

WEICK, K. E. and WESTLEY, F. (1996). 'Organizing for innovation'. In Clegg, S., Hardy, C. and Nord, W. (Eds), *Handbook of Organization Studies*. London: Sage, 424–40.

WESTENHOLZ, A. (1993). 'Paradoxical thinking and change in the frames of reference'. *Organization Studies*, **14**, 1, 37–58.

WOLFE, R. (1994). 'Organizational innovation: review, critique and suggested research directions'. *Journal of Management Studies*, **31**, 3, 405–31.

Part IV
Knowledge, Learning and Change

[16]

ORGANIZATION SCIENCE
Vol. 2, No. 1, February 1991
Printed in U.S.A.

ORGANIZATIONAL LEARNING AND COMMUNITIES-OF-PRACTICE: TOWARD A UNIFIED VIEW OF WORKING, LEARNING, AND INNOVATION*

JOHN SEELY BROWN AND PAUL DUGUID

Xerox Palo Alto Research Center and
Institute for Research on Learning, 2550 *Hanover Street*,
Palo Alto, *California* 94304
Institute for Research on Learning, 2550 *Hanover Street*,
Palo Alto, *California* 94304

Recent ethnographic studies of workplace practices indicate that the ways people actually work usually differ fundamentally from the ways organizations describe that work in manuals, training programs, organizational charts, and job descriptions. Nevertheless, organizations tend to rely on the latter in their attempts to understand and improve work practice. We examine one such study. We then relate its conclusions to compatible investigations of learning and of innovation to argue that conventional descriptions of jobs mask not only the ways people work, but also significant learning and innovation generated in the informal communities-of-practice in which they work. By reassessing work, learning, and innovation in the context of actual communities and actual practices, we suggest that the connections between these three become apparent. With a unified view of working, learning, and innovating, it should be possible to reconceive of and redesign organizations to improve all three.

(LEARNING; INNOVATION; GROUPS; DOWNSKILLING; ORGANIZATIONAL CULTURES NONCANONICAL PRACTICE)

Introduction

Working, learning, and innovating are closely related forms of human activity that are conventionally thought to conflict with each other. Work practice is generally viewed as conservative and resistant to change; learning is generally viewed as distinct from working and problematic in the face of change; and innovation is generally viewed as the disruptive but necessary imposition of change on the other two. To see that working, learning, and innovating are interrelated and compatible and thus potentially complementary, not conflicting forces requires a distinct conceptual shift. By bringing together recent research into working, learning, and innovating, we attempt to indicate the nature and explore the significance of such a shift.

The source of the oppositions perceived between working, learning, and innovating lies primarily in the gulf between precepts and practice. Formal descriptions of work (e.g., "office procedures") and of learning (e.g., "subject matter") are abstracted from actual practice. They inevitably and intentionally omit the details. In a society that attaches particular value to "abstract knowledge," the details of practice have come to be seen as nonessential, unimportant, and easily developed once the relevant abstractions have been grasped. Thus education, training, and technology design generally focus on abstract representations to the detriment, if not exclusion of actual practice. We, by contrast, suggest that practice is central to understanding work. Abstractions *detached from practice* distort or obscure intricacies of that practice. Without a clear understanding of those intricacies and the role they play, the practice itself cannot be well understood, engendered (through training), or enhanced (through innovation).

*Accepted by Lee S. Sproull and Michael D. Cohen.

1047-7039/91/0201/0040/$01.25

We begin by looking at the variance between a major organization's formal descriptions of work both in its training programs and manuals and the actual work practices performed by its members. Orr's (1990a, 1990b, 1987a, 1987b) detailed ethnographic studies of service technicians illustrate how an organization's view of work can overlook and even oppose what and who it takes to get a job done. Based on Orr's specific insights, we make the more general claim that reliance on espoused practice (which we refer to as *canonical practice*) can blind an organization's core to the actual, and usually valuable practices of its members (including *noncanonical practices*, such as "work arounds"). It is the actual practices, however, that determine the success or failure of organizations.

Next, we turn to learning and, in particular, to Lave and Wenger's (1990) practice-based theory of learning as "legitimate peripheral participation" in "communities-of-practice." Much conventional learning theory, including that implicit in most training courses, tends to endorse the valuation of abstract knowledge over actual practice and as a result to separate learning from working and, more significantly, learners from workers. Together Lave and Wenger's analysis and Orr's empirical investigation indicate that this knowledge–practice separation is unsound, both in theory and in practice. We argue that the composite concept of "learning-in-working" best represents the fluid evolution of learning through practice.

From this practice-based standpoint, we view learning as the bridge between working and innovating. We use Daft and Weick's (1984) interpretive account of "enacting" organizations to place innovation in the context of changes in a community's "way of seeing" or interpretive view. Both Orr's and Lave and Wenger's research emphasize that to understand working and learning, it is necessary to focus on the formation and change of the communities in which work takes place. Taking all three theories together, we argue that, through their constant adapting to changing membership and changing circumstances, evolving communities-of-practice are significant sites of innovating.

1. Working

a. *Canonical Practice*

Orr's (1990a, 1990b, 1987a, 1987b) ethnography of service technicians (reps) in training and at work in a large corporation paints a clear picture of the divergence between espoused practice and actual practice, of the ways this divergence develops, and of the trouble it can cause. His work provides a "thick" (see Geertz 1973), detailed description of the way work actually progresses. Orr contrasts his findings with the way the same work is thinly described in the corporation's manuals, training courses, and job descriptions.[1]

The importance of such an approach to work in progress is emphasized by Bourdieu (1973), who distinguishes the *modus operandi* from the *opus operatum* —that is, the way a task, as it unfolds over time, looks to someone at work on it, while many of the options and dilemmas remain unresolved, as opposed to the way it looks with hindsight as a finished task. (Ryle (1954) makes a similar point.) The *opus operatum*, the finished view, tends to see the action in terms of the task alone and cannot see the way in which the process of doing the task is actually structured by the constantly changing conditions of work and the world. Bourdieu makes a useful analogy with reference to a journey as actually carried out on the ground and as seen on a map ("an abstract space, devoid of any landmarks or any privileged centre" (p. 2)). The latter, like the *opus operatum*, inevitably smooths over the myriad

[1]For a historical overview of anthropology of the workplace, see Burawoy (1979).

decisions made with regard to changing conditions: road works, diversions, Memorial Day parades, earthquakes, personal fatigue, conflicting opinions, wrong-headed instructions, relations of authority, inaccuracies on the map, and the like. The map, though potentially useful, *by itself* provides little insight into how *ad hoc* decisions presented by changing conditions can be resolved (and, of course, each resolved decision changes the conditions once more). As a journey becomes more complex, the map increasingly conceals what is actually needed to make the journey. Thick description, by contrast, ascends from the abstraction to the concrete circumstances of actual practice, reconnecting the map and the mapped.

Orr's study shows how an organization's maps can dramatically distort its view of the routes its members take. This "misrecognition," as Bourdieu calls it, can be traced to many places, including pedagogic theory and practice. Often it has its more immediate cause in the strategy to downskill positions. Many organizations are willing to assume that complex tasks can be successfully mapped onto a set of simple, Tayloristic, canonical steps that can be followed without need of significant understanding or insight (and thus without need of significant investment in training or skilled technicians). But as Bourdieu, Suchman (1987a), and Orr show, actual practice inevitably involves tricky interpolations between abstract accounts and situated demands. Orr's reps' skills, for instance, are most evident in the improvised strategies they deploy to cope with the clash between prescriptive documentation and the sophisticated, yet unpredictable machines they work with. Nonetheless, in the corporation's eyes practices that deviate from the canonical are, by definition, deviant practices. Through a reliance on canonical descriptions (to the extent of overlooking even their own noncanonical improvisations), managers develop a conceptual outlook that cannot comprehend the importance of noncanonical practices. People are typically viewed as performing their jobs according to formal job descriptions, despite the fact that daily evidence points to the contrary (Suchman 1987b). They are held accountable to the map, not to road conditions.[2]

In Orr's case, the canonical map comes in the form of "directive" documentation aimed at "single point failures" of machines. Indeed, the documentation is less like a map than a single predetermined route with no alternatives: it provides a decision tree for diagnosis and repair that assumes both predictable machines and an unproblematic process of making diagnoses and repairs through blindly following diagnostic instructions. Both assumptions are mistaken. Abstractions of repair work fall short of the complexity of the actual practices from which they were abstracted. The account of actual practice we describe below is anything but the blind following of instructions.

The inadequacies of this corporation's directive approach actually make a rep's work more difficult to accomplish and thus perversely demands more, not fewer, improvisational skills. An ostensible downskilling and actual upskilling therefore proceed simultaneously. Although the documentation becomes more prescriptive and ostensibly more simple, in actuality the task becomes more improvisational and more complex. The reps develop sophisticated noncanonical practices to bridge the gulf between their corporation's canonical approach and successful work practices, laden with the dilemmas, inconsistencies, and unpredictability of everyday life. The directive documentation does not "deprive the workers of the skills they have;" rather, "it merely reduces the amount of information given them" (Orr 1990a, 26). The burden

[2]Not all the blame should be laid on the managers' desk. As several anthropologists, including Suchman (1987a) and Bourdieu (1977) point out, "informants" often describe their jobs in canonical terms though they carry them out in noncanonical ways. Lave (1988) argues that informants, like most people in our society, tend to privilege abstract knowledge. Thus they describe their actions in its terms.

of making up the difference between what is provided and what is needed then rests with the reps, who in bridging the gap actually protect the organization from its own shortsightedness. If the reps adhered to the canonical approach, their corporation's services would be in chaos.

Because this corporation's training programs follow a similar downskilling approach, the reps regard them as generally unhelpful. As a result, a wedge is driven between the corporation and its reps: the corporation assumes the reps are untrainable, uncooperative, and unskilled; whereas the reps view the overly simplistic training programs as a reflection of the corporation's low estimation of their worth and skills. In fact, their valuation is a testament to the depth of the rep's insight. They recognize the superficiality of the training because they are conscious of the full complexity of the technology and what it takes to keep it running. The corporation, on the other hand, blinkered by its implicit faith in formal training and canonical practice and its misinterpretation of the rep's behavior, is unable to appreciate either aspect of their insight.

In essence, Orr shows that in order to do their job the reps must—and do—learn to make better sense of the machines they work with than their employer either expects or allows. Thus they develop their understanding of the machine not in the training programs, but in the very conditions from which the programs separate them—the authentic activity of their daily work. For the reps (and for the corporation, though it is unaware of it), learning-in-working is an occupational necessity.

b. *Noncanonical Practice*

Orr's analyses of actual practice provide various examples of how the reps diverge from canonical descriptions. For example, on one service call (Orr 1990b, 1987b) a rep confronted a machine that produced copious raw information in the form of error codes and obligingly crashed when tested. But the error codes and the nature of the crashes did not tally. Such a case immediately fell outside the directive training and documentation provided by the organization, which tie errors to error codes. Unfortunately, the problem also fell outside the rep's accumulated, improvised experience. He summoned his technical specialist, whose job combines "trouble-shooting consultant, supervisor, and occasional instructor." The specialist was equally baffled. Yet, though the canonical approach to repair was exhausted, with their combined range of noncanonical practices, the rep and technical specialist still had options to pursue.

One option—indeed the only option left by canonical practice now that its strategies for repair had been quickly exhausted—was to abandon repair altogether and to replace the malfunctioning machine. But both the rep and the specialist realized that the resulting loss of face for the company, loss of the customer's faith in the reps, loss of their own credit within their organization, and loss of money to the corporation made this their last resort. Loss of face or faith has considerable ramifications beyond mere embarrassment. A rep's ability to enlist the future support of customers and colleagues is jeopardized. There is evidently strong social pressure from a variety of sources to solve problems without exchanging machines. The reps' work is not simply about maintaining machines; it is also and equally importantly, about maintaining social relations: "A large part of service work might better be described as repair and maintenance of the social setting" (Orr 1990b, 169). The training and documentation, of course, are about maintaining machines.

Solving the problem *in situ* required constructing a coherent account of the malfunction out of the incoherence of the data and documentation. To do this, the rep and the specialist embarked on a long story-telling procedure. The machine, with its erratic behavior, mixed with information from the user and memories from the technicians, provided essential ingredients that the two aimed to account for in a composite story. The process of forming a story was, centrally, one of diagnosis. This process, it should be noted, *begins* as well as ends in a communal understanding of the machine that is wholly unavailable from the canonical documents.

While they explored the machine or waited for it to crash, the rep and specialist (with contributions from the ethnographer) recalled and discussed other occasions on which they had encountered some of the present symptoms. Each story presented an exchangeable account that could be examined and reflected upon to provoke old memories and new insights. Yet more tests and more stories were thereby generated.

> The key element of diagnosis is the situated production of understanding through narration, in that the integration of the various facts of the situation is accomplished through a verbal consideration of those facts with a primary criterion of coherence. The process is situated, in Suchman's terms, in that both the damaged machine and the social context of the user site are essential resources for both the definition of the problem and its resolution . . . . They are faced with a failing machine displaying diagnostic information which has previously proved worthless and in which no one has any particular confidence this time. They do not know where they are going to find the information they need to understand and solve this problem. In their search for inspiration, they tell stories (Orr 1990b, 178–179).

The story-telling process continued throughout the morning, over lunch, and back in front of the machine, throughout the afternoon, forming a long but purposeful progression from incoherence to coherence: "The final trouble-shooting session was a five hour effort . . . . This session yielded a dozen anecdotes told during the trouble shooting, taking a variety of forms and serving a variety of purposes" (Orr 1990b, 10).

Ultimately, these stories generated sufficient interplay among memories, tests, the machine's responses, and the ensuing insights to lead to diagnosis and repair. The final diagnosis developed from what Orr calls an "antiphonal recitation" in which the two told different versions of the same story: "They are talking about personal encounters with the same problem, but the two versions are significantly different" (Orr 1987b, 177). Through story-telling, these separate experiences converged, leading to a shared diagnosis of certain previously encountered but unresolved symptoms. The two (and the ethnographer) had constructed a communal interpretation of hitherto uninterpretable data and individual experience. Rep and specialist were now in a position to modify previous stories and build a more insightful one. They both increased their own understanding and added to their community's collective knowledge. Such stories are passed around, becoming part of the repertoire available to all reps. Orr reports hearing a concise, assimilated version of this particular false error code passed among reps over a game of cribbage in the lunch room three months later (Orr 1990b, 181ff.). A story, once in the possession of the community, can then be used—and further modified—in similar diagnostic sessions.

c. *Central Features of Work Practice*

In this section, we analyze Orr's thick description of the rep's practice through the overlapping categories, "narration," "collaboration," and "social construction"—categories that get to the heart of what the reps do and yet which, significantly, have no place in the organization's abstracted, canonical accounts of their work.

Narration. The first aspect of the reps' practice worth highlighting is the extensive narration used. This way of working is quite distinct from following the branches of decision tree. Stories and their telling can reflect the complex social web within which work takes place and the relationship of the narrative, narrator, and audience to the specific events of practice. The stories have a flexible generality that makes them both adaptable and particular. They function, rather like the common law, as a usefully underconstrained means to interpret each new situation in the light of accumulated wisdom and constantly changing circumstances.

The practice of creating and exchanging of stories has two important aspects. First of all, telling stories helps to diagnose the state of a troublesome machine. Reps begin by extracting a history from the users of the machine, the users' story, and with this and the machine as their starting point, they construct their own account. If they cannot tell an adequate story on their own, then they seek help—either by summoning a specialist, as in the case above, or by discussing the problem with colleagues over coffee or lunch. If necessary, they work together at the machine, articulating hunches, insights, misconceptions, and the like, to dissect and augment their developing understanding. Story telling allows them to keep track of the sequences of behavior and of their theories, and thereby to work towards a coherent account of the current state of the machine. The reps try to impose coherence on an apparently random sequence of events in order that they can decide what to do next. Unlike the documentation, which tells reps *what* to do but not *why*, the reps' stories help them develop causal accounts of machines, which are essential when documentation breaks down. (As we have suggested, documentation, like machines, will always break down, however well it is designed.) What the reps do in their story telling is develop a causal map out of their experience to replace the impoverished directive route that they have been furnished by the corporation. In the absence of such support, the reps Orr studied cater to their own needs as well as they can. Their narratives yield a story of the machine fundamentally different from the prescriptive account provided by the documentation, a story that is built in response to the particulars of breakdown.

Despite the assumptions behind the downskilling process, to do their job in any significant sense, reps need these complex causal stories and they produce and circulate them as part of their regular noncanonical work practice. An important part of the reps' skill, though not recognized by the corporation, comprises the ability to create, to trade, and to understand highly elliptical, highly referential, and to the initiated, highly informative war stories. Zuboff (1988) in her analysis of the skills people develop working on complex systems describes similar cases of story telling and argues that it is a necessary practice for dealing with "smart" but unpredictable machines. The irony, as Orr points out, is that for purposes of diagnosis the reps have no smart machines, just inadequate documentation and "their own very traditional skills."

It is worth stressing at this point that we are not arguing that communities simply can and thus should work without assistance from trainers and the corporation in general. Indeed, we suggest in our conclusion that situations inevitably occur when group improvisation simply cannot bridge the gap between what the corporation supplies and what a particular community actually needs. What we are claiming is that corporations must provide support that corresponds to the real needs of the community rather than just to the abstract expectations of the corporation. And what those needs are can only be understood by understanding the details and sophistications of actual practice. In Orr's account, what the reps needed was the means to understand the machine causally and to relate this causal map to the inevitable intricacies of practice. To discern such needs, however, will require that corporations develop a less formal and more practice-based approach to communities and their work.

The second characteristic of story telling is that the stories also act as repositories of accumulated wisdom. In particular, community narratives protect the reps' ability to work from the ravages of modern idealizations of work and related downskilling practices. In Orr's example, the canonical decision trees, privileging the decontextualized over the situated, effectively sweep away the clutter of practice. But it is in the face of just this clutter that the reps' skills are needed. Improvisational skills that allow the reps to circumvent the inadequacies of both the machines and the documentation are not only developed but also preserved in community story telling.

Jordan's (1989) work similarly draws attention to the central, dual role of informal stories. She studied the clash between midwifery as it is prescribed by officials from Mexico City and as it is practiced in rural Yucatan. The officials ignore important details and realities of practice. For instance, the officials instruct the midwives in practices that demand sterile instruments though the midwives work in villages that lack adequate means for sterilization. The midwives' noncanonical practices, however, circumvent the possibility of surgical operations being carried out with unsterile instruments. These effective practices survive, despite the government's worryingly decontextualized attempts to replace them with canonical practices, through story telling. Jordan notes that the two aspects of story telling, diagnosis and preservation, are inseparable. Orr also suggests that "The use of story-telling both to preserve knowledge and to consider it in subsequent diagnoses coincides with the narrative character of diagnosis" (Orr 1990b, 178). We have pulled them apart for the purpose of analysis only.

Collaboration. Based as it is on shared narratives, a second important aspect of the reps' work is that it is obviously communal and thereby *collaborative*. In Orr's example, the rep and specialist went through a collective, not individual process. Not only is the learning in this case inseparable from working, but also individual learning is inseparable from collective learning. The insight accumulated is not a private substance, but socially constructed and distributed. Thus, faced with a difficult problem reps like to work together and to discuss problems in groups. In the case of this particular problem, the individual rep tried what he knew, failed, and there met his limits. With the specialist he was able to trade stories, develop insights, and construct new options. Each had a story about the condition of the machine, but it was in telling it antiphonally that the significance emerged.

While it might seem trivial, it is important to emphasize the collaborative work within the reps' community, for in the corporation's eyes their work is viewed individually. Their documentation and training implicitly maintain that the work is individual and the central relationship of the rep is that between an individual and the corporation:

> The activities defined by management are those which one worker will do, and work as the relationship of employment is discussed in terms of a single worker's relationship to the corporation. I suspect the incidence of workers alone in relations of employment is quite low, and the existence of coworkers must contribute to those activities done in the name of work.... The fact that work is commonly done by a group of workers together is only sometimes acknowledged in the literature, and the usual presence of such a community has not entered into the definition of work (Orr 1990a, 15).

In fact, as Orr's studies show, not only do reps work with specialists, as in the example given here, but throughout the day they meet for coffee or for meals and trade stories back and forth.

Social Construction. A third important aspect of Orr's account of practice, and one which is interfused with the previous two and separated here only to help in clarification, involves *social construction*. This has two parts. First and most evident in Orr's example, the reps constructed a shared understanding out of bountiful conflicting and confusing data. This constructed understanding reflects the reps' view of the world. They developed a *rep's* model of the machine, not a trainer's, which had already proved unsatisfactory, nor even an engineer's, which was not available to them (and might well have been unhelpful, though Orr interestingly points out that reps cultivate connections throughout the corporation to help them circumvent the barriers to understanding built by their documentation and training). The reps' view, evident in their stories, interweaves generalities about "this model" with particularities about "this site" and "this machine."

Such an approach is highly situated and highly improvisational. Reps respond to whatever the situation itself—both social and physical—throws at them, a process very similar to Levi-Strauss's (1966) concept of *bricolage*: the ability to "make do with 'whatever is to hand'" (p. 17). What reps need for *bricolage* are not the partial, rigid models of the sort directive documentation provides, but help to build, *ad hoc* and collaboratively, robust models that do justice to particular difficulties in which they find themselves. Hutchins, in his analysis of navigation teams in the U.S. Navy (in press, 1991), similarly notes the way in which understanding is constructed within and distributed throughout teams.

The second feature of social construction, as important but less evident than the first, is that in telling these stories an individual rep contributes to the construction and development of his or her own identity as a rep and reciprocally to the construction and development of the community of reps in which he or she works. Individually, in telling stories the rep is becoming a member. Orr notes, "this construction of their identity as technicians occurs both in doing the work and in their stories, and their stories of themselves fixing machines show their world in what they consider the appropriate perspective" (Orr 1990b, 187). Simultaneously and interdependently, the reps are contributing to the construction and evolution of the community that they are joining—what we might call a "community of interpretation," for it is through the continual development of these communities that the shared means for interpreting complex activity get formed, transformed, and transmitted.

The significance of both these points should become apparent in the following sections, first, as we turn to a theory of learning (Lave and Wenger's) that, like Orr's analysis of work, takes formation of identity and community membership as central units of analysis; and second as we argue that innovation can be seen as at base a function of changes in community values and views.

2. Learning

The theories of learning implicated in the documentation and training view learning from the abstract stance of pedagogy. Training is thought of as the *transmission* of explicit, abstract knowledge from the head of someone who knows to the head of someone who does not in surroundings that specifically exclude the complexities of practice and the communities of practitioners. The setting for learning is simply assumed not to matter.

Concepts of knowledge or information transfer, however, have been under increasing attack in recent years from a variety of sources (e.g., Reddy 1979). In particular, learning theorists (e.g. Lave 1988; Lave and Wenger 1990) have rejected transfer models, which isolate knowledge from practice, and developed a view of learning as social construction, putting knowledge back into the contexts in which it has meaning (see also Brown, Collins, and Duguid 1989; Brown and Duguid, in press; Pea 1990). From this perspective, learners can in one way or another be seen to construct their understanding out of a wide range of materials that include ambient social and physical circumstances and the histories and social relations of the people involved. Like a magpie with a nest, learning is built out of the materials to hand and in relation to the structuring resources of local conditions. (For the importance of including the structuring resources in any account of learning, see Lave 1988.) What is learned is profoundly connected to the conditions in which it is learned.

Lave and Wenger (1990), with their concept of *legitimate peripheral participation* (LPP), provide one of the most versatile accounts of this constructive view of learning. LPP, it must quickly be asserted, is *not* a method of education. It is an analytical category or tool for understanding learning across different methods, different historical periods, and different social and physical environments. It attempts to account for learning, not teaching or instruction. Thus this approach escapes problems that arise through examinations of learning from pedagogy's viewpoint. It makes the conditions of learning, rather than just abstract subject matter, central to understanding what is learned.

Learning, from the viewpoint of LPP, essentially involves becoming an "insider." Learners do not receive or even construct abstract, "objective," individual knowledge; rather, they learn to function in a community—be it a community of nuclear physicists, cabinet makers, high school classmates, street-corner society, or, as in the case under study, service technicians. They acquire that particular community's subjective viewpoint and learn to speak its language. In short, they are enculturated (Brown, Collins, and Duguid 1989). Learners are acquiring not explicit, formal "expert knowledge," but the embodied ability to behave as community members. For example, learners learn to tell and appreciate community-appropriate stories, discovering in doing so, all the narrative-based resources we outlined above. As Jordan (1989) argues in her analysis of midwifery, "To acquire a store of appropriate stories and, even more importantly, to know what are appropriate occasions for telling them, is then part of what it means to become a midwife" (p. 935).

Workplace learning is best understood, then, in terms of the communities being formed or joined and personal identities being changed. The central issue in learning is *becoming* a practitioner not learning *about* practice. This approach draws attention away from abstract knowledge and cranial processes and situates it in the practices and communities in which knowledge takes on significance. Learning about new devices, such as the machines Orr's technicians worked with, is best understood (and best achieved) in the context of the community in which the devices are used and that community's particular interpretive conventions. Lave and Wenger argue that learning, understanding, and interpretation involve a great deal that is not explicit or explicable, developed and framed in a crucially *communal* context.

Orr's study reveals this sort of learning going on in the process of and inseparable from work. The rep was not just an observer of the technical specialist. He was also an important participant in this process of diagnosis and story telling, whose participation could legitimately grow in from the periphery as a function of his developing understanding not of some extrinsically structured training. His legitimacy here is an important function of the social relations between the different levels of service technician, which are surprisingly egalitarian, perhaps as a result of the inherent incoherence of the problems this sort of technology presents: a specialist cannot hope to exert hierarchical control over knowledge that he or she must first construct cooperatively. "Occupational communities... have little hierarchy; the only real status is that of member" (Orr 1990a, 33).

a. *Groups and Communities*

Having characterized both working and learning in terms of communities, it is worth pausing to establish relations between our own account and recent work on groups in the workplace. Much important work has been done in this area (see, for example, the collections by Hackman (1990) and Goodman and Associates (1988)) and many of the findings support our own view of work activity. There is, however, a significant distinction between our views and this work. Group theory in general focuses on groups as canonical, bounded entities that lie within an organization and that are organized or at least sanctioned by that organization and its view of tasks. (See Hackman 1990, pp. 4–5.). The communities that we discern are, by contrast, often noncanonical and not recognized by the organization. They are more fluid and interpenetrative than bounded, often crossing the restrictive boundaries of the organization to incorporate people from outside. (Orr's reps can in an important sense be said to work in a community that includes both suppliers and customers.) Indeed, the canonical organization becomes a questionable unit of analysis from this perspective. And significantly, communities are emergent. That is to say their shape and membership emerges in the process of activity, as opposed to being created to carry out a task. (Note, by contrast, how much of the literature refers to the *design* or *creation* of new groups (e.g. Goodman and Associates 1988). From our viewpoint, the central questions more involve the *detection* and *support* of emergent or existing communities.)

If this distinction is correct then it has two particularly important corollaries. First, work practice and learning need to be understood not in terms of the groups that are ordained (e.g. "task forces" or "trainees"), but in terms of the communities that emerge. The latter are likely to be noncanonical (though not necessarily so) while the former are likely to be canonical. Looking only at canonical groups, whose configuration often conceals extremely influential interstitial communities, will not provide a clear picture of how work or learning is actually organized and accomplished. It will only reflect the dominant assumptions of the organizational core.

Second, attempts to introduce "teams" and "work groups" into the workplace to enhance learning or work practice are often based on an assumption that without impetus from above, an organization's members configure themselves as individuals. In fact, as we suggest, people work and learn collaboratively and vital interstitial communities are continually being formed and reformed. The reorganization of the workplace into canonical groups can wittingly or unwittingly disrupt these highly functional noncanonical—and therefore often invisible—communities. Orr argues:

> The process of working and learning together creates a work situation which the workers value, and they resist having it disrupted by their employers through events such as a reorganization of the work. This resistance can surprise employers who think of labor as a commodity to arrange to suit their ends. The problem for the workers is that this community which they have created was not part of the series of discrete employment agreements by which the employer populated the work place, nor is the role of the community in doing the work acknowledged. *The work can only continue free of disruption if the employer can be persuaded to see the community as necessary to accomplishing work* (Orr 1990, 48, emphasis added).

b. *Fostering Learning*

Given a community-based analysis of learning so congruent with Orr's analysis of working, the question arises, how is it possible to foster learning-in-working? The answer is inevitably complex, not least because all the intricacies of context, which the pedagogic approach has always assumed could be stripped away, now have to be taken back into consideration. On the other hand, the ability of people to learn *in situ*, suggests that as a fundamental principle for supporting learning, attempts to strip away context should be examined with caution. If learners need access to practitioners at work, it is essential to question didactic approaches, with their tendency to separate learners from the target community and the authentic work practices. Learning is fostered by fostering access to and membership of the target community-of-practice, not by explicating abstractions of individual practice. Thus central to the process are the recognition and legitimation of community practices.

Reliance on formal descriptions of work, explicit syllabuses for learning about it, and canonical groups to carry it out immediately set organizations at a disadvantage. This approach, as we have noted, can simply blind management to the practices and communities that actually make things happen. In particular, it can lead to the isolation of learners, who will then be unable to acquire the implicit practices required for work. Marshall (in Lave and Wenger 1990) describes a case of apprenticeship for butchers in which learning was extremely restricted because, among other things, "apprentices... could not watch journeymen cut and saw meat" (p. 19). Formal training in cutting and sawing is quite different from the understanding of practice gleaned through informal observation that copresence makes possible and absence obviously excludes. These trainees were simply denied the chance to become legitimate peripheral participants. If training is designed so that learners cannot observe the activity of practitioners, learning is inevitably impoverished.

Legitimacy and peripherality are intertwined in a complex way. Occasionally, learners (like the apprentice butchers) are granted legitimacy but are denied peripherality. Conversely, they can be granted peripherality but denied legitimacy. Martin (1982) gives examples of organizations in which legitimacy is explicitly denied in instances of "open door" management, where members come to realize that, though the door is open, it is wiser not to cross the threshold. If either legitimacy or peripherality is denied, learning will be significantly more difficult.

For learners, then, a position on the periphery of practice is important. It is also easily overlooked and increasingly risks being "designed out," leaving people physically or socially isolated and justifiably uncertain whether, for instance, their errors are inevitable or the result of personal inadequacies. It is a significant challenge for design to ensure that new collaborative technologies, designed as they so often are around formal descriptions of work, do not exclude this sort of implicit, extendable, informal periphery. Learners need legitimate access to the periphery of communication—to computer mail, to formal and informal meetings, to telephone conversations, etc., and, of course, to war stories. They pick up invaluable "know how"—not just information but also manner and technique—from being on the periphery of competent practitioners going about their business. Furthermore, it is important to consider the periphery not only because it is an important site of learning, but also because, as the next section proposes, it can be an important site for innovation.

3. Innovating

One of the central benefits of these small, self-constituting communities we have been describing is that they evade the ossifying tendencies of large organizations. Canonical accounts of work are not only hard to apply and hard to learn. They are also hard to change. Yet the actual behaviors of communities-of-practice are constantly changing both as newcomers replace old timers and as the demands of practice force the community to revise its relationship to its environment. Communities-of-practice like the reps' continue to develop a rich, fluid, noncanonical world view to bridge the gap between their organization's static canonical view and the challenge of changing practice. This process of development is inherently innovative. "Maverick" communities of this sort offer the core of a large organization a means and a model to examine the potential of alternative views of organizational activity through spontaneously occurring experiments that are simultaneously informed and checked by experience. These, it has been argued (Hedberg, Nystrom and Starbuck

1976; Schein 1990), drive innovation by allowing the parts of an organization to step outside the organization's inevitably limited core world view and simply try something new. Unfortunately, people in the core of large organizations too often regard these noncanonical practices (if they see them at all) as counterproductive.

For a theoretical account of this sort of innovation, we turn to Daft and Weick's (1984) discussion of interpretive innovation. They propose a matrix of four different kinds of organization, each characterized by its relationship to its environment. They name these relationships "undirected viewing," "conditioned viewing," "discovering," and "enacting." Only the last two concern us here. It is important to note that Daft and Weick too see the community and not the individual "inventor" as the central unit of analysis in understanding innovating practice.

The *discovering organization* is the archetype of the conventional innovative organization, one which responds—often with great efficiency—to changes it detects in its environment. The organization presupposes an essentially prestructured environment and implicitly assumes that there is a correct response to any condition it discovers there. By contrast, the *enacting organization* is proactive and highly interpretive. Not only does it respond to its environment, but also, in a fundamental way, it creates many of the conditions to which it must respond. Daft and Weick describe enacting organizations as follows:

> These organizations construct their own environments. They gather information by trying new behaviors and seeing what happens. They experiment, test, and stimulate, and they ignore precedent, rules, and traditional expectations (Daft and Weick 1984, p. 288).

Innovation, in this view, is not simply a response to empirical observations of the environment. The source of innovation lies on the interface between an organization and its environment. And the process of innovating involves actively constructing a conceptual framework, imposing it on the environment, and reflecting on their interaction. With few changes, this could be a description of the activity of inventive, noncanonical groups, such as Orr's reps, who similarly "ignore precedent, rules, and traditional expectations" and break conventional boundaries. Like story telling, enacting is a process of interpretive sense making and controlled change.

A brief example of enacting can be seen in the introduction of the IBM Mag-I memory typewriter "as a new way of organizing office work" (Pava cited in Barley 1988). In order to make sense and full use of the power of this typewriter, the conditions in which it was to be used had to be reconceived. In the old conception of office work, the potential of the machine could not be realized. In a newly conceived understanding of office practice, however, the machine could prove highly innovative. Though this new conception could not be achieved without the new machine, the new machine could not be fully realized without the conception. The two changes went along together. Neither is wholly either cause or effect. Enacting organizations differ from discovering ones in that in this reciprocal way, instead of waiting for changed practices to emerge and responding, they enable them to emerge and anticipate their effects.

Reregistering the environment is widely recognized as a powerful source of innovation that moves organizations beyond the paradigms in which they begin their analysis and within which, without such a reformation, they must inevitably end it. This is the problem which Deetz and Kersten (1983) describe as closure: "Many organizations fail because . . . closure prohibits adaptation to current social conditions" (p. 166). Putnam (1983) argues that closure-generating structures appear to be "fixtures that exist independent of the processes that create and transform them" (p. 36). Interpretive or enacting organizations, aware as they are that their environment is not a given, can potentially adopt new viewpoints that allow them to see beyond the closure-imposing boundary of a single world view.

The question remains, however, how is this reregistering brought about by organizations that seem inescapably trapped within their own world view? We are claiming that the actual noncanonical practices of interstitial communities are continually developing new interpretations of the world because they have a practical rather than formal connection to that world. (For a theoretical account of the way practice drives change in world view, see Bloch 1977.) To pursue our connection with the work of the reps, closure is the likely result of rigid adherence to the reps' training and documentation and the formal account of work that they encompass. In order to get on with their work, reps overcome closure by reregistering their interpretation of the machine and its ever changing milieu. Rejection of a canonical, predetermined view and the construction through narration of an alternative view, such as Orr describes, involve, at heart, the complex intuitive process of bringing the communicative, community schema into harmony with the environment by reformulating both. The potential of such innovation is, however, lost to an organization that remains blind to noncanonical practice.

An enacting organization must also be capable of reconceiving not only its environment but also its own identity, for in a significant sense the two are mutually constitutive. Again, this reconceptualization is something that people who develop noncanonical practices are continuously doing, forging their own and their community's identity in their own terms so that they can break out of the restrictive hold of the formal descriptions of practice. Enacting organizations similarly regard both their environment and themselves as in some sense unanalyzed and therefore malleable. They do not assume that there is an ineluctable structure, a "right" answer, or a universal view to be discovered; rather, they continually look for innovative ways to impose new structure, ask new questions, develop a new view, become a new organization. By asking different questions, by seeking different *sorts* of explanations, and by looking from different points of view, different answers emerge—indeed different environments and different organizations mutually reconstitute each other dialectically or reciprocally. Daft and Weick (1984) argue, the interpretation can "shape the environment more than the environment shapes the interpretation" (p. 287).

Carlson's attempts to interest people in the idea of dry photocopying—xerography—provide an example of organizational tendencies to resist enacting innovation. Carlson and the Batelle Institute, which backed his research, approached most of the major innovative corporations of the time—RCA, IBM, A. B. Dick, Kodak. All turned down the idea of a dry copier. They did not reject a flawed machine. Indeed, they all agreed that it worked. But they rejected the *concept* of an office copier. They could see no use for it. Even when Haloid bought the patent, the marketing firms they hired consistently reported that the new device had no role in office practice (Dessauer 1971). In some sense it was necessary both for Haloid to reconceive itself (as Xerox) and for Xerox's machine to help bring about a reconceptualization of an area of office practice for the new machine to be put into manufacture and use.

What the evaluations saw was that an expensive machine was not needed to make a record copy of original documents. For the most part, carbon paper already did that admirably and cheaply. What they failed to see was that a copier allowed the proliferation of copies and of copies of copies. The quantitative leap in copies and their importance independent of the original then produced a qualitative leap in the way they were used. They no longer served merely as records of an original. Instead, they participated in the productive interactions of organizations' members in a unprecedented way. (See Latour's (1986) description of the organizational role of "immutable mobiles.") Only in use in the office, enabling and enhancing new forms of work, did the copier forge the conceptual lenses under which its value became inescapable.

It is this process of seeing the world anew that allows organizations reciprocally to see themselves anew and to overcome discontinuities in their environment and their structure. As von Hippel (1988), Barley (1988), and others point out, innovating is not always radical. Incremental improvements occur throughout an innovative organization. Enacting and innovating can be conceived of as at root sense-making, congruence-seeking, identity-building activities of the sort engaged in by the reps. Innovating and learning in daily activity lie at one end of a continuum of innovating practices that stretches to radical innovation cultivated in research laboratories at the far end.

Alternative world views, then, do not lie in the laboratory or strategic planning office alone, condemning everyone else in the organization to submit to a unitary culture. Alternatives are inevitably distributed throughout all the different communities that make up the organization. For it is the organization's communities, at all levels, who are in contact with the environment and involved in interpretive sense making, congruence finding, and adapting. It is from any site of such interactions that new insights can be coproduced. If an organizational core overlooks or curtails the enacting in its midst by ignoring or disrupting its communities-of-practice, it threatens its own survival in two ways. It will not only threaten to destroy the very working and learning practices by which it, knowingly or unknowingly, survives. It will also cut itself off from a major source of potential innovation that inevitably arises in the course of that working and learning.

4. Conclusion: Organizations as Communities-of-Communities

The complex of contradictory forces that put an organization's assumptions and core beliefs in direct conflict with members' working, learning, and innovating arises from a thorough misunderstanding of what working, learning, and innovating are. As a result of such misunderstandings, many modern processes and technologies, particularly those designed to downskill, threaten the robust working, learning, and innovating communities and practice of the workplace. Between Braverman's (1974) pessimistic view and Adler's (1987) optimistic one, lies Barley's (1988) complex argument, pointing out that the intent to downskill does not *necessarily* lead to downskilling (as Orr's reps show). But the intent to downskill may first drive noncanonical practice and communities yet further underground so that the insights gained through work are more completely hidden from the organization as a whole. Then later changes or reorganizations, whether or not intended to downskill, may disrupt what they do not notice. The gap between espoused and actual practice may become too large for noncanonical practices to bridge.

To foster working, learning, and innovating, an organization must close that gap. To do so, it needs to reconceive of itself as a community-of-communities, acknowledging in the process the many noncanonical communities in its midst. It must see beyond its canonical abstractions of practice to the rich, full-blooded activities themselves. And it must legitimize and support the myriad enacting activities perpetrated by its different members. This support cannot be intrusive, or it risks merely bringing potential innovators under the restrictive influence of the existing canonical view. Rather, as others have argued (Nystrom and Starbuck 1984; Hedberg 1981; Schein 1990) communities-of-practice must be allowed some latitude to shake themselves free of received wisdom.

A major entailment of this argument may be quite surprising. Conventional wisdom tends to hold that large organizations are particularly poor at innovating and adapting. Tushman and Anderson (1988), for example, argue justifiably that the *typical*, large organization is unlikely to produce discontinuous innovation. But size may not be the single determining feature here. Large, *atypical*, enacting organizations have the potential to be highly innovative and adaptive. Within an organization perceived as a collective of communities, not simply of individuals, in which enacting experiments are legitimate, separate community perspectives can be amplified by interchanges among communities. Out of this friction of competing ideas can come the sort of improvisational sparks necessary for igniting organizational innovation. Thus large organizations, *reflectively structured*, are perhaps particularly well positioned to be highly innovative and to deal with discontinuities. If their internal communities have a reasonable degree of autonomy and independence from the dominant world view, large organizations might actually accelerate innovation. Such organizations are uniquely positioned to generate innovative discontinuities incrementally, thereby diminishing the disruptiveness of the periodic radical reorganization that Nadler calls "frame breaking" (Nadler 1988). This occurs when conventional organizations swing wholesale from one paradigm to another (see also Bartunek 1984). An organization whose core is aware that it is the synergistic aggregate of agile, semiautonomous, self-constituting communities and not a brittle monolith is likely to be capable of extensible "frame bending" well beyond conventional breaking point.

The important interplay of separate communities with independent (though interrelated) world views may in part account for von Hippel's (1988) account of the sources of innovation and other descriptions of the innovative nature of business alliances. Von Hippel argues that sources of innovation can lie outside an organization among its customers and suppliers. Emergent communities of the sort we have outlined that span the boundaries of an organization would then seem a likely conduit of external and innovative views into an organization. Similarly, the alliances Powell describes bring together different organizations with different interpretive schemes so that the composite group they make up has several enacting options to choose from. Because the separate communities enter as independent members of an alliance rather than as members of a rigid hierarchy, the alternative conceptual viewpoints are presumably legitimate and do not get hidden from the core. There is no concealed noncanonical practice where there is no concealing canonical practice.

The means to harness innovative energy in any enacting organization or alliance must ultimately be considered in the design of organizational architecture and the ways communities are linked to each other. This architecture should preserve and enhance the healthy autonomy of communities, while simultaneously building an interconnectedness through which to disseminate the results of separate communities' experiments. In some form or another the stories that support learning-in-working and innovation should be allowed to circulate. The technological potential to support this distribution—e-mail, bulletin boards, and other devices that are capable of supporting narrative exchanges—is available. But narratives, as we have argued, are embedded in the social system in which they arise and are used. They cannot simply be uprooted and repackaged for circulation without becoming prey to exactly those problems that beset the old abstracted canonical accounts. Moreover, information cannot be assumed to circulate freely just because technology to support circulation is available (Feldman and March 1981). Eckert (1989), for instance, argues that information travels differently within different socio-economic groups. Organizational assumptions that given the "right" medium people will exchange information freely overlook the way in which certain socio-economic groups, organizations, and in particular, corporations, implicitly treat information as a commodity to be hoarded and exchanged. Working-class groups, Eckert contends, do pass information freely and Orr (1990a) notes that the reps are remarkably open with each other about what they know. *Within* these communities, news travels fast; community knowledge is readily available to community members. But these communities must function within corporations that treat information as a commodity and that have superior bargaining power in negotiating the terms of exchange. In such unequal conditions, internal communities cannot reasonably be expected to surrender their knowledge freely.

As we have been arguing throughout, to understand the way information is constructed and travels within an organization, it is first necessary to understand the different communities that are formed within it and the distribution of power among them. Conceptual reorganization to accommodate learning-in-working and innovation, then, must stretch from the level of individual communities-of-practice and the technology and practices used there to the level of the overarching organizational architecture, the community-of-communities.

It has been our unstated assumption that a unified understanding of working, learning, and innovating is potentially highly beneficial, allowing, it seems likely, a synergistic collaboration rather than a conflicting separation among workers, learners, and innovators. But similarly, we have left unstated the companion assumption that attempts to foster such synergy through a conceptual reorganization will produce enormous difficulties from the perspective of the conventional workplace. Work and learning are set out in formal descriptions so that people (and organizations) can be held accountable; groups are organized to define responsibility; organizations are bounded to enhance concepts of competition; peripheries are closed off to maintain secrecy and privacy. Changing the way these things are arranged will produce problems as well as benefits. An examination of both problems and benefits has been left out of this paper, whose single purpose has been to show where constraints and resources lie, rather than the rewards and costs of deploying them. Our argument is simply that for working, learning, and innovating to thrive collectively depends on linking these three, in theory and in practice, more closely, more realistically, and more reflectively than is generally the case at present.

Acknowledgments

This paper was written at the Institute for Research on Learning with the invaluable help of many of our colleagues, in particular Jean Lave, Julian Orr, and Etienne Wenger, whose work, with that of Daft and Weick, provides the canonical texts on which we based our commentary.

References

ADLER, P. S. (1987), "Automation and Skill: New Directions," *International Journal of Technology Management* 2 [5/6], 761–771.

BARLEY, S. R. (1988), "Technology, Power, and the Social Organization of Work: Towards a Pragmatic Theory of Skilling and Deskilling," *Research in the Sociology of Organizations*, 6, 33–80.

BARTUNEK, J. M. (1984), "Changing Interpretive Schemes and Organizational Restructuring: The Example of a Religious Order," *Administrative Science Quarterly*, 29, 355–372.

BOURDIEU, P. (1977), *Outline of a Theory of Practice*, trans R. Nice. Cambridge: Cambridge University Press. (First published in French, 1973.)

BLOCH, M. (1977), "The Past and the Present in the Present," *Man*[*NS*], 12, 278–292.

BRAVERMAN, H. (1974), *Labor and Monopoly Capitalism*: *The Degradation of Work in the Twentieth Century*, New York: Monthly Review Press.

BROWN, J. S. AND P. DUGUID, (in press), "Enacting Design," in P. Adler (Ed.), *Designing Automation for Usability*, New York: Oxford University Press.

BROWN, J. S., A. COLLINS AND P. DUGUID (1989), "Situated Cognition and the Culture of Learning," *Education Researcher*, 18, 1, 32–42. (Also available in a fuller version as IRL Report 88-0008, Palo Alto, CA: Institute for Research on Learning.)

BURAWOY, M. (1979), "The Anthropology of Industrial Work," *Annual Review of Anthropology*, 8, 231–266.

DAFT, R. L. AND K. E. WEICK (1984), "Toward a Model of Organizations as Interpretation Systems," *Academy of Management Review*, 9, 2, 284–295.

DEETZ, S. A. AND A. KERSTEN (1983), "Critical Models of Interpretive Research," in L. L. Putnam and M. E. Pacanowsky (Eds.), *Communication and Organizations: An Interpretive Approach*, Beverly Hills, CA: Sage Publications.

DESSAUER, J. H. (1971), *My Years with Xerox: The Billions Nobody Wanted*, Garden City, Doubleday.

ECKERT, P. (1989), *Jocks and Burnouts*, New York: Teachers College Press.

FELDMAN, M. S. AND J. G. MARCH (1981), "Information in Organizations as Signal and Symbol," *Administrative Science Quarterly*, 26, 171–186.

GEERTZ, C. (1973), *Interpretation of Cultures: Selected Essays*, New York: Basic Books.

GOODMAN, P. AND ASSOCIATES (1988), *Designing Effective Work Groups*, San Francisco: Jossey-Bass.

HACKMAN, J. R. (Ed.) (1990), *Groups that Work (and Those that Don't)*, San Francisco: Jossey-Bass.

HEDBERG, B. (1981), "How Organizations Learn and Unlearn," in P. C. Nystrom and W. H. Starbuck, *Handbook of Organizational Design, Vol. 1: Adapting Organizations to their Environments*, New York: Oxford University Press.

________, P. C. NYSTROM AND W. H. STARBUCK (1976), "Designing Organizations to Match Tomorrow," in P. C. Nystrom and W. H. Starbuck (Eds.), *Prescriptive Models of Organizations*, Amsterdam, Netherlands: North-Holland Publishing Company.

HUTCHINS, E. (1991), "Organizing Work by Adaptation," *Organization Science*, 2, 1, 14–39.

________ (in press), "Learning to Navigate," in S. Chalkin and J. Lave (Eds.), *Situated Learning*, Cambridge: Cambridge University Press.

JORDAN, B. (1989), "Cosmopolitical Obstetrics: Some Insights from the Training of Traditional Midwives," *Social Science and Medicine*, 28, 9, 925–944. (Also available in slightly different form as *Modes of Teaching and Learning: Questions Raised by the Training of Traditional Birth Attendants*, IRL report 88-0004, Palo Alto, CA: Institute for Research on Learning.)

LATOUR, B. (1986), "Visualization and Cognition: Thinking with Eyes and Hands," *Knowledge and Society*, 6, 1–40.

LAVE J. (1988), *Cognition in Practice: Mind, Mathematics, and Culture in Everyday Life*, New York: Cambridge University Press.

________ AND E. WENGER (1990), *Situated Learning: Legitimate Peripheral Participation*, IRL report 90-0013, Palo Alto, CA.: Institute for Research on Learning. (Also forthcoming (1990) in a revised version, from Cambridge University Press.)

LEVI-STRAUSS, C. (1966), *The Savage Mind*, Chicago: Chicago University Press.

MARTIN, J. (1982), "Stories and Scripts in Organizational Settings," in A. H. Hastorf and A. M. Isen (Eds.), *Cognitive and Social Psychology*, Amsterdam: Elsevier.

NADLER, D. (1988), "Organizational Frame Bending: Types of Change in the Complex Organization," in R. H. Kilman, T. J. Covin, and associates (Eds.), *Corporate Transformation: Revitalizing Organizations for a Competitive World*, San Francisco: Jossey-Bass.

NYSTROM, P. C. AND W. H. STARBUCK (1984), "To Avoid Organizational Crises, Unlearn," *Organizational Dynamics*, Spring, 53–65.

ORR, J. (1990a), "Talking about Machines: An Ethnography of a Modern Job," Ph.D. Thesis, Cornell University.

________ (1990b), "Sharing Knowledge, Celebrating Identity: War Stories and Community Memory in a Service Culture," in D. S. Middleton and D. Edwards (Eds.), *Collective Remembering: Memory in Society*, Beverley Hills, CA: Sage Publications.

________ (1987a), "Narratives at Work: Story Telling as Cooperative Diagnostic Activity," *Field Service Manager*, June, 47–60.

________ (1987b), *Talking about Machines: Social Aspects of Expertise*, Report for the Intelligent Systems Laboratory, Xerox Palo Alto Research Center, Palo Alto, CA.

PEA, R. D. (1990), *Distributed Cognition*, IRL Report 90-0015, Palo Alto, CA: Institute for Research on Learning.

PUTNAM, L. L. (1983), "The Interpretive Perspective: An Alternative to Functionalism," in L. L. Putnam and M. E. Pacanowsky (Eds), *Communication and Organizations: An Interpretive Approach*, Beverley Hills, CA: Sage Publications.

REDDY, M. J. (1979), "The Conduit Metaphor," in Andrew Ortony (Ed.), *Metaphor and Thought*, Cambridge: Cambridge University Press, 284–324.

RYLE, G. (1954), *Dilemmas: The Tarner Lectures*, Cambridge: Cambridge University Press.

SCHEIN, E. H. (1990), "Organizational Culture," *American Psychologist*, 45, 2, 109–119.

SCHÖN, D. A. (1987), *Educating the Reflective Practitioner*, San Francisco: Jossey-Bass.

________ (1984), *The Reflective Practitioner*, New York: Basic Books.

SCHÖN, D. A. (1971), *Beyond the Stable State*, New York: Norton.

SCRIBNER, S. (1984), "Studying Working Intelligence," in B. Rogoff and J. Lave (Eds). *Everyday Cognition: Its Development in Social Context*, Cambridge, MA: Harvard University Press.

SUCHMAN, L. (1987a), *Plans and Situated Actions: The Problem of Human–Machine Communication*, New York: Cambridge University Press.

________ (1987b), "Common Sense in Interface Design," *Techné*, 1, 1, 38–40.

TUSHMAN, M. L. AND P. ANDERSON (1988), "Technological Discontinuities and Organization Environments," in A. M. Pettigrew (Ed.), *The Management of Strategic Change*, Oxford: Basil Blackwell.

VAN MAANEN, J. AND S. BARLEY (1984), "Occupational Communities: Culture and Control in Organizations," in B. Straw and L. Cummings (Eds), *Research in Organizational Behaviour*, London: JAI Press.

VON HIPPEL, E. (1988), *The Sources of Innovation*, New York: Oxford University Press.

ZUBOFF, S. (1988), *In the Age of the Smart Machine: The Future of Work and Power*, New York: Basic Books.

[17]

ELSEVIER

Research Policy 27 (1998) 237–253

'Knowledge management practices' and path-dependency in innovation

Rod Coombs [*,1], Richard Hull

ESRC Centre for Research on Innovation and Competition, Manchester M13 9QH, UK

Received 6 October 1997; revised 13 January 1998; accepted 13 March 1998

Keywords: Knowledge management; Path-dependency; Innovation

1. Introduction

An increasing number of researchers and commentators have recently been turning their attention to 'knowledge management', [2] and particularly the role of knowledge management in innovation. [3] It seems that there are two major underlying influences which are at work in these discussions and that they both have complementary and contradictory features.

The first of these influences can be seen as 'internal' to innovation research and it is the literature which synthesises the received findings of 'innovation studies' into an evolutionary economics perspective on technical change. [4] The central feature of this work for our purposes is its weaving together of the

* Corresponding author.

[1] Also at Manchester School of Management, UMIST, Manchester M60 1QD.

[2] See I. Nonaka, A dynamic theory of organizational knowledge creation, Organization Science, Vol. 5 (1), 1994, pp. 14–47; Andrew C. Inkpen, Creating knowledge through collaboration, California Management Review, Vol. 39 (1), 1996, pp. 123–140; Chris Marshall, Larry Prusak, David Shpilberg, Financial risk and the need for superior knowledge management, California Management Review, Vol. 38 (3), 1996, pp. 77–101; Economist Intelligence Unit, in co-operation with IBM Consulting Group, The Learning Organisation: Managing Knowledge for Business Success. The Economist Intelligence Unit, New York, 1996; Georg von Krogh, Johan Roos (Eds.), Managing Knowledge: Perspectives on Cooperation and Competition, Sage, London, 1996; Annie Brooking, Intellectual Capital: Core Asset for the Third Millenium Enterprise, International Thompson Business Press, London, 1996.

[3] In particular, see Dorothy Leonard-Barton, Wellsprings of Knowledge: Building and Sustaining the Sources of Innovation. Harvard Business School Press, Boston, 1995. See also Abdelkader Daghfous, George R. White, Information and innovation: a comprehensive representation, Research Policy, Vol. 23, 1994, pp. 267–280; Max H. Boisot, Is your firm a creative destroyer? Competitive learning and knowledge flows in the technological strategies of firms, Research Policy, Vol. 24, 1995, pp. 489–506; Inge C. Kerssens-van Drongelen, Petra C. de Weerd-Nederhof, Olaf A.M. Fisscher, Describing the issues of knowledge management in R&D: towards a communication and analysis tool, R&D Management, Vol. 26 (3), 1996, pp. 213–229. Many of these discussions are additionally informed by broadly economic perspectives on learning and innovation, especially Wesley M. Cohen, Daniel A. Levinthal, Absorptive capacity: a new perspective on learning and innovation, Administrative Science Quarterly, Vol. 35, 1990, pp. 128–152.

[4] Indeed, it could be argued that the major thrust of 'innovation studies' is *predicated* on the ideas enshrined in the concept of 'path-dependency'—namely, that innovation is evidently and observably not random; that it is, on the other hand, dependent on a variety of factors; that those factors to a certain extent determine a 'trajectory' or path for many classes of innovation; and that hence, one can make reasonable estimates about the future genesis and success of many classes of potential innovation.

PII S0048-7333(98)00036-5

observed path-dependency of innovation, with the firm-specificity of the routines which generate innovation. For example, Metcalfe and de Liso [5] elaborate the idea that a business unit will have a specific 'normal design configuration', a shared mental framework of fundamental design concepts relating to specific technologies, providing the 'operational route' to specific artefacts. Thus, the perspective in this literature links knowledge to innovation by focusing on firm-specific routines which stabilise certain bodies of knowledge, embed them in the shared understandings within the firm, and provide templates for deploying that knowledge to produce innovations which have a distinctive organisational 'signature'. [6]

The second underlying influence in the 'knowledge management' literature has arisen at the interface of innovation research and management research. It derives from the perceived increase in importance of knowledge as a factor of production and as a driving force in broader changes in the nature of contemporary economies, and in the enterprises which operate in those economies. One of the key reference points in the emergence of a new focus on 'knowledge management' in enterprises is the work of Nonaka. [7] Arising originally from empirical studies of new product development in Japanese firms, Nonaka has developed a model of the various ways in which organisations create knowledge and has suggested a style of management and an organisational structure for best managing the knowledge creation process, namely the 'hypertext organisation'. Central to the model (as indeed to much other work on knowledge management) is Michael Polanyi's distinction between tacit and explicit knowledge. Nonaka argues that tacit and explicit knowledge can be converted from one to the other and his main focus is managing the interactions between the four 'modes of knowledge conversion'. Another major contributor is Dorothy Leonard-Barton [8] who bases her discussion more firmly on the 'core competence' strategy literature and has a focus on what she calls "the *whole system* of knowledge management" (ibid, pp. 271–272, original emphasis), which is seen to be an integral element of competitive advantage, or 'core technological capability'. Her specific interest is in the 'key knowledge-building' activities—shared problem solving, implementing and integrating new technical processes and tools, experimenting and prototyping, and importing and absorbing technological and market knowledge.

In many ways, these two perspectives—the evolutionary economics perspective and the 'knowledge-centred-model of the enterprise'—are compatible with each other. [9] At the very least, it can be argued that they have considerable potential to enrich and illuminate each other. However, in one crucial respect they present different pictures of the nature of, and possibilities for, 'knowledge *management*' in

[5] Stanley J. Metcalfe, Nico de Liso, Innovation, Capabilities and Knowledge: The Epistemic Connection, paper presented to the 3rd international conference on Advances in Sociological and Economic Analysis of Technology (ASEAT), Manchester, September 1995. Forthcoming in Technology and Organisations, Rod Coombs, Ken Green, Albert Richards, Vivien Walsh (Eds.), Edward Elgar, London, 1998.

[6] We are grateful to one of the anonymous referees for pointing out that there are, of course, a great many studies which suggest links between knowledge and innovation through focusing on the routines and processes within R&D and product development. However, these have generally been post hoc categorisations, of particular routines and processes, as entailing a 'knowledge' element, such as knowledge dissemination. They have not been empirical studies of those routine activities and processes which are explicitly intended for, or understood as, 'knowledge management'.

[7] Nonaka, 1994, op. cit. See also I. Nonaka, The Knowledge Creating Company, Harvard Business Review, No. 69 (1991); and I. Nonaka, H. Takeuchi, The Knowledge Creating Company: How Japanese Companies Create The Dynamics of Innovation, Oxford University Press, Oxford, 1995.

[8] Leonard-Barton, op. cit., 1995.

[9] Assumptions and arguments for such potential compatibility (though limited to an evolutionary perspective of the *firm*, as opposed to a fully fledged evolutionary *economics*) can be found in many of the papers in Strategic Management Journal, Vol. 17, Winter 1996, Special Issue on Knowledge and the Firm, especially J.-C. Spender, Robert M. Grant, Knowledge and the firm: overview (Guest Editorial), pp. 5–9; Robert M. Grant, Towards a knowledge-based theory of the firm, pp. 109–122; J.-C. Spender, Making knowledge the basis of a dynamic theory of the firm, pp. 45–62; and, to a certain extent, Haridimos Tsoukas, The firms as a distributed knowledge system: a constructionist approach, pp. 11–25.

the business unit or firm.[10] This difference concerns the extent to which a firm is intrinsically limited in the degree to which it can modify the content and scope of its knowledge base. Simplifying somewhat, the Nonaka/Leonard-Barton perspective emphasises the potential openness of the firm to the acquisition of external knowledge and the possibility for the firm to increase its potential to create radically new knowledge. In a sense, it presents a relatively increased possibility of 'breaking free' of path-dependency. In contrast, the evolutionary economics perspective emphasises the way in which the knowledge base of a firm and its routines of operation *reinforce* path-dependency and limit the rate of integration of external knowledge or production of radically new knowledge. To put the problem in the language of evolutionary economics, the two perspectives pull in different directions on the question of the degree of variety generation which is possible *within the firm*. It is clear that variety generation within the firm is *constrained* variety generation—but the question which is posed in this discussion is the potential for *modifying* those constraints on its variety generation.[11]

This paper proposes an approach to understanding and researching knowledge management which is designed to explore this problem in more detail. The central feature of the approach is a theoretical and empirical focus on knowledge management *practices* in the firm,[12] which is in contrast to the focus, characteristic of a great deal of the current literature in this field, on categorising different types of knowledge.[13] In particular, it will be argued that it is vital to look not only at the effects of existing knowledge management practices on innovation within the firm, but also to account for the creation and maintenance of new knowledge management practices.

In Section 2 of the paper, the case for a focus on knowledge management practices is elaborated. In Section 3, a taxonomy of knowledge management practices is presented, with some illustrative exam-

---

[10] The unit of analysis is important here. Clearly, the predominant locus of path-dependency is the business unit. But there are also significant elements of path-dependency in the behaviour of a division, and of a corporation, the firm as a collection of business units. The degree of interactions between these loci of path-dependency will be influenced by, among other things, the corporate management style. These issues are discussed later in the paper in Sections 3 and 4. Until that point we will refer to 'the firm' as the unit of analysis.

[11] This question has recently been given a further dimension in debates on the validity of 'knowledge-based approaches to the theory of the firm'. See Nikolai J. Foss (a), Knowledge-based approaches to the theory of the firm: some critical comments, Organization Science, Vol. 7 (5), pp. 470–476, 1996; Kathleen R. Connor, C. K. Prahalad, A resource-based theory of the firm: knowledge versus opportunism, Organization Science, Vol. 7 (5), 1996, pp. 477–501; Bruce Kogut, Udo Zander, What firms do? coordination, identity, and learning, Organization Science, Vol. 7 (5), 1996, pp. 502–518; and Nikolai J. Foss (b), More critical comments on knowledge-based theories of the firm, Organization Science, Vol. 7 (5), pp. 519–523, 1996. The debate centres around the extent to which 'knowledge perspectives' can explain *why firms exist at all*; this has clear implications for the ways in which a 'knowledge perspective' may inform our understanding of the degree of variety generation that may be possible within a firm.

[12] In Section 2 of the paper we elaborate on our understanding of knowledge management practices as *routines* within the firm. It is worth pointing out here, however, that there is increasing interest in analysing 'practices' within a number of disciplines. See for instance Tsoukas, op. cit. for a focus on 'social practices' within the firm. Within sociology, see Stephen Turner, The Social Theory of Practices: Tradition, Tacit Knowledge, and Presuppositions, University of Chicago Press, Chicago, 1994. In the history and sociology of science and technology, see Andrew Pickering, The Mangle of Practice: Time, Agency and Science, University of Chicago Press, Chicago, 1995. Within social anthropology, Jean Lave has suggested a focus on 'communities of practice' (Jean Lave and E. Wenger, Situated Learning: Legitimate Peripheral Participation, Cambridge University Press, Cambridge, 1991). Lave's ideas are now being utilised by some within organisation studies, and interestingly by senior figures at the Rank Xerox Palo Alto Research Centre—see John Seely Brown, Paul Duguid, Organizational learning and communities-of-practice: towards a unified view of working, learning and innovation, Organization Science, Vol. 2 (1), 1991, pp. 40–57.

[13] Thus, we do not base our approach around discussion of the differences between tacit and explicit knowledge, or between 'individual', 'group' and 'organisational' knowledge. This approach in the event appeared justified, as many of the interviewees themselves discussed the difficulties they found with attempting to distinguish different types of knowledge when describing their knowledge management activities, and preferred to describe those activities in terms more relevant to their everyday work experience.

ples drawn from exploratory case studies. [14] In Section 4, the paper returns to the question of variety generation within the firm and considers how knowledge management practices create both the possibility of variety generation and the limits around that possibility.

2. The case for studying knowledge management practices

One starting point for the study of the role of knowledge in innovation at firm level is to focus on the various forms which knowledge can take and the modalities in which it plays a role in innovation. The pedigree for this approach goes back to Polanyi, as has already been noted. But, as Faulkner [15] demonstrates, a variety of innovation studies have for many years developed categorisations of the knowledge used in innovation which go beyond a simple distinction between tacit and explicit. For instance, Fleck and Tierney [16] distinguish seven knowledge types, ranging from 'metaknowledge', through 'formal' and 'informal' knowledge, to 'instrumentalities', whilst Vincenti [17] identified six rather different categories. Drawing together these and other categorisations, Faulkner [18] builds a 'composite typology' of 15 types, grouped according to the 'object' of the knowledge. Finally, the types can additionally be grouped along another axis concerning five distinct sets of 'characteristics' of knowledge: tacit vs. articulated; complex vs. simple; local vs. universal; specific vs. general, and understanding/information/skill.

This approach can clearly be fruitful if the research objective is to construct plausible accounts of the development of specific innovations and technologies within one firm or a network of firms. Different episodes, individuals, and arguments can be categorised in terms of these types of knowledge. However, it is less appropriate as a starting point if the objective is to move toward a more generalised account of the role of knowledge *management* in promoting innovation, through modifying the constraints on variety generation. In other words, regardless of the validity or otherwise of identifying distinct types of knowledge, members of organisations can only make use of these types of knowledge through specific tasks, sequences of tasks (i.e., processes), techniques, or through less formal activities. We propose then that knowledge management is best studied as a set of specific practices. [19] To stress this

[14] Exploratory case studies of KMPs in R&D and innovation activities, has been conducted in five companies. Each case involved semi-structured interviews with an average of 11 people, ranging from Executive Directors, R&D managers, R&D practitioners, to in-house Information Scientists, and several forms of feedback and validation with the participating firms. The five cases yielded a total of over 80 distinct KMPs. We are currently preparing a 'self-audit tool' on KMPs and innovation, as an additional outcome of these studies, which may be used for later surveys. This research has been supported by the UK Economic and Social Research Council, Grant No. L125251008.

[15] Wendy Faulkner, Conceptualizing knowledge used in innovation: a second look at the science–technology distinction and industrial innovation, Science, Technology and Human Values, Vol. 19 (4), 1994, pp. 425–458.

[16] James Fleck, Margaret Tierney, The management of expertise: knowledge, power and the economics of expert labour, Edinburgh PICT Working Paper, No. 29 (Research Centre for Social Science, University of Edinburgh, Edinburgh, 1991). See also James Fleck, Expertise: knowledge, power and tradeability, in: W. Faulkner, J. Fleck, R. Williams (Eds.), Exploring Expertise, Macmillan, 1998.

[17] W. Vincenti, What engineers know and how they know it: Analytical studies from aeronautical history, John Hopkins University Press, Baltimore, 1991.

[18] Faulkner, 1994, op. cit.

[19] There is of course a sense in which 'insights about types of knowledge' are sometimes utilised and brought to bear within organisations through specific artefacts, especially computers and telecommunications technologies, and their associated software, and we discuss some specific KMPs related to information and communication technologies in Section 3.2.5. It is worth noting here, though, that (a) there have been considerable attempts to pursue an 'IT-based' approach to knowledge management; (b) there are however considerable problems with 'IT-based' attempts at organisational change—see for instance Rod Coombs, Richard Hull, BPR as IT-enabled organisational change: an assessment, New Technology, Work and Employment, Vol. 10 (2), pp. 121–31; and (c) one element of those problems is the diversity of understandings and operationalisations of the concept of 'knowledge' within ICTs and computer science—see Richard Hull, Governing the conduct of computing: computer science, the social sciences, and frameworks of computing, Accounting, Management and Information Technologies, Vol. 7 (4), pp. 213–240.

point more clearly, it is worth briefly rehearsing some of the pertinent arguments within management research and organisation studies. [20]

One evident starting point is the long-running but recently revived interest in Organisational Learning, much of which can, of course, be traced back to Kenneth Arrow's essentially economic arguments in 1962 for a focus on 'learning by doing', and crystallised in the work of Chris Argyris and Donald Schön on organisational behaviour. [21] The current revival of interest is characterised by a variety of approaches—economic, psychological and organisational. A useful review by Mark Dodgson argues that much of the literature underestimates the complexities of the 'processes of learning', and Cohen and Levinthal argue for a focus on the 'internal mechanisms' within the firm that influence it's 'absorptive capacity' to learn. [22] Summarising these various works, it would seem fair to suggest that, despite the recent turn towards a prescriptive and rather rhetorical approach to Organisational Learning, the literature has always suggested an empirical focus first on the detailed activities within organisations. [23]

Another obvious reference point is the literature on 'knowledge work' and 'knowledge workers'. Once again, many of the origins of this literature can be found within debates during the late 1950's and 1960's which were constructed around the 'intellectual sector' and 'post-industrial society' (Bell), the 'production of knowledge' (Machlup), the 'knowledgeable society' (Lane), 'knowledge as a crucial resource' (Galbraith), and finally, Peter Drucker's focus on 'knowledge work'. [24] A useful presentation of the variety of current approaches points firstly to the need to contextualise the recent resurgence of interest in knowledge work within a broader picture of contemporary structural and cultural change; and secondly to the problems for empirical research, leading to the suggestion that 'knowledge work should not be defined in terms of what knowledge workers know... but in terms of what they do'. [25] In a later review, Blackler argues for a focus on 'knowing in practice', which has considerable similarities with the influential notion of 'communities of practice' from the anthropologist Jean Lave. [26] We learn

[20] In an earlier consultancy report for the ESRC (Rod Coombs, Richard Hull, Intelligent Organisations: A Review of the Literature, 1994) we have already shown that the 'knowledge-centred' literature combines in an eclectic but somewhat haphazard manner observations on 'old' management practices which are now being used in new ways to 'generate knowledge' and 'new knowledge management activities' and that this literature had no practical tools for mapping these various practices in real situations.

[21] K. Arrow, The implications of learning by doing, Review of Economic Studies, Vol. 26, pp. 166–170. A series of works by Chris Argyris, Organization and Innovation, Irwin and Illinois, 1965; Today's problems with tomorrow's organizations, Journal of Management Studies, Vol. 4 (1), 1967, pp. 31–55; Chris Argyris, Donald Schön, Theory in Practice, Jossey-Bass, San Francisco, 1974; Chris Argyris, Donald Schön, Organizational Learning, Addison-Wesley, 1978.

[22] Mark Dodgson, Organizational learning: a review of some literatures, Organization Studies, Vol. 14 (3), 1993, pp. 375–393; Wesley M. Cohen, Daniel A. Levinthal, Absorptive capacity: a new perspective on learning and innovation, Administrative Science Quarterly, Vol. 35, 1990, pp. 128–152. See also Daniel A. Levinthal, James G. March, The myopia of learning, Strategic Management Journal I, Vol. 14, 1993, pp. 95–112, which argues for some skepticism towards the optimistic expectations for 'organizational learning'.

[23] Another useful source is the literature on 'management learning' which augments the Organisational Learning approaches with perspectives and empirical research within Management Studies, much of which argues once again for detailed and skeptical examination of the everyday activities of managers. See for instance the 're-launch' of the journal Management Learning, Vol. 25 (1), 1994.

[24] Daniel Bell, The Coming of Post-Industrial Society, Heinemann, London, 1974, especially pp. 33–40, where he discusses his earlier contributions from 1959 onwards. Fritz Machlup, The Production and Distribution of Knowledge in the United States, Princeton University Press, Princeton, 1962. Robert Lane, The decline of politics and ideology in a knowledgeable society, American Sociological Review, Vol. 21 (5), 1966. J.K. Galbraith, The New Industrial State, Hamish Hamilton, London, 1967. Peter F. Drucker, The Age of Discontinuity: Guidelines to Our Changing Society, Harper and Row, New York, 1968. See also his earlier The Practice of Management, New York, 1954.

[25] Frank Blackler, Michael Reed, Alan Whitaker, Editorial epilogue: an agenda for research, Journal of Management Studies, Vol. 30 (6), pp. 1017–1020, Special Issue on Knowledge Workers and Contemporary Organizations, 1993.

[26] Frank Blackler, Knowledge, knowledge work and organizations: an overview and interpretation, Organization Studies, Vol. 16 (6), 1995, pp. 1021–1046; Craig Pritchard, A commentary on Blackler: knowledge, knowledge work and Organizations: an overview and interpretation, Organization Studies, Vol. 17 (5), 1996, pp. 857–858; Frank Blackler, Response to Pritchard's commentary, Organization Studies, Vol. 17 (5), 1996, pp. 858–860. Jean Lave, E. Wenger, op. cit.

from these discussions, then, that observations of shifts at the broad structural and social levels—which we may characterise in terms of the growing importance of knowledge resources and knowledge work—are not easily translatable into research projects at the detailed level of specific organisational settings, for which a more appropriate emphasis is 'what people do in practice'.

To recap: our focus is *not* on *all* of the relationships between knowledge and innovation, and the various practices or routines which may be thought to be important to those relationships—that form of focus, after all, has been central to a considerable body of research over the last 30 years. [27] Our focus is on the effects on innovation of knowledge management—an as yet rather loosely defined set of ideas, techniques, and prescriptions—and we suggest above that the most appropriate method for such a focus is upon what happens in practice, rather than types of knowledge. Broad examples of 'what happens in practice', which we may temporarily picture as 'mechanisms', include accumulation mechanisms which govern the content and location of the 'stocks of knowledge' in the firm; the interface mechanisms which govern the balance between, for example, internal and external sources of knowledge; and deployment mechanisms which govern the ways in which the stocks of knowledge are brought to bear within decision-making. Mechanisms such as these are important in defining the collective knowledge—of whatever type—in an organisation, which makes one firm's behaviour different, and *consistently different*, from another firm. In the next part of this discussion, we propose that the most fruitful way to investigate these mechanisms is to first re-examine the notion of path-dependency in innovation—since it is the idea of path-dependency which is at the heart of the contemporary understanding that innovation is a process which is intrinsically firm-specific.

2.1. The location of path-dependency

The notion of path-dependency is centred on the idea of positive returns. [28] Doing things in a particular way, whether it be designing, manufacturing or marketing a product, yields effects which pre-dispose the organisation to do (at least some) things in the same way the next time around. [29] If we consider the way the idea of path-dependency has been developed in studies of innovation and in evolutionary economics in recent times, it becomes plain that this manifestation of path-dependency is potentially 'located' in three different domains within the firm. The first domain, 'technology-as-hardware', comprises the specific technological artefacts such as products, machinery, equipment, software, etc. These items bear the impression of previous choices and chance events, and they shape future possibilities for the development of further artefacts.

The second domain in which path-dependency may be located is the 'knowledge base' of the firm. This knowledge base can be variously interpreted. For Metcalfe and de Liso, [30] the knowledge base is quite closely connected to the technologies and customers currently familiar to the firm, and consists of the 'shared mental framework of fundamental design concepts' mentioned above. However, for some writers in the evolutionary economics school, there are more aggregated levels of 'knowledge base' in the firm which shape action. Hodgson, [31] for example, argues that 'corporate culture' provides an explanation of the 'existence and relative efficiencies' of firms, an explanation that is superior to the transaction-costs approach to forms of co-ordination. Commencing with a discussion of the ways in which firms cope with 'radical uncertainty', and hence are required to ensure that learning takes place, it is

[27] We are grateful to one of the anonymous referees for pointing out this possible misinterpretation of the focus of this paper.

[28] See for instance Brian Arthur, Competing technologies, increasing returns, and lock-in by historical events, The Economic Journal, Vol. 99, 1989, pp. 116–131.

[29] See for instance, Richard Nelson, Sidney Winter, An Evolutionary Theory of Economic Change, Harvard University Press, Cambridge, 1982. See also Rod Coombs, Paolo Saviotti, Vivien Walsh, Introduction, in: Rod Coombs, Paolo Saviotti, Vivien Walsh (Eds.), Technological Change and Company Strategies: Economic and Sociological Perspectives, Academic Press, London, 1992.

[30] Metcalfe and de Liso, op. cit. 1995.

[31] Geoffrey M. Hodgson, Corporate Culture and the Nature of the Firm, Judge Institute of Management Studies Working Paper No. 14 (1993–94), University of Cambridge, Cambridge.

argued that maintaining the 'competencies' of groups and individuals requires that the firm has a capacity to 'mould the individual perceptions, preferences, abilities and actions of its personnel'. This capacity is operated partly through the ability of the firm to generate trust and loyalty, but more importantly through the 'transmission' of a corporate culture. This culture consists of 'shared information... practices and habits of thought'.

Path-dependency may therefore be seen as being located in the 'knowledge base' of the firm, as narrowly defined by the specific technologies and markets of which it has experience, or more broadly defined as the culture of the organisation, which includes but transcends the more narrow definition.

The third potential domain in which path-dependency might be located is the collection of *routines* which are carried out in the firm in order for it to conduct its regular business. Particularly important for our purposes of course are those routines which are related to innovation. These would include routines which *deploy* the existing knowledge base of the firm in order to make sense of particular problems in the area of product and process development. These would include routines which aim to characterise customer requirements; to identify feasible technical solutions; to establish projects and work plans to implement those solutions; and so on. These routines, by their sheer *repetition*, serve to reinforce the distinctiveness and legitimacy of *both* of the other domains mentioned—namely the knowledge base and the previously accumulated technology and hardware. However, these routines would also be capable of exposing perceived limitations and weaknesses in those areas, and thus open up (path-dependent) avenues through which those weaknesses are addressed.

From this discussion, it seems plain that the phenomenon of path-dependency may indeed be located in all three domains: in the 'technology-as-hardware', in the knowledge base, and in the routines of the firm. This follows from the way in which the three domains are bound up with and depend on each other. The knowledge base structures the routines, which in turn deploy knowledge to create the technology, which in turn underpins the knowledge, and so on. Where then should the focus of research be, if our aim is to explore the claimed potential for active 'knowledge management' to *modify* the limits on innovation posed by path-dependency? Should we focus on the technology, on the knowledge, or on the routines?

If we focus on the technology-as-hardware, we are restricted to looking at something which only reveals the traces of path-dependency once it has become an 'output' of the firm. [32] This may be valuable in the development of a sociology of technology, but is too limited as an approach to understanding knowledge management in real time in companies. If we focus on the knowledge base as a site of path-dependency, we are faced with the very difficult task of identifying those aspects of a company's knowledge base which confer firm-specificity on its activity. These are, by definition, often the most difficult to access. Furthermore, such an approach encounters the many difficulties of developing and applying metrics for knowledge which can be applied in empirical studies. [33] However, if we focus on the *routines* which are involved directly in the development and application of the knowledge base, we have a more tractable situation. [34] We can list some of the advantages of treating routines as the focus of analysis.

- The routines can be empirically observed as practical activities, such as the conceptual structuring and archiving of a technical document; or selecting external sources of knowledge to access and to disseminate internally.

[32] Indeed all 'failed' or aborted attempts at innovation would be hidden from view, however interesting in terms of knowledge management.

[33] Epistemological, ontological, and indeed political. See for instance: Frank Blackler, 1995 and 1996, and Pritchard, 1996, op. cit., (See also Scott D.N. Cook, John Seeley Brown, Bridging Epistemologies: The generative dance between organisational knowledge and organisational knowing, mimeo, Xerox Palo Alto Research Centre, CA, 1995), Some of these epistemological, ontological and political difficulties have, for many years, been highlighted within work on the sociology of scientific knowledge —see for instance Andrew Pickering (Ed.), Science as Practice and Culture, Chicago University Press, Chicago, 1992. Our focus on knowledge management practices as routines thus steps around many of these difficulties. See also Richard Hull, 'Knowledge' as a Unit of Analysis, and the Role of Critique in the Sociology of Scientific Knowledge, in Review for Social Studies of Science.

• The routines will have certain common features which 'transfer' from one firm setting to another, but which are also capable of being given a greater or lesser degree of importance by firms, or are capable of being implemented in a different way.

• The routines are (potentially) topics which are the subject of debate and change within a company, as it reflects on its performance and makes changes. This also makes them more visible to the researcher, and makes changes open to discussion in terms of reasons and rationales for change.

These points will be developed further below. However, to recap the argument so far, we suggest that the phenomenon of 'knowledge management' in the specific field of innovation lends itself to a research approach which focuses on the interplay of knowledge management and the generation and maintenance of path-dependency in the firm. In order to uncover this interplay, the most fruitful activities to examine are the routines which are explicitly intended, or believed, to involve 'knowledge management' within innovation processes. We propose to call these specific routines 'knowledge management practices' (KMPs), and they are evidently particularly important in shaping the knowledge base of the firm and making it available in the innovation process. A suggested taxonomy of KMPs is presented in the Section 3. [35]

[34] See [11] above. There is, of course, the familiar but still difficult question of the extent to which *reported* practices and routines are actually followed—an old and (we would argue) unresolved debate about rules, language and actions. See for instance the chapters by David Bloor, Michael Lynch in Pickering, 1992, op. cit.; and Tsoukas, 1996, op. cit. attempts an essentially ethnomethodological solution. A more pragmatic answer is to cite the practical advantages of focusing on routines and practices, as we have done here. But there is, in addition, an *ethical* response, which is to say that all we should *hope or attempt* to govern (through research, description, comparison or prescription) are the rules, practices, and routines within any organisation—the conduct—rather than any form of subjective experience, as for instance embodied in the concept of tacit knowledge—see Richard Hull, Actor Network and Conduct: The Discipline and Practices of Knowledge Management, in review for Organization, special issue on Actor Network Theory, 1999.

[35] We are thus developing and considerably refining the ad hoc broad identification of four critical 'knowledge management processes' by Inkpen, 1996, op. cit.

3. Types of Knowledge Management Practice

In this section, we first present a framework for understanding KMPs which is designed to guide empirical research. Section 3.1 first presents the framework in terms of the attributes of a KMP. In Section 3.2, we present some examples of KMPs we have identified, which have been grouped utilising those attributes and according to their relationship with some of the principal functional activities involved in innovation. A further group of KMPs is defined in terms of the enabling role being played by information technology applications which permit KMPs to be significantly modified, or indeed trigger the creation of new KMPs. In each case, the KMPs are briefly illustrated with examples drawn from five exploratory case-studies which are part of an ongoing research programme. [36] In Section 3.3, we then discuss the relationship between the varieties of the KMPs we have described.

3.1. The attributes of Knowledge Management Practices

Knowledge management practices take a variety of forms, and this creates a need for a flexible approach to describing and classifying them. The approach needs to be able to cope with practices which are both formal and informal; paper-based and electronic; people-driven or system-driven; wholly or only partially centred on knowledge management, and so on. It is first, worth offering a formal definition of practices at this point. We see practices as encompassing the variety of ways in which labour is regularised and routinised, whether formally in recognised tasks, processes- which are sequences of tasks- and techniques; or informally in acknowledged ways of 'getting by' and 'getting the work done'. We now propose a model of KMPs which has four components or attributes which are as follows: [37]

1. The 'knowledge processing' characteristics of the KMP—generation, transfer and utilisation, and a number of additional characteristics.

[36] See [13].

2. The knowledge domains or topics addressed by the KMP.
3. The part of the organisation's performance which, it is intended, will be most affected by the KMP.
4. The format, or degree of formality, of the KMP.

In some circumstances, it is also possible to identify the principal actor(s) involved in a KMP. However, we do not include the actor as a necessary part of the KMP itself, since in some cases agency is unclear or contested. [38]

Thus, a typical KMP may be carried out by an actor, but it will certainly relate to a specific knowledge domain. It will perform some action on the knowledge in a particular way, be conducted within a specific format, and have particular effects on the organisation. To give a specific example: the manager of a pilot plant for the manufacture of a polymer may prepare a technical report which captures operating data (the processing characteristic) on the efficiency of a new catalyst (the domain). The report may be rapidly through Lotus Notes (the format) to R&D personnel working on optimising the catalyst and may therefore improve the efficiency of the R&D process (the performance parameter).

We can now expand the description of each of these four elements of a KMP in turn.

3.1.1. *The processing characteristics of the KMP*

It has traditionally been assumed that there are three broad types of knowledge processing—*generation, transfer, and utilisation*. However, this is a somewhat narrow approach perhaps more appropriate to information processing (from which it derives) than to knowledge management. From reviews of the literature on types of knowledge (Faulkner op. cit.) and from our own empirical studies we propose the following additional processing characteristics: *identification* of knowledge that may be useful; *capture* or retrieval of knowledge; *altering the format* (for instance, *codifying* knowledge by transferring it onto paper or onto IT systems); *validation* of knowledge (for instance, through discussions with peers); *contextualising* and re-contextualising (for instance, looking for common aspects between the original context of the knowledge, and the intended context); and achieving *closure* (for instance, the processes of agreeing common definitions). Thus, the essential feature of a KMP can range from relatively 'routine' activities such as recording data, to more judgement-based and potentially contestable activities involving selection and contextualisation of knowledge.

3.1.2. *Domain*

There is often a specific knowledge focus for KMPs, involving a delimited area of knowledge targeted by that practice. Such areas may include: highly specified areas of scientific and/or technical knowledge and related to particular journals, conferences, or professional associations; knowledge of particular products or processes; knowledge of particular markets and customer bases; knowledge of particular features of the organisation; and knowledge of projects, project processes and project management. Thus, the broad categories of domain are *Technical* (both internal and external to the firm), *Market*, and *Organisational Procedures*.

[37] There are, of course, extensive methods and models for 'task analysis' within a variety of academic and operational fields; there are also methods and models within Organisation Studies which focus on categories of activities, most notably the 'Aston Studies' (see D.S. Pugh, The Aston Research Programme, in: A. Bryman (Ed.), Doing Research in Organisations, Routledge, London, 1988, pp. 123–35); and of course Weber's original characterisation of 'bureaucracy' rested on a large number of organisational variables, many of which concerned the nature of activities within organisations (see Stewart R. Clegg, Max Weber and the Sociology of Organisations, in: Larry J. Ray, Michael Reed (Eds.), Organizing Modernity: New Weberian Perspectives on Work, Organization and Society, Routledge, London, 1994, pp. 46–80). The Aston Studies, in adopting a limited set of Weber's 'organisational variables', identified formalisation, specialisation and standardisation as collectively the 'structuring of activities'. The pragmatic approach we have adopted—aimed primarily at developing a simple taxonomy of KMPs—can be characterised as delineating firstly three attributes to any practice—immediate goal, long-term aim, and degree of formality. Secondly, for KMPs, the immediate goal has been divided into two elements—the knowledge processing characteristics, and the domain of the KMP. Finally, the long-term aim is described here in terms of the intended impact on performance.

[38] Typical actors in an R&D setting include R&D scientists, project managers, gatekeepers (formal or informal); library personnel, patent and intellectual property specialists, technical marketing personnel, business development specialists, etc.

There may also be a more general focus for a KMP, which may include: knowledge that may arise unpredictably, for instance, through synergy or co-location; knowledge that is needed by new or younger personnel from time to time, for example, during personnel induction and continuing mentoring practices; and knowledge that others may find useful, for instance, the practice of publishing material on internal Web pages on an 'intranet'.

3.1.3. The intended effect on organisational performance variables

This is the most problematic one of the four elements to specify clearly. The reason for this is the well-known difficulty surrounding the creation of relevant and accepted measures for the efficiency and effectiveness of R&D and innovation. However, there are some 'micro-measures' of the performance of certain elements of the R&D function which provide a point of reference. For example, clever and prompt interpretation of competitors' patents and patent applications, and the communication of that knowledge to an R&D team, can identify the degree of *design freedom* available to that team and result in a better targeting of their effort. [39] In most circumstances, it is at least possible to identify an *intended* performance effect of a KMP, even if in practice it is often difficult to measure that effect.

3.1.4. The format

As already suggested above, particular KMPs may vary between 'formal' and 'informal'; from a highly specified and standardised job-role of specific individuals, through to a general expectation that people will carry out the practice (for instance, passing on useful knowledge). Any KMP may also be expected to take place at specific times or locations, for instance, during particular meetings, or during the 'demand analysis' phase of projects, or within the space where project teams are clustered together; it may be directed at enabling ad hoc, temporary or rapid arrangements, for instance, by establishing links and contacts between people with shared expertise or interests. Alternatively a particular KMP may be set up within MIS or ICT systems, and hence, be specified and constrained to varying degrees, so that for instance, e-mail discussion lists may be seen to be far less formal than a shared database or groupware system with strictly delimited field attributes.

This question of the format of KMPs is of particular topical concern at present. The rapid diffusion and refinement of IT techniques for the archiving and distribution of knowledge is now penetrating R&D functions in companies. Formal 'information management' procedures and personnel who have, up to now, been concerned with other areas of company activity are now turning their attention to R&D and innovation as an area where they can make a significant contribution. Furthermore, the significant growth of multi-site R&D and electronically-enabled virtual R&D project teams is providing a fruitful recruiting ground for their ideas.

3.2. The main groups of knowledge management practices.

In this section, we describe some of the KMPs we have identified from case studies. These are clustered into five main groups in terms of the relationships between particular KMPs and some of the main functional activities within innovation processes—R&D Management, Mapping Knowledge Relationships, [40] Human Resource Management, Managing Intellectual Property, and R&D Information Technology Management. The process of deciding on these main groups was essentially iterative, and proceeded first from the categorisation of KMPs in terms of the four attributes described above, which enabled similarities and differences between KMPs to be drawn based on the practices themselves, rather than on, for instance, theories about 'correct' knowledge management. Thus, the KMPs identified in each case-study were first grouped for that particular

[39] This example is taken from a case study in the R&D labs of a major manufacturer of electronic consumer and capital goods.

[40] Group B, Mapping Knowledge Relationships, is not immediately apparent as a main functional activity within innovation processes. However, it emerged from our case-studies as a strong focus for a considerable number of activities.

firm or unit, but as the studies progressed the groups we identified became more generic. [41]

Consequently, these groups should not be considered exhaustive, although they would appear to represent the main clusters of KMPs that might be encountered within the innovation processes of any 'innovation-active' firm. Secondly, it is in the nature of many practices within firms—especially those units with fairly loose functional boundaries—that any particular practice may have multiple functions. Thus, for instance, to take one of the examples described below, the secondment of R & D personnel to Product divisions is clearly an aspect of Human Resource Management in terms of enabling personnel to pursue a variety of career options, but is also an aspect of R & D Management in terms of ensuring effective communication between R & D and Divisions.

3.2.1. Group A: KMPs and the R & D management process

These are KMPs which are found to varying degrees in all R & D and innovation environments, and which often have other primary purposes. The main examples are mentioned below.

- Writing technical reports on outputs of R & D projects. This is a procedure often viewed as routine. In fact however, it depends fundamentally on the use of concepts, language, and cross-referencing processes, which are deeply influenced by the existing knowledge base of the firm, and which reinforce that knowledge base. Furthermore, the relevance of technical reports to knowledge management is being transformed in some companies by the placing of the reports in electronic archives and making them searchable by other R & D or marketing personnel (see Group E below).
- Periodic reviews of projects, departments, and other relevant organisational sub-units in an R & D lab. These procedures generate documents and shared knowledge which play an important role in contextualising knowledge and creating shared categories for identifying 'that which is important'. They also play a role in forming a formal or informal inventory of skills and capabilities in the R & D function.
- Physical clustering of R & D projects in cognate technological areas has a profound effect both on the generation and sharing of technical and market knowledge, and on the demand for relevant knowledge to be supplied to such groups by other internal services such as the library/information service department, and the IPR department.

In some companies, R & D activity centres around a small number of very large projects, which last a long time, and which are very context-specific. Examples would be the design and building of a chemical plant in another country; or the design and building of a large civil engineering project such as an airport terminal. For these companies, one of the difficulties in 'knowledge management' is that teams of people are assembled to do the work, and they acquire a great deal of experience and skill which appears to be very specific to 'getting that project done' but which, in fact, conceals some potentially generic and transferable lessons. But the culture of such R & D work is that the completion of the hardware is the driving force, and after that is complete, the teams are broken-up and there is low motivation to reflect on and document the transferable experience and re-use it in future projects. This leads to frequent instances of reinvented wheels. Such circumstance can give rise to a cluster of KMPs which constitute a quite highly developed solution to this problem.

- In one particular design and construction company, a large team of R & D personnel do nothing else but interrogate, contextualise, present and re-present 'project experience' in ways which try to 'fix' it as the accumulated current best practice of the company. Thus, on the question of, for example, how you specify appropriate acoustic insulation levels for offices in particular, geographic markets, and how you procure the appropriate (and sometimes quite varying) building materials in those markets to reach those acoustic levels, a set of guidelines and procedures will be formulated and made available to all technical personnel in the field. This cluster of

[41] So for instance, for some time we identified one group as being concerned with 'serial transfer of project experience', because that appeared as a major issue for the several of the early cases. However, it soon became apparent that such an issue was specific to firms engaging in large, extended projects, and that such issues could be more usefully considered as a sub-set of R&D management activities.

KMPs is currently largely paper-based in the form of manuals which project staff carry around with them. Interestingly, this is a case where, although the KMP is highly evolved, it is not being driven by IT enabling processes (as some other KMPs are) because the IT is still a less convenient format than paper for the very mobile character of the project staff who use the knowledge.

These KMPs in Group A are at the heart of the key 'knowledge circuits' in R&D. They grow directly out of the performance of the R&D work itself, and are typically embodied in the R&D scientists and their formal and informal communication patterns within and beyond the lab. The importance of such knowledge-centred activities has been recognised for many years, going back to the work of Allen [42] on gatekeepers. Some aspects of this set of KMPs have not changed fundamentally since then. Other aspects are changing rapidly as a result of the greater formality of R&D planning processes, and the opportunities to use information technology to change the range of options for the storage and dissemination of documents and data.

3.2.2. Group B: KMPs and the 'mapping' of knowledge relationships

R&D organisations are typically organised around project teams and around departments with specific technical expertise. Often, these two reference points for organisation form the two sides of the matrix in a matrix management structure. However, even with this type of structure, emergent nodes of technical expertise which develop around particular categories of problem can often be relatively 'invisible' and not formally located within one of the strong cells in the matrix. Similarly, emergent bodies of knowledge and experience about customers, competitors and market segments can arise in parts of the R&D organisation, but not be formally 'owned' by anyone in the management system. These 'orphan' fragments of knowledge can be even more numerous and difficult to locate if there are multiple R&D centres in a corporate structure, and multiple networks of contacts with business units, and with their customers. In many firms—especially large divisionalised corporations—a group of KMPs have emerged which are concerned with mapping these fields of knowledge and person-embodied skill, and making the resulting maps available to managers to provide new perspectives on the firm's innovation activities. These mapping KMPs can be subdivided into those which target internal technologies, external technologies, customers and market segments, and inter-company relationships. These are now discussed in turn.

3.2.2.1. B1: internal technology maps. There has been an increase in the development of specific KMPs designed to *identify and map* the range of specific domains of technology-centred knowledge in the R&D centres, and to similarly identify and map the parallel categories of 'market-centred' knowledge. In some cases, this activity may be organised as a formal 'technology audit'. In other cases it may be much more ad hoc, and dependent on particular groups or individuals taking an initiative from the bottom-up. The salient point in each case is that pockets of knowledge and skill which are not project or product-specific, by virtue of being named, take on a more solid existence.

It should be stressed that some of the items that find their way onto these maps are obvious and not surprising to anyone in senior management, but that others are surprising, and are then the cause of discussion and debate about whether 'anything should be done' about these pieces of knowledge in terms of their formal recognition as new parts of the lab structure, or in terms of the more active dissemination of the knowledge to others in the R&D unit or parent corporation who might make use of it.

3.2.2.2. B2: external technology maps. A major distinction within this group of KMPs is that between the mapping of *internal* knowledge within the firm, and the mapping of *external* knowledge in other firms, in research agencies, in universities, in the public literature, patents, and so on. The balance between these two types of mapping depends on firm-specific factors such as history and innovation

[42] T.J. Allen, Communications in the Research and Development Laboratory, Technology Review, Vol. 70 (1), pp. 31–37. T.J. Allen, Managing the Flow of Technology: Technology Transfer and the Dissemination of Technological Innovation within the R&D Organization, MIT Press, Cambridge, 1977. See also Stuart Macdonald, Christine Williams, The survival of the gatekeeper, Research Policy, Vol. 23, 1994, pp. 123–132.

posture. It also reflects the view of the firm regarding its degree of self-reliance or dependence on external technology. Where both internal and external mapping are highly developed this can result in a third sub-set of mapping KMPs which explore and establish *connections* between the firm's internal technologies and its external technical environment. This is clearly one of the most important categories of KMP in terms of the issue of variety generation and the modification of path-dependence.

These mapping initiatives are being taken by diverse groups in the R&D centres, but library and information science professionals are a strong promoter of the ideas. These groups have the special skills and technologies to monitor publications, grants, conferences, patents, etc., and to categorise them into relevant categories for presentation to research teams. But such activity is transformed from the merely administrative to the strategic if the categories chosen and the audiences addressed are linked directly into the fine-grained technological ideas which underpin actual R&D projects.

Examples of this trend are the increasing use of proactive dissemination of topic-centred news-sheets (often electronically delivered) which are placing company-specific items of technical and market intelligence in front of R&D scientists. The more radical versions of this development involve the formal use of company 'intranets' for this purpose, as well as judicious and secure use of internet access for external searching. Some companies now cite the issue of 'information failures' amongst R&D scientists as part of the justification for the expenditure on an 'intranet'.

Moreover, these mapping KMPs are not entirely conducted in virtual space. One of the frequent consequences of the mapping processes is that people in different parts of the organisation find that they have a common interest in a particular technology or application-centred topic, and form (either officially or unofficially) a new 'interest group' which can sometimes congeal into a formal new skill centre with a budget and a brief to develop the skill.

3.2.2.3. B3: market mapping. Mapping KMPs are not restricted to working with technical knowledge. The work of R&D staff in centres with a strong product development orientation is profoundly intertwined with assessment of customers and their reactions to the functionality of products and services, and to the products of competitors. This is done by marketing personnel in product development teams, by technical marketing staff in follow-up field work, and often by R&D staff directly in customer interactions. Consequently, it is possible to find significant mapping activities focused on markets, market segments, customer behaviour, future customer requirements, etc. This is not simply the 'market research' of the conventional marketing department (although that is relevant here as well), but is something more organically embedded in the 'innovation community' in the firm. This is centred on the R&D staff, but extends beyond them to a variety of more 'customer-involved' groups. These KMPs which generate and organise market knowledge, if articulated with the internal and external technology mapping KMPs, are a central part of the variety-generating potential of the firm. It is these routines especially, and the modification of these routines, which hold the key to the possibility of partially 'relaxing' the constraints of path-dependence in innovation.

3.2.2.4. B4: mapping inter-company relationships. In industrial sectors such as biotechnology, there are many complex inter-company relationships centred on technology transfer, licensing, joint R&D, and so on. Companies in these circumstances find it valuable to have separate mapping activities which track these alliances and relationships, often strongly linked in to their mapping of external technologies. The results of the relationship mapping can sometimes reveal the development of 'patent roadblocks' which make certain research directions less fruitful; they can also help in predicting changes in the strategic posture of competitors, and can assist in the evaluation of new options for alliances.

These four categories of mapping KMP (B1–B4) are a major aspect of emerging new knowledge management practice, with their own distinctive skills and techniques.

3.2.3. Group C: R&D Human Resource Management

This set of KMPs are concerned with motivating and rewarding R&D personnel. These are closely tied, to quite varying degrees, to the broader corporate Human Resource Management policies such as training and career development activities. R&D HRM will, in many cases, be confined to simple 'dual-ladder' policies, with procedures for enabling personnel to pursue either 'technical' or 'commercial' careers, but some R&D units have a particular focus on activities designed to encourage knowledge-sharing and the development of inter-disciplinary expertise and cross-boundary working, and indeed, there may often be conflicts between corporate and R&D HRM.

- Secondments are routinely made between staff in a company's R&D Lab and Product Divisions, typically lasting about 6 months. These are seen as aspects of career development, as well as seeking to achieve productive exchanges between different knowledge domains and to identify new areas of activity for R&D. In other cases, secondments will be made between R&D and Marketing, or between broadly defined project themes.
- R&D personnel are encouraged to offer consultancy to the company's business units and to answer queries over the phone or face-to-face. They keep a 'day book' when doing this to help identify emerging themes and issues. This provides important feedback from the market and external developments and helps to build a reputation of technical excellence for the R&D function.
- Heads of Departments in the corporate R&D laboratory maintain a 'Skills Matrix' which encapsulates the areas of expertise of each member of that unit. This is used during induction courses to help newcomers get assistance from specialists in a subject, as well as enabling project managers to build teams with an appropriate mix of skills.
- R&D units uses a policy of dual 'matrix management' of key R&D staff by project staff supervisors and departmental line managers with the aim of translating and disseminating knowledge between project-specific and functional departmental domains.
- Induction courses give technical overviews of all disciplines covered in the lab, supported by well-signposted and simple electronic access through an intranet and e-mail to relevant experts and knowledge sources. Ongoing training courses also provide opportunities for staff to learn skills outside their prime area of expertise.

3.2.4. Group D: KMPs for Managing Intellectual Property Positions

There are a number of KMPs in the field of intellectual property rights which reflect the fact that in-house IPR experts in R&D labs are becoming more pro-active. Instead of principally providing a service to formulate patent applications and maintain patents, it is now more common to find them actively distributing information about competitors' patent activity to R&D teams, with commentary on its implications for the strategic direction and detail of the company's own R&D. In some cases, this activity is conducted jointly with library staff to provide an electronically delivered 'Patent Watch' service available to the desktop of individual scientists.

A second major KMP in this group is the early involvement of IPR staff with R&D teams to formulate the IPR dimensions of emergent instances of novel technology. The distinguishing feature of this practice is that IPR expertise is being brought to bear on the direction of R&D technical activity in mid-project. In addition, there are often issues around the translation between the legal basis of IPR expertise, and the varieties of backgrounds to R&D expertise.

3.2.5. Group E: KMPs and R&D information technology management

As has already been mentioned, information technology applications can be a significant enabler of the emergence of new KMPs. Examples are the electronic archiving of technical documents which emerge from R&D work (Group A above); electronic 'Patent Watch' bulletins (Group D above), and Intranet approaches to the facilitation of clusters of R&D expertise making their skills available to previously unknown collaborators elsewhere in the corporate structure (Group B above). In the firms with large extended projects, it has already been noted that in the context of civil engineering, this is not necessarily dominated by electronic media, although they do have some role. In the context of the building of chemical plants however, the role of information technology-based modes of knowledge capture appears to be somewhat greater.

There is, however, a (somewhat non-rigorous) distinction to be made between those cases where IT *supports* a KMP which has a strong independent existence, and those cases where IT provides the trigger to create or change a KMP. [43] There is no doubt that e-mail availability has facilitated the emergence of new R&D virtual clusters of personnel, and that some of this activity is therefore, 'bottom-up' activity enabled by the unintentional consequences of e-mail availability. It is also our observation that the availability of groupware packages such as Lotus Notes has stimulated experiments in new ways of sharing knowledge in project teams that might not otherwise have been attempted. Similarly, the rapidly diffusing experience of individuals using the worldwide-web has raised expectations and interest concerning the potential of its corporate equivalent: the 'intranet'.

In addition to these changes in the availability of IT, we can also note the fact that R&D centres are now attracting the attention of information management specialists from the corporate centre, who have already cut their teeth on information systems to support operations management, finance, and marketing functions; and are now asking the question 'what is the strategic role of IT in R&D?'. This leads to the emergence of champions and of the relevant expertise to actually implement such projects as electronic archives of technical data, intranets, and the like.

3.3. Relationships between KMPs

In Sections 3.1 and 3.2, we have developed a framework for categorising knowledge management practices, based around four dimensions or attributes of KMPs. These dimensions have not been predicated on any particular understanding of the nature of knowledge or the desirability and techniques for knowledge management. Instead, we have developed a perspective that views KMPs as one instance of practices in general, and hence, described them in terms of their objectives (what is 'done' to knowledge, and what is the 'domain' of that knowledge, and what are the intended effects on firm performance), and in terms of the format or degree of structuring of the KMPs. We have then used these dimensions to describe and to classify some of the most common KMPs to be found in R&D and innovative activities. Whilst many of these have been established for some time and are clearly embedded as routine activities within R&D, others are emerging from within established sub-departments of R&D or across organisational boundaries, and they are either instigated at a senior level or appearing as bottom-up initiatives.

Despite the preliminary state of this taxonomy, it is nonetheless interesting to note that there are some broad patterns visible in the interactions of the KMPs in any given R&D unit. The *knowledge base* of a firm was identified in Section 2 of the paper as important to the understanding of path-dependent innovation within the evolutionary perspective. We suggest that knowledge management practices drawn from all 5 of the categories described above can be seen to contribute in three distinct ways to that knowledge base.

Firstly, the KMPs constitute and enable discussion of an evolving 'stock' of knowledge about technologies which the firm can deploy, and about the significance of those technologies. Furthermore, that stock is conceived as both internal and external to the firm.

Secondly, the same KMPs can contribute to a stock of market-based knowledge, concerning the requirements of customers, their behaviour, and the market opportunities which might be feasible in the future.

Thirdly, the KMPs create a stock of knowledge about the administrative, technical and management processes within the firm itself, through which it identifies and delivers both existing and new products and processes.

Now, it is clear that the various histories, choices and circumstances of firms influence the extent to which these three bodies of knowledge are thoroughly articulated and developed. In some firms, the technology stock is much more thoroughly developed as a genuine firm resource than in others,

[43] This raises the question of whether it is possible, in general, to distinguish between ICTs which support existing KMPs, and those which enable the creation of new or significantly changed KMPs. This would seem to be difficult, and such distinctions are perhaps more likely to be highly context-specific.

largely through the application of Group B1 or B1 and B2 KMPs. In other firms, the market knowledge stock can be more thoroughly developed; and in others, the process knowledge stock is better understood. [44] In addition, there may be marked differences between firms in terms of their focus upon KMPs for accumulating, interfacing or deploying their knowledge bases. Some of the reason for this variation lies in the specific nature of the companies and their industries; but all of them could, in principle, exploit all types of knowledge base management to a higher degree.

The potential for interaction between the major types of KMP can be illustrated by the case of one company, in particular, which produces a wide variety of electronic devices. An emergent new model of the strategic mission for the corporate R&D lab could be discerned in the discussions around KMPs. This took the form of a model in which the lab would try to fully exploit all three types of knowledge base (technology, market, and company process), and to *combine* them in such a way as to identify 'new business propositions' for the corporate parent. This is interesting because it is a role for the R&D unit which goes beyond simple innovation, and instead proposes corporate diversification options of strategic significance.

4. Conclusion

The preceding discussion demonstrates that knowledge management practices can vary from firm to firm in their number, detail, and mode of implementation. It also demonstrates that the 'menu' of available KMPs is in principle growing, and that firms can, if they chose, avail themselves of more and more sophisticated knowledge management options, even to the point of having knowledge management 'strategies'.

We have also seen that by focusing on KMPs rather than on the technology itself or on the actual forms of knowledge, we have penetrated quite deeply into both the *current* forms of path-dependence in a firm *and* the KMPs which are capable in principle of *changing* the constraints on innovation, and thus, *modifying* the path-dependence of a firm. This raises the issue, referred to in the introduction, of the potential for variety-generation *within* the firm. It was pointed out that the traditional evolutionary perspective emphasises the constraints on variety, whereas the new perspectives on knowledge management emphasise the possibility of partially *relaxing* the constraints on variety generation.

The analysis presented above suggests that there is some reason to move partially towards this second point of view. This is a qualified judgement however. Firms are clearly moving at different speeds to adopt new KMPs. Furthermore, it is not clear that all the new KMPs strengthen variety generation. It is possible to imagine a mode of implementing a highly IT-based set of KMPs which lead to a *strengthening* of that part of the knowledge base which maintains the current distinctive technological 'signature' of a firm, and does not promote more variety. Like many other aspects of management activity, the outcome is as much dependent on the implementation of changes as on their intended substance.

If it is true that knowledge management can modify the potential for variety generation within the firm, then this finding has significance for evolutionary economics in general. Currently, variety generation is seen very much as a phenomenon linked to populations of firms, and mediated through firm birth and firm death. An increase in the potential for intra-firm variety generation would shift the locus of variety generation away from the population to some extent.

Finally, it seems fruitful to continue to explore these issues through the lens of knowledge management *practices*, rather than only through categories

[44] This could be a case where the path-dependency of a particular firm was seen to be located strongly within its 'technology as hardware'—that is, the senior management sees the firm to be highly tied to its operational technologies, such as production lines or communications systems, and they deal with that through maintaining extensive knowledge of that hardware. In other words, in general, the relationship between KMPs as a location of path-dependency, and 'technology-as-hardware' as a location of path-dependency, will depend not just on differences between forms of 'technology-as-hardware', but also on the ways in which the 'process knowledge stock' is maintained and utilised.

of knowledge or technology. [45] These practices have the advantage that they can be mapped empirically, and that the particular combinations of KMPs in a given firm can be diagnosed and linked to the observed innovative activity. Furthermore, it seems that in mapping KMPs, one is laying bare a dimension of the way firms organise which does not relate mechanically to other reference points for organisation such as money, power or authority. [46] Focusing on KMPs allows us to access the sense in which firms are engaged in *organising* rather than simply exhibiting the properties of an organisation. This is a fruitful research agenda for the future.

Acknowledgements

The authors gratefully acknowledge the support of an ESRC Grant No. L125251008, within the ESRC Innovation Programme. Various drafts of this paper have been presented on a number of occasions and we have had many useful comments. We are especially grateful to the three anonymous referees, to Stan Metcalfe, Malcolm Peltu, Andy McMeekin, our colleagues in CRIC, and to the participants of seminars at SPRU, MKIRU, the BAM conference, and the EASST/4S conference.

[45] This is also in accordance with the observations of Foss, op. cit. 1996a and 1996b, who argues forcibly that 'knowledge-based approaches to the theory of the firm', although interesting, do not provide *sufficient* explanations for the existence of *firms*, rather than other forms of economic organisation such as markets. He further suggests that the basis of economic organisation may instead be found in the study of contracts and asset ownership. It could be surmised that such a focus would further tend to downplay the possibilities for relaxing the constraints on innovation.

[46] Thus, for instance, mapping the KMPs found within the innovation processes of a large divisionalised corporation may yield quite a different picture to that obtained through organisational charts, or the flows of finance and formal reporting. It is in such a context that the unit of analysis for understanding the locations of path-dependency become of critical importance.

[18]

Technology Analysis & Strategic Management, Vol. 8, No. 2, 1996 91

Tacit Knowledge, Innovation and Technology Transfer

JEREMY HOWELLS

ABSTRACT *Until recently, the concept of tacit knowledge has been neglected by academics and managers alike, but this has now changed as tacit know-how has become recognized as playing a key role in firm growth and economic competitiveness. Tacit knowledge forms an important element in a firm's knowledge base and has a central role in organizational learning. This paper analyzes what is meant by tacit knowledge and outlines its main parameters and traits. The analysis stresses the need to view tacit knowledge in a dynamic setting, and that tacit knowledge can be acquired and transferred on a variety of levels: individual, group, firm and inter-firm basis. The paper then explores the policy implications of technology transfer initiatives which seek to shift tacit know-how between firms and analyzes the ways that this can be achieved.*

Introduction

Just as technological innovation up until the 1960s was treated as an unexplained variance in economic growth and performance, so tacit knowledge as an element within technological innovation has, until recently, been seen in a similar way. Interest in tacit knowledge has grown rapidly as it has become increasingly acknowledged that the contribution of technological innovation to growth and economic performance is not just simply associated with embodied technologies, such as new plant and equipment, but is also highly dependent on disembodied, intangible assets and working practices.[1]

As such, there has been a growing recognition that the performance of economies and firms is dependent on qualities and attributes that are tacit in form.[2] In the management literature, the importance of tacit knowledge has also been acknowledged with the growing acceptance of the importance of the learning process within organizations as a means of corporate renewal and reinvigoration. As Pisano[3] has noted "... the proposition that competitive advantage stems from firm-specific skills and capabilities has made learning a focal point of concern ... ". Such interest has coalesced in studies outlining the creation and dynamics of the 'learning organization'.[4]

Definition

A central issue in any discussion about tacit knowledge is how it is defined and what are its key dimensions and attributes. This is the very reason that tacit knowledge is so difficult to define and quantify. Indeed, Olesko,[5] in the context of reviewing investigations into the history of science, suggests that even the hint that a scientific process involved some element or form of tacit knowledge led to its foreclosing as a scientific activity for study. As a consequence, the activity would remain a nebulous process to outsiders,

Jeremy Howells, Judge Institute of Management Studies/ESRC Centre for Business Research, University of Cambridge, UK. Current address: PREST, 8 John Adam Street, London WC2N 6EZ, UK.

0953-7325/96/020091-16

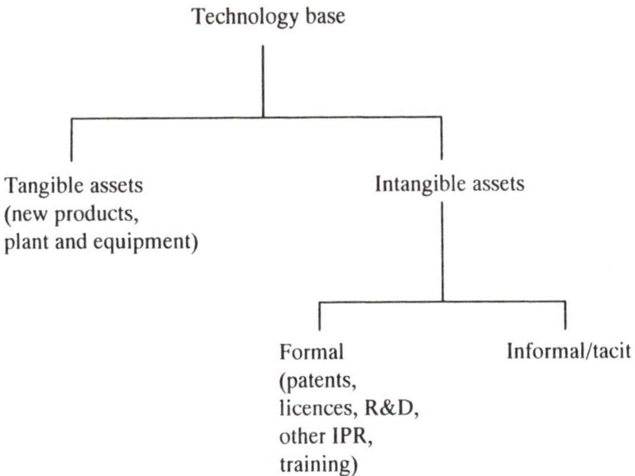

Figure 1. The technology profile of a firm.

ring-fenced by the title 'tacit knowledge'. This also explains why it has been a neglected subject for analysis, but also makes it of such interest.

How is tacit knowledge defined? It is generally accepted that tacit knowledge (as distinct from intangible investment more generally) is non-codified, disembodied know-how that is acquired via the informal take-up of learned behaviour and procedures. Learning in an unstructured or semi-structured way is a key process within tacit knowledge acquisition and transfer. In discussing tacit knowledge, it is important to posit it within the wider technology base of the firm (Figure 1). A major component of this is the tangible asset or resource base of the firm evident in embodied technologies associated with new products and equipment. However, another major element is the firm's intangible assets. Many non-tangible assets and investments are formalized in terms of patents, licences, research contracts or specific training programmes.[6] Research has begun on trying to measure and evaluate these more accurately, led by the work of the Organization for Economic Cooperation and Development (OECD),[7] but adequate measurement of technical non-tangible assets still remains a long way off. As such, tacit knowledge does not involve the generation and acquisition of tangible products and processes, or the more formal element of intangible knowledge flows associated with specific research, technical or training programmes.

However, much of the discussion about what tacit knowledge is has been influenced and based upon the work of Michael Polanyi.[8] Polanyi[9] describes tacit knowledge as involving two kinds of awareness: the 'subsidiary' and 'focal'. While we might focus our awareness on a particular object or process, we bring with that 'focal awareness' a 'subsidiary awareness' which is in turn associated with two types of clues: 'subliminal clues', which are clues we cannot directly experience ourselves (for example, a process which is too small to observe) and 'marginal clues', which are marginal to our field of awareness or vision but which impart some information. Both sets of clues are not intended to contribute directly to the reality of the object on which attention is focused. In turn, 'subsidiary' and 'focal' awareness, in combination, are fundamental to tacit apprehension and (as in wider gestalt theory) provide a functional appreciation which would not be possible if they were taken in isolation. However, although tacit knowing involves awareness, it is also combined with 'subception', learning without awareness.

This process can be associated with scientific intuition (see, for example, Ziman[10]) and the issue of serendipity in scientific discovery.

Elsewhere, Polanyi[11] sums up tacit knowing as an act of 'indwelling', the process of assimilating to ourselves things from outside. It also involves more innate values, such as skills. Thus:

> If I know how to ride a bicycle or keep afloat when swimming I may not have the slightest idea of how I do this or even an entirely wrong or grossly imperfect idea of it and yet I go cycling or swimming merrily. Nor can it be said that I know how to bicycle or swim and yet do not how to coordinate the complex pattern of muscular acts when I do my cycling or swimming. I both know how to carry out these performances as a whole and also know how to carry out the elementary acts which constitute them, though I cannot tell what these acts are. This is due to the fact that I am only subsidiarily aware of these things, and our awareness of a thing may not suffice to make it identifiable.[12]

In addition, it is generally accepted that tacit know-how cannot be directly or easily transmitted (see later), as knowledge and task performance are individual and specific and involve the acquirer making changes to existing behaviour. However, the degree of tacitness does vary. Within the range of tacit knowledge itself, the less explicit and codified the tacit know-how is, the more difficult it is for individuals and firms to assimilate it.[13] 'Learning by doing',[14] 'learning by using'[15] and 'learning to learn'[16] are seen as critical elements within tacit knowledge acquisition. Above all, there are no clear market mechanisms which facilitate the transfer of tacit knowledge directly or by which it can be adequately measured.

Academic and policy interest in tacit knowledge has come from two strands. One strand relates to work on technological innovation which has become increasingly interested in tacit knowledge through continued developments in trying to improve the measurement of technological change and in terms of its acknowledged role in industrial and corporate performance. Analysis here has focused either on specific technologies themselves or, on a more macro-level basis, trying to identify regularities between sectors or markets on their dependence on tacit knowledge for technical and competitive advantage.

The other strand has come from management and business studies investigating the management of change and core competencies of the firm,[17] as well as the role of learning (both individual, group and organization-wide) and knowledge in firm performance.[18] This interest has been heightened by the growth of Japanese competition and the spread of Japanese management techniques.[19] The strength of Japanese corporations was seen to reside not so much in research and development (R&D) or the scale and performance of the specific plant and machinery ('hard technology'), but in the way these operations were managed and configured and in the skills and flexibility of the workforce (i.e. 'soft technology'[20]). Increasingly, however, the two main strands of interest are coalescing in terms of their interest in tacit know-how and technological competitiveness.

This paper seeks to provide an overview of existing research into tacit knowledge, but more particularly aims to provide a more rigorous framework in which to analyze and codify the different dimensions and attributes of tacitness. Lastly, and most importantly, it will seek to outline some of the key conclusions and themes arising from this analysis.

Tacit Knowledge: Framework and Attributes

As noted earlier, there have been considerable advances in the measurement of embodied technologies associated with new products and processes. In contrast, tacit knowledge which is informal and non-tangible in character has still been largely neglected in the context of research and policy formulation. A major reason why this has been the case is that tacit knowledge remains a very nebulous concept and is extremely difficult to measure and evaluate; even compared with formal, non-tangible assets see earlier). The previous section provided a definition of what tacit knowledge is, but this mainly defined what tacit knowledge is in terms of what it is not.

To gain a better understanding of what tacitness is concerned with, it is useful to outline the different elements or attributes that tacit knowledge contains. These key dimensions or attributes of tacit knowledge cover:

(1) the different forms that tacit knowledge can take;
(2) tacit knowledge acquisition channels—the medium by which tacit knowledge is transferred and, related to this, organizational/firm level of flows;
(3) the locus and scale of tacit knowledge transfer;
(4) the length of time and periodicity of tacit knowledge flows;
(5) the degree of formality of tacit knowledge;
(6) the time period in the innovation process at which tacit knowledge is acquired and utilized.

The rest of this section will outline these different attributes of tacit knowledge in an attempt to improve our conceptual understanding of the phenomenon. However, it will also act as a precursor to raising a number of key strategic issues concerning tacit know-how, both at the firm/organizational level and also in terms of the wider economy as it relates to industrial competitiveness.

The Different Attributes of Tacit Knowledge

As noted earlier, previous definitions of tacit knowledge have described what it is not, i.e. explicit knowledge. Tacitness is something that cannot be easily codified or learnt. More specifically, are there different types of, or dimensions to, tacit knowledge? Zander and Zander,[21] in their analysis of imitation and tacitness in two Swedish companies, highlight the notion of degrees of tacitness based upon Polyani's three forms of tacit knowing. The first, the high 'speed and simultaneity' of information processing may force a learner of a new skill to work out the details of the coordination for himself/herself. In this case, the actual performance cannot be slowed down and practising cannot be done slowly. In the second form, it is sometimes difficult to 'articulate' all that is necessary to master a skill since the action is embedded in the context. If one of the many context variables changes too much there will be no performance and all the 'ifs' cannot be meaningfully expressed.

Lastly, the relationship between the details of a complex skill, even if articuable one by one, is sometimes lost in language, which due to its serial nature cannot simultaneously serve to describe relationships and characterize the things related. Zander and Zander[22] see this as leading to "our assertion that skills tend to be more articuable when the pace of the required performance is slow and pace variations tolerable, when a standardised, controlled context for the performance is somehow assured, and when the performance as a whole can be truly cut down to a set of simple parts that relate to one another only in very simple ways".

Tacit knowledge therefore involves learning and skill but in a way that cannot be communicated in any direct, codified way. 'Learning by doing' and 'learning by using' (and also 'learning to learn') are therefore crucial elements in tacit knowledge acquisition associated with direct, on-the-job contact with new equipment, work practice or operation. This directness is important whether it be at a person-to-machine, person-to-person or person-to-activity level. It is hard to conceive of situations where tacit knowledge can be acquired indirectly as this would involve some kind of codification and lack of direct experience.

Tacit Knowledge: Generation, Acquisition and Organizational Flows

A key element, particularly in corporate strategy and policy debates, is how tacit knowledge can be acquired. Since tacitness is something very much to do with direct experience and is person-embodied, it is not directly codifiable via artefacts. A firm or organization can possess tacit knowledge through its workforce or via the operational milieu that exists and is created and sustained within the organizational structure. As such, personnel within a firm can gain tacit knowledge via direct work experience in, for example, the production process, research laboratory or pilot plant. Tacit knowledge, however, is not a static stock of knowledge (see later). It is continually being built upon and learnt, involving intuition and trial and error. This can include improvements and modifications to new technology in terms of plant and machinery acquired from outside the firm (associated with 'learning by using'), or new machinery or work practices, involved with production or other corporate functions, developed within the firm (associated with 'learning by doing'). In either of these two cases, although the technology may be acquired from outside the firm, tacit knowledge is gained from experiences within the firm.

Tacit knowledge, however, can also be gained from outside the firm. It can involve staff working off-site collaborating with other firms in the same industry or sector (horizontal collaboration), or via collaboration backwards with suppliers, or forwards with firms further up the production or marketing chain. Tacit knowledge can also be gained through intermediaries, such as consultancies, that provide direct on-the-job training or undertake, for example, diagnostic or 'trouble-shooting' services.

Understanding the organizational level at which tacit know-how flows can occur is particularly useful in codifying support mechanisms and policy intervention levels. These can be classified as:

(1) *Intra-firm/intra-organizational flows*—involving the movement of tacit knowledge at individual, group, departmental and establishment level between sites and countries within the same organization.
(2) *Inter-firm flows: vertical*—covering the links between staff from firms in different industries collaborating on the same product, process or technology field (associated with comakership, buyer–supplier, vendor and subcontracting links).
(3) *Inter-firm flows: horizontal*—relating to the movement of, and contact with, staff between different firms working in the same industry and collaborating with each other.
(4) *Inter-institutional flows*—involving links and staff flows between firms, higher education institutes (HEIs), public research establishments (PREs) and other intermediaries.

All these acquisition channels, though they can cross firm or organizational boundaries, are associated with largely person-embodied acquisition patterns rooted in direct on-site learning and experience. Since tacit knowledge cannot be easily codified or stored it can, over time, be forgotten by individuals. Similarly, in a more general organizational context the conditions from which tacit knowledge can be gained can also be eroded over time if the right environmental context is dissipated. Tacit knowledge may also be lost by the hiring away of skilled staff by another firm (see later).

Locus and Scale of Tacit Knowledge

Much of the discussion about tacit knowledge has been about the individual. This is not surprising given that tacit knowledge is largely person-embodied. On this basis, is it appropriate to consider tacit knowledge operating at a firm level? Equally, how far can a firm be said to have a clear tacit knowledge profile of its own?

Certainly, individuals as a group can be involved in jointly acquiring tacit knowledge associated with the working conditions of the firm and its collaborative links. Some forms of tacit knowledge may indeed be only acquired within a group, collective learning context; for example, the working practices developed on the shopfloor, or in a particular research laboratory group. Many firms can be said to have such identifiable corporate cultures and learning capabilities,[23] and these might be considered to form the basis for a more corporate-wide tacit knowledge environment that can be sustained and nurtured.

Strategies and policies designed to improve tacit knowledge at the firm level need to consider both the individual, group, site, business unit and firm levels. How can the working environments within each of these levels be developed which can be sustained and improved in relation to tacit knowledge learning? Firms also need to consider net flows of tacit knowledge to and from the firm. There can indeed be outward flows of person-embodied, tacit know-how from the firm, via the hiring away of skilled staff, and inward flows, through the recruitment of new personnel (see later). Consideration of scale is therefore crucially important in terms of strategies and policies.

The Timing and Periodicity of Tacit Knowledge Flows

The time-scale and periodicity involved in personal contacts when transferring tacit know-how is also important. It can range from a one-off, face-to-face meeting, through to temporary staff-secondment and on to continuous interaction by staff working at the same site collaborating on a joint project. On an inter-organizational basis, tacit know-how links can also vary from one-off, infrequent contacts through to lengthy, long-term research or technical collaborative programmes. Short and/or infrequent visits, even when the organizations are formally committed to tacit know-how sharing, can be a poor mechanism for transferring tacit knowledge when the individuals from each of the organizations are unfamiliar with each other and as a consequence are reluctant to share information.[24]

Tacit Knowledge Acquisition and Stage in the Innovation Process

Related to this dimension, the stage at which tacit knowledge is gained and utilized in the innovation and production process is an important strategy and policy issue. Thus, tacit knowledge transfer can occur when:

- generating new scientific knowledge (associated with 'learning to learn');
- incorporating new knowledge in the design of a new product;
- when learning new production methods ('learning by doing');
- once the new product or process is being used internal to the firm or by external consumers ('learning by using'[25]).

It is important to emphasize that tacit knowledge is gained throughout the innovation and production chain of a company, not just on the shopfloor associated with direct manufacturing operations. Tacit know-how is therefore gained and utilized throughout all functions and stages of a firm's operations.

Formality of Tacit Knowledge Acquisition and Transfer

Although tacit knowledge cannot be formalized in the sense that it is fully codifiable or exactly reproducible, the conditions from which tacit knowledge can be acquired can vary substantially in terms of formality. They can range from planned on-the-job training schemes that are run by outside intermediaries to informal, chance contacts or via trail-and-error sessions by employees working on their own, perhaps in their spare time.

Tacit Knowledge: Imitation, Diffusion and Appropriability

It is paradoxical that policies that have been targeted at tacit knowledge have been aimed at improving the diffusion of tacit knowledge between firms, although it has been revealed that tacit knowledge has been a key barrier in the diffusion of technological innovation. A key element, therefore, is that tacit knowledge is difficult to codify and it is usually part of a long-term, accumulated learning process that often starts a more systematic scientific understanding of a technology or process.

Thus, studies on the growth of the US commercial aircraft industry have highlighted the incremental developments in aircraft and engine design associated with learning by using during the course of aircraft manufacture and the uncertainty involved in the complex integration of the whole range of aircraft subsystems. This can often be likened to a search process of testing and discovery. As such "a great deal of the knowledge that is important to the operation and improvement of a given process or product technology is 'tacit' that is, not easily embodied in a blueprint or operating manual".[26] This helps to explain observations of the industry in terms of the benefits of the steep learning curve related to the increasing number of total airframes built by a particular aircraft company.[27] This view has been taken up in more detail by Vincenti's[28] study of the aircraft industry and the development of flush-riveting in airplanes—aircraft companies required practical 'trial-and-error' experience (learning by using) to master fully the new technology and personal demonstration.[29]

Equally, many of the early developments in the chemical and pharmaceutical industries were dependent not on sound scientific theory, but on observation and experimentation and 'feel' for what was right in terms of, for example, how patients reacted to new medicines.[30] Thus, experimental methods in the 17th and 18th centuries laid the foundation for Paracelsian chemistry, which formed the basic framework of modern chemistry.[31] Similarly, early work in the use of insulin for treating diabetes was based on close observation of the effects of various pancreatic extracts on animals and humans.[32] It was often only subsequently that scientific discoveries and advances were able to explain and systematize the initial observations and practice that arose out of them in medicine.

Process equipment technology, particularly scientific instruments, machine tools and advanced manufacturing technologies, is also an area where tacit knowledge has had a profound role in technological development. The early development of scientific instruments (indeed up until recently) has been associated with staff in laboratories working together in a highly informal manner, 'tinkering' around with existing apparatus.[33] The work of Von Hippel[34] has amply illustrated the importance of the users' practical experiences in using scientific instruments, and the tacit knowledge gained from this, that has provided such a valuable input to the instrument makers in their further refinement and development of their products. Equally, Ehrnberg and Sjöberg,[35] in their study of diffusion of flexible manufacturing systems (FMSs) in machine tools, have also highlighted the role of tacit knowledge as a key, but indirect entry barrier into FMS technology for machine tool builders. Application knowledge, which was a core capability in developing competence in FMS, was highly tacit in nature and centred around the ability to specify and describe the order of events and the flow of information, tools and workpieces that could only be gained via interaction with advanced customers. For potential new entrants, lack of access to these advanced customers and hence the ability to gain tacit application knowledge meant they effectively remained blocked from gaining entry to the new technology. On a more general level, Leonard-Barton[36] has also acknowledged the role of tacit know-how in organizational learning, and this pivotal role played by tacit knowledge has in turn been supported by Bessant and Buckingham[37] in their study of organizational learning in the implementation of advanced manufacturing technology in three UK-based firms.

The *a posteriori* confirmation by science of practical technical and engineering results rather than providing *a priori* guidance to technical workers can also be seen in developments in metallurgy. As such "well into the twentieth century, metallurgy was a sector in which the technologists typically 'got there first', developing powerful new technologies in advance of systematic guidance by science".[38] This is echoed by Knoedler's study of the US steel industry in the 19th century and her analysis of the background of the individuals working on technological developments within the sector. Thus "innovations in the pre-1900 US steel industry were not developed by scientifically trained personnel who spent their days exploring the industry's scientific foundation; instead they were developed and executed through the efforts of 'rule of thumb' men, mainly through on the job modifications of traditional production techniques".[39]

This contrast between scientists and technologists in the way they operate (the scientist who is logical and whose work is capable of being codified and readily communicable to outsiders, compared with the technologist whose work is practical and involving 'hands on' tacit experience not readily communicable to outsiders) is one which is elaborated upon by Sørensen and Levold[40] in their portrayal of the role of Kristian Birkeland and Sam Eyde in the commercial development of nitrogen fertilizer and the establishment of Norsk Hydro. This contrast is summed up as 'scientific cunning' as against 'engineering stamina'.[41] However, although many of these studies continue to portray scientific work operating within a highly logical and formalized set of codes and frameworks, evidence from the pharmaceutical industry, cited above, and more generally by Ziman,[42] suggests that 'intuition', serendipity and 'craft skills'[43]—all based on tacit qualities—still play an important role in the process of scientific discovery.

All these examples serve to indicate that science does not always precede developments in technology and production. Moreover, it has been shown that science itself does not always follow a structured, codified path and that innovation is frequently associated with long-term accumulated knowledge that is difficult to acquire. The very strength and importance of tacit knowledge is that it is often very difficult for competitor firms to imitate it. Tacit knowledge is therefore often an important element in industrial collaboration, both as a factor initiating collaboration and in its success. On one hand, firms may seek to collaborate in a close and sharing manner because they acknowledge that tacit knowledge is a key factor in the competitive advantage of the collaboration or joint venture and this is the only way that tacit know-how can be transferred and shared. Ring[44] describes the environments created to enhance the transfer of new tacit know-how assets between firms in collaborative technology development as 'commensualistic environments', which are in turn dependent on a high degree of trust to be fully successful. Levels of trust, in turn, depend critically on the presence of certain institutional processes which reduce the risks inherent in agents trusting one another, associated with the development of norms and standards in a sector or technology.[45] Willingness to share tacit knowledge is also likely to be dependent on levels of reciprocity, with firms only trading information when they know it will be reciprocated.[46]

However, where a company is collaborating for other non-technical reasons, such as market access or cost sharing, and where it sees its tacit knowledge as a key factor in its competitiveness, it will go to great lengths to stop such tacit knowledge leaking out. Thus, Boeing has gone to great lengths to isolate much of its tacit know-how in airframe manufacturing and marketing from its Japanese collaborators in the 777 consortium.[47] Equally, work by Zander and Zander[48] has revealed that in the case of one innovation, a pulp flash dryer, tacit knowledge was important in restricting imitators. This was particularly true in the critical area of dryer dimensioning which required the exact tooling of different parts of the dryer and where competing firms found it difficult to replicate the process. Key know-how in this manufacturing process, therefore, proved to be highly effective in providing a long-term, competitive advantage for the firm who initially developed it.

However, tacitness by itself may not always restrict imitation. In another example from Zander and Zander's study, a hydraulic rock drill, there were a large number of imitators. This was in spite of a complex and partly tacit manufacturing process where reverse engineering and other methods to get hold of the production technology were strongly impaired. In the case of the pulp flash dryer, a key factor reducing imitation was not tacit knowledge itself but that this tacit know-how could not be held by a single individual or a small group of individuals who could then leave and set up for themselves or work for rival companies. The company achieved this by restricting the access and maintaining the secrecy of the accumulated learning as far as possible through combining bits of tacit knowledge (in part through the eventual codification of some of the critical knowledge) from local sources into one central place, Sweden, and not allowing this information then to be dispersed back down to these local units. Indeed, this is a good example of tacit know-how being shown to be a group-wide, firm-based, phenomenon rather than just being an individual-centred process (see earlier).

Tacit knowledge, therefore, may not in itself provide the basis for gaining competitive advantage over existing and potential competitors. However, in combination with making tacit know-how difficult to copy or replicate by competitors, via hiring away of key staff, reverse engineering or other means of getting hold of tacit knowledge and accumulated learning, it can be a powerful element in a firm's wider knowledge base[49] and competitive capability. For a firm to develop a successful strategy on the basis of its tacit knowledge skills, it therefore needs to enhance these capabilities by a range of other measures that will protect them from imitation. Above all, companies need continually to regenerate their tacit knowledge capabilities and enable them to be captured and enhanced at a business or firm level, rather than allow them to reside in a few individuals or groups of people who may then leave.

Tacit Knowledge: Key Issues

What has this review and analysis revealed about tacit knowledge itself and firms seeking to foster tacit know-how and transfer within their organization and between their organization and other organizations? Certainly, a number of significant points have arisen from this analysis of tacit knowledge, and are outlined in the following.

The Importance of Tacit Knowledge

This paper has highlighted the importance of tacit knowledge. Indeed, a recent survey of R&D workers in 23 firms revealed that tacit skills acquired largely on the job made a greater contribution to innovation than had formal knowledge acquired from literature and education.[50] However, equally, its role should not be overstated in terms of its universality and strength. Even in areas where tacit knowledge is significant, such as experiential learning, knowledge creation and scientific discovery, and where know-how cannot be codified or fully formalized, it should be seen within a wider framework of a more conscious process of learning.[51] This specific learning process can, in turn, form part of a wider organizational learning 'routine'[52] that can help to create and diffuse firm-specific competencies and knowledge sets.[53]

This theme is more strongly echoed by Pisano's[54] study of process development in the pharmaceutical industry. Although it is almost inescapable that firms will have to learn some things through 'learning by doing', it can often, where possible, be preferable to undertake 'learning before doing'. In Pisano's study, biotechnology firms were forced to carry out 'learning by doing' because they lacked experience, while longer established pharmaceutical firms could rely more on previous research that they had accumulated and retained within their technical knowledge base. Thus, although, as Pisano[55] notes, there is no best approach to learning ('learning by doing' versus 'learning before doing'), firms working in the same innovation environment are not automatically dependent on 'learning by doing'. Thus, alternatives do often exist for on-the-job acquisition of tacit know-how, at least for firms which have been able to accumulate the necessary technical and organizational knowledge.

Moreover, the importance of tacit knowledge does appear to vary significantly between sector, technology, market or product group.[56] The value and relevance of tacit knowledge may indeed vary significantly within an industry or even between products produced by the same firm. More research needs to be undertaken on why these inter-industry and inter-firm variations in the importance of tacit knowledge exist, and it would also help to reveal more about the nature of tacit knowledge itself. The possible substitution between tacit and non-tacit know-how acquisition and sectoral differences in the significance of tacit knowledge are therefore research areas where knowledge remains limited.

The Dynamics of Tacit Knowledge and the Competitive Stock of Knowledge

The issue of hiring away of key staff, noted earlier, highlights the importance of viewing tacit knowledge in terms of a dynamic process of knowledge generation and flows that alter the total stock and profile of tacit know-how that a firm holds at any one time. Tacit knowledge should therefore not be seen as a static phenomenon. It involves a stock of knowledge that is continually being added to through accumulated learning and eroded away via loss of staff, 'forgetting'[57] or through other companies attempting to capture similar tacit qualities. As such, this dynamic competence may be termed the 'competitive stock of tacit knowledge' of a firm and can be linked in with a wider body of literature that has attempted to describe the organizational capabilities of firms in this respect (see earlier).

More specifically, the 'competitive stock of tacit knowledge' a firm possesses at any point in time involves:

- assimilation (inflow) of tacit knowledge from outside the firm;
- net changes in the internal stock of tacit knowledge capabilities that a firm possesses

which varies according to (a) its generation and accumulation (increase) of know-how learning, as well as (b) its loss via institutional forgetting or misplacing;
- through leakage and imitation of tacit know-how to other firms leading to a loss in tacit know-how assets.

In this latter respect, it should be noted that the absolute stock of tacit knowledge that a firm holds does not go down when it is imitated by other firms, as information and knowledge once gained cannot be lost simply by sharing it[58] (although it can still be forgotten, abandoned or misplaced by the firm). In this sense, it represents a relative loss in the stock of tacit knowledge; however, in certain instances when key personnel that hold valuable tacit know-how are poached away by other competing firms this can therefore also mean an absolute loss of tacit knowledge to the firm.

Lastly, the time advantage a firm possesses is also an important element when considering competitive advantage relating to tacit knowledge. Here again, although the actual stock of tacit know-how a firm possesses may be large, its competitive stock of knowledge may not be large enough if it can be rapidly imitated by other competitors. Therefore the more a firm can lengthen the period between imitation and 'catching up' by other firms of tacit know-how the more it extends its 'competitive stock of knowledge'. In essence, it seeks to lengthen its 'quasi' or temporary monopoly in the generation and use of knowledge.[59]

Tacit knowledge may, therefore, not in itself confer major technical and competitive advantages for a firm. As noted earlier, in certain sectors, tacit know-how may not be particularly important. Even where it is, if tacit knowledge can be acquired or imitated fairly easily, the competitive advantage for the firm that has taken the lead in acquiring and developing it will not remain significant for very long.[60] A firm therefore needs to develop a dynamic tacit competence that is continually being refreshed and updated. As part of this strategy, firms need to consider ways in which the unplanned leakage of tacit know-how to other firms can be slowed down or halted.

The Locus of Tacit Knowledge Learning and Transfer

The importance of distinguishing between tacit knowledge learning and transfer at the individual, group and firm level was noted earlier. Individuals are significant sources, conduits and generators of tacit knowledge, but a firm's tacit knowledge and learning base is not just simply the sum of its individual employees. There is, as well as individual learning patterns, organizational tacit know-how learning led by key teams of managers and decision-makers throughout the firm, which help to steer the cognitive development of the firm and create an environment where tacit knowledge can be more successfully generated and sustained by individuals working within the firm. More particularly, the key components of how a new technology or product are designed or manufactured can often only be learnt or stored at the firm or group level. Thus, although individual workers may have contributed to that store of knowledge, they will not be able to hold all the necessary information and know-how for its successful utilization or recombination. More emphasis should be placed on investigating tacit knowledge learning and acquisition at the group or firm-wide level and not just to perceive it only operating at the individual level.

In terms of external links, firms should also be wary of finding suitable tacit knowledge skills and practices from other firms and organizations. As has been shown, evidence suggests that tacitness is highly specific not only at sector or technology level, but also within individual product groups or similar production processes. What may work for one industry, or one firm within an industry (or indeed one product being manufactured by a firm), may not work for other industries, firms or products. In this context, Faulkner[61] has noted "Learning is particularly crucial in relation to difficult-to-acquire tacit and skill-based knowledge, which may explain why tacit knowledge is often identified as being derived primarily from in-house capability and efforts". Despite this, there appears to have been too much emphasis in the past on trying to gain tacit knowledge and skills from other firms, instead of the firm first deciding what existing tacit knowledge capability it has itself and what improvements could be made to build up and enhance its accumulated learning and tacit know-how competence. This indeed should form part of a wider strategy by the firm to improve the learning process across the organization.[62] Consideration should also be given to how a firm can defend its competitive stock of tacit knowledge, thereby extending its temporary lead and response times over its competitors.

None the less, inter-firm and inter-organizational tacit know-how learning and acquisition should not be dismissed. Where possible, firms should be encouraged to share their tacit knowledge and learning skills with other firms in certain circumstances, although this is unlikely to be with firms in direct competition with them. Obviously, not all firms are competitors, and indeed sharing tacit skills may have long-term benefits to the providing firm. Such tacit knowledge flows relate most directly to encouraging know-how sharing with firms that are vertically related to the sharing or providing firm. This involves firms with which the tacit 'donor' company has backward or forward linkages and which reside in the same sector or technology. A number of 'lead firms', mainly from Japan but also latterly from the US, already seek to help their suppliers to achieve their corporate quality supply standards, or to speed up production and timeliness of delivery. These may be seen as the 'advanced customers' outlined by Ehrnberg and Sjöberg[63] in their study of FMS technology. Companies may also share their tacit competencies with firms more generally, but these are still likely to be external to their specific market ('non-rival firms'[64]). Such sharing of information and knowledge is usually more general in nature, but may provide guidelines to recipient firms on how they might adapt such principles to their particular situation.

Firms may even share tacit know-how on a horizontal basis with firms in the same industry or product market. This is likely to be more unusual but may occur between small and medium-sized enterprises and/or domestic companies operating in the same sector (sometimes encouraged by government policies such as the UK LINK scheme) who may be willing to share tacit information. This is particularly evident where trust and levels of reciprocity are relatively high, to help compete against larger, more powerful companies, often from overseas. Identification of such a common threat may galvanize such smaller companies into at least some mutual cooperation.

Lastly, inter-organizational tacit knowledge learning and transfer may cross institutional boundaries, involving links between firms and universities or firms and public research establishments. The process of workers moving from one job environment with its set of innate tacit skills to a different working environment often facilitates this tacit knowledge transfer, but also enhances new tacit know-how learning as well. Indeed, the Teaching Company Scheme (TCS) set up in the UK, focused on this approach by transferring workers employed in universities to firms, as a mechanism to improve industry–academic links.[65] The scheme involved selecting an 'associate' who was then jointly supervised by academics and industrialists on a specific project within the 'host' firm. In essence, therefore, the TCS has been "a mechanism designed to promote the movement of tacit knowledge from the site of its production to commercial enterprise, with the explicit aim of translating this knowledge into terms which will help the enterprise solve key problems".[66]

Conclusions

There are, perhaps, three conclusions to be made from this review and analysis of tacit knowledge in relation to technological innovation. Firstly, on a conceptual level, as more research is undertaken on tacit knowledge and it is no longer an area of study to be avoided,[67] it is likely that those areas of knowledge that are truly 'tacit' in nature are smaller than initially thought. More elements of tacit knowledge may in reality be, if not formally liable to codification, at least able to constitute an organizational routine that can be transferred between employees or groups of employees in a more structured framework that forms part of the firm's accumulated knowledge base. Firms may indeed discover that more may be learnt before doing and that those elements that have to be learnt by doing are fewer than was expected. The domain of truly tacit knowledge in a firm's knowledge base and learning profile may therefore be smaller than is currently conceived.

However, tacit knowledge will remain important and firms need to accept and incorporate it more into their learning regime so as to enhance and maintain their competitive advantage. This is not easy, though. Firms need to balance the need to spread tacit knowledge within the firm as quickly and effectively as possible, and the need to guard against these tacit skills and repertoires unintentionally leaking to other firms by individuals or groups walking away and setting up on their own or being poached by other firms. Above all, firms need to develop a dynamic tacit knowledge regime that continually renews and updates the organizations' tacit know-how skills.

Lastly, it was highlighted that strategies aimed at improving tacit knowledge learning and skills of firms are difficult to establish and implement by the very nature that the focus of such policies, tacitness, is difficult to codify, standardize and transfer. Tacit knowledge should not just be conceived of as simply a person-centred process, attention must also be paid to firm or group-level learning and transfer mechanisms. On an inter-organizational basis, a key issue is how far firms are willing to share tacit knowledge and with whom. There are some elements of tacit knowledge that are highly proprietary[68] and core to a firm's strategic competence that would make sharing, particularly in a horizontal network, highly unlikely. However, in other situations, such as in a vertical supply relationship or in more general, non-technical, but still important, activities (such as marketing, purchasing or financial operations), firms may be much more willing to be involved in supporting tacit knowledge networks. Above all, for the firm, learning about, dealing with and transferring tacit knowledge represent valuable tools for enhancing their competitive and technical profile, requiring little in terms of new resources or funding but having the potential to make substantial improvements to industrial performance.

Acknowledgements

Thanks go to Enrico Deiaco and two anonymous referees for their helpful comments on this paper. This paper is based on a number of earlier drafts, the first presented at a conference on 'Tacit Knowledge' organized by SPRINT-EIMS, part of DGXIII, Commission of the European Communities in Luxembourg in April 1993. The paper arises out of research funded by the UK Economic and Social Research Council, Grant No. R/000/23/1911.

References

1. D. R. Charles & J. R. Howells, *Technology Transfer in Europe: Public and Private Networks* (Chichester, Wiley, 1992), p. 3.
2. P. David, 'Knowledge, Property and System Dynamics of Technological Change', *Paper presented to the World Bank Annual Conference on Development Economics*, 30 April–1 May, 1992, Washington, DC, p. 9.
3. G. P. Pisano, 'Knowledge, Integration, and the Locus of Learning: An Empirical Analysis of Process Development', *Strategic Management Journal, 15*, 1994, p. 85.
4. R. S. Hayes, S. C. Wheelwright & K. Clark, *Dynamic Manufacturing* (New York, Free Press, 1988); P. Senge, 'The Leader's New Work: Building Learning Organisations', *Sloan Management Review, 32*, 1990, pp. 7–23.
5. K. M. Olesko, 'Tacit Knowledge and School Formation', *OSIRIS, 8*, 1993, pp. 16–29.
6. R. Hall, 'The Strategic Analysis of Intangible Resources', *Strategic Management Review, 13*, 1992, p. 136.
7. OECD, *Technology and the Economy: The Key Relationship* (Paris, OECD, 1992), pp. 114–133.
8. M. Polanyi, 'Knowing and Being', *Mind N. S., 70*, 1961, pp. 458–470; M. Polanyi, 'Tacit Knowing', *Review of Modern Physics, 34*, 1962, pp. 601–616; M. Polanyi, 'The Logic of Tacit Inference', *Philosophy, 41*, 1966, pp. 1–18; M. Polanyi, *The Tacit Dimension* (London, Routledge and Kegan Paul, 1967).
9. M. Polanyi, *op. cit.*, 1966, Ref. 8.
10. J. Ziman, *Reliable Knowledge: An Exploration of the Grounds for Belief in Science* (Cambridge, Cambridge University Press, 1978), p. 103.
11. Polanyi *op. cit.*, 1962, Ref. 8.
12. Polanyi *op. cit.*, 1966, Ref. 8, p. 4.
13. W. M. Cohen, & D. A. Levinthal, 'Absorptive Capacity: A New Perspective on Learning and Innovation', *Administrative Science Quarterly, 35*, 1990, p. 135; see also R. R. Nelson & S. G. Winter, *An Evolutionary Theory of Economic Change* (Cambridge, MA, Harvard University Press, 1982).
14. K. Arrow, 'The Economic Implications of Learning by Doing', *Review of Economic Studies, 29*, 1962, pp. 155–173.
15. N. Rosenberg, *Inside the Black Box: Technology and Economics* (Cambridge, Cambridge University Press, 1982).
16. H. C. Ellis, *Transfer of Learning* (New York, Macmillan, 1965); W. K. Estes, *Learning Theory and Mental Development* (New York, Academic Press, 1970); C. Argyris, & D. A. Schon, *Organisational Learning: A Theory of Action Perspective* (New York, Addison-Wesley, 1978), J. E. Stigilitz, 'Learning to Learn, Localised Learning and Technological Progress', in: P. Dasupta, & P. Stoneman (Eds), *Economic Policy and Technological Performance* (Cambridge, Cambridge University Press, 1987), pp. 125–153.
17. See, for example, S. Winter, 'Knowledge and Competence as Strategic Assets', in D. Teece (Ed.), *The Competitive Challenge: Strategies for Industrial Innovation and Renewal* (Cambridge, MA, Ballinger, 1987), pp. 159–183; C. Prahalad & G. Hamel, 'The Core Competence of the Corporation', *Harvard Business Review, 68*, 1990, pp. 79–91; K. Pavitt, 'Key Characteristics of the Large Innovating Firm', *British Journal of Management, 2*, 1991, pp. 41–50; P. Grindley, 'Managing Technology', in: P. Swann, (Ed.), *New Technologies and the Firm: Innovation and Competition* (London, Routledge, 1993), pp. 19–35; J. Kay, & P. William, 'Managing Technological Innovation', in: P. Swann, (Ed.), *New Technologies and the Firm: Innovation and Competition* (London, Routledge, 1993), pp. 26–53.
18. B. Hedberg, 'How Organisations Learn and Unlearn', in: P. C. Nystrom and W. H. Starbuck (Eds), *Handbook of Organisation Design* (Oxford, Oxford University Press, 1981), pp. 3–27; Nelson & Winter, *op. cit.*, Ref. 13; R. S. Hayes, S. C. Wheelwright & K. Clark, *op. cit.*, Ref. 4; J. S. Metcalfe & M. Gibbons, 'Technology, Variety and Organisation', in: R. Rosenbloom & R. Burgelman (Eds), *Research on Technological Innovation, Management and Policy: Volume 4* (Tokyo, JAI Press, 1989); P. Senge, 'The Leader's New Work: Building Learning Organisations', *Sloan Management Review, 32*, 1990, pp. 7–23.
19. S. M. Tatsuno, 'New Concepts of Innovation: The Japanese Approach', *Paper Presented to EIMS Workshop on Tacit Knowledge*, April 1993, SPRINT-EIMS, DGXIII, Commission of the European Communities, Luxembourg.

20. B. Morgan, 'Transferring Soft Technology', in: R. D. Robinson (Ed.), *The International Communication Technology* (New York, Taylor and Francis, 1990), pp. 149–166.
21. U. Zander & I. Zander, 'Innovation and Imitation in the Multinational Company—Preliminary Remarks on the Role of Tacitness', in: V. Simoes (Ed.), International Business and Europe after 1992, *Proceedings of the EIBA 19th Annual Conference*, Lisboa, December 1993, Volume *2*, CEDE, Lisboa, pp. 174–193.
22. Zander & Zander, *op. cit.*, Ref. 21, p. 186.
23. See, for example, D. Ulrich, T. Jick & M. A. Von Glinow, 'High Impact Learning: Building and Diffusing Learning Capability', *Organizational Dynamics*, *22*, 1993, pp. 52–66.
24. H. M. Collins, *Changing Order: Replication and Induction in Scientific Practice* (London, Sage Publications), p. 55.
25. See, for example, S. Slaughter, 'Innovation and Learning During Implementation: A Comparison of User and Manufacturer Innovations', *Research Policy*, *22*, 1993, pp. 81–95.
26. D. C. Mowery & N. Rosenberg, *Technology and the Pursuit of Economic Growth* (Cambridge, Cambridge University Press, 1989), p. 9; see also D. C. Mowery & N. Rosenberg, 'Technical Change in the Commercial Aircraft Industry, 1925–1975', in: N. Rosenberg (Ed.), *Inside the Black Box: Technology and Economics* (Cambridge, Cambridge University Press, 1982), pp. 165–177; D. C. Mowery & N. Rosenberg, 'Commercial Aircraft: Cooperation and Competition Between the US and Japan', *California Management Review*, *28*, 1985, pp. 70–97.
27. T. P. Wright, 'Factors Affecting the Cost of Airplanes', *Journal of Aeronautical Sciences*, *3*, 1936, pp. 122–128.
28. W. G. Vincenti, 'Technological Knowledge Without Science: The Innovation of Flush Riveting in American Airplanes', *Technology and Culture*, *25*, 1984, pp. 540–576.
29. Vincenti, *op. cit.*, Ref. 28, p. 563; see also W. G. Vincenti, *What Engineers Know and How They Know It* (Boston, MA. John Hopkins University Press).
30. J. M. Liebenau, 'International R&D in Pharmaceutical Firms in the Early Twentieth Century', *Business History*, *26*, 1984, pp. 329–346; P. Swann, *Academic Scientists and the Pharmaceutical Industry: Cooperative Research in Twentieth-Century America* (Boston, MA, John Hopkins University Press, 1984).
31. V. Klein, 'Origin of the Concept of Chemical Compound', *Science in Context*, *7*, 1994, pp. 163–204.
32. Swann, *op. cit.*, Ref. 30, p. 123.
33. D. J. de Solla Price, 'The Science/Technology Relationship, The Craft of Experimental Science and Policy for the Improvement of High Technology Innovation', *Research Policy*, *13*, 1984, pp. 11–12.
34. E. Von Hippel, 'The User's Role in Industrial Innovation in the Scientific Instrument Innovation Process', *Research Policy*, *5*, 1976, pp. 212–239; E. Von Hippel, 'The Dominant Role of the Users in the Semiconductor and Electronic Subassembly Process Innovation', *IEEE Transactions on Engineering Management*, EM24, 1977, pp. 60–71.
35. E. Ehrnberg & N. Sjöberg, 'Technological Discontinuities, Competition and Firm Performance', *Technology Analysis & Strategic Management*, *7*, 1995, p. 100.
36. D. Leonard-Barton, 'Implementation as Mutual Adaptation of Technology and Organisation', *Research Policy*, *17*, 1988, p. 254.
37. J. Bessant & J. Buckingham, 'Innovation and Organizational Learning: The Case of Computer-aided Production Management', *British Journal of Management*, *4*, 1993, pp. 219–234.
38. Mowery & Rosenberg, *op. cit.*, Ref. 26, p. 33.
39. J. T. Knoedler, 'Market Structure, Industrial Research, and Consumers of Innovation: Forging Backward Linkages to Research in the Turn-of-the-century US Steel Industry', *Business History Review*, *67*, 1993, pp. 98–139.
40. K. H. Sørensen & N. Levold, 'Tacit Networks, Heterogeneous Engineers and Embodied Technology', *Science, Technology and Human Values*, *17*, 1992, pp. 13–35.
41. Sørensen & Levold, *op. cit.*, Ref. 40, p. 21.
42. Ziman, *op. cit.*, Ref. 10.
43. J. R. Ravetz, *Scientific Knowledge and its Social Problems* (Oxford, Oxford University Press, 1971), p. 102.
44. P. S. Ring, 'Cooperating on Tacit Know-how Assets', *Paper presented at the First Annual Meeting of the International Federation of Scholarly Association of Management*, Tokyo, September 1992.

45. See H. M. Collins, 'The TEA Set: Tacit Knowledge and Scientific Networks', *Science Studies*, *4*, 1974, pp. 165–186; P. S. Ring & A. H. Van de Ven, 'Structuring Cooperative Relationships Between Organizations', *Strategic Management Journal*, *13*, 1992, pp. 483–498; M. Dodgson, 'Learning, Trust and Technological Collaboration', *Human Relations*, *46*, 1993, pp. 79 & 82–83; C. Lane & R. Bachman, 'Risk, Trust and Power: The Social Constitution of Supplier Relations in Britain and Germany', *ESRC Centre for Business Research, Working Paper No. 5*, University of Cambridge, 1995.
46. E. Von Hippel, 'Cooperation Between Rivals: Informal Know-how Trading', *Research Policy*, *16*, 1987, p. 295.
47. Ring, *op. cit.*, Ref. 44, p. 4.
48. Zander & Zander, *op. cit.*, Ref. 21.
49. Nelson & Winter, *op. cit.*, Ref. 13; Winter, *op. cit.*, Ref. 17; G. Dosi, 'Sources, Procedures and Micro-economics of Innovation', *Journal of Economic Literature*, *26*, 1988, pp. 1120–1171.
50. W. Faulkner, J. Senker with L. Velho, *Knowledge Frontiers: Industrial Innovation and Public Sector Research in Biotechnology, Engineering Ceramics and Parallel Computing* (Oxford, Clarendon Press, 1994).
51. P. Alder, 'Shared Learning', *Management Science*, *36*, 1990, pp. 938–957.
52. Nelson & Winter, *op. cit.*, Ref. 13.
53. B. Levitt & J. March, 'Organizational Learning', *Annual Review of Sociology*, *14*, 1988, pp. 319–340.
54. Pisano, *op. cit.*, Ref. 3.
55. Pisano, *op. cit.*, Ref. 3, p. 98.
56. Metcalfe & Gibbons, *op. cit.*, Ref. 18, p. 164.
57. M. Douglas, *How Institutions Think* (London, Routledge, 1987); B. Johnson, 'Institutional learning', in: B.-A. Lundvall (Ed.), *National Systems of Innovation* (London, Pinter, 1992), pp. 23–44.
58. G. Stigler, 'The Economics of Information', *Journal of Political Economy*, *69*, 1961, pp. 213–225; D. Lamberton, 'Information Economics and Technological Change', in: S. Macdonald, D. Lamberton & T. Manderville (Eds), *The Trouble with Technology: Explorations in the Process of Technological Change* (London, Pinter, 1983), pp. 75–92.
59. C. Tiler & M. Gibbons, 'A Case Study of Organizational Learning: The UK Teaching Company Scheme', *Industry and Higher Education*, *5*, 1991, p. 50.
60. E. Mansfield, 'How Rapidly Does New Industrial Technology Leak Out?', *Journal of Industrial Economics*, *34*, 1985, pp. 217–223.
61. W. Faulkner, 'Conceptualizing Knowledge used in Innovation: A Second Look at the Science–Technology Distinction and Industrial Innovation', *Science, Technology & Human Values*, *19*, 1994, p. 440.
62. H. Itami & T. W. Roehl, *Mobilizing Invisible Assets* (Cambridge, MA, Harvard University Press, 1987).
63. Ehrnberg & Sjöberg, *op. cit.*, Ref. 35, p. 100.
64. Von Hippel, *op. cit.*, Ref. 46, p. 301; see also Von Hippel, *Sources of Innovation* (Boston, MA, MIT Press, 1989).
65. Tiler & Gibbons, *op. cit.*, Ref. 59; see also P. Senker & J. Senker, 'Transferring Technology and Expertise from Universities to Industry: Britain's Teaching Company Scheme', *New Technology, Work and Employment*, *9*, 1994, pp. 81–92.
66. Tiler & Gibbons, *op. cit.*, Ref. 65, p. 51.
67. Olesko, *op. cit.*, Ref. 5.
68. J. S. Metcalfe, & M. Boden, 'Evolutionary Epistemology and the Nature of Technology Strategy', in: R. Coombs, P. Saviotti & V. Walsh (Eds), *Technological Change and Firm Strategies: Economic and Sociological Perspectives* (London, Academic Press, 1992), p. 58.

[19]

the dominant role of users in the scientific instrument innovation process*

by
Eric von HIPPEL
Alfred P. Sloan School of Management, Massachusetts Institute of Technology, Cambridge, Mass. 02139, USA

1. INTRODUCTION

Quantitative research into the industrial good innovation process has, over the last few years, demonstrated convincingly that:
(1) Approximately three out of four commercially successful industrial good innovation projects are initiated in response to a perception of user need for an innovation, rather than on the basis of a technological opportunity to achieve them**,
(2) Accurate understanding of user need is the factor which discriminates most strongly between commercially successful industrial good innovation projects and those which fail [2].
The studies which produced these findings were designed to test many hypotheses regarding the causes of successful industrial good innovation. Understandably, therefore, they are enticingly scant on detail regarding the "understanding of user need" hypothesis which showed such an encouraging correlation with innovation success. Among the interesting questions left unanswered are:
How does an innovating firm go about acquiring an "accurate understanding of user need"? Via an information input from the user? If so, should the

* The research reported on in this paper was supported by the Office of National R & D Assessment, NSF (Grant No. DA–44366) and the MIT Innovation Center. The author gratefully acknowledges intellectual stimulation and assistance rendered by Alan Berger, Allan Chambers, Neal Kaplan, Walter Lehman and Frank Spital, who served as Research Assistants during the project.

** Utterback [1] lists the quantitative findings of eight studies which support this point.

manufacturer take the initiative in seeking out such input, or will the user seek him out? And, what does a "need input" look like? Should one be on the alert for user complaints so vague that only a subtle-minded producer would think of using them as grist for a product specification? Or, perhaps, should one be touring user facilities on the alert for something as concrete as home-made devices which solve user-discerned problems, and which could be profitably copied and sold to other users facing similar problems?

Answers to questions such as these would be of clear utility to firms interested in producing innovative industrial goods and would also, we feel, be of interest to researchers working towards an improved understanding of the industrial good innovation process. The study which we are reporting on here was designed to forward this work.

Our report is organized into six sections. After this introductory section, we describe our methods of sample selection and collection of data in sect. 2. In sect. 3 we present our findings on the overall pattern characteristic of innovation in scientific instruments, and in sect. 4 we discuss the implications of these. Sections 5 and 6 are given over to the presentation and discussion of more detailed findings bearing on two aspects of the innovation process in scientific instruments, and sect. 7 is a summing up.

2. METHODS

2.1. The sample

The sample of industrial good innovations examined in this study consists of four important types or families of scientific instruments and the successful

Table 1
Sample composition

Instrument type	Basic innovations	Major improvements	Minor improvements	Total
Gas chromatography	1	11	–	12
Nuclear magnetic resonance spectrometry	1	14	–	15
Ultraviolet absorption spectrophotometry	1	5	–	6
Transmission electron microscopy	1	14	63	78
Total	4	44	63	111

major and minor improvement innovations involving these. The total sample size is 111, distributed as shown in table 1. We chose to select our entire sample from a relatively narrow class of industrial goods because previous studies have shown that characteristic patterns in the innovation process vary as a function of the type of good involved*. Given our sample size of 111 and the level of detail at which we want to examine "user input" and "accurate understanding of user need", discretion dictated the sample's narrow focus. Scientific instruments were selected as the class to be studied primarily because previous research on the innovation process had ascertained that innovation in response to user need was prominent in scientific instruments [3, 4]. This minimized the risk of choosing to study user need input in an industrial segment where, for some unforeseen reason, such input would turn out not to be salient. Gas–liquid partition chromatography, nuclear magnetic resonance spectrometry, ultraviolet spectrophotometry (absorption, photoelectric type), and transmission electron microscopy were the families of scientific instruments selected for study because:

– These instrument types have great *functional* value for scientific research as well as for day-to-day industrial uses such as process control**.

– First commercialization of all of these instrument types ranges from 1939 to 1954. This time period is recent enough so that some of the participants in the original commercialization processes are currently available to be interviewed. It is long enough ago, however, so that several major improvement innovations have been commercialized for each instrument type.

While neither annual sales of instrument types nor unit prices were used as a criterion for sample selection, the reader may find such data contextually useful and we have included it in table 2.

We should emphasize that our sample consists of more than 100 functionally significant improvements within but four instrument 'families.' This sample structure is considerably different from that used by previous studies of innovation in scientific instruments (cf. Shimshoni [4], Utterback [3], and

* Cf. Project SAPPHO's [2] innovation patterns in the chemical and instrument industries.

** National Research Council of the National Academy of Sciences [5] found the Gas–Liquid Partition Chromatograph, the Nuclear Magnetic Resonance Spectrometer, and the Ultraviolet Spectrophotometer to be three of the four instruments with the highest incidence of reported use in articles in "selected representative US chemical journals." Electron microscopy, of which transmission electron microscopy was the first, and until recently the only type, is the only way one can get a picture of something smaller than 1000 Angstroms in size. As such, it has been and is a key instrument type in fields ranging from genetics to metallurgy.

Table 2
Characterization of sample

Instrument type	Annual world-wide sales 1974[a)]	Per unit cost range[a)]	Approx. median unit cost[a)]	Utility measure[b)]	Date type was first commercialized
Gas chromatography	$100mm	3–15k	7k	17	1954
Nuclear magnetic resonance spectrometry	30mm	12–100k	NA	18	1953
Ultraviolet absorption spectrophotometry	120mm	2.7–26k	6k	21	1941
Transmission electron microscopy	20mm	30–90k	50k	–	1939

a) Source: Estimates by instrument company market research personnel.
b) Instance of use per 100 articles, 1964 (ref. [5], p. 88).

Achilladelis et al. [2]. While the authors of these studies found it appropriate for their purposes to assemble samples without regard for the instrument family membership involved, we felt it important that we limit our sample to a few instrument families. Our reasoning was that the "understanding of user need" pattern seen in this kind of a sample would be the one actually experienced by real-world firms. An instrument family or type tends to represent a product line for commercial firms, and clearly, firms tend to be interested in improvement innovations which impact instrument types which they are currently selling – not in a random mix of unrelated improvement innovations. Further, the fact that they are already in the business of selling an instrument type will impact the kind of incremental input they need to "accurately understand user need" for an improvement innovation, as well as how they go about acquiring that input – and these are precisely the issues which we wish to study here.

There is a negative consequence of our decision to choose a sample limited to a few instrument types. It is that often a single company with an established commercial position in, for example, Nuclear Magnetic Resonance equipment, will be the first company to commercialize several of the improvement innovations in our sample. This raises issues of sample independence which we must deal with in the data analysis.

2.2. Identification of sample members

As indicated in table 1, our sample of innovations is divided into three categories: "basic" innovations, "major improvement" innovations and "minor improvement" innovations. As will be discussed in detail below, innovations are assigned to one or another of these categories on the basis of the degree of increase in *functional* utility (basic, major improvement or minor improvement) which its addition to the basic instrument type (Gas–Liquid Partition Chromatograph, Nuclear Magnetic Resonance Spectrometer, Ultraviolet Spectrophotometer and the Transmission Electron Microscope) offers to the instrument user.

Sample selection criteria particular to a single category of innovation are discussed below in the context of that category. Selection criteria common to all three categories are:

– Only the first commercial introduction of an innovation is included in the sample. Later versions of the same innovation introduced by other manufacturers are not included.

– An innovation is included in the sample only if it is "commercially successful." Our definition of commercial success is: continued offering of an innovation (or a close functional equivalent) for sale, by at least one commercializing company, from the time of innovation until the present day.

2.2.1. Major improvement innovations

In setting out to identify major improvement innovations, we took as our base line features which appeared on the initially commercialized unit. Major innovations which were commercialized at a later data were eligible for inclusion in the sample. In our gas chromatography sample, for example, thirteen such innovations were identified. Capsule descriptions of the utility of two of these may serve to provide the reader with some feeling for what we term "major functional improvements."

Name of innovation	Functional utility to user
Temperature programming	Improves speed and resolution of analysis for samples containing components of widely differing boiling points
Argon ionization detector	Sensitivity 20–30 times greater than that attainable with thermal conductivity detector

We defined "major" improvement innovations as those innovations which made a major functional improvement in the instrument from the point of view of the instrument user. Thus, the above-mentioned Argon ionization detector, which improved the sensitivity of the instrument many fold over previous best practice, was judged a significant improvement in functional utility to the user. Transistorization of detector electronics, on the other hand, would not be included in the sample as a significant innovation because the functional impact of the change on the great majority* of users is minimal. From the user's point of view, inputs and outputs affecting him significantly remain undisturbed by the change.

The identity of "major" innovations in a family of instruments was ascertained by consensus among experts – both users and manufacturers in the field. More quantitative measures of significance were felt impractical given the different parameters impacted by the various innovations (How do you make the functional utility of an improvement in speed commensurate with an improvement in accuracy or with an increase in the range of compounds analysable?). The expert consensus method, while embarked on with some trepidation, turned out to yield remarkably uniform results. Either almost everyone contracted would agree that an innovation was of major functional utility – in which case it was included – or almost no one would – in which case it was rejected.

The experts consulted were, on the manufacturer side, senior scientists and/or R & D managers who had a long-time (approximately 20 years) specialization in the instrument family at issue and whose companies have (or, in the case of electron microscopy, once had) a share of the market for that instrument family. On the user side, users who were interested in instrumentation and/or had made major contributions to it were identified via publications in the field and suggestions from previously contacted experts.

Data were collected on *every* major improvement innovation identified by our consensus among experts.

2.2.2. Basic instrument innovations

The basic instrument innovations which we list in table 1 are basic in the sense that they are the first instruments of a given type to be commercialized.

* We say that the impact on the 'great majority' of users is small simply because there might be some few users – say those trying to fit a gas chromatograph into a space satellite, if there are such – to whom the increase in reliability and decrease in size occasioned by a switch from tube electronics to transistorized electronics might be very significant.

By definition, only four cases of 'basic innovation' are available to us within the sample space of four instrument types which we have allowed ourselves. These are: the first commercial Gas–Liquid Partition Chromatograph; the first Nuclear Magnetic Resonance Spectrometer; the first Ultraviolet Spectrophotometer; and the first Transmission Electron Microscope.

2.2.3. Minor improvement innovations

The criterion for inclusion in our sample of minor innovations (collected for Transmission Electron Microscopy only)* was simply that the innovation be of some functional utility to the user in the opinion of experts. This list of minor innovations is probably not exhaustive: it was initiated by asking user and manufacturer experts for a listing of all such innovations they could think of. This list was augmented by our own scanning of the catalogues of microscope manufacturers and of microscope accessory and supply houses for innovative features, accessories, specimen preparation equipment, etc. As in our sample of major improvement innovations, only minor improvements which were *not* present in an instrument type as initially commercialized were eligible for inclusion in the sample.

2.3. Data collection methods

Data were collected under four major headings:

(1) Description of the innovation and its functional significance;

(2) Innovation work done by the first firm to commercialize the innovation;

(3) What, if anything, relating to the innovation (e.g. need input, technology input, etc.) was transferred to the commercializing firm and how, why, etc.;

* Our initial plan was to collect a sample of minor improvement innovations for all four of the instrument types which we have been studying – not just Transmission Electron Microscopy. This plan was abandoned however, when our experience with the Transmission Electron Microscopy sample indicated to us that events surrounding minor innovations were not recalled by participants in them nearly so well as events surrounding major improvement innovations were recalled by the participants in those. The reason for this discrepancy appeared to be that participants in minor innovations generally had no feeling that they were participating in significant events – they were just doing a typical day's work. Asking them to recall specific aspects of those events perhaps ten years after they had occurred, therefore, was tantamount to asking them to describe details of a casual chat by the water cooler ten years ago – a bootless exercise.

(4) What was the nature of, focus of, reason for, etc. the innovation-related work done outside the commercializing firm and later transferred to it.

Our principal data sources were descriptions of instrument innovations in scientific journals and both face-to-face and telephone interviews. Insofar as possible, key individuals directly involved with an innovation, both inside and outside of the initial commercializing firm, were interviewed. Data collected by interview were written up and sent to the interviewees for verification of accuracy and correction as necessary.

3. RESULTS

3.1. Overview of the innovation process in scientific instruments

The central fact which emerges from our study of the innovation process in scientific instruments is that it is a *user*-dominated process. In 81% of all major improvement innovation cases, we find it is the *user* who:

– Perceives that an advance in instrumentation is required;
– Invents the instrument;
– Builds a prototype;
– Proves the prototype's value by applying it;

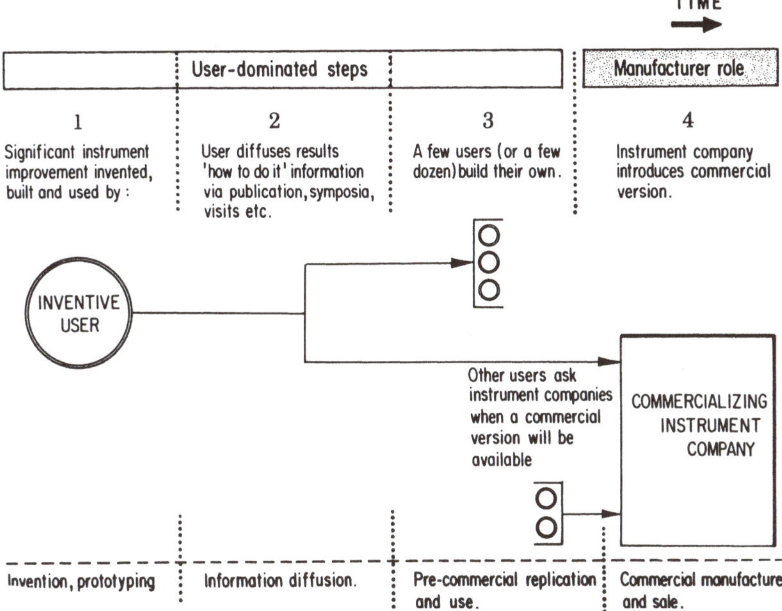

Fig.1. Typical steps in the invention and diffusion of a scientific instrument or instrument improvement.

– Diffuses detailed information on the value of his invention and how his prototype device may be replicated, via journals, symposia, informal visits, etc. to user colleagues and instrument companies alike.

Only when all of the above has transpired does the instrument manufacturer enter the innovation process. Typically, the manufacturer's contribution is then to:

– Perform product engineering work on the user's device to improve its reliability, convenience of operation, etc. (While this work may be extensive, it typically affects only the engineering embodiment of the user's invention, not its operating principles)*;

– Manufacture, market and sell the innovative product.

The frequency with which this "typical" user-dominated pattern was displayed in our sample of scientific instrument innovations was striking, as table 3 shows.

Interestingly, as table 4 indicates, this user-dominated pattern appeared typical also for innovations which were more "basic" than those in our main sample of major improvement innovations and for minor improvement innovations as well**.

Table 3
Frequency of user-dominated innovative processes by type of instrument

Major improvement innovations affecting	% User dominated	Innovation process dominated by: User	Manufacturer	NA	Total
Gas chromatography	82%	9	2	0	11
Nuclear magnetic resonance	79%	11	3	0	14
Ultraviolet spectrophotometry	100%	5	0	0	5
Transmission electron microscope	79%	11	3	0	14
Total	81%	36	8	0	44

We define the process leading to an ultimately commercialized innovation as "user dominated" only if a user performed all of the following innovation-related tasks prior to commercial manufacture of the device: invention, reduction to practice, first field use, publication of detailed experimental methods used and results obtained. The data indicate that when a user does one of these tasks, he tends to carry out the entire set. Where he fails to carry out any one of them, however, we take a conservative stand relative to the user-dominated pattern we are exploring and code that case as manufacturer dominated.

* Cf. first footnote in sect. 5 for an elaboration of this distinction.

** See sect. 2 for description of basic, major improvement and minor improvement innovations.

Table 4
Frequency of user-dominated innovative processes by type of innovation

Type of innovation	% User dominated	Innovation process dominated by User	Manufacturer	NA	Total
Basic instrument	100%	4	0	0	4
Major improvement	82%	36	8	0	44
Minor improvement (Transmission electron microscope only)	70%	32	14	17	63
Total	77%	72	22	17	111

The reader may have noted in table 4 a trend toward an increasing percentage of "manufacturer" dominated innovations as those innovations become less significant. Our attention was also attracted by this pattern, and we made several attempts to gather data on innovations far out on the incremental/trivial dimension to see if we could find indications that the trend continued. We were largely frustrated in our efforts because, typically, no one could recall who had first done something *that* trivial ("You expect *me* to remember who first did *that*?"). Interestingly, on those few occasions when we were able to approach the ultimate in trivia (e.g. specially-shaped tweezers useful for manipulating electron microscope samples), we found that a user was the inventor.

The user-dominated pattern we have described also appears to hold independent of the size – and thus, presumably, of the internal R & D potential – of the commercializing company. Only one out of the ten major improvement innovations in our sample which were first commercialized by companies with annual sales greater than one hundred million dollars (at the time of commercialization) was the result of a manufacturer dominated innovation process. Nine of the ten were the result of user-dominated innovation processes.

Finally, we observe that the pattern of a user-dominated innovation process appears to hold for companies who are established manufacturers of a given product line – manufacturers who "ought to know" about improvements needed in their present product line and be working on them – as well as for manufacturers for whom a given innovation represents their first entry into a product line new to them. Of the thirty-four major improvement innovations in our sample which represented additions to established product lines of the companies commercializing them, twenty-four were the result of user-dominated innovation processes and ten the result of manufacturer-dominated processes. *All* of the eight major improvement innovations which represented the commercializing companies' initial entry into a new product line and which we were able to code on this issue (the information was not available in a ninth case) were the result of user-dominated innovation. Indeed, it is our (unquantified) impression that users often have to take considerable initiative to bring a company to enter a product line new to it. (We here regard Gas Chromatography, Nuclear Magnetic Resonance Spectrometry, Ultraviolet Spectrophotometry, and Transmission Electron Microscopy as "product lines".) This is especially interesting when one notes that the degree of novelty involved in entering a new line was usually minimal for companies in our sample. Typically, a company would be introducing a new instrument type to its established customer base.

As we noted in sect. 2, our data contain several instances in which more than one major innovation was invented and/or first commercialized by the same instrument firm*. Also there are a few cases in which the same innovative user was responsible for the pre-commercial work on more than one major innovation**. This raises potentially troublesome issues of sample independence. We can easily demonstrate, however, by means of a subsample (table 5)

Table 5

A subsample of cases, which exclude all but the first chronological case in which a given user and/or firm plays a role, shows substantially the same pattern as did the total sample.

Major improvement innovations affecting:	% User Dominated	Innovation process dominated by User	Manufacturer	NA	Total
Gas chromatography	86%	6	1	0	7
Nuclear magnetic Resonance spectrometry	100%	5	0	0	5
Ultraviolet spectrophotometry	100%	2	0	0	2
Transmission electron microscopy	83%	5	1	0	6
Total	90%	18	2	0	20

* Specifically, the 111 innovations in our sample were first commercialized by only twenty-six companies as follows: Gas Chromatography; 12 innovations first commercialized by 8 companies. Nuclear Magnetic Resonance Spectrometry; 15 innovations first commercialized by 3 companies. Ultraviolet Absorption Spectrophotometry; 6 innovations, first commercialized by 2 companies. Transmission Electron Microscopy; 15 basic and major improvement innovations, first commercialized by 6 companies plus 63 minor innovations first commercialized by a total of 7 companies.

** Cf. table 8.

Table 6
Presence of homebuilts in the cases of user-dominated innovations, when the time-lag from publication of invention to first commercial model was greater / less than one year

	Greater than one year, were homebuilts present? % Yes	Yes	No	NA	One year or less, were homebuilts present? % Yes	Yes	No	NA
Gas chromatography	100%	5	0	0	0%	0	3	1
Nuclear magnetic resonance	100%	8	0	1	0%	0	1	1
Total	100%	13	0	1	0%	0	4	2

which excludes all but the *first* case, chronologically* in which a particular user or firm plays a role, that at least this source of possible sample interdependence is not responsible for the pattern of user-dominated innovation which we have observed.

The precommercial diffusion of significant user inventions via "homebuilt" replications of the inventor's prototype design by other users, shown schematically in fig. 1, appears to be a common feature of the scientific instrument innovation process. Literature searches and interviews in our Gas Chromatography and Nuclear Magnetic Resonance Spectrometry samples (we did not collect this particular item of information for our Ultraviolet Spectrophotometry and Transmission Electron Microscopy samples due to time constraints found by those assisting with the data-gathering effort) showed (table 6) that homebuilt replications of significant user inventions were made and used to produce publishable results in every case where more than a year elapsed between the initial publication of details regarding a significant new invention and the introduction of a commercial model by an instrument firm.

3.2. Sample cases

Abstracts of innovation case histories which display the user-dominated pattern we have observed may serve to give the reader a better feeling for the

* Employment of other decision rules (e.g., "exclude all but the last case in which a given firm or user plays a role") does not produce a significantly different outcome.

data we are presenting in this paper*. Accordingly, three such abstracts are presented below. The first of these illustrates a *user*-dominated innovation process leading to a major improvement innovation in the field of Nuclear Magnetic Resonance. The second illustrates a *manufacturer*-dominated innovation process leading to a major improvement in Transmission Electron Microscopes. The third illustrates a user-dominated innovation process resulting in a *minor* improvement in Transmission Electron Microscopy.

Case Outline 1: A major improvement innovation: spinning of a nuclear magnetic resonance sample (user-dominated innovation process)

Samples placed in a nuclear magnetic resonance spectrometer are subjected to a strong magnetic field. From a theoretical understanding of the nuclear magnetic resonance phenomenon it was known by both nuclear magnetic resonance spectrometer users and personnel of the only manufacturer of nuclear magnetic resonance equipment at that time (Varian, Incorporated, Palo Alto, Ca.) that increased homogeneity of that magnetic field would allow nuclear magnetic resonance equipment to produce more detailed spectra. Felix Bloch, a professor at Stanford University and the original discoverer of the nuclear magnetic resonance phenomena, suggested that one could improve the effective homogeneity of the field by rapidly spinning the sample in the field, thus 'averaging out' some inhomogeneities. Two students of Bloch's, W. A. Anderson and J. T. Arnold, built a prototype spinner and experimentally demonstrated the predicted result. Both Bloch's suggestion and Anderson and Arnold's verification were published in *Physical Review,* April, 1954.

Varian engineers went to Bloch's lab, examined his prototype sample spinner, developed a commercial model and introduced it into the market by December of 1954. The connection between Bloch and Varian was so good and Varian's commercialization of the improvement so rapid, that there was little time for other users to build homebuilt spinners prior to that commercialization.

* Readers interested in further material which reflects what we term a 'user-dominated' innovation pattern may wish to refer to Shimshoni [4]. Although Shimshoni focuses his analysis primarily on his hypothesis that "... innovation depends primarily on the mobility of enterprising and talented individuals," his data base is instrument industry innovations and he presents much rich case data and discussion which often includes a description of the role of users in particular instrument innovations. Although we did not use any data from Shimshoni's work because of our preference for primary sources, in some cases our sample and his overlapped. In such instances, we found his and our data in substantial agreement.

Case Outline 2: A major improvement innovation: well-regulated high-voltage power supplies for transmission electron microscopes (manufacturer-dominated innovation process).

The first electron microscope and the first few pre-commercial replications used batteries connected in series to supply the high voltages they required. The major inconvenience associated with this solution can be readily imagined by the reader when we note that voltages on the order of 80 000 volts were required – and that nearly 40 000 single cell batteries must be connected in series to provide this. A visitor to the laboratory of Marton, an early and outstanding experimenter in electron microscopy, recalls an entire room filled with batteries on floor to ceiling racks with a full-time technician employed to maintain them. An elaborate safety interlock system was in operation to insure that no one would walk in, touch something electrically live and depart this mortal sphere. Floating over all was the strong stench of the sulfuric acid contents of the batteries. Clearly, not a happy solution to the high-voltage problem.

The first commercial electron microscope, built by Siemens of Germany in 1939, substituted a 'power supply' for the batteries but could not make its output voltage as constant as could be done with batteries. This was a major problem because high stability in the high-voltage supply was a well-known prerequisite for achieving high resolution with an electron microscope.

When RCA decided to build an electron microscope, an RCA electrical engineer, Jack Vance, undertook to build a highly stable power supply and by several inventive means, achieved a stability almost good enough to eliminate voltage stability as a constraint on high-resolution microscope performance. This innovative power supply was commercialized in 1941 in RCA's first production microscope.

Case Outline 3: A minor improvement innovation: the self-cleaning electron beam aperture for electron microscopes (user-dominated innovation process)

Part of the electron optics system of an electron microscope is a pinhole-sized aperture through which the electron beam passes. After a period of microscope operation, this aperture tends to get 'dirty' – contaminated with carbon resulting from a breakdown of vacuum pump oils, etc. This carbon becomes electrically charged by the electron beam impinging on it and this charge, in turn, distorts the beam and degrades the microscope's optical performance. It was known that by heating the aperture one could boil off carbon deposits as rapidly as they formed and keep the aperture 'dynamically clean.' Some microscope manufacturers had installed electrically heated apertures to perform this job, but these solutions could not easily be retrofitted to existing microscopes.

In 1964, a microscope user at Harvard University gave a paper at EMSA (Electron Microscope Society of America) in which he described his inventive solution to the problem. He simply replaced the conventional aperture with one made of gold foil. The gold foil was so thin that the impinging electron beam made it hot enough to induce dynamic cleaning. Since no external power sources were involved, this design could be easily retrofitted by microscope users.

C. W. French, owner of a business which specializes in selling ancillary equipment and supplies to electron microscopists, read the paper, talked to the author/inventor and learned how to build the gold foil apertures. He first offered them for sale in 1964.

4. IMPLICATION OF THE OVERALL PATTERN OF INNOVATION IN SCIENTIFIC INSTRUMENTS: THE LOCUS OF INNOVATION AS AN INNOVATION PROCESS VARIABLE

We have seen that for both major and minor innovations in the field of scientific instruments, it is almost always the user, not the instrument manufacturer, who recognizes the need, solves the problem via an invention, builds a prototype and proves the prototype's value in use. Furthermore, it is the user who encourages and enables the diffusion of his invention by publishing information on its utility and instructions sufficient for its replication by other users – and by instrument manufacturers.

If we apply our study finding to the stages of the technical innovation process as described by Marquis and Meyers, we find, somewhat counterintuitively, that the locus of almost the entire scientific instrument innovation process is centered in the user. Only "commercial diffusion" is carried out by the manufacturer (fig.2).

This finding appears at odds with most of the prescriptive literature in the new product development process (e.g. the innovation process) directed to manufacturers. That literature characteristically states that the *manufacturer* starts with an "idea" or "proposal" and that the *manufacturer* must execute stages similar to those described by Marquis and Meyers in fig. 2 in order to arrive at a successful new product. For example, Booz, Allen, and Hamilton suggest that a manufacturer wishing an innovative new product should proceed through the following "stages of new product evolution" [7]:

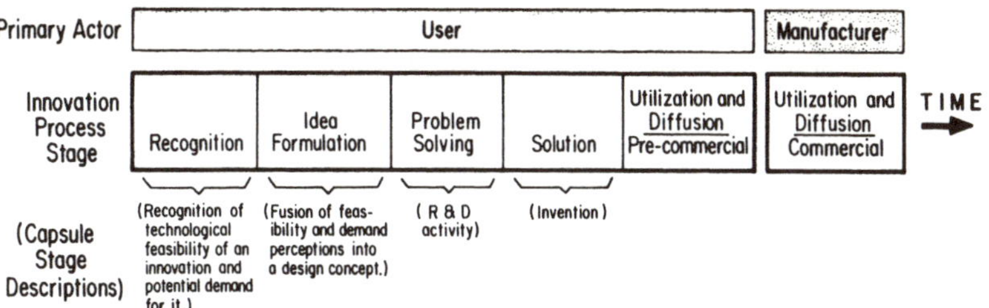

Fig. 2. The primary actor in each innovation process stage* in the scientific instrument innovation process.

> Exploration – the search for product ideas to meet company objectives.
> Screening – a quick analysis to determine which ideas are pertinent and merit more detailed study.
> Business Analysis – the expansion of the idea, through creative analysis, into a concrete business recommendation including product features and a program for the product.
> Development – turning the idea-on-paper into a product-in-hand, demonstrable and producible.
> Testing – the commercial experiments necessary to verify earlier business judgments.
> Commercialization – launching the product in full-scale production and sale, committing the company's reputation and resources.

As a second illustration from the new product development literature, the Conference Board, in their book, *Evaluating New Product Proposals,* devotes a chapter to "Early Stage Testing of Industrial Products." In it, they advise evaluation of industrial product concepts before much development work has been done by the firm, apparently assuming that this means that no prototype exists [8]] :

> Just what kinds of idea-pretesting is appropriate or feasible depends on the nature of the product and its market, secrecy requirements and many other factors. If – as many companies recommend – concept testing begins as early as possible, then dealing with abstract ideas poses an especially troublesome dilemma. Naturally, it is easier for the sponsor to

* The names of stages and the capsule descriptions of them used in fig. 2 are taken from Marquis and Meyers [6] with but one alteration: we have divided Marquis and Meyers' "Utilization and Diffusion" state into precommercial and commercial segments.

present the product idea meaningfully, and for the respondent to react meaningfully to it, if the project is at a more advanced stage where perhaps the respondent can review scale models or prototypes of the product. This is not always possible, but a number of companies have found ways of at least partially overcoming the difficulties of discussing a product that "exists" only as an idea.

Very early in a development project, concept testing may be carried out to weigh potential users' initial reactions to the product idea, whether a market need truly exists, or to gain some idea as to what commercial embodiment would have the greatest market appeal. Later, when a model or prototype has been developed, further testing may again be carried out . . .

It is perhaps natural to assume that most or all of the innovation process culminating in a new industrial good occurs within the commercializing firm. For many types of industrial goods, the locus of innovation *is* almost entirely within the firm which first manufactures that good for commercial sale*. Our findings that the scientific instrument innovation process doesn't follow such a within-manufacturer pattern does not invalidate that pattern — it simply indicates, we feel, that other patterns exist.

Some might feel alternatively that the scientific instrument data which we have presented is *not* evidence of an innovation pattern differing from the within-manufacturer 'norm' and that the Booz, Allen and Hamilton/ Conference Board scenarios can be made to fit the scientific instruments data. One might decide, for example, that the user-built prototype of an innovative instrument available to an instrument firm simply serves as a new product "idea" which that firm, in Marquis and Meyers' terminology, "recognizes". It would then follow that the stages coming after "recognition" in the Marquis and Meyers model also occur within the manufacturing firm. The "idea

* We have preliminary data, for example, which indicate that this would be an accurate description of the process of innovation in basis plastic polymers. Each of the seven basic polymers we have examined to date shows a history of innovation activity located almost entirely within the commercializing firm.
Some additional pressure in the direction of assuming a within-manufacturer innovation process pattern is universal may be exerted unintentionally via product advertising. Very naturally, in the course of marketing an innovation, manufacturing firms will advertise 'their' innovative device. These firms do not mean to imply that *they* invented, prototyped and field-tested the advertised innovation. But, in the absence of countervailing advertising by other contributors to the innovative process – advertising which they generally have no reason to engage in – it is easy to make the assumption.

formulation" stage, for example, would consist of the thinking devoted by manufacturer personnel to the commercial embodiment of the user prototype. "Problem solving" and "Solution" would be the engineering work leading to realization of the commercial embodiment.

Although one might make the argument outlined above, we ourselves find it rather thin and unproductive to do so: essentially the argument enshrines relatively minor activities within the manufacturer as the "innovation process" and relegates major activities by the user to the status of "input" to that process. If instead we look at the scientific instrument data afresh, we see something very interesting: an industry regarded as highly innovative in which the firms comprising the industry are not necessarily innovative in and of themselves. Indeed, we might plausibly look at instrument firms as simply the manufacturing function for an innovative set of user/customers. Or, less extremely, we might say that in approximately eight out of ten innovation cases in the scientific instrument industry (given that our sample is indeed representative of that industry), the innovation process work is shared by the user and manufacturer. Whatever the view, there are important implications for all those interested in the process:

– Government, desirous of promoting industrial good innovations as a means of enhancing exports, improving industrial productivity, etc., should consider users as well as manufacturers when designing incentive schemes for innovation.

– Instrument firms, finding that approximately eight out of ten successful instrument innovations come to them from users in the form of field tested prototypes, could optimize their innovation search and development organization for this kind of input.

– Researchers, interested in characterizing the innovation process, can shake their heads sadly at the realization that "locus of innovation activity" is yet another variable to contend with.

4.1. Other innovation patterns

We ourselves hope eventually to be able to model shifts in the locus of the innovation process as a function of a few product and industry characteristics and are extending our data gathering into a range of different industries toward that ultimate end. At the moment, however, we can only offer the reader some innovation cases which suggest, but do not prove, that the locus of innovation is in fact an innovation process variable. As is indicated in fig. 3, following, we identified cases in the literature appearing to display three clearly different innovation patterns. In one of these the user is

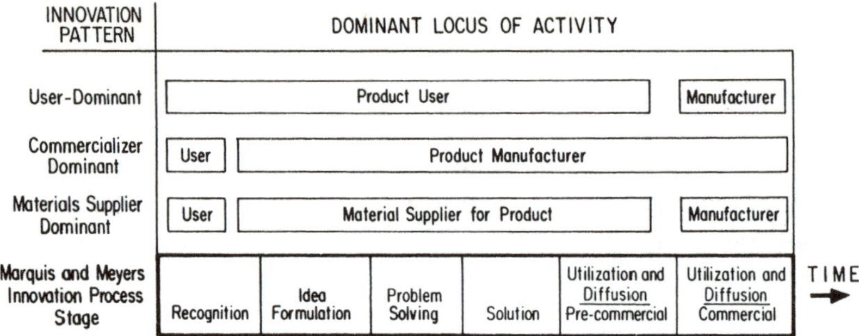

Fig.3. Innovation patterns displayed by some case histories.

dominant, in one the manufacturer is dominant and in the third pattern the suppliers of *material* to manufacturers of innovative products appear dominant. We hasten to add that at this point we by no means wish to suggest that the patterns which we will describe are in any sense "pure types" or represent an exhaustive listing of possible innovation patterns. We merely wish to offer these cases as interesting and suggestive of the possibility that a variety of patterns exist.

4.2. A user-dominated innovation pattern

A user-dominated innovation pattern is, as we have discussed, characteristic of scientific instruments used in laboratories and industrial process control. It is also, Project SAPPHO finds*, typical of chemical process innovation. On the basis of anecdotal evidence, we suspect that this pattern is also characteristic of medical and dental innovations (e.g. new dental equipment is usually invented, first used and perhaps discussed in journals by dentists prior to commercial manufacture being undertaken by a dental equipment firm).

* SAPPHO (Vol. I, p. 67), ". . . for process innovations, the first successful application is usually within the innovating organization." If (a) the process innovation involved innovative hardware for its execution and if (b) a non-using manufacturer manufactured this equipment for commercial sale to other chemical processors, the situation would parallel exactly the innovation pattern which we found in scientific instruments. Conditions (a) and/or (b) do not always hold in the case of chemical process innovations however. With respect to the innovative hardware condition for example: Innovative chemical processes can often be carried out using standard process hardware, just as a standard lab test tube can play a role in a novel chemical experiment.

Further, we have found that the pattern is at least occasionally present in the innovation of industrial process machinery*.
For examples illustrative of a user-dominated innovation pattern, the reader may refer to case outlines 1 and 3 in subsect. 3.2.

4.2.1. A manufacturer-dominated innovation pattern
Case outline 2 in subsect. 3.2 displays a manufacturer-dominated innovation pattern. Input from the user is restricted to a statement of a need, if that. All other innovation activity is carried out by the manufacturer who first commercializes the innovation.

4.2.2. A material supplier-dominated innovation pattern
Professor Corey of Harvard has written a fascinating book [9] in which he describes an innovation pattern apparently characteristic of suppliers of "new" materials. Essentially, when suppliers of such materials (e.g. plastic, aluminum, fiberglass) want to incorporate their material into a product but do not want to manufacture the product itself, they will often:
– design the product incorporating the new material;
– help an interested manufacturer with start-up problems;
– help market the manufacturer's new product to *his* customers.
The extent to which the materials supplier can be the locus of activity leading to innovative products commercialized by others is made clear in the following two examples from Corey:

> *(A) Vinyl floor tile* [10]
> Bakelite Company, a chemical company producing plastic materials did much of the pioneering work on the chemical technology of using vinyl resin in flooring and on the development of commercial processes for manufacturing various types of vinyl floor products . . .
> Bakelite had experimented with vinyl flooring as early as 1931. In 1933 Bakelite installed vinyl tile in its Vinylite Plastics House at the Chicago World's Fair to demonstrate the product and to get some indication of its wearing qualities. When the flooring was taken up at the close of the Fair, no measurable decrease in its thickness could be noted even though an estimated 20 million people had walked over this surface . . .

* An example is provided by a paint manufacturing firm which invented, built, and field tested a new type of paint mill. After debugging the prototype, it sent engineering drawings to a company specializing in heavy metal fabricating and ordered several for its own use. Later the fabricating company built many more of the innovative paint mills and sold them to other paint companies.

Bakelite Company personnel had attempted before World War II to interest leading linoleum manufacturers such as Armstrong Cork and Congoleum-Nairn in making continuous vinyl flooring. These efforts were to no avail . . .
The first company to take on the manufacture of continuous vinyl was Delaware Floor Products, Inc., a small concern located in Wilmington, Delaware . . .
One Bakelite engineer spent almost full time for six months in 1946 to help Delaware Floor Products personnel to iron out the "bugs" in the production processes

(B) Aluminum trailers for trucks [11]
Alcoa first attempted to promote the use of aluminum in vantype trailers in the late 1920's. In the early stages of market development, Alcoa representatives achieved the greatest success by working with fleet operators and persuading them to specify aluminum when ordering new trailers . . .
In the development of markets both for aluminum van trailers and for vinyl flooring, the materials producers assumed the burden of extensive technical development work. In the case of the aluminum van trailer, for example, it was an Alcoa engineer who developed the basic design for the monocoque trailer . . .
In addition to developing the basic monocoque design, Alcoa engineers assisted fleet operators in designing individual trailers and worked with trailer builders on the techniques of aluminum fabrication. When a fleet operator could be persuaded to specify aluminum in a new trailer, Alcoa prepared design drawings and bills of materials for him. Alcoa personnel then followed closely the construction of this unit by the trailer builder and provided the builder with engineering services during the period of construction.

5. FURTHER FINDINGS AND DISCUSSION

To this point we have restricted our presentation of findings to the overall pattern of the innovation process observed in scientific instruments. In the space remaining, we would like to present further findings and discussion bearing on two aspects of that innovation process. Specifically, we would like

to present*:
– A further characterization of the "inventive user";
– An attempt to discern what aspects of the information potentially derivable from a user's prototype instrument (one can find data bearing on both need and on solution technology by studying such a prototype) is actually new and useful information to commercializing firms.

5.1. Characterization of the inventive user

An instrument firm engulfed by users of its products might well be interested in knowing more about the characteristics of those likely to come up with prototype instruments of commercial potential. It might be modestly useful in this regard to note the organizational affiliations of the inventive users in our sample (table 7).

We might also note that we feel we can discern two quite different types of reasons why the user-inventors in our sample undertook to develope the basic or major improvement credited to them. Some needed the invention as a day-in, day-out functional tool for their work. They didn't care very much *how* the tool worked, only that it *did* work. An example of such a user might be a librarian who builds an information retrieval system of a certain type – because he/she needs it to retrieve information. Others were motivated to invent and reduce the invention to practice because *how* it performed was a

Table 7
Employment of inventive users

Major improvement innovation	University or institute	Private manufacturing firm	Self-employed	NA	Total
Gas chromatography	3	3	1	2	9
Nuclear magnetic resonance	9	0	0	2	11
Ultraviolet spectrophotometry	4	1	0	0	5
Transmission electron microscopy	10	0	0	1	11

* Obviously, there are many additional issues which it would be instructive to explore. We are currently addressing some of these in a real-time study of the instrument innovation process now being carried out by Frank Spital, a doctoral candidate at MIT's Sloan School. (The real-time feature of this study will allow one to study issues characterized by data too evanescent for retrospective examination.)

useful means of testing and deepening their understanding of the principles underlying its operation. Thus, a researcher attempting to understand how bits of information are interrelated might also build an information retrieval system – not because he wanted to retrieve information himself or help others to do so, but because he wanted to test an hypothesis. Note that a "user" inventor so motivated does use his creation although not necessarily for its nominal purpose.

We have not attempted to code our sample of users according to the motivational distinction outlined above because motivations are hard to judge and often change over time: A biologist might start out to improve gas chromatography apparatus in order to forward his work on membranes but later get fascinated by the process itself and continue to explore it for its own sake.

5.2. Multiple significant innovations by the same individual

The search process of instrument companies for user invented prototypes of commercial interest would be eased if the same non-instrument firm employees tended to come up with more than one such prototype. We went through our data and did find a few such cases as shown in table 8.

Those individuals who are responsible for more than one significant innovation in an instrument type are not unknown quantities to instruments firms who sell that type of instrument. Two out of the four individuals identified in table 8 had firmly established consulting relations with a single company.

Table 8
Multiple significant innovations by the same individual

Major improvement innovations affecting	Total major innovations by users	Instances of more than one major innovation invented by the same non-instrument firm employee
Gas chromatography	9	2 by one user
Nuclear magnetic resonance	11	3 by one user
Ultraviolet spectrophotometry	5	2 by one user
Transmission electron microscopy	11	4 by one user
Total	36	11

6. NON-REDUNDANT INFORMATION CONTENT OF USER PROTOTYPES

We introduced this paper with the observation that prior research into the innovation process had highlighted a strong correlation between innovation success and "accurate understanding of user need" on the part of the innovating firm. We further noted that prior research did not shed much light on how such "accurate understanding of user need" was obtained by innovating manufacturers and that the present study would explore this issue further in the particular context of scientific instrument innovations. On the basis of the broad brush findings we have set forth so far, we can see that scientific instrument companies typically are *not* constrained to accurately perceive user need as such. Instead, they have available to them a hardware *solution* to a need which a user has – hopefully accurately – perceived himself as having. The fact that a hardware solution (a user prototype) is typically available to the commercializing firm, however, does not mean that that firm will find all the information derivable from that prototype either novel or useful. Therefore, while a commercializing firm *can* derive data on both user need and on solution technology from a prototype instrument, it does not necessarily follow that the firm *will* use both – or either. (A firm utilizing the user *need content only,* will in effect respond to a user prototype by saying: "We didn't know that you needed something to do that. Now that we see the need, we'll sit down and design a solution better that the one used in your prototype." A firm using only the *solution content* of a user prototype will in effect be saying: "We already knew what you needed, but didn't know how to build a suitable device. Thanks for the design help." A firm using *both the need and solution content* of the user prototype will be saying in effect: "You need that? OK. We'll build some to your design.")

During the course of our retrospective data gathering work, we tried to explore this issue and determine the frequency with which the need and/or the solution content of a user prototype did in fact convey novel information to a commercializing firm participating in a user-dominated innovation process. Unfortunately, we found that we could not succeed in answering this question reliably insofar as the novelty of *need* input was concerned. Retrospectively gathered interview data is notoriously unreliable unless buttressed by memos or other forms of "hard" evidence generated contemporaneously with the events being discussed and, in the case of novelty of need input to a commercializing firm, we were unable to find any such supporting documentation. When we sought to determine the novelty of the *solution* content of a user prototype to a commercializing firm, however, we had better luck. We

Table 9
In those cases where a user prototype precedes a commercialized innovation, was the technical solution used by the prototype substantially replicated in the commercial device?

Major innovations	% Yes	Yes	No	Na	Total
Gas chromatography	78%	7	2	0	9
Nuclear magnetic resonance	82%	9	2	0	11
Ultraviolet spectrophotometry	100%	5	0	0	5
Transmission electron microscopy	64%	7	4	0	11
Total	78%	28	8	0	36

were able to buttress the recollection of our interviewees regarding the novelty and utility of the *solution* content of a user prototype by looking at contemporaneously generated hardware and publications and asking: Does the commercialized instrument display the same technological solution to the new problem as did its user prototype predecessor? When this test supported our interviewees' recollection regarding the novelty and utility of user prototype solution content to the commercializing firm, we felt able to use the data (table 9).

As we indicated earlier in this article when we described the product manufacturer's role in the innovation process as product engineering work which ". . . typically affects only the engineering embodiment of the user's invention, not its operating principles," the answer to the question is "Yes", the operating principle portion of the solution content of the user prototype is typically used*. Interestingly, in all cases where an instrument firm did not utilize the operating principles of a preceding user prototype in its com-

* The coding of this question involves some existence of technical judgment by the coder as no clear definitional boundary exists between the "operating principles" of an invention and its "engineering embodiment": Perhaps we can best convey a feeling for the two categories via an illustration. If we may refer to the example provided by Bloch's sample spinning innovation described in subsect. 3.2 of this paper: The *concept* of achieving an effective increase in magnetic field homogeneity via the "operating principle" of microscopically spinning the sample can have many "engineering embodiments" by which one achieves the desired spin. Thus one company's embodiment may use an electric motor to spin a sample holder mounted on ball bearings. Another might, in effect, make the sample holder into the rotor of a miniature air turbine, achieving both support and spin by means of a carefully designed flow of air around the holder.

mercial version, the operating principle involved lay within the purview of mechanical or electrical engineering rather than chemistry or physics.

7. SUGGESTIONS FOR FURTHER RESEARCH

The results and lack of results of the study we have reported on here lead us to suggest two research directions as being exciting and worth further work:
(1) We feel that the finding that the locus of innovation activity is *not* necessarily found within the commercializing firm, but rather may vary from industry to industry and very possibly also within a single industry is worth further exploration. An effort to map who carries out what role in the innovation process in various industries and structures might allow us to eventually model and understand the "locus of innovation". Such understanding would surely benefit those trying to manage the innovation process at the firm, industry or government level: knowing where innovation occurs would seem to be a minimum prerequisite for exerting effective control.
(2) In this study we keenly felt our inability to explore certain issues of interest within the context of the scientific instrument industry, due to limitations inherent in retrospectively gathered data. For example, we have been unable to "see" messages about and perceptions of user needs which were not documented contemporaneously. Also, we have not been able to determine how instrument firms select some user prototypes for commercialization from the many available (or do users with prototypes choose firms?). Better understanding of such issues should make it possible to make operationally useful suggestions regarding the scientific instrument innovation process, and we suggest that real time, rather than retrospective, research designs are most appropriate for addressing many of them.

REFERENCES

[1] J. Utterback, Innovation in Industry and the Diffusion of Technology, *Science* (February 15, 1974) p. 622, table 2.

[2] Achilladelis et al., *Project SAPPHO. A Study of Success and Failure in Industrial Innovation,* Vol. 1 (Center for the Study of Industrial Innovation, London, 1971) p. 66.

[3] J. Utterback, The Process of Innovation: A Study of the Origin and Development of Ideas for New Scientific Instruments, *IEEE Transactions on Engineering Management* (November 1971) 124.

[4] D. Shimshoni, *Aspects of Scientific Entrepreneurship* (unpublished doctoral dissertation, Harvard University, Cambridge, Massachusetts, May 1966).

[5] National Research Council of the National Academy of Sciences, *Chemistry: Opportunities and Needs* (Printing and Publishing Office, National Academy of Sciences, 2101 Constitution Avenue, Washington, D.C., 1965).

[6] D. Marquis and S. Meyers, *Successful Industrial Innovations* (National Science Foundation, May, 1969) p. 4, figure 1, "The Process of Technical Innovation".

[7] Booz, Allen & Hamilton, Inc., *Management of New Products* (Booz, Allen & Hamilton, Inc., New York, 1968) pp. 8–9.

[8] The Conference Board, *Evaluating New Product Proposals,* Report No. 604 (The Conference Board, New York, 1973 pp. 63–64.

[9] E. R. Corey, *The Development of Markets for New Materials* (Division of Research, Graduate School of Business Administration, Harvard University, Boston, Massachusetts, 1956).

[10] *Ibid.,* pp. 18, 21, 22.

[11] *Ibid.,* pp. 35, 36, 41, 42.

[20]

"Sticky Information" and the Locus of Problem Solving: Implications for Innovation

Eric von Hippel
Sloan School of Management, Massachusetts Institute of Technology, 50 Memorial Drive, Cambridge, Massachusetts 02139

To solve a problem, needed information and problem-solving capabilities must be brought together. Often the information used in technical problem solving is costly to acquire, transfer, and use in a new location—is, in our terms, "sticky." In this paper we explore the impact of information stickiness on the locus of innovation-related problem solving. We find, first, that when sticky information needed by problem solvers is held at one site only, problem solving will be carried out at that locus, other things being equal. Second, when more than one locus of sticky information is called upon by problem solvers, the locus of problem solving may iterate among these sites as problem solving proceeds. When the costs of such iteration are high, then, third, problems that draw upon multiple sites of sticky information will sometimes be "task partitioned" into subproblems that each draw on only one such locus, and / or, fourth, investments will be made to reduce the stickiness of information at some locations.

Information stickiness appears to affect a number of issues of importance to researchers and practitioners. Among these are patterns in the diffusion of information, the specialization of firms, the locus of innovation, and the nature of problems selected by problem solvers.
(*Sticky Information; Information Transfer Costs; Innovation; User Innovation; Technological Change; Problem Solving; Location of Problem Solving; Iteration*)

1. Introduction

To solve a problem, needed information and problem-solving capabilities must be brought together—physically or "virtually"—at a single locus. The need to transfer information from its point of origin to a specified problem-solving site will not affect the locus of problem-solving activity when that information can be shifted at no or little cost. However, when information is costly to acquire, transfer, and use—is, in our terms, "sticky"—we find that patterns in the distribution of problem solving can be affected in several significant ways. In this paper we explore this general matter within the specific context of technical, innovation-related problem solving.

It has not always been clear that technical information used by innovators in the course of their problem-solving work might be costly to transfer from place to place. Indeed, the central tendency in economic theorizing has been to view information as costlessly transferable, and much of the research on the special character of markets for information has been based precisely on this characteristic. Thus, Arrow observes that "the cost of transmitting a given body of information is frequently very low. . . . In the absence of special legal protection, the owner cannot, however, simply sell information on the open market. Any one purchaser can destroy the monopoly, since he can reproduce the information at little or no cost" (1962, p. 614–615). However, a number of scholars with an empirical as well as theoretical interest in the economics and diffusion of technological information have long argued, and to some extent shown, that the costs of information transfer in technical projects can vary significantly (Nelson 1959, 1982; Rosenberg 1982; Griliches 1957; Mansfield 1968; Pavitt 1987; and Teece 1977).

In this paper we first review and draw on the work of these scholars to provide a reasoned basis for our assumption that information used by technical problem

0025-1909/94/4004/0429$01.25

solvers is in fact often "sticky" (§2). We then explore four patterns in the locus of innovation-related problem solving that appear related to information stickiness. First, when information needed for innovation-related problem solving is held at one locus as sticky information, the locus of problem-solving activity will tend to take place at that site (§3). Second, when more than one locus of sticky information is called upon by problem solvers, the locus of problem-solving activity may move iteratively among such sites as innovation development work proceeds (§4). Third, when the costs of such iteration are high, problem-solving activities that draw upon multiple sites of sticky information will sometimes be "task partitioned" into subproblems that each draw on only one such locus (§5). Fourth, when the costs of iteration are high, efforts will sometimes be directed toward investing in "unsticking" or reducing the stickiness of information held at some sites (§6).

Finally, we will conclude the paper with a discussion of the likely impact of information stickiness on a number of issues of interest to innovation researchers and practitioners. For example, we will reason that the incentives to invest in reducing the stickiness of given information are affected by how frequently that information is a candidate for transfer. Such a pattern would, in turn, offer an economic explanation for a general shift of innovation-related problem solving toward users, as in the current trend in which the producers of software and other products seek to "empower" users by offering them tools that reduce the cost of problem solving and innovation carried out at user sites (§7).

2. "Sticky" Information

As an aid to exploring patterns in the locus of innovation-related problem solving as a function of information transfer costs, we coin the term "sticky" information. We define the stickiness of a given unit of information in a given instance as the incremental expenditure required to transfer that unit of information to a specified locus in a form usable by a given information seeker. When this cost is low, information stickiness is low; when it is high, stickiness is high. Note that in our definition, information stickiness involves not only attributes of the information itself, but attributes of and choices made by information seekers and information providers. For example, if a particular information seeker is inefficient or less able in acquiring information unit x (e.g., because of a lack of certain tools or complementary information), or if a particular information provider decides to charge for access to unit x, the stickiness of unit x will be higher than it might be under other conditions. The purpose of being inclusive with respect to causes of information stickiness in this definition is to allow us to focus on the impact of information stickiness independent of cause.

As noted earlier, a number of reasons have been advanced and explored as to why information might be sticky. Some reasons have to do with the nature of the information itself, some with the amount of information that must be transferred, and some with attributes of the seekers and providers of the information.

With respect to the impact of the nature of the information to be transferred on variations in information stickiness, consider that some information is encoded in explicit terms, while some is "tacit." Polanyi has pointed out that many human skills, and much human expertise, both extensively employed in technical problem solving, are of the latter sort. He observes that "the aim of a skilful performance is achieved by the observance of a set of rules which are not known as such to the person following them" (Polanyi 1958, p. 49, italicized in original). For example, swimmers are probably not aware of the rules they employ to keep afloat (e.g., in exhaling, they do not completely empty their lungs), nor are medical experts generally aware of the rules they follow in order to reach a diagnosis of various symptoms. "Indeed," Polanyi says, "even in modern industries the indefinable knowledge is still an essential part of technology." And, he reasons, "an art which cannot be specified in detail cannot be transmitted by prescription, since no prescription for it exists. It can be passed on only by example from master to apprentice . . ." — a relatively costly mode of transfer (Polanyi 1958, pp. 52–53).

Rosenberg (1982) argues that drawing on technologically useful information involves not just dealing with theoretical knowledge derived from science, but requires breaking open and examining what transpires "inside the black box" of technological phenomena. Indeed, much technological knowledge is costly, difficult, and slow to diffuse since it deals with "the specific and the particular," consists of "innumerable small increments . . . ," and may well be tacit (Rosenberg 1976, p. 78). Nelson argues that technological knowledge is "partly a private good and partly a public one," that is, (1) "a set of specific designs and practices," and (2) "a body of generic knowledge that surrounds these and provides understanding of how things work. . . ." (Nelson 1990; pp. 1, 8, 13). The former is often relatively costly and difficult to acquire, learn to use, and diffuse (Nelson 1982), and thus can be private to its creators in certain respects (Nelson and Winter 1982, Chapter 4). In contrast, "generic knowledge not only tends to be germane to a wide variety of uses and users. Such knowledge is the stock in trade of professionals in a field, and there tends to grow up a systematic way of describing and communicating such knowledge, so that when new generic knowledge is created anywhere, it is relatively costless to communicate to other professionals" (Nelson 1990, pp. 11–12).

The cost of transferring information sufficient to solve a given innovation-related problem can also vary according to the amount of information called for by a technical problem solver. Sometimes stickiness is high because a great deal of information with a nonzero transfer cost per unit is drawn upon to complete innovation development work. Thus, successful anticipation and avoidance of all field problems that might affect a new airplane (Rosenberg 1982, Chapter 6) or a new process machine (von Hippel and Tyre 1994) or a new type of laser (Collins 1982) would require that a very large amount of information about the use environment be transferred to the development lab—because one does not know in advance which subset of that information will be relevant to anticipating potential failures. Scientists trying to build a successful copy of a research apparatus often face great difficulties for the same reason. "It's very difficult to make a carbon copy [of a gravity wave detector]. You can make a near one, but if it turns out that what's critical is the way he glued his transducers, and he forgets to tell you that the technician always puts a copy of *Physical Review* on top of them for weight, well, it could make all the difference" (interviewee in Collins 1975, p. 213).

Information stickiness can also be high because organizations must typically have or acquire related information and skills to be able to use the new knowledge that may be transferred to them. (For example, artists seeking to generate computer art using the mathematics of fractals will not typically be aided by receipt of a software program designed for mathematicians. They must either get the information they seek in "user friendly" form [which in practice means that the transmitter must understand what the recipients already know or can easily learn and must adapt access to the new information accordingly] and/or the recipients must learn the additional complementary information needed to use the existing math program.) Thus, Pavitt points out that "even borrowers of technology must have their own skills, and make their own expenditures on development and production engineering; they cannot treat technology developed elsewhere as a free, or even very cheap, good" (Pavitt 1987, p. 186). Similarly, Cohen and Levinthal argue that a firm's learning or absorptive capacity with respect to new, outside technical information is "largely a function of the firm's prior related knowledge." This stock of knowledge includes not only "basic skills or even a shared language . . ." but also knowledge generated in the course of a firm's own R&D, marketing and manufacturing operations, and technical training programs (Cohen and Levinthal 1990, pp. 128–129). And, again similarly, Evenson and Kislev find in studies of the economic impact of scientific research on agricultural productivity that "little knowledge is borrowed if no indigenous research takes place" (Evenson and Kislev 1973, p. 1314).

Information stickiness can also vary due to other attributes of an information transmitter and receiver. For example, it has been shown that specialized personnel such as "technological gatekeepers" (Allen 1977, Katz and Allen 1982, Katz and Tushman 1980) and specialized organizational structures such as transfer groups (Katz and Allen 1988) can significantly affect the cost of transferring a given unit of information between organizations. And, of course, the decisions of information possessors as to the pricing of access to proprietary information also directly affect the stickiness of that information.

Evidence on the costs of transferring technical information from place to place during innovation-related problem solving also supports the view that technical information can be sticky. A number of empirical studies have been carried out on the costs of transferring a product or process technology from one firm or location to another with full cooperation on both sides. These show that the costs of information transfer do vary and can be significant. For example, Teece (1977) studied 26 international technology transfer projects and examined the costs of transmitting and absorbing all the relevant unembodied technological knowledge (i.e., information on methods of organization and operations, quality control, manufacturing procedures, and associated information, but not the knowledge embodied in capital goods, blueprints, or technical specifications). He found that transfer costs varied widely for the projects in his sample, ranging from 2 percent to 59 percent of total project costs, and averaging 19 percent—a considerable fraction (Teece 1977; pp. 245, 247).

In sum then, it does appear likely that information sought by technical problem solvers will often be sticky. Therefore it will be useful to examine the effects that information stickiness might have on the locus of innovation-related problem solving. In the following sections we identify four such effects.

3. Sticky Information and the Locus of Innovation-related Problem Solving

When information transfer costs are a significant component of the costs of the planned problem-solving work, it is reasonable that there will be a tendency to carry out innovation-related problem-solving activity at the locus of sticky information, other things being equal—just as, in the case of production, it is reasonable that a firm will seek to locate its factory at a location that will minimize transportation costs, other things being equal.

Evidence bearing on this matter can be found in a number of places. Thus, Rosenberg (1982, Chapter 6) describes "learning by using," which involves problem solving carried out in use environments by, typically, product users. For example, after a given jet engine had been in use for a decade, the cost of maintenance declined to only 30 percent of the initial level because users had learned to perform this task better (Rosenberg 1982, p. 131). Rosenberg argues that such learning by using must be carried out at the user locus because that is the site of the information drawn upon by problem solvers. Similarly, agricultural researchers seeking to develop new plant varieties that will flourish under given local conditions often find it efficient to shift problem solving to sites where such conditions exist. Griliches (1957), for example, observed that the complex, innovative process of developing hybrid corn seed was carried out separately by local agricultural experiment stations and private seed companies in order to incorporate unique location-specific factors (such as soil type, topography, length of growing season, fertilizer requirements, rainfall, and insect and disease resistance) required in a hybrid for that specific locality.

Finally, Mowery and Rosenberg (1989, Chapter 4) proposed that independent research contractors are most likely to supply research services that exploit little or no firm-specific knowledge because such knowledge is, in our terminology, sticky. To test their hypothesis, they examined the content of all projects carried out by three major independent R&D contracting firms (the Mellon Institute, the Battelle Memorial Institute, and Arthur D. Little, Inc.) between 1900 and 1940. They found that the bulk of the projects carried out by the independent R&D contractors were of a nature that required a relatively small amount of firm-specific knowledge, and reasoned that the projects requiring large amounts of such knowledge had been carried out in client firms' internal labs. This finding is what we would expect if the locus of problem solving is affected by the locus of sticky information.

4. Sticky Information and "Iteration"

When the solving of a given problem requires access to sticky information located at two or more sites, we propose that problem-solving activity will sometimes move iteratively among these sites. We base this proposal on the finding that problem solving in general (Baron 1988, pp. 43–47) and technical problem solving in particular (Marples 1961, Allen 1966) has trial and error as a prominent feature. If and as each cycle of a trial-and-error process requires access to sticky information located at more than one site, it seems reasonable that iterative shiftings of problem-solving activity among sticky information sites will occur as problem solving proceeds (von Hippel 1990a).

Iteration of the predicted type can often be observed in the problem solving involved in new product and service development. In these arenas two information bases located—at least, initially—in physically different places are typically important for successful problem solving. The first is information on need, located initially with the user. The second is information on solution technologies, located initially at the site of the manufacturer. If need information is sticky at the site of the potential product user, and if solution information is sticky at the site of the product developer, we may see a pattern in which problem-solving activity shuttles back and forth between these two sites.

Thus, as shown schematically in Figure 1, a problem solver may first draw on user need information to generate some attributes for a desired new product or service. Then, manufacturer information may be drawn upon in order to develop a prototype that appears responsive to the specification. The prototype is next tested within its proposed use context to verify function and the accuracy of the initially stated need. If the two do not match satisfactorily—and they often do not—the loci of need and / or capability information must be revisited in search of a closer match. This cycle may be repeated few or many times until an acceptable match is found.

This pattern of iterative shifting of innovation development activity from site to site will be less costly than the transfer of sticky information to a single problem-solving locus given a key condition: The intermediate outputs of problem solving conducted at each locus that *are* transferred between sites must be less sticky than the information operated upon to produce the outputs. Intuitively it seems reasonable that this will often be the case: Such an intermediate output may be in the form of nonembodied information transferable at low cost, or it may be in the form of a prototype that can be economically transferred. For example, an artist may not be able to transfer all information involved in the creative process that brings him or her to specify to a supplier, "I need a green paint of precisely X hue and luminance." However, that (nonembodied) need specification is very simple and precise, and it can be transferred at very low cost. Similarly, the responding paint manufacturer may be able to create and transfer the requested shade of green to the artist (embodied in a prototype or final product), but not be able to transfer the complex knowledge drawn on by that firm's chemists to achieve the feat.

Figure 1 **Iterative Problem-solving Pattern Often Encountered in New Product and Service Development**

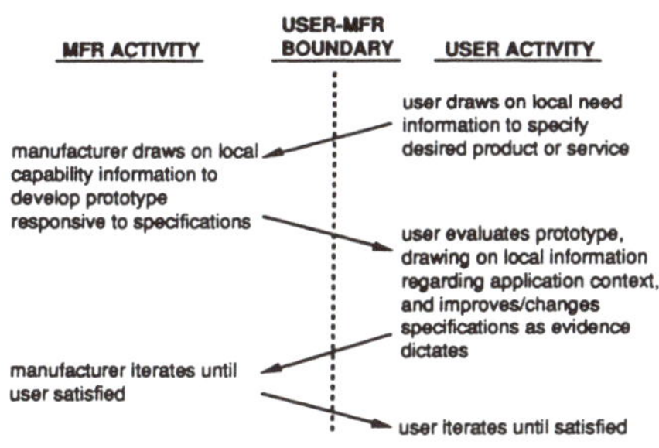

Figure 2 **Number of Shifts Between Plant and Lab During Problem Solving**

Source: Tyre and von Hippel 1993.

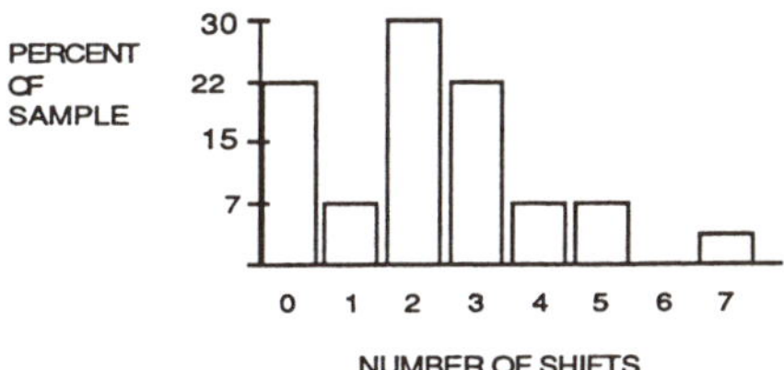

Recent empirical studies report the iterative problem-solving pattern described in Figure 1. Tyre and von Hippel (1993) explored the innovation-related problem solving involved in identifying and diagnosing 27 field failures in process equipment used to automatically assemble complex circuit boards. They observed repeated shifts in the locus of technical problem-solving activity occurring during this work, with the number of shifts found ranging from 0 to 7, and averaging about 2.3 times per problem identified and diagnosed (Figure 2). These shifts involved engineers traveling back and forth between development lab and plant (two to three hours by car), carrying out technical problem-solving activities at each site, and carrying intermediate findings back and forth in their minds and/or computer data disks. For example, to begin the diagnosis of a machine that was failing in the field, the designers of that particular machine would often visit the plant where it was being used in order to observe the malfunction in context and run diagnostic tests. Then they would return to the development lab (the site of specialized lab equipment, relevant expertise, and other types of information) to examine the test results and continue their diagnostic work. Often this work would lead to the need for a second trip to the field for more data collection, and so forth.

In this study, the cost of the iterative shifting of innovation-related problem-solving activity observed did appear to be less than the cost of transferring all information needed by technical problem solvers to a single locus—say, the development lab. While no particular item of information found useful for diagnosing a particular process machine malfunction was very costly to transfer from the plant to the development lab, the specific items needed by the lab could not be identified without problem-solving and trial-and-error activities conducted in the plant. As a consequence, shifting all information needed to diagnose field problems from plant to lab would have meant shifting a great deal of information—effectively the entire use environment—from plant to lab (von Hippel and Tyre 1994). Carrying out such a massive information transfer would have been much more costly than the iterative transfer of problem-solving activity between plant and lab that was found to have taken place.

In studying product innovation in the Danish food industry Kristensen (1992) observed a similar iterative pattern. Here, information is passed back and forth between Danish food producers and customers located in culturally, linguistically, and geographically distant markets. Often, prototypes are used as the medium for information transfer because, as Kristensen points out, "prototypes are not only inexpensive and fast to produce in the food products industry; they are also small and inexpensive to transport." When, for example, a Danish bakery firm was asked to develop a new frozen unbaked cake by a British retail food chain, the bakery's production department responded by developing several prototypes of the proposed cake and sending them to the customer to bake, taste, and smell, and to evaluate on the basis of "local tastes and the situation they were meant for—a type of social gathering not practised in Denmark." Comments on the baked cakes were sent back to the producer, who adjusted the recipes accordingly, "using his familarity with baking and with local raw materials." In total, "five successive revised generations were sent during the course of three months before the Danish producer and the United Kingdom retail chain's test kitchen reached the generation of satisfactory variations." Kristensen reports that over 40 percent of the 103 Danish food producers he studied had developed one or more products within the previous two years via such iterative interactions with customers (Kristensen 1992; pp. 204–205, 210).

The likely ubiquity of the iteration pattern we describe is suggested by the recent emergence of product development procedures specifically designed to implement such a pattern. For example "rapid prototyping" is a method of software development explicitly designed to shuttle repeatedly between manufacturer and users, replacing the traditional, specification-driven ("waterfall") method of software development. In that traditional method, systems analysts meet with users at the start of a project to determine user needs and agree on a written product requirements specification, and they then work isolated from further user contact until the completed product is delivered (in six to eight months or up to two years or more), all too often "late, overbudget and not what the customer wanted" (Zelkowitz 1980, p. 1037). In the rapid prototyping method, manufacturers respond to initial user need inputs by quickly developing and delivering to users (usually within weeks) an inexpensive, easy to modify, working model that simulates a lot of the functionality of the proposed new software. Users then learn by using the prototype in their own setting on their own data and clarify their needs, in part by drawing on their tacit knowledge and experience (Gronbaek 1989, pp. 114–116). Users then relay requests for changes or new features to the software developers, who respond by drawing on their own sticky information and tools to make modifications to the prototype. Some of these modifications are minor, such as altering report formats, and some are major, such as implementing a new feature or modifying the basic structure of the prototype (Feld 1990, p. 14). A revised prototype is then sent to the user, and this process of iteration between developer and user is repeated until an acceptable fit between need and solution is found. A number of individual case studies and experiments have shown that rapid prototyping methods are not only less costly than traditional, noniterative methods but are able to "better satisfy true user requirements and produce information and functionality that is more complete, more accurate, and more meaningful" (Connell and Shafer 1989, p. 15; Boehm et al. 1984; Gomaa 1983).

5. Sticky Information and "Task Partitioning"

When more than one locus of sticky information must be drawn upon to solve a problem, common experience suggests that even iteration can sometimes be very costly with respect to time and effort. For example, no patient likes the shuffling back and forth and time lags involved when a medical condition involves even routine diagnostic tests by and coordinated problem solving among several physicians in different specialties. And, similarly, no designer likes the cost in time and money and frustration involved in repeated redesign of a finished product or service as a result of new information uncovered in the course of test marketing conducted at user sites.

As a consequence, we reason that when the information transfer costs of iteration are high, innovation-related problem-solving activities that require access to multiple loci of sticky information will sometimes be "task partitioned" into subproblems that each draw on only one such locus of sticky information. Because there are many different ways to partition a given innovation project, the selection of a particular partitioning can have a very strong effect on how much information from one task must be drawn upon to solve another as the technical problem-solving work progresses (von Hippel 1990b). As a schematic illustration, consider two alternative ways of partitioning the project of designing a new airplane:

—"Firm X is responsible for the design of the aircraft body, and firm Y is responsible for the design of the engine,

and:

—"Firm X is responsible for designing the front half of both the aircraft body and engine, and firm Y is responsible for designing the back half of both.

Taken together, each of these proposed task partitionings has the same project outcome—a complete aircraft design. But the two differ greatly with respect to the level of information exchange and/or iterative relocation of problem-solving activities. Clearly, information transfer costs would be much higher in the second alternative than in the first: Many design decisions affecting the shape of the "front half" of an aircraft body would force related changes on the designers of the "back half" of the body, and vice versa, because the two halves cannot be considered independently with respect to aerodynamics.

As a real world example of the task partitioning of an innovation project, consider the problem-solving work involved in designing a silicon integrated circuit on a semiconductor chip for a custom application. In this design problem, two sticky data bases are central to the problem-solving work: (1) information at the circuit user locus involving a rich and complex understanding of both the overall application in which the custom integrated circuit will play a role and the specific function required of that circuit; (2) information at the circuit manufacturer locus involving a rich and complex understanding of the constraints and possibilities of the silicon fabrication process that the manufacturer uses to produce integrated circuits.

Traditionally, custom integrated circuits were developed in an iterative Figure 1-like process between a circuit user possessing sticky need information and an integrated circuit manufacturer possessing sticky information about designing and producing silicon integrated circuits. The process would begin with a user specifying the functions that the custom chip was to perform to a circuit design specialist employed by the integrated circuit manufacturer. The chip would then be designed at the manufacturer locus, and an (expensive) prototype would be produced and sent to the user. Testing by the user would typically reveal faults in the chip and/or the initial specification, responsive changes would be made, a new prototype built, and so forth.

More recently, the Application Specific Integrated Circuit (ASIC) method of making custom integrated circuits has come into wide practice. In the ASIC method, the overall problem of designing custom circuits is partitioned into subproblems that each draw on only one locus of sticky information, thereby eliminating the need to iterate between two such sites in the design process. The manufacturer of ASICs draws on its own sticky information to develop and improve the fabrication processes in its manufacturing plant, a "silicon foundry." The manufacturer also draws on its own sticky information to design "standard" silicon wafers that contain an array of unconnected circuit elements such as logic gates. These standard circuit elements arrays are designed by the manufacturer to be interconnectable into working integrated circuits by the later addition of custom interconnection layers designed in accordance with the needs of specific users. To facilitate this user task, the manufacturer provides custom circuit users with a user-friendly Computer-Aided Design (CAD) software package that enables them to design a custom interconnection layer that will meet their specific application needs and yet stay within the production capabilities of the manufacturer's silicon foundry. This CAD software also allows the user to simulate the function of the custom circuit under design, and to conduct trial-and-error experiments. Taken together, these capabilities allow the user to both design a circuit, and to refine need specifications and the desired circuit function through an iterative process that draws only on sticky information located at the user site. In sum, by partitioning the overall circuit design task somewhat differently than is done in the traditional method, the ASIC method of designing custom integrated circuits reduces the need for the iterative shifting of the locus of innovation-related problem solving between user and manufacturer.

6. Sticky Information and Investing in "Unsticking" Information

The stickiness of a given body of information is not immutable. Thus, when the costs of iteration are considered to be high, efforts will sometimes be directed toward investing in "unsticking" or reducing the stickiness of some of the information. For example, firms may reduce the stickiness of a critical form of technical expertise by investing in converting some of that expertise from tacit knowledge to the more explicit and easily transferable form of a software "expert system" (Davis 1986). Or they may invest in reducing the stickiness of information of interest to users by converting it into a remotely accessible and user-friendly computer data base. This is what the travel industry did, for example, when it invested substantial sums to put its various data bases for airline schedules, hotel reservations, and car rentals "on-line" in a user-accessible form.

However, incentives to unstick information can vary. For example, suppose that to solve a particular problem, two units of equally sticky information are required, one from a user and one from a manufacturer. In that case, there will be an equal incentive operating to unstick either of these units of information in order to reduce the cost of transfer, other things (such as the cost of unsticking) being equal. But now suppose that there is reason to expect that one of the units of information, say the manufacturer's, will be a candidate for transfer n times in the future, while the user's unit of information will be of interest to problem solvers only once. For example, suppose that a manufacturer expects to have the same technical information called on repeatedly to solve n user product application problems and each problem involves unique user information. In that case, the total incentive to unstick the manufacturer's information across the entire series of user problems is n times higher than the incentive for an individual user to unstick its problem-related information. And, as an important consequence, it is reasonable that the locus of problem-solving activity will tend to shift to the locus of the less frequently called-upon information—in the case of our example, to the user.

As illustration, recall the shift from the traditional iterative method of designing custom integrated circuits to the ASIC task-partitioning method that we described earlier. During the problem-solving work of circuit design, each circuit designer requires access to the same information about the constraints of the circuit manufacturing process, but requires different information about the specific application being designed for. As a consequence, the ASIC manufacturer found it economic to unstick the repeatedly called-upon production process information by investing in encoding it in a user-friendly CAD package. And, as a further consequence, the problem-solving activity of custom circuit design was shifted to the locus of sticky information regarding each unique application—the user.

The particular pattern just described will often hold in real-world problem solving, we suggest, because it offers a way for manufacturers to seek economies of scale by producing standard products, while at the same time enabling users to carry out the problem solving needed to adapt these to specific local needs and conditions. Consider, for example, the current trend in software (Feld 1990) toward "empowering users." To empower users, manufacturers invest in unsticking some of their programming expertise and information by offering user-friendly programming languages such as Object Oriented Programming (OOPs), and user-tailorable application programs or tool boxes. This has the effect of shifting the problem-solving activity involved in tailoring software to local conditions to the locus of sticky information regarding those local conditions—the user.

7. Discussion and Suggestions for Further Research

In this paper we have begun to explore the impact of sticky information on the locus of innovation-related problem solving, and we propose that further study of information stickiness can be of significant value and interest to both innovation researchers and innovation practitioners.

In the course of our initial work we have observed and discussed four patterns in the distribution of innovation-related problem solving associated with efforts made by technical problem solvers to reduce information transfer costs. First, when technical information that is costly to acquire, transfer, and use is held in one locus of sticky information, innovation-related problem-solving activities will tend to move to that locus; second, when more than one locus of sticky information is called upon to solve a problem, the locus of problem-solving activity will tend to iterate among these sticky information sites as innovation development work proceeds; third, when the costs of such iteration are high, innovation-related problem-solving activities that require access to multiple loci of sticky information will sometimes be "task partitioned" into subproblems that each draw on only one such locus of sticky information; and fourth, when the costs of iteration are high, investments may be made toward investing in "unsticking" or reducing the stickiness of information held at some sites.

This short list is not intended to be exhaustive, and further work may identify additional patterns as well as usefully elaborate on the four already identified. For example, in the present paper we have not examined patterns in the distribution of innovation-related problem solving that will be visible when a problem *can* be solved using only technical information that can be acquired, transferred, and used without cost or nearly so. We speculate that, in such cases, the locus of problem-solving activities will depend on the costs associated with locating the noninformation components necessary to the technical problem-solving work. Problems appropriate for problem solvers who "telecommute" can fall into this category because the data inputs and outputs called upon can be sent nearly anywhere at low cost over telecommunication networks. Therefore, telecommuters can locate themselves wherever they and their employers find it most cost-effective and convenient to carry out their problem-solving work.

Innovation practitioners may wish to use the information transfer patterns we have discussed in this paper to consciously manage their information transfer costs. The value of doing this in any particular circumstance will depend on these strategies not adversely affecting other innovation cost factors or an innovator's abilities to appropriate innovation-related benefit. We think this can often be the case even though, on the face of it, the latter condition seems problematic. After all, patents and trade secrecy and lead time can all be important to an innovator's ability to profit from an innovation (von Hippel 1988, Chapter 5), and these all depend on an innovator's maintaining at least some secrecy at least for a while. But how can one expect an innovating firm to keep secrets if it conducts problem solving not on the innovator's premises but at sites of sticky information? For example, would not a firm that wants to keep a chemical formula a trade secret be ill-advised to conduct some of the technical development work at a customer site?

Often, however, conducting innovation-related problem solving at remote sites need not compromise an innovator's ability to protect commercially important secrets. First, consider that firms can come to some legal arrangement that will maintain secrecy for problem solving done at another locus. Second, consider that firms routinely do locate some of this type of problem solving off their premises without taking legal precautions, and with no apparent impact on their ability to appropriate benefit from their innovations. In some instances, this is explicable because the innovation development task undertaken outside the firm is just a piece of the whole, and revealing a part does not reveal the whole to would-be imitators. Thus, firms routinely ask outside suppliers to develop components of an innovative product, engage in market research and product testing on customer sites, and so forth. In other instances, an innovation being worked upon without benefit of secrecy is nonetheless protected because it is tied in some way to a product or service or process that is protected. Thus, a supplier of a proprietary computer program may benefit from nonproprietary improvements to it, because the improvements will only operate in conjunction with the proprietary program.

The concept of information stickiness can also enable us to understand more about patterns of specialization among individuals and firms. Since an organizational boundary can add to the costs of information transfer, it seems likely that firms seeking to economize with respect to the transfer of sticky information will seek to align their organizational boundaries—and their specializations—with the partitionings dictated by the types of innovation-related problem-solving tasks that are important to them. For similar reasons, consideration of the impact of sticky information may be useful in studying the various collaborative innovation patterns that are being practiced by firms today (e.g., Gemunden 1980). We also propose that studies of sticky information can increase our understanding of how firms protect, sell, trade, diffuse, and appropriate benefit from information. Thus, stickiness can help the possessors of valuable information to prevent unintentional diffusion to competitors, but that same property may make it more costly to diffuse the information intentionally.

Studies that use information stickiness as a variable can also help researchers to explore patterns in the *nature* of problems selected by technical problem solvers. It seem reasonable that problems that involve low information transfer costs would tend to be selected preferentially. Thus, a firm may elect to develop new products that draw on local information in preference to those that require costly information transfers from suppliers or users or others. Similarly, responses to information transfer costs, such as a decision to partition problem-solving tasks in a different way, or to unstick certain information, can affect the kind of solutions that technical problem solvers may develop to a given problem. For example, the development of single-site "desktop publishing" (which removed the need for iterative problem solving among author, graphic designer, and printer) may well enable author/"publishers" to create very different documents as well as less expensive ones. And the development of home medical diagnosis kits (which reduce the need for information transfers among patient, doctor, and medical laboratory) may bring about qualitative and quantitative changes in the type of medical care that is demanded and the way it is delivered.

Finally, it is interesting to speculate about the patterns in the locus of innovation-related problem solving that will emerge as the computerization of problem-solving activities continues to make information even more accessible via computer networks and increasingly portable, inexpensive, and user-friendly computer equipment and software. Taken together, these trends can certainly facilitate "anywhere" problem solving when all of the information drawn upon to solve a technical problem is nonsticky, as in the instance of telecommuting discussed above. When information transfer costs vary and at least some of the needed information is sticky, however, these same trends can make the patterns discussed in this paper even more salient. Thus, researchers equipped with computers and network access will be free to transfer their work to and among field sites containing sticky information, managers will be free to move decision making to the sites of critical tasks, and product designers will be free to design products working directly with users at user sites. It will be an interesting world to develop and explore![1]

[1] I am very grateful to my colleagues Anne Carter, Bradley Feld, Dietmar Harhoff, Zvi Griliches, Ralph Katz, Richard Nelson, Nathan Rosenberg, Stephan Schrader, Stefan Thomke, Marcie Tyre, and Jessie von Hippel for their contributions to the ideas explored in this paper.

I thank the Sloan Foundation for funding the research reported on in this paper.

References

Allen, Thomas J., "Studies of the Problem-Solving Process in Engineering Design," *IEEE Transactions on Engineering Management*, EM-13, 2, June (1966), 72–83.

——, *Managing the Flow of Technology: Technology Transfer and the Dissemination of Technological Information Within the R&D Organization*, MIT Press, Cambridge, MA, 1977.

Arrow, Kenneth J. "Economic Welfare and the Allocation of Resources of Invention," in Richard R. Nelson (Ed.) *The Rate and Direction of Inventive Activity: Economic and Social Factors*, A Report of the National Bureau of Economic Research, Princeton University Press, Princeton, NJ, 1962, 609–625.

Baron, Jonathan, *Thinking and Deciding*, Cambridge University Press, New York, 1988.

Boehm, Barry W., Terence E. Gray, and Thomas Seewaldt, "Prototyping Versus Specifying: A Multiproject Experiment," *IEEE Transactions on Software Engineering*, SE-10, May (1984), 290–303.

Cohen, Wesley M. and Daniel A. Levinthal, "Absorptive Capacity: A New Perspective on Learning and Innovation," *Administrative Sci. Quarterly*, 35, 1, March (1990), 128–152.

Collins, H. M., "Tacit Knowledge and Scientific Networks," in Barry Barnes and David Edge (Eds.), *Science in Context: Readings in the Sociology of Science*, MIT Press, Cambridge, MA, 1974, 1982, 44–64.

——, "The Seven Sexes: A Study in the Sociology of a Phenomenon, or the Replication of Experiments in Physics," *Sociology*, 9, 2, May (1975), 205–224.

Connell, John L. and Linda Brice Shafer, *Structured Rapid Prototyping: An Evolutionary Approach to Software Development*, Prentice-Hall, Englewood Cliffs, NJ, 1989.

Davis, Randall, "Knowledge-Based Systems," *Science*, 231, 4741, February 28 (1986), 957–963.

Evenson, Robert E. and Yoav Kislev, *Agricultural Research and Productivity*, Yale University Press, New Haven, CT, 1975.

Feld, Bradley A., "The Changing Role of the User in the Development of Application Software," Working Paper No. BPS 3152-90, Sloan School of Management, Massachusetts Institute of Technology, Cambridge, MA, August 1990.

Gemunden, Hans Georg, "Efficient Interaction Strategies in Marketing of Capital Goods" (in English), Working Paper, Institut fur Angewandte Betriebswirtschaftslehre und Unternehmensfuhrung, University of Karlsruhe, Karlsruhe, Germany, n.d. Published as "Effiziente Interaktionsstrategien im Investitionsgutermarketing," *Marketing ZFP*, March (1980), 21–32.

Gomaa, Hassan, "The Impact of Rapid Prototyping on Specifying User Requirements," *ACM Sigsoft Software Engineering Notes*, 8, 2, April (1983), 17–28.

Griliches, Zvi, "Hybrid Corn: An Exploration in the Economics of Technical Change," *Econometrica*, 25, 4, October (1957), 501–522.

Gronbaek, Kaj, "Rapid Prototyping with Fourth Generation Systems—An Empirical Study," *Office: Technology and People*, 5, 2, September (1989), 105–125.

Katz, Ralph and Thomas J. Allen, "Investigating the Not Invented Here (NIH) Syndrome: A Look at the Performance, Tenure, and Communication Patterns of 50 R&D Project Groups," *R&D Management*, 12, 1, January (1982), 7–19.

—— and ——, "Organizational Issues in the Introduction of New Technologies," in Ralph Katz (Ed.), *Managing Professionals in Innovative Organizations*, Ballinger, Cambridge, MA, 1988, 442–456.

—— and Michael L. Tushman, "External Communication and Project Performance: An Investigation into the Role of Gatekeepers," *Management Sci.*, 26, 11, November (1980), 1071–1085.

Kristensen, Preben Sander, "Flying Prototypes: Production Departments' Direct Interaction with External Customers," *International J. Operations and Production Management*, 12, 7, 8 (1992), 195–211.

Mansfield, Edwin, *Industrial Research and Technological Innovation: An Econometric Analysis*, W. W. Norton, New York, 1968.

Marples, David L., "The Decisions of Engineering Design," *IRE Transactions on Engineering Management*, June (1961), 55–71.

Mowery, David C. and Nathan Rosenberg, *Technology and the Pursuit of Economic Growth*, Cambridge University Press, New York, 1989.

Nelson, Richard R., "The Simple Economics of Basic Scientific Research," *J. Political Economy*, 67, June (1959), 297–306.

——, "The Role of Knowledge in R&D Efficiency," *Quarterly J. Economics*, 97, 3, August (1982), 453–470.

——, "What is Public and What is Private About Technology?" Consortium on Competitiveness and Cooperation, Working Paper No. 90-9, Center for Research in Management, University of California at Berkeley, Berkeley, CA, April 1990.

—— and Sidney G. Winter, *An Evolutionary Theory of Economic Change*, Harvard University Press, Cambridge, MA, 1982.

Pavitt, Keith, "The Objectives of Technology Policy," *Science and Public Policy*, 14, 4, August (1987), 182–188.

Polanyi, Michael, *Personal Knowledge: Towards a Post-Critical Philosophy*, University of Chicago Press, Chicago, IL, 1958.

Rosenberg, Nathan, *Perspectives on Technology*, Cambridge University Press, New York, 1976.

——, *Inside the Black Box: Technology and Economics*, Cambridge University Press, New York, 1982.

Teece, David J., "Technology Transfer by Multinational Firms: The Resource Cost of Transferring Technological Know-How," *Economic J.*, 87, 346, June (1977), 242–261.

Tyre, Marcie J. and Eric von Hippel, "Locating Adaptive Learning: The Situated Nature of Adaptive Learning in Organizations," Working Paper No. BPS 3568-93, Sloan School of Management, Massachusetts Institute of Technology, Cambridge, MA, May 1993.

von Hippel, Eric, *The Sources of Innovation*, Oxford University Press, New York, 1988.

——, "The Impact of 'Sticky Information' on Innovation and Problem-Solving," Working Paper No. BPS 3147-90, Sloan School of Management, Massachusetts Institute of Technology, Cambridge, MA, April, 1990a (revised October 1991).

——, "Task Partitioning: An Innovation Process Variable," *Research Policy*, 19, 5, October (1990b), 407–418.

—— and Marcie J. Tyre, "How Learning by Doing Is Done: Problem Identification in Novel Process Equipment," *Research Policy*, forthcoming, (1994).

Zelkowitz, Marvin V., "A Case Study in Rapid Prototyping," *Software—Practice and Experience*, 10, 2, December (1980), 1037–1042.

Accepted by Ralph Katz; received January 1992. This paper has been with the author 11 months for 2 revisions.

Part V
Alliances and Networks

[21]

Journal of Management Studies 33:3 May 1996
0022-2380, pp. 333–359

THE ROLE OF NETWORKS IN THE DIFFUSION OF TECHNOLOGICAL INNOVATION*

MAXINE ROBERTSON
JACKY SWAN
SUE NEWELL

University of Warwick Business School

ABSTRACT

This research considers the diffusion of computer-aided production management (CAPM) technology in the UK manufacturing sector during the mid to late 1980s, focusing on the role of inter-organizational networks in the diffusion process. Research on innovation diffusion has tended to adopt a 'pro-innovation bias' such that adoption of prescribed best practice technologies is always considered to be the best policy. In the UK, one particular form of CAPM (MRP/MRPII) has been heavily promoted by technology suppliers as best practice. However, the notion of 'best practice' de-emphasizes the importance of decisions about technology design when users attempt to develop firm-specific solutions. Crucial to these decisions are the inter-organizational networks through which potential adopters learn about relevant technologies. Using three case companies, where the introduction of CAPM occurred at approximately the same time, decisions regarding adoption, design and subsequent implementation, are explored in order to establish the influence of inter-organizational networks on the diffusion and subsequent appropriation of CAPM technologies. These cases revealed that potential adopters engaged in a range of inter-organizational networks through which they learned about new technologies. However, the knowledge diffused through many of these networks was shaped by technology suppliers who were promoting similar ideas about best practice. Thus, while involvement in inter-organizational networks gave potential adopters access to information about new technology, this information tended to reinforce supplier images of best practice and did not always lead these firms to develop appropriate technological solutions. Problematic relationships between the suppliers of the technology and the users was seen here to limit the redesign and further diffusion of CAPM.

INTRODUCTION

In this paper we consider the diffusion of technological innovation from a communications perspective, whereby diffusion is seen as a social process of formal and informal information exchange among members of a social system (Rogers, 1983[1962]). This perspective emphasizes the importance of interpersonal

Address for reprints: Maxine Robertson, University of Warwick Business School, Coventry CV4 7AL, UK

networks in the diffusion process. As Rogers observes, 'we must understand the nature of networks if we are to comprehend the diffusion of innovations fully' (p. 293). We attempt to contribute further to this understanding by drawing upon this communications perspective, together with more recent literature on inter-organizational networks (e.g. Alter and Hage, 1993; Grandori and Soda, 1995) and innovation design (Clark and Staunton, 1989; Clark et al., 1992; Fleck et al., 1990; Scarbrough and Corbett, 1992), to explain diffusion of a particular technology to firms in the UK.

The technology that we focus on here is referred to as computer-aided production management (CAPM). CAPM is used to describe, collectively, various technologies for planning and controlling inventory levels and material flows, predominantly within manufacturing firms, although also in services and retail. One variant of CAPM is known as manufacturing resources planning, or MRPII (and, earlier, materials requirements planning – MRP). MRPII attempts to control production by integrating the information that is used across traditional functional areas in the logistics chain, and therefore has major organizational implications (Swan and Clark, 1992; Wilson et al., 1994). MRPII has been particularly prominent in the UK and in North America to the extent that the term 'CAPM' is sometimes used synonymously with 'MRPII' (Corke, 1985). MRPII has been presented by technology suppliers as 'the' best practice for computer-aided production management. However, as we will see later, there are alternative ways of designing CAPM technology and users face major problems in choosing and in designing firm-specific solutions (Clark et al., 1992).

CAPM has been the focus of numerous research papers and projects in the UK, and also in North America.[1] This is in large part because users have experienced major and costly difficulties when trying to implement these technologies (Bessant and Buckingham, 1993; Cooper and Zmud, 1989; Swan and Clark, 1992; Wilson et al., 1994). Thus, many of these projects have focused on intra-firm problems of implementation (e.g. Cooper and Zmud, 1989; Wilson et al., 1994).

Other research has examined the interface between the user, or adopting firm, and technology suppliers (Clark et al., 1992; Clark and Newell, 1993; Fleck et al., 1990; Newell et al., 1993; Webster and Williams, 1993). This research has suggested that the diffusion of CAPM, and the dominance of MRPII in the UK and North America, is strongly influenced by technology suppliers. Clark et al. (1992) have developed a theoretical framework, rooted in Rogers' (1983[1962]) communications perspective, to describe the diffusion and appropriation of CAPM. In this they highlight the importance of the user–supplier interface in shaping the availability and design of CAPM technologies. Appropriation occurs when users manage to unpack the technology as it is presented by the technology suppliers and reconfigure this in order to generate firm-specific solutions. Fleck et al. (1990) also recognize the importance of the supplier–user interface in their concept of 'innofusion'. This refers to the process by which technological solutions that evolve in user firms during implementation are picked up and further diffused by technology suppliers. Both these approaches to the diffusion of CAPM have parallels with Rogers' notion of innovation diffusion as involving a communication process of convergence whereby participants involved in social networks are mutually creating and sharing information. Rogers (1983) argues that diffusion is often better understood in this way, rather than as a one-way linear process whereby information is transferred en mass from one partner to another.

In this paper we report case study data from three manufacturing companies operating in closely related industrial sectors in the UK, which all chose to adopt a particular variant of CAPM during the late 1980s. However, rather than focus on problems of implementation which are already well documented in the literature, we consider problems of diffusion and design of CAPM technology. In this way, we hope to test and further inform the theoretical perspectives provided by Rogers (1983), Clark et al. (1992) and Fleck et al. (1990). One issue that has received relatively less attention in the diffusion literature has been the relevance of inter-organizational networks, other than those provided by the technology supplier–user interface. Where this issue has been investigated empirically, other networks, such as those provided by professional associations, have been found to have an important role in shaping the design and diffusion of CAPM technology (Swan and Newell, 1995). In particular, then, we use recent literature on inter-organizational networks in order to explore the roles that various inter-organizational networks, other than just supplier–user networks, play in the diffusion of new ideas about CAPM.

The paper will:

- Examine the extent to which different inter-organizational networks played a role in promoting the diffusion of particular computer-aided production management (CAPM) technologies to three manufacturing firms in the UK.
- Explore the extent to which outcomes of firms' attempts to implement the technology can be related to their involvement in the different kinds of inter-organizational networks through which information was diffused.
- Provide a test of and suggest developments in the theoretical perspectives offered by Clark et al. (1992) and Fleck et al. (1990) on the design and diffusion of technological innovation.

THEORETICAL BACKGROUND

The concept of inter-organizational networks is problematic in that definitions abound. It is necessary therefore to be clear about how the term 'network' is to be used here. Alter and Hage (1993) define networks as unbounded or bounded clusters of organizations that: 'constitute a basic social form that permits inter-organizational interactions of exchange, concerted action and joint production' (p. 46). Networking refers, therefore, to the activity of creating or maintaining this kind of organizational exchange. Organizations may engage in informational collection and exchange in order to reduce risk or uncertainty, or to share resources or expertise needed to develop innovative solutions, and networks provide the necessary vector for informational exchange (Alter and Hage, 1993). This approach relates well to the industrial network perspective (Axelsson and Easton, 1992) where the focus of research is the 'space' between organizations. This perspective recognizes that 'there are a number of types of relationship in a network where direct economic exchange is absent though other forms of relationship (primarily informational) may exist, e.g. between competitors' (Axelsson and Easton, 1992, p. 12). These definitions are useful in recognizing that employees within organizations are involved in a set of exchange relations and these can include the exchange of knowledge, information and expertise with other social actors, both within and across industrial sectors. They are also consistent with Rogers' (1983) view that interpersonal networks are central to innovation diffusion because they allow information to be communicated across organizational boundaries or, in Rogers' terms, across social 'cliques'. Individuals who are involved in networking are engaged both in the construction and also in the diffusion of knowledge. These individuals have the opportunity to learn about new technologies and may, as a consequence, make more informed decisions about technology design. These individuals are known in the literature as 'boundary spanners' (Tushman and Scanlan, 1981) and it is this boundary spanning activity and its influence on the early stages of innovation diffusion and design that are the focus of the case studies reported here.

Research on inter-organizational networks has tended to focus on relatively formal or contractual relationships among firms in industry such as strategic alliances (Contractor and Lorange, 1988; Mowery, 1988), joint ventures (Laage-Hellman, 1989; Moxon et al., 1988), or obligational linkages such as subcontracting or referrals (Hollingsworth, 1991). However, there are a variety of other, sometimes less formal, networks that may be important for the diffusion process. These may include collaboration among firms in industry and universities, professional associations, government and so forth (Alter and Hage, 1993; Grandori and Soda, 1995; Hauschlidt, 1992; Swan and Newell, 1995). Diffusion research has also recognized the importance of 'weak ties' among different social groups for diffusion of new ideas (Granovetter, 1973; Rogers, 1983).

Weak ties, such as sporadic meetings with distant acquaintances or former colleagues, link individuals who are associated only marginally in their usual activities. Rogers argues that individuals are unlikely to encounter new ideas through highly interconnected, close-knit social networks because individuals in the same social clique tend to possess similar information. In contrast, weak ties provide a link among individuals from different social cliques who possess different knowledge and information. These weak ties, then, are central to the diffusion process because they expose individuals to new ideas such that 'even though weak ties are not a frequent path for the flow of communication, the information that does flow through them plays a crucial role' (Rogers, 1983, p. 297). Rogers tends to focus on links among individuals or small groups but, at an organizational level, this analysis suggests that more distant, informal, or sporadic contact with other organizations from, for example, different occupational sectors, may be an important mechanism for the diffusion of new ideas.

Weak ties among organizations can also help to generate a climate of trust from which more formal collaborative networks can evolve and these collaborative networks are seen as central to the innovation process (Alter and Hage, 1993). Thus, where organizations are involved, through the activities of their employees, in networks with other organizations such as suppliers, competitors, universities or professional associations, they are likely to encounter new ideas that may then enable them to develop innovative solutions.

This paper builds from Rogers' second framework (Rogers, 1983) which recognizes that innovations are sometimes modified or redesigned by the user in a process that Rogers refers to as 're-invention'. There is a recognition here then that a notion of 'best practice' is oversimplified. Often technological innovations cannot necessarily be adopted by organizations as 'off-the-shelf' packages with fixed parameters and universal applicability. Rather, they are multifaceted bundles of knowledge, which may require modification and reconfiguration to make them suitable within specific organizational and societal contexts (Pinch and Bijker, 1989). Recent writers on technological innovation have referred to this process as 'appropriation' of innovation and have suggested that varying degrees of appropriation can occur within an organization (Clark, 1987).

The process of 'innofusion' as defined by Fleck et al. (1990) sits comfortably with notions of appropriation and reinvention (von Hippell, 1982). This research highlighted the ways in which technologies evolved and became further elaborated during implementation. It suggested that organizational knowledge bases were developed or enhanced during appropriation, and also that this learning enriched the knowledge of the suppliers of the technology. During the innofusion process suppliers, acting according to economic self-interest, become aware of the cumulative and progressive transformation of an innovation. They incorporate those aspects of re-invention which they believe enhance the innovation, and which may have general applicability, into new versions of the technology. Subsequent adopters of the innovation, it is suggested, then benefit from the incorporation of these modifications and this aids the diffusion process. The concepts of appropriation and innofusion are compatible with a social constructivist approach to technology which recognizes the relevance of social groups with different vested interests that influence the design and diffusion of (or opposition to) emergent technologies. The influence of such groups or networks is the focus of this paper.

The diffusion literature has been dominated by a perspective which assumes that rational adopters make technically efficient choices based on information that is received via diffusion networks (Rogers, 1983). However, this perspective underestimates the selective nature of the information provided to potential adopters by suppliers of innovations. It also fails to address sufficiently the institutional mechanisms which can lead organizations to adopt technically inefficient innovations (Abrahamson, 1991; DiMaggio and Powell, 1983). For example, DiMaggio and Powell's theory of institutionalized isomorphism suggests that, within industrial sectors characterized by a high degree of interconnectivity, coupled with poor understanding of technology and environmental uncertainty, organizations will develop homogeneously. Isomorphism refers to 'the constraining process that forces one unit in a population to resemble other units that face the same set of environmental conditions' (DiMaggio and Powell, 1983, p. 149). With respect to the diffusion of technological innovation, the implications of this theory are that potential adopters may base their decisions on one or more of the following: (i) they may mimic other organizations within their sector that they perceive to be successful (mimetic processes); (ii) they may experience pressure from other organizations upon which they are dependent to adopt particular technologies (coercive processes); and (iii) the norms established by professionals and professional associations may exert pressure on them to adopt particular technologies in order to be seen as legitimate (normative processes).

In terms of CAPM technology, MRPII has been diffused widely in the UK and North America as 'the' best practice, despite evidence to suggest that these technologies are technically inefficient for many organizations (Swan and Clark, 1992; Waterlow and Monniot, 1986). Researchers have acknowledged that, despite the promises of some technology suppliers, there is no generally accepted 'best way' to implement CAPM that will guarantee success (Roberts and Barrar, 1992; Turnispeed et al., 1992; Wilson et al., 1994). Therefore, the notion of 'best practice', with respect to this technology, is unhelpful and potentially misleading.

Other research has considered the role of professional associations in the diffusion of CAPM technology and supports the idea that normative processes may lead some organizations to adopt MRPII (Newell and Clark, 1990; Swan and Newell, 1995). Surveys and interviews were conducted with members of those professional associations most closely involved in production and inventory control in the UK (the British Production and Inventory Control Society – BPICS) and in North America (the American Production and Inventory Control Society – APICS in the USA, and its equivalent association in Canada). The findings suggested that these associations imparted knowledge through their formal activities (e.g. certification programmes and courses) that was used by practitioners in industry to develop CAPM technologies. These associations also provided weak linkages across organizations so that contact was made between practitioners and individuals from other sectors, such as technology suppliers, consultants, government bodies, academics etc. However, this research also found that, in the UK during the early to mid 1980s, BPICS promoted only one variant of CAPM which was MRPII.

MRPII technology is a highly centralized 'push' system of planning and control, developed in the USA and strongly influenced by American ideas about best practice (Clark and Newell, 1993). MRPII requires considerable levels of accuracy in basic data collection, input and maintenance. It also imposes a requirement on organizations, to adopt more integrated approaches to work organization and practices which makes appropriation of this technology problematic (Swan and Clark, 1992). This 'push' system contrasted sharply to the Japanese use of CAPM at the time, whereby MRPII was used in only a limited way to provide an overall framework of production tactics and detailed production control was provided by just-in-time (JIT) systems, which were based on a 'pull' philosophy. The different usage made of MRPII in the USA/UK and Japan, is an illustration of the different variants of CAPM technology that existed and of the societal embedding of these technologies (Clark, 1987; Clark and Newell, 1993). Particular professional associations may focus on only those variants that are considered normatively to be 'best practice' in that society at the time, and may thus diffuse information that is incomplete or not relevant for particular organizations (Swan and Newell, 1995).

That different variants of CAPM exist simultaneously reinforces the idea that a notion of fixed best practice is over simplified. Potential users of this technology need to make design decisions about which configuration to appropriate in order to solve their unique production control problems. The decision-episode framework (DEF), shown in figure 1, is an attempt to contextualize these decisions. The DEF was developed from Rogers' model of diffusion, initially by Clark and Staunton (1989), and then later by Clark et al. (1992) and Newell et al. (1993). An important difference is that, while Rogers focused on the needs of suppliers in

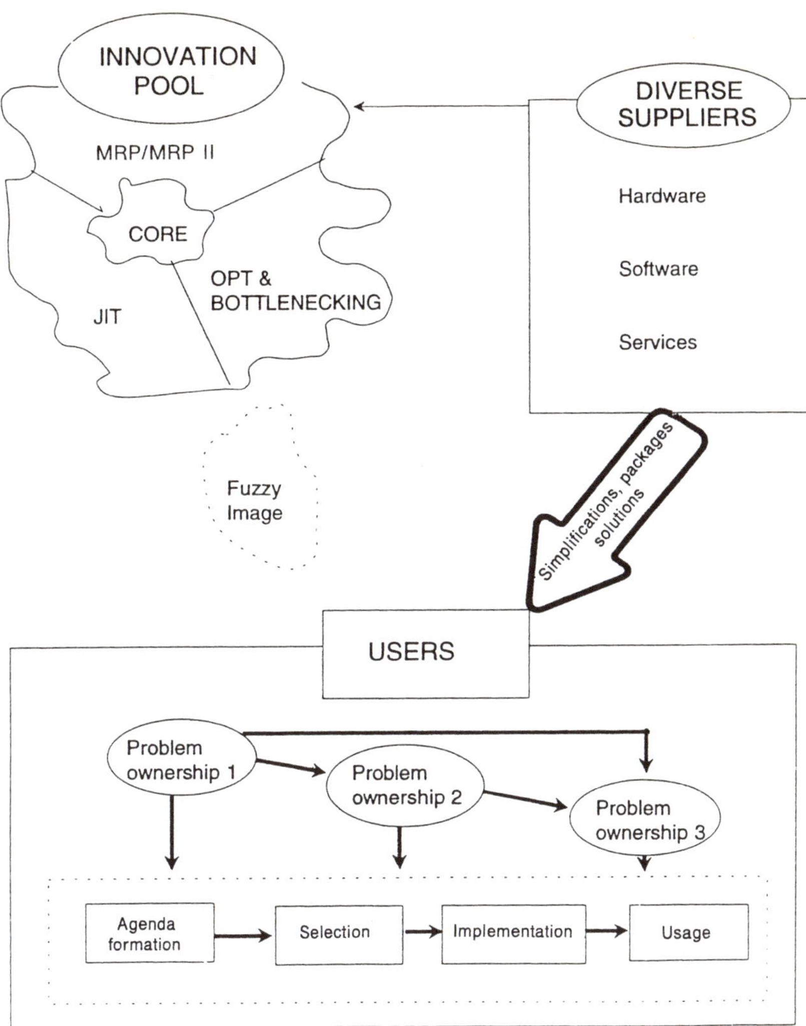

Source: Adapted from Clark et al., 1992.

Figure 1. The decision-episode framework: the context for user decisions

encouraging rapid diffusion of best practice, the DEF takes as its focus the design decisions that need to be made by users in choosing and appropriating these 'best practice' solutions. The framework is therefore useful because it contextualizes the problems faced by users in designing CAPM solutions and stresses the networks that link users and technology suppliers as central in shaping the diffusion of CAPM.

The DEF provides a base from which to explore the diffusion and design of

CAPM in each of the three case companies reported next. The framework consists of three interacting elements: the innovation pool; the supply side; and the users. The innovation pool comprises the major variants of CAPM technology which, at that time (i.e. during the mid/late 1980s) were, MRPII, JIT and optimized production technology (OPT), with an overlapping core illustrating some degree of commonality across these technologies. The technology supply side is portrayed as shaping availability of the technology to the users and consists of a diverse set of hardware, software and consultancy service vendors, all presenting a favourable and often simplified version of the particular technology they provide. The users are depicted as active in the diffusion process in making decisions about how to (re)design technologies. These decisions transgress four decision-episodes: agenda formation, selection, implementation and usage. The DEF recognizes the importance of political dimensions of the innovation process (Cooper and Zmud, 1989). Problem ownership within the firm can shift as the innovation process unfolds. For example, those individuals that are required to implement bought technologies may not have been involved in defining problems or potential solutions (Swan and Clark, 1992). The decision-making process is also understood as iterative, involving muddled and overlapping episodes, rather than as linear and sequential. For example, there may be instances of problems chasing solutions (Swan and Clark, 1992). The problems with adhering to sequential stage models of innovation are well documented and need not be repeated here (see, for example, Clark and Staunton, 1989; Ettlie, 1980; Tornatzky and Fleischer, 1990; Wolfe, 1994).

Here we focus on the roles of networks during the first two episodes of the DEF: agenda formation and selection. In these episodes users seek to match their unclear or 'fuzzy' image of the technology with their own unique requirements. Problems are defined and solutions are generated. The episodes of agenda formation and selection are crucial because here there are opportunities for users to redesign the innovation as presented by the supply side and this is important for subsequent implementation (Swan and Clark, 1992). However, while much research has focused on implementation and usage of CAPM technology (e.g. Bessant and Buckingham, 1993; Waterlow and Monniot, 1986; Wilson et al., 1994), less has focused on these earlier episodes of agenda formation and selection. This may be, in part, because the idea of best practice favoured by much of the innovation literature (see Wolfe, 1994, for a review) precludes the need to study problems in technology design: i.e. if there is a fixed best practice then there is no problem of design.

In the remainder of this paper we use this literature on innovation design and diffusion and on the role of inter-organizational networks to frame our analysis of three firms that made decisions to adopt CAPM technologies. This analysis also suggests modifications to the analytical frameworks, in particular the DEF, and these will be discussed later.

METHODOLOGY

Because of the problems associated with adopting a variance style approach to research on innovation diffusion, we adopted a process-oriented approach for our research (Mohr, 1982). Thus the focus here was to consider the processes by which diffusion occurred by describing sequences of events over time. This research does not attempt to identify causality between an exhaustive, generalizable set of variables and eventual success of CAPM implementation. Rather, it seeks to explore the nature of the relationships among social actors within inter-organizational networks and to ascertain what influence, if any, these relationships may have had on the diffusion process in these cases. Outcomes, in terms of the relative success or failure of implementation, were clearly established at the time of the research and could be used to anchor our discussion of antecedent events and the roles of particular networks. The explanatory power of this analysis comes from comparing these descriptive accounts in order to seek patterns of events, focusing on the roles of networks, that tended to precede outcomes (Pettigrew, 1992).

The main methodology used was semi-structured interviews with personnel involved in the decision-making process leading to implementation of CAPM in three manufacturing companies. In each company a project team was formally given the task of agenda formation and selection, and so key players were easily identifiable. The interviews focused specifically on agenda formation and selection and on the networks that informed decisions at that time although, inevitably, interviewees also discussed outcomes of their attempts to implement the chosen technologies.

In order to establish comparability, the three case companies were selected using the following criteria:

- Manufacturing profile.
- Establishment size.
- Approximate time period within which the decision-making process occurred.

There would be inherent problems of comparability if the research did not acknowledge a requirement to compare firms with similar manufacturing profiles. The importance of contextual embedding of CAPM technology highlighted above imposes a requirement to compare like with like. A company operating batch production techniques is not comparable to a company operating to a make-to-order profile: their CAPM requirements will be qualitatively different. The three companies selected were all characterized by a make-to-order profile and operated in the vehicle manufacturing sector in the UK. It was also important to compare companies of similar size and, for this research, large sized companies (N greater than 1,500) were selected. This is important because investment decisions in new technology and the management of change will be qualitatively different in a small sized establishment as compared to a medium or large sized establishment. CAPM typically entails heavy expenditure on hardware and/or software and this can be beyond the reach of some smaller firms (at least in terms of turnover). Chronologically, all three companies had embarked upon agenda formation and selection of CAPM technology during the late 1980s. Geographically, all three companies were based in the same region. It is therefore feasible to assume that the networks that were available at that time, and that had the potential to be exploited, were quite consistent across the three case companies.

Secondary sources in the form of minutes of meetings and company reports were also used to support interviewees' perceptions of the decision-making process in each of the case companies. Professional association and trade journals relating to production and inventory control over a period from the mid to late 1980s were also analysed in order to consider what influence they may have had on the diffusion of CAPM technology at that time. The analysis of these journals is reported in detail elsewhere (Newell et al., 1995) but are used here to inform our observations on the roles of professional association networks.

RESULTS

The cases will be described and presented here under three headings: antecedents, which describe the context surrounding each firm's decision to adopt CAPM (while protecting firms' anonymity); networks, especially those that were seen to have an important influence on design decisions during agenda formation and selection; and outcomes, of firms' decisions to adopt CAPM. A summary of the findings for the three cases under these headings is shown in table I. The discussion, later, uses comparisons across these cases in order to identify patterns in the ways in which inter-organizational networks shaped the diffusion of CAPM.

Outcomes are used to make meaningful comparisons of cases in terms of which were relatively successful in implementing CAPM. In studies of technological innovation, outcomes can be assessed in a variety of different ways so it is important to define how we assessed them here. Each of these case study firms chose to adopt some variant of MRPII technology. One classification scheme that assesses outcomes with this type of technology has been prescribed by the Oliver Wight organization (Wight, 1984). The Oliver Wight Group is a major US consultancy operating internationally and specializing in the provision of education and training in MRPII concepts both in the USA and Europe. Their classification scheme has been used for research on implementation of MRP/ MRPII (e.g. Wilson et al., 1994) and measures success on a scale of 'Class A' (highest) to 'Class D' (lowest). A problem with this type of classification is that it is heavily premised on notions of best practice. Companies are audited using a checklist that describes how the technology should be implemented. Those that fail to implement the technology exactly as prescribed by the technology suppliers are unable to attain Class A status. As noted previously, this notion of best practice with respect to CAPM is fundamentally flawed. Even within an MRPII variant of CAPM, firms adapt and redesign to the technology such that what they refer to as MRPII may be configured quite differently in different firms (Burcher, 1991). As seen, this process of redesign is an important feature both of appropriation of technological innovation and of the innofusion process, but it would not be recognized as legitimate in the classification scheme prescribed by Wight (1984).

As an alternative, we used Clark's (1987) description of degrees of appropriation of innovation to assess outcomes with CAPM. The notion of appropriation is not prescriptive about the precise configuration of technological innovation. Instead, outcomes are assessed in terms of the extent to which user firms manage to (re)design technological solutions that are appropriate for their own unique

Table I. Summary of case study findings

	ManCo	*LiveCo*	*JellCo*
Antecedents			
Composition of the project team	Managerial representatives: Special Projects Manager (Engineering) Logistics Manager	Managerial representatives: Logistics Sales & Marketing Manufacturing Systems Manufacturing engineering Operations management Consultant	Managerial representatives: Manufacturing systems Production control Materials management Manufacturing engineering Team leader (consultant)
Product market	Declining	Declining	Increasing
Reasons for adoption	Performance gaps	Performance gaps	Performance gaps Slack resources
Inter-organizational networks			
Professional associations	BPICS IPS	BPICS	IMechE IEE BPICS
Academic institutions	University MBA University course		
Other firms	Reference sites (arranged by suppliers)	Company visits (arranged via weak ties)	Reference sites (arranged by suppliers)
Technology suppliers	Consultants Software supplier	Consultants (×2) Software supplier	Consultants Software supplier
CAPM Solution	MRPII	MRPII + JIT	MRPII
Outcomes			
Degree of appropriation	Small scale modification	Appropriation	Failure
Degree of integration (start-finish)	1–2	1–4	1–1
User 'class' reached	Class B	Class A	Class D

problems. Degrees of appropriation are shown in table II(a) and range from failure, where the innovation actually disrupts existing competencies, to appropriation, where there is cumulative and progressive transformation of the innovation coupled with changes in the existing knowledge bases in the user organization.

Outcomes with MRPII are also assessed by the extent to which firms manage to integrate the technology, regardless of the precise configuration taken, using Waterlow and Monniot's (1986) scale of levels of integration. This is shown in table II(b), where 0 indicates no CAPM and 4 indicates complete integration.

Table II. Assessment of outcomes

(a) Degrees of appropriation (after Clark, 1987)	
Appropriation	Cumulative and progressive transformation of the innovation coupled with modifications to existing knowledge bases in the user organization
Limited reinvention	The innovation is slightly adapted but the organizational knowledge bases remain similar
Small Scale Modification	Low-level modification of the innovation only
Licensed reproduction	The innovation is used according to supplier specifications of uses. Only a heuristic knowledge is incorporated by the user
Failure	The innovation disrupts existing competencies
(b) Levels of integration (after Waterlow and Monniot, 1986)	
0 – No CAPM	No CAPM or CAPM presently being installed
1 – No integration	Several functions computerized but without regard to integration
2 – Partial integration	Several functions linked via common files and co-ordinated controls
3 – Full integration	All CAPM functions using common databases
4 – Integration of manufacturing systems	CAPM systems designed, in conjunction with material conversion handling and quality systems, against manufacturing strategy objectives

MRPII is only optimized when firms manage to integrate information and data usage across functional areas in the logistics chain. If integration is not the intended goal, then MRPII is not really an optimal solution. Therefore, these cases were also assessed using Waterlow and Monniot's (1986) scale. Table II describes each case in terms of start to finish level on this scale. As seen, each of the three firms had used computerized systems for some functions (indicated with a 1 on the scale) before attempting to adopt integrating systems.

A danger with any outcomes measure that is used to indicate success of implementation of a particular technology is that it may imply a 'pro-innovation bias' – there is a tendency to assume that a technology should be adopted by members of a social system and that a decision not to adopt represents failure (Rogers, 1983). With this in mind, the assessments of outcomes used here need to be qualified with the statement that scoring low on these measures indicates a failure only in the sense that these particular companies did not achieve outcomes that they themselves had intended. In these cases all three firms intended to implement integrated CAPM and some were relatively more successful in this respect than others. If integration had not been relevant or intended by a particular firm, a decision not to integrate would not be deemed 'failure'.

Company 1: ManCo

Antecedents. In 1986, ManCo recorded its first operating loss of $20 million. The North American parent corporation responded by demanding strategic change to improve efficiency and increase sales. The UK president decided that in order to increase sales, a greater product offering should be made available. The future product would be 'tailor-made' to customer specification. This strategy had considerable operating implications. The company was effectively moving away from mass production and introducing a more flexible form of production. The UK factory at the time was structured along traditional functional groupings and was characterized by highly centralized decision making. This change in production methods would require the introduction of different tools and techniques and impose substantial organizational change. At this point the North American parent decided to replace the majority of the UK board. The managing director was replaced by the existing finance director and other board positions were given to external candidates. Thus, ManCo experienced a significant change in leadership at the top, coupled with a requirement for operational and organizational change from the North American parent. It was recognized that existing manufacturing systems were incapable of supporting the introduction of more flexible production methods. The new managing director therefore appointed a small team to consider what form the replacement should take.

Networks and the decision making process. The project team comprised: a special projects manager – a qualified engineer with 23 years' service; a logistics manager – an IT professional who had worked across a range of functions and had two years' experience in ManCo and 15 years' prior experience. The logistics manager first became aware of MRPII when he attended a seminar in 1985 arranged by the British Production and Inventory Control Society (BPICS). He subsequently attended several more seminars, all of which were on the same theme and which were presented by software suppliers and consultants. The special projects manager first became aware of MRPII while completing a part-time MBA at a leading UK university, of which one of the course options was 'Manufacturing planning and control systems'. An external academic and consultant from the University of North Carolina lectured on this option for a term. He is co-author of a book called *Manufacturing Planning and Control Systems* (Vollman and Berry, 1985) which focuses on MRPII technology. The book is dedicated to the memory of Oliver Wight: 'a pioneer in manufacturing planning and control'. This book and the MBA option focused almost entirely on the use of MRPII as the optimal planning and inventory control tool.

Based on this initial awareness of MRPII, the team actively sought consultants in the UK who could more fully explain the concept of MRPII. Within their own organization they had access to a variety of professional association and trade journals and contacted the Oliver Wight Group reasoning that 'it was the one consultancy that appeared to be mentioned everywhere'. Arrangements were made for Oliver Wight consultants to present MRPII concepts and implications to the board.

The board of ManCo had limited background knowledge of MRPII. Several members had previously worked in companies that operated MRPII but had not been involved directly with the introduction of this technology. Another board member had been on a five-day course at another UK university which had included several sessions on MRPII. Following the presentation by the Oliver Wight Group, the board agreed to go on a short educational course. One board member voiced concern over the decision to adopt MRPII. This member was actively involved in the Institute of Purchase and Supply (IPS). The IPS were actively promoting JIT technology and the two technologies were not considered, at that time, to be compatible (Plenert and Best, 1986). Ultimately this team member's reservations were set aside. This was because the other board members considered them to be politically motivated and not useful to the decision-making process.

In 1987, the board took the decision to implement MRPII, using the following rationale:

- MRPII would provide an integrated approach to manufacturing and would support the firm's objectives for centralized planning and tighter control and flexible production methods.
- A software package had been purchased by ManCo four years previously, to aid planning and it appeared to 'fit' the MRPII concept. The board was believed that it was feasible to assume that there were going to be no significant software costs, if MRPII were to be implemented. The existing software could be adapted to run MRPII.

Outcomes. While it had been thought that the existing software could be adapted to meet ManCo's MRPII requirements, reality proved to the contrary. Implementation of the software was 'fraught' (logistics manager). The supplier of the original software was not particularly accommodating or prepared to work with ManCo. This was because the software had been purchased some years previously and the supplier was now incurring update costs that were both significant and unplanned. ManCo did not implement all of the functionality of MRPII technology. The majority of software modules were introduced but only partial integration across all functions (level 2 on the Waterlow and Monniot scale) was achieved. Using the classification system designed by Wight (1984), ManCo achieved Class B status. In terms of appropriation, ManCo eventually managed small-scale modification to the technology that enabled them to go some way to solving their own production problems. The overall consensus was that the original software actually imposed severe constraints on full implementation. As one implementation team member stated: 'If we had known what it was going to do to us, I don't think we would have ever have gone with it.' ManCo embarked on a programme of over 33,000 employee hours of training but failed to fully integrate or appropriate the system.

Company 2: LiveCo

Antecedents. During the early 1980s, LiveCo was facing an economic crisis. Sales were declining in all markets due to what LiveCo believed to be an outdated product range. Production was distributed over 14 sites in the UK, all operating independently and aiming to maximize their own efficiency using manufacturing systems that were considered to be outdated and inefficient. In 1983 a new managing director was appointed. He made changes to the composition of the board and ordered a complete review of commercial and manufacturing strategy. This review recommended that there should be consolidation and rationalization of all manufacturing operations on to one site and that existing manufacturing systems should be updated in line with this. Commercially, it was decided to upgrade existing product ranges and offer more choice to the customer by moving to a make-to-order system.

LiveCo was structured according to functional divisions, although it had a tradition of decision making that formally demanded input for policy decisions from senior managers across the various functions. In keeping with this tradition, the managing director set up a multi-disciplined project team to define a business system specification to update the manufacturing systems. This team included external support from a senior management consultant from a large management consultancy who had worked with the company in the past. The team recognized that, while a package solution was attractive, some bespoke development may be required.

Networks and the decision making process. The project team in LiveCo comprised: the logistics director as the team leader; plus managerial representatives from the manufacturing, engineering, marketing and purchasing functions. Information systems support was also provided by a specialist IT management consultancy who were used regularly by LiveCo. Initial awareness of MRPII within the team developed through team members' involvement in a number of networks. Some members of the team, specifically those in the logistics function, had developed an awareness of MRPII through their contact with software vendors and access to trade and professional journals. As one member of the logistics function commented, 'it was difficult to read or speak to anyone back then without MRPII being mentioned as the answer to all of our problems'. The logistics director was also an active member of BPICS at the time. He had developed an in-depth understanding of the MRPII concept through the association journal and attending BPICS events. The consultant involved in the team also advocated the adoption of MRPII technology and recommended that the Oliver Wight Group should present MRPII technology to the board.

However, with some understanding of MRPII technology at this stage in the decision-making process, the team were aware that their manufacturing profile did not comfortably 'fit' the MRPII concept. As a consequence, team members were encouraged to actively seek out other companies with a similar manufacturing profile and to arrange factory visits. These visits were arranged through informal contacts (for example, former colleagues) that individual team members had with other firms. These reference-site visits led the team to develop an awareness of other technologies for production control such as JIT and OPT which they were anxious to understand more fully. This proved to be difficult because team members found little information available on these technologies from the variety of sources that they approached, including software vendors, consultants and professional and trade journals. Ultimately their awareness of these technologies developed mainly from looking at other firms' usage of them.

The team in LiveCo was always conscious that the company's operations were not going to try and 'fit' the technology. The board accepted the recommendations of the team that MRPII be implemented in a limited capacity; for high-level centralized planning. Detailed shop-floor planning and control was to be achieved with a combination of in-house designed systems running on a mini-based system, interfacing with MRPII and a JIT *Kanban* system to control shop-floor flow of materials and components. It is worth noting that this approach was not generally recommended by technology suppliers or by trade and association journals in the UK at that time. It was not until later, during the 1990s, that some technology suppliers and journals began to recommend using MRPII alongside JIT as an optimal solution.

LiveCo selected software that was compatible with their existing operating environment from a supplier who could offer significant support. They decided to use a firm of consultants to initiate education and training, but the relationship was problematic. Senior team members who attended the consultant's courses were suspicious that they were being offered, 'a single point solution'. They were sufficiently confident of their 'pragmatic' approach to the development of their CAPM systems that they rejected much of the courses' content and developed in-house training courses.

Outcomes. LiveCo modified the software to accommodate their unique CAPM requirements. The software supplier acknowledged no interest in this development. At the time, they themselves were working on an upgrade to their MRPII package and did not consider developments that LiveCo were making as significant to their own software development. LiveCo fully implemented their new CAPM systems by the end of 1987. At the time, the company was aware that it could not achieve Class A status, based on the criteria established by the Oliver Wight Organisation. This was because LiveCo were using JIT for their shop-floor planning rather than MRPII modules prescribed by Oliver Wight as essential to achieve Class A status. However, LiveCo did manage to achieve full integration and appropriation of CAPM.

Company 3: JellCo

Antecedents. During the early part of the 1980s JellCo was enjoying unprecedented commercial success. However, the company was finding it increasingly difficult to satisfy demand. The company had surplus financial resources with which to invest in new technology and there was board support for investment in any technology that could increase overall capacity and efficiency. Various technological initiatives had been attempted during the early part of the 1980s. However, JellCo had experienced problems with some of these technologies. Notably, they had attempted to introduce a computer-integrated manufacturing (CIM) system but had abandoned it when they were unable to integrate the technology. JellCo had a functional structure whereby functional heads had considerable power and autonomy in their operational strategies. The failure of the CIM project was attributed largely to power struggles across functions and inter-functional conflict.

Manufacturing systems to support production control in JellCo were over 20 years old and were becoming less efficient in their attempts to handle increased production levels. In March 1985 the manufacturing director appointed a new manufacturing systems manager and a manufacturing systems strategy team was set up to consider the introduction of CAPM technology.

Networks and the decision making process. The project team comprised: an external IT consultant (familiar to JellCo) as team leader; plus managerial representatives from engineering, manufacturing, and manufacturing systems. With the failure to introduce CIM, the manufacturing director looked to appoint a project team leader who was objective and could remain 'above the politics of the company'.

The team members developed an awareness of MRPII through involvement in a number of inter-organizational networks. All of the team had attended mandatory in-house presentations given by an independent consultant from the USA on the subject of manufacturing control. The consultant was invited to speak in his capacity as a Fellow of the Institute of Mechanical Engineers (IMechE), to which several board members of JellCo also belonged. MRPII was not the focus of the presentations. However, it was discussed as a concept that could provide integration within manufacturing and across related functions. The consultant was also a Fellow in APICS and in the Institute of Industrial Engineers (IEE). Two members of the strategy team were also BPICS members and several of the team attended BPICS seminars where the concept of MRPII was discussed. These seminars were presented by MRPII vendors. However, those interviewed believed that these events were an opportunity to meet other users and potential users of MRPII and that this enhanced their understanding of the technology.

It followed that, while there was an awareness of MRPII technology and an acknowledgement that it may be able to provide the integration that JellCo required, further information was needed prior to recommending MRPII to the board. The project leader was aware that the Oliver Wight Group was a specialist MRPII consultancy. One of the systems managers on the team also became aware of the Oliver Wight Group as a source of MRPII expertise from reading trade journals. Consequently, the vice president of the Oliver Wight Group in the USA was invited to present MRPII to the JellCo board. Following this, and with the recommendation of the systems strategy team, the board gave their approval for investment in software, education and training to support the implementation of MRPII.

JellCo invited six software vendors to tender. The major criteria used to support decision making at this stage were the vendors' ability to demonstrate a large client base and a willingness to provide a significant amount of support during implementation. One of the software suppliers offered suitable reference sites and was also able to provide detailed education and training regarding overall MRPII philosophy. Board level approval was given to invest in this software package and a two-tier approach to education and training was adopted. The Oliver Wight Group was used for board and senior management education but the software supplier was used for the detailed training of all other employees affected by, and involved in, MRPII implementation and usage.

A full-time MRPII implementation project team was then set up, led by a director. The implementation team consisted of representatives from all of the major functions, e.g. finance, marketing, as well as engineering and manufacturing. As suggested by the DEF, problem ownership shifted during implementation to this group. Certain functional groups who had not been involved during agenda formation and selection were not committed to the MRPII solution. These groups illustrated this by nominating very junior members of their departments to be team members. While senior board members fully supported the introduction of MRPII, they were unable to champion the project. As one team member stated, 'they were too busy running the business'. This finding supports earlier findings that have illustrated that implementing MRPII entails political processes centred around ownership of the system and these can prove to be problematic. In particular, lack of broad-based support can severely impede implementation (Swan and Clark, 1992; Wilson et al., 1994).

Outcomes. The implementation team in JellCo experienced significant problems when they attempted to install the software and to introduce the organizational and operational changes required to implement MRPII. Not enough consideration had been given to the organizational changes required for successful MRPII implementation. As one implementation team member stated, 'culturally from day one we were on a hiding to nothing'. Initially the software supplier was supportive of any modifications required; however, this situation changed. As a supplier they were keen to use JellCo as a reference site, in order to promote their product. However, JellCo refused to be used for this purpose given the problems they were experiencing with implementation. A difficult relationship developed between the company and the suppliers and any changes made to the software were subsequently managed internally. Individual software modules were installed and interfaced with existing systems. However, overall, the pilot implementation project failed. MRPII was not appropriated and integration was not achieved.

DISCUSSION

This research revealed similarities between the antecedent contexts at ManCo and LiveCo. Both companies were experiencing a commercial and financial crisis and were operating at a loss. There was a gap between current performance and future performance which needed to be addressed if they were going to survive within their respective industries. This gap is one of the necessary preconditions for diffusion of innovation defined in Rogers' second framework (Rogers, 1983). Change occurred in both case companies with respect to leadership and business strategy as well as technologies. There was significant alteration in board membership and there was also a recognition by decision makers that in markets they were currently operating in, and in potential new markets, customers were becoming more demanding and desiring more choice. This highlighted a need to move to a more 'customized', flexible form of production characterized as post-Fordist (Thompson and McHugh, 1990). This market-led change required new tools/technologies to support it.

Changes in a firm's product market during implementation is an important external factor that may affect implementation of integrated manufacturing technologies but this influence does not appear to operate in a particular direction (Wilson et al., 1994). Wilson et al. reported firms that experienced difficulties implementing MRPII during periods where their product market is declining as well as firms that had problems during a rapid increase in their turnover. Here, two of the firms were facing market decline but one, none the less, managed to appropriate an integrated CAPM system. Another was experiencing rapid growth but failed to appropriate CAPM. A more important factor seemed to be the way in which change was managed within these companies. The antecedent context was similar for ManCo and LiveCo, the actual management of change differed across the two companies. The change process at LiveCo was more radical than that at ManCo in the sense that site rationalization at LiveCo imposed change on all employees, regardless of changes demanded by a new technology. At ManCo only those employees directly related to production were affected by the change process and organizational structure remained unchanged. Thus LiveCo introduced MRPII in conjunction with changes in the organizational infrastructure and experienced relatively fewer implementation problems than ManCo, who did not make major changes to their infrastructure. This pattern mirrors that obtained elsewhere where firms implementing technologies that altered existing organizational practices needed to make corresponding changes in their organizational structure (Swan and Clark, 1992).

The antecedent context at JellCo was somewhat different in that slack resources were available in terms of finances with which to invest in new technology. Slack resources have been identified as an important pre-condition in the diffusion process (Roberts and Barrar, 1992). From this case it can be seen that slack resources might encourage initial adoption of an innovation but this does not guarantee successful appropriation. There was also perceived to be a gap in JellCo, between existing practices and future performance, in that current manufacturing systems were unable to manage, support and control, increasing levels of production.

Common to all three companies was the need to update manufacturing systems. LiveCo were relatively more successful in this respect, managing to fully integrate and appropriate CAPM. But this company only achieved Class B status. This case illustrates the problems of using classifications based on notions of best practice to assess users' success. Using the Wight (1984) scheme, LiveCo were not fully successful because they failed to implement the technology as prescribed by the suppliers. However, LiveCo were successful in designing a variant of the technology that met their own unique requirements.

The decision-making process in these cases mirrored that outlined in the decision-episode framework (Clark et al., 1992) and included episodes of:

(i) Agenda formation – all three companies perceived a need to update their existing systems and set up a cross-functional project team to define their business requirements and to identify what form of technological innovation should be adopted.

(ii) Selection – in each company the project teams attempted to evaluate alternatives before selecting a particular solution. On the basis of the team's recommendations, all three companies' boards decided to adopt MRPII technology.

(iii) Implementation – each company set up a multi-functional implementation team responsible for software implementation and education and training using the services available from the consultants and/or software suppliers.

(iv) Usage – The outcome, however, i.e. the degree of appropriation of MRPII technology, varied significantly across the three companies.

Rational-choice perspectives highlight the importance of defining problems and searching for alternative solutions before selecting specific alternatives. In reality, though, decision-making rarely follows this pattern (Abrahamson, 1991). Here, all three firms appeared to adopt a rational approach to the adoption of CAPM technology by searching for alternative solutions. However, in reality, only one firm actually managed to develop an understanding of the various design forms for CAPM captured in the innovation pool in the DEF. An examination of the roles of inter-organizational networks helps to explain this apparent constraint on the innovation diffusion process.

Rogers' (1983) framework and the DEF developed by Clark et al. (1992) highlight the role of suppliers in shaping availability of CAPM technology but fail to include other networks that may shape availability of innovation and the role they play in the diffusion process. As noted earlier, empirical work on inter-organizational networks has tended to focus on relatively formal or contractual inter-firm networks (see Alter and Hage, 1993, for a review). This paper lends empirical support to recent literature on inter-organization that discusses the importance of a variety of different types of inter-organizational networks in diffusion of CAPM networks (e.g. Alter and Hage, 1993; Grandori and Soda, 1995). Those involved in decision making in these companies participated in at least three networks, in addition to the supplier network identified in the DEF, which shaped the design and diffusion of technology. These networks are summarized in table I and comprise: academic, professional association and inter-company, as well as technology suppliers. However, the information disseminated through these other networks was shaped by the involvement of technology suppliers who tended to promote a particular vision of best practice.

The significance of the academic network for the decision-making process was illustrated in the case of ManCo where a team member, in effect half the team, developed a perception of CAPM that was shaped solely by information provided on an MBA course. Similarly, a board member in this company had learned of MRPII via a university course. However, these academic courses tended to reinforce supplier images of MRPII as best practice. For example, in the case of the MBA course, this was delivered by a consultant who specialized in MRPII.

The role of professional association networks was shown in these cases by the involvement of team members with professional associations such as BPICS, the IMechE and the IPS. For example, in ManCo, team members engaged in an active search for 'expert knowledge' relating to CAPM which involved attendance at professional association seminars and the use of association journals. The role of professional associations in LiveCo was highlighted by the team leader's (Logistics Director) involvement with BPICS. At this time the focal professional production control associations (i.e. BPICS, APICS and the IMechE) were heavily promoting MRPII technology as best practice technology for production control. This process was aided informally by the involvement of technology suppliers and consultants who were also members of these professional associations and were able to use this as a way of legitimating their role as professionals. For example, in JellCo, everyone interviewed spoke highly of presentations they had attended which were given by a leading consultant. Comments were made such as 'he speaks a lot of sense' and 'he seems to have a genuine understanding of the problems we have on a day-to-day basis'. This individual had developed a relationship with board members through his involvement with the IMechE. He was subsequently invited to present in detail his ideas on manufacturing planning and control in his professional role of consultant. At these presentations MRPII was discussed as an appropriate tool for the control of production. All of those interviewed referenced this individual in relation to his involvement with the IMechE, rather than in his role as a management consultant. This professional involvement appeared to diminish the suspicions among users of the pro-innovation bias more usually associated with consultants and hence the content of his presentations was considered to be a useful source of 'unbiased' information.

These cases support Swan and Newell's (1995) findings which suggested that technology suppliers used their involvement in professional associations to promote particular technologies as best practice. The cases also mirror findings in the USA where it has been suggested that a major supplier (IBM) used members of the US professional association, APICS, to promote their vision of best practice to industry (Clark and Newell, 1992). In several cases, the team's initial awareness of MRPII technology developed through this route and was subsequently reinforced by the involvement of consultants with MRPII expertise. Thus professional associations provided weak social ties that later led to more formal collaboration among users and the technology suppliers (Grandori and Soda, 1995; Granovetter, 1973; Rogers, 1983).

The roles of these professional association networks need to be understood here from a political perspective. This has not been greatly emphasized in earlier work (though see Drazin, 1990). For example, on the basis of the typology suggested by Grandori and Soda (1995), professional associations are considered to be symmetric bureaucratic inter-firm networks. Later, Grandori (1995) describes professional associations as voluntary organizational democracies. Both of these typologies emphasize professional associations as networks that link firms in industry and which are not dominated by the interests of a particular player. However, here it can be seen that professional associations involve actors from multiple sectors (e.g. manufacturing industry, technology suppliers, academia) with multiple interests. For example, technology suppliers are interested in selling technology whereas manufacturing firms are interested in appropriating technology. These interests are sometimes incompatible. This could be seen in ManCo where the software supplier refused to make modifications to the software that the user needed in order to be able to appropriate CAPM. In this case the supplier had finished selling the technology and did not consider it in their own interests to spend time developing bespoke modifications for this particular user. Further, the interests of particular actors can play a dominant role in the activities of professional associations. The promotion of MRPII as best practice by APICS and BPICS may reflect the interests of suppliers who, although they comprise a minority of members, are actively involved in the dissemination activities of these associations (Newell et al., 1995). This suggests that professional associations may have characteristics typical of polyarchies as well as those of democracies (Grandori, 1995).

These cases also highlight the political processes inherent in the interaction among different professional groups, whereby attempts are made to exercise power and control over particular knowledge domains (Abbott, 1988; Drazin, 1990). This was illustrated in ManCo by the ways in which board members in different professional groups in the logistics chain (manufacturing and purchasing) that were aligned with different professional associations (BPICS or the IPS) disagreed in their perceptions of best practice for production control. At that time BPICS and the IPS were actively promoting different CAPM technologies as 'best practice' (Newell et al., 1995).

Inter-company networks, particularly collaborative inter-company networks, have been highlighted in the literature as central in shaping the design and diffusion of innovation (Alter and Hage, 1993; Jarillo, 1993). The role played by the inter-company network in ManCo was limited to the involvement of the new board, most of whom were external appointees who had learned about MRPII when they were employed by other companies. The extent to which ManCo actively sought information from other companies introducing CAPM technology was limited to visits to reference sites recommended by the consultants. Similarly, in JellCo, the project team were wary of the pro-innovation bias from suppliers and requested visits to reference sites. But it seems unlikely that suppliers would suggest visits to reference sites where MRPII had failed. Hence, this inter-company network was, in effect, shaped by consultants and suppliers and was therefore subject to a pro-innovation bias promoting MRPII as the best practice solution.

Inter-company networks played a different role at LiveCo. Here, members of the team actively sought to identify other firms with similar manufacturing profiles in order to establish what form of CAPM technology they were using, and arranged site visits. Contacts made through this network of weak ties did provide team members with an awareness of other CAPM technologies such as JIT and OPT and highlighted their applicability to particular parts of the production process. This information provided by other firms proved to be a useful input to the decision-making process. These firms were not those usually accessed via software suppliers, and as such did not constitute part of the supplier network. In support, those interviewed stated that further information regarding these technologies was not forthcoming from any of the consultants that they were involved with.

These cases provided empirical support for both Rogers' framework and the DEF in that a diverse range of technology suppliers shaped the diffusion and design of CAPM technology. In these cases decision makers' understanding about MRPII was heavily shaped by the simplified image being promoted by the supply side. However, this research has shown that the role played by three networks other than suppliers of technology (i.e. academic, professional association, and inter-firm) were also significant in the decision-making process in all three companies. However, interestingly, suppliers and consultants of MRPII technology had become actively involved in these networks, inter-penetrating some of them. The analysis illustrates that isomorphic pressures were generated by networks on the diffusion of CAPM technology in the late 1980s (DiMaggio and Powell, 1983). These included mimetic processes that led some firms to adopt MRPII because it was seen to be successful in other firms, for example in reference sites, and also normative pressures from professional associations and suppliers to adopt MRPII. For example, the award of Class A was sought by these firms because it would help to legitimate their status as 'world class' manufacturers. But this award, by definition (at least in the form prescribed by the

Oliver Wight Group) leads firms to adopt the same technology design, regardless of whether it is the most efficient for a particular firm's production problems.

All three companies were aware that suppliers and consultants shaped the availability of particular forms of CAPM technology and consequently actively sought alternative expert knowledge domains to aid the decision-making process. However, this research suggests that other networks accessed actually *reinforced* the availability of MRPII as best practice, being shaped by suppliers' and consultants' visions of best practice at that time. This is an example of networks of weak ties generating 'rhetorical closure' regarding the design of CAPM technology (Pinch and Bijker, 1989). There were linkages among all of these networks and the supplier/consultancy network. There was only one example of networking that was not shaped to some degree by supplier involvement – where at LiveCo individuals managed to obtain information from other firms through their informal contacts or 'weak ties'. This analysis suggests that an update to the DEF to include these other networks is timely and a revision of the DEF is given in figure 2. This shows diverse suppliers, academics, other firms and professional associations as all shaping availability of CAPM technology potentially in a highly favourable and simplified way. The relationship between the commercial supply side and these other networks is illustrated using feedback loops among the individual networks.

CAPM technology is a configurational technology, i.e. one that depends for its usage on a strong element of contextual embedding (Clark and Staunton, 1989). In these cases significant customization of the software occurred when the companies attempted to appropriate CAPM. However, while customization did occur, there was no evidence of innofusion of the technology (cf. Fleck et al., 1990). In each company the software was customized in an attempt to make it 'fit' the particular organizational context, but enhancements to the software were not made with the active co-operation of the suppliers. ManCo had a 'fraught' relationship with their software supplier which prevented innofusion occurring. The implementation team at LiveCo had a very clear idea of the customization required in order to interface with the bespoke systems they were developing. However, this again did not lead to innofusion of the technology as the supplier, already involved in their own major upgrade to their MRPII software, considered any modifications current users were making to be 'unimportant', relative to their own system upgrade. JellCo also had a difficult relationship with their software supplier. The supplier was keen to use JellCo as a reference site to promote their product but JellCo, having experienced severe implementation problems both organizationally and operationally, were anxious to avoid any publicity that would reflect badly on what was a very prestigious image at the time. Consequently JellCo refused to be used in this way and modifications to the software did not involve suppliers.

Recent research regarding innofusion (Webster and Williams, 1993) suggests that relationships exist between suppliers and users which are based on trust and co-operation, but these were not apparent here. The lack of innofusion here may be a reflection of the nature of the relationship that existed *at that time* between user and supplier. More recent examples of innofusion may reflect a significant change in the nature of that relationship, as suppliers have recognized the contribution users can make to the diffusion process of CAPM technology. Perhaps

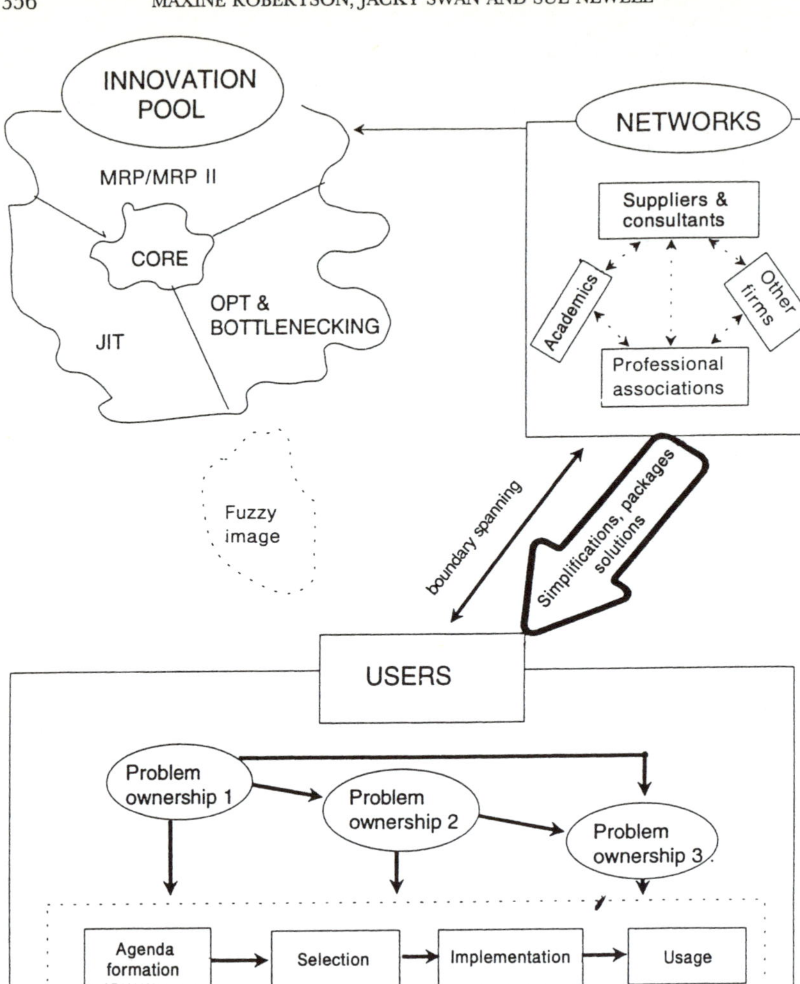

Figure 2. Update to the DEF

it would be useful to address ways in which the nature of supplier–user relationships in particular industrial sectors change and mediate the innofusion process.

CONCLUSION

This research has found that during the late 1980s, companies within the manufacturing sector were involved in networks of weak ties that promoted the diffusion of certain technologies over other variants. Using CAPM technology as an example, the research found that a variety of networks reinforced and shaped availability of MRPII. Other CAPM technologies existed at this time, e.g. JIT, OPT, yet were not actively promoted by these networks. Potential adopters of CAPM technology experienced difficulties in gaining access to networks which *did not* shape availability of the technology at this time. This research suggests that in industrial sectors characterized by a degree of institutionalized isomorphism (DiMaggio and Powell, 1983), diffusion rates of production control technologies cannot be predicted by adopting the efficient-choice perspective, which dominates the innovation diffusion literature (Rogers, 1971). Organizations through their network activity are subject to both mimetic and normative processes which act to influence the adoption decision. This research has therefore highlighted that while networks are valuable forums for the acquisition of information, it cannot be assumed that this information always makes a positive contribution to the innovation adoption decision.

While generalizations cannot be made across the population of adopters, the research found that the way in which MRPII diffused affected the degree of appropriation of the technology. More recent diffusion research (Webster and Williams, 1993) suggests that the innofusion process has further propelled the diffusion of MRPII and yet this research found no evidence of innofusion. This may in part be due to the time period in which the research was based. This research found that during the late 1980s relationships between suppliers and users were inherently commercial, often involving power and political dimensions, which precluded the development of relationships based on trust and co-operation. Subsequently, suppliers may have recognized the potential importance of users' knowledge and application of software such that innofusion occurs. This illustrates the importance of longitudinal research to the understanding of the diffusion process with respect to current technological innovation.

NOTES

*The authors would like to acknowledge the support of the Economic and Social Research Council (UK) in funding this research.

[1] Following operational problems with CAPM in the mid 1980s, the Engineering and Physical Science Research Council (EPSRC – formerly SERC) commissioned a number of projects specifically to investigate these problems in the UK.

REFERENCES

ABBOTT, A. (1988). *The System of Professions*. London: University of Chicago Press.

ABRAHAMSON, E. (1991). 'Managerial fads and fashions: the diffusion and rejection of innovations'. *Academy of Management Review*, **16**, 586–612.

ALTER, C. and HAGE, J. (1993). *Organizations Working Together*. Newbury Park, CA: Sage.

AXELSSON, B. and EASTON, G. (1992). *Industrial Networks. A New View of Reality*. London: Routledge.

BESSANT, J. and BUCKINGHAM, J. (1993). 'Innovation and organizational learning: the case of computer-aided production management'. *British Journal of Management*, **4**, 219–34.

Burcher, P. (1991). 'The use of capacity requirements planning in manufacturing planning and control systems'. Unpublished Ph.D. thesis, Aston University.

Clark, P. A. (1987). *Anglo-American Innovation.* New York: DeGruyter.

Clark, P., Bennett, D., Burcher, P., Newell, S., Swan, J. and Sharifi, S. (1992). 'The decision-episode framework and computer-aided production management (CAPM)'. *International Studies of Management and Organization*, **22**, 4, 69–80.

Clark, P. and Newell, S. (1993). 'Societal embedding of production and inventory control systems: American and Japanese influences on adaptive implementation in Britain'. *International Journal of Human Factors in Manufacturing*, **3**, 69–81.

Clark, P. A. and Staunton, N. (1989). *Innovation in Technology and Organization.* London: Routledge.

Cooper, R. B. and Zmud, R. W. (1989). 'Material requirements planning system infusion'. *OMEGA International Journal of Management Science*, **17**, 471–81.

Corke, D. (1985). *A Guide to CAPM.* London: Institute of Production Engineers.

Contractor, F. and Lorange, P. (Eds) (1988). *Cooperative Strategies in International Business.* Lexington, MA: Lexington Books.

DiMaggio, P. and Powell, W. (1983). 'The iron cage revisited: institutional isomorphism and collective rationality in organizational fields'. *American Sociological Review*, **48**, 147–60.

Drazin, R. (1990). 'Professionals and innovation: structural-functional versus radical-structural perspectives'. *Journal of Management Studies*, **27**, 3, 245–63.

Ettlie, J. E. (1980). 'Adequacy of stage models for decisions on adoption of stage models of innovation'. *Psychological Reports*, **46**, 991–95.

Fleck, J., Webster, J. and Williams, R. (1990). 'Dynamics of information technology implementation: a reassessment of paradigms and trajectories of development'. *Futures*, July/August, 618–40.

Grandori, A. (1995). 'The missing alternative in the organization of economic activities: modeling pluralistic governance'. Paper presented at the EGOS 12th Colloquium, July, Istanbul.

Grandori, A. and Soda, G. (1995). 'Inter-firm networks: antecedents, mechanisms and forms'. *Organization Studies*, **16**, 183–214.

Granovetter, M. S. (1973). 'The strength of weak ties'. *American Journal of Sociology*, **78**, 1360–80.

Hauschlidt, J. (1992). 'External acquisition of knowledge for innovations'. *R & D Management*, **22**, 105–10.

Hollingsworth, J. R. (1991). 'The logic of coordinating American manufacturing sectors'. In Hollingsworth, J. R. and Lindberg, L. N., *The Governance of the American Economy*. New York: Cambridge University Press, 35–74.

Jarillo, J. C. (1993). *Strategic Networks. Creating the Borderless Organization.* Oxford: Butterworth-Heinemann.

Laage-Hellman, J. (1989). *Technological Development in Industrial Networks.* Doctoral dissertation, Uppsala, Sweden: University of Uppsala Publishers.

Mohr, L. B. (1982). *Explaining Organizational Behavior.* San Francisco: Jossey-Bass.

Mowery, D. C. (Ed.) (1988). *International Collaborative Ventures in U.S. Manufacturing.* Cambridge, MA: Ballinger.

Moxon, R., Roehl, T. and Truitt, J. F. (1988). 'International cooperative ventures in the commercial aircraft industry: gains, sure, but what's my share?' In Contractor, F. and Lorange, P. (Eds), *Cooperative Strategies in International Business.* Lexington, MA: Lexington Books.

Newell, S. and Clark, P. A. (1990). 'The importance of extra-organizational networks in the diffusion and appropriation of new technologies'. *Knowledge: Creation, Diffusion, Utilization*, **12**, 199–212.

NEWELL, S., SWAN, J. and CLARK,. P. (1993). 'The importance of user design in the adoption of new information technologies: the example of PICS'. *International Journal of Operations and Production Management*, **13**, 2, 4–22.

NEWELL, S., SWAN, J. A. and ROBERTSON, M. (1995). 'Professional associations as forms of pluralistic organization and their role in the innovation process'. Paper presented at the EGOS 12th Colloquium, July, Istanbul.

PETTIGREW, A. (1992). 'The character and significance of strategy process research'. *Strategic Management Journal*, **13**, 5–16.

PINCH, T. P. and BIJKER, W. E. (1989). 'The social construction of facts and artifacts: or how the sociology of science and the sociology of technology might benefit each other'. In Bijker, W. E., Pinch, T. P. and Hughes, T. P. (Eds), *The Social Construction of Technological Systems*. Cambridge, MA: MIT Press.

PLENERT and BEST (1986). 'MRP, JIT or OPT. What's best?'. *Production and Inventory Management Journal*, **2**, 22–9.

ROBERTS, H. J. and BARRAR, P. (1992). 'MRPII implementation: key factors for success'. *Computer-integrated Manufacturing Systems*, **5**, 31–8.

ROGERS, E. M. (1983). *Diffusion of Innovations*, 3rd edn. First published 1962. New York: Free Press.

ROGERS, E. M. (1971). *Communication of Innovation*. New York: Free Press.

SCARBROUGH, H. and CORBETT, J. M. (1992). *Technology and Organization, Power, Meaning and Design*. London: Routledge.

SWAN, J. A. and CLARK, P. (1992). 'Organisational decision making in the appropriation of technological innovation: cognitive and political dimensions'. *European Work and Organizational Psychologist*, **2**, 2, 103–27.

SWAN, J. A. and NEWELL, S. (1995). 'The role of professional associations in technology diffusion'. *Organization Studies*, **16**, 5, 847–74.

THOMPSON, P. and MCHUGH, D. (1990). *Work Organizations: A Critical Introduction*. London: Macmillan.

TORNATZKY, L. G. and FLEISCHER, M. (1990). *The Process of Technological Innovation*. Lexington, MA: Lexington Books.

TURNISPEED, D. L., BURNS, O. M. and RIGGS, W. E. (1992). 'An implementation analysis of MRP systems: a focus on the human variable'. *Journal of the British Production and Inventory Control Society*, **33**, 1.

TUSHMAN, M. and SCANLAN, T. (1981). 'Boundary spanning individuals: their role in information transfer and their antecedents'. *Academy of Management Journal*, **24**, 289–305.

VOLLMAN, A. and BERRY, W. (1985). *Manufacturing Control*. Illinois: Dow Jones-Irwin.

VON HIPPELL, E. (1982). 'The customer-active paradigm for industrial products generation'. *Research Policy*, 240–66.

WATERLOW, G. and MONNIOT, J. (1986). *A Study of the State of the Art in Computer-Aided Production Management*. ACME Research Directorate Report, Swindon: SERC.

WEBSTER, J. and WILLIAMS, J. (1993). 'The success and failure of computer-aided production management – the implications for corporate and public policy'. *Edinburgh PICT Research Report No. 2*.

WILSON, F., DESMOND, J. and ROBERTS, H. (1994). 'Success and failure of MRPII implementation'. *British Journal of Management*, **5**, 221–40.

WIGHT, O. (1984). *Manufacturing Resource Planning: MRPII*. Vermont: Oliver Wight Publications.

WOLFE, R. A. (1994). 'Organizational innovation: review, critique and suggested research directions'. *Journal of Management Studies*, **31**, 405–31.

Knowledge management and innovation: networks and networking

Jacky Swan, Sue Newell, Harry Scarbrough and Donald Hislop

The authors

Jacky Swan is Reader in Organizational Behaviour, Warwick Business School, University of Warwick, UK (irobjs@wbs.warwick.ac.uk).
Sue Newell is Professor of Innovation and Organizational Behaviour, Nottingham Business School, Nottingham Trent University, UK (s.newell@ntu.ac.uk).
Harry Scarbrough is Professor of Organizational Analysis, Leicester University Management Centre, Leicester University, UK (hs28@le.ac.uk).
Donald Hislop is Senior Lecturer in Organizational Behaviour and Human Resource Management, Sheffield Business School, Sheffield Hallam University, UK (d.w.hislop@shu.ac.uk).

Keywords

Innovation, Knowledge management, Networking, Banking, Manufacturing

Abstract

Begins with a critical review of the literature on knowledge management, arguing that its focus on IT to create a network structure may limit its potential for encouraging knowledge sharing across social communities. Two cases of interactive innovation are contrasted. One focused almost entirely on using IT (intranet) for knowledge sharing, resulting in a plethora of independent intranets which reinforced existing organizational and social boundaries with electronic "fences". In the other, while IT was used to provide a network to encourage sharing, there was also recognition of the importance of face-to-face interaction for sharing tacit knowledge. The emphasis was on encouraging active networking among dispersed communities, rather than relying on IT networks. Argues for a community-based model of knowledge management for interactive innovation and contrasts this with the cognitive-based view that underpins many IT-led knowledge management initiatives.

Journal of Knowledge Management
Volume 3 · Number 4 · 1999 · pp. 262–275

Introduction

From the 1990s onwards an emphasis on innovation has been seen to replace efficiency and quality as the main source of competitive advantage for firms (Bolwijn and Kumpe, 1990). Reflecting this emphasis a huge body of literature has emerged which aims to identify "best practice" in both the diffusion of innovation to users, and in the implementation of innovation within user firms (for reviews, see Wolfe, 1994; Slappendel, 1996). This literature emphasises the importance of networks and networking for innovation. So for example, individual employee involvement in professional associations has been shown to facilitate the diffusion and adoption of new ideas (Swan *et al.*, forthcoming). Through such external networking activity individuals become aware of new technologies, which may be relevant to their own organizations. Individuals thus acquire knowledge and information through boundary spanning activity. It is also necessary to convince others within their organization of the potential advantages of the new technology and to bring together the necessary skills and knowledge needed to implement and appropriate it. So internal networking is also important. However, while networks and networking are clearly central to understanding innovation processes, there has been a change recently in how these processes are conceived.

The literature on innovation has been extremely broad incorporating perspectives as diverse as traditional structuralist approaches through to more process-oriented approaches. From the structuralist perspective, innovation is seen as a "thing" or entity with fixed parameters (e.g. a new technology or management practice) which is developed externally, packaged ("blackboxed") by suppliers and then transferred to potential users where it can be seen to offer them competitive advantage (Wolfe, 1994). Around this, models of innovation have been aimed, either at helping suppliers to diffuse the latest best practice innovations (e.g. Rogers, 1983), or at helping users to implement them (e.g. Damanpour, 1987). From this perspective then, networks are treated as structures

The research was supported by a grant from the Economic and Social Science Research Council, Swindon, UK.

Journal of Knowledge Management
Volume 3 · Number 4 · 1999 · 262–275

through which information and knowledge can be (unproblematically) transferred from suppliers to users so that the new "thing" can be adopted within the user firm.

Structuralist perspectives have been criticised for under-emphasising the dependency of innovation on the social and organizational context (Scarbrough and Corbett, 1992). In particular, the notion of "best practice" – i.e. of an objectifiable innovation which is universally applicable in all contexts – has been questioned for all but the most simple examples of innovation (Clark, 1987). In contrast, process perspectives argue that innovation should be seen, not simply as a "thing" to be transferred from place to place, but as a complex, time phased, politically-charged design and decision process often involving multiple social groups within organizations. For example, despite the grandiose claims of some proponents, technologies such as Business Process Re-engineering cannot simply be inserted into firms by top management. They are highly sensitive to the organizational context and depend on knowledge, skills and commitment of multiple groups and stakeholders. Process perspectives on innovation then extend structuralist perspectives by examining those more dynamic cognitive, social and political processes through which new ideas are developed, communicated, transferred and implemented over time within particular organizational contexts, and by identifying ways of facilitating these processes. According to this approach innovation may be defined as:

> the development and implementation of new ideas by people who over time engage in transactions with others in an institutional context (Van de Ven, 1986).

Networking as a social communication process, which encourages the sharing of knowledge among communities, is centre-stage in process perspectives and this is reflected in this definition.

This paper builds from a process perspective on innovation but argues that this too needs to be extended. This is because the unit of analysis in process research has tended to be localised to the single firm or business unit. Here we argue that, as firms enter the twenty-first century, the context for many is one of flatter, less bureaucratized and more decentralised, even virtual, organizational arrangements with key areas of expertise (e.g. IT) often being provided externally. This, coupled with ever more sophisticated information technologies and pressures for dealing with global customers, is placing a much greater emphasis on innovation that allows integration both within and across traditional organizational and inter-organizational boundaries. Thus many innovation processes are becoming increasingly interactive, requiring simultaneous networking across multiple "communities of practice" (e.g. functional groups, business units, IT suppliers) sometimes on a global scale. This networking involves negotiation among different social communities, which may have distinctive norms, cultural values and interests in the innovation process (Scarbrough and Corbett, 1992; Spender, 1989). Knowledge needed for innovation is therefore increasingly distributed both within organizations (e.g. across functions and geographically dislocated business units) and across organizations (e.g. across IT suppliers, consultants and user firms). This poses new challenges for innovating firms in terms of creating, sharing and managing knowledge and expertise. In these situations, knowledge has to be continuously negotiated through interactive social networking processes. This perspective recognises that the knowledge and skills needed for innovation cannot be unproblematically transferred through networks linking these multiple groups – there also needs to be what Kogut and Zander (1992, p. 389) termed a "common stock of knowledge", to facilitate such processes. That is, the communication of knowledge is only possible between people who, to some extent at least, share a system of meaning (Trompenaars, 1995). Knowledge then is not transferred but must be continuously created and recreated through networking as individuals come to share a common understanding or a common frame of reference. From this perspective then networking is seen not as a case of linear information transfer but as a process of interrelating and sense making (Weick, 1990).

This paper will argue that these insights appear to be relatively poorly understood in the existing knowledge management (hereafter KM) literature. Thus, the contribution of the KM literature to date in terms of understanding innovation has been limited by a rather narrow focus on IT-based tools and systems, premissed on a cognitive

Knowledge management and innovation: networks and networking
Jacky Swan, Sue Newell, Harry Scarbrough and Donald Hislop
Journal of Knowledge Management
Volume 3 · Number 4 · 1999 · 262–275

information-processing view of KM. These IT-based tools and systems create the structural networks but, as the cases below will demonstrate, do not necessarily encourage the social networking processes so necessary for communication and sense making. We therefore suggest that this IT emphasis needs to be balanced by an approach which takes greater account of localised communities of practice and the importance of social networking in KM. This is especially critical when trying to understand innovation processes, which are characteristically interactive.

The paper will begin with a brief overview of the literature on KM to date. This highlights an overwhelming emphasis on IT and major gaps in the treatment of people (Scarbrough *et al.*, 1999). Next, limits of IT-based approaches to KM in terms of understanding innovation will be considered, in particular focusing on processes of exploitation and exploration. Two case studies will be presented as empirical examples of interactive innovation. These demonstrate the limits of IT-based approaches to KM. The contrast between these two cases leads in the discussion to the development of two alternative models of KM:

(1) the cognitive network model; and
(2) the community networking model.

The community model emphasises dialogue and sense making occurring through active networking (some of which may be IT enabled) while the cognitive model (which underpins most of the KM literature) emphasises linear information flows through static IT-based networks. These cases strengthen the argument for moving towards the development of a community model of KM innovation for achieving interactive innovation.

Knowledge management and innovation – a review of the current position

One of the first things to be said about KM and innovation is that definitions abound. In this article KM is defined very broadly, encompassing any processes and practices concerned with the creation, acquisition, capture, sharing and use of knowledge, skills and expertise (Quintas *et al.*, 1996) whether these are explicitly labelled as "KM" or not. KM, then, is about harnessing the intellectual and social capital of individuals in order to improve organizational learning capabilities, recognising that knowledge, and not simply information, is the primary source of an organization's innovative potential (Marshall, 1997; Castells, 1996). The objective of KM can be to enhance exploitation (i.e. where existing knowledge is captured, transferred and deployed in other similar situations) or exploration (i.e. where knowledge is shared and synthesised and new knowledge is created (Levinthal and March, 1993)). The purpose of exploitation is to reduce problems of "reinventing the wheel" by using existing knowledge more efficiently. Although this is important for innovation, it is largely exploration through knowledge sharing that allows the development of genuinely new approaches.

Interest in the topic of "KM" has undoubtedly boomed over the last two to three years. A review of KM articles listed in searchable databases (e.g. Proquest Direct) during the period 1990 to 1998 compared the interest afforded to KM with that afforded to what might be expected to be related discourses of organizational learning and the "learning organization" (Scarbrough *et al.*, 1999). This showed that a decline in interest afforded to the learning organization since 1995 was mirrored by a sharp increase in references to KM. Indeed, there were more references (over 150) to KM in the first six months of 1998 than cumulatively in the previous five years. Interestingly, the profile reflected the normal distribution associated with management fads observed by Abrahamson (1996). KM could then be easily dismissed as yet another management fad. However, the growing emphasis on innovation through "knowledge work" and "knowledge workers" and on the leveraging of "knowledge assets" suggests that the need to manage knowledge will endure as a core business concern, even if the label may change (Drucker, 1993). This is not to say that knowledge was ever insignificant – what is distinctive about the current period is that knowledge now acts upon itself in an accelerating spiral of innovation and change. Castells (1996, p. 32) summarises this shift:

> What characterises the current technological revolution is not the centrality of knowledge and information but the application of such knowledge and information to knowledge generation

> and information processing/communication devices, in a cumulative feedback loop between innovation and the uses of innovation ... For the first time in history, the human mind is a direct productive force, not just a decisive element of a production system.

There are also clearly organizational trends which are aligned to this focus on KM in innovation. In organizational terms, the new "era" is typified by flatter structures, deburеaucratisation, decentralisation, and co-ordination through increasing use of information and communication technologies (ICT). However, as businesses are stretched across time and space, reorganized along process or product lines, and restructured around virtual teams, they lose opportunities for innovation through the casual sharing of knowledge and learning induced by physical proximity. As Prusak (1997) puts it:

> If the water cooler was a font of useful knowledge in the traditional firm, what constitutes a virtual one?

Gibbons (1994) notes further that "modes of knowledge production" are changing from the conventional (mode 1) disciplinary-based model, to a new (mode 2) model where knowledge is produced interactively at the point of application among heterogeneous groups. In short, innovation processes are becoming more interactive – more dependent on knowledge which is widely distributed – therefore KM is increasingly central. Although the term "KM" may ultimately become another fad, the impetus for it is the profound problems posed by new kinds of organization and innovation.

KM for interactive innovation has distinct implications for the deployment of ICTs as well as for the management of people and social networks. However, Scarbrough *et al.*'s (1999) review highlighted a major gap in the KM literature in terms of its treatment of people. They found that the learning organization literature had emphasised people management issues, such as selection, motivation and rewards, trust, organizational development and culture. However, the KM literature paid little attention to these issues and focused rather on IT and information systems (IS) to create the networks structures, which can link together individuals distributed across time and space. For example, IT/IS was the focus of nearly 70 per cent of all KM articles in 1998. Despite the odd observation that "the most dramatic improvements in KM capability in the next ten years will be human and managerial" (Davenport, 1995), many articles continued to focus on developing and implementing KM databases, tools (e.g. decision support tools) and techniques for the creation of "knowledge bases", "knowledge webs" and "knowledge exchanges" (Bank, 1996).

Behind this tools-based approach to KM lies a cognitive, information processing view of the firm where valuable knowledge located inside people's heads (i.e. the input) is identified, captured and processed via the use of IT tools so that it can be applied in new contexts (i.e. the output). The aim, then, is to make the knowledge inside people's heads (i.e. cognitive knowledge) widely available to reduce the threat of valuable knowledge assets literally "walking out of the door". Indeed the practice of KM is frequently reduced in the literature to the implementation of new IT systems for knowledge transfer:

> the idea behind KM is to stockpile workers' knowledge and make it accessible to others via a searchable application (Cole-Gomolski, 1997).

People do feature but only in as much as they need to be willing and able to use KM tools.

Great claims are made, then, in the literature for the use of sophisticated IT-based tools (such as intranets, e-mail, groupware, data warehousing) for knowledge capture, storage and sharing. However, these typically overestimate the utility of new ITs for delivering organizational performance improvements:

> There is increasing hype about the wonders delivered by the newest information technologies in an era characterised by knowledge as the critical resource for business activity (Malhotra, 1998).

This is supported by evidence, which demonstrates that there is no direct correlation between IT investment and business performance (Malhotra, 1998; Strassmann, 1998). The case examples that follow highlight the limits of IT-based approaches to KM in terms of their ability to facilitate interactive innovation processes.

Case examples

The cases outlined here are drawn from a larger study of the roles of networks and knowledge management in interactive innovation projects. An understanding of the

Journal of Knowledge Management
Volume 3 · Number 4 · 1999 · 262–275

processes involved was achieved by systematically studying the development of innovation in each case over real time. This involved a minimum of three one-week site visits to interview project members over a period of two years supported by documented evidence over that time. The purpose here is not to draw generalised prescriptions from direct case comparisons but rather to illustrate our main argument concerning the role of networks and networking for KM during interactive innovation processes.

Both cases represent examples of multinational firms, which had attempted to introduce innovation in the provision and delivery of services to clients. Both had grown rapidly in the past ten years mainly through acquisition. The organizations were structured, then, around geographically-dispersed business units which have in the past operated with a high degree of local autonomy. The need to provide common services to global customers had led the corporate centre in each case to launch innovation projects aimed at improving the uniformity of service delivery across their disparate business units through the introduction of common, integrated IT platforms. In the case of Ebank, this was via the development of a global intranet and in the case of Brightco it was via the development of a common enterprise resources planning (ERP) system. In both cases, the projects required interaction among communities which were very different, both in terms of local organizational culture and *modus operandi*, and in terms of national institutional context. The technical and organizational knowledge relevant to these innovation projects was thus widely distributed (e.g. across functional departments, business units, corporate staff and nations).

The case of Ebank – an example of "mad practice"

Ebank is located across 70 countries worldwide, and is one of Europe's largest investors in IT. Despite calling itself "the networked bank", the reality was quite different. Each country and each department operated relatively independently with its own systems, services and processes. Ebank's "Vision 2000" innovation project was launched in 1996 when a major client left the bank because they felt they were not getting an integrated service across countries. In addition, the feeling among top management was that resources were being wasted because different units and departments failed to learn from one another, thus continuously "reinventing the wheel". The vision from the top then was to develop a global network in order to integrate existing knowledge within the bank and to provide a global service portfolio. Key to this was to be the development of a world-wide communications infrastructure using intranet technology.

An intranet pilot project was launched, led by the corporate IT group and funded centrally. The pilot involved mostly technical (IT) specialists from different business units world-wide and was focused on creating a corporate intranet infrastructure which would allow far-flung business units to connect. This pilot highlighted the benefits of the intranet for knowledge sharing and so enthused those involved. They returned to their own divisions and persuaded them to develop their own intranet, resourced with local funds and people. Thus, the translation of the global KM vision was very much left to individuals working at the local level. The result was that the espoused objective of developing intranet technology to increase knowledge sharing across the functional and geographical boundaries within the bank was not achieved. Instead the actual outcome was an explosion of different and discrete intranet projects. Nobody could say exactly how many sites had been developed (although someone estimated that there were at least 150 different intranet sites), where, with what purpose, or how to access them.

The use of these independent intranet sites suggested that they resulted in very limited knowledge sharing even at the local level. For example, the IT division knew about the technical requirements of intranet and had managed to develop their own technically sophisticated intranet (iweb) specifically designed for knowledge sharing across the IT function. However, when asked what was actually shared via iweb the only examples they could cite were the company telephone directory and the corporate bus timetable. The latter gave information of the times of company buses running between different local sites every 20 minutes! Thus iweb was essentially being used as a digital repository of existing information which was used by some (but not all) of the staff within the division. There was no evidence that the intranet had promoted any sharing of knowledge or

Journal of Knowledge Management
Volume 3 · Number 4 · 1999 · 262–275

expertise relevant to improving business performance or innovation even within the IT division, let alone across the bank.

Moreover, the lessons learned in the development of this intranet (which looked impressive and technically worked well) were not shared with developers of intranets in other divisions even within the same region. There were countless examples where project teams had spent time and money on developing an application for their particular intranet only to find later that another group had done something very similar which they could have used instead. For example, a number of the intranet projects had used a particular firm of consultants and in each case there had been problems with the relationship and the service provided by this consultancy. However, given that there was limited (no) communication across the intranet projects, the same mistakes with this consultancy continued to be made. Reinvention, then, was extremely common in an innovation initiative specifically aimed at preventing such reinvention! Further, expertise was not shared across functional specialisms within the bank, especially business management and IT. The result was that some intranets (e.g. iweb) proved technically very sophisticated but offered little in the way of business-relevant innovation. In others, where business-relevant innovation (e.g. in the form of integrated service delivery) could have been achieved the intranets failed because of difficulties in appropriating the necessary technical expertise. For example, in one case failure to anticipate bandwidth problems led to the developed intranet being abandoned because it took nearly 20 seconds to turn a page.

In terms of the global KM vision, there was recognition, at least by a small corporate IT strategy team, that the various intranet projects needed to be more fully co-ordinated. To facilitate this an intranet steering committee was set up and a two-day global workshop was convened. The global workshop involved both technical experts who had the knowledge to design intranet systems and business managers who would be using the intranet system to manage their businesses. In this sense the workshop did attempt to integrate the knowledge from technical and business experts. The problem was that those with the business expertise discussed their needs and cultural differences in terms of knowledge sharing on the first day of the workshop and then left. On the second day, the technical experts soon reverted to detailed technical issues, specifically the development of a common "portal" based on a "one-stop-shopping" philosophy where different intranets could be accessed through the same common window. There was no real consideration of the kinds of organizational and cultural issues that had been discussed on day one. Again, ironically, the result of the global workshop was that on returning "to base", individual projects were set up to develop many different portal sites in the different areas of the bank.

The most important feature of this case was thus the lack of recognition of the need for creating some shared understanding through active and involved networking. Rather there was the view that as long as the networks were structurally in place, then knowledge sharing across the internal boundaries would happen almost effortlessly. Indeed, some active networking did occur but is was not systematically designed and occurred in a "scattergun" fashion, which was ineffective in promoting the active sense making necessary for knowledge sharing on a broad scale across the bank. The focus was on the technology (i.e. developing intranet systems and technical infrastructural networks) rather than people (i.e. encouraging employees to engage in active networking to share knowledge, taking account of local organizational and cultural differences). Individuals had not been encouraged to share their knowledge even within a division, never mind across the global organization. In many ways the emphasis on the technology had simply helped to reinforce existing divisions with electronic fences, rather than break down barriers as had been envisaged. Ironically, this made it more, rather than less, difficult for information to be exchanged across the organization. Adopting intranet technology had effectively created a series of knowledge silos. The bank had managed to create a network linking individuals and groups across the bank, but had patently failed to stimulate any networking and consequent knowledge sharing. Evidence suggests that this may not be uncommon in organizations, especially where functional and departmental boundaries remain strong. Thus:

> misused, an intranet can intensify mistrust, increase misinformation, and exacerbate turf wars (Cohen, 1998).

Journal of Knowledge Management
Volume 3 · Number 4 · 1999 · 262–275

The case of Brightco – an example of "good" practice

Brightco is one of the world's largest manufacturers and service providers of specialist materials handling equipment with its headquarters in Sweden and divisions spread across Europe, Asia and the USA. Approximately half of its business is in service rather than manufacturing. Brightco's sales services support project (SSP) was launched in response to a corporate study of business processes which pointed to a need to improve co-ordination and communication across Brightco's different businesses and to provide a more integrated service for global customers. A major vehicle for this would be the introduction of a common business information system, funded centrally and implemented across all of Brightco's European divisions. It was recognised that this would represent a major upheaval because, until then, the traditional culture had been one of divisional autonomy with each European division having its own, various IT systems. Investment in IT had been relatively low; for example, there were only ten full-time staff in the corporate IT department.

The SSP project was launched in 1996 with overall responsibility resting with the corporate IT function. The design and implementation of an integrated management information and planning system – essentially an ERP system – were its main focus. Initially a small group of senior managers was brought together to review and evaluate currently available systems on the market. They concluded that none of these could handle Brightco's core business portfolio, i.e. multisite, multinational and with a large proportion of rental service agreements. Following negotiations with various external IT suppliers, Brightco contracted a Swedish supplier, Intsoft, to design and develop a new version of their software jointly with Brightco personnel. Critically, the relationship was to take the form of a close partnership with both parties benefiting – Brightco because they would have an ERP system that fitted their business requirements, and Intsoft because they would have a new version of their system that they could market more widely to other similar businesses using Brightco as a reference site.

Although he did not specifically use the term, the project leader from IT recognised that KM would be a critical issue especially due to the limited resources available in the central IT function. For example, it was recognised early on that selection, recruitment and commitment would be critical in developing a project team with the necessary IT and business expertise. The human resources director was therefore called upon to help in designing the project management procedures to be used on the SSP prior to the work formally starting and continued to have close contact with the project leader (albeit informally) throughout. The project team was selected through informal consultation with senior managers from the different European divisions who suggested those divisional staff who had the most knowledge of the local systems they were currently using. These were often those with detailed knowledge of operating procedures (e.g. from finance) rather than IT specialists.

The design and development phase of the ERP system was intensive with Intsoft consultants working alongside Brightco business managers representing different functional areas (e.g. sales, finance, operations) and different European divisions brought together on one site in Sweden for approximately three days a week over a 12-week period. In addition, two (and later four) graduates with business and IT backgrounds were employed specifically to work on the SSP project. These were employed by Intsoft, but were offered the option of employment either with Intsoft or Brightco when the project ended (indicative of the close attention paid to HR issues in the project). These graduates worked partly on site at Brightco and partly in Intsoft so were important "link pins" in the relationship between Brightco and Intsoft and brought valuable expertise, acquiring detailed knowledge of both the Intsoft software and Brightco's operating context.

Implementation of the ERP system was managed by three co-ordinated project teams each of which was responsible for two to four different European sites. Each team comprised representatives from Intsoft, corporate IT managers and business managers who (where possible) were those that had been involved during the design phase. The teams were thus multi-skilled and, importantly, involved representatives from most of the different social communities that would be affected by the system and whose local knowledge was important. They were

Journal of Knowledge Management
Volume 3 · Number 4 · 1999 · 262–275

also selected (on an informal basis) to comprise different "personality" types. For example, where it was known informally that a team leader was less "dynamic" (but suitably senior) they would be complemented by one of the more active IT or Intsoft staff.

These teams travelled to the sites to deliver initial training in the software. However, it was continuously stressed that implementation itself had to be owned locally (hence the label "sales *support* project"). Therefore local divisions provided their own project managers who were seconded to the SSP project during implementation. Importantly, although the three teams travelled two weeks in three, these periods were, where possible, timed so that all three teams returned to Sweden on the third week.

This was specifically so that knowledge could be shared across the teams, and hence across the European divisions they were responsible for. E-mail was used extensively for communication both within and across teams and across divisions. This allowed lessons from implementation in one division to be codified, captured and transmitted to another. For example, an e-mail site which emerged initially informally for "frequently asked questions" provided an important network for users at local sites to learn from one another about implementation problems in other sites.

However, importantly this IT-based communication of written information was supported by a high degree of verbal communication, either face-to-face or by telephone (every team member was provided with a mobile phone). The SSP project, then, did use an IT network for communication and this encouraged exploitation. However, the project was characterised by a high degree of strategically co-ordinated formal and informal networking across those various widespread social communities whose knowledge was needed to develop and implement a common and business relevant information system and this encouraged innovation through exploration. It is too early to tell whether the SSP project would meet the initial vision of performance improvement via a more integrated business but Brightco were at least successful in implementing a common business information system which was being used by most of its European divisions.

Discussion – the problems with IT-led knowledge management for innovation

In each of the cases of interactive innovation presented here the role of IT for KM was considered. The Brightco case illustrates that the use of IT can provide a network to enable communication to facilitate KM in interactive innovation projects. However, this is where it is used alongside relevant people management and organizational practices, in particular those which encourage active networking across disparate social communities of practice. The active design and facilitation of social networking in this case provided the opportunity for the individuals involved to develop overlapping, rather than mutually exclusive task knowledge and expertise. Such overlapping knowledge is essential because it allows for what Hutchins (1990) calls "redundant representation" – the ability to envisage a social system of joint actions. This encourages individuals to take responsibility for all parts of the system to which they can make a contribution, not just their small "corner". Those involved in the Brightco project were able to develop this redundant representation because the conceptualisation of KM was broad, encompassing both the use of IT to develop the network structure and the encouragement of active social networking between individuals concerned with the sharing, development and utilization of knowledge, skills and expertise. Thus both exploitation and exploration were embraced by Brightco's approach to KM. In contrast, Ebank demonstrates the limitations of approaches to KM which rely too heavily on IT. Here there was no attempt to systematically encourage active networking across the internal divisions within the bank; thus the KM project was not able to overcome the narrowly focused and entrenched attitudes which had developed due to the dominant, historical culture of functional and business autonomy. Therefore the focus of the KM project on technical, infrastructural issues blinded them to the importance of the social and cultural aspects to change management necessary to facilitate the development of a truly global, knowledge sharing network. In the case of Ebank, the result was that even exploitation of existing knowledge was limited with what was published via the intranet adding little in terms of Ebank's potential to innovate.

This confirms arguments by recent critics

(including IS experts) that there has been far too much reliance on the idea that KM has to do with IT systems:

> successful KM requires a skilful blend of people, business processes and IT (Dash, 1998).

The "mad" practice at Ebank was thus the result of an inability to systematically create the networking opportunities that would allow those involved to attend to and communally make sense of the wider goals of knowledge sharing across the global bank. In contrast, a kind of heedful interrelating (Weick and Roberts, 1993) was possible at Brightco precisely because active networking was systematically planned for and encouraged attention to the broader needs and goals of the European enterprise.

These cases illustrate several fundamental problems with IT-driven approaches which are considered next. First, they assume that all, or most, relevant knowledge in an organization can be made explicit and codified. Second, they are underpinned by a partial view of KM, focusing more on processes of exploitation than on processes of exploration. Third, they are supply driven – assuming that if information is widely available it will be applied in new ways to develop innovation.

Problems of codification and the importance of tacit knowledge

The approach in Ebank was essentially to codify existing knowledge into explicit forms and share this widely via the use of IT tools. This emphasis is also clearly reflected in the literature on KM. However, it is argued that it is tacit rather than explicit knowledge which will typically be of more value to innovation processes (Grant, 1996; Hall, 1993). Yet tacit knowledge is knowledge which cannot be communicated, understood or used without the "knowing subject" (Popper, 1972; Lam, 1998). This suggests that KM that focuses on creating network structures to transfer only explicit forms of knowledge will be severely limited in terms of the contribution to innovation. There are a number of reasons why the most valuable tacit knowledge in a firm may not lend itself to capture via the use of IT networks. It may be too difficult to explain, too uncertain, considered unimportant to anyone else, too changeable, too contextually specific, too politically sensitive or too valuable to the individual or group concerned (Gardner, 1998). Therefore attempts to codify tacit knowledge may only produce knowledge which is: useless (if it is too difficult to explain); difficult to verify (if it is too uncertain); trivial (if it is too unimportant); redundant (if it is subject to continuous change); irrelevant to a wider audience (if it is too context dependent); politically naïve (if it is too politically sensitive); inaccurate (if it is too valuable and is therefore secreted by the "knower"). Tacit knowledge, therefore, cannot easily be articulated or transferred in explicit forms because it is personal and context-specific. Also, the activity-based nature of knowing and understanding in organizations, where knowing is considered to continuously evolve through an ongoing process of practice, application and experience (Blackler 1995; Brown and Duguid 1991), further limits its codifiability and transferability.

IT-led KM, which emphasises codification and the development of network structures, typically fails to consider these problems in sharing tacit knowledge. For example, in Ebank important tacit knowledge about how "good" particular consultants were may have been difficult to codify. In contrast, in Brightco, informal face-to-face networking was often used heavily precisely because the limits of IT networks, in terms of their ability to act as a medium for the exchange of valuable tacit knowledge, were recognised.

The sharing and exchange of tacit knowledge may arguably be even more difficult where innovation processes are interactive. This is because the communication of tacit knowledge requires some shared system of meaning so that it can be understood and applied (Nonaka, 1994). Interactive innovation, however, involves disparate social communities which can have very different systems of meaning. For example, in the cases, languages, behavioural norms, cultural symbols and organizational routines varied widely across business divisions and functional groupings. In such situations, "redundancy" for knowledge creation becomes even more crucial (Nonaka, 1994). That is, some knowledge must be possessed by individuals even if they do not regularly need it because it allows them to engage with and interpret or make sense of the knowledge of others (Weick, 1990). Although, Brightco's use of mobile, multi-skilled project teams who travelled across Europe was enormously

Journal of Knowledge Management
Volume 3 · Number 4 · 1999 · 262–275

time-consuming for those involved, it did allow them to develop a common "language" and to appreciate each other's world views. This then made it easier to develop a common sense of purpose and a common system that was actually seen as relevant across different communities and was therefore much more likely to encourage integration. In contrast in Ebank, the focus on IT and relative neglect of any considerations about systematically stimulating active networking, in order to manage interfaces among different communities of practice, meant that each group developed their own system which actually encouraged further disintegration.

Problems of exploitation versus exploration

Unnecessary reinvention is a common problem in many firms. The case of Brightco shows how IT-based networks (e.g. e-mail) may increase the exploitation of existing knowledge by recording and storing the lessons from one implementation attempt (in the form of "frequently asked questions") making these available to others. In this way IT-based tools were useful for processing information that already existed in the organization, and for transferring information between Brightco and their IT suppliers. However, exploitation of existing knowledge is only a small part of what constitutes KM in innovation projects. Also crucial are processes of exploration, whereby new knowledge is created (Levinthal and March, 1993). Exploration may be informed by lessons from the past, but should not be constrained by them.

In turbulent business environments the source of innovation is not merely the more efficient processing of existing information but the application of knowledge to knowledge itself (Drucker, 1993). This dilemma between efficiency and innovation has been noted in the organizational literature for some time (Clark and Staunton, 1989). Yet most of the emphasis in IT-driven approaches has been on increasing efficiency by exploitation of existing knowledge rather than on encouraging more explorative processes. In Ebank, for example, the intranet tool was KM (indeed the development of the intranet was even referred to as the KM project) and the focus was therefore almost entirely on developing the infrastructure to support the network structure. It is ironic then, that there was very little awareness of the difficulties of managing knowledge, particularly for encouraging exploration, in this KM project.

Moreover, as demonstrated in the case of Ebank, the building of networks to formalise knowledge sharing may introduce rigidities into the system and reinforce existing organizational boundaries that then make processes of knowledge sharing and creation which are central to interactive innovation projects more difficult. This is supported by evidence which demonstrates that there is no direct correlation between IT investment and business performance (Malhotra, 1998). As seen Ebank was one of Europe's biggest spenders on IT. Yet, the intranet(s) they developed actually appeared to offer little in terms of improving business performance through the provision of integrated services. The cases presented here demonstrate the varied and multiple impacts that the development of IT networks may have on KM in innovation projects. They demonstrate that building the physical, infrastructural networks without encouraging active, personal networking can have a negative rather than a positive impact on interactive innovation processes. Sharing and creating knowledge across heterogeneous organizational and social communities requires an investment in interpersonal interrelationship building, so that those involved can make sense of and envisage the broader goals of the system, which they are designing and developing.

Problems of supply and demand

In these cases it is possible to distinguish broadly between "supply-driven" (Ebank) and "demand-driven" (Brightco) approaches to KM. Supply-driven approaches focus on using IT-based tools to build networks for the supply of knowledge and information which will then, somehow miraculously, be applied and used to develop innovative solutions. This assumes that the problems of KM are to do with the flow of knowledge and information across the organization. The aim is to increase that flow by capturing, codifying and transmitting knowledge using IT-based networks. However, even where knowledge can be codified, stored and broadcast, it does not follow that this knowledge will be used or applied by others. For example, on the demand side a major problem many managers face is information overload. In order to manage knowledge for innovation there is a

Journal of Knowledge Management
Volume 3 · Number 4 · 1999 · 262–275

need to understand the difference between knowledge and competency or expertise. Competency or expertise is more than a "bucket of knowledge"; it is also the insight to be able to apply that knowledge (Dove, 1998). Supply-driven approaches therefore suffer from the drawbacks of IT-led approaches outlined above.

On the other hand, initiatives that are demand driven tend to be more concerned with the creation and application of knowledge in innovation projects. The motivation and attitudes of multiple stakeholders are seen as crucial and consequently there is a more focal concern with human networking processes which can encourage sharing and use of knowledge which is relevant for innovation. This is not to say that supply-driven initiatives ignore these factors but they are seen as peripheral to the problems associated with the technology rather than as core features of KM (Scarbrough *et al.*, 1999).

There are obvious implications, then, for KM in terms of facilitating innovation, of attending to networking processes that encourage knowledge sharing and exploration. Interestingly, the cases show how people management practices are often more fundamental to knowledge sharing than the use of IT. For example, even in Ebank where there were high levels of technical expertise and familiarity with systems and high expenditure on IT, IT was only used for fairly low-level information exchange (e.g. the digital telephone directory). In Brightco, face-to-face and verbal interaction were used for knowledge sharing, despite difficulties of international travel, with those involved recognising that deeply embedded tacit knowledge is difficult, if not impossible, to share through other medium particularly where local practices and cultures differ widely. However, although intense face-to-face networking was a crucial media for knowledge sharing, it could also be seen that this was extremely challenging for those involved. Working away from home, for example, for two weeks in three over a period of over a year, was generating significant stress. The challenge for IT developers, then, is not to develop systems that aim to replace people as the primary source of expertise. Rather, the aim should perhaps be to develop systems that allow experts to engage in active networking through creating environments that are media-rich enough to encourage knowledge sharing and organizational learning where it is relevant for innovation (Huber, 1991). The risk, however, is that installing network links between communities may actually undermine social networking processes seen as critical to innovation (Conway, 1995) because individuals in different groups no longer have the perceived need to be active in terms of their interaction. This occurred in Ebank where installing the network links reduced rather than increased active networking. This in turn reduced rather than increased knowledge sharing across the different communities.

Conclusions – developing a networking community view of knowledge management for innovation

A core assumption in the literature on KM is that technology can provide the network of links between geographically dispersed groups and individuals that enables effective knowledge sharing. However, this privileges an information processing view where knowledge is seen as cognitive abilities (inputs) which can be transferred and processed using technological networks to produce certain outputs. This equates knowledge to the skills and cognitive abilities of individuals and views the transfer of this knowledge through networks as unproblematic – a cognitive network model. Knowledge is assumed to "flow" fluidly between people through networks. In contrast, organizational theorists highlight the need to understand knowledge as also embedded in, and constructed from and through social relationships and interactions (Nonaka and Takeuchi, 1995; Blackler, 1995; Weick and Roberts, 1993) – a community networking model. According to this view, knowledge (unlike information) cannot simply be processed; rather it must be continuously re-created and re-constituted through dynamic, interactive and social networking activity. This is especially important for innovation processes that are interactive. Knowledge is inherently sticky and must be given meaning through active networking processes which allow those involved to engage in negotiation and sense-making (Weick, 1990). For example, the team working in Brightco was not simply moving knowledge around from person to person, it

Journal of Knowledge Management
Volume 3 · Number 4 · 1999 · 262–275

was also creating new knowledge and shared understandings through the synthesis and interaction of team members. The KM initiatives here then had focused on consciously and deliberately creating communities with an appropriate mix of skills, expertise and personality and then providing plenty of opportunity for intense interaction and interrelating. At Ebank, on the other hand, the focus had been on building the network links and the interaction needed to these links had been left to chance and individual inclination. This haphazard and unmanaged approach to the active networking needed for KM ultimately undermined the attempt to encourage knowledge creation and sharing across the bank. The cognitive network model appears to underpin most previous KM examples (and is illustrated again in Ebank) and certainly fits with most of what is written about KM tools. On the other hand, a community networking model perhaps summarises the more realistic view, certainly when considering the issue of knowledge exploration rather than knowledge exploitation. The core differences between the network and networking views of knowledge and KM are shown in Table I.

The community networking model highlights the importance of relationships, shared understandings and attitudes to knowledge formation and sharing within innovation processes (Spender, 1996). It is important to acknowledge these issues since they help to define the likely success or failure of attempts to implement KM practices that facilitate innovation. The community networking model suggests that, whilst it might be relatively easy to share knowledge where innovation is localised and groups are homogeneous, it is extremely difficult where the innovation is interactive and groups are heterogeneous. Yet, it is precisely the sharing of knowledge across functional or organizational boundaries, through using cross-functional and inter-organizational, inter-disciplinary and inter-organizational teams, that is seen as the key to the effective use of knowledge for innovation (Gibbons, 1994). Cognitive, IT-led approaches to KM typically fail to take into account the pre-existing organizational structures, norms and cultural values that lead different groups to have divergent, possibly even irreconcilable, interpretations of what needs to be done and how best to do it. They unrealistically assume that building networks that provide structural links between these different groups will somehow automatically produce knowledge creation and sharing. The community view recognises that knowledge has to be continuously negotiated through interactive social networking processes. Thus the community model emphasises dialogue occurring through active and systematic networking (which may be IT-enabled) rather than linear information flows.

Seeing knowledge as constructed through processes of social interaction and heedful interrelating among communities of practice means that issues of social networking, power and social inclusion/exclusion come to the forefront (Aldrich and von Glinow, 1992). Therefore a crucial feature raised by these cases is the importance of social co-ordination and networking (formal and informal) in

Table I Two contrasting views of the KM process

Cognitive network model (e.g. Ebank)	Community networking model (e.g. Brightco)
Knowledge for innovation is equal to objectively defined concepts and facts	Knowledge for innovation is socially constructed and based on experience
Knowledge can be codified and transferred through networks: information systems have a crucial role	Much knowledge is tacit and is shared and made sense of through active networking within and between occupational groups and teams
Gains from KM include exploitation through the recycling of existing knowledge	Gains from KM include exploration through the sharing and synthesis of knowledge among different social groups and communities
The primary function of KM is to codify, capture and transfer knowledge through networks	The primary function of KM is to encourage knowledge-sharing through networking
The critical success factor is technology	The critical success factor is trust and collaboration
The dominant metaphors are the human memory and the jigsaw (fitting pieces of knowledge together to produce a bigger picture in predictable ways)	The dominant metaphors are the human community and the kaleidoscope (creative interactions producing new knowledge in sometimes unpredictable ways)

Knowledge management and innovation: networks and networking
Jacky Swan, Sue Newell, Harry Scarbrough and Donald Hislop

Journal of Knowledge Management
Volume 3 · Number 4 · 1999 · 262–275

managing knowledge. In some cases (e.g. Brightco) communication technologies complement these processes by increasing the ability to communicate across boundaries of time and space. In other cases IT networks may actually undermine knowledge sharing and creation (e.g. in the case of Ebank) by reducing opportunities for informal contact or strengthening, electronically, the existing organizational walls, based on functional or geographical differentiation. Thus careful attention is needed to the potential impact of IT networks on KM for innovation in relation to existing communities within organizations. KM initiatives that encourage active networking are key to interactive innovation processes and an over-emphasis on building IT-based network links may ironically undermine rather than increase this.

References

Abrahamson (1996), "Management fashion", *Academy of Management Review*, Vol. 21, pp. 254-85.

Aldrich, H. and von Glinow, M.A. (1992), "Personal networks and infrastructure development", in Gibson, D.V., Kozmetsky, G. and Smilor, R.W. (Eds), *The Technopolis Phenomenon: Smart Cities, Fast Systems, Global Networks*, Rowman & Littlefield, New York, NY.

Bank, D. (1996), "Technology – know-it-alls – chief knowledge officers have a crucial job: putting the collective knowledge of a company at every worker's fingertips", *Wall Street Journal*, Eastern edition, November 18, p. 28.

Blackler, F. (1995), "Knowledge, knowledge work and organizations: an overview and interpretation", *Organization Studies*, Vol. 16 No. 6, pp. 16-36.

Bolwijn, P.T. and Kumpe, T. (1990), "Manufacturing in the 1990s – productivity, flexibility and innovation", *Long Range Planning*, Vol. 23, pp. 44-57.

Brown, J. and Duguid, P. (1991), "Organization learning and communities of practice: towards a unified view of working, learning and innovation", *Organization Science*, Vol. 2 No. 1, pp. 40-57.

Castells, M. (1996), *The Rise of the Network Society*, Blackwell, Oxford.

Clark, P.A. (1987), *Anglo-American Innovation*, De Gruyter, New York.

Clark, P. and Staunton, N. (1989), *Innovation in Technology and Organization*, Routledge, London.

Cohen, S. (1998), "Knowledge management's killer application", *Training and Development*, Vol. 52 No. 1, pp. 50-3.

Cole-Gomolski, B. (1997), "Users loath to share their know-how", *Computerworld*, Vol. 31 No. 46, p. 6.

Conway, S. (1995), "Informal boundary spanning communication in the innovation process: an empirical study", *Technology Analysis and Strategic Management*, Vol. 7, pp. 327-42.

Damanpour, F. (1987), "The adoption of technological, administrative and ancillary innovations: impact of organizational factors", *Journal of Management*, Vol. 13, pp. 675-88.

Dash, J. (1998), "Turning technology into TechKnowledgey", *Software Magazine*, Vol. 18 No. 3, pp. 64-73.

Davenport, T.H. (1995), "Think tank", *CIO*, Vol. 9 No. 6, pp. 30-2.

Dove, R. (1998), "A knowledge management framework", *Automotive Manufacturing and Production*, Vol. 110 No. 1, pp. 18-21.

Drucker, P. (1993), *Post-Capitalist Society*, Butterworth-Heinemann, Oxford.

Gardner, D. (1998), "Knowledge that won't fit in a database – people", *InfoWorld*, Vol. 20 No. 14, p. 98.

Gibbons, M. (1994), *The New Production of Knowledge: The Dynamics of Science and Research in Contemporary Societies*, Sage, London.

Grant, R. (1996), "Toward a knowledge based theory of the firm", *Strategic Management Journal*, Vol. 17, pp. 109-22.

Hall, R. (1993), "A framework for linking intangible resources and capabilities to sustainable competitive advantage", *Strategic Management Journal*, No. 14, pp. 607-18.

Huber, G.P. (1991), "Organizational learning: the contributing process and the literatures", *Organization Science*, Vol. 2 No. 1, pp. 88-115.

Hutchins, E. (1990), "The technology of team navigation", in Galegher, J., Kraut, R. and Egido, C. (Eds), *Intellectual Teamwork*, Erlbaum, Hillsdale, NJ, pp. 191-220.

Kogut, B. and Zander, U. (1992), "Knowledge of the firm, combinative capabilities, and the replication of technology", *Organization Science*, Vol. 3 No. 3, pp. 383-97.

Lam, A. (1998), "Tacit knowledge, organizational learning and innovation: a societal perspective", paper presented at the British Academy of Management Conference, Nottingham.

Levinthal, D. and March, J. (1993), "The myopia of learning", *Strategic Management Journal*, Vol. 14, pp. 95-112.

Malhotra, Y. (1998), "Tools at work: deciphering the knowledge management hype", *The Journal of Quality and Participation*, Vol. 21 No. 4, pp. 58-60.

Marshall, L. (1997), "Facilitating knowledge management and knowledge sharing: new opportunities for information professionals", *Online*, Vol. 21 No. 5, pp. 92-8.

Nonaka, I. (1994), "A dynamic theory of organizational knowledge creation", *Organization Sciences*, Vol. 5, pp. 14-37.

Nonaka, I. and Takeuchi, H. (1995), *The Knowledge Creating Company*, Oxford University Press, New York, NY.

Popper, K. (1972), *Objective Knowledge: An Evolutionary Approach*, Clarendon Press, Oxford.

Prusak, L. (1997), *Knowledge in Organizations*, Butterworth-Heinemann, Oxford.

Quintas, J.B., Anderson, P. and Finkelstein, S. (1996), "Managing professional intellect: making the most of the best", *Harvard Business Review*, Vol. 74, March-April, pp. 71-80.

Journal of Knowledge Management
Volume 3 · Number 4 · 1999 · 262–275

Rogers, E. (1983), *Diffusion of Innovations*, 3rd ed., Free Press, New York.

Scarbrough, H. and Corbett, J.M. (1992), *Technology and Organization: Power, Meaning and Design*, Routledge, London.

Scarbrough, H., Swan, J. and Preston, J. (1999), *Knowledge Management and the Learning Organization*, IPD, London.

Slappendel, C. (1996), "Perspectives on innovation in organizations", *Organization Studies*, Vol. 17 No. 1, pp. 107-29.

Spender, J.C. (1989), *Industry Recipes*, Blackwell, Oxford.

Spender, J.C. (1996), "Organizational knowledge, learning and memory: three concepts in search of a theory", *Journal of Organizational Change*, Vol. 9 No. 1, pp. 63-78.

Strassmann, P.A. (1998), "Taking a measure of knowledge assets", *Computerworld*, Vol. 32 No. 4, p. 74.

Swan, J., Newell, S. and Robertson, M. (forthcoming), "Central agencies in the diffusion and design of technology: a comparison of the UK and Sweden", *Organization Studies*.

Trompenaars, F. (1995), *Riding the Waves of Culture: Understanding Cultural Diversity in Business*, Nicholas Brealey, London.

Van de Ven, A.H. (1986), "Central problems in the management of innovation", *Management Science*, Vol. 32, pp. 590-607.

Weick, K.E. (1990), "Technology as *equivoque*: sensemaking in new technologies", in Goodman, P.S., Sproull, L.S. and Associates (Eds), *Technology and Organisations*, Jossey-Bass, Oxford.

Weick, K. and Roberts, K. (1993), "Collective minds in organizations: heedful interrelating on flight decks", *Administrative Science Quarterly*, Vol. 38, pp. 357-81.

Wolfe, R.A. (1994), "Organizational innovation: review, critique and suggested research directions", *Journal of Management Studies*, Vol. 31, pp. 405-31.

Further reading

Dwyer, L. (1990), "Factors affecting the proficient management of product innovation", *International Journal of Technology Management*, Vol. 5 No. 6, pp. 721-30.

Hibbard, J. and Carillo, K.M. (1998), "Knowledge revolution", *Informationweek*, Vol. 5 No. 663, pp. 49-54.

Hislop, D., Swan, J., Scarbrough, H. and Newell, S. (1998), "Boundary spanning: the importance of extra-organisational networking in the early stages of the innovation process", paper presented at British Academy of Management Conference, Nottingham, September.

Senge, P. (1990), *The Fifth Discipline: The Art and Practice of the Learning Organization*, Doubleday, London.

Tsoukas, H. (1996), "The firm as a distributed knowledge system: a constructionist perspective", *Strategic Management Journal*, Vol. 17, pp. 11-25.

Wegner, D., Erber, R. and Raymond, P. (1991), "Transactive memory in close relationships", *Journal of Personality and Social Psychology*, Vol. 61, pp. 923-9.

Journal of Management Studies 39:4 June 2002
0022-2380

INNOVATION, IDENTITIES AND RESISTANCE: THE SOCIAL CONSTRUCTION OF AN INNOVATION NETWORK

Denis Harrisson

Murielle Laberge

University of Québec in Hull

ABSTRACT

This paper explores the process of diffusion of a socio-technical innovation among workers of a large microelectronics firm. Actor–network theory (ANT), which draws on the sociology of science and technology, is applied to the analysis of socio-technical innovation in order to understand the actions of creating and putting the actors' arguments into action. Actors constructed and organized these arguments with the aim of diffusing innovation among workers whose support was essential to the project's success. The authors of the innovation project wanted to change the state of relations between different actors. In the present study, the aligment of identities was established according to the criteria defined by the managers and engineers but the expected benefits of the innovation, in this case, technology and teamwork, were not automatically accepted. Network analysis reveals how persuasive arguments that repudiate the old reality and justify steps to create the new reality are constructed. This article will reveal how innovation is constituted and the form it takes by following the chain of arguments and the responses of the actors involved.

INTRODUCTION

The aim of this article is to analyse the process of diffusion of a socio-technical innovation among workers of a large microelectronics firm. Actor–network theory (ANT), which draws on the sociology of science and technology, is applied to the analysis of socio-technical innovation in order to understand the actions of creating and putting the actors' arguments into action. Innovation is established through the construction of consent rather than through coercion (Tuckman, 1995). Actors constructed and organized these arguments with the aim of diffusing innovation among workers whose support was essential to the project's success. Innovation spread through a network whereby disparate elements were brought

Address for reprints: Denis Harrisson, Department of Industrial Relations, University of Québec in Hull, C.P. 1250, succursale B, Hull, Québec, Canada (denis_harrisson@uqah.uquebec.ca).

together by creating and putting into action a sequence of different types of arguments. This sometimes entailed appeals, persuasion or use of convincing language and, at other times, it involved more coercive methods, such as deception, power plays and the restructuring of contextual elements. Managers and engineers, the authors of the innovation project, wanted to change the state of relations between different actors. In the present study, the alignment of identities was established according to the criteria defined by the managers and engineers but the expected benefits of the innovation, in this case, technology and team work, were not automatically accepted. Innovation calls for a redistribution of power in the organization, which challenges the legitimacy of new forms of co-operation (Murakami, 1995). Studies on the innovation process have shown that it resembles an assembly of disparate elements that belong both to the new universe being built and to the former world that resists and reproduces itself in order to protect actors' interests (Alter, 1993; Barnett and Carroll, 1995; Gattiker, 1990; Heckscher et al., 1994; Pettigrew, 1985; Scarbrough and Corbett 1992; Van de ven and Poole, 1995). Network analysis reveals how persuasive arguments that repudiate the old reality and justify steps to create the new reality are constructed. This article will reveal how innovation is constituted and the form it takes by following the chain of arguments and the responses of the actors involved. It is hypothesized that innovation does not impose itself but is constructed through the interaction between members of an organization and the intermediaries that they introduce in order to legitimize the decisions made.

The article is divided into two parts. The first part presents actor–network theory (ANT) as a method that can be used to recreate the chain of translation of the interests and identity of members who are asked to join the network. Emphasis is put on the identity of the workers through whom co-operation is constructed but among whom resistance also emerges as the other aspect of innovation. The second part presents a case study of the development of innovation by the engineers and managers. This entailed the formation of a new socio-technical configuration based on new production technologies and team work and in which the mobilization of workers was crucial. The strategy of *interessement* and *enrolment* of workers will be analysed, as well as the ensuing ambiguity, as workers rejected the identity that others had created for them, thus limiting the scope of innovation. These are not viewed as two separate processes, one technical and the other social, but rather as a whole process that includes these two facets.

INNOVATION AND THE DEFINITION OF IDENTITIES

A suitable starting point is Schumpeter's definition of innovation, that is, the implementation of new combinations of different resources in the firm (Schumpeter, 1967). Studies of innovation generally distinguish between technological and social innovation. Technological innovation is often the result of a deliberate creation or invention while social innovation most often consists in the codification of a specific type of interaction. The former becomes irreversible once its influence begins to build up over time (Hughes, 1987) while the latter is a source of continuous tension. Despite these differences, it is suggested here that both types of innovation are assimilated at the moment when they are diffused in organizations. Indeed, according to ANT, the distinction between social and technical innovation is becoming increasingly tenuous. The process of implementing innovation disrupts the identities of the actors whose support for these new combinations of resources in the firm provokes rejection and resistance from workers. We will briefly examine how technology and social arrangements are viewed in the innovation process.

Relations between organizations and technologies have been curently analysed on the basis of three dominant theories: contingency theory (Woodward, 1965), control of the labour process (Braverman, 1986; Thompson, 1990) and strategic choice (Child, 1972; Zuboff, 1988). The latter theory can be used to examine how opposing interpretations of a technology affect its development and the interaction with the technology. The perspective of social construction of technologies shows how meanings surrounding technologies are created and defended (Bijker et al., 1987; Bloomfield, 1986; Woolgar, 1981). Other studies focus on aspects of the agents' interaction with the technology whose development may provide the opportunity to propose structural changes (Barley, 1986; Orlikowsi, 1992; Tyre and Orlikowski, 1994). From the perspective of social construction, technologies result from a structuring process which influences the construction of meaning by producing opposing cognitive models. By virtue of these models, certain actions are more consistent with social influences than other mechanisms. The role of social interaction has been underestimated in models of adoption of technologies (Fulk, 1993; Pinch and Bijker, 1987; Wilkinson, 1983). For example, computer systems are social constructions associated with ways of thinking and acting which significantly change the state of relations between agents (Bloomfield, 1986; Bloomfield and Coombs, 1992).

In organizations, technologies are now developed simultaneously with social arrangements of work organization as responses to market pressures to increase productivity (Appelbaum and Batt, 1994; Cappelli et al., 1997). Team work, as an archetype of social innovation, provides ways to react to the new economy of flexibility and quality in which communications become easier and hierarchy less necessary (Heller et al., 1998). However, applications of teamwork are disparate and appear to be inadequately compensated (Cunningham et al., 1996; Sinclair, 1992). Participation implies that decision-making will be shared, but control is no less present, albeit in more subtle forms which go against the identity of employees (Ezzamel and Willmott, 1998). A dual form of control also exists, one through electronic surveillance and the other through peer pressure (Sewell, 1998). Although the primary role of electronic equipment is to control production, it nevertheless involves surveillance of employees (Batt, 1999; McArdle et al., 1995; Zuboff, 1988). The translation of combined team principles to production technologies is far from automatic since employees are not necessarily eager to accept collective responsibility which, as will be seen below, is intertwined with increased technological control. It is therefore imperative to examine how innovation is presented, discussed and debated at the local level. The actors advance positions, they negotiate their role and induce the intermediaries to act in their favour. As is already known, distribution of social roles is asymmetrical in accordance with the institutional forms of domination. Therefore, it is important to discover how the arguments are presented and debated at the moment of innovation to create a new order of domination. It is crucial to observe behind-the-scenes interactions in order to understand this moment of construction. In fact, innovations is an intense period which is rich in information about the definition of identities and the establishment of social roles. The positionings of influence and power play a particularly important role at this moment. In these circumstances, the question of consent becomes crucial. To obtain the consent of actors and form an alliance with them, their desires and needs must be interpreted because their identities are significantly affected.

The process of innovation requires that identities change so that alliances can be formed (Munro, 1995). Actors are defined by their identities, a polysemous concept that synthesizes all individual and collective characteristics, allowing individuals, groups and collectivities to differentiate themselves from others (Jenkins, 1996; Michael, 1996). Identity is defined not only around objective criteria but also through awareness that the group exists with its own values, symbols and histories (Hogg and Abram, 1988). This article focuses on the collective identities of a particular group of workers. In the present case, ambiguities appeared, showing that the workers' identities had been evaluated incorrectly and that they were able to reject an identity that others had created for them, but which did not meet their expectations, needs or interests. Conflicts and resistance were manifested in various ways. Many studies show that attempts to increase control over work have always been identified with the managerial authority that imposes them. Resistance is generally aimed at the authors of such strategies. Resistance is an attempt to regain dignity in the face of forms of work organization which violate workers' interests, prerogatives and autonomy (Graham, 1993; Hodson, 1995; Jermier et al., 1994).

ANT provides the means to explain these exchanges, which involve both forms of adaptation, co-operation and accommodation, as well as conflict. Consent and co-operation should be treated in the same way as conflict, like a dialectical exchange between two sides of a coin (Kelly, 1998). Thus, workers are subject to the authority of managers and the need to plan production in accordance with the imperatives of the capitalist market. Employees do not only create opposition and resistance to managerial control but, in return, managers cannot unilaterally impose their vision on employees, who are not merely passive actors (Edwards, 1986). However, although hierarchical authority may appear to dictate rules, in reality, power can only be exercised if the actors accept it or decide not to obstruct it (Durkheim, 1950).

INNOVATION AND ACTOR–NETWORK THEORY

ANT focuses on how collective projects are constituted (Barley and Bechky, 1994; Hassard, 1994; Munro, 1995). Through ANT, the following type of sequence can be analysed: having designed an innovation project, an ad hoc group creates a provisional structure, develops arguments to legitimize the project and defines the necessary conditions for membership. A socio-technical innovation is established as a result of exchanges of knowledge and ideas by individual actors or groups mobilized through legitimization activities, depending on the given internal and external context (Pettigrew, 1985, 1990). Actors are the starting point of innovation. They join in the process or they oppose it, they protect interests and propose others. ANT shows how the network spreads. What are the dynamics for recruiting elements? Who joins the network? Who rejects the network? The foundations of actor–network theory draw on two contemporary sociological approaches: social constructivism and network analysis.

Social Construction

Although diversified, all social construction approaches examine local arrangements based on the methods of producing or constructing facts in their original place, facts that can be observed through human negotiations. According to this view, social reality is constructed by particular social actors, in particular places, at precise times. We always operate in local situations in the context of interactions (Knorr-Cetina, 1988). The macro context has a status of local representation, suggesting behavioural regularities. But how are these regularities accomplished? Should they be retraced? To understand its meaning, this reality must be interpreted, by clarifying the process through which meaning is constructed and by showing how meanings are incorporated into human actions. It is therefore necessary to focus on the practices that test the content resulting from social and cognitive co-production (Berger and Luckman, 1966; Gergen, 1985; Lincoln and Guba, 1985; Michael, 1996; Schwant, 1994). ANT is a post-structuralist approach (Law, 1994; Michael, 1996) which organizes the world through the narration of a story about how the actors define themselves and others.

A Network

Network analysis is not a unitary approach. The structuralist perspective emphasizes the positions of agents in the network without considering the values and ideals of the actors who construct them (Freeman, 1991; Galaskiewicz and Wasserman, 1994). Another approach consists of analysing the patterns of relations rather than simply considering ready-made categories. A network therefore becomes a series of social relations with a specific content (Emirbayer and Googwin, 1994). These are the phenomenological realities whose narratives describe links in the network (White, 1992). In this case, the analysis of a network refers to the voluntary aspects of social life and the capacity of the actors to transform or reproduce long-term structures. This latter meaning is used in the present article. Thus, the analysis of innovation through a network takes into account useful information in order to represent non-codified phenomena in an orderly way. At the start of innovation, the network of alliances is most important since the content of innovation is variable and open (Westphal et al., 1997). Innovation is thus conceived as a support network between innovating actors who negotiate and come to an agreement, thus making up for the inadequacy of institutional and organizational forces which primarily serve the status quo. Innovating means dismantling existing associations and creating and stabilizing new ones for a while (Callon, 1995). Innovation requires breaking free of the usual relations, even though there are often contradictions between innovation and the organization (Alter, 1993).

The Specificity of ANT

ANT is original because it views technical objects, scientific and natural facts and, by extension, knowledge, as network elements (Michael, 1996). ANT shows how one actor constructs the identity of the other actor by trying to make the latter act in accordance with his wishes. Certain actors make an innovative proposal, mobilize resources and try to translate the interests of others in an effort to enrol them. The network authorizes multilateral agreements that result from the translation of the actors' disparate interests, which will eventually converge. In contrast, there can also be resistance, for example, as the network becomes more complex and identities more ambiguous. Alternative, unforeseen translations may then take place.

Non-human contributions are important insofar as they produce effects on human components. ANT has been criticized for giving non-human objects a symmetrical role (Collins and Yearley, 1992). In response, Michel Callon (1992) has pointed out that the symmetry between humans and non-humans does not depend on an equivalent status but rather on the possibility of creating a chain made up of intermediaries, actors, texts, knowledge and scientific facts, each contributing in its own way to propagate innovation among those whom the network wishes to mobilize. Humans are distinguished from non-humans by laws, agreements and rules that guide their interactions. The principle of symmetry suggests that anything can be analysed in the same terms. There are no pre-established distinctions between elements and they all serve to introduce a new order. Thus, for John Law (1994), ANT gives the non-social a place in the social organization, which also has hierarchies and ranks that give rise to precise practices.

Information can be exchanged rapidly through the network and decision-making can be decentralized if the network's dynamics tend towards exchanges between members who co-operate and develop complementarities. However, criticisms by those who resist influence the process and can even change the outcome (Valente, 1996). Callon shows that when researchers carry out scientific activity, they make hypotheses about the identity of people, defining it according to their own wishes (Callon, 1986a, 1986b). Similarly, it can be said that managers and engineers make hypotheses about the identity of workers when they put forward a socio-technical innovation. ANT recommends that no judgement be made about the way in which actors analyse society. The observer follows the chain of arguments in order to determine how the actors define, associate and negotiate the elements that make up their social world. In the following pages, the method consists in following the actor, the *primens movens*, through an itinerary made up of four stages (Callon, 1986a, 1986b):

(1) The *construction of the problem* consists of formulating the problem and proposing solutions. How can productivity be increased, how can we modernize, how can we become the leader in a high-tech sector, or the world's best? The project's authors reply: by introducing innovation in products, technology, management, human resources and work co-ordination. They formulated questions and bring other actors and intermediaries into play: technologies, the market context, human resources managers, the workers they wish to recruit, the ideology of excellence, ISO standards and the principles of flexibility and quality. The had to show that the alliance was beneficial to each and every one of them.

(2) The mechanisms of *interessement* are defined as a set of actions through which the *primens movens* impose and stabilize the identity of other actors, promoting the pursuit of the objectives and goals that have been attributed to them. The invited actor may submit, or he may define his identity, aims, projects and interests differently. *Interessement* is an important stage in which the *primens movens* impose and stabilize the identity of the other actors as they have been defined in the construction of the problem. However, this is not always the first scenario. The *primens movens* will try to sever the links between

the interested and the others, that is, to isolate him so that he submits to the construction of the problem. This may involve negotiation or coercion. They are trying to build alliances and destroy competing associations, as in the case that follows, with the union or employees in other departments.

(3) *Enrolment* consists of defining a role and ensuring that it is played by the actor to whom it is proposed. In other words, it is the distribution and assignment of roles in the network. Technology is also included. It consists of speeding the production cycle as well as creating a space for teamwork. For the workers in the case below, this involved participating and finding solutions to quality, production and technological problems according to management principles. *Enrolment* is the result of successful *interessement.* It is the moment of acquiescence and consent, which may take the form of either conformity with rules or authentic commitment (Kerfoot and Knights, 1995).

(4) Finally, *mobilization of allies* is the stage in which ordering is transferred. Innovation becomes irreversible or, on the contrary, the network begins to fall apart. The *primens movens* take care of the interests of others and speak in their name, and get them to move from their initial position through intermediaries (meetings, training, information, privileged status, etc.). The actors are caught in a network of constraining links whose consensus limits each actor's room to manoeuvre. However, this representativeness may fail, resulting in dissidence and resistance. This shows that the network cannot ensure the interests of everyone and thus wavers.

THE CONSTRUCTION OF THE PROBLEM

At ELCOM, the innovation project was double-sided, involving both the use of information technology to remodel the production process and the introduction of teamwork to restructure the organization of work. These innovations were implemented as part of a single process, that is, not a superimposition of two different sequences of innovation but rather an amalgamation of technological and social arguments. These innovations followed a well-defined course of action as drawn up by the authors of the network. As spokespersons for the innovation project, the authors constructed the identities that they wanted the employees to adopt with the aim of enlisting their support and participation in the innovation. The spokespersons enacted a version of their desired organizational order which fit perfectly with the structure of innovations.

For three years, we followed the design of a new production system that sought to change the manufacturing of a new optonumerical card by introducing new technology and a new form of work organization. Forty-seven interviews were carried out with managers, union representatives, workers, supervisors and technical staff. The interviews focused on work carried out, work organization, communication, work coordination, the process of change, involvement in the process, problems raised by change, the resolution of disputes and tensions and the future of the establishment. We carried out a documentary analysis of the meetings' minutes, the directives and policies of the firm and the union newsletters. The case study was carried out in three phases of observation and interviews, conducted in 1994, 1995 and 1997. ELCOM, a major multinational manufacturer of electronic components for telecommunication products, owns 50 plants around the world. The Montreal plant, in which the case analysis was carried out, employs 2000 people. The 885 operators, 300 technicians, 100 skilled workers and 400 engineers were divided into two separate production units. To cope with competition, senior managers developed a four-pronged strategy: (a) sub-contracting the production of particular components and irregular production batches; (b) transferring mass production to Mexican plants where the production costs are cheaper when unskilled labour is required; (c) investing in R&D to gain an advantage over competitors in an industrial sector with rapid product obsolescence (three product generations in ten years); and (d) redesigning the workplace, drawing particularly on information technology and teamwork as sources of innovation. Our analysis will focus on these latter innovations.

The New Department: Opto World

The innovation began with the design of a new optonumerical card that increased the speed of telecommunications by handling up to 192 data/second. The card was now standardized and more uniform despite being produced in different sizes and forms. It was specifically designed to be produced in small batches and to be adapted easily to changes expected over the following 10 to 15 years. Rapid changes are also part of the product itself. To manufacture the new optonumerical cards, managers believed that a new department was needed. Flexibility would be increased by reducing the time to introduce the new production technology and by increasing the plant's production capacity. High quality would be achieved by documenting processes and involving employees in continuous improvement programmes. What exactly was involved in the new arrangements related to technology and teamwork will be examined below.

Integration of machines, computers and software. The new technology was an integration of machines, computers and software. First, an automatic conveyor linking different work stations was a major change. In particular, card trays were no longer carried from one station to another. The rhythm of work was no longer established by the handling of the trays but by the speed of the conveyor, thereby requiring tighter co-ordination and better communication among employees. The second technological change, computer-assisted design (CAD) meant that the card was designed in a laboratory located 200 kilometres away. Manufacturing information was then transferred to the Montreal factory and integrated into the manufacturing database, giving operators automatic access to the blueprints at their work station. Finally, procedures and methods were easily accessible through a computer program which enabled operators to consult their computer screen for manufacturing procedures and quality tests to be made on batches. The work design increased flexibility and decreased reaction time. Moreover, management had automatic access to all the information on the whole production process, the efficiency of each team and the volume of the conveyor. Technology is a non-human actor introduced into the network that has modified the traditional organization of work by transforming the operators' tasks and acting on modes of co-ordination. In technical terms, traditional work could be divided individually since each operator was given a tray with a precise number of electronic cards on which he would carry out pre-determined tasks. By adding a conveyor, products could circulate continuously. Rather than being set by the employees, the pace of work depended on the speed of the conveyor. Also, the uniform size of the printed circuit cards allowed for more flexible manufacturing of batches without having to modify equipment. Certain tests and verifications were computerized.

The introduction of CAM influenced the circulation of information, drawings and documentation, and instructions became available on-screen, eliminating the need for a human intermediary. Use of a bar code to number cards meant that batches could be quickly identified in order to access files and activate automatic operations. The operators used visual on-screen aids to carry out assembly operations and tests, quality control and product cycle times. Each work station therefore had a computer. The conveyor and CAM thus met the objective formulated, the manufacturing process became flexible. Performance and production volume on assembly lines were available. In addition, the activities were identified with the operator who carried them out.

The conveyor and CAM were designed to eliminate the individualization of work. The team thus co-ordinated activities according to the orders received on-screen. There were now fewer manual tasks required of the employee. He was at the interface between the screen and product. He was collectively responsible for the expected results in terms of quality, quantity and production cycle. The new technical work organization required more communication between production workers. The latter had to document the work and indicate the procedures followed. Upstream, the work of one employee directly affected another employee's work downstream. In addition, as regards the physical layout of the premises, the supervisors' offices were moved outside the department in order to foster teamwork that is not strictly supervised. Since it is technology that makes this possible, it was enrolled in the innovation network.

Social design of the shop floor. Another type of innovation affected the social design of the shop floor and was aimed at adding more flexibility to the production process. The 200 job descriptions that existed under the previous form of work organization were reduced to just ten by breaking them down into primary and secondary tasks. The operators are at the intersection of the computer and the product, between the production goals and the outcomes in terms of quality, quantity, time schedule and delivery time. For management, this requires obedience and conformity to the rules on the part of the operators. They have to adhere strictly to the procedures included in the computer program. Thus, the work process has become more formal than ever.

Teamwork cells, composed of operators and technicians, were made responsible for the complete assembly of the card. The members of the team also became responsible for assigning tasks amongst themselves as well as for the work schedule and quality control. Nonetheless, the goals in each of these areas were established by the managers, based on clients' orders. Supervisors were replaced by team leaders who acted as coaches. The innovations were created in accordance with a deliberate process in which employees were requested to passively accept their assigned role. This way of constructing the problem had an impact on the identity of workers because the concept of socio-technical design in itself reduces the autonomy of workers while managers continued to claim that it is increasing.

The enrolment of technology is important in at least two respects. Firstly, it is designed at a predetermined, not a haphazard moment in the chain of events. Technology establishes the elements of innovation that are stabilized and oblige others to support it. In this case study, if the workers had been mobilized before the technology was enrolled, innovation would have gone another way. Workers played a limited role at the moment when technology was designed. The Core Group avoided enrolling them too early since technology is not negotiable.

Secondly, within scientific and technical limits, technology establishes the role that is desired of others. Technology speaks for itself. It has its own identity and it controls mathematically modelled activities through algorithms. It intervenes by accelerating the pace of production, standardizing quality and reducing production cycles as well as set-up time. Technology thus had a number of characteristics that met the desired objectives at the point of *interessement* of workers by the Core Group. But the social characteristics of technology required an intermediary, or spokesperson. It was the Core Group that spread the idea that team work was the organizational form that comes with the technology. Human Resources managers created the conditions for team work that included autonomous, skilled, responsible and committed workers. Technology had a spokesperson that idealized what could be accomplished. Thus technology made this form of work organization possible but did not directly enrol the workers.

The activation of technology as a non-human actor in a symmetrical role is interesting in itself. What gives rise to criticism is the fact that this actor does not act alone, but is created, developed and interpreted by others who include in it their own conception of productivity and social order, as Bloomfield (1986) stated, through a typified representation of what it should be. Our focus in what follows will be the trajectory taken by this socio-technical innovation.

THE PROCESS OF *INTERESSMENT*: THE CONSTITUTION OF AN INNOVATION NETWORK

Innovation became a complex process comprising several different simultaneous change programmes, including the design of the card, the choice of information technology, and its integration with a new HR philosophy of team work. The firm's leaders adopted a dominant discourse based on Japanese experiences according to which it is necessary to involve those who are most knowledgeable about the product manufacturing process and can adequately meet the client's needs. A multidisciplinary team had a weekend meeting at a resort hotel to determine Opto World values and mission. In order to succeed in making these changes, the authors of the network launched an initial project involving workers who were prepared to support the innovation. The underlying logic of this strategy was that a success would promote innovation throughout the plant and serve as a means for *interessement* and *enrolment* of other employees. A senior manager commented on the goal in these terms:

> . . . Relying on a dynamic and committed team, to aim for excellence in the field of telecommunications so as to satisfy the needs of our clients and thus become the leader world-wide.

A special committee called the Core Group was created to put these innovations together. The members of the Core Group designed the technological and social facets of the workplace and then attempted to enlarge their influence by enrolling other members of management as well as workers. The Core Group was initially composed of engineers and managers who were supported and trusted by senior management. The ties within the Core Group were based on members' shared knowledge of how to build and support the innovation. Although there was no formal hierarchy in the network an informal hierarchy formed on the basis of status, which in turn depended on knowledge of technology, the production system and workplace innovation. An engineer who dealt with the technical aspects of innovation and a human resources advisor who dealt with the social aspects quickly became the project's leaders. Once the innovation was implemented, the project's chief engineer was appointed as one of the firm's vice-presidents. The Core Group received the financial support needed to set up the innovation. It began with the following general criterion: increased flexibility based on advanced technology, small batch production and quality improvement. In the logic of efficiency shared by the members of the network, teamwork became a means of adapting human resources to the technology and production requirements. The involvement of employees was a way to accomplish the change. The HR managers were dominant in this phase since HR was responsible for designing the teamwork structure as well as for selecting and training the employees. In this regard, the innovation also consisted of fostering a new attitude and behaviour within the workforce. However, employees did not react passively to the identities proposed by the authors. The Core Group therefore structured the issues around job security and set up two *interessement* mechanisms to win employee support for the innovation project: job security and wages.

Job Security

In 1974, 1000 of the 2000 employees were operators; by 1986 the number of operators had grown to 1200; by 1997, however, the number had dropped to 885. The downsizing consisted of a twofold plan. First, ELCOM management closed three of its four Montreal plants and transferred production to sub-contractors or to ELCOM establishments in other countries. Second, ELCOM management decided to cease the production of obsolete products and strengthen the units that made competitive products, such as the optonumerical cards. As a result, senior employees changed plants or departments, but employees with less seniority lost their jobs.

Consequently, job security became a major issue for the remaining employees and operated as a device to create support for the innovation. Indeed, the employees who were assigned to the Opto World work stations improved their chances of keeping their jobs. With huge production cost savings and higher efficiency and quality, Opto World had a brighter future than did the traditional departments. Traditionally, internal transfers depended on skills and seniority. Given equal skills, the worker with more seniority obtained the position. However, this rule was bypassed. Those in charge of human resources in the Core Group assigned new position numbers when the 200 job descriptions were reduced to ten. This protected the Opto World employees because qualification and, by extension, skill were exclusive to Opto World employees. No employee could displace them. In this context of downsizing, Opto World became attractive to employees who wished to have job security.

Wages

The union and ELCOM management concluded an agreement that provided a better classification system and wages that reached the top level of the salary scale. When the job descriptions were reorganized (from 200 to 10), those responsible for human resources in the Core Group integrated class 3 job descriptions into class 4. The reclassification therefore benefited employees, resulting in promotions and wage increases. The independent ELCOM union was advised of the changes when the project started, but because the Core Group was an ad hoc structure, they were excluded from it. The union's traditional role was limited to negotiating the collective agreement and thus at other times, it was unable to mobilize its members. Otherwise, the union did not take part in either the discussion or decision making regarding the design of the innovation. Hence, the union positioned itself as a satellite of the network, taking only low-profile actions regarding the innovation.

According to the translation precept of actor–network theory, these were two crucial mechanisms of *interessement*. They were led by the *primens movens* (the Core Group) with the aim of motivating workers to seal an alliance by becoming interested in the innovation and playing their assigned roles. Nonetheless, the transformation of shop floor work organization must be achieved through an implicit harmonization of managers' and employees' contributions. In sum, the innovation network was a heterogeneous system composed of engineers, HR managers, selected workers, the optonumerical card, the collective agreement, technology and new production concepts such as flexibility, quality and teamwork. The aim of the enlarged Core Group was now to attract designated employees, who would be invited to play a new but strictly limited role as members of work teams. This was more than a simple job transfer, and involved playing a new role. The authors of the network sought to reconstruct the workers' identity and have them take on characteristics such as involvement, the teamwork mindset, client satisfaction, quality, standardization of work methods, open communication, non-conflictual relations and conformism.

It was necessary to attract workers to the network mainly as members of the work teams, not as joint designers of innovation. The process of *enrolment* consisted of breaking the routines associated with the segmented jobs in the traditional production units and having workers accept new behaviours with additional responsibilities and a new work ethic. The knowledge, and especially the know-how of the operators, were useless to the core Group. Thus, it was not the operators from the former workplace who were engaged in the Network, but individuals with the teamwork mindset who could easily abandon old habits and take on a new challenge. This new identity was necessary, according to Core Group members, including the employees associated with it but whose representativeness was questionable. The construction of the problem led to the adoption of *interessement* strategies in which identities were defined but the primary aim was to impose and stabilize these identities. This stage only succeeds once the allies mobilize themselves; otherwise, the result is dissidence and resistance.

THE STRATEGY OF *ENROLMENT*

The selection of employees to work in the Opto World unit was a major phase of the workplace agreement. It consisted of selecting the 150 'best' employees on an individual basis. An intended consequence of this operation devised by the Core Group was to suppress the collective ties originating in the former pattern of work organization while building a new corporate identity that would embrace all categories of employees and managers. Tests of applicants' psychological traits and technical skills were developed to select the appropriate operators.

The Core Group wanted to create a competitive spirit among the employees, to challenge them to become a member of a model team that would lead the others towards 'Excellence'. The tests devised by the HR managers discriminated between the employees by classifying them into four categories: the *team players* and the *team leaders* were automatically selected and included as members of Opto World; but the *loners* and the *introverts* were rejected. As an HR manager expressed it: 'We didn't look only for the skills, but also for a mindset . . . people who like to work as a team and like to work with machines . . .'. The Core Group wanted high performance from workers, but only the 'best' workers who were already in favour of the innovation.

The design of the teamwork model and the selection of the first generation of teamwork employees were part of a strategy of legitimization. The arrangement was put in place to serve as an example of a new context of co-operation and a new way of dealing with employees in an increasingly competitive market. The Excellence and Ownership programme was particularly designed to instil a new attitude towards quality, continuous improvement and accountability based on client satisfaction. In fact, the Excellence and Ownership programme put the emphasis on management values, encouraging employees to think like entrepreneurs and develop their team and their job in accordance with the values of productivity, technology and efficiency. The aim of the programme was to make the employees' attitudes and behaviours a carbon copy of those of managers. An engineer commented on workers' attitudes in the following terms: '. . . the operators are not smart enough to learn the new concepts of production quickly, that's why they have to be educated on the new philosophy of production'. However, the programme put too much emphasis on the values of productivity to the detriment of collective values such as those rooted in the informal habits of operators. This is illustrated by the following comment by one of the managers:

> I am interested in competition and in ways of increasing our productivity; everything I do is driven only by efficiency criteria. Culture is not an aim . . . I leave culture to the communists!

The ideology of productivity underlying the Excellence and Ownership programme was subsequently replaced by ISO, which was more functionally-oriented. ISO was an instrumental guide put in place to reach the organization's goals. The employees internalized the new quality norms, accepting them as routine and conforming to them. The ISO norms matched their own work ethic since they made quality, as opposed to quantity and efficient work load, the ultimate goal of production.

The first year of the project proved the Core Group to be correct. The operators enrolled in the network consented to the new productivity and quality organization and the production cycle was shortened from 20 to 8 days. A member of the Core Group commented:

> . . . at the beginning of Opto World, it was a great success. We shared a team spirit, communication between different levels of the organization was very good, we knew where we were going, we shared the same goals, everyone knowing the expectations of the others. But we were only 150 people, we were a small organization at the time, it was more manageable than it is now and then . . . it was a real success!

A new spirit was created, but after a while, the translation process began to have the opposite result, contributing to a split in the plant between two distinct categories of employees – those in Opto World, derisively called 'Another World', and those in the rest of the plant. the analogy is by no means insignificant. It indicates that the workers in other departments were distancing themselves from the employees recruited by Opto World who, in their view, were more assimilated into the Core Group than their own employee group. The boundaries between 'Them' and 'Us' were drawn, temporarily, since the situation would later reverse itself.

MOBILIZATION AND RESISTANCE

After a while, a failure in the translation chain became apparent. The attempts of the Core Group to attract the 'top notch' operators through the use of ideological and functional arguments as well as psychological tests and exams were not as successful as had been expected. In particular, the Core Group underestimated the influence of past events and conventions. Even though the 'best' employees complied with the regulation, they repeated some behaviours from the former organizational structure of work. In the traditional production units, operators could receive up to 20 per cent of the first year's production savings resulting from their suggestions. However, the suggestion box was not implemented in Opto World. From the point of view of the Core Group, employees were part of the new design and it was their responsibility and role to try to improve the process by every means available. They had a moral obligation to make suggestions that could improve such things as work design and procedures. Moreover, they had a higher classification and better wages, meaning that they were already paid for improvements as a part of their task. Nevertheless, the employees felt that they were not treated fairly compared to the others, and so they refused to co-operate by withholding suggestions that might improve production and quality. It appears that cutting off the suggestion program created a significant obstacle to making employees more responsible.

> A lot of people said they had good ideas, but they'd keep them to themselves because they [the managers] didn't want to pay . . . Right now suggestions are being made, but I think people are holding back because everyone is waiting for the suggestions to pay off. (An operator)

For the Core Group, the new workplace had been created to cope with competition by increasing productivity through advanced technology and high-performance workers. For their part, unsatisfied employees asked for more economic incentives, by demanding financial rewards for their suggestions in the same way as other employees.

The Core Group was seeking to foster positive attitudes regarding involvement, empowerment and team thinking on the part of new employees. But the engineers and managers also had some qualms about employee input. They felt threatened when an operator made a suggestion, regarding it as a criticism of their ideas and arrangements. Opto World was a conformist world based on a non-adversarial relationship. In this environment of docility, any question could become a threat. The search for non-conflictual relationships gradually became an obstacle to the expansion of the network as seen by the Core Group. However, it had become part of the network, which meant that problems had to be overcome before going further. Each member of Opto World had come to develop his or her own way of coping with difficulties instead of finding a collective or consensual solution. The relentless pursuit of conformity translated directly from the technological design, blinding the network and obstructing any sort of negotiation between the actors.

The selection of the best employees did not prove sufficient to discipline the employees. The new values – such as respect, dignity, involvement, teamwork thinking, innovation and client satisfaction – were promoted by 'teamwork' but in the minds of employees they could not be implemented without direct negotiations. Moreover, the workers were not powerless. They came to the network with their own demands and expectations. They were certainly not the silent and docile members sought by the authors of the network. Instead of meeting the authors' expectations, they interpreted the innovation according to a logic specific to their identity as workers.

A new source of authority appeared as engineers gained influence over the technical organization of the shop floor and, as the principal designers of the department, increased their influence and power over social organization. Within the network, they became the spokespersons of high-tech design and of the productivist ideology. Their new authority increased managerial pressure and power over the employees. Their role changed from one of providing support and service to the assembly line to one of direct line management. They were part of the team, were present on the shop floor and took part in the everyday life of Opto World. As the work of the operators became less physical and more dependent on a keener knowledge of procedures, including knowledge of the software developed by the engineers, the engineers provided direct feedback to the operators in a paperless relationship. They became the experts of the socio-technical design of work, those who knew how to manage and regulate the complex mixture of the new product, the new process and the new production goals. There were signs of the rising influence of engineers over line managers and operators.

Technology was a disappointment for the operators. It did not play the role that the Core Group had said it would. In the language of ANT, it offered less than what was promised. Hence, the operators were making fewer decisions based on their judgement and on the informal know-how acquired by on-the-job experiences. As a consequence, when they could, the operators bypassed some of the procedures established by the engineers. With one accord, employees worked according to their own logical sequences and, with the exception of quality auditing, they organized their tasks according to their experience, skills and know-how. They eventually organized the work collectively, thereby rejecting the Core Group's vision of teamwork, that is, as no more than the sum of upgraded individuals. For its part, management bypassed the quality rules to meet tight schedules and increase production. Thus, an informal workplace organization was taking root and two distinct representations of the new work design were emerging, one held by the managers and engineers and the other by the employees. For the latter, the problem was the result of a number of specific circumstances that created disorder. First, the employees lost sight of the original concept. After a while, the operators reverted to the methods they had used previously in the traditional work organization. The identity that the Core Group had wished to establish vacillated, making way for an unexpected itinerary through with employees imposed new intermediaries. Second, the department grew too rapidly and the managers lost control over the training process. As a pilot project in work organization, Opto World started with 150 operators, but over the next three years it grew to 450 operators. Moreover, although employees continued to be selected on the basis of the same tests, the promotion cut-off point was lowered. As one engineer put it, '. . . this is the second string players, they are less responsible, less efficient . . .'. According to the logic promoted by the authors of the network, only individuals mattered. According to the Core Group member responsible for human resources, growth had been too rapid, not leaving her enough time to 'indoctrinate' the employees.

Gradually, the supposed advantages like responsibility, the satisfaction of working together as a team and increased influence over decision-making proved insufficient in themselves. The employees reported that, even though the department was modern and up-to-date, they did not feel more responsible or empowered. Employees were given no input into production rules or group norms; and they were given no say in decisions related to the work load, team members, work methods or tools. The gap between what was said and what was actually done was so great that the training received by employees was quickly forgotten. Instead, their contributions were limited to minor decisions such as the choice of ergonomic chairs for their work stations or electric screwdrivers. After a while, some of them started to stretch out their breaks, be absent more often, go outdoors for a cigarette or make personal phone calls on the job. Employees referred to Human Resources as 'Human Remains' in a derisory manner, indicating that Opto World workers had distanced themselves from the Core Group as spokesperson. Workers no longer identified with the Core Group and a boundary was drawn between the two, a sad reminder that the promises made as part of *interessement* had not been kept. Opto World had not been designed to control employees, but they felt that they had lost their autonomy and their identity in the name of better quality control, the procedures or the product itself. As one employee said:

> The work hasn't changed, the task hasn't changed, but what has changed is that we're asked for more information to improve the product. So, what has changed is quality management, not the work organization.

The employees soon began to develop informal production quotas and to slow down the speed of the conveyor by filling out ESR and DCR forms. Instead of combining the skills of employees with the special knowledge of engineers as a way of finding solutions to production and technical problems, a technocratic purpose was pursued with the introduction of the ESR (Engineering Services Request) and DCR (Document Changes Request) forms. In order to better control production interruptions, engineers introduced these forms, which had to be completed by operators when a problem occurred. These forms are seen by some operators as decreasing their decision-making autonomy. But for others, they were seen as a gain of influence over the production process since their requests were now written down and effective as long as the problem was not solved. The pace of work thus slowed down, enabling the operators to work extra hours at overtime rates. In the traditional production units, working overtime was considered substandard performance, as was a production slowdown. Thus, workers could still take initiatives after learning the ropes at Opto World and still take advantage of the informal organization. The patterns of behaviour that had been present in the older departments were slowly being reintroduced into Opto World.

The chain of translation was broken because the authors of innovation did not understand the real issues of concern to employees. After a while, employees began to complain about the inequity and the weight of the workload. Training was no longer a way of socializing, and the work cell information meetings became shorter and less frequent to avoid taking away from production time. Employees complained about this reduction since they had no time to meet, to socialize and to find solutions to technical and organizational difficulties.

Finally, both sides came to the same conclusion, though on the basis of very different arguments. The managers and engineers claimed that the employees did not understand the productivity and efficiency goals, whereas the employees criticized the weakness of collective and social means to create a genuine teamwork orientation. The failure of the project soon sparked a process of blaming the other side. Teamwork had no real roots. It was not designed as a collective way of working but rather as an individual way of linking skills and mind. According to the employees, teamwork ran into trouble because common sense was missing from a project which was too narrowly conceived and which had been implemented according to a logic of efficiency that did not take into consideration any real knowledge of the operators' relationships on the shop floor.

At the outset, the managers aimed to create a model of work methods and a teamwork attitude that would be extended to the entire plant, but eventually the opposite occurred. The traditional practices of the older forms of work organization were introduced into Opto World and gradually 'contaminated' the team spirit such as it was conceived by the initial Core Group. The argument of efficiency served as a guideline for other logics and, in the minds of the Core Group, the teamwork mindset should have been subordinated to that destiny. The desired merging of identities failed. Despite being chosen carefully, the employees had an identity that was much closer to that of their co-workers and workers in other departments than to the one proposed by the Core Group.

DISCUSSION: THE CONSEQUENCES OF THE INNOVATION PROCESS

Zuboff's study (1988) observed that workers' sense of their professional identity is marked by their understanding and attachment to tangible entities of their work. Technology distances them from this sensitivity. Thus, it may be said that the disenchantment created by Opto World did not only relate to the limited and unsatisfactory role of the workers *vis-à-vis* the socio-technical system, but also to what remained in terms of concrete tasks to be accomplished. The operator reacted. He first of all agreed, but then refused to do what he was told to do by the Core

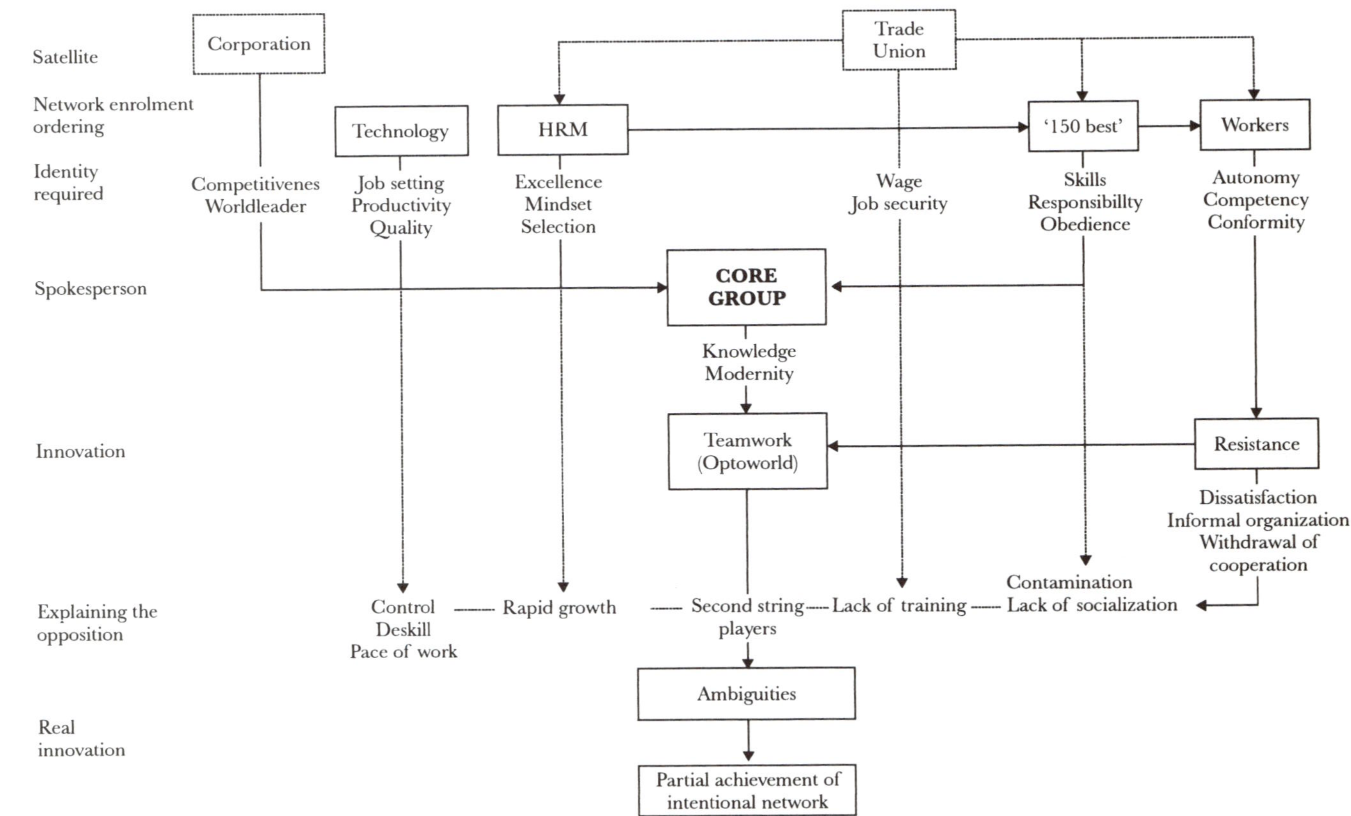

Figure 1. The constitution and ordering of an actor–network

Group. We came on the scene at that point and observed an episode of this process. Technology was already enrolled. It was already a component of the network, one that functioned based on its own properties as well as those imposed by the Core Group. Workers also played a role in the network, but their disappointment and subsequent disillusion revealed another facet of it. The workers were interested, then enrolled in a socio-technical whole. Thus, the reaction of the workers not only related to the technology but to this whole. A withdrawal of co-operation indicates disagreement concerning a project's direction by the rejection of rules that others accept. To be meaningful, a refusal to co-operate must lead to a realignment of the translation chain which, from then on, must follow this obligatory passageway of workers' patterns of relations and values. Otherwise, innovations will be slowed down. The Core Group planned what it thought was a perfect implementation of *interessement* mechanisms with the aim of enrolling workers, and imposing and stabilizing identities. The authors proposed several *interessement* mechanisms: restructuring the context by transferring production and downsizing; persuasion by increasing wages and classification; instillation of new ideas through training and meetings; forcing support through tests and exams; seduction with images such as 'You are the cream of the crop', and manipulation of identity with ideas such as 'Each employee is an entrepreneur'. These were the management's symbols and myths, which were driven by power, but wrapped up in an egalitarian discourse. However, this social dimension set by the Core Group had only a low level of legitimacy in the view of workers who were invited to support the network by conforming. Workers were not the docile agents that management made them out to be. By selecting workers who were compatible with their own representations, managers and engineers expected to rely on relationships of trust and thus save on costly bureaucratic controls. The authors represented identities without any real knowledge of workers' normative and cognitive systems. They believed that these representations were neutral and apolitical. In fact, the Core Group reified workers, treating them as a malleable components without history, social ties or any other membership in a collectivity outside the company. The Core Group's view resembled Olson's representation of agents, which suggests that individuals act out of a rational choice, solely in order to maximize their personal interests (Abel, 1995; Olson, 1982), and as if workers had no past, but only a future.

Workers were reluctant to support an innovation in which there was no place for an identity based on autonomy, socialization and solidarity. They were opposed to the psychologization of work and assimilation to corporate goals (McKinlay and Taylor, 1996). They introduced unanticipated and unwelcome activities and behaviours into the network, thus making it necessary to negotiate in order to counter resistance. The Core Group was not diverted by the employees' collective values nor by the inclusion of unfamiliar identity sources in the network. Instead, they wanted to construct the teamwork innovation on individuality and technological skills. This representation of workers' identity was deceptive. Employees did not adhere to arguments for efficiency and productivity, thinking that high-tech development would gradually contribute to the erosion of skills. Nor did employees believe in the social dimension of the innovation, which had been dictated by external realities such as the perceived need to increase sales, increase production capacity and develop the most modern plant in order to outdistance competitors. The workers did not see the Core Group as speaking for them.

Jenkins (1996) showed that identity is never simple, but rather it is constructed by objective criteria such as qualifications and classifications, which are the external signs of membership in an employee group. However, subjective criteria refer to a desire to belong to a specific group. We have shown that an identity cannot be created spontaneously, as the Core Croup would have liked, but that it involves a long process. This is particularly relevant in the present case since the Core Group was trying to form new identities by breaking down traditional boundaries between itself and workers and by creating similarities based on symbolic values of all the allied groups. However, what the workers saw were managers concerned about increasing productivity and they therefore projected an identity founded on differences. The interests of workers and managers are distinct (Kelly and Kelly, 1991) and workers are perfectly capable of making this distinction.

As an element of the network, high tech contributed to extending a production system in such a manner that it became an intermediary to anyone else who wanted to join the network. Technology possesses its own basic strengths, rooted in technical and scientific rationality (Scarbrough and Corbett, 1992). Conservative values – such as maintenance of the *status quo* in social structures and failure to recognize the human being as anything more than an instrument of production – are also connected to technology, itself reinforced by ideologies such as 'productivity', 'competitiveness' and 'efficiency'. Technology is allied to human beings who have particular social values to defend, as shown by Bloomfield (1986). It becomes a tie, becoming more and more inflexible as the alliance grows in the network. The process was complex because the Core Group did not want to treat the worker merely as an extension of the machine. They wanted to integrate the worker into the managerial function. The technology worked, the operator accomplished a number of tasks well, but he operated further downstream in the production process. His vision of work had to be integrated into that of the managers. Work knowledge was increasingly concentrated in the hands of the engineers and the commitment of the workers was achieved through management functions. This is why so much attention is paid to the selection, training, socialization and creation of a normative 'mindset'. In an innovation design network, anything is still possible, but the workers were excluded as a social group from this essential phase of innovation. The study examined an adoption network in which the actors' desired techniques and role were stabilized and in which the *primens movens* recruited new actors through the intervention of new intermediaries. The transformation itself is the product of judgements and decisions at different stages of the process technology (Clark et al., 1988). The actor who is interested and attracted by the innovation has to adhere to this alliance. The more it structures, the more technology becomes imperative and replaces other social components, such as solidarity and working-group collective identity. When it is enrolled in a network, technology spreads out quickly and becomes normal, as if it had always been there. This is precisely what the workers rejected.

The prescriptive design set by the Core Group breeds a culture of conformity and obedience. Indeed, it is not coincidental that employee participation in the design, choice and adoption of technology is very weak (Fulk, 1993; Reshef et al., 1994). Workers are only included in the decision-making process when they possess specific knowledge that is critical to the process. Usually, only the experts are concerned, knowledge being a precondition for participation. One of the engineers at ELCOM stated:

> We can't call a meeting just to see if there is some solution to problems . . . it doesn't matter anyway because problems are technical by nature and they can't be solved by this kind of participatory meeting.

The real innovation was not the blueprint that was initially drawn up by the Core Group. The new workplace is neither a carbon copy of idealized relationships based on excellence nor an informal setting in which employees gain some autonomy, but rather a workplace wherein power and influence are still at stake between management and labour. ANT explains how consent is established and how it ensures that some actors will have legitimacy and the right to speak. As Burawoy (1979) has pointed out, legitimacy is important because managers not only want to regulate or direct, but want to do it with workers' consent. Consent is achieved by organizing and aligning arguments that will lead workers to adopt a formal conduct that conforms to that sought by managers. Network analysis is a highly useful tool for examining the process of innovation through ordered representation of diffuse phenomena. In this regard, ANT is more heuristic than theoretical (Law, 1994; Michael, 1996) and can be use to reconstruct the sequence of translation of all the means and mechanisms used in the *interessement* of workers. It illustrates how the new dominant configuration was constituted through an *ad hoc* operating procedure which generated its own effectiveness through a series of decisions made in situations of uncertainty and according to the actors' reaction. As Law (1994) stated, ANT reveals how new hierarchies are formed and how traditional hierarchies are deconstructed. It would therefore be wrong to view the relations established through the innovation process as a simple continuation of previous relations. These mechanisms of *interessement* did not simply reproduce an already existing type of relations. Rather they legitimated domination, which took on a new face through differently organized language and symbols (Sewell, 1998). Subjectivity was manipulated and workers contributed to their own subordination while at the same time putting up resistance and refusing to legitimate the domination. What emerged here was the establishment of new rules of co-ordination and the rejection of former ones. Vallas and Beck (1996) have already shown how actors – in the present case engineers – develop skills which put them at the centre of relations of domination through the acquistion of new codified knowledge, mastery of technologies and control of the social arrangements which have been adopted.

CONCLUSION

The empirical data presented above are based on the conception of a network which was organized through authority, required unilateral support and in which consensus was forced. It was neither voluntary nor free. Participation was less unified than it appeared since the actors participated through plans which had been established in advance by a design network. Industrial organization is ruled by agreements and institutions which cannot be completely dismantled overnight by organizational innovations. In the case studied here, innovation was a top-down process which was driven by the structure of roles, was close to the hierarchy of knowledge and know-how and had little mutuality in the labour–management relationship. Innovation provided the opportunity to create new forms of co-operation through the interaction of actors and objects. Nevertheless, the alliances created in the network were weak and confined. The innovation network was also shaped by agreements and predetermined patterns of relations oriented by management and efficiency ideologies, as well as by workers' expectations about collective relationships. The reconstitution of the innovation process in terms of a chain of translation highlighted a network which members joined according to the representation of their identity. Technology was enrolled in the network as the bridgehead, meeting productivity needs and supporting the hegemonic place occupied by the engineers within the organization. The network's authors attempted to forge an identity for human beings, but this identity for the workers was controversial and was reinterpreted in an unexpected way, thereby breaking the planned series of innovation sequences.

REFERENCES

Abel, P. (1995). 'The new institutionalism and rational choice theory'. In Scott, R. W. and Christensen, S. (Eds), *The Institutional Construction of Organizations. International and Longitudinal Studies*. Thousand Oaks, London and New Delhi: Sage, 3–14.

Alter, N. (1993). 'Innovation et organisation deux légitimités en concurrence'. *Revue française de sociologie*, **XXXIX**, 2, 175–97.

Appelbaum, E. and Batt, R. (1994). *The New American Workplace*. Ithaca, NY: ILR Press.

Barley, S. (1986). 'Technology as an occasion for structuring: evidence from observations of CT scanners and the social order of radiology departments'. *Administrative Science Quarterly*, **35**, 61–103.

Barley, S. R. and Bechky, B. A. (1994). 'In the backroom of science: the work of technicians in science labs'. *Work and Occupations*, **21**, 1, 85–126.

Barnett, W. P. and Carroll, G. R. (1995). 'Modeling internal organizational change'. In Hagan, J. and Cook, K. S. (Eds), *Annual Review of Sociology*, **21**, 217–36.

Batt, R. (1999). 'Work organization, technology, and performance in customer service and sales'. *Industrial and Labor Relations Review*, **52**, 4, 539–64.

Berger, P. L. and Luckmann, T. (1966). *The Social Construction of Reality, A Treatise in the Sociology of Knowledge*. New-York, London, Toronto, Sydney, Auckland: Anchor Books, Doubleday.

Bijker, W., Hugues, T. and Pinch, T. (Eds) (1987). *The Social Construction of Technological Systems*. Cambridge, MA: MIT Press.

Bloomfield, B. P. (1986). *Modelling the World. The Social Constructions of Systems Analysts*. Oxford: Basil Blackwell.

Bloomfield, B. P. and Coombs, R. (1992). 'Information technology, control and power; the centralization and decentralization debate revisited'. *Journal of Management Studies*, **29**, 4, 459–84.

Braverman, H. (1986). *Labor and Monopoly Capital*. New York: Monthly Review Press.

Brown, A. D. (1998). 'Narrative, politics and legimacy in IT implementation'. *Journal of Management Studies*, **35**, 1, 35–58.

Burawoy, M. (1979). *Manufacturing Consent: Changes in the Labor Process under Monopoly Capitalism*. Chicago: The University of Chicago Press.

Callon, M. (1986a). 'Some elements in a sociology of translation: domestication of the scallops and fishermen of St Brieuc Bay'. In Law, J. (Ed.), *Action, Belief and Power*. London: Routledge, 196–233.

Callon, M. (1986b). 'The sociology of an actor-network: the case of the electric vehicle'. In Callon, M., Law, J. and Rip, A. (Eds), *Mapping the Dynamics of Science and Technology*. London: Routledge, 19–34.

CALLON, M. (1992). 'Variété et irréversabilité dans les réseaux de conception et d'adoption des techniques'. In Foray, D. and Freeman, C. (Eds), *Technologie et richesse des nations.* Paris: Economica, 275–324.

CALLON, M. (1995). 'L'innovation technologique et ses mythes' (Technological innovation and its myths). In Boucher, L. (Ed.), *La recherche sur l'innovation, une boîte de Pandore?* (*Reserch on Innovation. A Pandora's Box?*), Actes du colloque multidisciplinaire Recherche en innovation, tenu dans le cadre du congrès de l'Acfas à Montréal en mai 1994, Montreal: Acfas, Les cahiers scientifiques, 83, 5–29.

CALLON, M. and LATOUR, B. (1991). *La science telle qu'elle se fait – Anthologie de la sociologie des sciences de langue anglaise.* (*Science as it is made – Anthology of English Sociology of Science*). Paris: Editions La Découverte.

CAPPELLI, P., BASSI, L., KATZ, H., KNOKE, D., OSTERMAN, P. and USEEM, M. (1997). *Change at Work.* New York and Oxford: Oxford University Press.

CHILD, J. (1972). 'Organizational structure, environnement and performance: the role of strategic choice.' *Sociology*, **6**, 1–22.

CLARK, J., MCLAUGHLIN, I., ROSE, H. and KING, R. (1988). *The Process of Technological Change: New Technologies and Social Change in the Workplace.* Cambridge: Cambridge United Press.

COLLINS, H. M. and YEARLEY, S. (1992). 'Epistemological chicken'. In Pickering, A. (Ed.), *Science as Practice and Culture.* Chicago: Chicago University Press, 301–26.

COOKE, W. N. (1989). 'Improving productivity and quality through collaboration'. *Industrial Relations*, **28**, 2, 299–319.

CUNNINGHAM, I., HYMAN, J. and BALDRY C. (1996). 'Empowerment: the power to do what?'. *Industrial Relations Journal*, **27**, 2, 143–55.

DURAND, J.-P. (Ed.) (1994). *La fin du modèle suédois.* Paris: Syros.

DURKHEIM, E. (1950). *Leçons de sociologie. (Lessons of sociology).* Paris: Quadrige/Presses Universitaires de France (1995).

EDWARDS, P. (1986). *Conflict at Work.* Oxford: Basil Blackwell.

EMIRBAYER, M. and GOOGWIN, J. (1994). 'Network analysis, culture, and the problem of agency'. *American Journal of Sociology*, **99**, 6, 1411–54.

EZZAMEL, M. and WILLMOTT, H. (1998). 'Accounting for teamwork: a critical study of group-based systems of organizational control'. *Administrative Science Quarterly*, **43**, 358–96.

FREEMAN, C. (1991). 'Networks of innovators: a synthesis of research issues'. *Research Policies*, **20**, 499–514.

FULK, J. (1993). 'Social construction of communication technology'. *Academy of Management Journal*, **36**, 5, 921–50.

GALASKIEWICZ, J. and WASSERMAN, S. (1994). 'Introduction: advances in the social and behavioral sciences from social network analysis'. In Wasserman S. and Galaskiewicz, J. (Eds), *Advances in Social Network Analysis.* Thousand Oaks, London, New Delhi: Sage, xi–xvii.

GATTIKER, U. E. (1990). *Technology Management in Organizations.* Newbury Park, CA: Sage.

GERGEN, K. J. (1985). 'The social constructionist movement in modern psychology'. *American Psychologist*, **40**, 266–75.

GIDDENS, A. (1984). *The Constitution of Society*, Cambridge: Polity Press.

GRAHAM, L. (1993). 'Inside a Japanese transplant – a critical perspective'. *Work and Occupations*, **29**, 47–173.

GRIFFITH, L. (1999). 'Technology features as triggers for sensemaking'. *Academy of Management Review*, **24**, 3, 472–88.

HASSARD, J. (1994). 'Postmodern organisational analysis: toward a conceptual framework'. *Journal of Management Studies*, **31**, 3, 303–24.

HECKSCHER, C., EISENSTAT, R. A. and RICE, T. J. (1994). 'Transformational processes'. In Heckscher, C. and Donnelson, A. (Eds), *The Post-Bureaucratic Organization. New Perspectives on Organizational Change.* Thousand Oaks: Sage, 129–77.

HELLER, F. A., PUSIC, E., STRAUSS, G. and WILPERT, B. (1998). *Organizational Participation: Myth and Reality*. New York: Oxford University Press.

HODSON, R. (1995). 'Worker resistance: an underdeveloped concept in the sociology of work'. *Economic and Industrial Democracy*, **16**, 79–111.

HOGG, M. A. and ABRAM, D. (1988). *Social Identifications: A Social Psychology of Intergroup Relations and Group Processes.* London: Routledge.

HUGHES, T. P. (1987). 'The evolution of large technological systems'. In Bijker, W., Hughes T. and Pinch T. (Eds), *The Social Construction of Technological Systems.* Cambridge, MA: MIT Press, 51–82.

JENKINS, R. (1996). *Social Identity.* London: Routledge.

JERMIER, J. M., KNIGHTS, D. and NORD, W. R. (Eds) (1994). *Resistance and Power in Organizations.* London and New York: Routledge, 1–24.

KELLY, J. (1998). *Rethinking Industrial Relations. Mobilization, Collectivism and Long Waves.* London: Routledge and LSE.

KELLY, J. and KELLY, C. (1991). 'Them and us. Social psychology and the new industrial relations'. *British Journal of Industrial Relations*, **29**, 1, 25–48.

KERFOOT, D. and KNIGHTS, D. (1995). 'Empowering the "quality" worker? The seduction and contradiction of the total quality phenomenon'. In Wilkinson A. and Willmott H. (Eds), *Making Quality Critical. New Perspectives on Organizational Change.* New York and London: Routledge, 219–39.

KISSLER, L. (1994). 'Industrial modernization by workers' participation'. *Economic and Industrial Democracy*, **15**, 2, 179–211.

KNORR-CETINA, K. D. (1981). *The Manufacture of Knowledge: An Essay on The Constructivists and Contextual Nature of Science.* Oxford: Pergamon.

LATOUR, B. (1989). *La science en action.* (*Science in Action*). Paris: Éditions La découverte.

LATOUR, B. and WOOLGAR, S. (1979). *Laboratory Life: The Social Construction of Scientific Facts.* Beverly Hills, CA: Sage.

LAW, J. (1994). *Organizing Modernity*. Oxford and Cambridge: Blackwell.

LAW, J. and CALLON, M. (1988). 'Engineering and sociology in a military aircraft program: a network analysis of technical change'. *Social Problems*, **35**.

LINCOLN, Y. S. and GUBA, Y. (1985). *Naturalistic Inquiry.* Beverly Hills, CA: Sage.

LUTMAN, W. (1994). 'ISO 9000: can America demonstrate a commitment to quality?' *Production and Inventory Management Journal*, **35**, 2, 81–5.

MCARDLE, L., ROWLINSON, M., PROCTER, S., HASSARD, J. and FORRESTER, P. (1995). 'Total quality management and participation'. In Wilkinson A. and Willmott, H. (Eds), *Making Quality Critical. New Perspectives on Organizational Change.* New York and London: Routledge, 156–72.

MCKINLAY, A. and TAYLOR, P. (1996). 'Power, surveillance and resistance: inside the "factory of the future".' In Ackers, P., Smith, C. and Smith, P. (Eds), *The New Workplace and Trade Unionism.* London and New York: Routledge, 279–300.

MICHAEL, M. (1996). *Constructing Identities.* London, Thousand Oaks, New Delhi: Sage Publications.

MUNRO, R. (1995). 'Governing the new province of quality. Autonomy, accounting and the dissemination of accountability'. In Wilkinson, A. and Willmott, H. (Eds), *Making Quality Critical. New Perspectives on Organizational Change.* New York and London: Routledge, 127–55.

MURAKAMI, T. (1995). 'Introducing team working – a motor industry case study from Germany'. *Industrial Relations Journal*, **26**, 4, 293–305.

OLSON, M. (1982) *The Logic of Collective Action.* Cambridge, MA: Harvard University Press.

ORLIKOWSKI, W. J. (1992). 'The duality of technology: rethinking the concept of technology in organizations'. *Organisation Science*, **3**, 3, 398–427.

PETTIGREW, A. M. (1985). *The Awakening Giant. Continuity and Change in Imperial Chemical Industries.* Oxford: Basil Blackwell.

Pettigrew, A. M. (1990). 'Longitudinal field research on change: theory and practice'. *Organization Science*, **1**, 3, 267–92.

Pinch, T. J. and Bijker W. E. (1987). 'The social construction of facts and artifacts: or how the sociology of science and the sociology of technology might benefit each other'. In Bijker, W., Hughes, T. and Pinch, T. (Eds), *The Social Construction of Technological Systems*. Cambridge, MA: MIT Press, 17–50.

Peshef, Y., Stratton-Devine, K. and Bemmels, B. (1994). 'The impact of manufacturing employees on technological changes'. *Economic and Industrial Democracy*, **15**, 4, 505–31.

Sewell, G. (1998). 'The discipline of teams: the control of team-based industrial work through electronic and peer surveillance'. *Administrative Science Quarterly*, **43**, 397–428.

Scarbrough, H. and Corbett, J. M. (1992). *Technology and Organisation – Power, Meaning and Design*. London and New York: Routledge.

Schumpeter, J. A. (1967). *The Theory of Economic Development*. Oxford: Oxford University Press.

Schwandt, T. A. (1994). 'Constructivist, interpretivist approaches to human inquiry'. In Denzin, N. K. and Lincoln Y. S. (Eds), *Handbook of Qualitative Research*. Thousand Oaks, London, New Delhi: Sage, 118–37.

Sinclair, A. (1992). 'The tyranny of a team ideology'. *Organization Studies*, **13**, 4, 611–26.

Thompson, P. (1990). 'Crawling from the wreckage: the labour process and the politics of production'. In Knights, D. and Willmott, H. (Eds), *Labour Process Theory*. London: Macmillan, 95–124.

Trist, E. and Bamforth, K. W. (1951). 'Some social and psychological consequences of the long-wall method of coal-getting'. *Human Relations*, **4**, 1, 3–38.

Tuckman, A. (1995). 'Ideology, quality and TQM'. In Wilkinson, A. and Willmott, H. (Eds), *Making Quality Critical. New Perspectives on Organizational Change*. New York and London: Routledge, 54–81.

Tyre, M. J. and Orlikowski, W. J. (1994). 'Windows of opportunity: temporal patterns of technological adaptation in organizations'. *Organization Science*, **5**, 1, 98–119.

Valente, T. W. (1996). 'Social network thresholds in the diffusion of innovation'. *Social Network*, **18**, 68–89.

Vallas, S. P. and Beck, J. P. (1996). 'The transformation of work revisited: the limits of flexibility in American manufacturing'. *Social Problems*, **43**, 3, 339–61.

Vande Ven, A. H. and Poole, M. S. (1995). 'Methods for studying innovation development in the Minnesota Innovation Research Program'. In Huber, G. P. and Van de Ven, A. H. (Eds), *Longitudinal Field Research Methods. Studying Processes of Organizational Change*. Thousand Oaks: Sage Publications, 155–85.

Westphal, J. D., Gulati, B. and Shortell, S. M. (1997). 'Customization or conformity? An institutional and network perspective on the content and consequences of TQM adoption'. *Administrative Science Quarterly*, **42**, 366–94.

White, H. C. (1992). *Identity and Control*. Princeton, NJ: Princeton University Press.

Wilkinson, B. (1983). *The Shopfloor Politics of New Technology*. London: Heinemann Educational Books.

Wilkinson, A. and Willmott, H. (1995). 'Introduction'. In Wilkinson, A. and Willmott, H. (Eds), *Making Quality Critical. New Perspectives on Organizational Change*. New York and London: Routledge, 1–32.

Woodward, J. (1965). *Industrial Organization: Theory and Practice*. Oxford: Oxford University Press.

Woolgar, S. (1981). 'Interests and explanation in the social studies of science'. *Social Studies of Science*, **11**, 365–94.

Zehr, S. C. (1994). 'The centrality of scientists and the translation of interests in rain controversy'. *The Canadian Review of Sociology and Anthropology*, **31**, 3, 325–53.

Zuboff, S. (1988). *In the Age of the Smart Machine: The Future of Work and Power*. London: Oxford University Press and Heinemann.

International Journal of Innovation Management
Vol. 5, No. 3 (September 2001) pp. 275–298

WHAT'S THIS "TOSH"?: INNOVATION NETWORKS AND NEW PRODUCT DEVELOPMENT AS A POLITICAL PROCESS

IAN McLOUGHLIN
Newcastle School of Management, University of Newcastle
Newcastle upon Tyne, NE1 7RU, UK
e-mail: I.P.McLoughlin@ncl.ac.uk

CHRISTIAN KOCH
Department of Civil Engineering
Technical University of Denmark, Lyngby, Denmark
e-mail: ck@ifa.dtu.dk

KEITH DICKSON
School of Business and Management
Brunel University, Uxbridge, UB8 3PH, UK
e-mail: Keith.dickson@Brunel.ac.uk

Received 12 June 2001
Revised 5 May 2001
Accepted 5 May 2001

Innovation is increasingly seen as best conducted in networks and understood through a synthesis of evolutionary economic and sociological perspectives. This article contributes to this understanding by seeking to apply a political process perspective to collaboration between organisations engaged in new product development. It argues that the building of collaborative networks is a power-process and requires political action. Contrary to conventional views, power and politics are treated as an omnipresent feature of the creation of collaborative networks. It is concluded that mastering the political is a central element of the eventual success of any product development endeavour. This argument is illustrated by drawing upon the findings of an international study on collaboration in new product development (BiCoN). Here we focus on a UK and a Danish case of software development where two contrasting forms of collaboration between the software supplier, intermediaries and end user/customers are evident.

Keywords: collaboration, innovation networks, politics, new product development, software

Introduction

Technological innovation is increasingly seen as a phenomenon best regarded as conducted through network relationships (Jones *et al.*, 1998; Dodgson, 1993; Hislop *et al.*, 1997; Lawton Smith *et al.*, 1991; Senker & Faulkner, 1992). Perspectives on innovation networks range from institutional and evolutionary economics on the one hand through organisational analysis/theory to sociologically influenced constructivist positions on the other. There have also been attempts to bring about some convergence between these apparently diverse positions in the study of innovation networks (Coombs *et al.*, 1996; Green *et al.*, 1999). Rather than seeing sociological contributions as no more than studying the "tosh" of economic activity (Williamson cited by Ingham, 1996: 262), we appear to be moving to a more interesting position enabled by a synthesis of insights.

We wish to contribute to this development by seeking to apply a political process perspective to the analysis of innovation networks as exemplified by inter-firm collaboration in new product development (Harris *et al.*, 1999). The political process perspective views organisations as "fundamentally political entities", wherein organisational members pursue their own potentially conflicting interests (Pettigrew, 1985; Pfeffer, 1992; Dawson, 1994; Buchanan & Badham, 1999; McLoughlin *et al.*, 2000; Koch, 2000a). As such, the outcomes of technological change and innovation can be seen as shaped in significant ways by the exercise of power by participants, as they seek to advance and defend their positions through building coalitions and negotiating with others. By examining collaboration and coalition building within and between organisations (for example, when collaborating in new product development), we also broaden the traditional focus of the political process perspective, which has tended to focus on processes within the individual organisation. As Elg & Johansson (1997) note, networks of organisations can equally well be seen as structural arrangements fused by conflicting and mutual interests and, as such, a key dynamic of network development, will also be the desire to advance and defend self-interests on the part of participants.

The structure of our discussion is as follows. First, we provide a brief overview of the treatment of political process as one factor shaping innovation networks and collaboration within and between organisations engaged in new product development. Here, we suggest that the exercise of power through political activity is more central than is conventionally assumed. We then seek to demonstrate the role of political processes in collaboration to develop new products through a presentation of case study findings from a study of intra- and inter-firm collaboration in new product development in the UK, Denmark and Germany (BiCoN). Here, we confine ourselves to a discussion of one of the UK and one of the Danish case studies. Finally, we argue that mastering the political is a central element of the eventual success of any product development endeavour. Indeed, it may well cast new light on the so-called "management of innovation problem" (Storey, 2000).

Collaboration, Networks and the Politics of New Product Development

The growth of inter-organisational forms of technological collaboration has been identified as one means of risk-reduction in increasingly unstable global markets (Aoki, 1984; DeBresson & Amesse, 1991; Child & Faulkner, 1998). Given the manner in which technological advances and corporate restructuring increasingly derive from novel synergies and combinations of scientific and technical knowledge, such collaboration has also been identified as an essential aspect of a successful innovation strategy. This has been highlighted as a specific factor in the success of new product development in terms of the effectiveness of collaborative alliances within the firm (Dougherty & Hardy, 1996) and in terms of participation in external networks (Steward & Conway, 1996). Vergragt *et al.* (1982: 244) go as far as to state that technological development, "is made possible through the creation of internal coalitions or networks and by extension of these networks to include other organisations in the environment". Ford & Thomas (1997) claim that a new product development strategy is now inevitably a networking strategy, and Tidd (1997) claims that technological innovation is now best understood through a focus on networks of collaboration rather than the traditional single enterprise unit. It has also been argued that innovation networks, if regarded as a specific rather than a generic form of technological collaboration, may avoid many of the conventional problems of inter-firm collaboration — for example, "cultural mismatch" between collaborators (Child & Faulkner, 1998). Defined in these terms, collaborative networks can be regarded as new "hybrid" organisational form. Such organisational arrangements are able to both use and deploy new technologies to change inter-sectoral relationships as well as relationships between firm functions, suppliers, customers and other network actors (Freeman, 1991: 509–10).

Analysis of innovation networks informed by an evolutionary understanding of technological development have played a major role in studies of technological collaboration. As Coombs *et al.* (1996: 3) note, from this perspective, such collaborative networks are a source of variety and qualitative change in the economic system. The formation of networks occurs as a response to a range of incentives which encourage firms to develop strategies for collaboration with each other. The principal empirical focus in studies informed by this view has been on identifying the formal and contractual characteristics of collaborations and on attempts to map the dimensions and patterns of networking activity (Coombs *et al.*, 1996). Significantly for our concerns in this article, conflicts between institutions or actors experienced in the innovation process are frequently framed in terms of "communication failures", which prevent for instance, effective relationships between suppliers and users, or act as barriers to learning and trust-building in collaborative relationships. At worst, the intervention of the "political" is seen as unwelcome and negative (see Pavitt, 1990). In our view there is a basic resistance founded in the domain assumptions of the evolutionary approach to the notion of political process as having significant explanatory power beyond being a barrier to or constraint on innovation (McLoughlin, 1999). In contrast, we would suggest that political processes are the means by which innovation is actually brought about and therefore the "political" should not just be evoked in attempts to account for failures or difficulties in innovating. In this respect, we are reminded of Latour's (1988) criticism that economics-derived understandings of technological innovation are often akin in their explanation to observing a luminous rugby ball in a darkened stadium. The trajectory of the ball is clear, but the intentionality, motives, actions and behaviours of the actors which produce this movement are not illuminated. In our terms, politics — intentionality, motives, actions, behaviours — are crucial elements in explaining how the "ball" got to be a "ball" in the first place, not just to the problems which may prevent or hinder the "ball" moving around as intended.

Turning to literature, specifically concerning new product development, we find a small but growing interest in the role of political process within organisations in the creation of new products. These approaches are emerging in opposition to a dominant "rationalistic" perspective based on the assumption that "a product that is well-planned, implemented and appropriately supported will be a success" (Brown & Eisenhardt, 1995: 344). From this viewpoint, there is little room for consideration of the political other than a potentially disruptive barrier to innovation as noted above. However, research which has focused on the decision making process involved in new product development has drawn attention to the role of what has been termed "disciplined problem solving" (e.g. Imai *et al.*, 1985; Clark & Fujimoto, 1991). This suggests that effective new product development requires the exercise of "subtle control" by senior management, who must create a strong vision for a new product, to ensure outcomes fit with corporate objectives, but at the same time leave sufficient ambiguity for "experiential improvisation" within the development team. The work of this balancing is ascribed to "heavyweight" team leaders (Brown & Eisenhardt, 1995: 351). However, whilst suggestive of some kind of political process, as Brown and Eisenhardt point out, concepts such as "heavyweight" team leaders remain vague and lack "political realism" in the sense that such leaders are portrayed as almost "superhuman".

A more sophisticated understanding of the role of political processes is found in studies which focus on the significance of information flows and communication to successful product development (e.g. Allen, 1977; Ancona & Caldwell, 1992). This approach goes further in highlighting political activity in some sense by drawing attention to the means by which the resources required for successful product development are secured by project teams (Frost & Egri, 1991). In particular, "politically orientated external communication" has been shown in several studies to increase the resources flowing to a product development team. In similar fashion, high levels of internal communication are seen to improve team performance (Brown & Eisenhardt, 1998: 351). Finally, the political processes involved in learning and trust building in the context of developing new products and more general collaboration within and between firms has also been highlighted (e.g. Cohen *et al.*, 1998; Dickson, 1996; Sako, 1992, 1998).

In a significant contribution to this discussion, Dougherty & Hardy (1996) argue that a focus on the personal power of individual managers to control resources (budgets, information, expertise, etc.), "only scratches the surface of power dynamics" (Dougherty & Hardy, 1996: 1147). They suggest that power also resides in the processes through which innovation occurs. Sustained product innovation requires the building of organisational systems that permit effective collaboration, *which is not* dependent upon the actions of powerful individuals. Moreover, the power of the meaning supporting innovation is "crucial" since without this, the possession of resources "easily unravels" in the absence of significant legitimation of their deployment and use (Dougherty & Hardy, 1996: 1148). Drawing on concepts of power and political process derived from the work of Clegg (1989), Dougherty & Hardy draw attention to the *different levels* at which power may be exercised and political activity engaged in within the product development processes. They argue that sustained new product development requires: the winning of resources (finance, technology, knowledge, information); the creation of organisational processes and structures, which enable collaboration; and the establishment of clear linkages between product development and overall organisational strategy. However, these requirements are not easily fulfilled. In particular, problems may occur when trying to establish a smooth flow of resources. This requires project "champions" to build effective coalitions of support; changing existing organisational arrangements and routines which act as a constraint on effective collaboration; creating meanings which enable others to understand the strategic significance and value of a new product development. Indeed, from their own research, Dougherty & Hardy suggest that the most successful product innovators are those who were able to solve through political activity a *high proportion of the resource, change and creation of meaning problems.*

Some of these points are supported in the work of Midler (1993). He has drawn attention to the emergent, contingent and vulnerable character of the new product development process. For example, in an extended longitudinal study of the development of the new Renault "Twingo" car, he details a process of coalition building through which support for the new car concept is sought by its proponents within the organisation. This is presented as a complicated and "incomplete" process, where the project manager plays a core role in mobilising support. For our purposes, what is important here is the way in which the development of a new product can be seen as predicated on the building of a network of support through the enrolment of key supporters and interests. Our contention is that the majority of innovation processes can be construed in these terms, that is as constituting internal and external processes of alliance building and negotiation through which the product becomes "socially constituted and constructed".

Dougherty & Hardy and Midler's work is primarily concerned with internal collaboration and the problems of innovating in mature firms. Nevertheless, we suggest that their analysis provides a number of pointers to the nature of the power-processes that may be involved in new product development in general, including those involving inter-organisational, as well as intra-organisational collaboration. This brings us back to a consideration of the manner in which collaboration is built, not just within, but also between organisations engaged in new product development. There is no reason, as we have already indicated, to suppose that inter-firm interactions should not be shaped by power-processes in the same way as intra-firm processes are. This point is taken up by Elg & Johansson (1997) who develop upon earlier work by Frost & Egri (1991). Their concern is to examine decision making processes in asymmetrical relationships in inter-firm networks. The proposition — based on resource-dependency models — is that network participants will seek to influence the decision making process in ways that advance their specific interests and enhances their position within the network. For example, organisations with more powerful positions will seek to exploit and preserve this position, whilst weaker organisations will seek to alter the conditions of their dependency. Network participants will seek to advance such motives by seeking out potential sources of network support and then seeking to control interactions within the network in order to use these supportive structures. Much of this will involve the "observable" exercise of power by one party over another, for example as they use the resources derived from their structural position within a network to advance or defend their position. However, in a similar argument to Dougherty & Hardy (1996), it is suggested that more subtle political activity will involve the non-observable "hidden" exercise of power and the power embedded in "deep structures" of "taken for granted" norms, expectations and beliefs.

Summarising, the existing literature on collaboration stresses the importance of networks for innovation. The evolutionary underpinnings of this perspective tend to be resistant to attributing a central role to political processes in explaining such behaviour. Studies of the new product development within organisations have, though, increasingly drawn attention to such processes. To-date, most attention has been given to a "resource dependency" model and the significance of powerful individuals in securing vital organisational resources. However, as Thomas (1994) notes, whilst adequate for a single decision-event at a particular point in time, when examining the unfolding pattern of a series of decisions over time, such notions of the structural sources of power are less realistic. For this reason, we concur with those who suggest that power should be understood not just as something that is possessed, but should also be seen as encompassing the properties of relationships of interaction between actors (Hardy, 1994).

This draws attention to the importance of coalition building, enrolment and legitimation in mobilising and exerting power over time. Accordingly, in what follows, we deploy a threefold focus on resources, the process of coalition building and the role of deeper structure such as culture, as sources for creating of meaning. Moreover, our concern is not exclusively with collaboration within single organisational units but, as we have indicated, collaboration in new product development which embraces two or more enterprises.

Building Collaboration in New Product Development

In this section, we wish to provide some preliminary illustration of political processes in network building by examining findings from a study of building collaboration in new product development (BiCoN). The two cases considered in this article are software development projects (other BiCoN cases focused upon specific artifacts — a continuous process wok in food production; sonar equipment for submarines and communication systems; electronic data interchange and satellite tracking technologies). "*Hansen*" (a common Danish name) is the pseudonym we apply to the software house which is the nodal organisation in the Danish case and "*Frontier Systems*", the name for the software company in the UK case. The public utility which figures in this case we refer to as *EnergyCo*. We selected these cases as part of the BiCoN project as software presents a key exemplar of the challenges of new product development. In particular, the well-documented problems of developing software that meets customer requirements, suggest that imperatives for collaborative arrangement in developing software are high. At the same time, in engaging with this problem, software providers are increasingly required to learn a considerable amount about their customers' businesses and associated markets. Indeed, increasingly the software developed by such firms is "bundled" with a range of consulting services which may even extend to managing significant organisational and business transformation programmes.

For instance, the cases we consider here present contrasting examples of the market for software products and the associated organisation of software development that is involved. The *Hansen* case is an example of an organisation operating in a situation where a mass market has emerged for a software product — in this case enterprise resource planning (ERP) packages (Koch, 2000b; Clausen & Koch, 1999). In this type of situation, the relationship between the software developer and the end-user/customer is typically highly mediated with a range of intermediaries between the two parties involved. These may be involved in translating and understanding customer requirements, assisting them in implementing a complex product (by providing training), and in a growing number of instances customising a generic software product to fit the customer's specific circumstances. The *Frontier Systems* case is illustrative of a different kind of situation where the market require bespoke software solutions to meet specific business needs — in this case, the updating of legacy systems and development of new software applications. These situations tend to be characterised by a dynamic of close collaboration between the software supplier and the customer/end-user in what are essentially "one off" development projects and implementations (Kyng & Mathiassen, 1997). In this case, many of the activities and functions that might devolve to intermediaries in a mass market for a software product are integrated within the supplying organisation. As we will see, in each situation, the imperatives for and dynamics of tend to be different.

The primary field work for both case studies was conducted between 1998 and 1999. Research methods in each of the case studies were primarily based on semi-structured interviews, supporting documentation and informal discussions with a variety of company personnel ranging from senior executives; functional specialists (e.g. human resources and legal specialists); project managers; through to project team members. Whilst not coterminous with length of the product development processes being studied, each case study contained a longitudinal element, which allowed us to some degree to construct a picture of the process as it emerged over time. Interviews were normally initiated with key project management personnel in the nodal organisations of each collaborative network. "Snow ball" sampling was then used to generate links to key personnel both in the project teams within the nodal enterprise and thence to key informants in other network member organisations. Interviews were normally conducted by one or two researchers and recorded in note form or by tape. Typically interviews lasted from one to two hours. Interviews were transcribed in summary form and their content analysed. First, in relation to emergent themes within the specific case study; second, in comparison to the other case studies being conducted by the particular country research team; and finally, in relation to the case studies being conducted across the three countries in the project as a whole. The latter analysis was executed through quarterly two- or three-day project workshops attended by the entire research team and held throughout the funded part of the research programme.

In the Danish case, it was possible to interview and conduct interviews at the level of individual product teams as well as senior project management. Access difficulties prevented this in the case of *Frontier Systems* and so we were unable to explore the operation of discrete elements of the overall product development process in the detail we would have wished. These difficulties arose because of broader corporate changes affecting *Frontier Systems*. These changes also meant *Frontier* became increasingly sensitive during the fieldwork to the fact that we were also collecting data from the client organisation "*EnergyCo*". This eventually resulted in our termination of data collection at the product development site and subsequently within *Frontier* as a whole. However, by this time, our planned programme of intial interviews was largely completed and it was the detailed exploration at the level of product development teams, and final follow-up interviews at the end of the fieldwork period, that could not be conducted. Some sensitivities, although not as significant in terms of data collection, also existed in relation to aspects of the research conducted at *Hansen* which found itself operating in an increasingly fierce competitive environment during the period of our research. In both cases, therefore, albeit to varying degrees, we are somewhat constrained in terms of the range of data we are able to bring, to bear in published form to illustrate the political process dimensions of the collaborations concerned. Accordingly, in the following, we have taken particular steps to preserve the confidentiality of our sources and have had to be more circumspect than we would have liked in the direct quotation and attribution of respondent views. Whilst presenting obvious drawbacks in terms of our stated objectives in this article, the difficulties alluded to in themselves, demonstrate the nature of the political process dimensions of networks. Indeed, on occasion, our activity as researchers was shaped and influenced by these very processes.

Case 1: Collaboration in software development within the UK energy industry

Frontier Systems was founded in the late 1960s. It was a young, dynamic and entrepreneurial company with something of a "frontier" ethos and an extremely charismatic and "hands-on" CEO who was the founder of the organisation. The core values *Frontier Systems* emphasised are "integrity, innovation, risk taking, flexibility and tenacity" in its dealings with clients. It viewed its own employees as a "resource" to be "treasured". Its core business was information technology systems integration, applications development, outsourcing and "business transformation". At the core of these activities was the application of what it represented to the market as tailor-made "state-of-the-art" IT systems to improve business processes in client organisations. *Frontier System's* rapid growth had been built around the establishment of partnerships with key clients in a number of industry sectors, including financial services, health care, travel and, as we will see in this instance, the energy sector. *Frontier Systems* targeted these sectors because they were characterised by radical changes requiring organisations operating within them to fundamentally rethink business operations and processes. In the case of the UK energy industry, for example, changes in technology and privatisation required formerly publicly-owned electricity supply companies to develop new strategies, processes and systems in order to compete in a deregulated market place (Russell, 1996). This case concerns the development and customisation of one such electricity company's computer and information systems (CIS) and associated adaptation of legacy systems by *Frontier Systems*.

For *EnergyCo* privatisation meant developing a strategic response to enable it to compete in the newly deregulated market. Like other supply companies, developing technological systems and infrastructure was identified as a key source of competitive advantage. *EnergyCo* did not see the operation and maintenance of its computer systems as one of its core tasks and decided, in 1992, to embark upon a 12-year outsourcing agreement with *Frontier Systems*. This arrangement subsequently provided the basis for an extension of the collaboration between *Frontier Systems* and *EnergyCo* to embrace two software systems development and modification projects.

In its relatively short existence, *Frontier Systems* had evolved an approach to developing new software products (which in its view embraced "total business solutions") in close collaboration with its customers. This collaboration was focused on the creation of client-specific organisational arrangements. In the contract with *EnergyCo*, this involved establishing a temporary project organisation at the client site comprising personnel from both *Frontier Systems* and former *EnergyCo*. This arrangement was the outcome of a lengthy period of "pre-contract relationship building". During this period, a process of what was termed "body shopping" occurred during which *Frontier Systems* personnel were based within the prospective client organisation to provide a detailed assessment of their expertise; to identify personnel with core technical and business knowledge; and to build credibility with the client through "troubleshooting" activities. Once the relationship with the client was formalised (in the *EnergyCo* case via the outsourcing agreement), *Frontier Systems* would offer employment to key client personnel in a project-based organisation to which its own personnel would also be seconded. Typically this "hybrid" organisation was located at the client site. In the *EnergyCo* case, this organisation grew rapidly to involve 650 personnel (around 70 of whom were former *EnergyCo* employees, largely from the information and computing systems area).

As in the case of most of its client partners, *Frontier Systems* was very different to *EnergyCo* in its way of organising, operating and in terms of its culture. *EnergyCo* was an organisation which had a history in the public sector and whose prior development had been based on a public service ethos, and involved bureaucratic forms of organisation, management style, and collective regulation in industrial relations. In contrast, *Frontier Systems* was a small but rapidly growing organisation with a flat structure. It had an innovative approach to business development. This was manifested in a strong orientation towards the customer; a highly individualistic and paternalist concept of employment relations (employees were termed "associates" and much emphasis was placed on integrity and trust in relationships both at work and in associates' "personal lives"); an emphasis on flexibility and a willingness to take risks; and a strong encouragement to employees to take the initiative and to try new ideas.

The "Deregulation Project"

This began in 1996 and was termed the "Deregulation Project" due to the intended completion for early 1998 when the UK electricity market was to be fully deregulated. This meant customers would be able to purchase electricity from a supply company whose existing customer-base was in another region of the country. In order to facilitate this, major adaptation and development was required of the information and computing systems of the energy supply companies. This work was essential in order to permit the new market to operate (the national cost of this development work was estimated at £1 billion). The "Deregulation Project" involved both changes to legacy systems, development of new software, and "re-engineering" of business processes for *EnergyCo*. This would then enable, for example, the exchange of customer information with other electricity supply companies in order to allow customers who chose to do so to switch suppliers, as the new market demanded.

Early adaptation of business processes and information systems would allow *EnergyCo* to enter the deregulated market place ahead of many of its competitors and thereby capture vital new market share and extend its customer-base. Accordingly, the development of its information and computing systems was seen by *EnergyCo's* Managing Director as a critical resource for future commercial success. The outsourcing arrangement with *Frontier Systems* was viewed as a means of reducing uncertainty by ensuring that this resource was available to the organisation. At the same time, it is envisaged that such an arrangement could be the basis for a joint-venture that would create a new organisation able to market its services and expertise elsewhere in the energy industry. *Frontier Systems* was precluded by its agreement with *EnergyCo* from working with other UK energy suppliers, but was allowed to undertake similar ventures in the UK with non-competitors. Part of *Frontier System's* longer-term strategy of learning about the UK energy market was the anticipation that considerable business could be gained in the future if the US market was deregulated in a similar manner.

During the early stages of the "Deregulation Project" problems of "cultural mismatch" became apparent. These were manifested both within the new hybrid project organisation and between the project organisation and the client — *EnergyCo*. For example, despite locating at the client site, cultural differences came to be symbolised by a bridge walkway linking the offices of the client with *Frontier System's* project organisation. The latter's offices were marked by an "open-plan, primary-colours and pot-plant" ambience, whilst the client organisation retained the "Kafka-esque" image of a public sector bureaucracy. *Frontier System's* lack of hierarchy also posed problems for *EnergyCo* personnel who found it difficult to identify opposite numbers with whom they could communicate. Within the "hybrid organisation" ex-*EnergyCo* employees, who were used to working in a bureaucratised and more formal environment, experienced assimilation problems within the new organisation with its more informal and less clearly defined work roles and responsibilities. In fact, a small group of *EnergyCo* staff declined to transfer their employment to the hybrid organisation and preferred a secondment arrangement. They had to be managed according to union rules, and formed a distinct group within the new organisation.

More fundamentally, relationships between *Frontier Systems* and *EnergyCo* in this period were characterised by low levels of trust and quickly became adversarial. One interviewee referred to the difficulty experienced by *EnergyCo* at this time as one of managing "all of the warring factions". For example, it was reported by some *EnergyCo* interviewees that *Frontier Systems* regarded its client in the early stages of the project as "naïve" in its decision to hand over full control of computing operations. As such, *Frontier Systems* felt it was able, in the words of one respondent, to "milk" the account for revenue. XZY managers talked in terms of "costs, budgets and constraints" whilst *Frontier Systems* spoke a new language of "business values, return-on-investment and business solutions". One of our *Frontier Systems* interviewees made the point more succinctly: *EnergyCo* had "not a competitive idea in its brain". Consequently, *EnergyCo* felt that *Frontier Systems* had failed to treat both their client and the collaboration responsibilities seriously by being unwilling to transfer vital technical knowledge and relying too much on junior staff to manage the relationship between the two companies. This led to tensions, documented by a frequent exchange of letters between the two companies spelling out each other's contractual obligations and threatening legal action for non-compliance.

However, despite these problems, the "hybrid" organisation began to make significant progress with the "Deregulation project". Software was updated, new applications developed and the complex structure of *EnergyCo* was simplified into a number of regional business units. *Frontier Systems* introduced its own organisation charts detailing a structure that *EnergyCo* could relate to when addressing problems. This did not reflect a strategy of organisational change within *Frontier Systems* as much as an accommodation to the needs of the client; *Frontier Systems* staff paid little attention to the "hierarchy" described on paper. As the hybrid organisation expanded, a human resources function was established. This used sophisticated recruitment and selection techniques to ensure a closer "fit" between an individual's profile and the organisation's culture as additional staff were recruited. *Frontier Systems* introduced a more commercial business attitude into *EnergyCo*. This meant that the value added by the collaboration became recognised throughout *EnergyCo*, and no longer depended largely upon the support of the CEO, who retired in the mid-90s.

The latter event coincided with a major review of the collaboration after four years. Acknowledgement of the dependency upon *Frontier Systems* expertise, and the increasing need for innovative systems in order to compete effectively, were both influential in ensuring the continuation of the relationship between the two companies, despite the previous problems. Ironically, the application of newly-acquired commercial acumen — in part provided through the existing collaboration with *Frontier Systems* — also allowed *EnergyCo* to negotiate far more favourable terms than had originally been the case, when it had seemingly meekly acquiesced to the contract terms drawn up by *Frontier Systems*. This victory illustrated the extent of learning that had taken place at *EnergyCo*. Its bargaining power had been enhanced by the recent recruitment of a new Finance Director and senior staff with IT knowledge, in a somewhat belated attempt to regain in-house technical knowledge and reduce the dependence on *Frontier Systems*.

Six years after the signing of the initial outsourcing agreement and with employment levels and workload at their peak, a *Frontier Systems* subsidiary outside of Europe was contracted to carry out testing alongside other *Frontier Systems* staff-based in its overseas headquarters. This enhanced the "virtual" dimension of the "hybrid" organisation as development teams began to collaborate across three continents in what amounted to a 24-hour software development cycle. At this time *Frontier Systems* also began work on a second major project to ensure *EnergyCo* systems were year 2000 compliant.

However, in the late 1990s both *EnergyCo* and *Frontier Systems* experienced further changes in their business environments. *EnergyCo* was the subject of a takeover by another energy company. At the same time *Frontier Systems* became a publicly-quoted company. In early 1999 (after our research relationship had terminated) *EnergyCo*, now under new ownership, gave public notice of its intention to terminate the relationship with *Frontier Systems*. The collaboration agreement was therefore ended as of late 1999, five years short of the agreed 12-year contract. This was said, in press releases from *EnergyCo*, to be the result of a "strategic business decision", to "return control of key elements of IT infrastructure and systems in-house" and to "provide the flexibility for IT to support [*EnergyCo's* new owner's] strategy. This strategy was to acquire and merge with power companies in the United Kingdom, United States and worldwide". The official view of *EnergyCo's* new owners, as reported in the press, was that this decision was not a reflection on the quality of *Frontier System's* performance in the seven years of the collaboration. However, press reports also referred to "leaked" internal memos that inferred the reasons for termination were less amicable.

Case 2: Collaboration in software development by a Danish software house

The company in the centre of the network is a software house named "*Hansen*". The software product is a generic enterprise resource planning (ERP) package. This comprises customisable modules covering various aspects of business functionality (finance, human resources, etc.). The installed base of these systems covers more than 50,000 customers within Denmark and more than 15,000 abroad. The system is sold in more than 20 countries.

The development, sale and implementation of this software have evolved over a 10-year period to involve a complex collaboration between *Hansen* itself and a network of value added resellers (VARs) and a small number of major customers in the private and public sectors. Many of the VARs had several times the turnover of *Hansen* itself and the network itself was continuing to develop with new entrants, existing members leaving, and other restructuring effects (mergers between VARs and so on).

The VARs both cooperated and competed within this framework. Many had overlapping customer groups, whilst others focused on more restricted market niches. Within this framework a range of additional services had been developed and "bundled" with the main software product, such as consulting, training and additional software modules. Within Denmark the network of VARs consists of over 100 companies. Internationally, there are approximately another 500 VARs linked to *Hansen*. These are legally independent companies with various types of formalised relationships with *Hansen* and "end-user" customer enterprises.

It is important to note therefore that, in contrast with *Frontier System's* close relationship with *EnergyCo* in the above case, *Hansen* does not have a direct relationship with most of its customers. It sought to use such inter-organisational collaborations as a means of "outsourcing" sales and implementation, whilst maintaining product development activities in-house. However, the larger and some of the more specialised VARs started developing additional software. The result was a distributed system of new product development. In this case, we focus on the development of the third generation of the ERP system (MARK III) and a specific module within this. This project involved the development of collaborative networks within *Hansen* itself, which then interacted with the broader network of VARs and selected customers.

The third generation ("MARK III") ERP system/XAS module

The MARK III product development process was initiated in the mid-90s. It is a clear example of "classical product development" where innovations in the technical content of the product predominated, building on experience of developing and using experience with the earlier generation of the product gained by the VARs and end users. The overall business objective behind these technical developments was to make the product more appropriate for use by middle-sized (not just small) enterprises and to expand in the international market.

The organisation of the product development process was based upon the Microsoft Solutions Framework (MSF) (Cusomano *et al.*, 1995). This represented a shift from a traditional functional project organisation to a form of matrix organisation. This involved the decentralisation of decision making to product teams and the shortening of development cycles. The principal objective behind these changes to project organisation was to achieve a reduction in "time-to-market". Second, there was a realisation that sustaining the growth of the company was dependent upon finding new ways in which to "leverage" the skills, expertise and knowledge of programmers and system developers during the product development process.

The formation of teams for the MARK III project broadly followed the MSF process model. This recommends that software development is divided into four phases: *vision phase* — intended to produce a vision scope and a series of approved project milestones; *planning phase* — through which a project schedule and resource allocation is agreed between project teams and project management;

development — where the first version (a beta version) of the intended software product is built; *test* — where the software is gradually "stabilised" through debugging and so on. Several cycles through these phases are undertaken until the product is deemed to be stable. In effect, when the number of newly discovered bugs declines the stabilisation of the product is confirmed.

One of the teams (responsible for the XAS module — one element of the overall MARK III development process) was followed through repeat interviews during this process. This revealed that, within the MSF process, the team was particularly successful in negotiating with the overall project management an appropriate fit of its task to available resources. The team were able to limit the scope of the tasks they were required to undertake and were able to persuade the project management to take a task away from the team. Similarly, in the planning phase, the team was able to take the initiative in prioritising certain tasks and downplaying others. Subsequently, the team was able to win additional human resources. *Internal* communications within the team also appeared to work relatively effectively; as specified by MSF, the team included a product manager, recruited externally, who had practical experience in the domain the software module was to address. In most of the MSF phases, the team was able to agree internally most of its priorities and design and to resist "interference" from outside. At "post mortem" meetings held at the end of each cycle of the MSF, several activities were evaluated by the team. These included a critical evaluation of the internal collaboration within the team itself and how their respective roles were functioning.

The team also established *external* communication about the customer requirement with the external intermediary network of VARs and significant major customers. In the first phase, there were informal interactions between the team and the external VAR network. Here three VARs and one significant end user/customer were consulted. These largely informal linkages served to open up information and communication channels between the VARs (who had a more direct experience of customer requirements) and the team (who were also able to manage the VARs' expectations as to what the new module would actually deliver). In a parallel process, the VARs were more "formally" consulted. A committee of VARs held three meetings before project management decided to halt the activity. This reflected a continuing debate within *Hansen* on the role of the VARs. Several different departments of *Hansen* articulated different views on this issue. Within the team studied, some members proffered an interpretation that "listening to the customers is in contradiction with being ahead of the competitors". The beta version of the module from this first cycle was released against the wishes of the team. This resulted in a heavy bombardment of telephone calls to the team from VAR representatives and others, who wanted specific details incorporated in the next cycle.

Two further forums served to facilitate the flow of information between *Hansen* and the VARs and between the VARs and end user/customers. These were monthly strategic meetings with both the *Hansen* distribution function and project management and project development workshops organised by the VARs for their customers which have in some instances resulted in joint specification of requirements. However, from the point of view of the VARs network the overall development process posed a number of problems. Whilst all VARs were keen to inform and support the development of the new ERP-package, not all were convinced that the end product was superior to competitor offerings. In some cases, VARs chose to develop their own additional modules in order to make their total offer more competitive from their viewpoint. Some VARs indicated that early product releases lacked the necessary quality and created problems with customers. By the end of our research period, there were still some VARs who would not implement the main releases of the ERP-package because of perceived quality problems. Several VARs express consternation regarding infrequent releases of service packs for servicing the existing base, and some mentioned the lack of help from *Hansen* in creating sales arguments in relation to competing systems. To this end, VARs used informal networks and contacts with software development project teams to gain product information of this type. In some cases, these flows of information contradicted internal structures and procedures within *Hansen*. Such tensions also highlight a differentiation between VARs. Many are "total systems solutions" providers where additional tailor-made programming for their customers is a central capability. Some have a role as developers, whereas others are mere implementers of a standardised system. If the VARs, which are developers and total systems solutions providers, flourish this will be problematic for *Hansen* in the long term in so far as the company is primarily interested in branding its ERP product as a very flexible standard solution with little need of subsequent customisation.

Comparative Discussion: Pro-Innovation Network Configurations?

In their study of product innovation in mature firms, Dougherty & Hardy talk of the predominance of "anti-innovation organisational configurations", where if product innovation did occur, it did so because of individual efforts to "buck the system" and win resources, create their own systems and structures to support collaboration, and to give meaning and value to the product development project (1996: 1144–1145). If proponents of network organisational forms are correct in their assertion that a new product development strategy is now inevitably a networking strategy, then how far have we observed in our two case examples of "pro-innovation network configurations"?

Our argument in this section is that the answer to this question in both cases is given by the political processes that underpin the building of the collaborative networks concerned. As indicated in our opening discussion, these dynamics can be demonstrated in terms of a threefold focus on: resources, the process of coalition building within the networks; and the role of deeper structures, such as culture, as sources for creating of meaning and value to the product development process. The extent to which the collaborative networks observed, acted to promote innovation rests ultimately, we would suggest, on the degree of embededness within the network configuration of the organisational power necessary to deliver resources, processes and meanings which sustain and reproduce innovation over time.

One aspect of the political dynamic involved here is revealed by the insights offered by the resource dependency perspective. This suggests that participants in networks will seek to build and/or maintain positions of strength within a network or overcome positions of weakness through seeking to change the structure of network relationships (Elg & Johannsen, 1997). Similarly, it has been argued that learning to deal competently with "assymmetries in the balance of power" is critical in successful collaboration (Lawton Smith *et al.*, 1996). Indeed, a significant characteristic of the collaboration between *Frontier Systems* and *EnergyCo* and between *Hansen* and the VARs seems to be a struggle to define the collaboration — the relationship between the partners and their respective roles and responsibilities — in such a way that one party rather than the other is able to control the development of the network.

However, whilst an attractive starting point the resource-dependency position is, as we have already noted, limited as an explanation of the dynamics of this process. Structural position within a network provides no more than a "starting point" for interpreting the intentionality and motivations of organisations and other network actors; it does not determine patterns of collaboration and network development (Elg & Johannsen, 1997: 362) or the actual outcomes of attempts to mobilise and win resources. Indeed, what is interesting about the two cases is how the intentions of the collaborators shifted over time in the face of changing contextual conditions and developments and the growing sophistication towards collaboration of the network actors concerned.

For example, under the outsourcing arrangement, it would seem that initially *EnergyCo* was in the stronger structural position but in fact, the pattern of interactions which subsequently occurred quickly allowed *Frontier Systems* to develop a position of considerable strength. This, as we have seen, was achieved through the appropriation of technological and business knowledge which *EnergyCo* had correctly identified as a key competitive competence in a deregulated market. As such, *Frontier Systems* was able to direct and control the development of the product development process. Ironically, success in this respect sharpened the sophistication of *EnergyCo's* business strategy. The organisation subsequently sought to exercise greater control over the relationship with *Frontier Systems* through tighter formal contractual and service level controls and by mobilising new sources of network support. The latter in the form of consultants to manage the project and by contracting third party software developers to second source some development work. Many of these "policing" arrangements were resisted to some extent by *Frontier Systems*. However, they had the effect of generating improvements in performance, not least because a revised formal contract linked part of *Frontier System's* fees to measurable business benefits accrued by *EnergyCo*. The collaboration also appeared to be moved onto a stronger footing when senior executives with considerable project management experience from *Frontier System's* overseas operations were seconded to the project and charged with re-building relationships with *EnergyCo*.

In the *Hansen* case, the nodal software house seemed to have a non-contestable structural position as the dominant party in the network. *Hansen* was thus able to set the agenda of the third generation of the ERP software and set out to build the necessary internal and external supporting organisational arrangements. However, some VARs, did not need to wait for *Hansen* to develop their system and new modules but chose to start alternative processes of developing parallel modules and other modules, thus changing the relative importance of the *Hansen* development process. Moreover, the internal network within *Hansen* around the MARK III and XAS module did not stay aligned throughout the process. Rather, tensions developed between development teams and sales/consulting representatives. For example, project management sought early release of the new product against product teams wishes as in the case of the first beta version of the XAS module.

Finally, a third level of power-processes is important in the cases. Here, we refer to what Elg & Johannsen term the "deep structures" of power embedded in values, cultures and meaning. As we noted above, Dougherty & Hardy suggest the 'power of meanings' supporting innovation is also "crucial". This seems to resonate with the new product development as a "disciplined problem solving" perspective discussed above, where strong visions and values link innovation to corporate objectives but leave sufficient ambiguity for "experiential improvisation" within development teams. *Hansen* and *Frontier System's* processes for organising software development work and the culture through which they encourage sense-making, can be seen as imbued with the power-capacities of processes which enable collaboration and meaning systems which seek to ensure "product integrity".

In the *Frontier Systems* case, this is illustrated by the centrality of the "hybrid organisational" form as the means of seeking to bridge the gap between the software developer and the end user/customer. In effect, the approach sought to extract from the customer domain key employees who were carriers of technical expertise and "re-socialise" them, so that they could rethink the application of their knowledge in the rather different context and business ethos of *Frontier Systems* in its effort to fashion a new business solution for its client organisation.

The *Hansen* case demonstrates more traditional ways of using organisational boundaries to enable product development. In contrast to *Frontier Systems*, the role of product teams is defined more by the means deemed necessary to organise and compartmentalise a large and complicated product development task. *Hansen* mass produce software and the introduction of MSF is clearly a strong symbolic tool to balance out the need for creativity and teamwork with the requirements of large scale projects organised to deliver high quality outputs within shorter and shorter lead-teams. In this respect, MSF was used as a tool to downplay tendencies in more conventional arrangements for product teams to engage in "over the wall" development and not align their activity with a broader project vision.

In sum, we would suggest that the political action observed in both cases of network building can be seen as more or less successful attempts to find organisational processes, systems and structures which would improve communication and information flows that in turn would support knowledge exchange and synthesis through collaboration. In both instances, the parties concerned struggled to find and embed effective organisational arrangements that would deliver this. In the case of *Frontier Systems*, *Hansen* and the VARs, this was done in the context of a "pro-innovation organisational configuration" and cannot be viewed as the "buck the system" activities of isolated innovators. The picture of *EnergyCo*, of course, is more complex, and it is a moot point as to whether the termination of the collaboration by the new owner of the company was ultimately the product of a failure to overcome the "anti-innovation configuration" of the organisation. This, in turn, raises the question of whether a political failure occurred in the manner in which the coalitions of interest which established the hybrid project organisation managed the building process. The management challenge in this respect is neatly set out in this quotation from the CEO of *Frontier Systems* made in a company publication:

> *In a world where the lines between companies, industries, and even nations get blurred, a leader builds an effective organization around values and work style. And a leader learns to define success in business as both producing financial strength and generating a team of people who support and nurture each other.*

Conclusion

Our analysis has demonstrated the emergent character and political dynamics of the product development process in networks of inter-firm collaborations. In general, the findings of the BiCoN project point to what can be termed as the "paradox of networking". That is, technological (and indeed other forms of) collaboration are normally presented as predicated on organisational intentions to seek a reduction in uncertainty in changing and unpredictable market and technological conditions. However, on the other hand, such behaviour exposes the organisation and its incumbents to new risks and uncertainties. These are associated with the complexities of forging collaborative relationships and the potentially novel (for the participants) organisational arrangements that may arise. Thus, whilst being a source of risk reduction, collaboration in innovation networks may expose collaborators to new sources of vulnerability associated with building and managing network relationships and new organisational forms (e.g. Dodgson, 2000: 171).

As we have tried to show here, the building of collaborative networks can usefully be viewed as a power-process that requires political action. Such action can be conceptualised in terms of resource dependencies as a source of structuring in network relationships; the manner and means through which coalition building contributes to network formation and maintenance; and the role of deeper structures such as culture as sources for creating common and shared meanings and values in relation to the product development process. Seen in this way, politics is not necessarily or inevitably a disruptive feature for innovation; neither is it antithetical to collaboration, trust-building, or learning. Indeed, we would contend that it is the means through which innovation in new product development involving collaborative networking is brought about and achieved. As such, we consider mastering (rather than minimising or avoiding) the political to be a central element of the eventual success of any product development endeavour.

Acknowledgements

This data is derived from a European Union funded project — "Building Collaborative Networks in New Product Development (BiCoN) — funded through Phase Two of the Targeted Socio-Economic Research Programme under contract number PL97–1084. The funding period was January 1998 to December 1999. The project involved research teams in the UK (led by Keith Dickson and Ian McLoughlin); Denmark (led by Christian Koch); and Germany (led by Fred Manske). Other project researchers were Lisa Harris, Anne-Marie Coles and Ruth McNally (UK); Allan Pleman, Ole Broberg, Henrik A.B. Hansen and Per Richard Hansen (Denmark); and Yonggap Moon (Germany). Primary responsibility for writing this article rests with Ian McLoughlin and Christian Koch. An earlier version of this paper was presented at the CISTEMA Conference on "Bringing Materiality (Back) Into Management", Copenhagen October 21–23, 1999. The project team would like to thank the EU Commission and all of the organisations and individual participants in the program-me for their help and assistance in conducting this research, as well as the article's anonymous reviewers for their helpful and constructive comments. The "torso lives"!

References

Aoki, A. (1984) *The Cooperative Game Theory of the Firm*. Oxford: Clarendon Press

Badham, R., McLoughlin, I.P. & Couchman, P. (1997) Implementing vulnerable socio-technical change projects. In *Innovation, Organisational Change and Technology*, ed. I.P. McLoughlin & M. Harris. London: ITB Press

Brown, S. & Eisenhardt, K.M. (1995) Produce development: Past research, present findings and future directions. *Academy of Management Review*, **20**(2), 343–379

Buchanan, D. & Badham, R. (1999) *Power, Politics and Organisational Change*. London: Sage

Child, J. & Faulkner, D. (1998) *Strategies of Cooperation*. Oxford: Oxford University Press

Clark, K. & Fujimoto, T. (1991) *Product Development Performance: Strategy, Management and Organisation in the World Automobile Industry*. Boston: Harvard Business School Press

Clausen, C. & Koch, C. (1999) The role of occasions and spaces in the transformation of information technologies. *Technology Analysis and Strategic Management*, **11**(3), 463–482

Clegg, S.R. (1989) *Frameworks of Power*. London: Sage

Cohen, C., Walsh, V. & Richards, A. (1998) Learning by designer-user interactions: An analysis of usability activities as coordination mechanisms in the product development process. In *Management and Technology*, EC Cost A3, **5**, ed. C. Garcia & L. Sanz-Menéndez, pp. 61–78

Conway, S. & Steward, F. (1998) Mapping innovation networks. *International Journal of Innovation Management*, **2**(2), 223–254

Coombs, R., Richards, A., Saviotti, P. & Walsh, V. (eds.) (1996) *Technological Collaboration: The Dynamics of Cooperation in Industrial Innovation*. Cheltenham: Edward Elgar

Cusumano, M.A. & Selby, R.W. (1995) *Microsoft Secrets: How the World's Most Powerful Software Company Creates Technology, Shapes Markets and Manages People*. New York: The Free Press

Dawson, P. (1984) *Organisational Change: A Processual Perspective*. London: Paul Chapman

DeBresson, C. & Amesse, F. (1991) Networks of innovators: A synthesis of research issues. *Research Policy*, **20**(5), 363–379

Dickson, K. (1996) How informal can you be? Trust and reciprocity within cooperative and collaborative relationships. *International Journal of Technology Management*, **11**(1–2), 129–139

Dodgson, M. (1993) *Technological Collaboration in Industry*, London: Routledge

Dodgson, M. (2000) *The Management of Technological Innovation*. Oxford: Oxford University Press

Dougherty, D. & Hardy, C. (1996) Sustained product innovation in large mature organisations: Overcoming innovation to organisation problems. *Academy of Management Journal*, **39**(5), 1120–1153

Elg, U. & Johansson, U. (1997). Decision making in inter-firm networks as political process. *Organisation Studies*, **18**(3), 361–384

Ford, D. & Thomas, R. (1997) Technology strategy in networks. *International Journal of Technology Management*, **14**(6–8), 596–612

Freeman, C. (1991) Networks of innovators: A synthesis of research issues. *Research Policy*, **20**(5), 499–514

Frost, P. & Egri, C. (1991) The political process of innovation. *Research in Organisational Behaviour*, **13**, 229–295

Green, K., Hull, R., McMeekin, A. & Walsh, V. (1999) Construction of the techno-economic: Networks vs. paradigms. *Research Policy*

Harris, L., Coles, A.M., Dickson, K. & McLoughlin, I.P. (1999) Building collaborative networks: New product development across organisational boundaries. In *Virtual Working: Social and Organisational Dynamics*, ed. P. Jackson. London: Routledge

Hislop, D., Newell, S., Scarborough, H. & Swann, J. (1997) *Innovation and Networks*, paper given at British Academy of Management Conference, London

Ingham, G. (1996) Critical survey: Some recent changes in the relationship between economics and sociology. *Cambridge Journal of Economics*, **20**, 243–275

Jones, O., Conway, S. & Steward, F. (1998) Introduction: Social interaction and innovation networks. *International Journal of Innovation Management*, **2**(2), 123–136

Koch, C. (2000a) The ventriloquist's dummy? — The role of technology in political processes. *Technology Analysis and Strategic Management*, **12**(1), 119–138

Koch, C. (2000b) *ERP Software Packages — Between Mass Production Communities and Intra-organisational Political Processes*. Paper prepared for the EGOS-colloquium: Sub-theme 11 Technological Change and Organisational Action. Helsinki

Kyng, M. & Mathiassen, L. (1997) *Computers and Design in Context*. Cambridge Mass.: MIT Press

Latour, B. (1988) *Science in Action*. London: Sage

Lawton Smith, H., Dickson, K. & Smith, S. (1991) There are two sides to every story: Innovation and collaboration with networks of small and large firms. *Research Policy*, **20**(5), 457–468

Lawton Smith, H., Dickson, K. & Coles, A.M. (1996) Adapting to new realities: Learning by doing in inter-firm collaboration. In *Knowledge, Technology and Innovative Organisations*, ed. S. Piccaluga & R. Butler. Italy: Guerni e associati

McLoughlin, I.P. (1999) *Creative Technological Change: The Shaping of Technology and Organisation*. London: Routledge

McLoughlin, I.P. & Dawson, P. (1999) *Twenty Years of Schooling, Still on the Day Shift? A Review of Research on New Technology, Work and Organisation.* Unpublished paper

McLoughlin, I.P., Badham, R. & Couchman, P. (2000) Configurations and frames: Rethinking the political process perspective. *Technology Analysis and Strategic Management*, **12**(1)

Midler, C.(1993) *L'auto qui n'existait Pas.* Paris: Intereditions

Miles, R.E. & Snow, C.C. (1986) Network organisation: New concepts for new forms. *The McKinsey Quarterly*, Autumn

Pavitt, K. (1990) Strategic management in the innovating firm. In *Frontiers of Management*, ed. R. Mansfield. London: Routledge

Pettigrew, A. (1985) *The Awakening Giant.* Oxford: Blackwell

Pfeffer, J. (1992) *Managing with Power: Politics and Influence in Organisations.* Boston, Mass.: Harvard Business Press

Russell, S. (1996) *At the Margin: British Electricity Generation after Nationalisation and Privatisation, and the Fortunes of Combined Heat and Power.* SHOT '96. *http://www.uow.edu.au/arts/sts/srussell*

Sako, M. (1992) *Prices, Quality and Trust: Inter-firm relations in Britain and Japan.* Cambridge: Cambridge University Press

Sako, M. (1998) *Trust Within and Between Organisations.* Oxford: Oxford University Press

Senker, J. & Faulkner, W. (1992) Networks, tacit knowledge and innovation. In *Technological Collaboration: The Dynamics of Cooperation in Industrial Innovation*, ed. R. Coombs, A. Richards, P. Saviotti & V. Walsh. Cheltenham: Edward Elgar

Steward, F. & Conway, S. (1996) Informal networks in the origination of successful innovations. In *Technological Collaboration: The Dynamics of Cooperation in Industrial Innovation*, ed. R. Coombs, A. Richards, P.P. Saviotti & V. Walsh. Cheltenham: Edward Elgar

Storey, J. (2000) The management of innovation problem. *International Journal of Innovation Management*, **4**(3), 347–369

Thomas, R. (1994) *What Machines Can't Do.* Berkeley: University of California Press

Tidd, J. (1997) Complexity, networks and learning: Integrative themes for research on the management of innovation. *International Journal of Innovation Management*, **1**(1), 1–19

Vergragt, P.J., Groenewegen, P. & Mulder, K.F. (1992) Industrial technological innovation: Interrelationships between technological, economic and sociological analysis. In *Technological Change and Company Strategies: Economic and Sociological Perspectives*, ed. R. Coombs, A. Richards, P. Saviotti & V. Walsh

ELSEVIER

Research Policy 24 (1995) 543–562

Innovation, networks, and vertical integration ☆

Paul L. Robertson [a,*], Richard N. Langlois [b]

[a] *Department of Economics and Management University College, University of New South Wales, ADFA, Campbell, A.C.T. 2600, Australia*

[b] *Department of Economics, The University of Connecticut, U63 Storrs, CT 06269-1063, USA*

Final version received March 1994

Abstract

A central debate in industrial policy today is that between proponents of large vertically integrated firms on the one hand and those of networks of small specialized producers on the other. This paper argues that neither institutional structure is the panacea its supporters claim. The menu of institutional alternatives is in fact quite large, and both firms and networks, of which there are several kinds, can be successful, growth-promoting adaptations to the competitive environment. Industrial structures vary in their ability to coordinate information flows necessary for innovation and to overcome power relationships adverse to innovation. The relative desirability of the various structures, then, depends on the nature and scope of technological change in the industry and on the effects of various product life-cycle patterns. The principal policy conclusion of this analysis is that the government's role ought to be facilitating rather than narrow and prescriptive, allowing scope for firms to develop organizational forms that are best adapted to their particular environments.

1. Introduction

The debate over the institutional forms most conducive to economic growth has intensified in recent years. In the mid-1980s, Michael Piore, Charles Sabel, and Jonathan Zeitlin challenged the notion that the growth of large businesses in twentieth-century Britain and the United States had been either necessary or desirable. On the basis of developments in Continental Europe, they have contended that communities of skilled craftsmen are as capable of generating high standards of living as are giant, vertically integrated firms (Piore and Sabel, 1984; Sabel and Zeitlin, 1985; Sabel et al., 1987; Sabel, 1989). Moreover, they claim, small firms are more flexible and thus better adapted to engendering and adopting innovations. To take advantage of these capabilities, they recommend reorienting the American economy towards small, craft-based firms that operate in a cooperative environment. Michael Best (1990) has reinforced this call, questioning the efficiency of both vertically integrated Western firms and Japanese networks and arguing

☆ An earlier version of this paper was presented at the Euro-Conference on Evolutionary and Neoclassical Perspectives on Market Structure and Economic Growth, held in Athens on 24–25 September 1993, at the Columbia University workshop on Comparative Corporate Governance, Industrial Organization, and Competitive Performance, 22 November 1993, and to seminars at the Australian National University and the University of Manchester. We particularly wish to thank David Audretsch and Dick Nelson for their help and encouragement.

* Corresponding author.

SSDI 0048-7333(94)00786-7

instead for the growth of geographical concentrations of small firms organized cooperatively along the lines of the 'Third Italy.' [1]

Other writers believe that large vertically integrated firms are in the best position to develop and exploit innovations. In contrast to Piore and Sabel and Best, William Lazonick contends that economies of scale will remain overwhelmingly important and that small firms will not be able to compete effectively in many areas. As a result, Lazonick believes, growth must be based on giant organizations that are able to combine strategic flexibility with access to economies of scale. But to survive, such organizations must have 'privileged access to resources,' including control of marketing and the supply of inputs, in order to provide the security to justify investments in large production facilities (Lazonick, 1990 and 1991a).

Richard Florida and Martin Kenney also believe that a high degree of vertical integration is desirable, but stress the need to coordinate basic research and development activities with product development and manufacturing in order to gain maximum benefits from scientific and engineering breakthroughs (Florida and Kenney, 1990a). Florida and Kenney and Lazonick are critical of Piore and Sabel and of current American developments in Silicon Valley and along Route 128 in Massachusetts because, they claim, small firms cannot fully realize the potential that seminal discoveries offer. As a result, well-articulated Japanese and Korean industrial conglomerates are appropriating the bulk of the benefits of American discoveries and, increasingly, are themselves making the important breakthroughs on which future growth will be based (Florida, 1990a, chapter 6). [2]

An intermediate position has been staked out by Michael E. Porter. Porter believes that, in order to be successful in international markets, firms must first develop the knack of competing domestically. To achieve this, he advocates a high degree of rivalry among firms in their home markets. He also cites the importance of networks of suppliers to provide inexpensive and flexible access to inputs (Porter, 1990). And, like Piore and Sabel, Porter believes that geographic concentrations of producers can increase productivity by enhancing access to knowledge and other factors of production. Although Lazonick (1991b) has criticized Porter's support for a high degree of domestic competition and networks of support firms, it is clear that, in contrast to Piore and Sabel, Porter is not advocating the establishment of ateliers when economies of scale are present.

There appear to be two basic differences between Porter and Lazonick. First, Porter believes that the American economy is large enough in most industries to justify competition among several large firms, while Lazonick supports monopolies or very tight oligopolies in the domestic economy. To Lazonick, the most important rivalry is on the international stage and industries on the national level should conserve their strength for competition with firms from other countries. Second, Porter believes that an extensive web of outside suppliers and regional agglomerations of producers provide flexibility to cushion downturns and give broad access to technical improvements, whereas Lazonick emphasizes the security that arises from maintaining resources under centralized control.

Prescriptions for government industrial policy also vary among analysts. Lazonick (1990, 1991a, 1991b), for example, contends that governments should promote centralization and concentration

[1] The 'Third Italy' is the area of northeast Italy centering on the regions of Emilia-Romagna and Tuscany. Although a number of substantial cities, such as Bologna, Modena, Florence, and Reggio-Emilia, are in the area, much of the industry is located in smaller towns that specialize in the production of various items including ceramic tiles, textiles, and machine tools. These local industries are frequently organized in government-sponsored cooperatives that provide access to cheap capital and to services in marketing, accounting, etc. Initiative in design and other fields, however, is retained by the member firms, that are commonly family-owned and have twenty or fewer employees. See also Lazerson (1988), Brusco (1982), and Hatch (1987).

[2] This chapter is reproduced in Florida and Kenney (1990b). See also Lazonick (1991b).

to permit firms to meet competitive challenges from large foreign firms. Piore and Sabel (1984) and Best (1990), on the other hand, recommend that governments actively support the growth of small firms and industrial districts by generating policies that simultaneously promote competition and cooperation. Finally, Porter (1990) believes that governments should emphasize the creation of environments that encourage domestic and international competition by promoting technological change, but that governments are in general ill-equipped to provide detailed economic direction.

All of these authors are grappling with the same problem of locating the patterns of industrial and firm organization that are most efficient in permitting a nation to innovate and gain or maintain productive superiority. [3] They have nevertheless reached a variety of contradictory prescriptions. The fundamental reasons for this confusion are twofold: the authors define firms and networks in fuzzy and inconsistent ways; and they provide sweepingly general recommendations to cover a variety of cases that are in many ways dissimilar.

In this paper, we examine the relationship between innovation and industry and firm structure to determine whether flexibility and the scope for change vary across environments. We conclude that the ability of various types of organizational structures to support innovation successfully depends crucially on the scope of the innovation and the relative maturity of the industries involved. As a result of the wide range of variations present in advanced industrial economies, any generalized government policy towards innovation is likely to be unsuitable for the needs of many sectors.

2. The lessons of history?

Lazonick and Piore, Sabel, and Zeitlin have all used historical evidence to support their policy recommendations. Lazonick draws heavily on the work of Alfred D. Chandler, Jr. to demonstrate that the growth of manufacturing since the late nineteenth century has been closely correlated to the degree of horizontal and vertical integration in 'cutting-edge' industries. In *The Visible Hand* (1977), Chandler showed that the rapid growth of firms in a number of American industries between 1870 and 1940 was based on significant and continuing increases in economies of scale. In order to take advantage of these scale economies, small firms that had been restricted to local markets merged to serve regional or even national markets. Horizontal integration in itself was rarely if ever enough to guarantee viability, however, because such collections of small enterprises could not gain the benefit of scale economies unless they were rationalized into larger units under central control. Thus the 'visible hand' of management was needed to initiate and direct the new giant firms. Moreover, because of the larger investments in fixed capital which were required, enormous size entailed greater risk. As a result, managers attempted to shield giant firms from market uncertainties by integrating forwards and backwards in the hope of ensuring supplies of inputs and, in particular, increasing the demand for finished products to keep pace with growing productive capabilities.

More recently, Chandler has extended his analysis to British and German history. He states, for example, that Britain's relative decline as a manufacturing power after 1870 occurred because "British entrepreneurs failed to make the essential three-pronged investment in manufac-

[3] Lazonick, Piore and Sabel, Best, and Florida and Kenney are also explicitly interested in finding ways of providing more interesting work, greater job stability, and better wages for the industrial labor force than currently prevails in the United States. In general, they recommend that this can be accomplished by increasing the intellectual content of factory employment and the scope for decision-making available to individual workers. Florida and Kenney, for example, "see the Japanese model as a successor to Fordism that uses new organizational forms to harness the intellectual as well as the physical capabilities of workers." (1991, p. 383.) Here, however, we concentrate on the authors' proposals concerning firm and industrial organization.

turing, marketing, and management in a number of the capital-intensive industries of the Second Industrial Revolution." [4] In other words, the British erred in not building large facilities or, when they did, in continuing to rely on market mechanisms and not providing adequate internal marketing and management skills to coordinate and protect their investments.

This, essentially, is the model that Lazonick projects into the future. He believes that to prosper nations must take advantage of substantial economies of scale in major industries, and that this requires centralized management and a high degree of vertical integration to overcome market deficiencies. To the extent that American firms are inhibited, either through government policy, market fragmentation, or managerial ineptitude, from matching the control that foreign competitors hold over resources, they will, he feels, lose out in a world of increasing returns.

Piore, Sabel, and Zeitlin provide a very different view of recent developments. [5] To them, the adoption of the paradigm of mass production represents the triumph of an idea rather than an economic necessity. Because of the highly publicized triumphs of producers such as Henry Ford, large firms came to be regarded as the norm. Nevertheless, craft production retained advantages in flexibility and variety that were overlooked as Britain and the United States moved towards gargantuan factories in the twentieth century. As counter-examples, Sabel and Zeitlin cite certain industries in France and Italy that maintained their craft traditions and prospered as a result. Piore, Sabel, and Zeitlin maintain that large firms often fail to cope successfully with the accelerating rate of innovation that they perceive, or to take advantage of the flexibility permitted by new production technologies. They recommend instead that the American economy be reoriented towards smaller firms, clustered in industrial districts, similar to those in the Third Italy, where they can develop symbiotically.

It is clear that Lazonick and Piore, Sabel, and Zeitlin are all correct in the sense that both large and small firms have thrived historically and continue to exist. But neither set of examples precludes the other because different industries are involved. In certain industries, such as iron and steel, automobile manufacturing and some branches of chemicals, economies of scale proved so strong that small firms were virtually wiped out in the first half of the twentieth century. [6] Chandler, however, probably overestimates the importance of these industries (Supple, 1991; Landes, 1991). In many other cases, economies of scale were limited, although increases in productivity may nevertheless have been great. In these latter industries, which include some branches of machinery manufacture, clothing, and retailing, small, highly competitive firms have been able to retain strong positions. Thus, if history is a guide to the future, then either the Lazonick or the Piore and Sabel scenario is feasible.

But it is a fundamentally ahistorical procedure to project future developments on the basis of supposed past, or even current, trends. Each experience occurs within its own context. The patterns outlined by Lazonick and Sabel and Zeitlin are essentially compressions of the experiences of many institutions (firms or industries) within their own environments. Not only is there reason to believe that the context of future developments will be different from that of the past, but there will be a variety of different contexts within which

[4] Chandler (1990), p. 236. Chandler explains the three prongs in more detail on p. 8.

[5] The historical material in chapter 2 of Piore and Sabel (1984) is a reworking of an article by Sabel and Zeitlin (1985). See also Sabel (1989) and Sabel et al. (1987). The latter article contrasts the recent decline of large textile machinery firms based in Massachusetts and the prosperity of similar but much smaller firms in Baden-Wurttemberg.

[6] Except, of course, for a few specialist firms such as Rolls Royce that could produce in small volumes because customers were willing to pay premium prices for high quality or distinctive features.

future firms and industries will be developing simultaneously. [7]

What is needed, therefore, is a way of predicting how these institutions will behave within their particular environments rather than an overarching model that may be inadequate to deal with the needs of any particular institution. It is to this that we now turn.

3. Networks and networks

Vertically integrated firms and loose webs of small producers are only two of types of networks operating in modern economies. [8] One way of classifying networks is according to their degree of formal articulation. When examined in this way, they range along a spectrum from market-based systems, with each transaction between components being conducted separately, to unified concerns that, as far as possible, internalize their activities through common ownership and control of the functions of supply, research, operations, and marketing. This way of casting the spectrum from 'market' to 'firm' goes back at least to Coase (1937) and is implicit (and sometimes explicit) in most of the modern transaction-cost literature. [9] Although useful for many purposes, however, this unidimensional characterization lacks much of the subtlety needed to think carefully about networks. There are in fact many dimensions along which various forms of industrial organization differ from one another. For the moment, we suggest that expansion from one dimension to two will yield a high marginal increase in explanatory power. [10]

There is something of a debate in the present-day economics of organization between the nexus-of-contracts view of the firm (Cheung, 1983) and the property-rights view (Hart, 1989). The former holds that organization within a firm is no less a contractual matter than organization through markets, and a 'firm' is nothing more than a particularly dense intersection of contracts. What differs between market and firm is the nature of the contracts involved, with contracts within the firm having an ongoing and more open-ended character (Ben-Porath, 1980). Such contracts require various degrees of conscious, ongoing administrative coordination among the parties. We might say, then, that the essence of the firm in this view is the nature of the coordination involved. In the property rights view, by contrast, ownership is the issue. The boundaries of the firm, rather fuzzy under the 'nexus' view, are here brightly illuminated by the title to ownable assets, and two stages of production are held to be vertically integrated when the assets involved are under common ownership.

Rather than debating which view best captures the essence of the notion of vertical integration, we can recognize that each captures an aspect of what integration means. Moreover, these two aspects are potentially separable. A major automobile firm can be integrated into the production of a particular part in the sense that it owns a company producing such parts, even if the parent deals with the subsidiary largely through the market on a more-or-less equal footing with other suppliers. At the same time, two distinct legal entities may be engaged in an ongoing develop-

[7] Lazonick (1991a, pp. 271–273) contends that an historical approach to development is preferable to the pared-down methodology of conventional economists, who have sacrificed much of the explanatory complexity of reality to produce 'an economic theory that is not bound by time and place.' Even if one accepts Lazonick's critique of 'conventional' economics, however, the fact remains that immersion in historical complexity will not, in itself, lead to good predictions if the conditions pertaining in the past were significantly different from those of the future.

[8] For a summary of the literature surrounding networks, see Bureau of Industry Economics (1991).

[9] For example, Williamson, 1985.

[10] Powell (1990, pp. 296–300) suggests that the notion that there is a 'continuum' of organizational forms ranging from markets through networks to vertically integrated firms is both inaccurate and analytically unhelpful. We feel that there are systematic relationships between organizational forms and various exogenous and endogenous conditions which can usefully be represented as spectra. We do concede, however, that as in Fig. 2 below, the order in which the organizational forms appear along a given spectrum may vary depending on which other factors are under consideration.

ment project that involves exclusive dealing, significant exchange of information, and administrative coordination.

We thus have two dimensions along which to analyze organizational forms. One dimension is the degree of ownership integration, the other is the degree of coordination integration. (see Fig. 1). We can use this construct to revisit various kinds of actually existing networks.

The loosest type of network is the Marshallian industrial district. Alfred Marshall (1961) based this concept on a pattern of organization that was common in late nineteenth century Britain in which firms concentrating on the manufacture of certain products were geographically clustered. In some cases, these clusters were highly specialized. While Lancashire as a whole was the center of cotton textile production, for example, individual towns within the county concentrated on spinning or weaving and on specific counts of yarn or styles of fabric. Similarly, different shipbuilding districts specialized in particular classes of vessels, and various Midlands cities such as Birmingham and Coventry became centers of different branches of the engineering industry. The characteristics of Marshallian industrial districts are similar to the "social structures of innovation" listed by Florida and Kenney: "integrative systems comprised of ... technology-oriented enterprise, highly skilled labor, considerable ... private R&D expenditures, extensive networks of suppliers, manufacturers and vendors, support firms such as law firms and consultants ..., strong entrepreneurial networks, and informal mechanisms for information exchange and technology transfer." (1988, p. 130.)

The two dominant characteristics of a Marshallian industrial district are high degrees of vertical and horizontal specialization and a very heavy reliance on market mechanisms for exchange. Firms tend to be small and to focus on a single function in the production chain. Suppliers of intermediate goods commonly sell their stocks locally, within the district, although the final products may be marketed internationally. Firms located in industrial districts are also highly competitive in the neoclassical sense, and in many cases there is little product differentiation. The major advantages of Marshallian industrial districts therefore arise from simple propinquity of

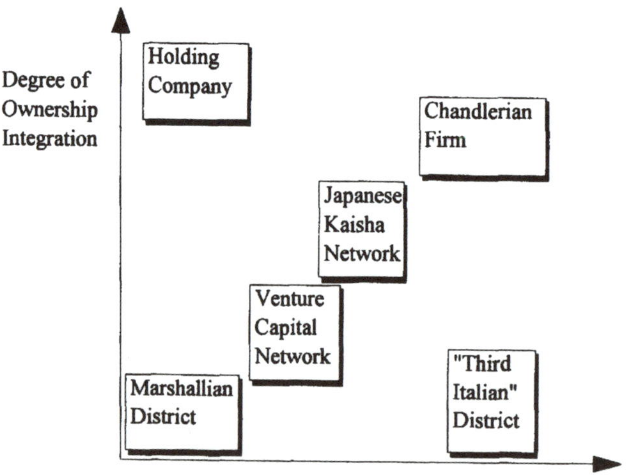

Fig. 1. Two dimensions of integration.

firms, which allows easier recruitment of skilled labor and rapid exchanges of commercial and technical information through informal channels. As Marshall described them, industrial districts illustrate competitive capitalism at its most efficient, with transaction costs reduced to a practical minimum; but they are feasible only when economies of scale are limited.

Recent commentators have revived the term 'industrial district' to describe somewhat different types of organizational arrangements. As applied to the 'Third Italy', the term indicates a higher degree of cooperative coordination than would be present in a Marshallian industrial district. In this part of Italy, vertical and horizontal specialization are again high and firms are generally small. Competition is high and barriers to entry and exit are low. Competition is limited to certain spheres of activity, however, in which firms might be expected to develop distinctive competences (Lazerson, 1988). [11] In general, this means design, especially in industries such as ceramics and textiles. For those activities in which economies of scale extend beyond the range of individual small firms and the degree of standardization is high, firms in industrial districts in Italy tend to favor cooperative arrangements, which are normally government sanctioned. Cooperation is common in such activities as business services, including bookkeeping; sponsorship of trade fairs and other domestic and, in particular, international marketing ventures; and the provision of utilities and other infrastructure. [12] Cooperation also extends to the provision of capital, which the banks lend directly to official cooperatives, who guarantee the loans and determine the distribution of funds among member firms (Brusco and Righi, 1987). As a result, small firms are able to sell their output in world markets and to gain some of the benefits of scale economies while continuing to compete strongly with each other.

Because of the legal advantages that pertain to small firms, many producers in the 'Third Italy' are reluctant to employ directly more than 15 or so workers. To avoid expanding too far, however, firms do take ownership positions in 'satellite firms' that maintain legal independence. Interestingly, the satellite firms are not generally used to expand output and increase market control, but to protect the core competences of the original enterprise by providing intermediate goods at lower cost or with greater security. The acquisition of satellites is also used to gain control over complementary design capabilities. The networks of satellites therefore represent small islands of ownership and control integration within the larger horizontally integrated networks of the cooperatives (Lazerson, 1988).

A second recent variation on the industrial district is the innovative network, as represented by Silicon Valley and Route 128. As in Marshallian industrial districts, coordination integration is low in these districts, [13] but some coordination is supplied by the venture capitalists who put up the initial seed money. The venture capitalists are specialist investors who have close connections throughout the districts and are also able to provide new firms with entrepreneurial and managerial guidance and connections with potential suppliers and customers (Florida and Kenney, 1988). [14] Under this arrangement, there are two networks, one of producers that approximates the

[11] This is consistent with the analysis that Bettis, Bradley, and Hamel (1992, pp. 18–20) present of outsourcing by Western firms, in which they indicate that firms should protect their core competences by producing them internally and that they should restrict outsourcing to peripheral activities. Sabel et al. (1987) describe similar conditions in Baden-Württemberg. Sabel (1989, p. 53) also discusses the role of distinctive competences in networking situations.

[12] Good descriptions of the operation of Italian industrial districts is given in Best (1990) and Lazerson (1988). Similar arrangements prevail in certain American agricultural cooperatives such Land-o-Lakes or Ocean Spray that provide infrastructure and processing and marketing facilities for members.

[13] According to Saxenian (1991), however, in Silicon Valley there is now considerable cooperation among vertically specialized firms in the computer systems industry.

[14] Although Florida and Kenney are moderately well disposed towards venture capitalists in their article, they are far more negative in chapter 4 of their 1990 book on *The Breakthrough Illusion*.

market orientation of the Marshallian industrial district, and a second network of venture capitalists that is superimposed on the network of produçers. In addition, the degree of local focus is frequently reduced to the extent that the venture capitalists come from other regions.

Although there is stronger orientation towards cooperation in the 'Third Italy' than in Marshallian industrial districts, both models are based on organic growth. Even the government sponsorship of collective action in Italy is a reinforcement of a socialist ethos that has been the dominant attitude among small producers in Emilia-Romagna for nearly a century. Thus the emphasis in both models is on competition within an appropriate institutional context. In such innovative networks as Silicon Valley and along Route 128, there has been a similar organic growth: The development of nuclei of isolated firms into large clusters required more than two decades (Dorfman, 1983; Miller and Côté, 1985). The imposition of a network of venture capitalists, however, marks a significant step in the direction of centralization and outside control. As a consequence, the organic nature of competition in the local industries is reduced and industrial districts dominated by venture capitalism represent a movement along the dimensions of both coordination integration and ownership consolidation, even if such arrangements fall far short of vertical integration in the Chandlerian vein.

Modularity is a form of organization that is related conceptually to industrial districts. When there are few economies of scale in assembly and consumers prefer the ability to choose components rather than pre-packaged sets, vertical specialization will occur, with firms concentrating on individual modules. But while firms retain significant independence in design, manufacturing, and marketing, they cannot be totally oblivious to the practices of either their competitors or of manufacturers of other modules because assembly requires a high degree of standardization to permit compatibility. When there is modularity, therefore, both vertical and horizontal networks may arise, perhaps with government enforcement as in the case of radio frequencies (Langlois and Robertson, 1992).

Writers like Piore and Sabel extol industrial districts for their 'flexible specialization,' which allows swift adaptation to market changes and permits the realization of a wide range of separate visions as manufacturers concentrate on product niches (Piore and Sabel, 1984; Saxenian, 1990). Industrial districts are less appropriate, however, when there are potentially large economies of scale or high transaction costs. Under these conditions, different types of organization are needed.

One possibility is the establishment of core networks. As the name implies, these are organized around a single firm, which is usually a large assembler. The satellite firms supply intermediate inputs to the core, which effectively coordinates the network as a whole. The relationships between US and Japanese automobile manufacturers and their assemblers illustrate two types of core networks. US auto firms have traditionally dealt with suppliers at 'arm's length,' using short-term contracts and exacting discipline by switching to other sources if they are dissatisfied with price, quality, or regularity of delivery. Suppliers fill orders as detailed by the core purchasers and are seldom given any discretion over design (Helper, 1991).

American core networks often approximate monopsonistic market relationships. Although, in theory, suppliers may serve a variety of firms, in practice this may be precluded by asset specificity, as dies and other capital equipment cannot be readily transferred to other uses. As a result, large US firms are able to use their bargaining power to exact low prices when dealing with small suppliers operating in competitive markets. The transaction costs of maintaining impersonal market relationships may be great, however, as the willingness of US core firms to switch suppliers engenders little loyalty from the latter, who therefore tend to stick to the letter of contracts and are reluctant to offer help when they are able. In any case, given the centralized nature of decision-making, there is only a slim chance that suggestions emanating from suppliers, including internal captive suppliers, would attract any attention at the core.

By contrast, the networks of Japanese automobile firms arguably serve to reduce transaction costs by establishing what Florida and Kenney (1991, p. 395) have termed "tightly networked production complexes." One aspect of this networking lies along the coordination dimension. As Smitka (1991) and others have argued, the longer-term 'relational' contracts among Japanese assemblers and suppliers, supported by rational, economically motivated structures of trust, reduce the transaction costs of bilateral monopoly. Moreover, such contracts, by encouraging the sharing of information, spur supplier-generated innovation in a way foreclosed to the American firms. Another, less-noticed, aspect of Japanese automotive networks is that they represent a more effective decentralization scheme. Rather than hoarding most technical and design knowledge inhouse, Japanese lead auto firms parcel out discrete modules to suppliers. "Typically," as Helper and Levine (1992, p. 563) write, "a Japanese automaker will not undertake the design of a part that it requires for a new model. Instead it will specify exterior dimensions and performance characteristics, and allow a specialist supplier to design the part to best match its process." For example, an American firm typically assembles a car seat from parts supplied by some 25 different subcontractors. By contrast, a Japanese firm will subcontract the entire seat to a 'first-tier' subcontractor, who will then assume primary responsibility for design, quality, and compatibility (Womack, Jones, and Roos, 1990). This efficient modularization also serves to reduce transaction costs, allowing the network of outside suppliers to achieve a higher level of productive capabilities than in the American system. The suppliers respond in Japan by increasing product specialization to a high degree (Odaka, Ono, and Adachi, 1988), giving the system some of the character of a Marshallian network. [15]

Another aspect of the Japanese supplier network in automobiles lies along the ownership dimension. Although Japanese core firms directly produce a smaller proportion of their components than do their American competitors and have a far smaller number of workers per unit produced, they often own a substantial stake in their suppliers, who are therefore not truly independent. Japanese suppliers are also provided with help in finding land close to the core factory to facilitate just-in-time deliveries. In part, the virtues of this ownership quasi-integration derive from the coordination integration it facilitates. Because of their close financial connections, Japanese core firms have an interest in the prosperity of their suppliers and an incentive to engage in reciprocal cooperation that is not present in America. But a dynamic perspective casts the ownership aspects of the network in a somewhat different light. Such ownership ties are part of efforts by the lead firms to create and cultivate the network of suppliers rather than efforts to manage the network once created. The strategy of creating an external network rather than producing in-house has long been a conscious strategy in the Japanese auto industry, albeit one forced on the industry in part in response to labor unrest in the early 1950s (Smitka, 1991).

Formal vertical integration is at the far end of our spectrum. Here, stages of production are under common ownership, and administrative coordination prevails over arm's-length coordination. Again, ownership integration does not by itself lead to centralized control, as firms may choose to have divisions deal with each other on an arm's-length basis to simulate market transactions. Alternatively, central management may through oversight or weakness lose control over internal divisions, which are then able to act independently. Indeed, it is important to remember that the innovation of the multi-divisional (M-form) structure was in one sense an innovation in decentralization. What made the large vertically integrated firms possible was an efficient parceling out of knowledge and control to modular subunits, with the core retaining only higher-level strategic functions. [16] This system is

[15] On networks in Japan from a native's perspective, see Imai and Itami (1984) and Imai (1989).

[16] Williamson (1985) discusses this decentralization in cybernetic terms: that it permits a separation of control over disturbances in degree (day-to-day management) from control of disturbances in kind (strategic management).

thus rather closer to the Japanese core network than one might think, except that strategic control is arguably greater in the M-form firm and, as Williamson argues in theory and students of industry have confirmed in practice, [17] internal supply divisions lack the 'high-powered incentives' of a financially independent (or at least quasi-independent) relationship.

Thus, in practice, the degrees of vertical integration available to producers are finely graded and may be chosen according to needs. There is no single degree of integration, or form of firm or industry organization, that suits all purposes. In some cases, firms may even mix forms as in the case of taper integration, in which firms produce a proportion of their needs for a given input internally and purchase the remainder from outside suppliers (Harrigan, 1983).

The degree of horizontal integration is also important in determining how effectively an innovation is adopted. The ability to generate research funds, for example, and the variety of options that might be tried in an uncertain research environment may be affected by the size of firms and their ability to cooperate. Small firms are often lauded for their responsiveness to the need for change. Moreover, many independent research efforts may generate more ideas than a few larger teams (Nelson and Winter, 1977). When research is expensive, however, small firms may be unable to pay the price of admission while large firms and consortia can tap greater pools of resources.

Forms of horizontal integration also vary. In a Marshallian industrial district, firms are independent for most purposes. [18] Formal horizontal combinations characterize the industrial districts of the 'Third Italy', however, and ad hoc horizontal combinations promoted by venture capitalists operate in American industrial districts that feature Innovative Networks. In general, large US firms are discouraged by antitrust laws and other regulations from horizontal cooperation, but this is less true in Japan and Europe. As in the case of vertical integration, the most efficient form of horizontal integration for promoting innovation depends on the circumstances of the particular case.

4. Specialization and appropriability

Specialization and the appropriability of benefits also exert conflicting influences on the choice of organizational form in an innovative environment. The advantages that flow from specialization and the division of labor should lead to a low degree of vertical and horizontal integration. The ability of an originator to appropriate the benefits arising from an innovation may be constrained, however, if the adoption and use of the innovation depend significantly on the activities of other firms, either at the same or different stages in the production process. When there are important appropriability problems (when the benefits flowing from an innovation are likely to elude the originator and fall into the pockets of others), increases in horizontal and vertical integration may therefore enhance the probability of both origination and adoption.

The advantages of specialization for promoting innovation are well-known. Adam Smith believed that workers would become more alert to improvements as they concentrated on performing fewer activities. By analogy, vertically specialized firms would also be expected to be more adept than integrated firms at isolating and solving problems. Horizontal specialization could also foster innovation by increasing the number of competing units searching for solutions to a given problem. Whereas there would be only a few groups of problem solvers in an oligopolistic market and the number of firms in which innovations could be implemented and tested would be limited, competition among a large number of firms could generate significantly more ideas and provide more opportunities for trial and adoption. Furthermore, if firms were clustered and the mobility of personnel high, as in an industrial district, rapid exchanges of information would

[17] For example, Womack, Jones, and Roos (1990), p. 143.

[18] Although even in nineteenth-century Britain certain kinds of collective action were common, especially employers' associations to combat unions.

speed up the sorting process leading to the identification of the best solution.

However, this method of problem solving might be inappropriate for certain types of systemic innovation. When the innovation involves changes that span stages of production or even industries, the same sort of concentration of activity that Smith praises could make it less likely that linkages would be discovered—that information would flow to where it is needed. As a result, specialization could retard recognition that an innovation produced for one purpose could serve other needs. Moreover, innovations adopted at one stage of a production chain could prove to be suboptimal for efficiency at other stages. Thus excessive specialization might hamper both the development and adoption of innovations. Development, for example, would appear less attractive if only a portion of a wide variety of potential uses were envisioned initially; and adoption would be less likely if potential users were unaware of innovations that were developed for other purposes but might be of use to them.

Such factors underlie the appropriability problems discussed by David J. Teece (1986) and Will Mitchell (1989; 1991). There are two essential sets of barriers that could keep the developer of an innovation from gaining a high enough share of the benefits to make development worthwhile. These barriers correspond to our two dimensions of coordination and ownership. The first, as we have just discussed, is imperfect information flows. When people are unaware either of the existence of suitable solutions for their problems or of problems that can be beneficially treated by particular solutions, then the payoff to, and incentive for, innovative activity will be reduced. The second set of barriers concern power relationships. Discovers of a breakthrough who are not directly involved in the industry to which the innovation is to be applied may have very limited bargaining power because they cannot themselves bring about implementation. In order to gain any benefits, they may therefore be forced to sell or license the innovation at a small fraction of its ultimate value to the user if they are to gain any profits at all. Moreover, if imitation is easy—if patents or trade secrets do not effectively protect the innovator—an innovating firm may be at the mercy or competitor (or even supplier) firms who can enter quickly and take cheap advantage of the capabilities created at high cost by the innovator. To profit well from innovation in such circumstances, the innovator would have to own many of the assets complementary to the innovation.

Both of these kinds of obstacles point towards vertical integration as a means of speeding up the rate of innovation. Information impactedness (to use Williamson's term) can be reduced if the developer of an innovation and the user are in the same organization. Users—marketing or production teams—can make R & D experts (whether within their own organizations or elsewhere in the network) aware of specific commercial needs to which they should devote attention. On the other hand, if researchers in such a network come up with an unanticipated development, they can easily alert others in the extended organization who might be able to use it. In the absence of coordination integration, potential benefits might be lost altogether or ceded to others. It is arguable, for instance, that the relative decline of many mature industries in Western economies in recent decades is in part the result of their stark separation from many industries, particularly in semiconductors, in which relevant innovations have been generated. In the more coordinated keiretsu system of Japan, however, the separation has been muted and manufacturers of mature products have had better access to the information needed for innovation.

Vertical integration can also redress adverse power relationships. Under joint ownership, the owners or their immediate delegees can reorganize capabilities because they have ultimate (though not necessarily day-to-day) control. They can buy and sell and hire and fire. When the same organization is both the developer and the user of an innovation, then, the benefits are internalized and appropriability is no longer a problem. Potential developers would not be deterred by the prospect of surrendering a high proportion of the payoff. Notice, however, that this argument applies to ownership integration, not coordination integration, since in principle the innovator need only take financial positions in the complementary assets—long positions in those likely to appreciate and short positions in those likely to depreciate. [19] How much coordination integration is necessary will depend on the pure information costs of informing and persuading those with de facto control over cooperating assets. Ownership integration itself does not guarantee enough coordination to solve the problem of information fragmentation, which could in principle be solved by a closely linked network that was not integrated in ownership.

Morris Silver (1984) has provided a further explanation of the role of vertical integration in promoting innovation. According to Silver, innovating firms sometimes are forced to integrate forwards or backwards because they cannot find specialists who appreciate the full potential of the innovation and are willing to associate themselves with a new product. This may be either because they literally cannot understand what the innovators need or because they do not believe that the innovation is commercially viable. In these cases, in order to implement their ideas, innovators may have to engage in tasks they would rather delegate to existing specialists through market mechanisms. For example, when developing the assembly line, the Ford Motor Company was obliged to produce the prototypes for many of its new dedicated machines because it could not convince machine tools firms that it was practicable to build machines of the required specifications (Langlois and Robertson, 1989).

One implication of this is that the desirability of vertical integration may depend on the existing array of capabilities already available in the economy. When the existing arrangement of decentralized capabilities is very different from that required by a major systemic innovation, vertical integration, which permits a quicker and cheaper creation of new capabilities, may prove superior (Langlois, 1992b). This may indeed help explain the prevalence of large vertically integrated companies in the historical periods that Chandler chronicles. The major rearrangements of capabilities enabled by rapid economic growth and the rapid decline of transportation and communications costs in the nineteenth century were refractory to the existing system of decentralized capabilities. Change came from large integrated firms who could sweep away ill-adapted structures in a wave of 'creative destruction.' At other times and in other places, however, entrenched vertical integration can prove just as refractory to change (Robertson and Langlois, 1992). In the pre-war American automobile industry, for example, the strategic move by General Motors to the annual model change, along with product innovations emanating from smaller, less-integrated auto makers, forced Ford reluctantly into the production of a new model (the Model A), whose development disrupted the firm's entrenched internal sourcing chain and forced considerable vertical disintegration (Abernathy, 1978; Langlois and Robertson, 1989). One can make the case that the overall American problem in dealing with Japanese and other foreign competition since the 1970s has had much the same character.

5. Networks and economic change

Bound up in the preceding discussion were two distinct characteristics of innovation that affect the appropriateness of organizational forms, namely, the systemic character of the innovation and its radicalness. These two factors often ride together, but in principle they are separable. Following Teece (1986), we can talk about an innovation as systemic if change in one part of the system (one stage of production, for example) necessitates corresponding change in other parts; by contrast, an innovation is autonomous if change in one part can proceed without materially affecting the rest of the system. The conventional view, which we have followed so far, is that decentralized networks of innovation do well under conditions of autonomous innovation but that systemic innovation calls for integration of both ownership and coordination in order to surmount adverse power relationships and avoid information impactedness. Moreover, one would typically think

[19] On this point, see also Mark Casson (1982), pp. 206–8.

of systemic innovation as more 'radical' than autonomous, since changing many parts of a system is clearly a relatively drastic procedure, whereas adjusting only a part seems to be necessarily an incremental business. But there is an often-forgotten sense in which autonomous innovation can be the most radical of all; or rather, in which the most radical of innovations is necessarily autonomous.

Consider an innovation that most would view as radical: the personal computer. This innovation required bringing together information from many diverse areas: semiconductors, programming, electronic assembly, etc. Yet this innovation was not the work of large vertically integrated firms whose capabilities spanned many disciplines. Rather, it was the work of small firms, whose early attempts to get the large organizations to take them seriously were persistently rebuffed. Many large firms failed miserably in the business, and even the success of IBM came as the result of almost completely abandoning its internal capabilities in favor of those of the market (Langlois, 1992a).

Although the radicalness to which internal organization is adapted may be greater than that to which certain kinds of market-based networks are adapted, there is in the end a kind of radicalness (or newness or uncertainty) that large organizations do not handle well. For this type of uncertainty, a decentralized network does much better (Langlois and Everett 1992). But such a network may be very different from the kind of decentralized network adapted to slow or incremental change. Consider the following distinctions. (See Fig. 2). At one end of a spectrum we might think of parametric change, that is, change of certain known variables within a known framework. [20] For example, it may be highly uncertain which grade of cloth or which style of tile will be demanded this season, but it is well known to all what it means to produce a grade of cloth or a style of tile. For this kind of uncertainty, Marshallian and Third-Italian structures arguably work well. A more radical kind of uncertainty or change we might call strategic. This would typically involve rearranging capabilities in fairly drastic ways, but within known boundaries. Here a vertically integrated firm may have an advantage over a pure market network, for many of the reasons detailed above. Once the dynamic random-access memory chip became a known commodity, for instance, large Japanese (and more recently, Korean) firms were able strategically to redirect capabilities into their mass production more decisively than less-integrated American firms. At the most radical extreme, however, is what we may call structural change. The personal computer may be an example. Here the ability of a decentralized Innovative Network to generate a wide diversity of information signals and to move rapidly may be an overwhelming advantage. Of course, as time passes, the same technology will change status, suggesting, as we develop more fully below, that the appropriateness of organizational structures varies over the product life cycle. [21]

Marshallian and Italian Districts	Chandlerian Firms	Japanese Networks	Innovative Networks
Parametric	**Strategic**		**Structural**

Fig. 2. Degrees of radicalness of uncertainty.

[20] The distinction between parametric and structural follows Langlois (1984).

[21] Contrary to widespread prediction to the contrary, however, the personal computer industry has not matured in such a way that advantage has fallen to large vertically integrated concerns, Rather, the industry has arguably matured into a high-volume mass-production network akin to nineteenth-century Lancashire in cotton textiles. Large firms continue to be singularly unsuccessful, and those large firm that do play in the market do so by emulating their vertically decentralized competitors. The Japanese and Koreans have made few inroads despite dominance in certain high-tech components like flat-panel displays and CD drives. The most successful firms in the industry are Intel and Microsoft, both of whom essentially limit their integration to some strategic alliances. Overall, unit costs and industrial concentration continue to fall hand in hand. (Langlois, 1992a.)

6. Industry structure and the scope of innovation

If, as we have outlined, there is a trade-off between the diversity of ideas that specialization and fragmentation may encourage, on the one hand, and the ease of implementation and internalization of returns permitted by vertical integration, on the other, then the choice of an appropriate industry structure will vary depending on the market forces operating within and upon the industry. When, for example, appropriability is not a problem, vertical specialization will be favored more strongly than when the originators are unlikely to capture the returns to an innovation themselves. The optimal degree of horizontal integration is also a function of specific influences surrounding an innovation, especially when development costs are beyond the resources of small firms.

Our discussion here concentrates on two factors that we consider to be particularly important. In this section, we investigate the ways in which the range of uses of an innovation, i.e. its scope, might influence the pattern of industrial structure that maximizes the benefits derived from the innovation. In the next section, we consider the effects of different product life-cycle patterns in the using industries on the adoption of an innovation.

Most innovations have a limited number of uses. This is true of much incremental change and also applies to significant innovations that are confined to one or a few industries. When the scope of an innovation is limited, the need for communication between developers and users is restricted to a narrow and easily-definable group. In these circumstances, information exchange is especially easy when there are existing channels of communication, as in an industrial district in which suppliers and customers deal with each other regularly and have a good idea of their respective needs. Even without geographic clustering, established market mechanisms can work well when the scope of innovation is confined. For example, specialist machine manufacturers who supply a particular industry may have good national or international connections that allow them to provide information on new models to potential customers quickly and cheaply. Another channel for communication would be the trade press, which can pick up news on developments from diverse sources and supply it to other interested firms.

There are, however, limits to the ability of firms to use markets effectively. When there is product differentiation, the producing firms are relatively small, and the population of customers is diverse and geographically dispersed, as in the ceramic tile, clothing, or textile industries, information problems may be overwhelming. Under these circumstances, the costs of spreading and acquiring information about innovations might be beyond the resources of both suppliers and buyers. Institutional arrangements like those in the 'Third Italy' can help to overcome the problem. Very few individual tile manufacturers are capable of advertising their distinctive patterns worldwide, and very few tile distributors abroad have the time or money to visit the manufacturers to inform themselves on available styles. As the prosperity of the industry depends heavily on exports, one of the major functions of the producer cooperatives is to arrange with small manufacturers to provide centralized exhibits and organize participation in international trade fairs. As a result, quasi-horizontal integration, the producer cooperative, forms the basis of quasi-vertical integration, as the producers are able to add marketing expertise to their distinctive competences in design (Best, 1990; Porter, 1990). [22]

When an innovation has a wide scope of uses, small firms operating in established channels may be less successful at communicating their discoveries because the problem of gaining credibility expands as the developer needs to attract attention among firms in unfamiliar sectors. Potential users may also experience difficulties in locating

[22] These arrangements result in important two-way channels of information because they reduce the cost to producers of collecting information on customers' preferences as well as spreading information on the producers' wares.

innovations from diverse sources if the initial applications are in different industries.

Major economy-wide changes like electrification or the use of semiconductors or railroads are extremely rare, but innovation across several industries occurs frequently. If discoveries are made by specialists, in line with the Smithian model, the developers may have neither knowledge of nor interest in applications in other industries. In other words, the very institutional framework that encourages the innovation in the first place can also retard its spread. Inventors with a wider perspective, however, who set out from the beginning to make discoveries with broad applicability, may not have the contacts with users required to gain adoption in any single industry, let alone in a variety of sectors.

These and similar institutional complications may account for the relatively slow spread of discoveries across industries. It took several decades, for example, for the diffusion of electricity for domestic, industrial, and traction purposes (Hughes, 1983), and the spread of applications of electronic components is still gaining pace more than four decades after the invention of the transistor. The search for suitable institutions is again important because, the longer the time period involved in diffusion, the more difficult it becomes for the initial developers of an innovation to appropriate the gains. [23] If the gains are uncertain, this may mean not only a disincentive to development in the first place, but also a loss to the country of development if the innovation is captured to a degree by foreign producers who recognize uses that were not apparent to potential users in the country of development. When the eventual adoption by foreigners is significantly greater than in the country of origin, even the original core industry may migrate internationally (Robertson and Langlois, 1992).

[23] The need for (vertical) ownership integration may be strengthened by the limited time period allowed to holders of patents. If potential users of an innovation cannot be recruited quickly, the effective life of patents, as measured by the profits to their holders, is shortened significantly.

7. Innovation and the product life cycle

The choice of suitable forms of internal and external organization to promote innovation and capture the resultant gains depends as well on the product life cycles (PLCs) of industries that might adopt or be affected by the innovation. It is well known that uncertainty varies over the stages of the PLC, in general reducing as the product progresses from the introductory stage to maturity. Uncertainty can again increase in mature industries, however, if the impact of an innovation is so high that it greatly affects the nature of the product or the production process. The choice of an appropriate structure will therefore depend on which stages of the PLC the source and user industries are at.

When an innovation is adopted by an industry that is in the introductory and growth phases of the PLC, the degree of uncertainty in both the source and user industries is very high. There are unlikely to be established channels of communication that the firms in the source industry can tap because the nature of the user industry is amorphous, with a high turnover of firms and lack of knowledge as to the nature of the users' products until a standard variation is finally decided upon by users. In such cases, it is very difficult to economize on information costs for both the user and the source because the necessary information might be coming from many directions at once.

Coordination integration is unsuitable in such an environment because it increases 'certainty' within an organization (a firm or closely articulated network) by artificially reducing the number of sources of information that are treated as credible. Innovations from external or non-accredited sources tend to be ignored or downgraded when there is coordination integration. When the flow of innovative ideas is high and the form of the user product in flux, it is crucial to be able to tap as many options as possible.

This implies the use of an innovative network, or 'network of networks,' that allows rapid exchanges in which both the source and user firms draw on the widest range of information available, consistent with a reasonable cost of collec-

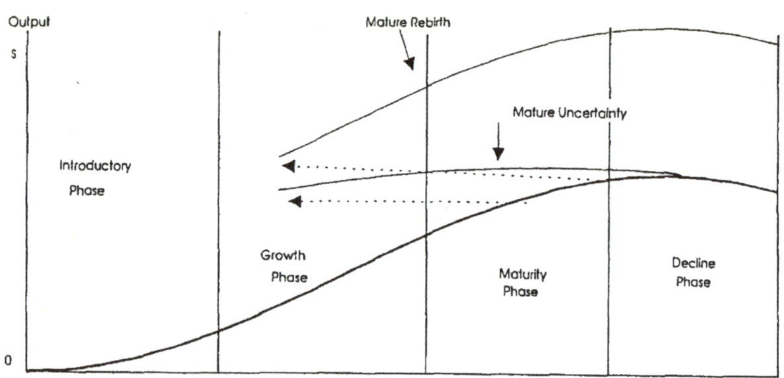

Fig. 3. The effect of innovation on the product life cycle.

tion and processing. The performance of such innovative networks is enhanced if they can draw on various types of clearing house activities provided by trade associations and similar groups. Government organizations such as MITI in Japan can also perform generalized information services.

When the user industry is mature and the innovation is largely autonomous in that it does not require drastic changes to the product or the production process, then a Marshallian or Third-Italian type of network would be most appropriate. These minor, or parametric, changes do not justify the cost involved in establishing elaborate information networks and coordination integration is also unnecessary because the cost to the would-be users is very low if they are not among the first to learn about a particular innovation.

Change along the product life cycle, however, is not necessarily unidirectional (Moenaer et al., 1990). The most interesting case in many ways (and one that receives much attention from Lazonick, Florida and Kenney, and Porter) occurs when an innovation has a systemic impact on a mature product that, as a consequence, requires substantial revamping of other aspects of that product or its manufacturing process. When this occurs, the path of the user industry is deflected from the usual 'S' curve of the PLC into either mature uncertainty or mature growth, as in Fig. 3. In both cases, the mature rebirth is returned to a stage of higher uncertainty similar to that in the growth stage of the PLC. [24]

Examples of these structural or strategic changes range from the incorporation of micro-components into existing types of machinery to the adoption of just-in-time manufacturing methods. Because such an innovation requires a total rethinking of the nature of the product and/or the manufacturing process, users must have a detailed knowledge of the technology of the innovation and of the varieties available. This can best be achieved through substantial coordination integration as provided by a vertically integrated Chandlerian firm or a Japanese network, because these are the forms of organization that (for a price) give users access to detailed information commensurate with the high importance of their requirements.

The choice between Chandlerian or Japanese network organizations will, in turn, be a function of degree of maturity and hence the extent of uncertainty prevailing in the industry supplying the innovation. If the supplying industry is in the

[24] The major difference between Mature Uncertainty and Mature Rebirth centers on the elasticity of demand for the product. When elasticity is high, a systemic innovation in a mature product may result in a renewed acceleration of growth, or 'rebirth,' but if demand is inelastic the innovation will result only in greater uncertainty. See Cheah and Robertson (1992).

early growth stage of the PLC and uncertainty concerning the nature of the innovation itself is high, the Japanese network solution is probably more appropriate because it permits the user of the innovation to collect information on a broader range of options. But when the innovation is near the end of the growth phase and the number of viable options has been narrowed, the Chandlerian solution is more suitable because the user firm does not need to spread its information net as widely and can therefore put more emphasis on coordination integration to make sure that the innovation is incorporated efficiently into the user product.

In either the Japanese network or Chandlerian case, however, the benefits of the innovation, as employed in that user industry, are likely to be appropriated by the user. This is because the other capabilities associated with the product are going to be held closely by the user firms which are already established. These user capabilities are particularly important in established oligopolies and include patents relevant to other aspects of the product or process, marketing skills, and the production of complementary products (Mitchell, 1989 and 1991). [25]

The distinction between mature and innovative user industries is illustrated by the effects of the adoption of semiconductors on the consumer appliance and computer industries. Recent major changes in refrigerator technology, for example, have significantly increased the reliance of manufacturers on external sources of knowledge. Whereas refrigerator firms previously had internal knowledge of all important aspects of their product, they must now conduct outside searches to obtain information on essential new technologies (Granstrand et al., 1992). Similarly, Florida and Kenncy (1990a) cite the decay of the mature consumer electronics industry as a major problem for American semiconductor manufacturers. In Japan, semiconductor researchers can work together with producers of washing machines and other white goods in environments with a high degree of coordination integration to find new uses for chips, as well as ways of introducing improvements into the appliances. In the US, however, opportunities are lost for semiconductor applications because developers and users are separated, resulting in lost efficiency to both groups. [26]

By contrast, there have been significant reciprocal advantages for parts of the US semiconductor industry, particularly microprocessors, and producers in such areas as microcomputers, work stations, and other computer-based systems (Langlois et al., 1988). In the latter case, both the source and user industries are in the growth phases of their PLCs and face considerable uncertainty. Thus the innovative network in Silicon Valley is well-adapted to their needs (Saxenian, 1991). Conversely, the more centralized organizational arrangements in Japan have contributed to the relative lack of success by Japanese firms in microprocessors and computers (*The Economist*, 1992; Zachary and Yoder, 1993).

8. Conclusion

The primary message that flows from our analysis is that the context of innovation is complex and varied. This may seem a mundane assertion, until one notices that many if not most of the leading theorists and commentators on industrial competitiveness have implied otherwise.

When there is innovation, the most efficient relationship between source and user firms will depend on, inter alia, the prior existence of information networks, the scope of the innovation, its

[25] If the innovation is truly revolutionary, however, existing firms may not possess sufficient capabilities to absorb it. Indeed, other firms, with different capabilities, may be better equipped than established firms to adopt the innovation and thus win a niche in the industry or even come to dominate it. See Robertson and Langlois (1992).

[26] This is, in fact, the anticipated outcome for a mature industry that undergoes vertical disintegration and comes to rely so heavily on outside suppliers that it suffers degradation of its basic competences and can no longer respond adequately to changes in its environment. See Bettis, Bradley, and Hamel (1992).

impact on various user industries, the presence or absence of economies of scale, and the stages of the product life cycle reached by both the innovating product and any product into which it might be incorporated. It seems, therefore, that no single government policy designed to facilitate change in one or another of these environments will be suitable for all. In fact, the number of permutations and combinations of efficient relationships is so large that it is improbable that any policy, or even group of policies, would be suitable for more than a small fraction of a nation's industries. Attempts to implement broadbrush policies may therefore be destructive because they can upset useful forms of organization in industries that are relatively unaffected by a particular innovation. For example, even if one accepts the contention of Piore and Sabel and Best that small firms operating in networks are more likely than other types of firms to be innovative and conducive to flexible specialization in the future, most modern industrial economies are still highly dependent on industries with significant economies of scale whose existing capabilities, and therefore their ability to serve the public, would be severely damaged if they were to be broken up in a search for faster rates of change.

On the other hand, the wide assortment of useful forms of organization that we have discussed also casts doubt on the wisdom of antitrust laws and other broad policies that prohibit firms from freely entering into relationships that allow them to operate more efficiently and effectively. If coordinated networks like those in the Third Italy or Japan are needed to encourage and diffuse innovation, attempts to ban them can cause significant harm (Bower and Rhenman, 1985; *Business Week*, 1992).

Overall, then, the most acceptable view of those canvassed here is Porter's. Government policy should be facilitating rather than narrow and prescriptive in that it should offer scope for firms to develop the organizational forms that are best adapted to their particular environments. This requires the provision of infrastructure and whatever regulations are needed to prevent anti-social activities and to channel rent-seeking behavior in productive directions; but it also entails self-discipline on the part of legislators and bureaucrats to resist the temptation to second guess firms and enforce overarching strategies.

References

Abernathy, W., 1978, The productivity dilemma: Roadblock to innovation in the American automobile industry (The Johns Hopkins University Press, Baltimore).

Ben-Porath, Y., 1980, The F-Connection: Families, friends, and firms in the organization of exchange, Population and Development Review, 6, 1–30.

Best, M.H., 1990, The new competition: Institutions of industrial restructuring (Harvard University Press, Cambridge, MA).

Bettis, R.A, S.P. Bradley and G. Hamel, 1992, Outsourcing and industrial decline, Academy of Management Executive, 6, 7–22.

Bower, J.L. and E.A. Rhenman, 1985, Benevolent cartels, Harvard Business Review, 63, July–August, 124–32.

Brusco, S., 1982, The Emilian model: Productive decentralisation and social integration, Cambridge Journal of Economics, 6, 167–84.

Brusco, S. and E. Righi, 1987, The loan guarantee consortia, Entrepreneurial Economy, 6, July–August, 11–13.

Bureau of Industry Economics, 1991, Networks: A third form of organisation, Discussion Paper 14, Australian Government Publishing Service, Canberra.

Business Week International, 1992, Learning from Japan, January 27, 38–44.

Casson, M., 1982, The entrepreneur: An economic theory (Barnes and Noble, Towota, N.J.).

Chandler, A.D., Jr., 1977, The visible hand: The managerial revolution in American business. (Harvard University Press, Cambridge, MA).

Chandler, A.D., Jr., 1990, Scale and scope: The dynamics of industrial capitalism. (Harvard University Press, Cambridge, MA).

Cheah, H.B. and P.L. Robertson, 1992, The entrepreneurial process and innovation in the product life cycle, Paper presented to a meeting of the International Joseph A. Schumpeter Society, Kyoto, Japan, August 19–22, 1992, Department of Economics and Management, University College, University of New South Wales.

Cheung, S.N.S., 1983, The contractual nature of the firm, Journal of Law and Economics, 26, 386–405.

Coase, R.H., 1937, The nature of the firm, Economica, n.s., 4, 386–405.

Dorfman, N., 1983, Route 128: The development of a regional high technology economy, Research Policy, 12, 299–316.

Economist, 1992, Japan's less-than-invincible computer makers, January 11, 59–60.

Florida, R. and M. Kenney, 1988, Venture capital-financed innovation and technological change in the USA, Research Policy, 17, 119–37.

Florida, R. and M. Kenney, 1990a, The breakthrough illusion: Corporate America's failure to move from innovation to mass production (Basic Books, New York).

Florida, R. and M. Kenney, 1990b, Silicon Valley and Route 128 won't save us, California Management Review, Fall, 68–88.

Florida, R. and M. Kenney, 1991, Transplanted organizations: The transfer of Japanese industrial organization to the US, American Sociological Review, 56, 381–98.

Granstrand, O., E. Bohlin, C. Oskarsson, and N. Sjoberg, 1992, External technology acquisition in large multi-technology corporations, R & D Management, 22, 111–133.

Harrigan, K.R., 1983, A framework for looking at vertical integration, Journal of Business Strategy, 3, 30–37.

Hart, O.D., 1989, An economist's perspective on the theory of the firm, Columbia Law Review, 89, 1757–1774.

Hatch, C.R., 1987, Learning from Italy's industrial renaissance, Entrepreneurial Economy, 6, 4–11.

Helper, S., 1991, Strategy and irreversibility in supplier relations: The case of the US automobile industry, Business History Review, 65, 781–82 (Winter).

Helper, S. and D.I. Levine, 1992, Long-term supplier relations and product market structure: An exit-voice approach, Journal of Law, Economics, and Organization, 8, 561–581.

Hughes, T.P., 1983, Networks of power: Electrification in western society 1880–1930, (The Johns Hopkins University Press, Baltimore).

Imai, K., 1989, Network industrial organization in Japan, in Bo Carlsson, ed., Industrial Dynamics: Technological, Organizational, and Structural Changes in Industries and Firms (Kluwer Academic Publishers, Dordrecht) 123–55.

Imai, K. and H. Itami, 1984, Interpenetration of organization and market: Japan's firm and market in comparison with the US, International Journal of Industrial Organization, 2, 285–310.

Landes, D.S., 1991, Introduction: On technology and growth, in Patrice Higonnet, David S. Landes, and Henry Rosovsky, Editors, Favorites of fortune: Technology, growth, and economic development since the industrial revolution. (Harvard University Press, Cambridge, MA), 1–29.

Langlois, R.N., 1984, Internal organization in a dynamic context: Some theoretical considerations, in M. Jussawalla and H. Ebenfield, Editors, Communication and information economics: new perspectives (North Holland, Amsterdam), 23–49.

Langlois, R.N., 1992a, External economies and economic progress: The case of the microcomputer industry, Business History Review, 66, 1–50.

Langlois, R.N., 1992b, Transaction-cost economics in real time, Industrial and Corporate Change, 1, 9–127.

Langlois, R.N., and M.J. Everett, 1992, Complexity, genuine uncertainty, and the theory of organization, Human Systems Management, 11, 67–75.

Langlois, R.N., T.A. Pugel, C.S. Haklisch, R.R. Nelson, and W.G. Egelhoff, 1988, Microelectronics: An industry in transition (Unwin Hyman, London).

Langlois, R.N., and P.L. Robertson, 1989, Explaining vertical integration: Lessons from the American automobile industry, Journal of Economic History, 49, 361–75.

Langlois, R.N., and P.L. Robertson, 1992, Networks and innovation in a modular system: Lessons from the microcomputer and stereo component industries, Research Policy, 21, 297–313.

Lazerson, M.H., 1988, Organizational growth of small firms: An outcome of markets and hierarchies? American Sociological Review, 53, 330–42.

Lazonick, W., 1990, Competitive advantage on the shop floor (Harvard University Press, Cambridge, MA).

Lazonick, W., 1991a, Business organization and the myth of the market economy, (Cambridge University Press, Cambridge).

Lazonick, W., 1991b, The enterprise, the community, and the nation: Social organization as a source of global competitive advantage, Paper presented at the Business History Seminar, Harvard Business School, November 25, 1991.

Marshall, A., 1961, Principles of Economics, 9th (variorum) Ed. (Macmillan, London).

Miller, R. and M. Côté, 1985, Growing the next silicon valley, Harvard Business Review, 63, 114–123.

Mitchell, W., 1989, Whether and when? Probability and timing of incumbents' entry into emerging industrial subfields, Administrative Science Quarterly, 34, 208–30.

Mitchell, W., 1991, Dual clocks: Entry order influences on incumbent and newcomer market share and survival when specialized assets retain their value, Strategic Management Journal, 12, 85–100.

Moenaert, R., J. Barbe, D. Deschoolmeester and Arnoud De Meyer 1990, Turnaround strategies for strategic business units with an ageing technology, in Ray Loveridge and Martyn Pitt, Editors, The strategic management of technological innovation, (John Wiley, New York).

Nelson, R.R. and S.G. Winter, 1977, In search of a more useful theory of innovation, Research Policy, 5, 36–76.

Odaka, K., K. Ono and F. Adachi, 1988, The automobile industry in Japan: A study in ancillary firm development (Oxford University Press, Oxford).

Piore, M.J. and C.F. Sabel 1984, The second industrial divide: Possibilities for prosperity, (Basic Books, New York).

Porter, M.E., 1990, The competitive advantage of nations, (The Free Press, New York).

Powell, W.W., 1990, Neither market nor hierarchy: Network forms of organization, Research in Organizational Behavior, 12, 295–336.

Robertson, P.L. and R.N. Langlois, 1992, Institutions, inertia, and changing industrial leadership, Department of Economics and Management, University College, University of New South Wales.

Sabel, C.F., 1989, Flexible specialization and the re-emergence of regional economies, in Paul Hirst and Jonathan Zeitlin, Editors, Reversing industrial decline? Industrial structure and policy in Britain and her competitors, (Berg, Oxford), 17–70.

Sabel, C.F., G. Herrigel, R. Kazis, and R. Deeg, 1987, How to keep mature industries innovative, Technology Review, 90, 26–35.

Sabel, C.F. and J. Zeitlin, 1985, Historical alternatives to mass production: Politics, markets, and technology in nineteenth-century industrialization, Past and Present, 108, 133–76.

Saxenian, A. 1990, 'Regional networks and the resurgence of Silicon Valley,' California Management Review, Fall, 89–112.

Saxenian, A., 1991, 'The origins and dynamics of production networks in Silicon Valley,' Research Policy, 20, 423–437.

Silver, M., 1984, Enterprise and the scope of the firm. (Martin Robertson, London)

Smitka, M.J., 1991, Competitive ties: Subcontracting in the Japanese automotive industry (Columbia University Press, New York).

Supple, B., 1991, 'Scale and scope: Alfred Chandler and the dynamics of industrial capitalism,' Economic History Review, 44, 500–514.

Teece, D.J., 1986, 'Profiting from technological innovation: Implications for integration, collaboration, licensing, and public policy,' Research Policy, 15, 285–305.

Williamson, O.E., 1985, The economic institutions of capitalism: Firms, markets, relational contracting (The Free Fress, New York)

Womack, J.P., D.T. Jones, and D. Roos, 1990, The machine that changed the world, (Rawson Associates, New York)

Zachary, G.P., and S.K. Yoder 1993, 'Order from chaos: Computer industry divides into camps of winners and losers,' The Wall Street Journal, January 27, p. A1.

[26]

© Academy of Management Journal
2001, Vol. 44, No. 5, 996–1004.

KNOWLEDGE TRANSFER IN INTRAORGANIZATIONAL NETWORKS: EFFECTS OF NETWORK POSITION AND ABSORPTIVE CAPACITY ON BUSINESS UNIT INNOVATION AND PERFORMANCE

WENPIN TSAI
Pennsylvania State University

Drawing on a network perspective on organizational learning, I argue that organizational units can produce more innovations and enjoy better performance if they occupy central network positions that provide access to new knowledge developed by other units. This effect, however, depends on units' absorptive capacity, or ability to successfully replicate new knowledge. Data from 24 business units in a petrochemical company and 36 business units in a food-manufacturing company show that the interaction between absorptive capacity and network position has significant, positive effects on business unit innovation and performance.

Inside a multiunit organization, units can learn from each other and benefit from new knowledge developed by other units. Knowledge transfer among organizational units provides opportunities for mutual learning and interunit cooperation that stimulate the creation of new knowledge and, at the same time, contribute to organizational units' ability to innovate (e.g., Kogut & Zander, 1992; Tsai & Ghoshal, 1998). However, knowledge is often "sticky" and difficult to spread (Szulanski, 1996; Von Hippel, 1994). How can an organizational unit gain useful knowledge from other units to enhance its innovation and performance?

Prior research has suggested that organizational units not only hold specialized knowledge but also have the opportunity to learn from other units (Huber, 1991). However, not every unit can learn from all other units in the same organization. A unit may want to obtain knowledge from other units but may not be able to access it. Even though the knowledge is available, the unit may not have the capacity to absorb and apply it for its own use. Organizational units require external access and internal capacity to learn from their peers. Because of their differential external access and internal capacity, organizational units differ in their abilities to leverage and benefit from knowledge developed by other units.

Although the organizational learning literature has highlighted the importance of the capacity to absorb knowledge by increasing R&D intensity (e.g., Cohen & Levinthal, 1990), much less attention has been focused on the process of gaining knowledge access. Getting access to new knowledge requires networking effort that is different from investing in R&D. In a multiunit organization, a unit can access new knowledge through a network of interunit links (Hansen, 1999). In this research, I conceptualize an organization as a network arrangement and investigate a unit's access to knowledge by analyzing its network position in its intraorganizational network. In addition, I argue that both external knowledge access and internal learning capacity are important for a unit's innovation and performance. Although a central network position allows a unit to access new knowledge developed by many other units, high learning capacity permits a unit to successfully apply or replicate new knowledge.

ORGANIZATIONAL LEARNING AND INTERUNIT KNOWLEDGE TRANSFER: A NETWORK PERSPECTIVE

Inside an organization, learning involves the transfer of knowledge among different organizational units. Such knowledge transfer occurs in a shared social context in which different units are linked to one another. Organizational units are embedded in a network coordinated through processes of knowledge transfer and resource sharing (Galbraith, 1977; Gresov & Stephens, 1993). Such a network of interunit links enables organizational units to gain critical competencies that contribute to their competitiveness in the marketplace.

Interunit links and networks are an important part of a learning process in which organizational units discover new opportunities and obtain new

The author would like to thank Don Bergh, Dan Brass, Sumantra Ghoshal, Ranjay Gulati, Mathew Hayward, Martin Kilduff, Harry Korine, Don Sull, Kevin Steensma, Linda Treviño, Anne Tsui, Greg Northcraft, and three anonymous reviewers for their very helpful comments and suggestions on drafts.

knowledge through interacting with one another. The importance of interunit links has been documented in the strategy literature. For example, research on diversification has emphasized the benefits, for multiunit companies, of pursuing synergy through knowledge transfer and resource sharing among their strategic business units (SBUs). As Gupta and Govindarajan noted, "The potential for synergistic benefits from resource sharing varies across strategic contexts, and the realization of these potential synergistic benefits depends on how effectively linkages between SBUs are actually managed" (1986: 696). In addition, research on the knowledge-based view of the firm has suggested that social networks facilitate the creation of new knowledge within organizations (e.g., Kogut & Zander, 1992; Tsai, 2000). Through the development of interunit network links, horizontal transfer of knowledge broadens organizational learning. As Huber (1991) suggested, a learning organization is characterized by motivated units that are intimately connected to one another. By linking different units together, a network arrangement provides a flexible learning structure that replaces old hierarchical structures.

Drawing on a network perspective on organizational learning, I examined two important concepts, *network position* and *absorptive capacity*, that determine the effectiveness of interunit learning and knowledge transfer. Network position, a unit's location in an interunit network, describes its access to knowledge; absorptive capacity, a unit's R&D investment, describes its capacity to learn. Organizational units are not identically capable of acquiring knowledge; they are not equally efficient or effective learners. Because of differences in their knowledge access and learning capacity, organizational units have differing learning capabilities that in turn have a significant impact on their innovation and performance.

Network Position

Different network positions represent different opportunities for a unit to access new knowledge that is critical to developing new products or innovative ideas. An organizational unit's network position reveals its ability to access external information and knowledge. By occupying a central position in the interunit network, a unit is likely to access desired strategic resources. Such resources will fuel the unit's innovative activities by providing the external information necessary to generate new ideas. Equally, the innovative work of the unit will benefit from access to the new knowledge necessary to resolve design and manufacturing problems (e.g., Dougherty & Hardy, 1996; Ibarra, 1993; Van de Ven, 1986). However, such knowledge is usually distributed unevenly within an organization. As Szulanski (1996) argued, knowledge is difficult to spread across different units within an organization in which preexisting relationships among units are absent. Indeed, innovative ideas are often at the nexus of interunit links. To foster innovation, information and knowledge should be deliberately distributed. A network of interunit links provides channels for distributing information and knowledge in such a way as to stimulate and support innovative activities. A central network position is associated with innovation outcomes for individual units within an organization. As several scholars have argued, a unit's network position is an important aspect of "social structure" that can enhance the unit's ability to create new value and to achieve economic goals (e.g., Coleman, 1990; Tsai & Ghoshal, 1998). An organizational unit occupying a more central position in its intraorganizational network is likely to produce more innovations. Hence,

Hypothesis 1a. The centrality of an organizational unit's network position is positively related to its innovation.

Organizational units differ in their internal knowledge, practices, and capabilities. Networks of interunit links allow organizational units to access new knowledge from each other and may increase their cost efficiency through dissemination of "best practices" within organizations. As Hill, Hitt, and Hoskisson noted, networks of knowledge transfer among organizational units "enable the diversified firm either to reduce overall operating costs in one or more of its divisions, or to better differentiate the products of one or more of its divisions" (1992: 502). The centrality of a unit in the intraorganizational network may determine the unit's access to different knowledge, thus affecting its ability to recognize and respond to new market opportunities. A unit occupying a central network position can gain competitive advantages in the marketplace because of its unique access to other units' knowledge or practices. Such a central unit may enhance its profitability by applying other units' knowledge or practices to adapt its products to market needs, to respond to emerging market trends, and to deal with competitive challenges. Moreover, a central unit is likely to improve its business operations as it can enjoy the benefits of scope economies by sharing the knowledge developed by other units. As a result, performance differences among organizational units may be attributable to the differences in their intraorganizational network positions. Hence,

Hypothesis 1b. The centrality of an organizational unit's network position is positively related to its business performance.

Absorptive Capacity

Organizational units also differ in their ability to assimilate and replicate new knowledge gained from external sources. Cohen and Levinthal (1990) labeled such ability "absorptive capacity." In discussing how it contributes to innovation, they argue that absorptive capacity tends to develop cumulatively and builds on prior related knowledge. Organizational units that possess relevant prior knowledge are likely to have a better understanding of new technology that can generate new ideas and develop new products. Organizational units with a high level of absorptive capacity are likely to harness new knowledge from other units to help their innovative activities. Organizational units must have the capacity to absorb inputs in order to generate outputs. Without such capacity, they cannot learn or transfer knowledge from one unit to another. For example, in a study of 122 "best practice" transfers in eight companies, Szulanski (1996) found that lack of absorptive capacity was a major barrier to internal knowledge transfer within organizations. Absorptive capacity results from a prolonged process of investment and knowledge accumulation. An organizational unit's absorptive capacity for learning depends on its endowment of relevant technology-based capabilities (Mowery, Oxley, & Silverman, 1996). R&D investment is a necessary condition for the creation of absorptive capacity. As Cohen and Levinthal suggested, the ability to utilize external knowledge is often a by-product of R&D investment. Organizational units with a high level of absorptive capacity invest more in their own R&D and have the ability to produce more innovations. Hence,

Hypothesis 2a. An organizational unit's absorptive capacity is positively related to its innovation.

An organizational unit's absorptive capacity also affects its business performance. According to Cohen and Levinthal (1990), absorptive capacity involves not only the ability to assimilate new external knowledge, but also the ability to apply such knowledge to commercial ends and, thus, create the opportunity for profits. Having good research and development, a unit with high absorptive capacity is likely to successfully commercialize its new products. In addition, a unit with high absorptive capacity is likely to apply new knowledge to improve its business operations. Increments to an organizational unit's knowledge base enhance the unit's business performance in that it can profit from the new knowledge it has absorbed. As a result, higher absorptive capacity is related to better business performance. Accordingly,

Hypothesis 2b. An organizational unit's absorptive capacity is positively related to its business performance.

Interaction between Network Position and Absorptive Capacity

Absorptive capacity is also likely to moderate the effect of network position on business unit innovation and performance. Although a central network position provides important access to new knowledge, its impact on business unit innovation and performance may depend on the extent to which a unit can absorb such new knowledge. A unit may be able to access certain new knowledge, but not enhance its innovation and performance if it does not have enough capacity to absorb such knowledge. The better a unit can access other units' knowledge, the more it needs absorptive capacity to benefit from such knowledge. An organizational unit occupying a central network position can access new knowledge from many other units. Such a central network position will have a more positive impact on the unit's innovation output and business performance if the unit has high absorptive capacity with which to effectively transfer knowledge from other units. The interaction between network position and absorptive capacity is critical to intraorganizational knowledge sharing. Without a simultaneous consideration of its network position and absorptive capacity, a unit is likely to encounter a "search-transfer problem" in which it cannot transfer the knowledge it identified through its network search (Hansen, 1999). The more central a unit is in an intraorganizational network, the broader the knowledge sources the unit has and the higher the absorptive capacity needed to transfer such knowledge. Hence,

Hypothesis 3a. The centrality of an organizational unit's network position is more positively related to innovation when the unit has high absorptive capacity than when the unit has low absorptive capacity.

Hypothesis 3b. The centrality of an organizational unit's network position is more positively related to business performance when

the unit has high absorptive capacity than when the unit has low absorptive capacity.

METHODS

Data Collection and Research Site

This research was conducted in two large multinational corporations, here given the fictitious names Taiplex Corporation and Resident Enterprise. Each had a typical multiunit organizational structure in which each unit was responsible for developing, manufacturing, and selling products. Although similar in organizational structure, the two companies specialized in different businesses and thus differed in many aspects of their operations. Taiplex specialized in the petrochemical industry and had annual revenues of $10.7 billion and total assets of $15 billion at the time of the study. Resident specialized in food manufacturing and had annual revenues of $4.1 billion and total assets of $3.8 billion. The two companies also targeted very different markets. Taiplex's products, which were mainly for industrial markets, included plastic raw materials, plastic secondary products, and industrial equipment. Resident's products, which were mainly for consumer markets, included edible oil, beverages, fast foods, and dairy products.

A questionnaire was distributed to all business units in the two companies in 1996. I used sociometric techniques in the questionnaire to collect relational data that described how units interacted with one another within each company. At the time of the survey, Taiplex had 24 business units and Resident had 36 business units. For each of these units, I contacted two individuals, the director and the most senior deputy director, to respond to my questionnaire. Therefore, I had a total of 120 potential respondents. Because top management in both companies approved and supported the study, all the contacts completed and returned my questionnaire. To ensure confidentiality, I promised that I would not reveal the true names of the companies, the units, and the respondents involved in this research. Respondents were asked to return their completed questionnaires directly to me instead of routing them through corporate headquarters. In addition to the questionnaire survey, corporate internal records were also used to collect data on business unit R&D intensity, innovation, and performance.

Because I had multiple respondents in each unit, I calculated interrater agreement to examine how responses varied within each unit. I used the mean percentage agreement, as suggested by Tsai and Ghoshal (1998), to measure interrater agreement for relational data. The mean percentage agreement is defined as the number of responses selected by both respondents in a unit divided by the number of responses selected by at least one of the two respondents in a unit. The value of the mean percentage agreement can range from 0.0 (perfect inconsistency) to 1.0 (perfect consistency). In this study, the mean percentage agreement was 0.93 in Taiplex and 0.77 in Resident for my network measure. The mean percentage agreement was calculated before I cross-validated the responses. For my statistical analyses, only validated data were used. The method for data cross-validation is detailed in the next section.

Dependent Variables

There were two dependent variables in this study: innovation and performance. Both were measured at the business unit level. Because units may specialize in different industries and have different strategic priorities, innovation and performance data needed to be adjusted to evaluate each unit (Gupta & Govindarajan, 1984). To do so, I used an innovation achieved rate, or the number of new products introduced in a unit in a particular year divided by the unit's target number in that year, and a profitability achieved rate—a unit's return on investment in a particular year divided by its target return in that year—to measure innovation and performance, respectively. The innovation and profitability targets were assessed and negotiated between unit managers and corporate managers each year. These managers considered business unit strategic priorities and industry-related factors when they set the targets. The achieved rates for all the units in this study were collected for the time period 1997–98 through corporate internal records.

Independent Variables

Absorptive capacity. Following Cohen and Levinthal (1990), I used R&D intensity (defined as R&D expenditure divided by sales) to measure absorptive capacity at the business unit level. Data on R&D expenditure and unit sales were obtained through corporate internal records. Consistent with the data collection period of other independent variables in this study, 1996 R&D intensity was used here.

Network position. To identify a business unit's intraorganizational network position, I developed a questionnaire item asking the respondents, "Which units provide your unit with new knowledge or expertise when your unit is seeking technical advice inside your organization?" A list of all the units was provided in the questionnaire, allowing respondents to simply select their answers from the list. To validate the data, I also asked the opposite question, that is, who came to them for new knowledge or expertise. I ascertained that there was a knowledge transfer relationship between units *i* and *j* if unit *i* indicated it had provided its knowledge to unit *j* and unit *j* also confirmed receiving knowledge from unit *i* (cf. Hansen, 1999; Krackhardt, 1990). Because I had multiple respondents per unit, I considered data valid if a knowledge transfer relationship (indicated by any respondent of the knowledge source unit) was confirmed by any respondent of the knowledge recipient unit. Using validated data, I constructed a relational matrix of interunit links for each company—a 24 by 24 matrix for Taiplex and a 36 by 36 matrix for Resident. In each matrix, the *i, j*th cell is coded 1 if unit *i* provided its knowledge to unit *j*.

Drawing on these relational matrixes of interunit links, I calculated in-degree centrality for each unit. In-degree centrality represents the total number of units from which a focal unit has received knowledge. The higher a unit's in-degree centrality, the more knowledge sources the unit has. As Freeman (1979) argued, in-degree centrality is the most suitable centrality measure for capturing an individual actor's information or knowledge access.

Control Variables

Size can affect a unit's innovation and performance. Large units tend to have more resources with which to enhance their innovation and performance. They are also usually more powerful than small units and have some advantages in gaining the headquarters' support for their business operations and innovation activities. In this study, I used the logarithms of unit sales and the number of employees in each unit as indicators of unit size. Since the two size indicators were correlated, I averaged them to create a composite measure. The Cronbach's alpha for this composite measure was .94 in Taiplex and .95 in Resident.

Local competition is another variable that can affect innovation and performance. To assess the extent of competition in different local markets, I used these two items: "Competition is intense in our local environment" and "Our unit has strong competitors in the marketplace" (1 = "strongly disagree," 7 = "strongly agree"; $\alpha = .82$, Taiplex, and .89, Resident; $r_{wg} = .92$, Taiplex, and .88, Resident).

I also controlled for past innovation and past performance. Business units with a strong history of innovation tend to continue producing many innovations. Likewise, business units that performed very well in the past are likely to keep up a good performance. Hence, I included the innovation and performance measures for previous years (1993–96) in my statistical analyses.

RESULTS

Table 1 shows the mean values, standard deviations, and correlations for all the measured variables for both companies. Since I had two research sites, I performed a Chow test to examine the consistency of results; it indicated that the levels of significance found for my independent variables were not statistically different across the two companies (business unit innovation, $F_{4,\ 52} = 0.95$, $p = 0.44$; business unit performance, $F_{4,\ 52} = 0.88$, $p = 0.48$). Given the result of the Chow test, I pooled the data for all subsequent analyses. To see how much additional variance was explained by the independent variables after controls, I tested my hypotheses with hierarchical regression analysis, entering control variables in step 1, independent variables in step 2, and interactions in step 3 and tracing change in the multiple squared correlation coefficient (R^2) from step to step.

Table 2 shows the results of hierarchical regression analyses estimating the effects of absorptive capacity and network position on business-unit innovation. Hypothesis 1a states that a unit occupying a more central network position is likely to be more innovative. As shown in Table 2, the coefficient for network position is positive and significant ($p < .01$), indicating that a unit's centrality in its intraorganizational network contributes to its innovation. Hence, Hypothesis 1a is supported. Hypothesis 2a predicts a direct effect of absorptive capacity on business unit innovation. The coefficient for absorptive capacity is positive and significant ($p < .01$), indicating that a unit with high absorptive capacity is likely to be more innovative. Hypothesis 2a is confirmed. Hypothesis 3a states that absorptive capacity will moderate the relationship between network position and innovation. To test this hypothesis, I multiplied network position and absorptive capacity and entered the multiplicative interaction item into the regression. Following Aiken and West (1991), I mean-centered the variables (transforming the data into deviation score form with means equal to zero) and reran the regression to minimize the distortion due to high correlations between the interaction term and its component variables. As predicted, the coefficient of the interaction was positive and significant ($p < .01$), indicating that the effect of network position

TABLE 1
Means, Standard Deviations, and Correlations

Variable	Mean	s.d.	1	2	3	4	5	6	7
Taiplex									
1. Network position	24.64	17.47							
2. Absorptive capacity	8.52	4.64	.27						
3. Unit size	5.24	0.44	−.28	.20					
4. Competition	4.05	1.63	−.30	−.20	.05				
5. Prior innovation	94.24	49.78	−.16	.28	.38	.07			
6. Innovation	92.04	51.27	.36	.60**	.29	−.15	.49*		
7. Prior performance	113.83	15.55	.20	−.28	−.04	−.49*	.08	−.09	
8. Performance	115.29	23.95	.34	.33	−.34	−.39	−.07	.13	.16
Resident									
1. Network position	23.49	20.11							
2. Absorptive capacity	9.28	3.94	.09						
3. Unit size	3.76	0.43	.64**	−.06					
4. Competition	4.22	1.76	−.26	.19	−.07				
5. Prior innovation	106.50	71.44	.31	.37*	.23	−.22			
6. Innovation	101.39	40.11	.56**	.45**	.56**	.06	.46**		
7. Prior performance	103.97	14.67	.16	−.08	.13	−.43**	.21	.03	
8. Performance	105.11	18.16	.36*	.24	.22	−.47**	.41*	.31	−.08

*$p < .05$
**$p < .01$
Two-tailed tests.

on innovation is dependent on a unit's absorptive capacity. Hence, Hypothesis 3a is supported.

Hypothesis 1b states that a unit occupying a more central network position is likely to perform better than a unit in a less central position. As shown in Table 2, the coefficient for network position is not statistically significant, indicating that a unit's centrality in its intraorganizational network does not contribute to its performance. Hence, Hypothesis 1b is not supported. Hypothesis 2b predicts a direct effect of absorptive capacity on business-unit performance. The coefficient for absorptive capacity is positive and significant ($p < .05$), indicating that a unit with high absorptive capacity is likely to have good performance. Hypothesis 2b is confirmed. Hypothesis 3b states that absorptive capacity will moderate the relationship between network position and performance. The interaction coefficient is significant ($p < .05$), indicating that the effect of network position on performance is dependent on a

TABLE 2
Results of Hierarchical Regression Analysis: Effects of Network Position and Absorptive Capacity[a]

	Business-Unit Innovation			Business-Unit Performance		
Variable	1	2	3	1	2	3
Unit size	34.50**	27.20**	32.30**	−2.41	−6.25	−4.51
Local competition	0.65	2.06	2.56	−5.72**	−4.93**	−4.69**
Company	57.33**	47.56**	57.78**	−10.49	−17.03	−13.63
Prior innovation	0.25**	0.14*	0.13*			
Prior performance				0.19	0.13	0.12
Network position		0.73**	0.60**		0.24	0.19
Absorptive capacity		4.12**	4.09**		1.27	1.24*
Network position × absorptive capacity			0.18**			0.06*
R^2	0.31	0.56	0.63	0.25	0.37	0.42
ΔR^2		0.24	0.08		0.12	0.05
ΔF		14.62**	11.01**		4.97**	4.41*

[a] $n = 60$. Data for the two research sites were pooled.
*$p < .05$
**$p < .01$

unit's absorptive capacity. Hypothesis 3b is supported.

To better explain the form of interactions reported in the above hierarchical regression analysis, I plotted the interaction effects in the graphs shown in Figure 1, using one standard deviation above and below the mean to capture high and low absorptive capacity (Cohen & Cohen, 1983).

Additional Analyses

In the above statistical analyses, a business unit's network position was measured as its in-degree centrality in its firm's intraorganizational network. I also performed additional analyses using an alternative measure of network position based on the similarity of ties among business units (e.g., Burt, 1976, 1987). To identify the similarity of ties, I ran structural equivalence analysis using UCINET IV (Borgatti, Everett, & Freeman, 1992). This alternative measure yielded the same pattern of results.

Finally, I also tested whether the effects of network position and absorptive capacity on business units' performance are mediated by their effects on business units' innovation by entering business-unit innovation as an additional control variable in the business unit performance analysis. The results show that absorptive capacity and its interaction with network position remain significant ($p < .05$) when business unit innovation has been entered as a control, indicating that the effects of network position and absorptive capacity on business-unit performance were not mediated by business-unit innovation in this study.

FIGURE 1
Interaction Results

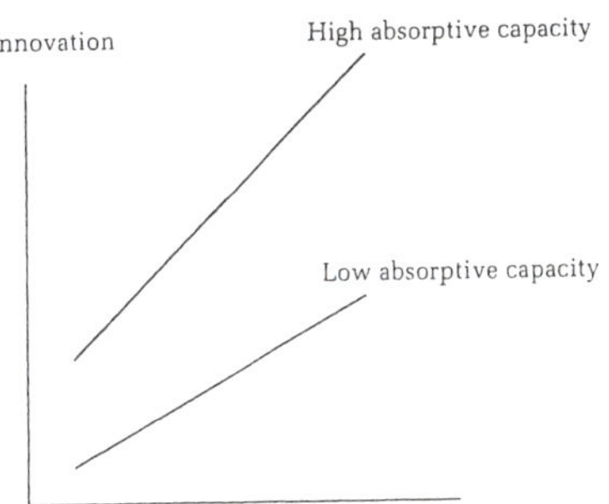

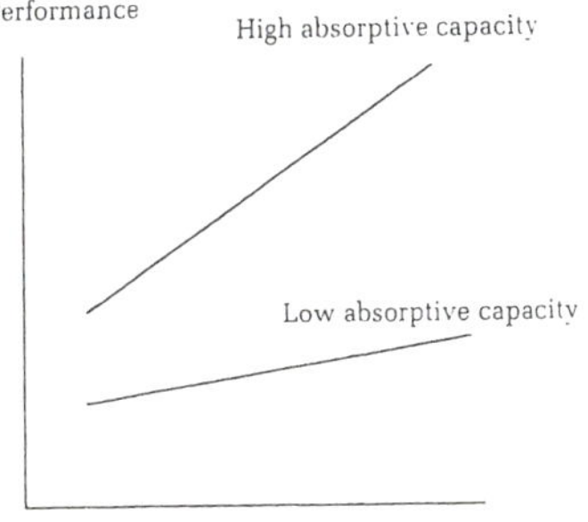

DISCUSSION AND CONCLUSION

How can an organizational unit gain useful knowledge from other units to enhance its innovation and performance? This research suggests that a unit's external knowledge access and internal learning capacity are critical to answering this question.

A unit's external knowledge access is characterized by its network position. By occupying a central network position, a unit is likely to access useful knowledge from other units. The result of this research indicates that a unit's innovative capability is significantly increased by its centrality in the intraorganizational network, which provides opportunities for shared learning, knowledge transfer, and information exchange. The result demonstrates the importance of gaining access to knowledge through networks and, at the same time, contributes to the literature on networks and innovations (e.g., Ibarra, 1993). Given that vigorous innovative activities usually take place in organizational units, it is indispensable to examine how internal social processes within organizations affect innovation at the organizational unit level. By showing how network position affects innovation in business units, this research provides motivation to study innovation processes within multiunit organizations. This research, however, does not show a significant association between a unit's network position and its business performance. It seems that the benefits of centrality may not always outweigh its costs. Although a central unit can gain a lot of information benefits, maintaining a central position may require intensive coordination efforts that lead to high administrative costs. More research is needed to investigate the net effect of a unit's network position on its performance.

An organizational unit's internal learning capacity determines the extent to which it can absorb new knowledge from other units (Cohen & Levinthal, 1990). Investing in absorptive capacity allows a unit to effectively assimilate and apply external knowledge for its own use. This research demonstrates that absorptive capacity significantly affects business units' innovation as well as their performance. The result suggests that high absorptive capacity is associated with a better chance to successfully apply new knowledge toward commercial ends, producing more innovations and better business performance. The result contributes to the research on business unit strategy, given that improving business performance is one of the most important objectives for business units in large, complex organizations (e.g., Gupta & Govindarajan, 1986).

This research also shows that the interaction between network position and absorptive capacity significantly affects business units' innovation and performance. This finding is interesting, given that previous research has focused on the direct effect of network structure in explaining business outcomes only, without addressing whether the effect might be dependent on the extent to which a unit can absorb knowledge (e.g., Tsai & Ghoshal, 1998). A central unit may be able to access knowledge through its network links but may not have sufficient capacity to absorb such knowledge. Hence, the better a unit can access other units' knowledge, the higher the absorptive capacity the unit should have. The result suggests that a unit has to invest significantly in its absorptive capacity when expanding its network links.

In this study, I focused on how the interaction between network position and absorptive capacity affected innovation and performance, respectively. Innovation may mediate the effects of absorptive capacity and network position on performance. However, this study does not demonstrate this potential mediation effect. It is possible that there is a significant time lag between innovation and a positive impact on performance. Future studies, including full longitudinal histories of business unit performance, could further explore this issue.

Although previous research has elaborated the concept of organizational learning, there is little systematic understanding of the social processes that underlie how organizational units learn from each other. Critical insights and ideas reside in organizational units. However, knowledge generated by individual units does not come to bear on an organization independently (Crossan, Lane, & White, 1999). Knowledge and ideas are shared and common meanings are developed through interactions. Knowledge is socially constructed, and organizational learning involves a complex social process in which different units interact with each other (Berger & Luckmann, 1966; Huber, 1991). An organization is a repository of knowledge. The ability to access knowledge and to integrate it effectively is truly a source of competitive advantage. By examining the pattern of intraorganizational knowledge transfer and its performance implications, this research contributes to the organizational learning literature and highlights the importance of sharing firm-specific knowledge within organizations.

Providing further evidence that networks play an important role in shaping business outcomes, this research has significant implications for the growing body of research on networks. Specifically, it indicates that network position can promote social learning that makes linked units more astute collectively than they are individually (Kraatz, 1998). Using network analysis, this research indicates a way of exploring the relational profiles of organizational units and the patterns of interunit knowledge transfer. Although a few other studies have examined attributes of interunit networks, their findings are limited to a specific organization because of a one-site sampling scheme (e.g., Hansen, 1999). In contrast, this research examined network structures in two multinational companies specializing in different industries. The present results are stronger given that a similar pattern was found in two different interunit networks.

An organizational unit's network position and absorptive capacity represent its ability to leverage useful knowledge residing in other parts of its organization. A unit's network position reveals its relative strength in gaining access to new knowledge, a unit's absorptive capacity reveals its ability to replicate or apply such new knowledge. The present results show a positive association between network position and business unit innovation, and confirm the moderating role of absorptive capacity in this association. The influence of both network position and absorptive capacity should be studied simultaneously. Investing in absorptive capacity while expanding network links is critical to the success of organizational units in learning new knowledge that eventually leads to competitive advantage. Investigating network position and absorptive capacity also provides useful information a multiunit firm's corporate headquarters can use to understand the relational profiles and learning potential of its units. Although this research focuses on learning outcomes at the unit level, collectively these outcomes may influence the evolutionary path of an entire organization. Interesting results may accrue from examining how interunit learning affects the development of organizational capabilities and organization-level outcomes. Future research pursuing this line of inquiry has great potential to make significant contributions to management research.

REFERENCES

Aiken, L. S., & West, S. G. 1991. ***Multiple regression: Testing and interpreting interactions.*** Newbury Park, CA: Sage.

Berger, P., & Luckmann, T. 1966. ***The social construction of reality: A treatise in the sociology of knowledge.*** Garden City, NY: Anchor Books.

Borgatti, S. P., Everett, M. G., & Freeman, L. C. 1992. ***UCINET IV Version 1.00.*** Columbia, SC: Analytical Technologies.

Burt, R. S. 1976. Positions in networks. ***Social Forces,*** 55: 93–122.

Burt, R. S. 1987. Social contagion and innovation: Cohesion versus structural equivalence. ***American Journal of Sociology,*** 92: 1287–1335.

Chow, G. 1960. Tests of equality between sets of coefficients in two linear regressions. ***Econometrica,*** 28: 591–605.

Cohen, J., & Cohen, P. 1983. ***Applied multiple regression/correlation analysis for the behavioral sciences*** (2nd ed.). Hillsdale, NJ: Erlbaum.

Cohen, W., & Levinthal, D. 1990. Absorptive capacity: A new perspective on learning and innovation. ***Administrative Science Quarterly,*** 35: 128–152.

Coleman, J. S. 1990. ***Foundations of social theory.*** Cambridge, MA: Harvard University Press.

Crossan, M. M., Lane, H. W., & White, R. E. 1999. An organizational learning framework: From intuition to institution. ***Academy of Management Review,*** 24: 522–537.

Dougherty, D., & Hardy, C. 1996. Sustained product innovation in large, mature organizations: Overcoming innovation-to-organization problems. ***Academy of Management Journal,*** 39: 1120–1153.

Freeman, L. C. 1979. Centrality in social networks: Conceptual clarification. ***Social Networks,*** 1: 215–239.

Galbraith, J. R. 1977. ***Organizational design.*** Reading, MA: Addison-Wesley.

Gresov, C., & Stephens, C. 1993. The context of interunit influence attempts. ***Administrative Science Quarterly,*** 38: 252–276.

Gupta, A. K., & Govindarajan, V. G. 1984. Business unit strategy, managerial characteristics, and business unit level effectiveness at strategy implementation. ***Academy of Management Journal,*** 27: 25–41.

Gupta, A. K., & Govindarajan, V. G. 1986. Resource sharing among SBUs: Strategic antecedents and administrative implications. ***Academy of Management Journal,*** 29: 895–714.

Hansen, M. T. 1999. The search-transfer problem: The role of weak ties in sharing knowledge across organizational subunits. ***Administrative Science Quarterly,*** 44: 82–111.

Hill, C. W. L., Hitt, M. A., & Hoskisson, R. E. 1992. Cooperative versus competitive structures in related and unrelated diversified firms. ***Organization Science*** 3: 501–521.

Huber, G. P. 1991. Organizational learning: The contributing processes and the literatures. ***Organization Science,*** 2: 88–125.

Ibarra, H. 1993. Network, centrality, power, and innovation involvement: Determinants of technical and administrative roles. ***Academy of Management Journal,*** 36: 471–501.

James, L. R., Demaree, R. G., & Wolf, G. 1993. r_{wg}: An assessment of within-group interrater agreement. ***Journal of Applied Psychology,*** 78: 306–309.

Kogut, B., & Zander, U. 1992. Knowledge of the firm, combinative capacities and the replication of technology. ***Organization Science,*** 3: 383–397.

Kraatz, M. S. 1998. Learning by association? Interorganizational networks and adaptation to environmental change. ***Academy of Management Journal,*** 41: 621–643.

Krackhardt, D. 1990. Assessing the political landscape: Structure, cognition and power in organizations. ***Administrative Science Quarterly,*** 35: 342–369.

Mowery, D. C., Oxley, J. E., Silverman, B. S. 1996. Strategic alliances and interfirm knowledge transfer. ***Strategic Management Journal,*** 17: 77–91.

Szulanski, G. 1996. Exploring stickiness: impediments to the transfer of best practice within the firm. ***Strategic Management Journal,*** 17(winter special issue): 27–43.

Tsai, W. 2000. Social capital, strategic relatedness and the formation of intraorganizational linkages. ***Strategic Management Journal,*** 21: 925–939.

Tsai, W., & Ghoshal, S. 1998. Social capital and value creation: The role of intrafirm networks. ***Academy of Management Journal,*** 41: 464–476.

Van de Ven, A. 1986. Central problems in the management of innovation. ***Management Science,*** 32: 590–607.

Von Hippel, E. 1994. "Sticky information" and the locus of problem solving: Implications for innovation. ***Management Science,*** 40: 429–430.

Wenpin Tsai (*wtsai@psu.edu*) is an assistant professor of management in the Smeal College of Business Administration at the Pennsylvania State University. He received his Ph.D. in strategic and international management at the London Business School. His current research interests include social capital, organizational learning, business unit strategy, and the evolution of intra- and interorganizational networks.

Name Index

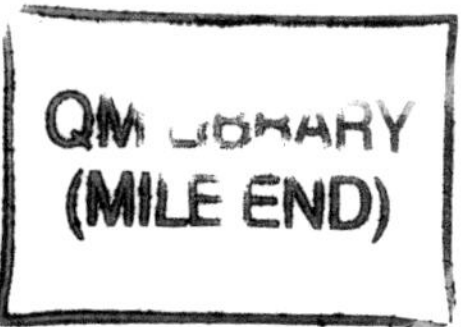